THE LAW AND ETHICS OF DEMENTIA

Dementia is a topic of enormous human, medical, economic, legal and ethical importance. Its importance grows as more of us live longer. The legal and ethical problems it raises are complex, intertwined and under-discussed. This book brings together contributions from clinicians, lawyers and ethicists—all of them world leaders in the field of dementia—and is a comprehensive, scholarly yet accessible library of all the main (and many of the fringe) perspectives. It begins with the medical facts: what is dementia? Who gets it? What are the current and future therapeutic and palliative options? What are the main challenges for medical and nursing care? The story is then taken up by the ethicists, who grapple with questions such as: is it legitimate to lie to dementia patients if that is a kind thing to do? Who is the person whose memory, preferences and personality have all been transformed by their disease? Should any constraints be placed on the sexual activity of patients? Are GPS tracking devices an unpardonable interference with the patient's freedom? These issues, and many more, are then examined through legal lenses. The book closes with accounts from dementia sufferers and their carers. It is the first and only book of its kind, and the authoritative text.

The Law and Ethics of Dementia

Edited by
Charles Foster
Jonathan Herring
and
Israel Doron

OXFORD AND PORTLAND, OREGON
2014

Published in the United Kingdom by Hart Publishing Ltd
16C Worcester Place, Oxford, OX1 2JW
Telephone: +44 (0)1865 517530
Fax: +44 (0)1865 510710
E-mail: mail@hartpub.co.uk
Website: http://www.hartpub.co.uk

Published in North America (US and Canada) by
Hart Publishing
c/o International Specialized Book Services
920 NE 58th Avenue, Suite 300
Portland, OR 97213-3786
USA
Tel: +1 503 287 3093 or toll-free: (1) 800 944 6190
Fax: +1 503 280 8832
E-mail: orders@isbs.com
Website: http://www.isbs.com

Hart Publishing is an imprint of Bloomsbury Publishing plc.

British Library Cataloguing in Publication Data
Data Available

ISBN: 978-1-84946-417-8

Typeset by Compuscript Ltd, Shannon
Printed and bound in Great Britain by
Lightning Source UK Ltd

Acknowledgements

Dr Rupert McShane, who gave invaluable help in shaping the book and suggesting contributors.

Preface

Dementia is one of the great and growing facts of our age. Modern medicine has spared us to grow old, and when we grow old, dementia is waiting for many of us. It will steal our neurones, our memories, our independence and our ability to perceive our relationships (if not the relationships themselves). It may even (there's an important debate about this) rob us of ourselves, or allow us to remake ourselves. By and large Western governments, seeing the scary demographics of dementia, have buried their heads in the sand. Insufficient money has been set aside to deal with dementia. It often seems as if, since patients with dementia can't complain, or can't complain on the statutory forms, they are presumed not to exist. Even when dementia is acknowledged, it is precisely that—dementia: the problem—that is acknowledged, rather than the people who have the condition. It is attitudes as well as organic disease which steal personhood.

So: dementia is unfashionable and frightening. Law and philosophy are slavish followers of fashion. They haven't given dementia and its victims (patients, carers, communities, all of us) anything like the attention they deserve. That's a shame. A shame not just for the governments (which can use all the help they can get), and for the victims (for whom even wrong-headed attention would be a comfort), but for the lawyers and the philosophers. They're missing some fascinating, deeply repercussive problems: problems that take us deep into what it means to be human; what it means to legislate; when it is appropriate for the state or anyone else to step into the shoes of another. And doctors, too, are forced by dementia to face the questions that their usual busy-ness helps them ignore: why treat at all? Whom should we treat? Who, indeed, *is* the patient lying in the hospital bed?

This book is an attempt to confront these questions. It has to be a big book, and it has to be a multidisciplinary book. Such work as there has been on the law and ethics of dementia has often suffered because the lawyers haven't read the ethicists, the ethicists haven't read the lawyers, neither have read the doctors and even many of the doctors have never had to break the news of the diagnosis to a patient or a spouse, or deal in the early hours with a patient who has started to masturbate in front of the nurses.

Some of the juxtapositions will jar. Good. Details of drug doses rub shoulders with Kant. That's how it should be. They need each other for credibility. An essay about the ethics of dangling therapeutic hopes before the noses of desperate patients is better for sharing space with a piece about what those hopes actually are.

Dementia diagnosis, therapy, care, philosophy, economics and law are all in their infancy. Most of the leading thinkers in the field (which includes all of the contributors to this book) are finding their way. Rarely is there any definitively right or wrong answer. That means that the book contains opinions, unreferenced assertions, debates and downright contradictions. If it didn't, it wouldn't represent the subject properly. The diseases called, generically, dementia, are mysterious. They generate baffling problems. There are no Ariadnes and no reliable threads in this labyrinth. We would like to think that by putting all this material between two covers we have contributed a little to the cross-fertilization which alone can produce the holistic scholarship fit for its enormous subject.

All that said, the book had to have some structure. You can only have a decent cocktail if you're clear at the start about the elements that are going into it. Part I deals with the medical facts about dementia, on the sadly contentious basis that the facts should ground the law and the ethics. Part II deals with the ethics, on the basis that many ethical reflections find their way into legal thinking, and discussion of the law makes more sense if one knows the ethical language in which much of the legal debate is couched. Part III deals with the law, following generally, but not always, the structure of the ethical part: one can often, therefore, look at exactly parallel ethical and legal discussions of the same issue. Where there are no parallel chapters, it is because we thought it would make for unacceptable repetition. Part IV looks at social perspectives—discrimination, physical, financial and other abuse, driving and voting and political participation. Part V is a collection of highly personal pieces—perspectives from carers and a patient. It could be argued strongly that these should have come first, and that by putting them at the end we are giving the impression that patients and carers are less important than the doctors, lawyers and ethicists who discuss them. That is the very opposite of our view. We wanted to give the final word to those most intimately affected by dementia. We hope that readers will come to those perspectives after having read the academic discussion, and in the light of the patient/carer views will sling out—or at least revisit—any misapprehensions into which they have been seduced by the academic sophistry.

Contents

List of Contributors

Charlotte L Allan, BA (Hons), MBChB, MRCPsych, Academic Clinical Lecturer, Department of Psychiatry, University of Oxford, UK.

Elissa L Ash, MD, PhD, Director, Center for Memory and Attention Disorders, Department of Neurology, Tel Aviv Sourasky Medical Center, Tel Aviv, Israel.

Peter Ashley

Matthew L Baum, MD, PhD Trainee, Harvard-MIT Division of Health Science and Technology, Harvard Medical School, USA.

Aileen Beatty, RMN, Clinical Lead Challenging Behaviour Team, Northumbria Healthcare NHS Foundation Trust, UK.

Sophie Behrman, BA, BM, BCh, MRCPsych, CT3 in Psychiatry, Oxford Deanery, UK.

Rob Berkeley

Sue Berkeley

Phil Bielby, LLB, PCHE, PhD, Lecturer in Law, University of Hull, UK.

Andrew Billen

Natalia Blaja-Lisnic, MD, PhD, Cognitive Clinic, Department of Geriatrics, Carmel Medical Center, Haifa, Israel.

Noa Bregman, MD, Memory and Attention Disorders Center, Department of Neurology, Tel Aviv Medical Center, Tel Aviv, Israel.

E-Shien Chang, MA, Chinese Health, Aging and Policy Program, Rush Institute for Healthy Aging, Rush University Medical Center, Chicago, IL, USA.

Ruijia Chen, MS, Chinese Health, Aging and Policy Program, Rush Institute for Healthy Aging, Rush University Medical Center, Chicago, IL, USA.

Carolyn Chew-Graham, MD, FRCGP, Professor of General Practice Research, Research Institute—Primary Care and Health Sciences, Keele University, UK.

XinQi Dong, MD, MPH, Director, Chinese Health, Aging and Policy Program, Associate Director, Rush Institute for Healthy Aging, Associate Professor of Medicine, Nursing and Behavioral Sciences, Rush University Medical Center, Chicago, IL, USA.

Israel (Issi) Doron, PhD, LLM, LLB, Head of the Department of Gerontology, University of Haifa, Haifa, Israel.

Mary Donnelly, PhD, Senior Lecturer, Faculty of Law, University College Cork, Eire.

Claudia Dunlop, MRCPsych, Specialist Registrar in Old Age Psychiatry, Oxleas NHS Foundation Trust, London, UK.

Michael Dunn, MA, PhD, The Ethox Centre, Nuffield Department of Population Health, University of Oxford, UK.

Klaus P Ebmeier, MD, Foundation Chair of Old Age Psychiatry, Department of Psychiatry, University of Oxford, UK.

Karen Eltis, BCL, LLB-BA, LLM, LLD, Professor of Law, University of Ottawa, Canada, and Columbia Law School, USA.

Charles Foster, PhD, Fellow, Green Templeton College, University of Oxford, UK.

Chris Fox, MD, MRCPsych, MMedSci, BSc, Clinical Senior Lecturer in Old Age Psychiatry, Norwich Medical School, Faculty of Medicine and Health Sciences, University of East Anglia, UK.

Ofra G Golan, LLD, The Ethics Committee Coordinator, Maccabi Healthcare Services, Israel. Formerly Senior Researcher at the Unit for Genetic Policy & Bioethics, Gertner Institute for Epidemiology & Health Policy Research, Sheba Medical Center, Israel.

Michael Gordon, MD, MSc, FRCPC, Medical Program Director, Palliative Care, Geriatric Health Care System, Professor of Medicine, University of Toronto, Canada.

Margaret Isabel Hall, LLB, LLM, Assistant Professor, Faculty of Law, Thompson Rivers University, British Columbia, Canada.

Rosie Harding, LLB, LLM, PhD, Senior Lecturer in Law, University of Birmingham, UK.

Jonathan Herring, BA, BCL, Professor of Law, University of Oxford, UK.

Andrea Hilton, BPharm, MSc, PhD, MRPharmS, PGCHE, FHEA, Lecturer, Faculty of Health and Social Care, University of Hull, UK.

U Hla Htay

Caroline J Huang, doctoral candidate, The Ethox Centre, Nuffield Department of Population Health, University of Oxford, UK.

Julian C Hughes, MA, MB, ChB, PhD, FRCPsych, Consultant and Honorary Professor of Philosophy of Ageing, Northumbria Healthcare NHS Foundation Trust and Institute for Ageing and Health, Newcastle University, UK.

Lesley King, LLB (Hons), Dip Crim, Solicitor, Professor and Professional Development Consultant with the University of Law, and Director of LK Law Ltd, UK.

Nina A Kohn, JD Harvard, AB Princeton, Professor, Syracuse University College of Law, Syracuse, New York, USA.

Amos D Korczyn, Professor Emiritus, Department of Neurology, Tel Aviv University, Israel.

Daniel Lasserson, MA (Hons) (Cantab), MBBS (Hons) MD (Cantab), MRCP (UK), MRCPE, MRCGP, Department of Primary Care Health Sciences, University of Oxford, UK.

Ian Maidment, Senior Lecturer, Pharmacy, Aston Research Centre for Healthy Ageing (ARCHA), Medicines and Devices in Ageing Cluster Lead School of Life and Health Sciences, Aston University, UK.

Andrew McGee, PhD, Health Law Research Centre, Faculty of Law, Queensland University of Technology, Brisbane, Australia.

José Miola, LLB (Hons), PhD, Professor of Medical Law, University of Leicester, UK.

Orna Moore, RN, MA, Nurse Consultant, Memory and Attention Disorders Center, Department of Neurology, Tel Aviv Medical Center, Israel.

Shirley Nurock

Desmond O'Neill, MD, FRCPI, Professor of Medical Gerontology, Trinity College, Dublin, Eire.

Michael Parker, Professor of Bioethics, The Ethox Centre, Nuffield Department of Population Health, University of Oxford, UK.

Bridget Penhale, BA (Hons), MSc, Reader in Mental Health of Older People, University of East Anglia, UK.

Leah Rand, MA, graduate student, The Ethox Centre, Nuffield Department of Population Health, University of Oxford, UK.

Peter Richards

Maartje Schermer, MD, PhD, Professor of the Philosophy of Medicine, Department of Medical Ethics and Philosophy of Medicine, Erasmus MC University Medical Center, Rotterdam, Netherlands.

Michael Schindler, PhD, Faculty of Law, Bar-Ilan University, Israel.

Winsor C Schmidt, JD, LLM, Endowed Chair/Distinguished Scholar in Urban Health Policy, Professor of Psychiatry and Behavioral Sciences, Professor of Family and Geriatric Medicine, Professor of Health Management and Systems Sciences, Department of Family and Geriatric Medicine, University of Louisville School of Medicine, USA.

Hugh Series, DM, FRCPsych, MA, MB, BS, Consultant Old Age Psychiatrist and Honorary Senior Clinical Lecturer, Department of Psychiatry, University of Oxford, UK.

Mark Sheehan, PhD, Oxford BRC Ethics Fellow, The Ethox Centre, Nuffield Department of Population Health, University of Oxford, UK.

Jeanette Shippen, RMN, Challenging Behaviour Nurse Specialist, Northumbria Healthcare NHS Foundation Trust, UK.

Melissa Simon, MD, MPH, Vice Chair of Clinical Research, Department of OB/GYN, Associate Professor of OB/GYN, Preventive Medicine and Medical Social Sciences, Chicago, IL, USA.

Gary Sinoff, MD, PhD, Past Director, Cognitive Clinic, Department of Geriatrics, Carmel Medical Center, Haifa, Israel; Senior Lecturer, Department of Gerontology,

Faculty of Social Welfare and Health Sciences, University of Haifa, Israel; Assistant Professor, Faculty of Medicine, Technion-Israel Institute of Technology, Haifa, Israel.

Doug Surtees, LLM, LLB, Associate Professor of Law, College of Law, University of Saskatchewan, Canada.

Keith Syrett, BA, MA, PhD, Professor of Public Health Law, Cardiff Law School, UK.

Adrian Treloar, MRCPsych, FRCP, MRCGP, Consultant and Senior Lecturer in Old Age Psychiatry, Oxleas NHS Foundation Trust, London, UK.

Veronika Vakhapova, MD, Consultant Neurologist, Maccabee Health Services, Israel.

Yael Waksman, LLB, LLM, LLD candidate, Faculty of Law, The Hebrew University of Jerusalem, Israel.

Jesse Wall, BA, LLB (Otago), BCL, MPhil, DPhil (Oxon) Junior Research Fellow, Merton College, University of Oxford, UK.

Perla Werner, PhD, Vice Rector and Head, Center for Research and Study of Aging, University of Haifa, Israel.

Emma Wolverson, ClinPsyD Bsc, Academic Tutor, Department of Clinical Psychology and Psychological Therapies, University of Hull, UK.

Table of Cases

Australia

Canada

Colombia

European Court and Commission of Human Rights,

Ireland

Israel

Netherlands

New Zealand

South Africa

United Kingdom

United States of America

Table of Legislation

Australia

Belgium

Brazil

Bulgaria

Canada

China

Czech Republic

European Union

Directives

Finland

Greece

Ireland

Israel

Kenya

Latvia

Lithuania

Luxembourg

Netherlands

New Zealand

Poland

Slovenia

Taiwan

United Kingdom

Statutory Instruments

United States of America

Constitution

Table of Conventions

Part I

Medical Fundamentals

1

What is Dementia?

ELISSA L ASH

DEFINING DEMENTIA

DEMENTIA IS NOT a single disease, but rather a clinical state where a decline in cognitive function, such as loss of memory, judgement, language, complex motor skills and other intellectual functions, leads to a decline in independent daily function.

The word dementia is derived from the Latin *de* (without) and *ment* (mind), and reflects a decline in mental functioning in a previously unimpaired or less impaired individual. According to the *Diagnostic and Statistical Manual of Mental Disorders IV*, revised text (DSM-IV-TR) (American Psychiatric Association, 2000), the standard classification of mental disorders used by mental health professionals in the United States through 2013, Dementia is defined as

> A. The development of multiple cognitive deficits manifested by both (1) memory impairment (impaired ability to learn new information or to recall previously learned information) and (2) one (or more) of the following cognitive disturbances: (a) aphasia (language disturbance); (b) apraxia (impaired ability to carry out motor activities despite intact motor function); (c) agnosia (failure to recognize or identify objects despite intact sensory function); (d) disturbance in executive functioning (ie, planning, organizing, sequencing, abstracting). B. The cognitive deficits in Criteria A1 and A2 each cause significant impairment in social or occupational functioning and represent a significant decline from a previous level of functioning. C. The deficits do not occur exclusively during the course of a delirium (acute change in mental functioning associated with variation in level of consciousness). D. The disturbance is not better accounted for by another disorder.

Dementia is differentiated from delirium, which is defined as a sudden and significant decline in mental functioning, not better accounted for by a pre-existing or evolving dementia, which occurs in the setting of a disturbance of consciousness (ie, reduced clarity of awareness of the environment), with reduced ability to focus, sustain or shift attention (DSM-IV-TR) (American Psychiatric Association, 2000). In delirium, the cognitive disturbance develops over a short period (usually hours to days), tends to fluctuate during the course of the day and is seen as a direct physiologic consequence of a general medical, neurological or psychiatric condition, an intoxicating substance, medication use or has more than one cause.

The ICD-10 criteria (World Health Organisation, 1992) for dementia are quite similar to the DSM-IV-TR (American Psychiatric Association, 2000). They include criteria of memory impairment (visual or verbal), as well as additional criteria of 'a decline in other cognitive abilities characterized by deterioration in judgment and thinking, such as planning and organizing, and in the general processing of information'. The diagnosis is further supported by evidence of damage to other higher cortical functions, such as aphasia, agnosia or apraxia. Additional criteria include a decline in emotional control or motivation, or a change in social behaviour, manifest as at least one of the following: (1) emotional lability; (2) irritability; (3) apathy; (4) coarsening of social behaviour. Preserved awareness of the environment (ie, absence of clouding of consciousness) must be established during a period of time long enough to enable the unequivocal demonstration of the cognitive impairment. When there are superimposed episodes of delirium the diagnosis of dementia should be deferred. The ICD-10 (World Health Organisation, 1992) includes a time frame for diagnosis: for a confident clinical diagnosis, cognitive impairment should have been present for at least six months; if the period since the manifest onset is shorter, the diagnosis can only be tentative. An emphasis is also placed on the need for objective verification of the criteria by obtaining a reliable history from an informant, supplemented, if possible, by neuropsychological tests or quantified cognitive assessments. Further, it is suggested that judgement about independent living or the development of dependence (upon others) need to take account of the cultural expectation and context. The ICD-10 (World Health Organisation, 1992) also provides guidelines for the diagnosis of dementia severity, with criteria for mild, moderate and severe dementia, which is an important diagnostic issue for determining the need for ancillary services or external support.

These criteria have been criticized for the inclusion of memory impairment as part of the necessary criteria for the dementia diagnosis in that they resemble the criteria for dementia of Alzheimer's disease. Not all dementias involve memory impairment; the presence of dementing disorders such as the fronto-temporal dementias that primarily involve the frontal lobes leading to decline in language, executive or behavioural functions without necessarily the involvement of memory, bring this criterion into question.

In 2011, a work group of neurologists and dementia experts from the National Institute on Aging and the Alzheimer's Association recommended a revised set of criteria for the diagnosis of dementia (Mckhann et al, 2011). According to their recommendations, dementia is diagnosed when there are cognitive or behavioural (neuropsychiatric) symptoms that:

1. interfere with the ability to function at work or at usual activities; and
2. represent a decline from previous levels of functioning and performing; and
3. are not explained by delirium or major psychiatric disorder.
4. Cognitive impairment is detected and diagnosed through a combination of (1) history-taking from the patient and a knowledgeable informant and (2) an objective cognitive assessment, either a 'bedside' mental status examination or neuropsychological testing. Neuropsychological testing should be performed when the routine history and bedside mental status examination cannot provide a confident diagnosis.
5. The cognitive or behavioural impairment involves a minimum of two of the following domains:
   a. Impaired ability to acquire and remember new information—symptoms include repetitive questions or conversations, misplacing personal belongings, forgetting events or appointments, getting lost on a familiar route.

b. Impaired reasoning and handling of complex tasks, poor judgement—symptoms include poor understanding of safety risks, inability to manage finances, poor decision-making ability, inability to plan complex or sequential activities.
c. Impaired visuospatial abilities—symptoms include inability to recognize faces or common objects or to find objects in direct view despite good acuity, inability to operate simple implements, or orient clothing to the body.
d. Impaired language functions (speaking, reading, writing)—symptoms include difficulty thinking of common words while speaking, hesitations; speech, spelling and writing errors.
e. Changes in personality, behaviour or comportment—symptoms include uncharacteristic mood fluctuations such as agitation, impaired motivation, initiative, apathy, loss of drive, social withdrawal, decreased interest in previous activities, loss of empathy, compulsive or obsessive behaviours, socially unacceptable behaviours.

This issue has been readdressed in the psychiatric community as well with the introduction of *The Diagnostic and Statistical Manual of Mental Disorders* (DSM-5) (American Psychiatric Association, 2013); the concept of dementia has been reformulated as 'Major Neurocognitive Disorder' (NCD). The revised criteria for NCD require decline in only one (or more) cognitive domains, and are similar to those of the National Institute on Aging (NIA) work group in that memory impairment need not be a feature of the clinical syndrome. Major NCD is defined by the requirement of (1) clear deficits in objective assessment of the relevant domain (typically >2.0 standard deviations (SD) below the mean [or below the 2.5th percentile] of an appropriate reference population [ie, age, gender, education, pre-morbid intellect and culturally adjusted]), and (2) cognitive deficits are sufficient to interfere with independence (for example, at a minimum requiring assistance with instrumental activities of daily living, ie, more complex tasks such as finances or managing medications). This assessment is inherently problematic in that relatively few patients undergo strict neuropsychological testing that would provide the appropriate data to assess the criterion of >2 SD below the mean in a given cognitive domain.

DEFINING MILD COGNITIVE IMPAIRMENT

The DSM-5 now recognizes a less severe level of cognitive impairment: mild NCD, a new definition that permits the diagnosis of less disabling syndromes that may nonetheless be the focus of concern and treatment. The criteria for mild NCD are similar to those that have been suggested for 'Mild Cognitive Impairment' (MCI), a syndrome that has been investigated as a possible prodromal state to dementia. The widely accepted criteria for MCI, suggested by Petersen et al (1999) and further refined by the workgroup of the NIA in 2011 (Albert et al, 2011) are:

1. concern regarding a change in cognition—this concern may be transmitted by the patient or by a reliable informant who knows the patient well, or by a skilled clinician who has been following the patient;

2. impairment in one or more cognitive domains—there should be evidence of lower performance in one or more cognitive domains that is greater than would be expected for the patient's age and educational background and if repeated assessments are available, then a decline in performance should be evident over time;
3. preservation of independence in functional abilities—persons with MCI commonly have mild problems performing complex functional tasks which they used to perform previously, such as paying bills, preparing a meal or shopping and may take more time, be less efficient and make more errors at performing such activities than in the past. Nevertheless, they generally maintain their independence of function in daily life, with minimal aids or assistance;
4. not demented—these cognitive changes should be sufficiently mild that there is no evidence of a significant impairment in social or occupational functioning. It should be emphasized that the diagnosis of MCI requires evidence of intra-individual change. If an individual has only been evaluated once, change will need to be inferred from the history and/or evidence that cognitive performance is impaired beyond what would have been expected for that individual. Serial evaluations are of course optimal, but may not be feasible in a particular circumstance.

MCI appears to be a significant phenomenon in older populations, although incidence rates are widely variable depending on clinical criteria (see below), with estimates as high as 76.5 per 1000 person-years (Luck et al, 2010). MCI has been evaluated as a possible precursor state to dementia. An overall probability of conversion from MCI to dementia was estimated at approximately 10–15% per year (Ritchie, 2004) which has been more recently revised to 3–15% per year (Petersen et al, 2009) within the first five years of diagnosis. Significant differences exist, probably depending on the population studied and the criteria used for MCI and dementia, as well as the duration of follow-up. It remains that not all subjects diagnosed with MCI go on to develop dementia syndromes, suggesting that this population is heterogeneous in nature and likely includes other pathophysiologic states besides dementing disorders.

It is important to emphasize that both dementia and MCI are clinical syndromes. Diagnosis of dementia or MCI, while important for understanding the condition of, addressing the needs of and providing the appropriate services to the patient, does not provide the pathophysiological cause of the disorder causing cognitive dysfunction. Further evaluation is often required to arrive at an etiology of the disorder, as described further below.

CHARACTERISTICS OF DEMENTIA

Dementia can be further defined by reference to several clinical characteristics. These characteristics may be of use by clinicians in attempting to diagnose the etiology of the underlying disorder that is causing the dementia state.

Onset

While in most dementing disorders the onset is usually insidious, some dementias may present with acute onset, such as post-traumatic states. Age of onset is also an important determining factor. Dementia can also be categorized as pre-senile if occurring before the age of 60, or senile dementia if occurring after the age of 60. While the cut-off age of 60 is relatively arbitrary, this categorization is useful in the diagnosis of neurodegenerative diseases, as they generally present in the population over age 60. Less than 5% of Alzheimer's disease is diagnosed before the age of 60, and in this population there is often a strong familial component. A myriad of neurological and systemic disorders can cause dementia in young persons, including genetic, toxic, metabolic, inflammatory and neoplastic conditions.

Clinical Features

Understanding the clinical presentation of the dementing disorder and the cognitive domains affected most early in the disease course are important factors for diagnostic purposes, as well as for evaluating the extent of cognitive and functional deficits. Memory deficits are usually first evident as a decline in working or short-term memory function, where the processes of attending to and encoding new information are affected. This may be experienced as a deficit in episodic memory, where recent events are not recalled. With advancing dementia, long-term memory deficits may become apparent, such as forgetting the names of family members or previously learned facts. Verbal and visuospatial memory functions can be evaluated using basic neuropsychological tests (word-lists, word pairs, stories; learning of complex figures or the placement of objects). Language production deficits can be identified by reductions in verbal fluency, word-finding deficits, inaccurate word choice; language comprehension deficits may manifest as difficulty in understanding written or spoken language. Decline in executive functions may be evidenced by a lack of ability to negotiate new or complex tasks, and/or loss of judgement and reasoning skills. Personality changes, including apathy and anxiety, or behavioural changes, including irritability or even psychotic features such as hallucinations or delusions, may become evident.

Course

Dementia can be considered rapidly progressive or slowly progressive based on the rate of cognitive and functional decline. The course is usually related to the underlying disorder causing the dementia state. Dementia due to neurodegenerative causes is usually slowly progressive, in that the clinical and functional symptoms progress over a period of years. In rapidly progressive dementia, however, there is a more rapid cognitive and functional decline that occurs usually over days/weeks to months, and is often associated with other causes of dementia such as infections, inflammatory disorders, neoplastic or para-neoplastic disorders or abnormal metabolic states. Dementia can also present as a static condition, as in post-traumatic states or dementia due to stroke, which can be static or can also progress in a 'step-wise' fashion, presumably due to the accumulation of additional damage to cortical or subcortical structures from additional strokes or other factors.

Etiological Subtypes

Alzheimer's Disease

Nearly any process affecting the brain and other systemic processes affecting the body and brain can lead to dementia or dementia-like symptoms. Over the age of 60, neurodegenerative diseases tend to become a prominent etiological factor in dementia. Not all degenerative disorders appear in old age, however, and may need to be considered before the age of 60 in patients with the appropriate clinical presentation. Of the neurodegenerative disorders leading to dementia, Alzheimer's disease (AD) is the most prominent due to its widespread prevalence in the ageing population. In 2012, an estimated 5.4 million Americans had Alzheimer's disease (Alzheimer's Association, 2012). A 2005 consensus study (Ferri et al, 2005) estimated that 24 million people worldwide had dementia in 2001. According to predictions of increasing prevalence, mostly due to ageing of the population together with the lack of good treatments to lower incidence, this number is expected to quadruple over the next 40 years. The financial burden of caring for individuals with a diagnosis of AD is similar to that of cancer or heart disease (Hurd et al, 2013). The clinical criteria for diagnosing AD were proposed in 1984 by a work group from the NINCDS-ADRDA (McKhann et al, 1984), and these criteria are still widely used today. An update of the criteria has recently been proposed by the NIA work group (McKhann et al, 2011). While decline in memory functions was considered the clinical hallmark in the diagnosis of AD, the revised criteria include amnesic and non-amnesic presentations of AD, either language (typically logopenic aphasia with impaired fluency, word retrieval and repetition but spared single-word comprehension) or visual-spatial perceptive decline (also known as Posterior Cortical Atrophy). In all cases, memory impairments become evident over time. Decline must be evident in more than one cognitive domain, leading to a decline in daily functioning, typically evidenced by a decline in instrumental activities of daily living (iADL). AD is designated as 'probable' or 'possible' when there is no histopathological information available, and can only be considered 'definite' when there is a sample of brain tissue that exemplifies the histopathological hallmarks of the disease, namely amyloid plaques and neurofibrillary tangles. As most patients who develop dementia do not undergo brain biopsy, the diagnosis of AD is thus usually considered 'probable' or 'possible' as per the clinical presentation. In order for the diagnosis of probable AD to be established, the absence of systemic or neurological disorders that in and of themselves could account for the cognitive deficits must be determined. This criterion has been refined to include the absence of significant cerebrovascular disease as based on clinical history and brain imaging, and the absence of core clinical features of other dementia syndromes, such as early onset of parkinsonism or cognitive fluctuations as seen in Lewy Body Dementia (LBD), or prominent language or behavioural deficits in the absence of memory or other impairments as seen in the variants of Fronto-Temporal Dementia (FTD). The diagnosis of AD may be considered 'possible' if the clinical syndrome is appropriate but there are additional factors present that may also explain dementia, or if core features of other dementia syndromes are evident. In fact, the most recent post-mortem histopathological studies of dementia patients has taught us that the most common cause of dementia is often 'mixed dementia', where brain changes due to more than one pathophysiological process (plaques and tangles, stroke or ischemic changes, Lewy bodies) are evident at the same time.

Concerted research efforts have been focused on the identification of biomarkers that can strengthen the probability of AD diagnosis. These efforts have mainly focused on imaging techniques and identification of biochemical markers in blood or cerebrospinal fluid (CSF). Loss of brain volume in the medial temporal lobes or brain atrophy, as measured by enlargement of the lateral ventricles via volumetric analysis, has been shown to correlate with the onset of AD (Scheltens et al, 1992; Westman et al, 2011). Functional imaging techniques including FDG-PET and HMPAO-SPECT may provide evidence for impaired brain metabolism or perfusion in medial temporal brain structures including the hippocampus and parahippocampal gyrus, or in associated brain regions, and may be useful in helping to differentiate the underlying dementia syndromes (Devous, 2002). Raised levels of CSF Tau protein (an intracellular neuronal protein that when increased in the CSF may indicate neuronal damage) or phosphorylated-Tau, a more specific AD marker, correlate with AD, as do decreased levels of CSF Aβ1-42, the component of amyloid plaques (Blennow et al, 2010). The ratio of these proteins has been identified as a sensitive and specific indicator of AD (Shaw et al, 2009). Most recently, amyloid imaging techniques using PET and a tracer called Pittsburgh Imaging Compound B (PIB), which binds to amyloid plaques in vivo, have been developed that allow for the in vivo identification of amyloid plaques and plaque burden (Klunk et al, 2004). While the PIB-PET technology has improved diagnostic accuracy, it has also proved cumbersome and expensive, which has limited its diagnostic use. The recent development of Florebetapir-PET as an amyloid imaging study may however change this issue in the future (Lister-James et al, 2011). Furthermore, in research settings, PIB-PET scans or CSF biomarker analyses may identify signs of amyloid burden or other abnormalities in subjects without cognitive dysfunction. This condition is often referred to as 'incipient', 'pre-clinical', or 'prodromal' AD (Dubois, 2000), as it is assumed that these subjects will eventually develop clinical symptoms of AD, and many but not all studies bear this out (Mattsson et al, 2009). It should be mentioned, however, that no ancillary tests provide 100% diagnostic accuracy, and the diagnosis of AD is still made clinically, with varying degrees of probability, unless there is histopathological evidence confirming the definite diagnosis of AD. The presence of a family history of AD and the establishment of continued cognitive and functional decline support the AD diagnosis.

OTHER CAUSES OF DEMENTIA

While AD is the most common cause of dementia in the ageing population, many other neurodegenerative diseases also cause dementia syndromes. These include vascular dementia, Parkinson's disease related dementia (PDD) and dementia with Lewy bodies (DLB), FTD and Huntington's disease (HD). Other neurological disorders such as mass lesions, multiple sclerosis, stroke, haemorrhage and epilepsy may lead to cognitive decline and dementia states. Dementia may be seen in patients who have suffered from traumatic brain injury or multiple concussions (McKee et al, 2013), or in the setting of autoimmune states such as limbic encephalitis or Hashimoto's encephalopathy.

Several infectious diseases can cause dementia, often rapidly progressive (eg Creutzfeld-Jacob disease (CJD)), or fungal infections; or more slowly (eg syphilis or HIV). Chronic drug or alcohol use has been associated with dementia states as is chronic deficiency in vitamins B1, B12 or folic acid. Medications can be associated with cognitive decline and conditions mimicking dementia, including anti-cholinergic medications, benzodiazepines and opioid pain relievers.

Dementia can be diagnosed in the context of genetic disorders, both in children and in adults, including the adrenoleukodystrophies and additional disorders too numerous to mention in this review. A genetic disorder should be suspected when dementia occurs at a relatively young age, is associated with a family history of similar disorders and occurs in conjunction with other neurological or systemic findings. In these conditions, dementia should be differentiated from developmental disorders such as mental retardation, where cognitive milestones are delayed or never achieved. Psychiatric disorders such as depression or schizophrenia can produce states of cognitive and functional decline. Another condition that is often considered in patients with gait disorders, incontinence and cognitive decline is that of Normal Pressure Hydrocephalus (NPH), which is associated with enlarged lateral ventricles and frontal lobe dysfunction.

THE EVALUATION OF A PATIENT WITH SUSPECTED DEMENTIA

Several factors must be considered when performing a medical evaluation of a patient with suspected dementia or cognitive decline. In addition to understanding the history of the symptoms obtained from the patient, it is critical that additional historical information is obtained from an independent observer who is in close contact with the patient and can provide an unbiased and objective account of his or her condition. This point is understandable, as in the setting of dementia the cognitive dysfunction may interfere with the patient's ability to provide relevant historical information. It is quite common for patients with cognitive decline to have impaired insight and awareness as to the nature or severity of the condition. A history of all elements of cognitive function is mandatory, as not all dementia syndromes have an associated memory dysfunction. A history of changes in language function, personality, mood or behaviour can provide insight into the nature and the location of cognitive dysfunction. A thorough history regarding all these elements should be obtained, including a careful analysis of the patient's previous medical history, medications and family history.

As part of the medical evaluation for dementia, an assessment of the patient's functional status is essential, as establishing functional decline is part of the criteria for diagnosis. Functional assessments are divided into two categories: basic activities of daily living (bADL), which are basic self-care tasks, including dressing, washing, toileting, cooking and are the ADL most often affected when there is a disability of motor function, and instrumental activities of daily living (iADL), which are daily activities that are related to higher cognitive ability and ability to function independently, such as organizing the home and performing housework, taking medications as prescribed, managing financial matters, shopping for groceries or clothing (buying the appropriate items), use of the telephone or other form of communication or technology, navigating successfully modes of transportation within the community and participation in community activities or hobbies.

One of the areas that should not be overlooked is the ability to manage one's health care needs (filling prescriptions, fulfilling doctors' recommendations), which may often be a 'red flag' for functional decline. Several iADL scales are in use (Lawton and Brody, 1969; reviewed in Sikkes et al, 2009). Pre-morbid levels of functioning need to be clearly established in order to identify decline.

Functional assessments need to be tailored to each patient in a personal manner; a retiree who is having trouble remembering what to buy at the grocery store or a 'CEO' of a company who needs to rely on her secretary to remember appointments may both be indicators of significant impairment. There may also be a cultural bias to the assessment of functional status; the role of taking care of elders in certain cultures may lead to the oversight of meaningful cognitive and functional impairments. These problems may only become evident when the patient is removed from his or her natural environment, such as on vacation in an unfamiliar place or hospitalization, or when an additional functional stressor is present, but with careful questioning, a preceding history of functional impairment may often be identified.

Cognitive testing is essential as part of the medical evaluation of dementia. A systematic assessment of memory, language, executive and visuospatial functions should be obtained. Typical 'bedside' or in-office, cognitive evaluations include the Mini-Mental State Examination (MMSE), which was devised as a simple cognitive test to grade the severity of cognitive dysfunction in dementia patients (Folstein et al, 1975). The MMSE is widely used to diagnose dementia but may not be an appropriate diagnostic test in many different settings, either missing the presence of significant cognitive decline in highly educated patients (ceiling effect), or overestimating impairments in patients with limited schooling or limited literacy. The MMSE is useful for assessing cognitive function and documenting subsequent decline. Additional tests have been developed to diagnose cognitive decline at earlier stages. These tests include the Montreal Cognitive Assessment (MOCA), which has been validated as an effective tool in screening for MCI and early dementia (Nazreddine et al, 2005). Other similar tests include the the St Louis University Mental Status Exam (SLUMS) (Tariq, 2006) and the short test of mental status (STMS) (Tang-Wai et al, 2003). Additional or more detailed cognitive or neuropsychological testing may be required in particular patients, especially when there is concern for underlying or co-morbid psychiatric disease.

In patients with suspected cognitive decline or dementia, a neurological examination is often performed in order to assess for signs and symptoms of co-morbid neurological disease that may assist in attaining an accurate diagnosis of the underlying disorder responsible for cognitive decline. Attention is paid to cortical and subcortical brain functions, sign of pyramidal or extrapyramidal tract dysfunction or other pertinent neurological findings that may point physicians in the direction of the offending disease process. Ancillary testing is also important in ruling out potentially treatable causes of cognitive decline. According to 2010 guidelines published by the European Federation of Neurological Societies (EFNS), most expert opinion advises screening for vitamin B12, folate, thyroid stimulating hormone, calcium, glucose, complete blood cell count and renal and liver function abnormalities. Serological tests for syphilis, Borrelia and HIV should be considered in individual cases at high risk or where there are suggestive clinical features (Hort et al, 2010). Most experts also agree that a brain imaging procedure, either CT or MRI, should be performed to assess for space occupying lesions or other treatable disorders. The role of functional neuroimaging is controversial in diagnosing dementia and is not part of the routine assessment, but may improve diagnostic accuracy in some patients. Other tests, including EEG or lumbar puncture, may be indicated in particular cases. Genetic testing is not routinely performed, but may be recommended in cases with early onset and familial pattern of inheritance (Goldman et al, 2011).

DIAGNOSING DEMENTIA: ETHICAL CONSIDERATIONS

Several important ethical questions are involved in the diagnosis of dementia. As discussed above, the diagnosis of dementia relies on having an accurate historical account of the patient's cognitive and daily functioning to establish a pattern of decline. The accuracy of the diagnosis necessarily depends on the accuracy of the information provided to the health care provider, and accuracy may be influenced by the source of information. Bias can hide in several forms, from the doting family member who underestimates the degree of decline to the family member with a potential conflict of interest if there is the possibility of financial gain. Errors in diagnosis may have far-reaching implications, from the inappropriate invalidation of a driver's licence in cases of transient disorders misdiagnosed as dementia, to the inability to access appropriate support services in patients with advancing dementia that is not identified. To minimize diagnostic error, the diagnosis of dementia should be made by a physician with experience in diagnosing dementia, usually a neurologist, a geriatrician or a geriatric psychiatrist. All efforts should be made by the treating physician to identify and collect data from objective data providers who know the patient well and will provide an unbiased accounting of the patient's situation. Special attention should be given to the patient's state of insight and awareness of their condition. These may be impaired in dementia, resulting in a patient not perceiving themselves as ill. Family member's accounts are also sometimes unreliable, and may be distorted by conflicts of interest. Long-term follow up by an experienced physician is recommended in order to minimize diagnostic error.

REFERENCES

Albert, MS et al (2011) 'The diagnosis of mild cognitive impairment due to Alzheimer's disease: Recommendations from the National Institute on Aging—Alzheimer's Association workgroups on diagnostic guidelines for Alzheimer's disease' 7 *Alzheimer's & Dementia* 270–79.

Alzheimer's Association Report (2012) *Alzheimer's Disease: Facts and Figures*.

American Psychiatric Association (2000) *Diagnostic and Statistical Manual of Mental Disorders*, 4th edn, text rev (Washington, DC, American Psychiatric Publishing).

—— (2013) *Diagnostic and Statistical Manual of Mental Disorders*, 5th edn (Arlington, VA, American Psychiatric Publishing).

Blennow, K et al (2010) 'Cerebrospinal fluid and plasma biomarkers in Alzheimer disease' 6 *Nature Reviews Neurology* 131–44.

Devous, MD (2002) 'Functional brain imaging in the dementias: role in early detection, differential diagnosis, and longitudinal studies' 29 *European Journal of Nuclear Medicine and Molecular Imaging* 1685–96.

Dubois, B (2000) 'Prodromal Alzheimer's disease: a more useful concept than mild cognitive impairment?' 13 *Current Opinion in Neurology* 367–69.

Ferri, CP et al (2005) Alzheimer's Disease International. 'Global prevalence of dementia: a Delphi consensus study' 366 *Lancet* 2112–17.

Folstein, MF, Folstein, SE and McHugh, PR (1975) '"Mini-mental state". A practical method for grading the cognitive state of patients for the clinician' 12 *Journal of Psychiatric Research* 189–98.

Goldman, JS et al (2011) 'Genetic counselling and testing for Alzheimer disease: joint practice guidelines of the American College of Medical Genetics and the National Society of Genetic Counsellors' 13 *Genetics in Medicine* 597–605.

Hort, J et al (2010) EFNS Scientist Panel on Dementia. 'EFNS guidelines for the diagnosis and management of Alzheimer's disease' 17 *European Journal of Neurology* 1236–48.

Hurd, MD et al (2013) 'Monetary Costs of Dementia in the United States' 368(14) *New England Journal of Medicine* 1326–34.

Klunk, et al (2004) 'Imaging brain amyloid in Alzheimer's disease with Pittsburgh Compound-B' 55 *Annals of Neurology* 306–19.

Lawton, MP and Brody, EM (1969) 'Assessment of older people: Self-maintaining and instrumental activities of daily living' 9 *The Gerontologist* 179–86.

Lister-James, J et al (2011) 'Florbetapir F-18: a histopathologically validated beta-amyloid positron emission tomography imaging agent' 41 *Seminars in Nuclear Medicine* 300–04.

Luck, T et al (2010) 'Incidence of mild cognitive impairment: a systematic review' 29 *Dementia and Geriatric Cognitive Disorders* 164–75.

Mattsson, N et al (2009) 'CSF biomarkers and incipient Alzheimer disease in patients with mild cognitive impairment' 302 *The Journal of the American Medical Association* 385–93.

McKee, AC et al (2013) 'The spectrum of disease in chronic traumatic encephalopathy' 136 *Brain* 43–64.

McKhann, G et al (1984) 'Clinical diagnosis of Alzheimer's disease: report of the NINCDS-ADRDA Work Group under the auspices of Department of Health and Human Services Task Force on Alzheimer's Disease' 34 *Neurology* 939–44.

—— (2011) 'The diagnosis of dementia due to Alzheimer's disease: Recommendations from the National Institute on Aging and the Alzheimer's Association workgroup' 7 *Alzheimer's & Dementia* 263–69.

Nazreddine, ZS et al (2005) 'The Montreal Cognitive Assessment, MoCA: A Brief Screening Tool for Mild Cognitive Impairment' 53 *Journal of the American Geriatrics Society* 695–99.

Petersen, RC et al (1999) 'Mild cognitive impairment: clinical characterization and outcome' 56 *Archives of Neurology* 303–08.

—— (2009) 'Mild cognitive impairment: ten years later' 66 *Archives of Neurology* 1447–55.

Ritchie, K (2004) 'Mild cognitive impairment: an epidemiological perspective' 6 *Dialogues in Clinical Neuroscience* 401–08.

Scheltens, P et al (1992) 'Atrophy of medial temporal lobes on MRI in "probable" Alzheimer's disease and normal ageing: diagnostic value and neuropsychological correlates' 55 *Journal of Neurology, Neurosurgery & Psychiatry* 967–72.

Shaw, LM et al (2009) 'Cerebrospinal fluid biomarker signature in Alzheimer's disease neuroimaging initiative subjects' 65 *Annals of Neurology* 403–13.
Sikkes, SAM et al (2009) 'A systematic review of Instrumental Activities of Daily Living scales in dementia: room for improvement' 80 *Journal of Neurology Neurosurgery & Psychiatry* 7–12.
Tang-Wai, DF et al (2003) 'Comparison of the Short Test of Mental Status and the Mini-Mental State Examination in Mild Cognitive Impairment' 60 *Archives of Neurology* 1777–81.
Tariq, SH et al (2006) 'Comparison of the Saint Louis University mental status examination and the mini-mental state examination for detecting dementia and mild neurocognitive disorder: a pilot study' 14 *American Journal of Geriatric Psychiatry* 900–10.
Westman, E et al (2011) 'Sensitivity and Specificity of Medial Temporal Lobe Visual Ratings and Multivariate Regional MRI Classification in Alzheimer's Disease' 6(7) *PLoS One.* Published online: 21 July 2011.
World Health Organisation (1992) *ICD-10 Classifications of Mental and Behavioural Disorder: Clinical Descriptions and Diagnostic Guidelines* (Geneva, World Health Organisation).

2

The Demographics of Dementia

ISRAEL (ISSI) DORON

AN AGEING WORLD: DIVERSITY IN AGEING

THE WORLD IS ageing. This is usually attributed to several factors, including declining fertility rates and increasing life expectancy. In some countries these trends are strengthened by either young-age or old-age immigration. Population has wide ranging health-related consequences: in particular, older persons are at risk of a number of common chronic conditions that are relatively rare among younger persons. Dementia—and Alzheimer's disease (AD) in particular—are among the most common age-related conditions. This chapter sets out what is currently known about the prevalence and socio-demographic characteristics of these conditions.

THE PREVALENCE OF DEMENTIA

Accurate national and international measurements and estimates of the current and future prevalence of dementia are essential for the effective planning of long-term care and social policy. However, in reality, such measurements and estimates are not easy, and until recent years, not many reliable data or estimates were available. Often there have been no systematic data collection systems. Sometimes the conditions themselves have, by wilful or negligent blindness, been invisible to official bodies, and sometimes difficulties in diagnosis or dispute about the medical definitions of particular conditions have made hard the collection of meaningful data. The various types of dementia are notoriously difficult to define and diagnose.

One likely source for variation among estimates of the prevalence of dementia is the use of different criteria for defining and diagnosing dementia. Some studies have used criteria that do not require evidence of impaired functional performance, while most use criteria requiring significant impairment in social or occupational functioning (Plassman et al, 2007). These methodological and conceptual difficulties are even more extreme than the usual issues concerning medical definitions. As noted by Bennet (2007: 134), the dichotomous system used many times to classify persons as having dementia (by which you either have or do not have dementia) obscures the fact that most dementias, especially AD, do not fall neatly into distinct categories. Moreover, dementia does not develop over minutes or hours like a myocardial infarction or stroke; rather, it develops over many months or years. During this time, affected persons typically go through a phase during which cognition is impaired and it is unclear whether a formal diagnosis of dementia can be made. Hence, any attempt to 'measure' accurately the prevalence or characteristics of dementia is inherently problematic.

Another difficulty is the fact that like other significant medical conditions (for example, stroke or cancer) there are major regional variations in the occurrence of these conditions—not only between different global regions, but between countries and sometimes even within different regions in a single country. Finally, another factor that might contribute to differences in prevalence estimates is bias due to non-participation. As noted by Bennett (2007), persons who decline to participate are likely to be more impaired than those who participate. Hence, actual prevalence rates may in fact be higher than those reported.

Before presenting the actual numbers, however, a word of caution is required about future predictions and estimates. As noted by Mura et al (2010), any prediction based on current incidence rates of dementia is problematic: we already know that certain dementia protective factors, such as education and management of cardiovascular risk factors, are likely to be very different in the coming generations. Further, a recent American study showed a drop in the prevalence of cognitive impairment between 1993 and 2002 (Langa et al, 2008). According to this study, the drop could be due partly to an increase in the educational level of the older population between these two times. It is therefore clear that any future predictions are susceptible to potential change (for example, as a result of changing educational levels or changes in broader health conditions) that may significantly alter the actual incidence rates of dementia in the future.

Once we have taken these constraints into account, we can consider the key data. There have been many studies and estimates of the prevalence of dementia. Notably, there was the ADAMS study in the United States (Plassman et al, 2007), the EURODEM studies in Europe (Fratiglioni et al, 2000), the Delphi Consensus Study (Ferri et al, 2005) and finally, the meta-analysis carried out by Alzheimer's Disease International (World Alzheimer Report, 2009).

We begin by presenting some figures taken from the World Alzheimer Report (2009). The summary of these estimates is:

> Having applied the age-specific, or age- and gender specific prevalence estimates to the UN population projections ... we estimate that 35.6 million people worldwide will be living with dementia in 2010. ... This number will almost double every 20 years, to 65.7 million in 2030 and 115.4 million in 2050. Much of the increase is clearly attributable to increases in the numbers of people with dementia in low and middle income countries (World Alzheimer Report, 2009: 38).

Table 1: Meta-Analysis Estimates of Dementia

Meta-analysed estimates or dementia prevalence, generated from Poisson random effects models, by GBD region

Global Burden of Disease region	Number of studies		Gender	Age group							Standardised prevalence[1], for those aged 60 and over
	Potentially eligible studies	Used in meta-analysis (age-specific, age- and gender specific)		60–64	65–69	70–74	75–79	80–84	85–89	90+	
ASIA											
Australasia	4	3, 0	All	1.8	2.8	4.5	7.5	12.5	20.3	38.3	6 01*
Asia Pacific, High Income	22	14, 10	M	1.4	2.3	3.8	6.4	10.9	18	34.9	6.30*
			F	0.9	1.7	3.1	6.0	11.7	21.7	49.2	
			All	1.0	1.7	2.9	5.5	10.3	18.5	40.1	5.57
Asia, East	34	34, 31	M	0.8	1.3	2.2	4.0	7.3	16.7	26.4	4.98*
			F	0.9	1.6	2.9	5.3	10.0	17.9	38.7	
			All	0.7	1.2	3.1	4.0	7.4	13.3	28.7	4.19
Asia, South	8	7, 6	M	1.0	1.7	2.9	5.3	9.4	16.4	33.7	5.65*
			F	1.5	2.3	3.8	6.5	11	18.1	35.1	
			All	1.3	2.1	3.5	6.1	10.6	17.8	35.4	5.78
Asia, Southeast	6	5, 2	M	1.7	2.6	4.0	6.2	9.8	15	26.4	7.63
			F	1.8	3.0	5.1	9.0	15.9	27.2	54.9	
			All	1.6	2.6	4.2	6.9	11.6	18.7	35.4	6.38*
EUROPE											
Europe, Western	56	52, 46	M	1.4	2.3	3.7	6.3	10.6	17.4	33.4	7.29*
			F	1.9	3.0	5.0	8.6	14.8	24.7	48.3	
			All	1.6	2.6	43	7.4	12.9	21.7	43.1	6.92
THE AMERICAS											
North America (USA only)	11	8, 6	M	13	2.1	3.7	6.8	123	21.6	45.2	6.77*
			F	1.0	1.8	3.3	6.4	12.5	23.2	52.7	
			All	1.1	1.9	3.4	6.3	11.9	21.7	47.5	646
Latin America	11	11, 10	M	1.0	1.9	3.7	7.0	13.0	24.3	55.0	8.50*
			F	1.0	2.0	4.2	8.4	16.4	32.5	79.5	
			All	1.3	2.4	4.5	8.4	15.4	28.6	63.9	8.48

THE DIFFERENT TYPES OF DEMENTIA

Dementia is an umbrella term, covering different types of dementia. In general, studies suggest that Alzheimer's disease comprises the majority of dementia cases. For example, the findings of the US ADAMS study showed that

> overall, AD [Alzheimer's Dementia] accounted for approximately 69.9% of all dementia, while VD [Vascular Dementia] accounted for 17.4%. Other types of dementia such as dementia of 'undetermined etiology', Parkinson's dementia, normal-pressure hydrocephalus, frontal lobe dementia, alcoholic dementia, traumatic brain injury and Lewy body dementia accounted for the remaining 12.7% of cases. With increasing age, AD accounted

> for progressively more of the dementia cases so that in the age 90+ group, AD accounted for 79.5% of the dementia cases compared to 46.7% among those aged 71–79 years (Plassman et al, 2007: 128).

Although in most studies, AD comprised the majority of dementia cases, in some countries, the rates of Vascular Dementia (VD) were found in the past to be higher (for example, in Japan: Kiyohara et al, 1994). It should be noted, however, that it is not always easy to distinguish clinically between AD and VD.

THE AGE–DEMENTIA CORRELATION

Age is the strongest predictor of dementia (both AD as well as other kinds of dementia). As can be seen in Table 1, while prevalence rates of dementia for persons aged 65–69 years range from 1.2% (in East Asia) to 2.6% (in Western Europe and Southeast Asia) and 2.8% (Australasia), this figure increases significantly in persons aged 90+ years, where the corresponding figures are 28.7%, 43.1%, 35.4% and 38.3% respectively. This age–dementia relationship and the exponential increase in dementia with advancing age were consistently found in prevalence studies (for example, Lee et al, 2002).

This means that as society ages, and as more and more people enter their eighties or nineties, more than a quarter of them will be subject to dementia. A society with a sub-group of older persons where every fourth member is experiencing dementia is a very challenging social reality. While there are differences between the countries and regions (see below), the overall trend of a significant increase in prevalence rates, especially in the 'older old' groups, crosses boundaries and societies.

EDUCATION

Many studies have found that the duration of education correlated negatively with dementia risk (for example, the EURODEM study—Launer et al, 1999; the Rotterdam Study—Ott et al, 1995). For example, in the Seoul study of the prevalence of dementia in older people in an urban Korean population (Lee et al, 2002), it was found that while the prevalence of dementia for older persons with seven years of education or more was 2.1%, for persons with between one and six years of education or no education it was 7.7% and 13.1% respectively. The correlation between higher education and lower rates of dementia is perhaps also reflected in the studies showing a lower degree of reduction in Mini-Mental State Examination scores between the ages of 85 and 88 in the more highly educated (Aevarsson and Skoog, 2000). It seems that, after chronological age, the level of education is one of the best predictors of dementia.

GENDER

Several studies have reported that females are at greater risk of AD than males (Bachman et al, 1992; Canadian Study, 1994; the EURODEM study—Launer et al, 1999). For example, in the Seoul study (Lee et al, 2002) the rate of dementia for women was 10.4% while for men it was 4.5%; however, others have reported no such difference (Hebert et al, 2001; Paykel et al, 1994). In the United States, the ADAMS study findings showed that while the percentage of older women with dementia was higher than for men (15.74% and 11.14% respectively); however, a logistical model that included age and gender found that women were not at higher risk of AD and other dementias (Plassman et al, 2007).

A Dutch study (Ruitenberg et al, 2001), which tried to find out whether women were at a higher risk of dementia than men, found that, overall, dementia incidence was similar for men and women. However, after 90 years of age, dementia incidence declined in men but not in women (in particular for AD). Furthermore, the overall incidence of vascular dementia was lower in women than in men.

It seems that while the scientific debate about the impact of gender on prevalence rates of dementia continues, there is evidence to suggest that gender has an impact on the different risk factors that influence the progression to dementia. Therefore, gender differences should be taken into account in the context of policy and treatment for dementia (Artero et al, 2008).

RACE

As with other background variables, there are conflicting views of the significance of race. Some studies reported a higher frequency of AD and other dementias among African-Americans compared with Caucasians (Perkins et al, 1997; Tang et al, 2001; Husaini et al, 2003), while another reported no such difference (Fillenbaum et al, 1998). In the ADAMS study (Plassman et al, 2007), African-Americans had a higher frequency of AD and other dementias, but once education, gender and APOE genotype were controlled, the contribution of race was no longer statistically significant.

There is still no consensus about the impact of race on the prevalence of dementia. There are methodological difficulties, for example, the under-representation of African-Americans in various research settings. However, Miles and colleagues (Miles et al, 2001) argue that preliminary findings indicate that the clinical and molecular aetiologies of dementia indeed differ between races. African-Americans have a higher prevalence of vascular dementia and a lower prevalence of Parkinsonian dementia than do Caucasians. The genetic aetiologies of Alzheimer's-type dementia appear to differ between African-Americans and Caucasians. Hence, there is a need to develop racially appropriate cognitive assessment methods and to develop preventive and treatment aetiologies tailored to the racial background of individual patients.

NURSING HOME RESIDENTS

A unique and important sub-population of the older persons group is residents of nursing homes. Surprisingly little is known about the prevalence of dementia in this population and even less is known about its health characteristics and care needs (Magaziner et al, 2000).

As described by Magaziner et al (2000), early studies of dementia prevalence in nursing homes suggest that between 25% and 74% of all residents have dementia (Garrard et al, 1993), with rates for new admissions as high as 67% (German et al, 1992; Rovner et al, 1990). Magaziner's (2000) study in the United States found that nearly half (48.2%) of newly admitted patients were diagnosed with dementia. It was concluded that 31.5% of newly admitted residents did not have dementia, and a firm diagnosis could not be reached in 20.3% of cases. The prevalence of dementia was higher in small facilities and in facilities located in metropolitan areas. Similar results were found in a British study, based on data from England and Wales, where 48.5% of residents had a definitive diagnosis of dementia (Matthews and Dening, 2002). A study from Glasgow (Lithgow et al, 2012), that found a prevalence of 58%, stressed that if one presumed that the undiagnosed or equivocally diagnosed patients (31.8% in their study) had dementia, the prevalence would be nearly 90%. However, a Chinese study found that only 36.7% of its nursing home population was diagnosed with dementia (Mingxian et al, 2012), which may be explained by the regional differences in dementia characteristics (see below).

These findings suggest that the issue of dementia in nursing homes is very important, since the prevalence in this setting is much higher than in the general older population. Future trends in long-term care (the ageing of the nursing home population, the success of community-based programmes to delay institutionalization and the availability of public support to community-based long-term care), may increase the proportion of residents in nursing homes with dementia.

GEOGRAPHICAL VARIATION IN PREVALENCE

The correlation between age and dementia affects the dementia prevalence in different parts of the world. Where the proportion of older people is predicted to increase, dementia rates are expected to increase correspondingly. A review article analyzing the prevalence and risk factors of dementia in developing countries (Kalaria et al, 2008) revealed the existence of significant variations within these countries. For example:

> Surprisingly, countries in Latin America, such as Venezuela and Argentina, bear a higher burden of over 5% prevalence of dementia. By contrast, a systematic analysis of six Indian studies suggests low prevalence (2–3%) of all dementias, with marginally fewer cases in urban compared with rural areas and in the northern versus southern states. Pooled analysis of 25 Chinese studies by Dong and colleagues, comprising a total population of more than 76,000, suggested that the overall prevalence of dementia was 3.1%, indicating a significant rise from 1980 to 2004. However, a recent survey of over 34,807 Han Chinese residents aged at least 55 years in 79 rural and 58 urban communities of four distant areas reported a crude prevalence estimate of 5.0%, and 6.8% after adjustment for negative screening (Kalaria et al, 2008: 814; references omitted).

The Alzheimer's Global Report (2009) contains the following meta-analysis of the different estimates of dementia in different regions of the world:

Table 2: Estimated Prevalence of Dementia by World Region

Total population over 60, crude estimated prevalence of dementia (2010), estimated number of people with dementia (2010, 2030 and 2050) and proportionate increases (2010–2030 and 2010–2050) by GBD world region

GBD Region	Over 60 population (millions)	Crude estimated prevalence (%)	Number of people with dementia (millions)			Proportionate increases (%)	
	2010	2010	2010	2030	2050	2010–2030	2010–2050
ASIA	406.55	3.9	15.94	33.04	60.92	107	282
Australasia	4.82	6.4	0.31	0.53	0.79	71	157
Asia Pacific	46.63	6.1	2.83	5.36	7.03	89	148
Oceania	0.49	4.0	0.02	0.04	0.10	100	400
Asia, Central	7.16	4.6	0.33	0.56	1.19	70	261
Asia, East	171.61	3.2	5.49	11.93	22.54	117	311
Asia, South	124.61	3.6	4.48	9.31	18.12	108	304
Asia. Southeast	51.22	4.8	2.48	5.30	11.13	114	349
EUROPE	160.18	6.2	9.95	13.95	18.65	40	87
Europe, Western	97.27	7.2	6.98	10.03	13.44	44	93
Europe, Central	23.61	4.7	1.10	1.57	2.10	43	91
Europe, East	39.30	4.8	1.87	2.36	3.10	26	66
THE AMERICAS	120.74	6.5	7.82	14.78	27.08	89	246
North America	63.67	6.9	4.38	7.13	11.01	63	151
Caribbean	5.06	6.5	0.33	0.62	1.04	88	215
Latin America, Andean	4.51	5.6	0.25	0.59	1.29	136	416
Latin America, Central	19.54	6.1	1.19	2.79	6.37	134	435
Latin America, Southern	8.74	7.0	0.61	1.08	1.83	77	200
Latin America, Tropical	19.23	5.5	1.05	2.58	5.54	146	428
AFRICA	71.07	2.6	1.86	3.92	8.74	111	370
North Africa/Middle East	31.11	3.7	1.15	2.59	6.19	125	438
Sub-Saharan Africa, Central	3.93	1.8	0.07	0.12	0.24	71	243
Sub-Saharan Africa, East	16.03	2.3	0.36	0.69	1.38	92	283
Sub-Saharan Africa, Southen	4.66	2.1	0.10	0.17	0.20	70	100
Sub-Saharan Africa, West	15.33	1.2	0.18	0.35	0.72	94	300
WORLD	758.54	4.7	35.56	65.69	115.38	85	225

There are significant differences not only in total numbers and the prevalence rates, but also in the proportional increases through time. Compare, for example, the proportionate increase of people with dementia in Europe between 2010 and 2050 (87%) with that of Africa (370%). This suggests that the experience and challenges of dementia will be very different in different places around the world.

However, it is hard to make broad generalizations about the likely future prevalence of dementia in countries which are still in a process of modernization and social change. On the one hand, in light of the expected ageing pattern in developing countries, it can be reasonably projected that the overall prevalence of dementia will increase significantly in coming years. On the other hand, the demographic picture seems more complicated, as some regions (for example, India and sub-Saharan Africa) experience lower prevalence rates. Moreover, as developing countries experience modernization processes they may also experience an increased incidence of vascular disease which will add to the burden of dementia. Finally, more research will be needed to examine the specific influences of local and traditional health-related practices (for example, using herbal medicines) to prevent or slow down dementia progression in different societies around the world (Kalaria et al, 2008).

CONCLUSION

Existing data and new and updated estimates regarding existing and future estimates of dementia prevalence clearly indicate that dementia is already a very large public health problem. It is also clear that the problem is going to increase markedly in the coming decades. For example, by 2040, an estimated 80 million persons worldwide will have dementia (Ferri et al, 2005). Finally, these new estimates and surveys provide important information about specific sub-groups within the population whose dementia prevalence is higher, for example, people with lower education, residents of specific regions and older persons living in institutional settings.

However, although in recent years there has been an impressive growth of literature about the demographics of dementia around the world, there is still much work to be done. In some countries there is a wealth of data, whereas in others there is very little, or the existing data is very poor (for example, based on small, non-representative sampling). It is still hard to make meaningful comparisons between different countries and regions, since there is little consistency in study methodology and disease definition.

From a policy perspective, applying the existing knowledge of the socio-demographic predictors of dementia can be very important. For example, to the extent that personal socio-demographic variables are relevant to dementia, existing findings support improving the education of the general population as a means of lowering the risk of dementia. Similarly, improving health conditions which prevent or decrease the risk of stroke or cerebrovascular diseases may reduce the rate of vascular dementia.

REFERENCES

Aevarsson, O and Skoog, I (2000). 'A longitudinal population study of the mini-mental state examination in the very old: relation to dementia and education' 11 *Dementia and Geriatric Cognitive Disorders* 166–75.

Artero, S et al (2008) 'Risk profiles for mild cognitive impairment and progression to dementia are gender specific' 79 *Journal of Neurology, Neurosurgery & Psychiatry* 979–84.

Bachman, DL et al (1992) 'Prevalence of dementia and probable senile dementia of the Alzheimer type in the Framingham Study' 42 *Neurology* 115–19.

Bennet, DA (2007) Editorial comment on 'Prevalence of dementia in the United States: The Aging, Demographics, and Memory Study' by Plassman et al 29 *Neuroepidemiology* 133–35.

Canadian Study of Health and Aging Working Group (1994) 'Canadian Study of Health and Aging: study methods and prevalence of dementia' 150 *Canadian Medical Association Journal* 899–913.

Ferri, CP et al (2005) 'Global prevalence of dementia: a Delphi consensus study' 366 *Lancet* 2112–17.

Fillenbaum, GG et al (1998) 'The prevalence and 3-year incidence of dementia in older Black and White community residents' 51 *Journal of Clinical Epidemiology* 587–95.

Fratiglioni, L et al (2000) 'Incidence of dementia and major subtypes in Europe: a collaborative study of population-based cohorts. Neurologic Diseases in the Elderly Research Group' 54 *Neurology* S10–15.

Garrard, J et al (1993). 'Differences between nursing home admissions and residents' 48 *The Journal of Gerontology* S301–09.

German, PS et al (1992) 'The role of mental morbidity in the nursing home experience' 32 *The Gerontologist* 152–58.

Hebert, LE et al (2001) 'Is the risk of developing Alzheimer's disease greater for women than for men?' 153 *American Journal of Epidemiology* 132–36.

Husaini, BA et al (2003) 'Racial differences in the diagnosis of dementia and in its effects on the use and costs of health care services' 54(1) *Psychiatric Services* 54.

Kalaria, RN et al (2008) 'Alzheimer's disease and vascular dementia in developing countries: prevalence, management, and risk factor' 7 *The Lancet* 812–26.

Kiyohara, Y et al (1994) 'Changing patterns in the prevalence of dementia in a Japanese community: The Hisayama study' 40 *Gerontology* 29–35.

Langa, KM et al (2008) 'Trends in the prevalence and mortality of cognitive impairment in the United States: is there evidence of a compression of cognitive morbidity?' 4 *Alzheimer's & Dementia* 134–44.

Launer, LJ et al (1999) 'Rates and risk factors for dementia and Alzheimer's disease: results from EURODEM pooled analysis' 52(1) *Neurology* 78.

Lee, DY et al (2002). 'The prevalence of dementia in older people in an urban population of Korea: The Seoul Study' 50 *Journal of the American Geriatrics Society* 123–1239.

Lithgow, S, Jackson, GA and Browne, D (2012) 'Estimating the prevalence of dementia: cognitive screening in Glasgow nursing homes' 27 *International Journal of Geriatric Psychiatry* 785–91.

Magaziner, J et al (2000) 'The prevalence of dementia in a Statewide sample of new nursing homes admissions age 65 and older: diagnosis by expert panel' 40 *The Gerontologist* 663–72.

Matthews, FE and Dening, T (2002) 'Prevalence of dementia in institutional care' 360 *Lancet* 225–26.

Miles, TP et al (2001) 'Dementia and race: are there differences between African Americans and Caucasians? 49 *Journal of the American Geriatric Society* 477–84.

Mingxian, G et al (2012) 'Prevalence of dementia and mild cognitive impairment in the elderly living in nursing and veteran care homes in Xi' an, China' 312 *Journal of the Neurological Sciences* 39–44.

Mura, T, Dartigues, JF and Berr, C (2010) 'How many dementia cases in France and Europe? Alternative projections and scenarios 2010–2050' 17 *European Journal of Neurology* 252–59.

Ott, A et al (1995) 'Prevalence of Alzheimer's disease and vascular dementia: association with education. The Rotterdam study' 310 *British Medical Journal* 970–73.

Paykel, ES et al (1994) 'Incidence of dementia in a population older than 75 years in the United Kingdom' 51 *Archives of General Psychiatry* 325–32.

Perkins, P et al (1997) 'Incidence and prevalence of dementia in a multiethnic cohort of municipal retirees' 49 *Neurology* 44–50.

Plassman, BL et al (2007) 'Prevalence of dementia in the United States: The Aging, Demographics, and Memory Study' 29 *Neuroepidemiology* 125–32.

Rovner, BW et al (1990) 'The prevalence and management of dementia and other psychiatric disorders in nursing homes' 2 *International Psychogeriatrics* 13–24.

Ruitenberg, A et al (2001) 'Incidence of dementia: does gender make a difference?' 22(4) *Neurobiology of Aging* 575–80.

Tang, MX et al (2001) 'Incidence of AD in African-Americans, Caribbean Hispanics, and Caucasians in northern Manhattan' 56 *Neurology* 49–56.

World Alzheimer Report 2009: The Global Prevalence of Dementia. London: Alzheimer's Disease International.

3

The Genetics of Dementia

SOPHIE BEHRMAN, KLAUS P EBMEIER AND CHARLOTTE L ALLAN

INTRODUCTION

THE IDEA OF traits or characteristics of an organism being passed on from one generation to another is commonly attributed to Gregor Mendel in the mid 1800s, gaining him the title 'father of modern genetics'. It was another one hundred years before the structure of DNA (deoxyribonucleic acid) was discovered, and this started the much anticipated genetics revolution. The intricacies of recent genetic research and theories are rapidly expanding, and are beyond the scope of this book, but the basics of genetic theory and its relevance to dementia are discussed in this chapter.

Traits passed on from generation to generation include a plethora of attributes, such as susceptibility to diseases; this *genotype* is coded within *genes*. Traits the individual actually exhibits are termed *phenotype*. Individuals inherit genes from both parents, and these parallel genes are termed *alleles*. Alleles may be *dominant* or *recessive*, meaning that if an individual inherits one of each, the dominant allele will win out over the recessive form, and the dominant phenotype will be expressed. For example, red hair is coded for by a recessive gene, therefore a person will only inherit red hair if both parents pass a red hair allele to their offspring. If one parent passes a 'brown hair' allele (for example), the brown hair allele, being dominant, will dominate, and the offspring will have brown hair. Most traits and diseases, however, involve several genes, which interact with the environment, so inheritance is rarely so straightforward.

A gene is a length of DNA, typically coding for one protein. Millions of genes are packaged into one *chromosome*. Humans have 23 pairs of chromosomes, making a total of 46 (ie, 23 from each parent: 22 non-sex-chromosomes or autosomes, and one X or Y chromosome each, which determines gender). Each chromosome contains millions of genes as well as a great deal of non-coding DNA. Some DNA is structural, holding the chromosome in shape, some affects how the genes are expressed and some does not (currently) appear to have a use. Genes work by coding for proteins, which form the structure of organisms. Within each gene, a sequence of three *nucleotides* codes for one amino acid (the building blocks of protein). Nucleotides are therefore a core component of DNA, and there are four types: adenine (A), guanine (G), cytosine (C) and thymine (T). The nucleotide sequence is read in groups of three, termed a codon. The chain of nucleotides is copied (transcribed) into a mirror chain of nucleotides, termed *messenger-RNA* or mRNA. This contains copied sequences of nucleotides, termed *exons*, that code for amino acids, and sequences of nucleotides, termed *introns*, which do not code for amino acids. Introns need to be spliced out before the mRNA can be translated into a chain of amino acids that is then folded into a protein. A few specific codons mark the start and end of the exon.

Some of the genetic variation seen within a species is the result of the substitution of a single nucleotide, termed a *single nucleotide polymorphism* (SNP). If this change is in a coding region of DNA, this may code for a different amino acid and may change the protein's structure and function (termed a *missense mutation*) or it may trigger a premature stop signal, leading to arrested protein translation (*nonsense mutation*). Many of these SNPs will however be in non-coding regions, resulting in no biological effects. Genome wide association studies, which compare the DNA of patients with the DNA of healthy controls, look for differences in SNPs. These can identify candidate genes, which may increase the risk of an individual developing a disease.

The DNA nucleotide sequence may be slightly altered, or mutate, as it is passed from one generation to the next due to copying errors in the production of germ (egg and sperm) cells. The chemical structure of DNA (rather than the code itself) can also be modified at any time by certain environmental factors, leading to changes in gene expression, referred to as *epigenetic* changes. Epigenetic changes can be passed on to offspring, but can also be subject to further modification. The interaction between genes and environment is a complex field, and we are still a long way from being able to predict prognosis for patients based solely on their genetic information.

ALZHEIMER'S DISEASE

Alzheimer's disease is thought to be the most common form of dementia in the elderly (Bettens et al, 2013) but the exact aetiology of the disease is not known. Brain scans show loss of brain cells, or atrophy, particularly around the hippocampus, which is thought to be responsible for converting short-term memory to long-term memory. Post-mortem studies show abnormal protein plaques made from beta-amyloid protein accumulating between cells; these are thought to contribute to cell death. Beta-amyloid is a by-product formed from the breaking up of amyloid precursor protein (APP) by enzymes, in particular β-secretase and γ-secretase. There are different forms of β-amyloid, including β-amyloid 40 (the most common) and β-amyloid 42 (more prone to accumulating in plaques).

Cells contain microtubules, which support the structure of the cell and provide lines of internal transport. Microtubules are usually supported by a phosphorylated (ie, chemically modified) form of the tau protein. In brain cells affected by Alzheimer's disease the tau protein is phosphorylated in excess, and therefore microtubules stick together leading to neurofibrillary tangles which lead to cell death. Plaques and tangles are not specific to Alzheimer's disease and are seen in other forms of dementia and with normal ageing. However, in Alzheimer's disease there tends to be a greater concentration of the plaques and tangles, particularly in the areas of the brain associated with memory.

Most cases of Alzheimer's disease are sporadic, meaning there is no clear pattern of inheritance. There are, however, some rare early forms of the disease, which tend to present before the age of 65, with an autosomal dominant inheritance pattern. The gene coding for amyloid precursor protein, also called APP, can be disrupted in a number of ways, but most commonly there is a missense mutation in or near the exons coding for β-amyloid, which shows a dominant inheritance pattern. Other mutations in APP include duplications of the gene, small deletions and other missense mutations, which result in altered β-amyloid production or an increase in the ratio of β-amyloid 42 to β-amyloid 40 (Bettens et al, 2013). These mutations lead to early-onset and highly heritable forms of Alzheimer's disease. People with Down's syndrome tend to develop an early-onset dementia of Alzheimer's type. This may be explained by the genetics of Down's syndrome, where people receive an extra chromosome number 21 (ie, they have three copies rather than the usual two). The gene for APP is located on chromosome 21, so it is likely that having an extra copy of this gene leads to increased production and therefore accumulation of β-amyloid.

The genes PSEN1 (Presenilin-1) and PSEN2 (Presenilin-2), located respectively on chromosomes 14 and 2, are also implicated in very rare cases of early-onset, autosomal dominant forms of Alzheimer's disease. These presenilin genes code for γ-secretase, one of the enzymes that breaks down APP to make β-amyloid. Missense mutations and splicing errors in these genes lead to an increase in the ratio of β-amyloid 42 to 40 (Bettens et al, 2013).

Although Alzheimer's disease shows clear links between inheritance pattern, genotype and phenotype, autosomal dominant inheritance accounts for only 13% of early-onset Alzheimer's disease, or less than 0.01% of all Alzheimer's disease (McGuffin et al, 2004). The more common form of Alzheimer's disease tends to present in the elderly and does not have such a strong genetic link. The most important risk gene identified is the gene coding for Apolipoprotein E (APOE), which is a gene on chromosome 19 with a number of different forms or alleles: APOEε2, APOEε3 and APOEε4. People with one copy of APOEε4 have three times the risk, and those with two copies (ie, one from each parent) have fifteen times the risk of developing Alzheimer's disease compared with people with two copies of APOEε3 (the most common allele) (Bettens et al, 2013). Apolipoprotein E is a protein with roles in tissue repair and metabolism of lipids; it is not clear how the different alleles confer different levels of risk, but APOE has been shown to have a role both in the deposition of beta-amyloid and phosphorylation of tau (Bettens et al, 2013).

Genome wide association studies have given rise to a number of other genes associated with increased risk of developing Alzheimer's disease. One such gene, CLU, located on chromosome 8 and coding for clusterin or apolipoprotein J, is involved in tissue repair. CLU mRNA is found at higher concentration in areas of the brain affected by Alzheimer's disease, when compared with brains of normal controls (Guerreiro et al, 2010). A polymorphism in an intron in this gene is more common in Alzheimer's disease than normal controls, but it is important to note that the risk conferred from this will be very slight compared with the other genes discussed above. Other genes associated with slight increased risk have been identified by genome wide association studies (see Table 1) and further work is required to see if subgroups of patients with a similar genetic pattern share a similar phenotype, and whether these genes shed any light on the pathophysiology of Alzheimer's disease. If subgroups within Alzheimer's disease can be identified it may be possible to develop treatments specific to these.

Table 1: Summary of inheritance patterns and relevant genes

	Inheritance	Relevant genes
Alzheimer's disease Early onset	Some autosomal dominant cases Rarer cases of autosomal recessive	APP, chromosome 21 PSEN1, chromosome 14 PSEN2, chromosome 2
Alzheimer's disease Late onset	Most cases sporadic Some risk genes identified	APOE, chromosome 19 CLU, chromosome 8 CR1, chromosome 1 PICALM, chromosome 11
Vascular dementia	Most cases sporadic	APP, chromosome 21 Cystatin C, chromosome 21 Notch 3, chromosome 19
Fronto-temporal dementia	50% have positive family history	C9orf72, chromosome 9 GRN, chromosome 17 MAPT, chromosome 17
Dementia with Lewy bodies	Most cases sporadic Not strongly inherited	APOE, chromosome 19 APP, chromosome 21 GBA, chromosome 1 LRRK2, chromosome 12 PARK1, chromosome 4 PSEN1, chromosome 14 PSEN2, chromosome 2 SNCA, chromosome 4
Huntington's disease	Autosomal dominant with a tricnucleotide repeat expansion	HTT, chromosome 4
Prion disease	Most cases sporadic Some familial, autosomal dominant	PRNP, chromosome 20

In summary, some early-onset Alzheimer's disease has an autosomal dominant inheritance pattern, with mutations in the APP, PSEN1 and PSEN2 genes. Identification of these mutations has been important in increasing understanding of the pathophysiology of the disease. In late-onset disease, multiple genes each of small effect may have a role in the aetiology of Alzheimer's disease. The most important finding has been the discovery of the APOE4 allele, which confers a significant increase in the risk of developing Alzheimer's disease, but does not determine who will develop the condition.

VASCULAR DEMENTIA

Vascular dementia is a broad term covering cognitive impairment following any kind of insult that compromises the blood supply to the brain. At its most dramatic, a large cerebrovascular event (stroke) caused by either a blood clot (infarct) or bleeding (haemorrhage) in the brain will cause widespread cell death, which may result in cognitive impairment. Some patients suffer transient ischaemic attacks (TIAs), which are mini-strokes; in these the patient will make a full physical recovery, but may have some residual cognitive impairment. Some TIAs are so small there will be no obvious symptoms but sufferers may notice a gradual—and sometimes step-wise—deterioration in their cognitive function. It is common for small and large lesions to coexist and a mixed dementia with features of Alzheimer's and vascular disease is relatively common.

Most vascular dementia occurs in parallel with cardiovascular disease, together with heart attacks, strokes and some circulation problems. The risk factors for developing cardiovascular disease are largely environmental (ie, smoking, diet, exercise). There is some evidence that genetic predisposition is important in the epidemiology of cerebrovascular disease, although so far very few specific genes have been identified (Markus, 2010). Putative genetic markers of risk are being identified, particularly in genes linked to high blood pressure, diabetes and cholesterol (Day and Wilson, 2001).

Some rare and highly heritable forms of vascular dementia have recently been discovered. In general, the more genetic forms of vascular dementia tend to present at younger ages and are more aggressive than subtypes with a more environmental aetiology. Cerebral Autosomal Dominant Arteriopathy with Subcortical Infarcts and Leucoencephalopathy (CADASIL) is a form of dementia due to dominant transmission of an aberrant form of the Notch3 gene on chromosome 19, which is expressed as a receptor on blood vessel walls (Iemolo et al, 2009). The exact mechanism is not clear, but people with CADASIL present with headaches, strokes and often an early-onset dementia. They are found to have numerous infarctions, particularly in the white matter of the brain, unrelated to the typical vascular risk factors described above.

Hereditary Cerebral Haemorrhage with Amyloidosis-Dutch Type (HCHWA-D) Dementia has been linked to an error in the gene for amyloid precursor protein. Abnormal deposition of amyloid in the small blood vessels in the brain results in recurrent haemorrhages (small bleeds) in the brain, which can lead to strokes and dementia (Iemolo et al, 2009). A similar disorder is found in the Icelandic population (Hereditary Cerebral Haemorrhage with Amyloidosis-Icelandic Type (HCHWA-I) with onset in early adulthood, which is caused by a missense mutation in the gene for cystatin C on chromosome 21. Cystatin C is found in blood vessel walls; the mutant form becomes unstable at high temperatures and aggregates, which can lead to haemorrhages. Prompt treatment of febrile illness in carriers of the mutant gene may improve their prognosis (McGuffin et al, 2004).

The APOE alleles discussed above relating to Alzheimer's disease are also thought to contribute to the risk of developing vascular dementia, although the absolute risk is difficult to assess due to the prevalence of mixed dementia and the clinical uncertainty of the aetiology of a patient's dementia until histopathological examination at post-mortem.

In summary, vascular dementia arises as a result of cardiovascular disease. Environmental factors are important determinants of cardiovascular disease, and therefore of vascular dementia, although genes linked to high blood pressure, diabetes and cholesterol may be important. There are a few, rare cases of vascular dementia which have an autosomal pattern of inheritance.

FRONTO-TEMPORAL DEMENTIA

Fronto-temporal dementia covers a range of disease processes and clinical presentations. Fronto-temporal refers to the lobes of the brain (frontal and temporal) that are mainly affected by this form of dementia. Patients with damage to the frontal lobes are likely to have a behavioural variant, with symptoms such as a lack of social awareness, increasing impulsivity and rigid patterns of thinking. Patients with more damage in the temporal lobes will have more language problems. This may manifest either as semantic dementia where the meaning of words is lost, or as non-fluent aphasia where understanding of meaning may be preserved but the ability to produce words and construct sentences is impaired. A form of fronto-temporal dementia is seen in 10% of patients with motor neurone disease, and a small proportion of patients who present with fronto-temporal dementia go on to develop symptoms consistent with motor neurone disease (Graham and Hodges, 2008).

Histopathological features of fronto-temporal dementia include abnormal protein inclusions in the cells' nuclei and cytoplasm that disrupt function and lead to cell death. These are called Pick's bodies and contain the protein ubiquitin and hyperphosphorylated tau. Some inclusions do not contain tau and more recently have been shown to be heterogeneous, containing a DNA binding protein (TDP-43) or other proteins, which are still yet to be characterised (Sieben et al, 2012). Correlations between inclusion body type and subtype of fronto-temporal dementia have been found, but no causal links have been identified.

Fronto-temporal dementia tends to present earlier than the more common forms of dementia and is more heritable with 50% of patients having a family history of fronto-temporal dementia, of which 10–20% show an autosomal inheritance pattern (Paulson and Igo, 2011). The first gene identified as causing fronto-temporal dementia was the tau gene, MAPT, on chromosome 17. A number of different dominantly inherited MAPT mutations have been observed. Mutations cause the tau protein to accumulate and form connections within the neurons, leading to cell death (Paulson and Igo, 2011). The gene for progranulin, GRN, is located near the MAPT gene on chromosome 17 and has also been linked to fronto-temporal dementia, as nonsense mutations and full gene deletions leads to accumulation of TDP-43 inclusions. Progranulin is converted into granulin which is involved in nurturing neurones and inflammatory pathways, so it is not clear why a lack of one of these alleles should cause TDP-43 accumulation (Paulson and Igo, 2011).

Linkage studies have also implicated the gene C9orf72, on chromosome 9, which encodes a protein of unknown function. The non-coding region of this gene contains a sequence of six nucleotides which is repeated between three and twenty-five times in healthy controls, but over sixty times in some patients with fronto-temporal dementia: this results in the gene not being expressed, and the build up of the faulty

RNA transcribed from the DNA, which may be toxic to the cell (Sieben et al, 2012). This nucleotide sequence expansion is seen in familial and sporadic cases of fronto-temporal dementia (Sieben et al, 2012).

In summary, fronto-temporal dementia is a heritable condition, and up to 20% of cases have an autosomal dominant pattern of inheritance. Mutations on chromosome 17 are important, and there may be overlap in genetic risk factors for motor neurone disease.

DEMENTIA WITH LEWY BODIES

Dementia with Lewy bodies (DLB) presents with progressive cognitive decline, particularly in attention and visuospatial functions. On a day-to-day basis there is usually significant fluctuation in cognitive symptoms. Common features include detailed visual hallucinations and parkinsonism (gait disorder, bradykinesia and limb rigidity). Other features include sleep disorder, falls and extreme sensitivity to neuroleptic medication (for example, anti-psychotic medication).

The anatomical hallmark of the disease is the presence of Lewy bodies, which are found throughout the brain. Lewy bodies are aggregates of protein found inside neurones. They are composed of abnormally phosphorylated, neurofilament proteins, predominantly of α-synuclein—a small soluble protein—although ubiquitin is also present (McKeith, 2002). Lewy bodies are not unique to DLB, and are also found in patients with Parkinson's disease, where they are primarily located in the brain stem, particularly the substantia nigra, and in Parkinson's disease dementia. Patients with DLB show degeneration in substantia nigra, which is more severe than that found in healthy controls, but not as marked as changes in Parkinson's disease. Other pathological features include pathology similar to Alzheimer's dementia, with degeneration of cholinergic neurones, amyloid plaques and fibrillary tangles.

DLB is not strongly associated with genetic factors (Paulson and Igo, 2011), but people with DLB commonly have a family history of dementia (Woodruff et al, 2006), and symptoms are more severe in those with at least two family members with DLB (Nervi et al, 2008). These, and other similar studies, have strengthened the hypothesis that genetic factors are relevant to DLB (Meeus et al, 2012). Given that there is considerable overlap in pathology with Parkinson's disease and Parkinson's disease dementia, genetic approaches to DLB have focused on shared genetic risk factors with Parkinson's disease and Parkinson's disease dementia.

The most promising candidate gene in DLB is the gene coding for α-synuclein, the core component of Lewy bodies. Mutations of the α-synuclein gene on chromosome 4 (SNCA and PARK1), including multiplication, polymorphisms and missense mutations, are relatively common variants, which have been implicated in the aetiology of a spectrum of diseases associated with Lewy body formation, including DLB (Meeus et al, 2012; Nalls et al, 2011). These genetic variations either increase expression of α-synuclein, or reduce its degradation, in both cases potentially increasing the number of Lewy bodies.

Similar to Alzheimer's disease, the ε4 allele of the APOE gene is a risk factor for DLB, increasing the risk of the disorder by a factor of three (Kobayashi et al, 2011). The biological mechanism for this may be due to increased β-amyloid deposition, which is found in people with DLB. A few studies, albeit with small numbers of patients, have demonstrated that mutations in the three genes that lead to early-onset Alzheimer's disease (APP, PSEN1 and PSEN2) cause widespread Lewy body pathology in some patients (Meeus et al, 2012). There may be a synergistic mechanism between amyloid and Lewy body pathologies, which act as an additional risk factor for DLB.

Leucine-rich repeat kinase 2 (LRRK2) and glucocerebrosidase mutations have also been implicated (Bonifati, 2008; Lashuel et al, 2013). Mutations in the LRRK2 gene (for example, PARK8) on chromosome 12 are predominantly seen in Parkinson's disease and may be relevant in the development of Lewy body pathology and the phenotype of DLB (Bonifati, 2008). Mutations in the glucocerebrosidae (GBA) gene on chromosome 1 are low frequency variants that have an intermediate effect, causing lysosomal protein degradation and altered processing of α-synuclein. GBA mutations can lead to α-synuclein accumulation in a dose and time dependent manner (Cullen et al, 2011), and may lead to more extensive cortical Lewy bodies (Clark et al, 2009). Whilst these mutations increase susceptibility to DLB, the frequency of mutation carriers with DLB is low, and therefore the population attributable risk is very small (3%) (Mata et al, 2008).

In summary, DLB is not a strongly inherited disease, and occurs sporadically in most cases. The high degree of clinical and neuropathological heterogeneity in DLB makes it unlikely that a major genetic determinant of DLB will be discovered soon (Tsuang et al, 2002). Some genes have been identified as relevant to its pathology; each has a small effect and it is clear that there is significant overlap with genetic determinants of Parkinson's disease, and Parkinson's disease dementia.

HUNTINGTON'S DISEASE

Huntington's disease is a rare dementia with an autosomal dominant pattern of inheritance due to an abnormal single gene. Clinically, Huntington's disease presents with a triad of progressive psychiatric features, motor disturbance and cognitive impairment. The age at onset is typically in the fourth or fifth decades, thus often after having children. Since it is a dominant gene, and fully penetrant (ie, if the gene is present it will lead to the Huntington's disease phenotype), 50% of children will inherit it. A diagnosis of Huntington's disease may therefore present a range of complex ethical and legal difficulties for the individual and their wider family. It should also be noted that sporadic or new mutations do occur, and so it is possible for it to present with no family history (Paulson and Igo, 2011).

The affected gene is the Huntington gene, HTT, located on chromosome 4 (Bucan et al, 1990) which codes for the Huntington protein. In Huntington's disease there is an abnormality in the first exon of the gene, with an abnormal tricnucleotide repeat expansion (CAG), coding for glutamine. This means that the Huntington protein produced by the gene is abnormal, and has an expanded poly-glutamine section and altered protein structure. This protein aggregates within neuronal nuclei forming intra-nuclear inclusion bodies, and can also be found in other parts of the cell. The abnormal Huntington protein alters cellular metabolism, has toxic effects on the cell and can be cleaved to produce small, toxic protein fragments (Ross and Tabrizi, 2011). These processes contribute to neuronal dysfunction and cell death.

In unaffected individuals the HTT gene contains fewer than 30 CAG repeats; in those with Huntington's disease there are over 35 repeats. The greater the number of repeats, the more severe is the clinical phenotype (Ross and Tabrizi, 2011). People with repeat expansions in the intermediate zone (27–39 CAG repeats) may only develop symptoms much later in life, and the disease may only be expressed if the individual lives a long life. Due to the phenomenon of anticipation, successive generations inheriting the affected gene tend to have a higher number of CAG repeats, and therefore present with an earlier age at onset and a more severe form of the disease. Although the length of the CAG repeat is associated with an earlier age at onset, it cannot be used to accurately predict when this will be. This suggests that other genetic (or environmental) factors may influence the clinical phenotype. For example, the genes HAP1, GRIK2 and TCERG1 produce proteins which interact with Huntington and may affect disease progression (Ross and Tabrizi, 2011; Tome et al, 2013).

In summary, Huntington's disease is a single gene disorder that is highly heritable. It is caused by a repeat expansion on the HTT gene, and the larger this repeat section, the more severe the disease.

PRION DISEASE

The prion diseases are a group of disorders characterised by rapidly progressive dementia associated with myoclonic jerks (involuntary muscle twitching). These clinical changes are accompanied by widespread spongiform change in the cortex with neuronal loss and gliosis. The majority of cases occur spontaneously, although the disease can be inherited or acquired. For this reason, prion disorders were previously called Transmissible Spongiform Encephalopathies (TSE).

Prion protein exists in two forms. Cellular prion protein (PrP^{C}) is produced normally in cells and is not pathogenic. Its function remains unclear, but it may influence other cellular processes, particularly relating to cell membranes or ion channels. Abnormal prion protein (PrP^{SC}) has a different structure, cannot be degraded by normal cellular processes and therefore accumulates in the brain, leading to neurodegeneration. It is also an infectious agent that can be transmitted between individuals and between species.

The gene coding for prion protein (PRNP) is located on chromosome 20. Genetic mutations in this gene (either spontaneous or inherited) can lead to altered prion protein production, so that cells produce PrP^{SC} rather than PrP^{C}. Once one unit of PrP^{SC} is produced, this abnormal protein continues to be propagated by protein–protein interaction, further exacerbating the adverse effects (Brown and Mastrianni, 2010).

The majority of cases of prion disease are sporadic, with no PRNP mutation (for example, sporadic Creutzfeldt-Jakob disease). Sporadic cases can however be caused by a point mutation at codon 129 in the PRNP gene, which changes the amino acid coded from valine to methionine. The nature of the polymorphism, can be used to classify different subtypes of sporadic prion disease (Puoti et al, 2012;

Sikorska et al, 2012). Some patients show different PrP^{SC} variants in different brain regions leading to mixed types of disease.

Familial patterns of inheritance are found in 10–15% of cases. There are three main types of familial disease: familial Creutzfeldt-Jakob disease (fCJD), Gerstmann-Straussler-Scheinker (GSS) syndrome and familial fatal insomnia (FFI). These are associated with an autosomal dominant mutation in PRNP, which is highly penetrant (Brown and Mastrianni, 2010). A number of genetic changes in PRNP can lead to altered protein production, including single base pair changes, insertion of base pair repeat segments and early stop codons (Brown and Mastrianni, 2010; Mead et al, 2006). Similar to sporadic disease, polymorphisms at codon 129 of PRNP are important in determining the risk and phenotype of familial prion diseases.

Prion protein disease can be acquired through the oral route of infection. In the United Kingdom, despite significant population exposure to contaminated meat, the number of acquired cases of prion disease in the form of variant CJD remains small (225 cases worldwide) (Saba and Booth, 2013). Exposure to the contaminant itself is not sufficient to develop the disease, and it seems likely that there is a range of individual and environmental factors which determine disease onset. Polymorphisms at codon 129 on the PRNP gene have an important influence on the susceptibility for variant CJD, and other PRNP mutations seem likely to confer resistance or increase susceptibility (Saba and Booth, 2013).

In summary, most prion disorders occur spontaneously and are not associated with genetic polymorphisms. However, some sporadic prion diseases are caused by point mutations in the prion protein gene, PRNP. Familial prion disease accounts for 10–15% of cases and these show autosomal dominant patterns of inheritance, again related to point mutations in the PRNP gene. Finally, abnormal prion protein, PrP^{SC} is an infectious agent which is transmissible between humans and between species.

CONCLUSION

Genetic factors have an important, causal role in the aetiology of dementia in a minority of cases. Most notably, early-onset Alzheimer's disease and Huntington's disease are both caused by genes inherited in an autosomal dominant manner. Genes for these disorders determine the clinical phenotype, and identification of at-risk individuals raises complex legal and ethical issues. The APOE4 allele, although not deterministic for dementia, is a common gene, which is associated with an increased risk and reduced age at onset. In population terms it has a significant effect because of the large number of people who carry the allele. In the majority of cases, there are a relatively large number of genetic variants contributing to a small increase in risk of dementia. Identifying these genes of small effect has, however, been important in terms of understanding the biological and molecular mechanisms of disease, and may inform the development of new treatment strategies.

REFERENCES

Bettens, K, Sleegers, K and Van Broeckhoven, C (2013) 'Genetic insights in Alzheimer's disease' 12(1) *Lancet Neurology* 92–104. doi: 10.1016/s1474-4422(12)70259-4.

Bonifati, V (2008) 'Recent advances in the genetics of dementia with lewy bodies' 8(3) *Current Neurology and Neuroscience Reports* 187–89.

Brown, K and Mastrianni, JA (2010) 'The prion diseases' 23(4) *Journal of Geriatric Psychiatry and Neurology* 277–98. doi: 10.1177/0891988710383576.

Bucan, M et al (1990) 'Physical maps of 4p16.3, the area expected to contain the Huntington disease mutation' 6(1) *Genomics* 1–15.

Clark, LN et al (2009) 'Association of glucocerebrosidase mutations with dementia with lewy bodies' 66(5) *Archives of Neurology* 578–83. doi: 10.1001/archneurol.2009.54.

Cullen, V et al (2011) 'Acid beta-glucosidase mutants linked to Gaucher disease, Parkinson disease, and Lewy body dementia alter alpha-synuclein processing' 69(6) *Annals of Neurology* 940–53. doi: 10.1002/ana.22400.

Day, IN and Wilson, DI (2001) 'Science, medicine, and the future: Genetics and cardiovascular risk' 323(7326) *British Medical Journal* 1409–12.

Graham, A and Hodges, JR (2008) 'Frontotemporal dementia' 7(1) *Psychiatry* 24–28. doi: dx.doi.org/10.1016/j.mppsy.2007.11.008.

Guerreiro, RJ et al (2010) 'Genetic variability in CLU and its association with Alzheimer's disease' 5(3) *PLoS One* e9510. doi: 10.1371/journal.pone.0009510.

Iemolo, F et al (2009) 'Pathophysiology of vascular dementia' 6 *Immunity & Ageing* 13. doi: 10.1186/1742-4933-6-13.

Kobayashi, S et al (2011) 'Apolipoprotein E4 frequencies in a Japanese population with Alzheimer's disease and dementia with Lewy bodies' 6(4) *PLoS One* e18569. doi: 10.1371/journal.pone.0018569.

Lashuel, HA et al (2013) 'The many faces of alpha-synuclein: from structure and toxicity to therapeutic target' 14(1) *Nature Reviews Neuroscience* 38–48. doi: 10.1038/nrn3406.

Markus, HS (2010) 'Unravelling the genetics of ischaemic stroke' 7(3) *PLoS Medicine* e1000225. doi: 10.1371/journal.pmed.1000225.

Mata, IF et al (2008) 'Glucocerebrosidase gene mutations: a risk factor for Lewy body disorders' 65(3) *Archives of Neurology* 379–82. doi: 10.1001/archneurol.2007.68.

McGuffin, P, Owen, M and Gottesman, I (2004) *Psychiatric Genetics and Genomics* (Oxford, Oxford University Press).

McKeith, IG (2002) 'Dementia with Lewy bodies' 180 *British Journal of Psychiatry* 144–47.

Mead, S et al (2006) 'Inherited prion disease with six octapeptide repeat insertional mutation – molecular analysis of phenotypic heterogeneity' 129(9) *Brain* 2297–317. doi: 10.1093/brain/awl226.

Meeus, B, Theuns, J and Van Broeckhoven, C (2012) 'The genetics of dementia with Lewy bodies: what are we missing?' 69(9) *Archives of Neurology* 1113–18. doi: 10.1001/archneurol.2011.3678.

Nalls, MA et al (2011) 'Imputation of sequence variants for identification of genetic risks for Parkinson's disease: a meta-analysis of genome-wide association studies' 377(9766) *Lancet* 641–49. doi: 10.1016/s0140-6736(10)62345-8.

Nervi, A et al (2008) 'Comparison of clinical manifestations in Alzheimer disease and dementia with Lewy bodies' 65(12) *Archives of Neurology* 1634–39. doi: 10.1001/archneur.65.12.1634.

Paulson, HL and Igo, I (2011) 'Genetics of dementia' 31(5) *Seminars in Neurology* 449–60. doi: 10.1055/s-0031-1299784.

Puoti, G et al (2012) 'Sporadic human prion diseases: molecular insights and diagnosis' 11(7) *Lancet Neurology* 618–28. doi: 10.1016/s1474-4422(12)70063-7.

Ross, CA and Tabrizi, SJ (2011) 'Huntington's disease: from molecular pathogenesis to clinical treatment' 10(1) *Lancet Neurology* 83–98. doi: 10.1016/s1474-4422(10)70245-3.

Saba, R and Booth, SA (2013) 'The genetics of susceptibility to variant Creutzfeldt-Jakob disease' 16(1–2) *Public Health Genomics* 17–24. doi: 10.1159/000345203.

Sieben, A et al (2012) 'The genetics and neuropathology of frontotemporal lobar degeneration' 124(3) *Acta Neuropathologica* 353–72. doi: 10.1007/s00401-012-1029-x.

Sikorska, B et al (2012) 'Creutzfeldt-Jakob disease' 724 *Advances in Experimental Medicine & Biology* 76–90. doi: 10.1007/978-1-4614-0653-2_6.

Tome, S et al (2013) 'MSH3 polymorphisms and protein levels affect CAG repeat instability in Huntington's disease mice' 9(2) *PLoS Genetics* e1003280. doi: 10.1371/journal.pgen.1003280.

Tsuang, DW et al (2002) 'Familial dementia with lewy bodies: a clinical and neuropathological study of 2 families' 59(10) *Archives of Neurology* 1622–30.

Woodruff, BK et al (2006) 'Family history of dementia is a risk factor for Lewy body disease' 66(12) *Neurology* 1949–50. doi: 10.1212/01.wnl.0000219812.20616.b3.

GLOSSARY OF TERMS

Allele	An alternative form of the gene. On autosomes each gene has two alleles, one maternally inherited and one paternally inherited.
Anticipation	The tendency for disorders to become more severe and occur earlier in offspring.
Base pair	The building block of DNA. There are 4 bases: adenine (A), guanine (G), cytosine (C) and thymine (T). A always pairs with T, and C with G.
Chromosomes	Contain all the genetic information, and are composed of millions of genes. In humans there are 46 chromosomes (23 pairs). Each chromosome has a short arm (p) and a long arm (q).
Codon	A section of 3 base pairs which code for an amino acid.
Dominant	A dominant gene will always be expressed, regardless of the second allele.
DNA	Deoxyribonucleic acid. This is a double helix structure composed of base pairs.
Epigenetics	The study of differential expression of genes which may occur due to environmental or other factors, even when the genetic code (DNA) remains the same.
Exon	Section of DNA which codes for amino acids.
Gene	A section of DNA found on a chromosome containing hundreds or thousands of base pairs. Each gene codes for a protein.
Genotype	The genetic sequence of an individual.

Genome wide association studies (GWAS)	Compare the DNA of patients with the DNA of healthy controls, searching for differences in SNPs.
Intron	Section of DNA which does not code for amino acids, ie, non-coding.
Mutation	A change in the sequence of base pairs.
Nucleotide	Part of the DNA molecule which contains a phosphate molecule and a sugar molecule (which form the 'backbone' of DNA), and a base (either A, T, C or G).
Penetrance	A gene which is fully penetrant is always expressed in the first filial generation. One that is partially penetrant may, or may not be expressed.
Phenotype	An individual's observable, clinical characteristics.
Polymorphism	This is a point mutation where one base pair changes. This may change the amino acid that a codon produces, therefore changing the protein which is produced.
Protein	Multiple amino acids combine to form a larger structure called a protein.
Recessive	A recessive gene will only be expressed if both alleles are recessive.
Single nucleotide polymorphism	A single base substitution which may change the amino acid that a codon codes for, therefore changing the protein which is produced (missense mutation) or stopping full expression of the protein (nonsense mutation).

4

Can Dementia be Prevented?

AMOS D KORCZYN AND VERONIKA VAKHAPOVA

THE NUMBER OF demented people has increased dramatically in the last decades. Global prevalence data have been documented, and projection estimates suggest that the frequency will double between 1990 and 2020 (Fratiglioni et al, 1999; Sloane et al, 2002). However, the increase is unlikely to stop there. This increase in prevalence is not limited to developed parts of the world; economically disadvantaged populations show the same trend (Ferri et al, 2005; Prince et al, 2003). Even more remarkable is the relative increase—caused by the reduced birth rate in many developed and developing populations—which will be reflected by an even higher proportion of elderly individuals in the future. In spite of its non-infectious etiology, it is justifiable to think of the great number of cases as constituting an epidemic, or rather a pandemic. The effects on the affected individuals and their families are easily appreciated, since we see tragic examples all around us. The economic implications are likely to be extreme, not only to the affected individuals and their families but also to society, with alarming consequences (Leung et al, 2003; Fillit and Hill, 2005).

Most of the world's epidemics have been of infectious diseases. These came, and went away, leaving behind suffering and devastation. Dementia is not an infectious disease, and needs to be addressed differently. But we cannot afford to sit by and wait for it to disappear, because it will not; we have to fight it, and of course epidemics cannot be dealt with primarily by treating the affected.

The last epidemic fought with outstanding success was the poliomyelitis epidemic. In order to win that war, the first step was to identify the cause—the polio virus. The next step, achieved within a few years, was to develop methods of cultivating the virus. John F Enders, Thomas H Weller and Frederick C Robbins were awarded the Nobel prize in 1954 for this important discovery, which led to the development of immunization methods by Albert B Sabin and Jonas E Salk.

Another example is the AIDS epidemic. The discovery of the HIV virus led to extensive research into the biology of the virus and the development of drugs which can inhibit its proliferation. While the use of these drugs, individually and particularly as a 'cocktail' can suppress the virus, the only effective method of preventing the spread of AIDS is a preventative method, ie, exercising safe sex through the use of condoms and similar methods. It was epidemiology—not basic virological research—which proved crucial in containing the epidemic in those places where it has been contained.

To beat dementia we must use a similar strategy. First, the enemy must be evaluated. We have to define it and understand the nosology. Unlike polio, dementia is not a disease but rather a syndrome, and there are multiple etiologies—some infectious (like syphilis or HIV) and some traumatic. However, the majority are degenerative. Scholars frequently claim that the most common cause of dementia is Alzheimer's disease (AD), followed by vascular brain disease, vascular dementia (VaD). But things are not quite so simple (Korczyn et al, 2012).

In most cases, demented patients suffer from a combination of neurodegenerative and vascular lesions. Mixed dementia is probably the most common type of dementia (Korczyn, 2002a; Korczyn, 2002b: 7–9; Roman, 2005). The fact that most elderly demented individuals have several different lesions affecting their brains, some vascular and some neurodegenerative, has been demonstrated in several neuropathological studies (Kalaria, 2002; Neuropathology Group, 2001; Jellinger, 2006; Chui et al, 2006; Jellinger, 2002).

Even vascular dementia cannot be considered a single nosologic entity. There are many causes of vascular damage to the brain, mostly atherosclerotic, some genetic (for example, CADASIL), some thromboembolic, some hemorrhagic, etc (Korczyn, 2002a). The spectrum of ischemic changes in the brain is large, and includes large cortical strokes and white matter changes (leucoaraiosis). Each vascular cause of dementia may result from any of a number of pathogenic mechanisms. Many vascular mechanisms may similarly be in play even when a diagnosis of AD is made (Kivipelto et al, 2005; Magri et al, 2006; Roman, 2002).

It thus seems that from an epidemiologic point of view, an important way to curb the dementia epidemic is through strict attention to vascular risk factors (Kivipelto et al, 2005). In fact, several studies have confirmed that good control of hypertension can prevent dementia (both AD and vascular) and treatment with statins also may have the same effect (DeKosky, 2005; Sparks et al, 2005; Masse et al, 2005).

Obviously, even strict attention to these risk factors will not be able to prevent dementia altogether. The most important vascular risk factor is probably age, which still cannot be manipulated. And the data concerning the reduction of the incidence of dementia should better be interpreted as delay in the onset rather than prevention.

However, because the prevalence of dementia doubles every five years, delay in the onset of dementia by five years is equivalent to a reduction of the prevalence by half in any given age group.

Another important issue is the difference between primary and secondary prevention. Most epidemiologic studies suggest that the risk factors mentioned in Table 1 are relevant if they occur in middle age, not after the onset of dementia. This is also logical. The effects of hypertension in increasing the risk of dementia are not immediate, but rather slowly cumulative, over many years. Therefore, treatment of these vascular risk factors should be initiated when problems are observed for the first time, usually in mid life.

Reducing the blood pressure of an elderly person could in fact be more dangerous since it may be that the auto-regulation of the cerebrovascular tree is impaired, and thus hypotensive drugs may cause ischemic episodes (Miklossy, 2003). Similarly, it has been demonstrated that statin use is not beneficial to patients who are already suffering from dementia (Hoyer and Riederer, 2007).

Epidemiological studies have confirmed the old belief, *mens sana in corpora sano*: 'a healthy mind in a healthy body'. Physical well-being and activity are important

Table 1: Risk factors for dementia

— Age
— Female gender
— Head trauma
— Low education
— Smoking
— Diabetes mellitus
— Hypertension
— Apolipoprotein E status
— Coronary artery disease
— High dietary saturated fat and cholesterol
— Midlife cholesterol
— Hyperhomocysteinemia

and so is social interaction. Intellectual stimulation has also been found to delay the onset of dementia, and cognitive training using computer programmes has been shown to be effective, at least for some time (Peretz et al, 2011).

Older people frequently face isolation. Forced or voluntary retirement from work, loss of friends through death, disease or changed residence and transfer to a nursing home, are frequent causes. In addition, older people may be incapacitated and limited in their ability to communicate with others due to impaired mobility, poor vision or hearing. Reduced social interaction is among the common factors associated with cognitive decline. These can and should be addressed. Community clubs as well as transfer to suitable assisted living facilities are highly recommended.

Yet another important factor is cognitive stimulation. It has long been observed that people who are engaged in cognitively demanding activities are relatively protected from cognitive decline in old age. Such activities include, for example, playing bridge (which is additionally helpful because it demands social interaction), reading books, etc.

In the computer age, being able to communicate by email and posting messages are also important. Lately, several studies have demonstrated some benefit of computerized cognitive training. Obviously not all programmes are the same, and there is need to develop personalized programmes of cognitive training which will benefit individual subjects.

In conclusion, the dementia epidemic which we face needs to be addressed. We are unlikely to discover a cure—namely a method that will reverse brain ageing. The most promising method is through the prevention of cognitive decline. Lifestyle changes (Table 2) and drugs (Table 3) should be employed to delay the onset of dementia throughout the world. Social networking, physical activity and cognitive stimulation should also be encouraged.

Table 2: Lifestyle changes

— Smoking cessation
— Overweight reduction
— Physical activity
— Cognitive activity
— 'Healthy' diet
— Mild/moderate alcohol use
— Sleep apnoea

Table 3: Drugs which may prevent dementia

— Antihypertensive therapy
— Lipid lowering drugs
— NSAIDs
— Folic acid/vitamin B12
— Antioxidants

CONCLUSION

Alzheimer's disease (AD) is considered to be the most common dementing disorder. The understanding of this disorder has greatly advanced over the past few years, and new therapeutic options have been developed. Another disorder, vascular dementia (VaD), is a syndrome with multiple etiologies operating through a variety of different mechanisms resulting in brain ischemia or haemorrhages. AD and VaD pathologies frequently coexist in the same person, making mixed dementia the most common type of dementia. Risk factors for VaD consist primarily of common vascular risk factors. Interestingly, the same risk factors are known to apply also to AD.

Therefore, attention to risk factors, such as hypertension, hyperglycemia, hyperlipidemia and smoking could reduce or delay the incidence of dementia, both vascular and Alzheimer's disease.

Another important risk factor is social isolation. Social interaction and cognitive stimulation may reduce the risk of dementia.

REFERENCES

Chui, HC et al (2006) 'Cognitive impact of subcortical vascular and Alzheimer's disease pathology' 60 *Annals of Neurology* 677–87.

DeKosky, ST (2005) 'Statin therapy in the treatment of Alzheimer disease: what is the rationale?' 118 *American Journal of Medicine* (Supplement 12A) 48–53.

Ferri, CP et al (2005) Alzheimer's Disease International 'Global prevalence of dementia: a Delphi consensus study' 366 *Lancet* 2112–17.

Fillit, H and Hill, J (2005) 'Economics of dementia and pharmacoeconomics of dementia therapy' 3 *American Journal of GeriatricPharmacotherapy* 39–49.

Fratiglioni, L, De Ronchi, D and Aguero-Torres, H (1999) 'Worldwide prevalence and incidence of dementia' 5 *Drugs & Aging* 365–75.

Hoyer, S and Riederer, P (2007) 'Alzheimer disease – No target for statin treatment. A mini review' 32 *Neurochemical Research* 695–706.

Jellinger, KA (2002) 'Vascular-ischemic dementia: an update' 62 *Journal of Neural Transmission* (Suppl) 1–23.

——(2006) 'Clinicopathological analysis of dementia disorders in the elderly – an update' 9(3) *Journal of Alzheimer's Disease* (Suppl) 61–70.

Kalaria, RN (2002) 'Small vessel disease and Alzheimer's dementia: pathological considerations' 2 *Cerebrovascular Diseases* (Suppl) 48–52.

Kivipelto, M et al (2005) 'Obesity and vascular risk factors at midlife and the risk of dementia and Alzheimer disease' 62 *Archives of Neurology* 1556–60.

Korczyn, AD (2002a) 'Mixed dementia – the most common cause of dementia' 977 *Annals of the New York Academy of Sciences* 129–34.

——(2002b) 'The complex nosological concept of vascular dementia' 203–04 *Journal of the Neurological Sciences* 3–6.

Korczyn, AD, Vakhapova, V and Grinberg, LT (2012) 'Vascular dementia' 322 *Journal of the Neurological Sciences* 2–10.

Leung, GM et al (2003) 'The economics of Alzheimer disease' 15 *Dementia and Geriatric Cognitive Disorders* 34–43.

Magri, F et al (2006) 'Stress and dementia: the role of the hypothalamicpituitary-adrenal axis' 18 *Aging Clinical and Experimental Research* 167–70.

Masse, I et al (2005) 'Lipid lowering agents are associated with a slower cognitive decline in Alzheimer's disease' 76 *Journal of Neurology, Neurosurgery & Psychiatry* 1624–29.

Miklossy, J (2003) 'Cerebral hypoperfusion induces cortical watershed microinfarcts which may further aggravate cognitive decline in Alzheimer's disease' 25 *Neurological Research* 605–10.

Neuropathology Group of the Medical Research Council, Cognitive Function and Ageing Study (MRC CFAS) (2001) 'Pathological correlates of late-onset dementia in a multicentre, community-based population in England and Wales' 357 *Lancet* 169–75.

Peretz, C et al (2011) 'Computer-based, personalized cognitive training versus classical computer games: a randomized double-blind prospective trial of cognitive stimulation' 36 *Neuroepidemiology* 91–99.

Prince, M et al 10/66 Dementia Research Group (2003) 'Dementia diagnosis in developing countries: a cross-cultural validation study' 361 *Lancet* 909–17.

Roman, GC (2002) 'Vascular dementia may be the most common form of dementia in the elderly' 203–04 *Journal of the Neurological Sciences* 7–10.

——(2005) 'Vascular dementia prevention: a risk factor analysis' 20 *Cerebrovascular Diseases* (Suppl 2) 91–100.

Sloane, PD et al (2002) 'The public health impact of Alzheimer's disease, 2000–2050: potential implication of treatment advances' 23 *Annual Review of Public Health* 213–31.

Sparks, DL et al (2005) 'Atorvastatin for the treatment of mild to moderate Alzheimer disease: preliminary results' 62 *Archives of Neurology* 753–57.

5

Clinical Management of Dementia: An Overview (1)

NOA BREGMAN AND ORNA MOORE

INTRODUCTION

THIS CHAPTER SETS out a perspective on the management of dementia based on experience in Israel. The corresponding chapter based on UK experience is chapter six.

The management of patients with dementia requires a comprehensive plan that includes a partnership between doctors, health care workers and families (Brodaty and Donkin, 2009). The needs of individuals with dementia are extensive, often requiring care beyond traditional bounds of medical practice, including pharmacologic and non-pharmacologic management interventions (Grand et al, 2011).

Current clinical practice encourages open discussion of the diagnosis of dementia with patients and their caregivers to facilitate early implementation of treatment strategies, and to allow families to plan for the future.

An integrated approach involving both pharmacological and psychosocial strategies is essential for effective care and management. This approach often includes community support services, professional support groups and associations, specialized dementia clinics and geriatric outreach services.

PHARMACOLOGICAL INTERVENTIONS IN DEMENTIA

These are reviewed in detail in chapter six. What follows is a shorter discussion, intended primarily to indicate the place that pharmacological interventions have in the overall treatment of dementia.

Alzheimer's Disease (AD)

There are currently five medications approved by the US Food and Drug Administration (FDA) for the treatment of AD. The cholinesterase inhibitors tacrine, donepezil, rivastigmine and galantamine were approved by the FDA for marketing in the United States for the treatment of AD in 1993, 1996, 2000 and 2001, respectively. Memantine was approved by the FDA in 2003 for the indication of moderately severe to severe AD.

The use of cholinesterase inhibitors for AD is based on the cholinergic hypothesis of memory impairment. The hypothesis implies that cholinergic deficits are responsible for cognitive and behavioural changes in patients with dementia and age-related memory impairment and, further, that pharmacologic augmentation of central cholinergic function will improve cognitive function.

Tacrine is a centrally-acting anticholinesterase and indirect cholinergic agonist (parasympathomimetic). It was the first centrally-acting cholinesterase inhibitor approved for the treatment of AD (Qizilbash et al, 1998). Tacrine has been discontinued in the US.

Donepezil is a long acting reversible acetylcholinesterase inhibitor. Two phase 3 clinical trials showed evidence of efficacy for FDA approval. Additional randomized clinical trials were completed and include trials of six and twelve months' duration and in severely impaired and nursing home patients, as reviewed in a Cochrane review (Birks and Harvey, 2006). One non-industry sponsored, randomized, placebo-controlled trial followed patients over several years and reported modest cognitive effects over two years but no significant effects on loss of function, nursing home placement, or health economic measures (Courtney et al, 2004). Donepezil is the only cholinesterase inhibitor specifically labelled for patients with severe AD. On three six-month, randomized, placebo-controlled clinical trials, the effect was shown to be modest (McArthur et al, 2010).

Rivastigmine is a pseudo-irreversible cholinesterase inhibitor that is selective for acetylcholinesterase and butyrylcholinesterase. Two published trials showed efficacy (Rosler et al, 1999). A transdermal patch formulation has been marketed based on a placebo-controlled study (Winblad et al, 2007). All formulations showed efficacy, but fewer adverse events occurred with the patch formulations.

Galantamine is a reversible competitive acetylcholinesterase inhibitor with relatively less butyrylcholinesterase inhibition compared with rivastigmine. Competitive inhibitors potentially are less active in brain areas that have remaining high acetylcholine levels and more active in other areas. Galantamine also functions as an allosteric modulator of nicotinic receptors, possibly enhancing cholinergic transmission by presynaptic nicotinic stimulation.

A Cochrane review concluded that galantamine shows consistent positive effects of three to six months' duration with no additional improvement with doses over 16 mg/d and that the frequency of gastrointestinal adverse events is similar to other cholinesterase inhibitors (Loy and Schneider, 2006).

Most investigations of drugs that demonstrate efficacy for AD have been done in three or six-month trials in patients with mild to moderate AD. Despite differences in the mechanism of action and dosing levels, there is no evidence for efficacy differences between the three cholinesterase inhibitors. A Cochrane review found that the drugs are associated with a mild clinical effect on cognition (Birks, 2006). Although clearly some patients improved substantially with cholinesterase inhibitors, some also worsened to a greater extent than those treated with a placebo.

The most common adverse events due to cholinesterase inhibitors are cholinergically mediated and include nausea, diarrhoea, vomiting, anorexia and weight loss.

The long-term safety of cholinesterase inhibitors has not been systematically studied. One analysis of medical and prescription records indicated that patients on cholinesterase inhibitors (mainly donepezil) were hospitalized for syncope nearly twice as often as people with dementia who did not receive these drugs. Moreover, they showed an increased risk to patients of bradycardia, of having a pacemaker implanted and suffering hip fractures (Farlow et al, 2010).

Overall, the use of cholinesterase inhibitors involves balancing the modest expectations of benefit, with the potential for the adverse effects of the drugs and with considerable clinical judgement.

Memantine was approved by the FDA in late 2003 for moderate to severe AD. It is characterized as a moderate-affinity, uncompetitive N-methyl-D-aspartate (NMDA) receptor antagonist; a rationale for its use is that it may protect against overstimulation of NMDA receptors that may occur in AD as well as consequent glutamate and calcium mediated neurotoxicity. The basis for approval was positive outcomes in three placebo-controlled clinical trials (Reisberg et al, 2003; Tariot et al, 2004; van Dyck et al, 2007).

Two out of four trials of memantine in mild to moderate AD showed statistically significant cognitive and global improvement (Peskind et al, 2006; Bakchine and Loft, 2008). Two others did not show significant drug–placebo differences (McShane et al, 2006; Porsteinsson et al, 2008) and in pooled analyses did not show efficacy for mild AD (Schneider et al, 2011a). Hence, memantine has not been approved by the FDA for patients with mild AD. Controlled clinical trials of memantine are summarized in a Cochrane review that concluded that memantine had a small beneficial effect in moderate to severe AD and was well tolerated (McShane et al, 2006). Adverse events are infrequent but can include headache, dizziness, confusion, somnolence and infrequent hallucinations. In clinical practice, memantine is either prescribed alone or added to a cholinesterase inhibitor, often after the latter has been used for a time (Schneider et al, 2011b; Reisberg et al, 2006; Schneider, 2006; Lopez et al, 2009; Rountree et al, 2009).

Non-Alzheimer's Dementias

With only a few exceptions, there are no established pharmacological treatments approved for non-Alzheimer's dementias.

Dementia Associated with Lewy Bodies (DLB) and Parkinson's Disease Dementia (PDD)

The Cochrane Library review on Cholinesterase Inhibitors (ChEIs) treatment in PDD included only the EXPRESS study and concluded there was evidence that rivastigmine had had a moderate effect on cognition. However, concerns about rivastigmine tolerability were stated (Maidment et al, 2006).

There are two randomized controlled trials (RCTs) with memantine in the treatment of PDD and one RCT which also examined the efficacy of memantine in DLB patients. In the first, smaller RCT, a significantly smaller proportion of memantine-treated PDD patients deteriorated globally compared with those treated with a placebo (Leroi et al, 2009). In the second, medium-sized RCT, at the end of the study, the PDD patients in the memantine group had significantly better global scores (Aarsland et al, 2009). The larger RCT observed significant benefits for memantine on the global measure for DLB and PDD patients. No statistically significant differences were observed for individual cognitive tests (Emre et al, 2010).

Whilst patients with DLB respond to cholinesterase inhibitors with an improvement in cognitive and psychiatric symptoms, they show a propensity to have exaggerated adverse reactions to neuroleptic drugs, with a significantly increased morbidity and mortality (Maidment et al, 2006). There are no Cochrane Library reviews on memantine in DLB or PDD yet.

Frontotemporal Lobar Degeneration (FTLD)

To date there is no approved treatment for FTLD of any subtype. Even so, and despite the lack of evidence from randomized, placebo-controlled clinical trials, off-label use of cholinesterase inhibitors (ChEIs) and memantine is common in the behavioural subtype of FTLD (Bei et al, 2010). There are only few open-label studies with each of the ChEIs (Moretti et al, 2004; Kertesz et al, 2008), and with memantine in FTLD (Boxer et al, 2009): all studies have failed to provide robust evidence for efficacy in FTLD.

A systematic review found that antidepressant treatment significantly improves behavioural symptoms in FTLD, but most studies reviewed were small and uncontrolled; serotonergic treatments with Selective Serotonin Reuptake Inhibitors (SSRIs) appeared to provide inconsistent improvement in the behavioural but not cognitive symptoms of FTLD (Deakin et al, 2004; Huey et al, 2006). Dopaminergic replacement in FTLD ameliorates only the motor symptoms with no evident effect on cognition (Rabinovici and Miller, 2010).

Corticobasal Syndrome (CBS) and Progressive Supranuclear Palsy (PSP)

One open-label study (Fabbrini et al, 2001) and one RCT (Litvan et al, 2001) in PSP showed no conclusive evidence in favour of donepezil. No evidence exists for CBS.

Huntington's Disease (HD)

There is a Cochrane Library review which includes 22 randomized, double-blinded, placebo-controlled clinical trials conducted on any symptomatic therapy used for HD. It was concluded in this review that there were no data for the treatment of cognitive impairment (Mestre et al, 2009). The Cochrane Library has also reviewed eight studies with agents with possible disease-modifying properties (ie, vitamin E, idebenone, baclofen, lamotrigine, creatine, coenzyme Q10+, remacemide, ethyl-eicosapentanoic acid) and found no effect on outcome measures (Mestre et al, 2009).

Prion Diseases

A systematic review (Stewart et al, 2008) found 33 published studies describing the use of 14 drugs, 10 of which had been reported in single studies of three or fewer patients. There are no Cochrane Library reviews. A recent observational study with the anti-malarial drug Quinacrine (Collinge et al, 2009) showed that it was reasonably tolerated but did not significantly affect the clinical course of prion disease. Further studies are ongoing (Zerr, 2009). No specific treatment for prion diseases can be recommended at the present time.

Normal Pressure Hydrocephalus (NPH)

Normal pressure hydrocephalus (NPH) is a rise in cerebrospinal fluid (CSF) in the brain that affects brain function. However, the pressure of the fluid is usually normal. NPH may be caused by any condition that blocks the flow of CSF or may have no known cause. As CSF fluid builds up in the brain, the fluid-filled chambers (ventricles) of the brain swell. This causes pressure on brain tissue which can damage or destroy parts of the brain. The symptoms often begin slowly. A person needs to have three symptoms to be diagnosed with NPH: headache, changes in gait (gait apraxia) or slowing of mental function such as forgetfulness, difficulty in paying attention, apathy or urinary incontinence. Diagnosis is based on clinical evaluation, imaging (head CT or MRI) and a lumbar puncture (spinal tap) with careful testing of walking before and after the spinal tap.

The treatment of choice is surgery to place a shunt that routes the excess CSF out of the brain ventricles. NPH is sometimes considered a treatable form of dementia; however, it is difficult to decide whether a patient would benefit from a shunting procedure (Esmonde and Cooke, 2002). Surgery seems to be more helpful in the cases that did not start with dementia, have milder cognitive impairment, no aphasia and short duration, or where a drainage test is positive. Cortical atrophy reduces but does not eliminate the chance of improvement with surgery. Surgical treatment carries considerable short and long-term risks (Marmarou et al, 2005). There are no class-I studies comparing operative versus conservative management of NPH, and therefore surgical treatment cannot be considered as a standard approach. The online 2008 assessment of the 2002 Cochrane intervention review has (to date) concluded that there is no evidence to indicate whether the placement of a shunt is effective in the management of NPH (Esmonde and Cooke, 2002).

THE PHARMACOLOGICAL TREATMENT OF MOOD AND BEHAVIOURAL DISORDERS IN DEMENTIA PATIENTS

Pharmacological interventions are necessary when non-pharmacological strategies fail to reduce behavioural symptoms sufficiently. Depression is common in older adults, including those with AD, and is often undiagnosed and untreated. The efficacy of antidepressants in patients with AD who also suffer from depression has been demonstrated in clinical trials; the most useful medications are those with minimal anticholinergic side effects. SSRIs seem to be effective and have fewer side effects compared with other antidepressants, and as such they are considered to be the agents of choice for the treatment of depression in patients with dementia (Lyketsos et al, 2000; Cummings et al, 2002).

Antipsychotic medications, typical and atypical agents, have been increasingly utilized in clinical practice for aggression, psychosis and agitation (Ballard and Corbett, 2010), but only a small number of clinical studies have investigated their relative cost–benefit ratio. Moreover, these benefits have to be considered in the context of significant adverse events, including extrapyramidal symptoms, accelerated cognitive decline, stroke and even death (Ballard and Corbett, 2010).

Atypical antipsychotic drugs have been commonly used off-label in clinical practice for the treatment of serious, dementia-associated agitation and aggression, although they are not approved by the FDA for such use. In addition, these agents have a black box warning of increased mortality among elderly patients with dementia-related psychosis. A meta–analysis assessed the evidence for increased mortality from atypical antipsychotic drug treatment for people with dementia. Results demonstrated that atypical antipsychotics may be associated with a 50% increased risk of death from all causes, which is similar to older antipsychotics (Schneider et al, 2005). If antipsychotics are indicated, then it is recommended that they are used at the lowest effective dose, with dosage reduced or treatment discontinuation considered on a regular basis (Christensen and Lin, 2007).

Cholinesterase inhibitors and memantine were also studied for treating behavioural disorders in AD. In a summary analysis of 14 cholinesterase inhibitor trials that assessed effects on behaviour in post hoc analyses, only three showed significant effects for improving behaviour (Rodda et al, 2009); none of these effects was large (Birks, 2006). Another meta-analysis reported significant but trivial effects on behaviour in the more mildly cognitively impaired patients, but no effect in the more severely impaired (Campbell et al, 2008).

NON-PHARMACOLOGICAL INTERVENTIONS AND NURSING MANAGEMENT

Non-Pharmacological Interventions

Various non-pharmacological therapeutic approaches are available to help manage complex behaviours and improve the quality of life of persons with dementia (Cohen-Mansfield, 2001; Logsdon et al, 2007a). A wide range of non-pharmacological interventions have been proposed or studied, although few have sufficient evidence supporting their effectiveness in improving quality of life or reducing behavioural symptoms such as depression, apathy, wandering, sleep disturbances, agitation and aggression (Thies and Bleiler, 2013).

Several therapies have been suggested including cognitive-based therapies, psychosocial therapies, physical therapies and sensorial therapies. These strategies may be implemented in a variety of settings (home, institutional care facility) and treatment modalities (individual or group-based therapy). Consequently, a comprehensive and integrated approach, which addresses the needs of the individual with dementia, the caregivers and the physical and psychosocial environment, is highly recommended (Curtin, 2010; Grand et al, 2011).

Physical activity therapy and exercise can be used as a therapeutic approach in a wide range of target populations including healthy ageing adults and individuals with dementia. The benefits of physical activity have been demonstrated in terms of mood, quality of life, falls, cardiovascular function and disability rates. Regular exercise can also slow down or help prevent functional decline associated with ageing, improve muscle mass, arterial compliance, energy metabolism, cardiovascular fitness and overall functional capacity.

An individual's overall physical fitness is composed of several components including cardio-respiratory and muscular fitness, flexibility and balance. Physical activity can also reduce behavioural symptoms and improve functional ability. Additional benefits of a sustained walking or exercise programme are decreased wandering and improved sleep quality and mood (Hulme et al, 2010).

Psychotherapeutic interventions may be beneficial for patients in the early stages of dementia. Psychodynamic approaches may be helpful in reorganizing the person to incorporate the disease process, replace inadequate coping with adequate coping and reduce emotional distress. Supportive psychotherapy is a particularly useful strategy that can play an important role in positively influencing the quality of life in the early stages of dementia. The aims of supportive therapy are to promote patients' best possible psychological and social adaptation by restoring and reinforcing their abilities to cope with the vicissitudes and challenges of life; to bolster self-esteem and self-confidence by highlighting assets and achievements, in addition to making patients aware of the reality of their life situation, for example, of their own limitations and those of treatment and what can and cannot be achieved; and to forestall a relapse of their clinical condition thus trying to prevent deterioration or rehospitalisation. Furthermore, to enable patients to require only the degree of professional support that will result in their best possible adaptation, and so prevent undue dependency to transfer the source of support from professionals to relatives or friends (Kasl-Godley and Gatz, 2000).

Cognitive interventions for dementia rely on the plasticity hypothesis, which theorizes that the brain is able to achieve neural and functional improvements by reorganizing its constituent elements and internal network connectivity according to environmental constraints (Lovden et al, 2010).

Cognitive training and cognitive rehabilitation are the two most commonly applied non-pharmacological strategies implemented in the early stages of dementia. These interventions involve targeted practice and training of specific cognitive domains, with a primary emphasis on memory, attention and executive functions. Cognitive training is a more individualized therapeutic approach, and its goals are to enhance functioning in everyday life, rather than improve performance of cognitive tasks. A recent Cochrane Database review showed that cognitive training was not associated with positive or negative effects in relation to any reported outcomes. The overall quality of the trials was low to moderate. The single RCT of cognitive rehabilitation found promising results in relation to a number of participant and caregiver outcomes, and was generally of high quality. Further, well-designed studies of cognitive training and cognitive rehabilitation are required in order to obtain more definitive evidence (Bahar-Fuchs et al, 2013).

Reminiscence therapy is a common psychosocial intervention in dementia care. This approach is based on evocation and discussion: to think about and revisit past events, experiences and activities. It often involves the use of objects and supports (for example, photographs, personal belongings, music) to help trigger specific memories. Very few randomized controlled trials have assessed reminiscence strategies in dementia. Cochrane meta-analysis by Woods et al (2005) showed significant improvements in behavioural functioning, as well as cognitive and depressive symptoms, compared with no-treatment and social-contact control groups, with sustained effects four to six weeks after cessation of the intervention.

Validation therapy is another form of psychosocial intervention for dementia. The goal is to promote and stimulate communication skills and to provide the individual with insights into their external reality. A Cochrane review by Neal and Briggs (2003) found little evidence supporting this form of intervention.

Stimulation-oriented approaches include various sensory-based therapies such as aroma therapy, bright light, movement, multi-sensory, music and touch therapies. These activities are generally offered as part of the therapeutic environment in long-term care.

Multi-sensory stimulation (MSS) environments or Snoezelen stimulate the senses through providing therapeutic objects of un-patterned visual, auditory, olfactory and tactile stimuli in a specially designed room or environment. Evidence demonstrates that MSS might help to reduce apathy in the latter stages of the disease, but many of the positive results were not statistically significant and the benefits were not sustained over time (Curtin, 2010).

Music therapy and the use of musical elements (voice, sound, rhythm) by a qualified music therapist promote non-verbal communication, relationships, learning and expression and improve emotional, social and cognitive functioning through increased quality of life. A review of ten studies found that music and music therapy were effective in reducing behavioural symptoms, but the impact did not persist over time (Hulme et al, 2010). Several randomized controlled trials of music therapy in dementia have recently been conducted, and significant positive effects have been found in the reduction of behavioural and psychological symptoms of dementia (BPSD). Background music has also been shown to be effective in reducing agitation (Grand et al, 2011).

Non-pharmacological strategies have demonstrated modest efficacy in improving mood and reducing behavioural disturbances in long-term care residents with dementia. Interventions that reduce behavioural symptoms, maximize the person's function and improve quality of life are potentially cost-effective and safe alternatives to pharmacological treatments.

Support groups assist early stage individuals, focusing on building coping strategies and reducing psychological distress. Support groups vary in structure, format and content which make it difficult to draw conclusions about their use as a whole. As a psychosocial intervention, the assumption is that when individuals who have experienced a similar diagnosis gather together to share their concerns, they can cope better than on their own. The group supplies: (a) emotional bonding that creates closeness and reduces feelings of isolation; (b) enhanced self-esteem in having information to share about current coping strategies; and (c) information exchange that creates a sense of hope and efficacy.

General guidelines are recommended for facilitating support groups for individuals with dementia: an effective group should create a safe, comfortable atmosphere; communicate interest, empathy and acceptance; encourage group decision-making; and foster members to interaction. Suggested techniques include: (a) introducing one question at a time; (b) being concrete and specific in restating themes and providing explanations; (c) remaining tolerant and providing reassurance if anxiety or confusion occur; (d) acknowledging limitations; and (e) being prepared to adopt an increasingly active role over time.

One significant variation in the format is to hold a support group for demented individuals and one for their care providers, concurrently, and then have the members from each group coming together for part of the time. This format allows the respective participants to address their independent, individual needs, while using their conjoint time to enhance communication and to educate caregivers about the impaired family member's capabilities (Kasl-Godley and Gatz, 2000).

Multidisciplinary team approaches to dementia care include management strategies for the treatment of cognitive impairments, functional deficits and behavioural and psychological symptoms of dementia. Multiple studies have shown the benefits of collaborative and integrated care to people with dementia.

The goals of a multidisciplinary team approach are to maximize functional and cognitive abilities for as long as possible, and enhance the safety and comfort of persons with AD and their families.

An integrated multidisciplinary approach to diagnosing and managing dementia is highly recommended in clinical practice because no single health care specialty has the expertise to deal with the complex range of cognitive, physical, social and emotional problems associated with dementia.

Managing dementia presents unique challenges to the practising clinician, and effective care hinges on a collaborative team approach. This approach relies less on standard pharmacologically based medical practice and more on the integration of therapies from a wide range of health care providers and community professionals. To implement this approach effectively, the clinician must understand the disease processes involved and the clinical presentation of dementia, and also appreciate the caregiving experience and how it affects patient care.

Using a multidisciplinary approach can be complex, but it benefits both the patient and the clinician. It allows clinicians to focus on the issues most relevant to their area of expertise, and it facilitates management of patient problems that are likely to require valuable health care resources (Grand et al, 2011).

The best approach to the care of individuals affected by dementia includes support from multiple sources. These may be integrated, parallel, or a combination of both. It is ideal for patients and caregivers to seek a blend of multidisciplinary services that come from various health care providers, social service agencies and professionals from outside the field of health care.

Multidisciplinary teams involved in dementia care tend to be based primarily on the availability of service resources, in addition to the social and cultural context of the community. Team members often include neurologists, geriatricians, neuropsychologists, nurse practitioners, physical/occupational therapists, nutritionists and social workers (Crooks and Geldmacher, 2004).

Nursing Management of Dementia

Nurses have a central role in the assessment and management of individuals with progressive dementia. The nurse's primary role is to assess and manage the dementia patient and their caregivers' responses to the disease process. This includes monitoring symptom presentation, responding to medication issues, providing education and relevant information to family members and assisting them in preparing for disease progression.

Nursing care should be given according to its cause, onset of illness and severity. The main aim of nursing care is to maintain quality of life, to reduce the caregiver burden by helping the family to adjust to life and coping with the disease and to delay nursing home placement and achieve a peaceful death.

Nursing assessment domains include cognitive, functional, behavioural, physical, caregiver and environment. Similarly, any intervention should assess and examine the physical and psychological effects of dementia care, describe the factors that help determine the nature and magnitude of these effects and discuss several approaches to caregiver intervention designed to reduce the negative impact of this challenging role. Such approaches should take into account the socio-demographic characteristics like gender, relationship to the patient, culture, race or ethnicity, caregiver resources like coping, social support, availability of a companion animal and also personal characteristics (Connell et al, 2001).

Nurses play a key role in the education of the patient and family about what to expect in terms of prognosis and disease progression, involving the patient and family in treatment goals tailored to the patient's current level of cognitive function and providing appropriate cognitive enhancement techniques and social engagement.

One of the important interventions of nurses is to encourage family communication early on and discussion about signs or symptoms that would indicate it is time for transition to another care setting. Signs may include incontinence, wandering or chronic or high levels of caregiver stress.

According to the nursing Standard of Practice Protocol (Fletcher, 2012), nurses should raise awareness of safety issues that will need to be addressed as the disease progresses. These include driving, operating tools and kitchen appliances and handling household poisons, firearms and other dangerous items.

Maintaining the patient's daily activities and social engagement is one of the main goals of the nurse, encouraging the family to maintain the patient's physical activity and social engagement to the greatest extent possible. As well as maximizing the functional capacity of the patient, it is also important to: maintain mobility and encourage independence for as long as possible; provide graded assistance as needed with activities of daily living (ADL) and instrumental activities of daily living (IADL); provide scheduled toileting and prompted voiding to reduce urinary incontinence; encourage an exercise routine that expends energy and promotes fatigue at bedtime; establish a bedtime routine and rituals; and, in addition, to ensure adequate rest, sleep, fluid, nutrition, elimination, pain control and comfort measures.

Key environmental features mainly in nursing homes include architectural elements, such as room layout and size (for example, smaller social spaces); interior design features, such as furniture type and arrangement (for example, homelike furnishing, familiar objects and personalized rooms); and sensory attributes (for example, noise, lighting and visual accessibility) (Grand et al, 2011). Grand et al state that adaptations of these environmental features have been found to reduce anxiety, increase a sense of emotional well-being and enhance social interaction for individuals with dementia.

Preventing complications is vital in ensuring a therapeutic and safe environment that is modestly stimulating and avoids over-stimulation that can cause agitation and increase confusion, and under-stimulation that can cause sensory deprivation and withdrawal. Further measures can include: utilizing patient identifiers (name tags), medic alert systems and bracelets, locks and wander guards; eliminating any environmental hazards and modifying the environment to enhance safety; providing environmental cues or sensory aides that facilitate cognition; maintaining consistency in caregivers and approaches; and, above all, monitoring the effectiveness and potential side effects of medications given to improve cognitive function or delay cognitive decline.

Management of behavioural disorder is also important as dementia is usually a slow, progressive condition and therefore sudden changes in behaviour or in cognitive abilities are likely to be caused by other problems. These include infection, other illness or even discomfort from constipation or arthritic pain. The person may have difficulty explaining this and therefore health care professionals must look out for the possibility that these problems are the cause of the changed behaviour and address them accordingly.

The most challenging part of managing treatment may come during the middle stages, when either families or clinicians begin to feel that some interventions are no longer appropriate. Patients at this stage may have problems complying with the treatment plan or have difficulty understanding its purpose.

Addressing behavioural issues is one of the complex issues that the family with dementia faces. Nurses can help out: by identifying environmental triggers, medical conditions or caregiver–patient conflict that may be causing the behaviour; by defining the target symptom (ie, agitation, aggression, wandering) and pharmacological (psychotropics) and non-pharmacological (manage affect, limit stimuli, respect space, distract, redirect) approaches and providing reassurance; and by referring to appropriate mental health care professionals as indicated (Fletcher, 2012).

Behavioural strategies are the most commonly used intervention in dementia care. The general principles include: creating a structured environment with a daily routine; simplifying tasks; providing one-step instructions; and using a non-confrontational approach. Sometimes behavioural issues appear to be triggered by environmental factors; interventions aimed at modifying the individual's environment may be the most effective means of addressing the behaviours.

Caregiver training is essential issue for nurses to address by providing education, information and support, while at the same time respecting the family systems/dynamics and avoiding making judgements. Here also a nurse can encourage open dialogue, emphasize the patient's residual strengths, provide access to experienced professionals and teach caregivers the skills of caregiving. According to the Standard of Practice Protocol, nurses should integrate community resources into the plan of care to meet the needs for patient and caregiver information; identify and facilitate both formal (for example, Alzheimer's associations, respite care, specialized long-term care) and informal (for example, churches, neighbours, extended family/friends) support systems.

Education and training programmes for family caregivers have been found to be effective in the reduction of BPSD in both nursing home environments and the community. The aim of caregiver training is to increase formal and informal caregiver understanding of BPSD and improve skills in managing and responding to problem behaviours. Individualized treatment plans developed according to the unique needs of the individual with dementia, combined with caregiver problem-solving techniques, are key features of successful education and training interventions (Grand et al, 2011).

Palliative care may be required as dementia frequently results in immobility, decreased physical conditioning, loss of muscle strength and tone and poor coordination. Impaired ambulation is common and increases the risk of falls and injury. Nursing care strategies that rely on the Progressively Lowered Stress Threshold (PLST) provide a framework for the care of families with dementia and include encouraging and supporting advance care planning and explaining the trajectory of progressive dementia, treatment options and advance directives. In addition, as well as providing appropriate end-of-life care in the terminal phase, they provide comfort measures, including adequate pain management and also weigh the benefits/risks of the use of aggressive treatment (for example, tube feeding, antibiotic therapy).

Nurses play an integral part in orchestrating end-of-life care, particularly in nursing homes. Family caregivers often seek nurses' guidance in end-of-life care decisions which can help to ensure that family caregivers are satisfied with the end-of-life care provided by nurse practitioners working in nursing homes.

To deliver good quality end-of-life care, significant improvement is needed in recognizing, understanding and including dementia in a palliative care approach. An emphasis on advance care planning and partnership working with palliative care is also advocated. Recent initiatives in end-of-life care include adopting best practice tools such as the Preferred Place of Care document, the Liverpool Care Pathway and the Gold Standards Framework. As end-of-life care in dementia develops, clearer pathways may help nurses to plan and deliver supportive palliative approaches earlier, leading to improved involvement, better symptom control and a more positive experience at the end of life (Hoe and Thompson, 2010).

Meeting the needs of people with dementia and supporting their families can be challenging. Nurses have a responsibility to ensure that they keep abreast of the changes and that improvements are integrated into the clinical setting (Hoe and Thompson, 2010). Early detection and management may prevent the overuse of costly health care resources and allow affected individuals and caregivers time to prepare for future medical, financial and emotional challenges.

THE FRAMEWORK OF FAMILY-CENTRED CARE

Caregivers play a critical role in the diagnosis and treatment of patients with dementia. Because caregivers have around-the-clock access to patient behaviour and the knowledge base to identify significant changes in patient functioning, they serve as a critical source of information for the clinical assessment of the patient (Schulz and Martire, 2004).

Caring for a person with AD and other dementias poses special challenges with the progression of the dementia: the care required of family members can result in family caregivers' experiencing increased emotional stress, depression, impaired immune system response, health impairments, lost wages resulting from disruptions in employment and depleted income and finances.

Nurses are key advocates in helping the family to begin the sensitive process of open communication in order to document advance care planning. As part of the care plan, it is important for the patient and family caregiver to establish advance directives as soon as possible (McCulloch et al, 2009–13).

Family caregivers of people with dementia—often called the invisible second patients—are critical to the quality of life of the care recipients. The effects of being a family caregiver, though sometimes positive, are generally negative, with high rates of burden and psychological morbidity as well as social isolation, physical ill-health and financial hardship. Caregivers vulnerable to adverse effects can be identified, as can factors which ameliorate or exacerbate burden and strain (Brodaty and Donkin, 2009).

For some caregivers, the demands of caregiving may cause a decline in their own health. They may experience a greater risk of chronic disease, physiological impairments, increased health care use and mortality than those who are not caregivers. According to the *Alzheimer's disease facts and figures* (2013) (Thies and Bleiler, 2013) 43% of caregivers of people with AD and other dementias reported that the physical impact of caregiving was high to very high. The chronic stress of caregiving is associated with physiological changes that indicate risk of developing chronic conditions. For example, a series of recent studies found that, under certain conditions, some AD caregivers were more likely to have elevated biomarkers of cardiovascular disease risk and impaired kidney function risk than those who were not caregivers (Thies and Bleiler, 2013).

Caregivers face many obstacles as they balance caregiving with other demands, including child rearing, career and relationships. The effects on caregivers are diverse and complex, and there are many other factors that may exacerbate or ameliorate how caregivers react and feel as a result of their role.

Caregiving typically involves a significant expenditure of time, energy and money over potentially long periods of time; it involves tasks that may be unpleasant and uncomfortable and are psychologically stressful and physically exhausting. Therefore, family caregivers experience high levels of stress and depression in caring for the person with dementia at home. Nursing home placement typically occurs after families have exhausted their financial, physical and emotional resources (Curtin, 2010).

Some research has suggested that caregivers are at increased risk of serious illness, and are also at increased risk of mortality (Schulz and Martire, 2004). Overall, the convergence of evidence from these studies indicates that a meaningful risk for adverse psychiatric and physical health outcomes exists for a subgroup of caregivers who sustain high levels of caregiving demands, experience chronic stress associated with caregiving, are physiologically compromised and have a history of psychiatric illness. Kesselring et al (2001) reported that with reference to burden, tolerance, mutuality and feelings of closeness between caregiver and patient that caregivers are mainly spouses (67%) and female (73%). These caregivers have been found to experience predominantly negative effects on their physical and mental health, rest and sleep, leisure time and social life, taking us to the conclusion that caring for dementia patients has a bio-psychosocial impact; the closeness between caregiver and patient being the key factor in deciding the long-term outcome.

The chronic and often severe stress associated with dementia caregiving may exert a substantial risk of the development of dementia in spouse caregivers. Norton et al (2010) examined the effects of caring for a spouse with dementia on the caregiver's risk of developing incident dementia. They found that a subject whose spouse experienced incident dementia onset had a six times greater risk of incident dementia compared with those subjects whose spouses were dementia free.

There is evidence to support the use of comprehensive caregiver care and support in reducing institutionalization. In one study, 65% of the intervention group was living at home after 30 months compared with 26% in the control group (Brodaty and Donkin, 2009).

In a Finnish study, the median time of residing in the community following a programme of systematic comprehensive support by a nurse or dementia family care coordinator was 647 days in the intervention group and 396 days in the control group (Eloniemi-Sulkava et al, 2001).

The clinical impact of this treatment on the patient was minimal and time-limited, with greatest benefit to those with severe dementia.

Caregivers should receive comprehensive training on interventions that are effective for people with dementia (Brodaty and Donkin, 2009). Psychosocial interventions have been shown to reduce caregiver burden and depression and delay nursing home admission. Comprehensive management of the patient with dementia includes building a partnership between health professionals and family caregivers, referral to Alzheimer's associations and psychosocial interventions where indicated (Brodaty and Donkin, 2009).

Interventions that may improve caregiver outcomes aim to lessen negative aspects of caregiving with the goal of improving the health outcomes of dementia caregivers. Characteristics of effective caregiver interventions include programmes that are administered over long periods of time, interventions that approach dementia care as an issue for the entire family and interventions that train dementia caregivers in the management of behavioural problems (Logsdon et al, 2007b; Logsdon, 2008). Multidimensional interventions appear particularly effective. These approaches combine individual consultation, family sessions and support and ongoing assistance to help dementia caregivers manage changes that occur as the disease progresses.

One important example of multidimensional interventions is the New York University Caregiver Intervention. Current analyses of data collected by Mittelman et al (2006) over an 18-year period indicate that the enhanced caregiver support intervention developed for spouse caregivers at NYU led to significant delays in nursing home placement. Their results suggest that with sufficient counselling and support, it is possible to achieve outcomes that are beneficial to most family caregivers, older patients and society. While nursing home placement may be necessary when caregivers are unable or unwilling to manage the care of their relatives at home, it typically does not reduce caregiver distress.

Nurses can play a pivotal role in the health and well-being of persons with dementia and their family caregivers. It is imperative that nurses take a proactive role in providing this anticipatory guidance for the family during the course of the disease, by using nursing interventions for the development and implementation of clinical and educational approaches.

Our Experience: Caregivers' Clinic in Israel

Over the years the medical community has became more and more aware of the importance and unique role of family members as caregivers of patients with chronic diseases, and especially in patients with neurodegenerative diseases (including Parkinson's disease, Alzheimer's disease, Huntingtons, LBD) and more than a decade ago, this led us to open a special clinic with a multidisciplinary approach for family caregivers. Relatives, particularly spouses and children, visit the clinic at the Memory Center in Tel Aviv Medical Hospital. The clinic is run by a consultant nurse specialist, together with neurologists, social workers and neuropsychologists.

Interventions provided include the following: assessment of the caregiver's status; providing information about the disease with emotional support; giving advice as to how to manage physical problems and deal with daily living difficulties; teaching coping skills and improving skills in managing and responding to problem behaviours, as well as giving instructions on how to prevent complications. In addition, we provide counselling on how to reduce and manage the stress associated with caregiving while preserving physical health and well-being and, over and above, enhance and provide social and emotional support for caregivers. In the meetings, caregivers can release their distress, fear and anger and share their feelings. In addition, we encourage caregivers to join support groups, and if necessary seek help from a psychiatrist, a family physician or psychologist. Further consultation, as needed, from sexologist, occupational therapist, dietician or social worker in the community. The process is supported by telephone contact and consultation.

Caregivers seek consultations mainly during the first years after diagnosis and also when neuropsychiatric symptoms appear and when ADL and mobility significantly decline, and as a result home assistance may be required. Most caregivers needed up to three visits to the clinic combined with on-going telephone consultations. The majority of the caregivers showed better coping skills and reported high satisfaction with, as well as gratitude for, the professional consultations and support they got.

In conclusion, caregivers are a population at risk, unrecognized as patients who require special attention, emotional, professional and social support. Clinicians and health professionals must be able to recognize factors associated with a caregiver's stress, burden and to refer them to consultation. Attending clinics for caregivers at the Memory Center has been shown to be an effective mode of intervention, for the benefit of the entire family coping with AD and other dementias.

REFERENCES

Aarsland, D et al (2009) 'Memantine in patients with Parkinson's disease dementia or dementia with Lewy bodies: a double-blind, placebo-controlled, multicentre trial' 8(7) *Lancet Neurology* 613–18.

Bahar-Fuchs, A et al (2013) 'Cognitive training and cognitive rehabilitation for mild to moderate Alzheimer's disease and vascular dementia' 6 *Cochrane Database of Systematic Reviews* CD003260.

Bakchine, S and Loft, H (2008) 'Memantine treatment in patients with mild to moderate Alzheimer's disease: results of a randomised, double-blind, placebo-controlled 6-month study' 13(1) *Journal of Alzheimer's Disease* 97–107.

Ballard, C and Corbett, A (2010) 'Management of neuropsychiatric symptoms in people with dementia' 24(9) *CNS Drugs* 729–39.

Bei, H et al (2010) 'Off-label medication use in frontotemporal dementia' 25(2) *American Journal of Alzheimer's Disease & Other Dementias* 128–33.

Birks, J (2006) 'Cholinesterase inhibitors for Alzheimer's disease' 1 *Cochrane Database of Systematic Reviews* CD005593.

Birks, J and Harvey, RJ (2006) 'Donepezil for dementia due to Alzheimer's disease' 1 *Cochrane Database of Systematic Reviews* CD001190.

Boxer, AL et al (2009) 'An open-label study of memantine treatment in 3 subtypes of frontotemporal lobar degeneration' 23(3) *Alzheimer Disease and Associated Disorders* 211–17.

Brodaty, H and Donkin, M (2009) 'Family caregivers of people with dementia' 11(2) *Dialogues in Clinical Neuroscience* 217–28.

Campbell, N et al (2008) 'Impact of cholinesterase inhibitors on behavioral and psychological symptoms of Alzheimer's disease: a meta-analysis' 3(4) *Journal of Clinical Interventions in Aging* 719–28.

Christensen, DD and Lin, P (2007) 'Practical treatment strategies for patients with Alzheimer's disease' 56 *Journal of Family Practice* (12 Suppl New) S17–23.

Cohen-Mansfield, J (2001) 'Nonpharmacologic interventions for inappropriate behaviors in dementia: a review, summary, and critique' 9(4) *American Journal of Geriatric Psychiatry* 361–81.

Collinge, J et al (2009) 'Safety and efficacy of quinacrine in human prion disease (PRION-1 study): a patient-preference trial' 8(4) *Lancet Neurology* 334–44.

Connell, CM et al (2001) 'The costs of caring: impact of dementia on family caregivers' 14(4) *Journal of Geriatric Psychiatry and Neurology* 179–87.

Courtney, C et al (2004) 'Long-term donepezil treatment in 565 patients with Alzheimer's disease (AD2000): randomised double-blind trial' 363(9427) *Lancet* 2105–15.

Crooks, EA and Geldmacher, DS (2004) 'Interdisciplinary approaches to Alzheimer's disease management' 20(1) *Clinics in Geriatric Medicine* 121–39.

Cummings, JL et al (2002) 'Guidelines for managing Alzheimer's disease: part I. Assessment' 65(11) *American Family Physician* 2263–72.

Curtin, AJ (2010) 'Non-pharmacological approaches to dementia in the long-term care setting' 93(12) *Medicine and Health Rhode Island* 369–71.

Deakin, JB et al (2004) 'Paroxetine does not improve symptoms and impairs cognition in frontotemporal dementia: a double-blind randomized controlled trial' 172(4) *Psychopharmacology (Berl)* 400–08.

Eloniemi-Sulkava, U et al (2001) 'Effects of supporting community-living demented patients and their caregivers: a randomized trial' 49(10) *Journal of the American Geriatrics Society* 1282–87.

Emre, M et al (2010) 'Memantine for patients with Parkinson's disease dementia or dementia with Lewy bodies: a randomised, double-blind, placebo-controlled trial' 9(10) *Lancet Neurology* 969–77.

Esmonde, T and Cooke, S (2002) 'Shunting for normal pressure hydrocephalus (NPH)' 3 *Cochrane Database of Systematic Reviews* CD003157.

Fabbrini, G et al (2001) 'Donepezil in the treatment of progressive supranuclear palsy' 103(2) *Acta Neurologica Scandinavica* 123–25.

Farlow, MR et al (2010) 'Effectiveness and tolerability of high-dose (23 mg/d) versus standard-dose (10 mg/d) donepezil in moderate to severe Alzheimer's disease: A 24-week, randomized, double-blind study' 32(7) *Clinical Therapeutics* 1234–51.

Fletcher, NK (updated August 2012) *Evidence-Based Content – Nursing Standard of Practice Protocol: Recognition and Management of Dementia.*

Grand, JH et al (2011) 'Clinical features and multidisciplinary approaches to dementia care' 4 *Journal of Multidisciplinary Healthcare* 125–47.

Hoe, J and Thompson, R (2010) 'Promoting positive approaches to dementia care in nursing' 25(4) *Nursing Standard* 47–56; quiz 58.

Huey, ED et al (2006) 'A systematic review of neurotransmitter deficits and treatments in frontotemporal dementia' 66(1) *Neurology* 17–22.

Hulme, C et al (2010) 'Non-pharmacological approaches for dementia that informal carers might try or access: a systematic review' 25(7) *International Journal of Geriatric Psychiatry* 756–63.

Kasl-Godley, J and Gatz, M (2000) 'Psychosocial interventions for individuals with dementia: an integration of theory, therapy, and a clinical understanding of dementia' 20(6) *Clinical Psychology Review* 755–82.

Kertesz, A et al (2008) 'Galantamine in frontotemporal dementia and primary progressive aphasia' 25(2) *Dementia and Geriatric Cognitive Disorders* 178–85.

Kesselring, A et al (2001) 'Emotional and physical demands on caregivers in home care to the elderly in Switzerland and their relationship to nursing home admission' 11(3) *European Journal of Public Health* 267–73.

Leroi, I et al (2009) 'Randomized controlled trial of memantine in dementia associated with Parkinson's disease' 24(8) *Movement Disorders* 1217–21.

Litvan, I et al (2001) 'Randomized placebo-controlled trial of donepezil in patients with progressive supranuclear palsy' 57(3) *Neurology* 467–73.

Logsdon, RG (2008) 'Dementia: psychosocial interventions for family caregivers' 372(9634) *Lancet* 182–83.

Logsdon, RG, et al (2007a) 'Evidence-based interventions to improve quality of life for individuals with dementia' *Alzheimer's Care Today* 8(4) 309–18.

—— (2007b) 'Evidence-based psychological treatments for disruptive behaviors in individuals with dementia' 22(1) *Psychology and Aging* 28–36.

Lopez, OL et al (2009) 'Long-term effects of the concomitant use of memantine with cholinesterase inhibition in Alzheimer disease' 80(6) *Journal of Neurology, Neurosurgery & Psychiatry* 600–07.

Lovden, M et al (2010) 'A theoretical framework for the study of adult cognitive plasticity' 136(4) *Psychological Bulletin* 659–76.

Loy, C and Schneider, L (2006) 'Galantamine for Alzheimer's disease and mild cognitive impairment' 1 *Cochrane Databaseof Systematic Reviews* CD001747.

Lyketsos, CG et al (2000) 'Randomized, placebo-controlled, double-blind clinical trial of sertraline in the treatment of depression complicating Alzheimer's disease: initial results from the Depression in Alzheimer's Disease study' 157(10) *American Journal of Psychiatry* 1686–89.

Maidment, I et al (2006) 'Cholinesterase inhibitors for Parkinson's disease dementia' 1 *Cochrane Database of Systematic Reviews* CD004747.

Marmarou, A et al (2005) 'Development of guidelines for idiopathic normal-pressure hydrocephalus: introduction' 57(3) *Neurosurgery* (Suppl) S1-3; discussion ii-v.

McArthur, RA et al (2010) 'Cognitive effects of muscarinic M1 functional agonists in non-human primates and clinical trials' 11(7) *Current Opinion in Investigational Drugs* 740–60.

McCulloch, DK et al (2009–2013) *Dementia and Cognitive Impairment Diagnosis and Treatment Guideline* (Group Health Cooperative).

McShane, R et al (2006) 'Memantine for dementia' 2 *Cochrane Database of Systematic Reviews* CD003154.
Mestre, T et al (2009) 'Therapeutic interventions for disease progression in Huntington's disease' 3 *Cochrane Database of Systematic Reviews* CD006455.
Mittelman, MS et al (2006) 'Improving caregiver well-being delays nursing home placement of patients with Alzheimer disease' 67(9) *Neurology* 1592–99.
Moretti, R et al (2004) 'Rivastigmine in frontotemporal dementia: an open-label study' 21(14) *Drugs & Aging* 931–37.
Neal, M and Briggs, M (2003) 'Validation therapy for dementia' 3 *Cochrane Database of Systematic Reviews* CD001394.
Norton, MC et al (2010) 'Greater risk of dementia when spouse has dementia? The Cache County study' 58(5) *Journal of the American Geriatrics Society* 895–900.
Peskind, ER et al (2006) 'Memantine treatment in mild to moderate Alzheimer disease: a 24-week randomized, controlled trial' 14(8) *American Journal of Geriatric Psychiatry* 704–15.
Porsteinsson, AP et al (2008) 'Memantine treatment in patients with mild to moderate Alzheimer's disease already receiving a cholinesterase inhibitor: a randomized, double-blind, placebo-controlled trial' 5(1) *Current Alzheimer Research* 83–89.
Rabinovici, GD and Miller, BL (2010) 'Frontotemporal lobar degeneration: epidemiology, pathophysiology, diagnosis and management' 24(5) *CNS Drugs* 375–98.
Reisberg, B et al (2003) 'Memantine in moderate-to-severe Alzheimer's disease' 348(14) *New England Journal of Medicine* 1333–41.
—— (2006) 'A 24-week open-label extension study of memantine in moderate to severe Alzheimer disease' 63(1) *Archives of Neurology* 49–54.
Rodda, J et al (2009) 'Are cholinesterase inhibitors effective in the management of the behavioral and psychological symptoms of dementia in Alzheimer's disease? A systematic review of randomized, placebo-controlled trials of donepezil, rivastigmine and galantamine' 21(5) *International Psychogeriatrics* 813–24.
Rosler, M et al (1999) 'Efficacy and safety of rivastigmine in patients with Alzheimer's disease: international randomised controlled trial' 318(7184) *British Medical Journal* 633–38.
Rountree, S et al (2009) 'Persistent treatment with cholinesterase inhibitors and/or memantine slows clinical progression of Alzheimer disease' 1(2) *Alzheimer's Research & Therapy* 7.
Schneider, LS (2006) 'Open-label extension studies and misinformation' 63(7) *Archives of Neurology* 1036; author reply 1036–37.
Schneider, LS et al (2005) 'Risk of death with atypical antipsychotic drug treatment for dementia: meta-analysis of randomized placebo-controlled trials' 294(15) *Journal of the American Medical Association* 1934–43.
—— (2011a) 'Lack of evidence for the efficacy of memantine in mild Alzheimer disease' 68(8) *Archives of Neurology* 991–98.
—— (2011b) 'Treatment with cholinesterase inhibitors and memantine of patients in the Alzheimer's Disease Neuroimaging Initiative' 68(1) *Archives of Neurology* 58–66.
Schulz, R and Martire, LM (2004) 'Family caregiving of persons with dementia: prevalence, health effects, and support strategies' 12(3) *American Journal of Geriatric Psychiatry* 240–49.
Stewart, LA et al (2008) 'Systematic review of therapeutic interventions in human prion disease' 70(15) *Neurology* 1272–81.
Tariot, PN et al (2004) 'Memantine treatment in patients with moderate to severe Alzheimer disease already receiving donepezil: a randomized controlled trial' 291(3) *Journal of the American Medical Association* 317–24.
Thies, W and Bleiler, L (2013) '2013 Alzheimer's disease facts and figures' 9(2) *Alzheimer's & Dementia* 208–45.

van Dyck, C et al (2007) 'A 24-week randomized, controlled trial of memantine in patients with moderate-to-severe Alzheimer disease' 21(2) *Alzheimer Disease & Associated Disorders* 136–43.
Winblad, BG et al (2007) 'IDEAL: a 6-month, double-blind, placebo-controlled study of the first skin patch for Alzheimer disease' 69(4) *Neurology* (Suppl 1) S14–22.
Woods, B et al (2005) 'Reminiscence therapy for dementia' 2 *Cochrane Database of Systematic Reviews* CD001120.
Zerr, I (2009) 'Therapeutic trials in human transmissible spongiform encephalo-pathies: recent advances and problems to address' 9(1) *Infectious Disorders – Drug Targets* 92–99.
Qizilbash N et al (1998) 'Cholinesterase inhibition for Alzheimer disease: a meta-analysis of the tacrine trials. Dementia Trialists' Collaboration' 280(20) *Journal of the American Medical Association* 1777–82.

6

Clinical Management of Dementia: An Overview (2)

CHRIS FOX, CAROLYN CHEW-GRAHAM, EMMA WOLVERSON, IAN MAIDMENT AND ANDREA HILTON

THIS CHAPTER SETS out a perspective on the management of dementia based on experience in the United Kingdom. The corresponding chapter based on experience in Israel is chapter five.

In 2010, it was estimated that 35.6 million people lived with dementia worldwide, with numbers expected to almost double every 20 years, to 65.7 million in 2030 and 115.4 million in 2050 (Prince et al, 2013). In 2010, 58% of all people with dementia lived in countries with low or middle incomes, with this proportion anticipated to rise to 63% in 2030 and 71% in 2050 (Prince et al, 2013). Dementia has an enormous economic impact with global expenditure of US$604 billion in 2010 (World Health Organization and Alzheimer's Disease International, 2012). There are at present no disease-modifying treatments.

This chapter reviews: (a) the role of primary care in dementia (and is supplemented by the perspective in chapter ten); (b) current and future potential pharmacological interventions (introduced in chapter five; (c) the use of medication in behavioural and psychological symptoms in dementia (introduced in chapter five); (d) psychosocial interventions in dementia (introduced in chapter five); and (e) medication concordance and appropriateness in dementia. The focus is on practice in the UK.

THE ROLE OF PRIMARY CARE

Primary Care in the UK

In the UK, primary care services are an integral part of the National Health Service (NHS) in which general practitioners (GPs) work as independent contractors. People are required to register as patients with a general practice; currently, a practice determines its boundaries and accepts patients who reside within this area. The GP works as a generalist and a provider of personal, primary and continuing care to individuals, families and a practice population, irrespective of age, gender, ethnicity and problem.

GPs work with a range of other health care professionals in a multidisciplinary primary health care team, which is essential in order to manage the complex demands of caring for an increasingly ageing population with chronic and multiple health problems. Greater emphasis on preventative care, the transfer of clinical responsibility for some chronic diseases from secondary to primary care and the shift in service provision in order to deliver care closer to patients' homes has contributed to these demands.

The implementation of a new General Medical Services (GMS) contract in 2004 changed the way in which GPs work in the UK. The contract defines essential primary care services and optional enhanced services that are additionally remunerated. The contract links achievements in clinical and non-clinical care quality to financial rewards, through a Quality and Outcomes Framework (QOF) derived from evidence-based care (NHS Confederation, 2011). The system encourages the delivery of optimum care in clinical domains, with emphasis on chronic disease management (Lester et al, 2006).

Evidence for Early Diagnosis

The National Dementia Strategy for England advocates earlier, more timely, diagnosis and there is evidence that patients and carers wish to know when a diagnosis of dementia is likely (Robinson et al, 2011). An Alzheimer's report (2012) suggested that 68% of patients waited for a year between onset of symptoms and diagnosis, and 8% waited for five years. Earlier diagnosis gives time for patients and carers to make plans for future care, whilst the patient still has the capacity to do this; in addition, early diagnosis can delay admission to residential or nursing care, and is therefore cost-saving for health and social care (Banerjee and Wittenberg, 2009).

In the NHS, the Quality and Outcomes Framework (2013) recognizes the need to make the diagnosis early, and that certain groups are at risk, for example, patients with diabetes and cardiovascular disease. It also includes a 'Directed Enhanced Service' for 'Testing for Dementia in at-risk groups'. The scope of this assessment is currently being refined, but is likely to include an initial enquiry about memory problems followed by a specific test. There will also be a focus on prompt diagnosis so that patients with the condition can be brought into the care pathway earlier.

Making the Diagnosis

The problem of memory loss is likely to be presented first to the GP by the patient or a carer. In the initial consultation a careful history from the patient and their main carer is needed, with relevant information (for example, risk factors and family history) from the patient's notes (Box 1).

Box 1. Diagnosing all-cause dementia, core clinical criteria:

Interferes with abilities to function at work or normal activities

AND represents a clear decline from previous levels of function and performance
AND symptoms are not explained by delirium or major psychiatric disorder.

Cognitive or behavioural impairment involves a minimum of two of the following domains:

1. Impaired ability to acquire and remember new information.
2. Impaired reasoning and handling of complex tasks, poor judgement.
3. Impaired visuo-spatial abilities.
4. Impaired language functions.
5. Changes in personality, behaviour or comportment.

Source: Albert et al, 2011

A physical examination with baseline investigations and an objective cognitive assessment should be also carried out by the GP (National Collaborating Centre for Mental Health, 2007; Young et al, 2011). The first step is to exclude a potentially treatable illness or a reversible cause of the dementia (Box 2). A review of medication may identify incorrect dosage or drug interactions that are causing cognitive impairment. These may include sedatives, tranquillizers, antiparkinsonian agents and hypotensives; adjustment or withdrawal of these will clarify the diagnosis. Normal pressure hydrocephalus, hypothyroidism, syphilis, hypercalcaemia and vitamin deficiencies as the cause of conditions mimicking dementia are rarities in practice. Older people with depression can present with memory loss ('pseudodementia'). Depression is probably the most common differential diagnosis of memory loss and should always be considered, and, if suspected, a trial of antidepressants may be indicated.

Box 2. Reversible causes of cognitive impairment:

- Infections: neurosyphilis, HIV.
- Anoxia: anaemia, congestive cardiac failure, chronic respiratory failure.
- Metabolic: liver failure, uraemia.
- Endocrine: hypothyroidism, Addison's disease, parathyroid disease.
- Vitamin deficiency: B12, folic acid, thiamine, nicotinic acid.
- Toxic: alcohol, barbiturates.
- Space occupying lesions: cerebral tumours, subdural haematomas, normal pressure hydrocephalus.

Several simple tools are available for use in the community to make an initial assessment of a person's cognitive function (National Collaborating Centre for Mental Health, 2007). The most commonly used cognitive assessment tool is the Mini-Mental State Examination (MMSE) (Folstein et al, 1975) marked out of 30: a score of less than 25 is suggestive of dementia. However, this can take up to 20 minutes to complete and may not be practical for use within a 10-minute primary care consultation. The General Practitioner Assessment of Cognition (GPCOG) (Brodaty et al, 2002) is clinically and psychometrically robust and more appropriate for use in primary care than the MMSE (Milne et al, 2008). The GPCOG is estimated to take between five and seven minutes to complete, with questions for both the patient and family carer, and thus may be more useful for primary care physicians (Brodaty et al, 2002).

Confirming the Diagnosis and Initiating Management

If the GP suspects a diagnosis of dementia, or the patient or carer is concerned about symptoms of memory loss, the patient should be referred for a specialist multidisciplinary assessment to either an old age psychiatry team or, if available, a memory clinic (National Collaborating Centre for Mental Health, 2007). Increasingly, old age psychiatry and memory clinics have access to CT and specialist scanning facilities to enable not only a diagnosis of dementia to be made, but also a specialist subtype of dementia to be confirmed. The advantages of early referral include: relief at acquiring an explanation for distressing symptoms; access to anticholinesterase inhibitor drugs and specialist cognitive rehabilitation and/or psychological interventions; advice on appropriate information and support services, including day care; carer assessment and support; and the ability to undertake advance care planning (Robinson et al, 2010).

Ongoing Management in Primary Care

The QOF currently dictates that practices keep a 'dementia register' and review patients at least every 12 months (Box 3).

Box 3. Components of the annual dementia review:

Appropriate physical and mental health review for the patient, including exploring new symptoms such as behavioural changes which may be caused by:

- Concurrent physical conditions (for example, joint pain or intercurrent infections).
- The new appearance of features intrinsic to the disorder (for example, wandering) and delusions or hallucinations due to the dementia or as a result of caring behaviour (for example, being dressed by a carer).

Review of medication:

- The prescribing of anticholinesterase inhibitors is initiated by the specialist, but the GP usually takes over prescribing and monitoring after about three months.
- If applicable, the carer's needs for information commensurate with the stage of the illness and his or her and the patient's health and social care needs.
- If applicable, the impact of caring on the caregiver.
- Communication and coordination arrangements with specialist health care and social care.

Source: NHS Confederation (2013) Quality and Outcomes Framework

Male carers are less likely to complain spontaneously, and the impact of caring is dependent on the presentation of the dementia, for example, on factors such as behaviour and affect. If the carer is not registered at the practice, but the GP is concerned about issues raised in the patient consultation, then, with appropriate permissions, they can contact the carer's own GP.

Advance Care Planning

People with dementia and their families often wish to plan ahead for when, in the future, they cannot make decisions and wish their decisions to be known. This process has recently been termed advance care planning (ACP) and should be discussed with the person with dementia whilst he or she still has the capacity to make decisions (National Institute for Health and Clinical Excellence, 2006). GPs need to inform people with dementia and their carers about advocacy services and voluntary support available to both parties together or independently. Whilst they still have the capacity, discussion of the use of advance directives to refuse treatment, lasting powers of attorney and a preferred place of care plan (National Institute for Health and Clinical Excellence, 2006) should occur.

CURRENT AND FUTURE POTENTIAL PHARMACOLOGICAL INTERVENTIONS

Currently there are four licensed medications for Alzheimer's dementia. Of these, three are called cholinesterase inhibitors (Donepezil, Rivastigmine and Galantamine) and the fourth is an N-methyl-D-aspartate receptor (NMDA) antagonist called Memantine. There is an older cholinesterase inhibitor called Tacrine which is hepatotoxic and has a complicated dosing regime. This is used rarely, and never in the UK.

Cholinesterase Inhibitors

The cholinergic hypothesis in Alzheimer's suggests that impairment in the cholinergic function of particular brain areas is of critical importance. The brain areas of particular importance are those dealing with learning, memory, behaviour and emotional responses, and include the neocortex and the hippocampus. Acetylcholinesterase (AChE) is an enzyme which is important in the breaking down of acetylcholine. According to the 'amyloid hypothesis' AChE produces secondary non-cholinergic functions that include promotion of beta-amyloid (Ab) deposition in the form of senile plaques/neurofibrillary tangles in the brain. This is a key part both of the initiation and the progression of Alzheimer's disease. The increasing activity of Butyrylcholinesterase (BuChE) plays an important role in Ab-aggregation. Inhibition of these enzymes increases the availability of acetylcholine in the brain regions, and decreases Ab deposition. This, it is said, is the mechanism of action of the cholinesterase inhibitors. The currently available cholinesterase inhibitors are for symptomatic patients and do not decelerate or prevent the progression of the disease. However, these therapies demonstrate modest but consistent benefit for cognition, global status and functional ability (Herrmann et al, 2011). As a group they are contraindicated in hypersensitivity.

Donepezil

This is a reversible AChE inhibitor and was first licensed in 1997. It has been available as a generic drug since 2012. It was licensed for mild, moderate and severe Alzheimer's dementia.

The side effects of the cholinesterase inhibitors are all similar. Gastrointestinal symptoms are the commonest (for example, nausea and loose stools) but are usually mild and transient. Vivid nightmares are another side effect which should be mentioned. Muscle cramps and diaphoresis are reported. Caution should be exercised in those with a slow heart rate. The current approved dose is 5 mg up to 10 mg. In the US a 23 mg dose is approved. The dose has to be titrated up from 5 mg/day. ECG is advisable before commencement.

Galantamine

This was approved in 2001 for mild to moderate Alzheimer's dementia. It is a reversible competitive inhibitor of AChE. It is derived from the snowdrop variety of the daffodil. It is an allosteric modulator of the nicotinic acetylcholine receptor. Although the nicotinic effect may increase cholinergic transmission, the clinical impact is theoretical.

There is a slow release form. The dose is for the standard version is 4 mg twice daily, increased after one month to 8 mg twice daily. The dose may be increased to 12 mg twice daily depending on the response. Prescription of the slow release form starts at 8 mg per day, and after one month can be increased to 16 mg per day and, ultimately, to an option of 24 mg per day. It should be taken with food to minimize gastrointestinal side effects. The side effects are similar to Donepezil but the gastrointestinal effects may be more significant. ECG is advisable before commencement.

Rivastigmine

This was approved in 2000, and is a reversible inhibitor of both AChE and BuChE. The clinical significance of the latter is uncertain. It is approved for mild to moderate Alzheimer's. In 2007, a patch was released which has fewer gastrointestinal effects. Gastrointestinal side effects for the non-patch version are higher. Rare cases of rupture of the oesophagus have been reported when starting at too high a dose. The oral version should be consumed with food. ECG is advisable before commencement.

Prescription starts at 1.5 mg twice daily. Every two weeks the dose is increased in 1.5 mg twice daily increments to a maximum of 6 mg twice daily. Reducing dose adjustment to four-weekly dose change and taking with food may increase tolerability. The patch starts at 4.6 mg per day and after one month can be increased to 9.5 mg. A delay is not usually necessary when switching between oral and patch administration.

There is some limited evidence that switching non-responders to another cholinesterase inhibitor may be of benefit.

Most physicians recommend a trial of six months to see if the drug helps. If there is no stabilization or improvement in the patient's condition, then a trial off the drug is indicated, with monitoring. If no difference is seen when the patient is off the drug, the clinician should consider switching to another cholinesterase inhibitor.

Acetylcholinesterase Inhibitors and the UK NICE Guidance (NICE Clinical Guideline 42)

The three acetylcholinesterase inhibitors are recommended as options in Alzheimer's disease of moderate severity only (that is, those with an MMSE score of between 10 and 20 points), and under the following conditions:

- — Only specialists in the care of people with dementia (that is, psychiatrists including those specializing in learning disability, neurologists and physicians specializing in the care of the elderly) should initiate treatment. Carers' views on the patient's condition at baseline should be sought.
- — Patients who continue on the drug should be reviewed every six months by MMSE score and global, functional and behavioural assessment. Carers' views on the patient's condition at follow-up should be sought. The drug should only be continued while the patient's MMSE score remains at or above 10 points and their global, functional and behavioural condition remains at a level where the drug is considered to be having a worthwhile effect. Any review involving MMSE assessment should be undertaken by an appropriate specialist team, unless there are locally agreed protocols for shared care.

Health care professionals should not rely on the MMSE score in certain circumstances. These are:

- — In those with an MMSE score greater than 20, who have moderate dementia as judged by significant impairments in functional ability and personal and social function compared with premorbid ability.
- — In those with an MMSE score less than 10 because of a low premorbid attainment or ability or linguistic difficulties, who have moderate dementia as judged by an assessment tool sensitive to their level of competence.
- — In people with learning disabilities.
- — In people who are not fluent in spoken English or in the language in which the MMSE is applied.

Memantine

Memantine is a non-competitive antagonist of the N-methyl-D-aspartate receptor of glutamate. The theory is that injured glutamate producing neurons release excessive glutamate which harms other neurons via calcium channel activation. Memantine protects these neurons by preventing the cascade. It was approved in 2003 for the treatment of moderate to severe Alzheimer's dementia. It is well tolerated and adverse effects are uncommon. The adverse effects include dizziness, constipation and headaches. Severe renal impairment is a contraindication, and the dose should be reduced in moderate renal dysfunction.

The dose starts at 5 mg per day and increases weekly until 20 mg per day is reached.

Memantine is recommended as an option for managing moderate Alzheimer's disease for people who cannot take acetylcholinesterase inhibitors, and as an option for managing severe Alzheimer's disease (NICE, 2011: Clinical Guide 42). In the US it is commonly prescribed with a cholinesterase inhibitor. In Europe mono-therapy is more common.

Natural Products

There is increasing interest in natural products for the treatment of dementia. Many are from traditional Chinese medicines. Proposed mechanisms include scavenging free radicals, inhibiting lipid peroxidation, suppressing neuronal apoptosis, enhancing the function of cholinergic neurons and/or improving behavioural abnormalities in experimental animal models. Some flavonoids, alkaloids, phenylpropanoids, triterpenoid saponins and polysaccharides were demonstrated to have potential efficacies against AD (Gao et al, 2013). This is an area of potential development as most studies have only been undertaken in vitro or in animals.

Nutritional Products

Souvenaid is a drink which is classed as a food for special medicinal purposes for the dietary management of early Alzheimer's disease. The evidence for benefit is weak and if there is a benefit, it seems to be short-lived (Scheltens et al, 2012).

In the US, Axona is available as a prescription medical food. It targets the diminished cerebral glucose metabolism (also known as glucose hypometabolism) which is an underlying pathological change in the Alzheimer's brain. This leaves neurons less able to utilize glucose for fuel, leading to an energy shortage in the brain. This process occurs early in the disease and may contribute to symptoms and disease progression. Axona helps to redress this deficiency by providing ketones as an alternative fuel source for neurons (Henderson et al, 2009).

Future Treatments

There are ongoing trials targeting amyloid, tau and other mechanisms.

Drugs Interfering with Amyloid β (Aβ) Deposition

The hypothesis that aggregation of Aβ leads to toxic oligomers has driven research into studying compounds that could prevent this aggregation. Several chelators of zinc and copper have been shown to inhibit Aβ aggregation in vitro and in animal studies.

Aβ is generated through proteolytic processing of the transmembrane peptide APP. APP can be cleaved by two competing proteases, α-secretase and β-secretase.

Only β-secretase, followed by γ-secretase cleavage, which in AD is the dominant pathway, will lead to the production of Aβ40 and Aβ42. By inhibiting these, or by increasing α-secretase cleavage, Aβ production may be reduced. There are problems in avoiding an impact on physiological function and large inhibitor targets—for example with the β-secretase enzyme BACE1. γ-secretase is a nucleoprotein complex with at least four different proteins from which presenilin PS-1 and PS-2 seem to be responsible for the enzymatic action on APP.

Unfortunately, besides APP, γ-secretase has many other substrates and cleaves several other transmembrane proteins which could result in toxic effects. α-secretase potentiation stimulates the neurotrophic α-secretase (nonamyloidogenic) pathway and inhibits Aβ-induced neuronal death, providing symptomatic relief and modifying the progression of disease.

Immunotherapy is one of the strategies being studied by many pharmaceutical companies, but to date trials have failed to show a sufficient benefit for the drugs to be made clinically available.

The mechanism of amyloid clearance by immunotherapy is unclear. The suggestions include:

- Direct disassembly of plaques by conformation-selective antibodies; antibody-induced activation of microglial cells and phagocytosis of pathological protein deposits.
- Non-complement-mediated phagocytosis activation of microglial cells.
- Neutralization of toxic soluble oligomers;
- A shift in equilibrium towards efflux of specific proteins from the brain, creating a peripheral sink by clearance of circulating Aβ cell-mediated immune responses; and immunoglobulin M (IgM)-mediated hydrolysis.

Drugs that Modulate Tau Deposition

Many compounds have been identified and current research is looking at the following:

- Interfering with tau deposition: methylene blue.
- Interfering with tau phosphorylation: lithium.
- Immunotherapy: vaccination (difficult as the target is intracellular).

Drugs that Modulate Inflammation and Oxidative Damage

Epidemiological evidence suggests that long-term use of non-steroidal anti-inflammatory drugs protects against the development of Alzheimer's dementia, but trials have not confirmed this. Potentially helpful antioxidants include mitoquinone, vitamin E, ginkgo biloba, natural polyphenols such as green tea, wine, blueberries and curcumin, omega-3 fatty acids, folate, vitamin B6 and vitamin B12 supplementation, but more research is needed. Substances that inhibit Tumour Necrosis factor via effects on cytokines could be of benefit, but there have been no trials yet.

THE USE OF MEDICATION TO CONTROL BEHAVIOURAL AND PSYCHOLOGICAL SYMPTOMS IN DEMENTIA

Behavioural and psychological symptoms in dementia (BPSD) are very common: 50% of people with dementia may experience such symptoms (Ballard and Waite, 2006). BPSD are among the most difficult symptoms to treat. They are strongly associated with caregiver stress, burden and depression and with placement breakdown and residential care utilisation (Child et al, 2012).

BPSD have traditionally been treated with anti-psychotics, but caution is needed: anti-psychotics are implicated in approximately 1800 deaths a year in the UK. The inappropriate use of anti-psychotics in people with dementia has been identified as a worldwide public health issue (Department of Health, 2009). In 1987 the US introduced the Omnibus Budget Reconciliation Act (OBRA), which set minimum standards for Medicare and Medicaid funded care homes and placed an emphasis on quality of life to ensure that residents achieved the 'highest practicable physical, mental and psychosocial well-being' (National Long Term Care Ombudsman Resource Center, 1987). The Act limited the use of anti-psychotics and reduced anti-psychotic usage by about 30%.

More recently, the UK National Dementia Strategy set a target of reducing by two-thirds the use of anti-psychotics (Department of Health, 2009). However, if treatment for BPSD is required, clinicians should follow the advice of the Alzheimer's Society and the product licences of the relevant pharmaceutical compounds. Medication should only be used where there is a risk of harm to the person with dementia, or others. Currently, the only approved medication for BPSD is the anti-psychotic, Risperidone. Treatment should be started at a low dose, reviewed regularly and continued for a maximum of six weeks.

The inappropriate use of medication in dementia may be much broader than anti-psychotics. Sometimes, BPSD need to be treated acutely, and if national guidance focuses solely on anti-psychotics other equally inappropriate treatments may be used in place of anti-psychotics. Evidence both from the US and UK has identified that benzodiazepines, and in particular Lorazepam, represent one likely substitute treatment; post-OBRA one study found that the usage of regular anxiolytics increased by 48.6% and 'as required' anxiolytics by 27.5% (Maidment et al, 2011; Borson and Doane, 1997). Indeed, Clinical Knowledge Summaries, which are widely used by primary care in the UK, recommend Lorazepam for the management of extreme agitation or aggression in dementia even though there is limited evidence to support such a recommendation (Clinical Knowledge Summaries, 2010). Unfortunately, the recent national UK audit of the treatment of BPSD did not capture Lorazepam usage, and it is not clear if rates of Lorazepam usage have increased as anti-psychotic rates have decreased (Health and Social Care Information Centre, 2012). Any future audits should record the use of all possible alternative treatments to anti-psychotics for BPSD, including Lorazepam and other benzodiazepines, trazodone and sedative antihistamines.

One wider issue is that national audit data may overestimate the extent of the reduction in anti-psychotic prescription rates for BPSD (Health and Social Care Information Centre, 2012). The national audit found a 51.8% decrease in the number of people with dementia receiving a prescription for an anti-psychotic between

2008 and 2011. However, only 45.7% of GP surgeries took part in the national audit—mainly because of insufficient resources for data extraction, or technical problems (Health and Social Care Information Centre, 2012). One project, which collected data from 98.3% of practices in a single PCT (Primary Care Trust) found that 15.3% of people with dementia were receiving an anti-psychotic (Child et al, 2012). This compares with the national audit, which collected data from 17.5% of practices in the same PCT, and found that 10.5% of people with dementia were receiving anti-psychotics. However, both projects relied upon the accuracy of dementia registers. Research by the Alzheimer's Society found that such registers may only capture 40% of the population with dementia.

People with dementia may receive complex medication regimens containing physical medicines in addition to psychotropics. Laxatives, painkillers containing opiates and antihistamines may be the most common classes of physical medicines prescribed inappropriately to people with dementia (Maidment et al, 2012). Whilst these medicines might appear to be relatively benign, the consequences of inappropriate usage can be significant; laxatives can cause diarrhoea, opiates can worsen any psychotic symptoms present in someone with dementia and antihistamines with anti-cholinergic activity are associated with worsening cognitive function and potentially an increase in mortality (Fox et al, 2011). There is therefore a need to develop interventions to limit such inappropriate medication use. One such intervention could be a comprehensive medication review, focusing on the treatment of BPSD and involving specialists in medication management for people with dementia.

PSYCHOSOCIAL INTERVENTIONS IN DEMENTIA

The value of psychosocial interventions in supporting people with dementia and their families is becoming increasingly recognized. The term encompasses a range of interventions that centre on interactions between people and aim to improve quality of life and maximize function in the context of existing deficits (American Psychiatric Association, 2007). Psychosocial interventions recognize that the emotional adjustment of people living with dementia is as important as cognitive function; a key aim is to reduce the excess disability commonly encountered in dementia as a result of fear and stigma. Informed by the emerging literature exploring the lived experiences of people with dementia, psychosocial interventions recognize that people with dementia, alongside their families, are active agents who seek to cope with and manage their illness. Psychosocial interventions therefore play an important role in engendering hope for people with dementia and their families. Many of the interventions are prophylactic: they do not target those who are already distressed, and can also be used with those with mild cognitive impairment (Moniz-Cook and Manthorpe, 2008).

There is growing evidence for the effectiveness of psychosocial interventions within dementia care, although it is recognized that the evidence base for specific interventions is mixed and, at times, limited. Indeed, few psychosocial interventions have reached the stage of rigorous evaluation. It has often been hard to find scientifically acceptable methods of evaluation, and funding has also been hard to find. However, it seems that positive effects are demonstrable, including effects on cognition, quality of life for family carers and on neuropsychiatric symptoms (Vasse et al, 2011). Impressively, psychosocial interventions with family carers have also been shown to be effective in postponing and decreasing the odds of entry to residential care (Spijker et al, 2008), but no such effects have been found in relation to other current treatment options. Moreover, unlike available pharmacological treatments, psychosocial interventions are not limited to specific types of dementia and have no obvious side effects. Despite this emerging evidence, the inclusion of psychosocial interventions within dementia guidelines across Europe is limited (Vasse et al, 2011) and within the UK the availability of such interventions varies hugely dependent upon location, often as a result of clinician knowledge and expertise.

There is a vast and ever-increasing range of psychosocial approaches offered. They include approaches delivered on an individual basis and in groups. Psychosocial interventions have been employed across the stages of dementia severity and with caregivers. For the purposes of this chapter, the approaches have been broadly divided into: those commonly delivered within the community; those delivered within residential care; and those used with caregivers. We have not presented an exhaustive list of approaches, but have instead selected a few as examples. It is also important to mention that 'standard' psychological approaches—such as cognitive behavioural therapy and psychotherapeutic groups—can be adapted and utilized for people living with dementia and their caregivers.

Community-Based Psychosocial Interventions

In the UK, cognitive stimulation is currently the only non-pharmacological therapy recommended by the National Institute for Health and Clinical Excellence Guidelines (NICE, 2006), reflecting the fact that its evidence base is well established (Spector et al, 2002). It involves taking part in exercises and activities that aim first to preserve cognition function and second to increase a person's self-worth, confidence and motivation: both aims are seen as co-dependent. Cognitive stimulation is traditionally carried out in a group but there is ongoing research to establish the evidence base for multimedia-based cognitive stimulation (Tarraga et al, 2006) and also individual programmes (Orrell et al, 2012).

Cognitive rehabilitation refers to approaches that aim to build on remaining memory skills and finding ways of compensating for impaired aspects of memory (Clare and Wilson, 1997). Programmes are tailored to an individual's strengths and weaknesses and seek to develop strategies to reach mutually-agreed realistic goals. Research into the success of such approaches is ongoing but such approaches seem to offer some gains in the short term.

Another popular psychosocial intervention is reminiscence, which is broadly concerned with the retrieval and recording of past pleasant experiences and sharing these memories in order to bring change to a person's current life—such as increased conversation. Reminiscence activities can take many forms. The most popular include individual life story work and group-based reminiscence programmes. Despite its popularity, the compelling informal evidence suggesting its effectiveness and the wealth of training materials available, reminiscence interventions have been difficult to evaluate. For example, a recent multicentre, randomized controlled trial in the UK found limited evidence for the effectiveness and cost-effectiveness of joint reminiscence groups for people with dementia and their family caregivers (Woods et al, 2012). Further work is needed to understand fully the value of such approaches in dementia care.

Finally, it should be mentioned that there is a growth of interest in the use of health technologies for people with dementia that can be utilized to promote quality of life and independence. For a review of current technologies, see chapter twenty-one of this book, and Bharucha et al (2009).

Psychosocial Interventions in Residential Care Settings

Many psychosocial approaches can be used to promote well-being in residential care. They include art therapies, music therapy, structured activity and exercise programmes. The use of cognitive stimulation and reminiscence approaches (see above) is also well established in residential care.

Reality orientation has been one of the most widely utilized approaches within residential settings. It employs rehearsal and physical prompts in an attempt to orientate people to their environment in the hope that providing the person with a greater understanding of their surroundings may result in an improved sense of control and self-esteem. It can be used both with individuals and with groups. However, there is some debate regarding the efficacy of the approach as there are concerns that it can remind the participants of their deterioration and subsequently lower mood, though the evidence does suggest that there are some benefits on both cognition and behaviour (Spector et al, 2001).

Validation therapy, rather than bringing people into the present, is concerned with trying to enter a person's world, wherever that may be. It assumes that people often retreat into the past as a way of coping with a present that is difficult or painful. It works on the principle that even the most confused behaviour has some meaning for the person with dementia. However, unlike reality orientation, there is at present a lack of research to assess its efficacy.

An often overlooked component of psychosocial approaches in residential settings is the environment. There is increasing recognition that people with dementia are particularly sensitive to their psychosocial environment, and good environmental design is now widely regarded as critical to care. The environment can be used as a therapeutic tool to compensate for disability—for example, a consistent and familiar environment can reinforce a person's identity and affect orientation and social interactions between people with dementia (Day and Calkins, 2002).

Caregiver Interventions

Historically most of the research on psychosocial interventions has been related to supporting caregivers. Most people living with dementia are cared for in the community by a family member. Providing care for someone with cognitive problems is thought to be more difficult than providing physical care alone (Davis, 1992).

Family carers are usually spouses and therefore often elderly themselves and with their own health problems. It is unsurprising, then, that rates of depression and poor physical health are high in this carer population (Schulz et al, 1990).

Caregiver interventions include emotional support, education, problem solving, stress management and behaviour management. In those studies which have shown improvements in caregiver well-being, key elements appear to be social components which aim to improve the quality and quantity of relationships, used in addition to cognitive components such as problem-solving (Bourgeois et al, 1996). In addition to family caregiver interventions, there is a growing corpus of research dealing with the effectiveness of interventions targeting formal care staff. Such interventions often involve staff training in an attempt to change attitudes and behaviours.

Future Work

With such a wide range of psychosocial approaches offered it is increasingly important to establish a robust evidence base. A key area for the future is developing an understanding of how to 'target' interventions in order to achieve the best possible outcomes. There is emerging evidence to suggest that, like pharmacological interventions, there may be a 'critical window' for psychosocial interventions, so that, for example, offering something too early in a person's illness may actually increase support needs (Moniz-Cook and Manthorpe, 2008). Further understanding is needed of how to match individuals to interventions. As the research allows better targeting of such interventions, evidence for their effectiveness is likely to increase.

MEDICATION APPROPRIATENESS AND CONCORDANCE IN DEMENTIA

Appropriateness

When people ask whether a particular medication is appropriate for their condition, what do they actually mean? And how do health care professionals assess this in order to answer the question?

Much has been written about appropriateness or, more correctly, inappropriateness. It is often easier to highlight inappropriate practice or prescribing. In 1997, Buetow and colleagues (Buetow et al, 1997) reviewed the application of appropriateness to clinical practice: 'appropriateness is also a judgement and an exclusionary criterion'. 'Sophisticated definitions of appropriateness have been suggested for health care in general but none provides a solidly unequivocal conceptualisation'.

If we apply the term 'appropriateness' to prescribing medication, 'inappropriate prescribing' is defined as an 'overuse, irrational choice or under use of drugs' (Oborne et al, 1997). Any medication which is prescribed should be the right medication, for the right patient at the right time, as highlighted by the National Patient Safety Agency.

Appropriate medication is often thought of as that where there is a clinical indication for the prescribing. For example, if a person has hypertension (high blood pressure) you would expect to have an antihypertensive medication; but there are many different classes of antihypertensive medication and not all will be appropriate for everybody. Often we will say simply that a particular prescription is right or wrong, but life is much more complex than that.

There are many different ways of measuring inappropriateness/inappropriate prescribing, such as:

— Drugs to avoid.
— Drug utilisation reviews.
— Explicit criteria.
(Hanlon et al, 2001).

Explicit methods involve a rigid structure to their answers, usually developed from literature reviews, expert opinion or consensus. Implicit methods are based around clinical judgement.

Many explicit measures have been developed, including:

1. The 'Beers criteria' (Beers et al, 1997) which was the first explicit publication identifying inappropriate medication and was carried out in a nursing environment in 1991. These criteria have been updated several times to become more generalized and include new medication, in 1997, 2002–03 and 2012. The Beers criteria is widely used within the US and included in several research trials as an outcome measure.
2. The 'Screening Tool of Older Persons; Potentially inappropriate Prescriptions' (STOPP) and the 'Screening Tool to Alert doctors to the Right Treatment' (START) which were validated in 2008 using a delphi consensus methodology of 18 UK and Ireland experts. There are 65 STOPP criteria (Gallagher et al, 2008; Hamilton et al, 2011).

The issue with all tools which use specific clinical examples is currency (for example, when clinical practice changes or there are safety concerns with a particular medication).

A mixture of both implicit and explicit criteria is often stated as being better. An example of a tool which adopts both approaches is the Medication Appropriateness Index (MAI). The index was developed based on the clinical experience of a clinical pharmacist (Hanlon) and geriatrician (Schmader) and employing a literature review (Hanlon et al, 1992). The US MAI is used to assess the overall appropriateness of medication against ten criteria. However, the MAI requires a comprehensive list of clinical details, including full details about drug history, past medical history, disease history and the assessor must have the ability to provide a clinical judgement and have an appreciation of the costs of medicines. The MAI was revalidated and underwent reliability work for use in the UK and as the primary outcome measure for the RESPECT trial:

> The RESPECT trial (Randomised Evaluation of Shared Prescribing for Elderly people in the Community over Time) was designed to estimate the effect of pharmaceutical care on the appropriateness of prescribing; patients' knowledge, adherence, and quality of life; and the incidence of adverse events in a randomised controlled trial (RESPECT trial team, 2010).

Box 4. MAI Comparison

US MAI version	UK MAI version
1. Is there an indication for the drug?	1. Is the drug indicated?
2. Is the medication effective for the condition?	2. Is it (the drug) effective for the condition?
3. Is the dosage correct?	3. Is the dosage correct?
4. Are the directions correct?	4. Are the directions correct?
5. Are the directions practical?	5. Are the directions practical, clear and unambiguous for this patient?
6. Are there clinically significant drug–drug interactions?	6. Are there clinically significant drug to drug interactions?
7. Are there clinically significant drug–disease/condition interactions?	7. Are there any clinically significant drug–disease/ condition interactions?
8. Is there unnecessary duplication with other drugs?	8. Is there unnecessary duplication with other drugs?
9. Is the duration of therapy acceptable?	9. Is the duration of therapy acceptable?
10. Is this drug the least expensive alternative compared with others of equal utility?	10. Is the drug you are assessing less expensive than alternative drugs of equal efficacy?

Specific tools are useful for assessing people's medications collectively, ie, to give an overall assessment of the medications people are taking. However, within the diagnosis of dementia some medications are appropriate only for a short period of time, for example, benzodiazepines; other medication may be completely inappropriate such as long-term anti-psychotics. Even when prescribed medication is completely appropriate, this may change the next day—for instance because of an interaction with a new drug being started.

Most general practices will undertake a medication review as part of an annual process: 'A structured, critical examination of a patient's medicines with the objective of reaching an agreement with the patient about treatment, optimising the impact of medicines, minimising the number of medication-related problems and reducing waste' (Room for Review, 2002). However, there are different levels of medication review. Level 1 is a prescription review, usually without access to the clinical notes. Level 2 is a treatment review which normally takes place under the direction of a doctor, nurse or pharmacist, but often without the patient—for instance, removal of unwanted items from the repeat medicines list and dose adjustments (Room for Review, 2002). A Level 3 review requires access to the patient's notes, a full record of prescriptions, non-drug care and results from laboratory tests. The review should include the complete repeat prescription as well as over-the-counter and complementary remedies. The patient should be involved fully, and their beliefs and views considered (Room for Review, 2002).

Involving Patients in Decision Making

A whole chapter or more could be devoted to the discussion on involving patients in decision making. We merely note, to conclude this section on medication appropriateness, that 'treatment and care should take into account patients' needs and preferences and patients should have the opportunity to make informed decisions about their care and treatment, in partnership with their healthcare professionals' (National Institute for Health and Clinical Excellence (NICE) 2009).

CONCLUSIONS

GPs have a vital and central role to play in both establishing a diagnosis of dementia, securing timely referral and ensuring regular review, and support, of the person with dementia and their carers. The medication available is of limited benefit, but that will not always be the case. A number of promising possibilities are being pursued.

The management of behavioural disturbance in dementia is difficult, and a staged approach with assessment is required. Non-medication approaches in dementia have shown promise and should be included in care. The use of any medication for people with dementia requires careful consideration of appropriateness and concordance.

There are numerous potential developments under test in the management of people with dementia which will hopefully prove beneficial and improve care.

REFERENCES

Albert, MS et al (2011) 'The diagnosis of mild cognitive impairment due to Alzheimer's disease: Recommendations from the National Institute on Aging-Alzheimer's Association workgroups on diagnostic guidelines for Alzheimer's disease' 7 *Alzheimer's & Dementia* 270–79. doi: 10.1016/j.jalz.2011.03.008.

Alzheimer's Society (2012) *Dementia 2012: A National Challenge.* Available at: www.alzheimers.org.uk/site/scripts/download_info.php?fileID=1389.

American Psychiatric Association (APA) (2007) *Practice guideline for the treatment of patients with Alzheimer's disease and other dementias* (Arlington, VA, American Psychiatric Association).

Ballard, C and Waite, J (2006) 'Atypical anti-psychotics for aggression and psychosis in Alzheimer's disease' 1 *Cochrane Database of Systematic Reviews* (Cochrane Collaboration, John Wiley & Sons, Ltd). doi: 10.1002/14651858.CD003476.pub2.

Banerjee, S and Wittenberg, R (2009) 'Clinical and cost effectiveness of services for early diagnosis and intervention in dementia' 24(7) *International Journal of Geriatric Psychiatry* 748–54. doi: 10.1002/gps.2191.

Beers, MH et al (1997) 'Explicit Criteria for Determining Potentially Inappropriate Medication Use by the Elderly: An Update' 157 *Archives of Internal Medicine* 1531–36.

Bharucha, A et al (2009) 'Intelligent Assistive Technology Applications to Dementia Care: Current Capabilities, Limitations, and Future Challenges' 17(2) *American Journal of Geriatric Psychiatry* 88–104. Available at: bma.org.uk/working-for-change/negotiating-for-the-profession/gp-contract/gp-contract-new-des.

Borson, S and Doane, K (1997) 'The Impact of OBRA-87 on Psychotropic Drug Prescribing in Skilled Nursing Facilities' 48 *Psychiatric Services* 1289–96.

Bourgeois, M, Schulz, R and Burgio, L (1996) 'Interventions for Caregivers of Patients with Alzheimer's Disease: A Review and Analysis of Content, Process and Outcomes' 43(1) *International Journal of Ageing and Human Development* 35–92.

Brodaty, H et al (2002) 'The GPCOG: a new screening test for dementia designed for general practice' 50 *Journal of the American Geriatrics Society* 530–34.

Buetow, SA et al (1997) 'Appropriateness in health care: Application to prescribing' 45(2) *Social Science & Medicine* 261–71.

Child, A et al (2012) 'A pharmacy led program to review anti-psychotic prescribing for people with dementia' 12 *BMC Psychiatry* 155. doi: 10.1186/1471-244X-12-155. Available at: www.biomedcentral.com/1471-244X/12/155.

Clare, L and Wilson, BA (1997) *Coping with memory problems: A practical guide for people with memory impairments and their relatives and friends* (Bury St Edmunds, Thames Valley Test Company).

Clinical Knowledge Summaries (2010) 'Dementia – extreme agitation or aggression'. Available at: cks.nice.org.uk/dementia#!scenarioclarification:4.

Davis, L (1992) 'Building a science of caring for family caregivers' 15 *Family and Community Health* 1–9.

Day, K and Calkins, MP (2002) 'Design and Dementia' in R Bechtel and A Churchman (eds), *Handbook of Environmental Psychology* (New York, John Wiley & Sons).

Department of Health (2009) *The use of antipsychotic medication for people with dementia: Time for action Living well with dementia: A National Dementia Strategy* (London, Department of Health). Available at: www.dh.gov.uk/en/Publicationsandstatistics/Publications/PublicationsPolicyAndGuidance/DH108303.

Folstein, MF, Folstein, SE and McHugh, PR (1975) '"Mini-Mental State": a practical method for grading the cognitive state of patients for the clinician' 12 *Journal of Psychiatric Research* 189–98.

Fox, C et al (2011) 'Anticholinergic medication use and cognitive impairment in the older population: The Medical Research Council Cognitive Function and Ageing Study (CFAS)' 59(8) *Journal of the American Geriatrics Society*. doi: 10.1111/j.1532-5415.2011.03491.x.

Gallagher, P et al (2008) 'STOPP (Screening Tool of Older Person's Prescriptions) and START (Screening Tool to Alert doctors to Right Treatment). Consensus validation' 46(2) *International Journal of Clinical Pharmacology and Therapeutics* 72–83.

Gao, J et al (2013) 'Research progress on natural products from traditional Chinese medicine in treatment of Alzheimer's disease' 7(2) *Drug Discoveries & Therapeutics* 46–57.

Hamilton H et al (2011) 'Potentially Inappropriate Medications defined by STOPP Criteria and the Risk of Adverse Drug Events in Older Hospitalized Patients' 171(11) *Archives of Internal Medicine* 1013–19.

Hanlon, JT et al (1992) 'A Method for Assessing Drug Therapy Appropriateness' 45(10) *Journal of Clinical Epidemiology* 1045–51.

—— (2001) 'Suboptimal Prescribing in Older Inpatients and Outpatients' 49(2) *Journal of the American Geriatrics Society* 200–09.

Health and Social Care Information Centre (HSCIC) (2012) National Dementia and Antipsychotic Prescribing Audit. Available at: www.ic.nhs.uk/dementiaaudit.

Henderson, ST et al (2009) 'Study of the ketogenic agent AC-1202 in mild to moderate Alzheimer's disease: a randomized, double-blind, placebo-controlled, multicenter trial' 6 *Nutrition & Metabolism* 31.

Herrmann, N et al (2011) 'Current and emerging drug treatment options for Alzheimer's disease: a systematic review' 71 *Drugs* 2031–65.

Lester, H et al (2006) 'The quality outcomes framework of the GMS Contract' 56 *British Journal of General Practice* 245–46.

Maidment, I et al (2011) 'An evaluation of an outreach role for specialist mental health pharmacists' (Paris, ICAD international meeting).

—— (2012) 'Medication review in care homes by Mental Health Pharmacist: a feasibility study' (Birmingham, MHRN conference; Manchester, Health Services Research Conference).

Milne, A et al (2008) 'Screening for dementia in primary care: a review of the use, efficacy and quality of measures' 3 *International Psychogeriatrics* 431–58.

Moniz-Cook, E and Manthorpe, J (2008) *Early Psychosocial Interventions in Dementia: Evidence Based Practice* (London, Jessica Kingsley Publishers).

National Collaborating Centre for Mental Health (2007) *Dementia. A NICE–SCIE Guideline on supporting people with dementia and their carers in health and social care. National Clinical Practice Guideline Number 42* (Leicester and London, British Psychological Society and the Royal College of Psychiatrists).

National Institute for Health and Clinical Excellence and the Social Care Institute for Excellence (NICE-SCIE) (2006) *Dementia: supporting people with dementia and their carers in health and social care. Clinical Guideline 42* (London, NICE-SCIE).

National Institute for Health and Clinical Excellence (NICE) (2009) *Medicines adherence; involving patients in decisions about prescribed medicines and supporting adherence. Clinical Guidance CG 76* (London, NICE).

National Institute for Health and Clinical Excellence (NICE) (2011) 'Alzheimer's disease – donepezil, galantamine, rivastigmine and memantine (TA217)', Technology Appraisal, March 2011.

National Long Term Care Ombudsman Resource Center (1987) OBRA '87 SUMMARY. Available at: www.allhealth.org/briefingmaterials/OBRA87Summary-984.pdf.

NHS Confederation (2013) *Quality and Outcomes Framework*. Available at: www.nhsemployers.org/PayAndContracts/GeneralMedicalServicesContract/QOF/Pages/QualityOutcomesFramework.aspx.

Oborne, AC et al (1997) 'Development of prescribing indicators for elderly medical inpatients' 43 *British Journal of Clinical Pharmacology* 91–97.

O'Connor, MN, Gallagher, P and O'Mahony, D (2012) 'Inappropriate prescribing: Criteria, Detection and Prevention' 29(6) *Drugs &Aging* 437–52.

Orrell, M et al (2012) 'Individual Cognitive Stimulation Therapy for dementia (iCST): study protocol for a randomized controlled trial' 13 *Trials* 172.

Prince, M et al (2013) 'The global prevalence of dementia: A systematic review and meta-analysis' 9(1) *Alzheimer's & Dementia* 63–75.

Respect Trial Team (2010) 'Effectiveness of shared pharmaceutical care for older patients: RESPECT trial findings' 60(570) *British Journal of General Practice* e10–e19.

Robinson, L et al (2010) 'Patient preferences for future care – how can advance care planning become embedded into dementia care: a study protocol' 10 *BMC Geriatrics* 1471–76.

—— (2011) 'The transition to dementia-individual and family experiences of receiving a diagnosis: a review' 23(7) *International Psychogeriatrics* 1026–43. doi: 10.1017/S1041610210002437.

Scheltens, P et al (2012) 'Efficacy of Souvenaid in mild Alzheimer's disease: results from a randomized, controlled trial' 31(1) *Journal of Alzheimer's Disease* 225–36. doi: 10.3233/JAD-2012-121189.

Schulz, R, Visintainer, P and Williamson, GM (1990) 'Psychiatric and Physical Morbidity Effects of Caregiving' 45 *Journals of Gerontology*: Physical Sciences 181–91.

Spijker, A et al (2008) 'Effectiveness of nonpharmacological interventions in delaying the institutionalization of patients with dementia: a meta-analysis' 56 *Journal of the American Geriatrics Society* 1116–28.

Spector, A et al (2001) 'Can reality orientation be rehabilitated? Development and piloting of an evidence-based programme of cognition-based therapies for people with dementia' 11 *Neuropsychological Rehabilitation* 377–97.

—— (2002) 'Efficacy of an evidence-based cognitive stimulation therapy programme for people with dementia: Randomized controlled trial' 183 *British Journal of Psychiatry* 248–54.

Tarraga, L et al (2006) 'A randomized pilot study to assess the efficacy of an interactive, multimedia tool of cognitive stimulation in Alzheimer's disease' 77(10) *Journal of Neurology, Neurosurgery & Psychiatry* 1116–21.

Task Force on Medicines Partnership and The National Collaborative Medicines Management Services Programme (2002) *Room for Review. A guide to medication review: the agenda for patients, practitioners and managers* (London, Medicines Partnership).

Young, J, Meagher, D and MacLullich, A (2011) 'Cognitive assessment of older people' 343 *British Medical Journal* (Clinical Review) 1–7.

Vasse, E et al (2011) 'Guidelines for psychosocial interventions in dementia care: A European survey and comparison' 27 *International Journal of Geriatric Psychiatry* 40–48.

World Health Organization and Alzheimer's Disease International (2012) *Dementia: A Public Health Priority* (Geneva, WHO Press).

Woods, R et al (2012) 'REMCARE: reminiscence groups for people with dementia and their family caregivers – effectiveness and cost-effectiveness pragmatic multicentre randomised trial' 16(48) *Health Technology Assessment*.

7

Best Interests Determination: A Medical Perspective

HUGH SERIES

'BEST INTERESTS' HAS come to be the basis on which decisions are made on behalf of those who lack the mental capacity to make them for themselves. In England and Wales, this is now written into statute in the Mental Capacity Act 2005 (MCA). That best interests ought to have such a central role is not at all self-evident: chapter twelve describes another possible approach—substituted judgement (the attempt to conclude what the person might have wanted had he had capacity either at the relevant time, or at the actual point at which he last had capacity (Hope et al, 2009)). Chapters thirteen and twenty-six of this volume deal with decisions made by proxies.

For such a key concept as best interests, much about it remains uncertain. Who should decide on where the best interests lie? When should they decide? How should they decide? What should they do in the event of a disagreement? At what point should the matter be referred to a court? Perhaps surprisingly, most of the time these problems do not arise, although best interests determinations are made constantly in caring for people who cannot decide for themselves. Even the decision to give an incapacitous patient, who cannot himself express a preference, one type of sandwich rather than another, is technically a best interests determination under the MCA. This chapter takes a pragmatic look at how, when, by whom and why such decisions are made in the context of the English legislation. For clarity, I refer to the subject of the best interests decision as 'he', and the principal decision-maker as 'she'.

HOW ARE MEDICAL DECISIONS MADE?

When a doctor sees a new patient she assesses him by taking a history, carrying out an examination and appropriate investigations, reaching a view of what is likely to be wrong (diagnosis) and, if appropriate, offering some treatment. Doctors are encouraged to discuss with the patient the range of treatment options which may be available, and then to invite the patient to choose the one he prefers. Very little is known about what drives patient choice in this area, though one might speculate that important factors include the perceived effectiveness, safety and tolerability of each of the treatments offered. No doubt a range of other factors come into the decision: prior attitudes, beliefs and experiences and advice from friends or family.

The range is wide. People do not always make choices which their doctor considers to be wise.

Doctors, on the other hand, are expected to make treatment decisions on the basis of the best available evidence as to safety and efficacy. The advice they give should be based on evidence, interpreted and applied to the current situation. In order to support this type of decision-making, the National Institute for Health and Care Excellence (NICE) is the national body charged with evaluating treatments and publishing guidance in order to make clear which ones are known to be effective and good value. 'Good value' in this context has a rather precise meaning describing those treatments whose use is known to produce, on average, an improvement in the quality of life within an agreed envelope of cost. Quality of life may be measured in quality-adjusted-life-years (QALYs), a utilitarian attempt to put a financial value on the quality of life. In other words, NICE recommends only those treatments which it considers to be based upon good evidence of effectiveness, and can (or should) be afforded within the NHS. It could be said to be an attempt to ensure that public money allocated for health is spent wisely. It can happen that a patient might want and might benefit from a particular treatment, although because of its cost it is not recommended by NICE. This is one way in which a treatment recommended by NICE may not always coincide with a patient's best interests.

The process of the doctor offering and the patient choosing a treatment strikes a balance between the medical expertise advising which treatments are likely to work and be safe, and the autonomy of the patient in choosing the treatment he prefers.

WHO MAKES THE DECISION WHEN THE PATIENT IS UNABLE TO DO SO?

Where the patient lacks the mental capacity to understand, retain and weigh up the choices available, someone else has to make the decision about treatment. There are complex provisions relating to the treatment and non-treatment of children, which do not concern us here. The MCA applies to patients over the age of 18, and the MCA Code of Practice (Mental Capacity Act Code of Practice, 2007) explains at paragraph 5.8 that:

> Under the Act, many different people may be required to make decisions or act on behalf of someone who lacks capacity to make decisions for themselves. The person making the decision is referred to throughout this chapter, and in other parts of the Code, as the 'decision-maker', and it is the decision-maker's responsibility to work out what would be in the best interests of the person who lacks capacity.
>
> — For most day-to-day actions or decisions, the decision-maker will be the carer most directly involved with the person at the time.
> — Where the decision involves the provision of medical treatment, the doctor or other member of healthcare staff responsible for carrying out the particular treatment or procedure is the decision-maker.
> — Where nursing or paid care is provided, the nurse or paid carer will be the decision-maker.
> — If a Lasting Power of Attorney (or Enduring Power of Attorney) has been made and registered, or a deputy has been appointed under a court order, the attorney or deputy will be the decision-maker, for decisions within the scope of their authority.

Paragraph 5.11 adds:

> There are also times when a joint decision might be made by a number of people. For example, when a care plan for a person who lacks capacity to make relevant decisions is being put together, different healthcare or social care staff might be involved in making decisions or recommendations about the person's care package. Sometimes these decisions will be made by a team of healthcare or social care staff as a whole. At other times, the decision will be made by a specific individual within the team. A different member of the team may then implement that decision, based on what the team has worked out to be the person's best interests.

This is reasonable and sensible advice. Often professionals will not be involved in major decisions purportedly made in a patient's best interests. This might be the case in a decision about whether or when an elderly person with dementia should be moved into a care home. If the cost of the placement is met through private funds, and there has been no local authority assessment of need, it may well be that no professional is involved. There may be no scrutiny of this decision, and nothing to ensure that it is made in the person's best interests. This is not to suggest that families make bad decisions, but as it is likely to be the family that is under pressure as a result of the often considerable care needs or behaviours of the person concerned, these can be hard to deal with, leading to a pressure to place the person concerned in a care home. A pressure in the opposite direction may arise from an understandable wish to save the cost of a care home placement for as long as possible. Professional staff are perhaps less likely to be subject to these kinds of pressures. They may, however, be subject to other pressures, for example the need to move a person out of a hospital bed as soon as possible after the immediate medical treatment has been completed, or a reluctance to put the necessary time, energy and resources into complex plans to support a person at a high level of need and risk in the community, when it might be very much easier and less risky to arrange for the person to be admitted to a care home where their care and safety will be someone else's concern. The public sector is usually highly risk-averse, and it can take a great deal of courage and experience to adopt a more risky care plan in the belief that, despite the higher risk, it may be better for the patient: As Lord Justice Munby has put it:

> The fact is that all life involves risk, and the elderly and the vulnerable are exposed to additional risks and to risks they are less well equipped than others to cope with. But just as wise parents resist the temptation to keep their children metaphorically wrapped up in cotton wool, so too we must avoid the temptation always to put the physical health and safety of the elderly and the vulnerable before everything else. Often it will be appropriate to do so, but not always. Physical health and safety can sometimes be bought at too high a price in happiness and emotional welfare. The emphasis must be on sensible risk appraisal, not striving to avoid all risk, whatever the price, but instead seeking a proper balance and being willing to tolerate manageable or acceptable risks as the price appropriately to be paid in order to achieve some other good—in particular to achieve the vital good of the elderly or vulnerable person's happiness. What good is it making someone safer if it merely makes them miserable? (Munby, 2010).

Where the issue is a medical treatment the decision-maker will usually be the doctor. Consequently, the doctor may have to do both jobs: provide the advice on treatment options, and make the choice for the patient. The doctor will often need to involve others in the decision-making. As doctors often work in teams they are likely to discuss the options with the rest of the team and with others who have a legitimate interest, such as the family.

In some circumstances someone other than the doctor or other involved professional makes the final decision on treatment. Many jurisdictions have procedures by which a person who has capacity can appoint an attorney to make decisions on their behalf at some future time when they may have lost capacity. In England and Wales the procedure is a Lasting Power of Attorney (LPA), which is a creature of the MCA. There are two types. An LPA Health and Welfare deals with aspects of care and treatment and includes, though is not restricted to, medical treatment. An LPA Property and Affairs deals with financial and property matters. An attorney appointed under one power does not thereby have authority under the other. This can create difficulties because it is more common to make an LPA Property and Affairs than a Health and Welfare LPA, and an attorney created under the former power may be surprised to discover that their authority does not extend to treatment decisions. Scotland has similar legislation.

Alternatively a person can make an advance decision setting out the types of treatment which he may or may not wish to receive in future if he should lose capacity (MCA sections 24–26). As a patient does not have a right to demand a particular treatment, but only to accept or refuse one that is offered, such advance decisions are in effect advance refusals of treatment, but may contain (non-binding) expressions of treatment preferences.

One limitation of these processes is that if those making a best interests decision are not aware of the existence of an LPA or advance decision then it cannot be used in the decision. It is possible to check with the Office of the Public Guardian whether or not an LPA exists for a given person, but there is no such national register for advance decisions. Indeed, the MCA does not prescribe any particular form for an advance decision, and, save for decisions to refuse life-sustaining treatment, it need neither be in writing nor witnessed. This may leave a very substantial difficulty in evidencing an advance decision; for instance if the family says that the person 'always said that he wanted/did not want X', what weight is the decision-maker to put on this?

WHAT ARE BEST INTERESTS?

For a concept that is so central in decision-making about people who lack capacity, there is a surprising lack of definition as to what constitutes best interests. Section 4 of the MCA describes those things which the person making the decision should consider— this is known as the statutory checklist. This is described in more detail elsewhere in this volume (see especially chapter twenty-five), but paraphrasing:

- A determination of best interests must not be based on the person's age, appearance or condition or behaviour (MCA section 4(1)).
- The person making the determination must consider all the relevant circumstances including whether the person might be able to make the decision at some future time (MCA section 4(3)).
- He must encourage so far as is possible the participation of the person concerned (MCA section 4(4)).

— He must not be motivated by a desire to bring about the person's death (MCA section 4(5)).
— He must consider the person's past and present wishes and feelings, his beliefs and values relevant to the decision and the other factors which the person concerned would have been likely to consider if he were able to do so (MCA section 4(6)).
— He must take into account, if it is practicable and appropriate to consult them, the views of:
  a. anyone named by the person as someone to be consulted on the matter in question or on matters of that kind;
  b. anyone engaged in caring for the person or interested in his welfare;
  c. any donee of a lasting power of attorney granted by the person;
  d. any deputy appointed for the person by the court;

  as to what would be in the person's best interests and, in particular, as to the matters mentioned in subsection (6) (MCA section 4(7)).

The MCA itself in the checklist above, the Code of Practice and case law has emphasised that decision-makers need to consider a much wider range of factors than just medical outcomes.

HOW ARE BEST INTERESTS ESTABLISHED?

A large number of decisions will arise every day in the life of a person who lacks capacity. Some will be relatively inconsequential: what to have for breakfast; when to have a bath; whether to go out for a walk. Others will be much more significant: whether to move house; whether to have a particular medical procedure; how to invest a large sum of money. Doctors will generally be involved only in decision-making about medical procedures, though they may have an important role in assessing capacity for other kinds of decisions. Some doctors such as GPs and psychiatrists may have a role in making wider decisions, particularly concerning where and how those lacking capacity should be cared for. While the MCA requires that all decisions made on behalf of a mentally incapacitated person should be based on a process of establishing incapacity followed by a consideration of best interests using the statutory checklist, plainly not all (indeed not most) decisions will be made by a formal consideration of the MCA criteria. It is clearly impractical to convene a best interests meeting for every decision, no matter how small. In practice, the person making the best interests decision will take a view on whether they themselves can make the decision, or whether a wider consultation is required. This will be guided by the significance of the decision, the risks arising from it and the experience and qualifications of the potential decision-maker.

Where a decision requires careful discussion and consideration, it is common practice to convene a best interests meeting. There is no statutory guidance on how, when or by whom this should be done, but such a meeting will require clear goals and preparation. The process is very helpfully explored in detail in Joyce (2007). A best interests meeting should be convened only for a person who lacks capacity to make a particular decision. An assessment of capacity therefore needs to have taken place before the meeting. If the person concerned has capacity, then that person should make the decision, and no meeting will be necessary. It is important to clarify what the goal of the meeting will be, ie, what is the decision that needs to be made, and who are the people who need to be part of making the decision. The MCA Code of Practice (chapter 4) says that the decision-maker should consult widely, and so a best interests meeting may need to include significant family members and/or friends, one or more doctors or other health professionals concerned with the treatment, social care staff and others who may have relevant knowledge or responsibility. In the event that the person is 'unbefriended', ie, has no one other than paid carers to speak for him, and the decision concerns serious medical treatment, or staying in hospital longer than 28 days, or placement in a care home for longer than eight weeks, the MCA requires that an Independent Mental Capacity Advocate (IMCA) is appointed (MCA Code chapter 10). Wherever possible, the person lacking capacity should be involved in the meeting.

After making introductions it will be helpful for the chair of the meeting to explain the purpose of the meeting, namely the decision which needs to be made and the framework of best interests to be considered. Those unfamiliar with the MCA may find the approach to be different from their own decision-making, and they may need to be encouraged not to reach a view before they have heard all the relevant information.

It may be helpful to follow the scheme of the statutory checklist described above. It will be necessary to confirm that the person has been assessed as lacking capacity, and that everything has been done to assist him to regain capacity. Consideration will need to be given to whether he is likely to regain capacity, and if so whether the relevant decision can be postponed. Great attention will need to be given to compiling the checklist of factors which bear on the decision. Williams et al (2012) give several helpful examples of scenarios for which checklists have been compiled. It is desirable that a consensus decision should be reached, but if not, the decision-maker will need to consider whether it is justified for her to take the decision in the absence of agreement, or whether other steps need to be taken which might include referring the matter to a court (in England and Wales this would be the Court of Protection).

The meeting will need to be minuted, and the minutes distributed appropriately and kept in the person's notes.

WHAT TRIGGERS A BEST INTERESTS MEETING?

In practice it is unrealistic for every best interests decision to be determined at a best interests meeting. It is also unnecessary where the decision is minor and of little enduring consequence for the person involved. To plan, assemble, conduct and minute a best interests meeting takes a substantial amount of time and resource which is often difficult to achieve in many health or social care settings. An empirical study commissioned by the Department of Health provides detailed information on the practice of best interests determinations in England in 2010–11 (Williams et al, 2012). As it is one of the very few published studies of how best interests decisions are in practice carried out it is worth examining in some detail.

The survey was carried out in four areas of England amongst health, social care and legal professionals by means of an online survey, telephone and face to face interviews. Over 400 professionals took part. The most common stated reasons for making a best interests decision were serious deterioration in health, discharge from hospital and change of accommodation. The majority of best interests decisions did, as required, follow an assessment that the person lacked capacity, but one in ten did not. In about half of cases, the assessment of capacity happened on the same day as the best interests decision. In about a quarter of cases, decisions on capacity appeared to have been made, contrary to the MCA, on the basis of history, diagnosis, disability, age, appearance, behaviour or the fact the someone was making an unwise decision. The authors comment that 'this seemed to indicate a reasonably widespread lack of understanding of the MCA'.

Over half of all decisions involved a series of meetings between the decision-maker, the person and usually others who knew the person. Specially convened best interests meetings could take many forms. They worked best if there had been good preparation and consultation beforehand. Sometimes best interests decisions were not made through meetings but informally, such as during conversations round a bedside. Best interests decision-making was often incorporated in the agenda of multidisciplinary team meetings, and was sometimes considered in other processes such as safeguarding. Successful decision-making processes were undertaken when the decision-maker or leader was clear about stating the parameters of the decision to be made, and when the person lacking capacity had already been prepared or consulted outside the meeting.

Almost half of the best interests decisions in the survey related to health care, while about a quarter concerned personal welfare or safety. Of the health care decisions, 40% concerned serious physical health care treatment. Some related to a Deprivation of Liberty Safeguards (DOLS) assessment. Almost half of the treatment decisions involved restrictions being put on the person, including the use of medication or staff control over the person. Only 7% were about property or financial matters. The views of the doctor did not always prevail. In one example, a consultant had recommended that a man with profound learning disabilities who had been in and out of hospital with aspiration respiratory difficulties should have a PEG feeding tube inserted through the skin of the abdomen into his stomach to ensure that he could be given food safely without risk of aspiration into his lungs. The outcome of a best interests process involving the man's parents and others was that PEG feeding was decided against since the process of eating food by mouth was so important to the quality of his life, despite the risk involved.

In a number of cases, a deterioration in health triggered a best interests process which then identified a series of other issues which also needed to be resolved. For example, a cognitively impaired older lady was admitted to hospital with an infection, but then concerns emerged about her safety at home, and so a decision needed to be made about whether or not she should be admitted to a care home. Frequently it was not easy to separate best interests decisions neatly into health and social care issues. As capacity is specific to a particular decision, this can create significant complexity. It is not unusual for a patient to be referred simply for 'an assessment of capacity' when it is not specified what the decision in question actually involves.

People with dementia accounted for 40% of those discussed in the online survey. Most of the social care decisions about people with dementia related to a change of accommodation and only a minority related to safeguarding, and accordingly social care practitioners were the largest single group of professionals who led best interests decisions on behalf of people with dementia. Capacity assessments of people with dementia typically took place in repeated attempts to assess over a period of up to several weeks. Sometimes standardised tests were mentioned as if they were tools for assessing capacity, and in some cases it appeared that doctors were inclined to conclude that a person lacked capacity simply because he had dementia.

Assessment of capacity emerged from this study as being the most difficult and sensitive area for practitioners. Many assessments of capacity were carried out by more than one professional, either as a joint assessment, or by discussion with colleagues afterwards. In only a minority of the interview cases (9 out of 25) did the same person take responsibility both for assessing capacity and leading the best interests decision. In a significant minority of cases, contrary to the MCA, a best interests decision was made even though the person concerned had not been assessed as lacking capacity. A common pattern was that inability to manage one's own independence and care was confused with inability to make a decision. It was rare that an older person was assessed as lacking capacity but also deemed able to live independently with support. In some people who had a strong personality and were able to speak up for themselves it was easy to overestimate capacity, while the opposite was also true, that capacity might be underestimated in people who are reluctant to speak up for themselves.

In medical best interests decisions, record keeping was mostly carried out by a detailed note. Some decisions were recorded formally using standardised pro formas, though these were more common in social care decisions. Overall, about a third of respondents said that a detailed note was used, and another third said that a pro forma was used. In a few cases, the pro forma provided was so short as to be extremely limiting in the information recorded. People often felt frustrated by how inadequately records were shared.

A wide range of professionals was recorded in the survey as taking part in making best interests decisions, though only 7% claimed to be the sole decision-maker. The survey data do not make clear how many were doctors as opposed to other health care professionals, but in the case scenarios discussed in the survey, it is clear that many professionals besides doctors led the process or took responsibility for the decision. In a minority of cases, Independent Mental Capacity Advocates (IMCAs) were involved in the process, but this worked best where they were involved early in the process. Consensus decision-making was generally preferred to individual responsibility. Some felt that doctors should be responsible for medical decisions in health care settings, but even then a meeting could be a helpful way of holding doctors to account for those decisions. A meeting could also be a helpful way for doctors to hear the views and personal knowledge of others involved in the patient's care before making a best interests decision. The two functions of leading the best interests process and taking responsibility for the decision were not necessarily always carried out by the same person. In a few situations, perhaps where there was a need for an urgent decision, it was helpful to have a single decision-maker.

The MCA makes provision for several specific formal processes in which best interests are decided. Where an LPA has been made which covers the decision in question, or there is a court appointed deputy, then that person has a clear responsibility to make the decision. This does not mean that there should be no discussion of best interests with others; on the contrary, the Act requires the attorney or deputy who is the decision-maker to consult widely in order to arrive at a best interests decision. For assessments for Deprivation of Liberty authorisations, at least two professionals must be involved, one of whom must be an appropriately trained doctor. In the survey, these formal processes formed a small minority of the best interests assessments carried out.

It may be helpful to articulate some practical guidance on making best interests decisions:

1. Assess capacity carefully and record the assessment.
2. Collect information relating to best interests.
3. Some decisions are either straightforward or relatively insignificant and may not require much formal discussion.
4. Where decisions are more complex, a meeting or series of meetings may be required. These need to be carefully prepared, chaired and minuted. The role of the chair should include setting out the purpose of the meeting, and explaining the relevant legal and ethical framework.
5. The decision to be made should be identified early, and information relevant to it shared. It may be the case that there is more than one decision, or one major decision and a group of consequential decisions.
6. It is helpful, too, for the meeting to be multidisciplinary, with the involvement of professionals, family, friends or others.
7. A decision needs to be made on whether or not it is desirable to invite the person lacking capacity to the meeting.

The guidance produced by the British Psychological Society (Joyce, 2007), supported by the Department of Health, contains a detailed and helpful account of conducting best interests meetings.

MEDICAL DECISION-MAKING

Doctors are involved in many kinds of best interests decision, ranging from life-sustaining treatment, DOLS assessments and decisions about discharge from hospital. Psychiatric treatments involving compulsion are more likely to be dealt with under the Mental Health Act 1983 (MHA) than the MCA; the MHA itself does not refer to best interests, and the majority of references to best interests in the MHA Code of Practice relate to the MCA or to consultation with other people about the patient. In the survey, health care decisions were slightly more likely than others to be taken at a single meeting that did not involve the person lacking capacity. In some cases, the decision-maker (the medical consultant or practitioner) was not present at the best interests meeting. Medical decisions, particularly those made in hospital, were nearly always driven by a desire to preserve life. While there were examples of doctors making decisions unilaterally—and with little apparent consideration of wider issues than just medical outcomes—there was much to suggest that doctors worked in a multidisciplinary team model, taking into account social and personal life issues as well as medical ones.

In England and Wales, the person certifying capacity to make an LPA may be (but does not have to be) a doctor. For an application for deputyship to the Court of Protection, form COP3 must be completed by a doctor as evidence of incapacity.

DISAGREEMENTS

In the survey, a minority of respondents reported that there had been some sort of disagreement about the person's best interests. Disagreements could be between professionals, or with family members and were often between the person lacking capacity and those making a decision for him. In a few cases the disagreements related to suspicions of financial abuse by relatives. Sometimes the needs of family carers needed to be weighed against the needs of the person lacking capacity, although the MCA itself allows only for consideration of the best interests of the person lacking capacity. There was only limited information in the survey about the views of families about best interests processes, but in a number of cases, the family member felt disempowered or excluded from the decision. IMCAs can have a helpful role in mediating disagreements, although this is not part of their statutory role.

BEST INTERESTS: A COHERENT CONCEPT?

Doctors are accustomed to making decisions on behalf of patients who cannot do so for themselves. They are not always very good at recording evidence of incapacity before they do so, and there is a perception that doctors do not always take sufficient account of non-medical factors in decision-making (though the study cited above found little evidence to support this). Patients themselves rarely follow a best interests process in their own decision-making. Other jurisdictions, notably the United States, make more use of concepts other than best interests, such as some form of substituted judgement to make decisions.

Particular difficulties can arise in determining capacity reliably. It may not be clear who ought to be the decision-maker, and there is no formal process for challenging a best interests decision other than an application to the Court of Protection. Best interests itself is a complex concept which draws on very many aspects of a person's situation. It is not always easy to balance such a wide range of complex factors. Where the issue relates to allowing someone to die, both doctors and the courts have a strong presumption in favour of preserving life, and it is far from clear that this adequately reflects the priorities of the wider public.

On the other hand, the framework of best interests does provide a logical structure for approaching decision-making for people who lack capacity, and the MCA and Code of Practice provide directions which are admirably clear and sensible, and go to great lengths to put the wishes, needs and circumstances of the incapacitated person at the heart of the decision. The Act tries hard to promote autonomy, and the mechanisms of LPA and—arguably—advance decisions provide a clear and helpful path for a person to choose for themselves who should make decisions for them and how. Doctors may have critical roles in these decisions, both in assessing capacity and in determining best interests and, as in the rest of medical practice, they need to be mindful of the wider social context in which medical decision-making takes place.

REFERENCES

Hope, T, Slowther, A and Eccles, J (2009) 'Best interests, dementia and the Mental Capacity Act (2005)' 35(12) *Journal of Medical Ethics* 733–38. doi: 10.1136/jme.2009.030783.

Joyce, T (2007) *Best Interests: Guidance on determining the best interests of adults who lack the capacity to make a decision (or decisions) for themselves* (The British Psychological Society/Department of Health).

Munby, J (2010) Keynote address. Paper presented at Taking Stock: The Mental Health & Capacity Reforms conference, Manchester.

Williams, V et al (2012) *Making Best Interests Decisions: People and Processes* (Mental Health Foundation).

LEGISLATION

The Mental Health Act, 1983
The Mental Capacity Act, 2005
Mental Capacity Act Code of Practice, 2007

8

Advance Decisions and Proxy Decision-Making in the Elderly: A Medical Perspective

GARY SINOFF AND NATALIA BLAJA-LISNIC

COMPARATIVE PERSPECTIVES

WHILE MANY ELDERLY remain healthy in advanced age, the dramatic increase in the number of elderly has brought with it an increase in those with cognitive impairment. This makes the basic right of decision-making about health care complicated. This basic concept includes the right to accept or refuse treatment. However in the presence of cognitive impairment, the person may lose this ability to participate in the decision-making process. This process of decision-making differs from country to country. Understanding the perspective from other countries allows physicians to relate to the complexity of the problem.

The Mental Capacity Act 2005 (England and Wales) enables patients to make legally binding arrangements to refuse specific treatments in advance or to appoint another to make decisions on their behalf (Kerrigan and Ormerod, 2010). Such advance directives seem at the moment to be uncommon. Bond and Lowton (2011) found that physicians expressed discomfort about following an advance directive relating to the withdrawal or withholding of life-sustaining treatment if in their professional opinion it did not represent the patient's best interests. Physicians also expressed concerns in relation to patient understanding of the role and limits of these documents.

In the United States, Silveira, Scott and Langa (2010) reported that almost half of patients prior to death needed to make decisions in relation to their treatment, yet 70% were incapable of making them. Of these, 67.6% had advance directives—a much higher proportion than, for instance, the United Kingdom.

In most jurisdictions, both lawyers and medical regulators expect surrogate decision-makers to be guided by the previously recorded preferences of the incapacitous patient.

The ethical problems associated with substituted judgement were described by Kapp (2010). One of the main concerns is the difficulty of thinking oneself accurately into the mind of another: there is hence a danger of assuming that the patient would have decided in the same way as the decision-maker.

In many countries, medical decisions are increasingly made using a shared decision-making model, by which physicians help patients to clarify their values and reach consensus about treatment courses consistent with the patient's wishes. Formal ethical consultations, perhaps involving a clinical ethicist, can be helpful in resolving conflicts when physicians and families disagree over decisions, especially in treatment plans for the end of life (Luce, 2010).

In Germany, many ethicists and lawyers have proposed models for retaining respect for patient autonomy at the end of life (Bauer, 2009), but many German physicians remain oblivious to the ethical imperative to involve patients in their decisions about medical care. These decisions may impinge not only on medical care, but relate to much wider issues. Shared decision-making, decision supports and decision aids empower patients to collaborate with their physicians in making informed medical decisions that lead to the best treatment outcomes (Drake and Deegan, 2009).

ADVANCE CARE PLANNING

The desired outcome of an Advance Care Plan (ACP) is a relevant, applicable advance directive, consistent with any other oral or written directives that exist. An ACP should include discussions about the illness and prognosis, the care and treatment options available, the individual's concerns, fears, wishes, goals, beliefs and values and take into account these preferences for future care and treatment and preferences for religious, spiritual or other personal support. Any discussion about particular treatments, which the patient in certain circumstances would refuse, must be documented (Moore, 2012).

Although there are no universally accepted standards for establishing the ability of individuals to consent/refuse medical treatment, a number of measures have been developed to assess decision-making capacity. Such assessment involves determining an individual's ability to understand and retain relevant information, appreciate the nature and consequences of the decision and express his decision. Additionally, the decision must be voluntary and free from coercion or undue influence (Fisher et al, 2009).

There is a cultural aspect to the process of decision-making. The approaches of different ethnic groups differ, and are related to the cultural values, demographic characteristics, level of acculturation and knowledge of end-of-life treatment options (Kwak and Haley, 2005).

The decision-making process may also be age-dependent. Puchalski et al (2000) found that most elderly in-patients would not want to be resuscitated in the event of a cardio/respiratory arrest, if prior to that arrest they had lost their decision-making capacity. Most patients prefer that their family and/or physician make such decisions for them.

In fact, it is hard to predict patients' preferences. Covinsky and Fuller (2000) found that patients who were older, had cancer, were women, believed their prognoses to be poor and were more dependent in activities of daily living function were less likely to want cardio-pulmonary resuscitation (CPR). Most patients do not discuss their preferences with their physicians, and for about only half of patients refusing CPR, is the 'Do Not Attempt Resuscitation' (DNAR) order recorded (Covinsky and Fuller, 2000).

Factors other than patients' preferences which determine whether DNAR orders were placed in the notes were the patient's age, the physician's specialty and the geographic site of care. However, there was no evidence that increasing the rate of documentation of advance directives resulted in care that was more consistent with patients' preferences. Bond and Lowton (2011) found that physicians and surrogates/proxies are often unaware of their patients' preferences. The end result is that the care provided to patients is often inconsistent with patients' preferences and is associated with factors other than preference. Improving these deficiencies in end-of-life care requires a systematic change: no simple intervention will cure the problem (Bond and Lowton, 2011).

As expected, spouses were more accurate in their substituted judgement than adult children. Surrogates/proxies who perceived a high degree of family conflict tended to be less accurate than those with lower degrees of family conflict. Physicians should be aware of these family factors when discussing advance care planning (Parks et al, 2011).

Even with advance care planning, there was a decreased reliance on patient preferences with increasing age. This may reflect the problem of ageism: the preferences of the elderly are often seen as less important than those of younger adults. Although studies have shown that patients want physicians/family members to have some part in the decision-making process, it is reported that surrogates and physicians are not good at predicting patients' wishes (Torke et al, 2010).

Making treatment decisions for older people is difficult, not only because of the complex interplay of multiple co-morbidities, but also because of the fine balance of risks versus benefit in any management plan (Aw et al, 2011). MacPherson and fellow researchers (MacPherson et al, 2013) studied this in those persons with chronic obstructive pulmonary disease. Advance care planning was recommended for these patients, with the aim of reducing unwanted interventions, but was rarely executed. Patients wanted more information about the diagnosis and prognosis, and most importantly wanted to be involved in ACP. Their expectations were that the initiation would come from the health care team. Accordingly health care professionals should take responsibility for initiating these discussions to improve relationships between them and their patients, as well as enabling patients to be more involved in current decisions about their care (MacPherson et al, 2013).

COGNITIVE IMPAIRMENT/DEMENTIA AND ADVANCE CARE PLANNING

Any neurological illnesses can leave patients unable to make valid decisions about their medical treatment (Kerrigan and Ormerod, 2010). This becomes more evident in persons with cognitive impairment. Because health care providers have both legal and ethical obligations to ensure that appropriate consent for treatment has been obtained, two issues arise: how to determine whether an individual can provide consent and how to make care decisions when he is incapable (Fisher et al, 2009).

Persons diagnosed as suffering from cognitive decline, especially in the early stages, are often concerned about how decisions about their future medical treatment would be made if they become incapable. They fear that they would be forced to receive life-sustaining or life-prolonging treatments against their will. The loss of the ability to make informed decisions is gradual, so the point at which they are no longer able to make a decision is quite difficult to pinpoint.

Dementia raises special issues because of the kind of suffering it engenders. Loss of control over both self and the environment is an inherent feature of all dementias, often producing anguish. In addition, demented persons may suffer when undergoing invasive medical interventions since they are incapable of understanding what is happening.

How one assesses a patient with cognitive decline and possible dementia is a complex problem. Undergoing extensive neuropsychological testing may be an answer, but this is unlikely to be routinely practicable for most patients. Gregory et al (2007) used the Mini-Mental State Examination (MMSE) screening tool for assessment of clinical capacity in patients with Alzheimer's disease, and suggested that a score of 18 out of 30 was an important watershed. This study reinforced previous studies which had shown the effectiveness of MMSE scores for assessing capacity (Molloy et al, 1996; Pucci et al, 2001).

Physicians will continue to be the locus of decision-making for individuals with dementia. Discussions with family members about the care of the demented person if he becomes incapacitated and unable to make decisions should be held and reviewed periodically (Triplett et al, 2008). Unfortunately, even in the earlier stages where the individual is able to express his wishes, these discussions are often not held (Garand et al, 2011; Lingler et al, 2008).

Whether patients' surrogates/proxies are involved in the ACP process or actually making a decision about treatment, reasonable decision-making presupposes a good understanding of the nature of the disease. The process of clarifying the nature of disease, eliciting the goal of care and translating the goal into specific interventions will allow for the provision of appropriate care for individuals with advanced dementia in the coming decades (Gillick, 2012).

CONCLUSIONS

Advance care planning helps with decision-making, based on the documented preferences of what the patient would have wanted while still with capacity. However, such documents are still the exception rather than the rule. Health care professionals are often wary of them (Aw et al, 2011).

The difficulties inherent in all advance decisions require flexibility in the law so that individuals are not bound in ways that they did not foresee and would not wish.

Misrepresentation of these decisions as being absolutely and incontestably binding will concern and frustrate patients and families who believe them to be obligatory and then discover they are not. It may also discourage physicians from engaging in the ACP process, if they mistakenly believe it will require them to act in ways contrary to their ethical and professional codes of practice. ACP will never eliminate the need for these decisions, but it should improve the process and provide valuable assistance to those involved.

With the growing enthusiasm for proxy decision-making, ethical doubts have arisen about whether proxies are really opting for what the patient would have selected (Emanuel and Emanuel, 1992). Unfortunately, timely advance medical planning will often not have occurred, leaving many uncertainties about what decisions are appropriate (Kapp, 2010). Proxies often resort to decisions based on the perceived 'best interests' of the individual, but this carries its own risks. Best interests are difficult to determine and may involve the value judgements of the decision-maker. Relying on physician recommendations has its appeal because doctors have clinical experience regarding prognosis, but medical training does not qualify physicians to judge which set of outcomes is more desirable, and physicians may inject their own values and preferences into the process.

One solution is to focus less on the outcome of decisions and more on the process. Procedural fairness depends on input from physicians, the balancing of burdens and benefits and the participation of all relevant stakeholders. Although doing so does not assure a good outcome, it does share the burden of decision-making and reduces isolation. Little information is available on how proxies determine what the individual wants and what constitutes the best interests of a person (Fisher et al, 2009).

Arguments against advance decision-making are based on problems with prediction, adaptation, extrapolation and the nature of surrogate decision-making. Patients' treatment preferences change all the time. Patients often cannot envisage living with disability and accordingly opt for aggressive treatments. However, patients vacillate.

It can be difficult for patients and surrogates to consider all the implications entailed in treatment decisions. Many do not want to think about issues related to illness, death and dying, and may not want to participate in decision-making. Clinicians do not have the time for lengthy advance care planning discussions, and physicians often feel compelled either to weight patient preference heavily in surrogate decision-making or to consider whether the ethical framework for surrogate decisions should be modified to allow for balancing multiple decision-making factors (Sudore and Fried, 2010).

REFERENCES

Age UK (2012) *Advance Decisions, advance statements and living wills.* Factsheet 72.

Aw, D et al (2011) 'Advance care planning and the older patient' 105(3) *QJM: An International Journal of Medicine* 225–30.

Bauer, AW (2009) 'Chances and limitations of patients' advance decisions at the end of life' 159 (17–18) *Wiener Medizinsche Wochenschrift* 431–38.

Beecher, HK (1970) *Research and the Individual: Human Studies*, 1st edn (Boston, Little, Brown and Company).

Berdon, V (2012) *Code of Medical and Human Experimental Ethics.* Available at: poynter.indiana.edu/sas/lb/codes.html.

Bond, CJ and Lowton, K (2011) 'Geriatricians' views of advance decisions and their use in clinical care in England: qualitative study' 40(4) *Age and Ageing* 450–56.

Buchanan, A (2004) 'Mental capacity, legal competence and consent to treatment' 97(9) *Journal of the Royal Society of Medicine* 415–20.

Cedars Sinai US (2013) *Advance Directives.* Available at: www.cedars-sinai.edu/Patients/Programs-and-Services/Healthcare-Ethics-/Advance-Directives.aspx.

Colorado Probate Code (2010) *Proxy decision-makers for medical treatment.* Section 25 of ch 374, Session Laws of Colorado 2010. Entire article added, p 1985, § 3, effective 4 June.

L. 94: (8) amended, p 2647 115, effective 1 July. L 2008: (2) and (3) amended, p 125, § 5, effective 1 January 2009. L 2009: (1) amended (HB 09-1260), ch 107, p 446, § 13, effective 1 July. L 2010: (1) effective 1 July.

Covinsky, KE and Fuller, JD (2000) 'Communication and decision-making in seriously ill patients: findings of the SUPPORT project' 48 *Journal of the American Geriatrics Society* (5 Suppl) S187–93.

Drake, RE and Deegan, PE (2009) 'Shared decision making is an ethical imperative' 60(8) *Psychiatric Services* 1007.

Emanuel, EJ and Emanuel, LL (1992) 'Proxy decision making for incompetent patients. An ethical and empirical analysis' 267(15) *Journal of the American Medical Association* 2067–71.

Fisher, KM et al (2009) 'Proxy healthcare decision-making for persons with intellectual disability: perspectives of residential-agency directors' 114(6) *American Journal on Intellectual and Developmental Disabilities* 401–10.

Garand, L et al (2011) 'Incidence and predictors of advance care planning among persons with cognitive impairment' 19(8) *American Journal of Geriatric Psychiatry* 712–20.

Gillick, MR (2012) 'The Graying of America: Challenges and Controversies. Doing the right thing: a geriatrician's perspective on medical care for the person with advanced dementia' 40(1) *Journal of Law, Medicine and Ethics* 51–56.

Gregory, R et al (2007) 'Is the degree of cognitive impairment in patients with Alzheimer's disease related to their capacity to appoint an enduring power of attorney?' 36 *Age and Ageing* 527–31.

Kapp, MB (2010) 'Medical decision-making for incapacitated elders: A "therapeutic interests" standard' 33 *International Journal of Law and Psychiatry* 369–74.

Kerrigan, S and Ormerod, I (2010) 'Advance planning in end-of-life care: Legal and ethical considerations for neurologists' 10 *Practical Neurology* 140–44.

Kwak, J and Haley, W (2005) 'Current research findings on end-of-life decision making among racially or ethnically diverse groups' 45(5) *The Gerontologist* 634–41.

Lingler, JH et al (2008) 'Frequency and correlates of advanced planning among cognitively impaired older adults' 16(8) *American Journal of Geriatric Psychiatry* 643–49.

Luce, JM (2010) 'End-of-Life decision making in the intensive care unit' 182(1) *American Journal of Respiratory Critical Care Medicine* 6–11.

MacPherson, A et al (2013) 'The views of patients with severe chronic obstructive pulmonary disease on advance care planning: a qualitative study' 27(3) *Palliative Medicine* 265–72.

Molloy, DW et al (1996) 'Measuring capacity to complete an advance directive' 44 *Journal of the American Geriatrics Society* 660–64.

Moore, ML (2012) Advance Care Planning (13th Annual Medical Law Conference, Wellington, New Zealand, March 2012).

National Institute of Health (1979) *The National Commission for the Protection of Human Subjects of Biomedical and Behavioral Research* (the Belmont Report). Available at: www.hhs.gov/ohrp/humansubjects/guidance/belmont.html.

Parks, SM et al (2011) 'Family factors in end-of-life decision-making: Family conflict and proxy relationship' 14(2) *Journal of Palliative Medicine* 179–84.

Pucci, E et al (2001) 'Information and competency for consent to pharmacological clinical trials in Alzheimer disease: An empirical analysis in patients and family caregivers' 15 *Alzheimer Disease and Associated Disorders* 146–54.

Puchalski, CM et al (2000) 'Patients who want their family and physician to make resuscitation decisions for them: observations from SUPPORT and HELP. Study to Understand Prognoses and Preferences for Outcomes and Risks of Treatment' 48 *Journal of the American Geriatrics Society* (5 Suppl) S84–90.

Silveira, MJ, Scott, YHK and Langa, KM (2010) 'Advance directives and outcomes of surrogate decision making before death' 362 *New England Journal of Medicine* 1211–18.

Sudore, RL and Fried, TR (2010) 'Redefining the "planning" in advance care planning: Preparing for end-of-life decision making' 153(4) *Annals of Internal Medicine* 256–61.
Torke, AM et al (2010) 'Physicians' views on the importance of patient preferences in surrogate decision-making' 58(3) *Journal of the American Geriatrics Society* 533–38.
Triplett, P et al (2008) 'Content of advance directives for individuals with advanced dementia' 20(5) *Journal of Aging Health* 583–96.
World Medical Association (2009) *Declaration of Helsinki. Ethical Principles for Medical Research Involving human Subjects*. Available at: www.wma.net/en/30publications/10policies/b3/17c.pdf.

9

The Happy Dementia Patient

HUGH SERIES

IN 1991 A medical student, Andrew Firlik, published an account of a woman he had got to know over the course of several visits to her apartment in New York. She had had Alzheimer's disease for at least five years and was very disabled by it since she needed a live-in carer, and had to be locked inside her apartment in case she got into difficulty outside. But she puzzled Firlik:

> Despite her illness, or may be somehow because of it, Margo is undeniably one of the happiest people I have known. There is something graceful about the degeneration her mind is undergoing, leaving her carefree, always cheerful. Do her problems, whatever she may perceive them to be, simply fail to make it to the worry centers of her brain? How does Margo maintain her sense of self? When a person can no longer accumulate new memories as the old rapidly fade, what remains? Who is Margo? (Firlik, 1991)

Margo has continued to puzzle and provoke a large number of commentators, and there is now a substantial literature debating what can be learnt from her situation about the nature of dementia and the nature of personhood.

This chapter examines how much we know about what it feels like to have dementia, whether some people with dementia are happy, how people with dementia communicate how they feel, whether there are differences between different types of dementia and what can be concluded about how we care for those with dementia.

There have been three main approaches to investigating quality of life in people with dementia. First, the opinions of carers have been given. Second, outwardly observable behaviours of people with dementia have been studied. Third, people with dementia themselves have been asked or have given accounts of their own. Perhaps surprisingly, given the substantial investment in research on the scientific basis of dementia as well as its impact on carers, there is much less research on this third approach, the views of those with dementia. For a long time there seems to have been a largely implicit assumption that people with dementia were not able to express their own views in a way which made it appropriate to ask them.

TWO MODELS OF DEMENTIA

Before reviewing the findings of each of these approaches it is worth considering why what is perhaps the most obvious approach—to ask people with dementia themselves—has been the least deeply explored. Alzheimer's disease itself was first described by Alois Alzheimer, a neurologist who was interested in the physical changes in the brain that lay behind the condition he described (Alzheimer, 1911; Möller and Graeber, 1998). He shared with colleagues a fascination with the microscopical study of brain tissue, and was able to take advantage of a newly discovered method of staining thin slices of brain with silver to make visible the characteristic plaques and tangles which are still regarded as defining the pathology of Alzheimer's disease. He, and thousands of doctors and researchers after him, regarded Alzheimer's disease as a fundamentally medical condition which led to progressive and inexorable deterioration of brain tissue, and as a result of that physical process to the outward signs and symptoms of dementia.

This view has enabled a remarkable development in our understanding of the causes of Alzheimer's, and led to vastly improved diagnostic methods and to the development of pharmacological treatments, albeit ones which currently have only modest efficacy. It has been a very productive approach and places the study of dementia firmly in the domain of medical science. But it also portrays dementia as a disease which steadily erodes the brain, leaving the physical shell of a person lacking the inner machinery of the person. If the person is no longer there, then there is no point in asking the shell about its experiences and beliefs, and no point in expecting the shell to be able to make meaningful decisions about how it should live or be cared for. The shell becomes an object of care and study, but not a person to be consulted.

This is not the only way of understanding dementia. A very different view has been developed by Tom Kitwood and others:

> Briefly, it suggests that the clinical presentation of dementia is far from being a direct consequence of a degenerative process in nervous tissue. Rather, the dementing process should be viewed as the outcome of a dialectical interplay between two tendencies. The first is neurological impairment, which does indeed set upper limits to how a person can perform. The second is the personal psychology an individual has accrued, together with the social psychology with which he or she is surrounded. Such a dialectical account can, in principle, rationalize the whole range of phenomena associated with dementia better than one derived simply from medical science ... Crucial to this account is a recognition of the 'malignant social psychology' which often bears down powerfully on those who are aged and confused: a psychology in which the others involved are usually well-intentioned but lacking in insight (Kitwood and Bredin, 1992).

On this account, the neurological impairment need not necessarily undermine the ability of a person with dementia to feel happiness or sadness or to communicate feelings with others. The patient is not to be seen as a diseased object, but rather as a person like any other. The disease may change how one communicates with the person, but it does not remove the need or the possibility of doing so. Good care is constantly mindful of the person, and with appropriate person-centred care much of the negative impact of the disease can be minimised.

Kitwood and others have described how it is often not so much the impairment itself, but the response of society around the person that creates much of the misery and suffering of dementia. True, the neurological impairment creates great difficulties for both sufferer and carers, but it is possible to respond in a much more positive way to minimise the damage and in doing so to enhance the experience, quality of life and level of function of the person affected. On occasion it is possible partially to reverse some of the measured impairments, giving the lie to the notion that the course of the disease is inexorably downwards. A wide range of approaches have been described, but the size of the task is immense, and patience, skill and time are required. Kitwood (1997) reviews some of these approaches and gives examples of the benefits that can follow.

THE EXPERIENCE OF DEMENTIA

In a study of 27 people with dementia and 28 relatives, Aggarwal et al (2003) found that people with dementia often described feelings of loss of independence (100% of those with dementia), communication difficulties (96%), frustration or anger (56%) and sadness or depression (48%). People with dementia were very critical of residential homes for their lack of choice and lack of activity, though their relatives were more positive: 'There are no activities at all. I'll be downstairs and sleep a lot and read my papers and then I go up and watch television and read my papers and so on and then I go downstairs again'. Some residents put their unhappiness more strongly: 'I hate it here, I hate it—this bloody place—suppose I've got to spend the rest of my life here'. Two residents, however, spoke of being relatively happy: 'I was happy to be brought here, because I'm not alone here and it's a pleasure not to be alone'. Generally, comments made about day care as opposed to residential care were much more positive.

In the same study, relatives also spoke of distress and burden: 'I've got to the stage now, where I think I'm almost beyond the crying. I've cried so much, I've cried an ocean I think'. Another said: 'It's awful. A terrible situation. Each phase is a terrible phase. You sort of have a plateau going along and then something else stops and it's a big hurdle you have to get over and then you go along on another plateau'. Intense loneliness, feelings of depression and social isolation were common features experienced by relatives.

In contrast, Cahill and colleagues (Cahill et al, 2004) used the Brod Quality of Life Tool to investigate the views of 98 people with dementia living in their own homes. The majority of respondents reported positive affects either very often, often or sometimes. These included feelings of happiness, cheerfulness, contentment, hopefulness and finding things to laugh and joke about with others: 'I am happy with what I've got. I like where I live, I generally get up in good humour. I worked all my life and am happy now just to relax and appreciate what I have and relax' (Ireland, male, 80 years). Most people with dementia reported high levels of self-esteem, and many referred to pleasure from the company of friends and family. Over 70% of the sample said that they enjoyed good, very good or excellent quality of life, with only 15% reporting their quality of life as bad. Ill-feeling was experienced only seldom or sometimes. A common worry was anxiety over health and future dependency. Those in this study were living in their own homes, and were on average only mildly or moderately impaired by their dementia.

It might be tempting to conclude that quality of life is high early in the course of dementia, but deteriorates as the condition progresses, particularly at the point where the person moves into a care home. However, in a study of 101 people with dementia, 99 of whom had family carers, Banerjee et al (2006) found that quality of life did not correlate with severity of dementia or functional limitation. Quality of life was poorer in those people with agitation, depression, anxiety, disinhibition and irritability.

BEHAVIOURAL MANIFESTATIONS

The setting of care is important. In a careful study of residents in ten NHS facilities and seven private sector facilities using dementia care mapping, an observational method in which trained observers sat for six-hour periods in each home, recording behaviours of residents with dementia every five minutes and categorising them according to their perceived value, there was a marked lack of positive activity:

> Over the six hour daytime period of observation, people spent 61 minutes (17%) asleep and 108 minutes (30%) either socially withdrawn or not actively engaged in any form of basic or constructive activity. Only 50 minutes (14%) were spent talking (or communicating in other ways) with staff or other residents, and less than 12 minutes (3%) were spent engaged in everyday constructive activities other than watching television (11 minutes (3%). The remaining 33% of the observation period was spent engaged in basic activities such as eating, going to the toilet, etc (Ballard et al, 2001).

Disturbances in behaviour include apathy, agitation, aggression and depression. Hallucinations and delusions are often associated with these behaviours. Together, these changes are often referred to as neuropsychiatric problems, or behavioural and psychological symptoms of dementia. They are common, occurring in 60–95% of groups studied. They are correlated with increased rates of institutionalisation, cost of care and carer stress. They correlate less well with cognitive impairment.

The pattern of neuropsychiatric problems differs between the different forms of dementia and is helpfully reviewed by Teng et al (2009). These problems have been most fully studied in Alzheimer's disease, where the commonest are apathy, aggression and anxiety. They tend to increase with severity, occurring in 80–90% of those with severe Alzheimer's.

Vascular dementia is a much less homogeneous disorder than Alzheimer's disease, and many different types of cerebrovascular pathology have been reported, so perhaps it is not surprising that there is considerable variation in the neuropsychiatric symptoms seen. Aggression, anxiety, apathy and irritability are relatively common (up to about 70%). There have been some attempts to relate symptoms to areas of the brain which are involved in the dementia process. It has been suggested that depression is more likely to be associated with frontal lobe problems, and that pathology involving subcortical structures of the brain is more likely to produce slowness of thought, and difficulties with speech and motor function.

Fronto-temporal lobar degeneration is a complex group of types of dementia which affect particularly the frontal and temporal lobes of the brain. Behavioural changes are very common, and are included as core diagnostic features. Apathy, hyperactivity, disinhibition, loss of social awareness and hyperphagia (eating too much and indiscriminately) are diagnostic features of fronto-temporal dementia. Speech problems are common and severe in semantic dementia, but disinhibition, aggression and altered motor activity are also common.

Delusions and hallucinations are common in people with dementia with Lewy bodies and Parkinson's disease dementia. Hallucinations, fluctuation and sleep disturbance are amongst the diagnostic criteria for dementia with Lewy bodies. Apathy is common but disinhibition and irritability tend to be less common than in other forms of dementia.

CONCLUSION

Is it possible to be happy with dementia? Yes, anecdotes and research studies indicate that it clearly is. Many factors affect this, including the type of dementia that one has, its severity, one's previous personality and way of adapting (or not) to the disorder. Perhaps most significant of all is the reaction of those around one, and how long one is able to continue to live at home. It is possible to continue to enjoy many of the same things that one previously did, and one can find continued pleasure in friends and family. One's interests and enjoyments may change. All these things tend to get more difficult as the disease progresses, but the range of ways of coping and reacting is as varied as the personalities of those affected.

Dementia is sometimes portrayed as an inexorable descent into a mindless, dreadful existence, placing a severe burden of care on those around the person affected. It can be like this, but it is not always so. Perhaps surprisingly, the research discussed earlier indicates that it is not so much severity that determines quality of life in dementia, but is much more to do with the personality of the person concerned, the reaction of those around him or her, and whether or not the person is still able to live at home. Margo was content because of who she was and how she lived, even though she was suffering from dementia of significant severity.

REFERENCES

Aggarwal, N et al (2003) 'People with dementia and their relatives: personal experiences of Alzheimer's and of the provision of care' 10(2) *Journal of Psychiatric and Mental Health Nursing* 187–97.

Alzheimer, A (1911) 'Uber einartige Krankheitsfalle des spateren Alters' 4 *Zeitschrift fur die Gesamte Neurologie und Psychiatrie* 356–85.

Ballard, C et al (2001) 'Quality of care in private sector and NHS facilities for people with dementia: cross sectional survey' 323(7310) *British Medical Journal* 426–27. doi: 10.1136/bmj.323.7310.426.

Banerjee, S et al (2006) 'Quality of life in dementia: more than just cognition. An analysis of associations with quality of life in dementia' 77(2) *Journal of Neurology, Neurosurgery & Psychiatry* 146–48. doi: 10.1136/jnnp.2005.072983.

Cahill, S et al (2004) '"I know where this is going and I know it won't go back". Hearing the individual's voice in dementia quality of life assessments' 3(3) *Dementia* 313–330.

Firlik, AD (1991) 'Margo's logo' 265(2) *Journal of the American Medical Association* 201–01. doi: 10.1001/jama.1991.03460020055013.

Kitwood, TM (1997) 'Personhood maintained' in TM Kitwood, *Dementia Reconsidered: The Person Comes First* (Buckingham, Open University Press).

Kitwood, T and Bredin, K (1992) 'Towards a theory of dementia care: personhood and well-being' 12(3) *Ageing and Society* 269–87.

Möller, HJ and Graeber, MB (1998) 'The case described by Alois Alzheimer in 1911' 248(3) *European Archives of Psychiatry and Clinical Neurosciences* 111–22. doi: 10.1007/s004060050027.

Teng, E, Marshall, GA and Cummings, JL (2009) 'Neuropsychiatric features of dementia' in BL Miller and BF Boeve (eds), *The Behavioral Neurology of Dementia* (Cambridge, Cambridge Univerity Press).

10

Dementia: A Perspective from Primary Care

DANIEL LASSERSON

THE CRISIS PRESENTATION

PRIMARY CARE PHYSICIANS are very familiar with the following scenario. A call comes to the practice late on a Friday afternoon. John, an 82-year-old man who has previously been seen in the memory clinic run by the local hospital elderly care service, seems upset and his wife, who has poor mobility from arthritis, feels she can't cope with him. John also has hypertension and type 2 diabetes and started insulin a year ago as tablets were not controlling his glucose levels. The injections are delivered daily by a visiting community nurse. John and his wife live in a house that is always neat. Their only daughter has her own family and lives a two-hour drive away.

After evening surgery finishes, the primary care physician duly visits and finds that the patient, who she knows well, is indeed agitated, unhappy and suspicious in his familiar surroundings and is not keen on a physical examination that might help to determine if there is an organic explanation for his signs and symptoms. His wife has noticed that he has 'not been himself' for several days but she 'didn't want to bother the doctor' as she knows she is busy. But now she is concerned as it is Friday and she knows that there is little help available over the weekend. Three months ago John was prescribed rivastigmine by the memory clinic, and one month ago he was admitted to the local general hospital after an episode of increasing confusion, presumed to be due to a urinary tract infection. During that hospital admission he experienced significant distress on the ward and was sedated several times. His wife feels that he should not go back into hospital as 'they made him worse'. He has not been seen by the psycho-geriatric service as there have been no mood or behavioural problems noted at his memory clinic reviews, and, for the same reason, the primary care physician has not felt the need to involve specialist mental health community services either. While the primary care physician is there, the daughter rings to find out what has happened, asks to speak to the doctor and communicates her concerns about her father's safety and the likely (significant) impact on her mother if he is to remain at home in his current condition.

What constitutes 'help' in this situation? Who needs help? How should a health and social care service deliver it?

The social and family contexts are key areas to consider in primary care when considering the support of a patient with declining cognition. However, in crisis presentations, even if an underlying cause has been identified and treatment initiated by a primary care physician, there are often no resources available for increasing supervision and care and so reducing the risks to the patient and the impact on a spouse or carer. There are a handful of pilot initiatives in the UK for rapid, capable, urgent responses in such situations, but the community services that are typically available to a primary care physician generally do not respond within urgent time frames: in many cases greater access to diagnostic tests and subsequent delivery of appropriate medical and nursing interventions is required, which usually necessitates transfer from the home environment.

Whilst there may be clinicians at practices who know patients and their clinical histories very well, they are generally not available 24 hours a day. Hence crisis presentations, which do not respect the boundaries of the working week, are dealt with by many different providers of urgent care, often without adequate knowledge of current medications or previously tried and poorly tolerated treatments, or the social context in which chronic conditions and their exacerbations are managed on a daily basis. For example, for an individual with worsening confusion on a Saturday evening a carer, spouse, relative or worried neighbour could call an 'out of hours' primary care service for a review by a primary care physician or emergency nurse practitioner (in the patient's own home or at an emergency primary care base), call for an emergency ambulance staffed by paramedics or take the patient directly to an emergency department. These emergency services have differing degrees of clinical skill, access to investigations, and differing degrees of perceptions of the threat posed by a suspicious and disorientated patient, but they all share a lack of information about previous medical history, about the medications that may have worsened confusion and about the social circumstances and support structures that may facilitate or hinder delivery of ambulatory care, ie, care outside a hospital.

Crisis presentations of worsening confusion are complex. The confusion may be due to an intercurrent illness that demands diagnosis and treatment, to psychological causes, or may represent a progression of dementia. Determining the cause and appropriate treatment needs a detailed assessment with rapid access to investigations; traditional primary care has limited ability to deliver this. The temptation to use bed-based services at the point of crisis is therefore great but this in itself carries risk. Patients with confusion in hospital environments have a poor prognosis (usually related to the underlying causes). The management of behavioural disturbance in bed-based environments can include pharmacological sedation alongside environmental interventions; such medical intervention is not without its own risks such as falls with consequent fractures.

THE CONTEMPORARY OLDER PATIENT

John's scenario illustrates many of the challenges for primary care in delivering care centred on the patient and their family and carers in the context of declining cognition. First, cognitive impairment in older age is very rarely present alone: there are other long term conditions which increase in prevalence as we age. Many of these increase the risk of cognitive impairment. Examples include chronic kidney disease, hypertension and cerebrovascular disease. The presence of co-morbidities has bidirectional effects. Physiological and biochemical disruption (for example, from heart failure, or rapidly changing glucose levels due to diabetes and its treatment) are likely to result in changes in behaviour and cognition which often increase the risk of harm, either due to inability to conduct activities of daily living, or because the risks associated with them have been inappropriately assessed. Conversely, as cognition declines, so often does the patient's ability to tolerate the treatment needed to maintain control of long-term conditions—either because of difficulties in adhering to complex prescribing regimens or because of the unwanted effects on cognition from medication targeted at chronic physical illness.

Second, there is a limited evidence base to guide management of crisis presentations of increased confusion and altered behaviour such as the one described above. Once the crucial step of ruling out an underlying acute disease process has been undertaken, there are uncertainties over how best to manage the increased confusion itself. In many developed health care systems, services that can rapidly diagnose the conditions that exacerbate confusion in patients with dementia are predominantly based in acute hospital settings, and even if no underlying cause is found (with the consequent presumption that deterioration in cognition represents dementia progression), the presence of increased confusion is deemed to pose a significant risk, and as a result clinical teams may be reluctant to send patients home without being able to set up an appropriate monitoring or ongoing treatment regime. Therefore, for the majority of patients who are assessed as being confused in primary care without an obvious cause that can be treated in the community, or patients in respect of whom there are felt to be risks from inadequate supervision, a hospital admission is highly likely. This leads to the additional problems associated with managing confusion on a hospital ward, as the environmental support that is needed is resource intensive and nursing staff to patient ratios may not be ideal for the provision of continuous one-to-one care. Primary care physicians are well aware of the potential harms of hospital admission in terms of increased agitation and the difficulties that this poses for the patient, relatives, carers and hospital clinicians, but when it is necessary to exclude significant physical illness rapidly, there is often no alternative.

Most developed health care systems have a primary care service; this is the predominant first contact in relation to health concerns that are not life threatening. The generalist clinicians who operate within such systems have sub-specialist levels of competence for the assessment of urgent care presentations and the formulation of treatment plans. Another key function of primary care is the management of long-term conditions: much of the evidence base for the treatment of such conditions comes from studies of younger patients with single conditions. However, the modern older patient now has multiple long-term conditions and is prescribed an increasing number of medications. Treating one long-term condition either chronically to maintain good control, or acutely to reduce the effects of an exacerbation, can affect other conditions: very often the competing priorities of one condition may impact on another. A good example is the combination of chronic kidney disease and heart failure, where the need to reduce fluid overload in heart failure is dealt with by increasing the intensity of diuretic treatment, which can further reduce chronically impaired kidney function.

However, appropriately responding to the complexity of the older patient with declining cognition is made more difficult by health care provision. Medicine tends, in its organisation, towards an inflexible dualism. Mental health services are often separate health care providers from physical health services, with different staff working in different buildings—so a patient may have their diabetes and ischaemic heart disease managed in one facility, and then will need to go elsewhere to address issues of mood or disturbance of thinking and cognition. Dementia services can also fragment along the border of physical and mental health, with services provided by elderly care physicians or old age psychiatrists. The allocation to a particular specialty may be dictated by local health service configurations or commissioning arrangements.

This unhelpful dualism is reflected, too, in the training and consequent skills and mindsets of clinicians. Mental health competencies in medicine are developed in those training to be psychiatrists, who then work within organisations of mental health providers. Similarly, physical health competencies are developed in those training to be physicians who then work within physical health institutions or networks. Although primary care as a generalist discipline aims to bridge a mental and physical divide, training is short in comparison to the complexity of need, and to be cost effective primary care providers typically require a high throughput across their registered population, thereby reducing both consultation and thinking time. Given that the typical modern older patient is now more complex and represents an increasing proportion of the community, does primary care service need to be redesigned? If so, this would entail a new type of doctor and therefore a new type of training. An appropriate evidence base to inform optimal decision-making would also need to ensure that the most complex patients were recruited in research studies. This would be facilitated if such patients were identified and routinely cared for in a more bespoke health system.

PATIENTS AT THE INTERFACE OF PRIMARY AND SECONDARY CARE

The patient who lives with physical, cognitive and social frailty is at the interface of primary and secondary care. Exacerbations of existing long-term conditions or intercurrent infections result in decompensation of physical and cognitive function, often presenting as a global decline, and primary care physicians will often judge that the current living environment is temporarily unable to meet an acute increase in needs. Traditionally configured primary care services have little to offer in such situations and secondary care requires that patients are investigated and treated in unfamiliar institutional environments in order to deliver rapid, efficient diagnostic and multidisciplinary interventions.

Community based emergency multidisciplinary units are being set up to address this gap in care between a predominantly office hours chronic disease management service (primary care) and a centralised institution delivering round-the-clock emergency care focused on physical health (secondary care). Such units incorporate therapist capability for physical and self-care functional assessments (physiotherapy, occupational therapy) and social workers alongside nursing and medical staff. In order to reduce the dependence of medical staff on centralised laboratory services for diagnostic tests, these community units utilise advances in point of care diagnostic technology. Thus, within minutes of a patient arriving on a community unit, a biochemical and haematological profile is available for rapid diagnostic decisions and appropriate interventions can be initiated, typically at an earlier time along the disease trajectory than if the patient had attended a traditionally configured emergency department supported by a separate laboratory service. A decentralised emergency multidisciplinary capability can also treat patients closer to their own home which minimises the disruption that results from longer transit times to large, busy emergency departments.

For the patient with dementia and acutely progressing confusion, such units offer a process of care that is more tailored to need, both in terms of speed of assessment and decision making and also in acute care environment. Along the chain of health care professionals delivering the service, all have specific expertise in the older patient with multiple conditions and without the intrusive noise and multiple changes of location of care that are components of the patient's experience in large emergency departments. The flexibility of the intensity of monitoring and treatment is also an advantage and contributes to the design of individualised packages of care. Patients can be sent home on the same day as they had their initial rapid assessment, and then reviewed within a 24-hour time frame. Risk can be mitigated by the provision of community-based nursing and social care teams to support and monitor individuals in their current living environment when the patient is not being directly observed on the unit. These features enable the rapid deployment of diagnostic and therapist assessment functions to stratify risk for decisions about location of care during treatment and recovery, as well as the identification or exclusion of acute physical illness as a cause of the syndromic dysfunctions that patients with dementia and their carers frequently encounter. This can therefore be achieved whilst minimising the disorientating effects resulting from temporarily altering the physical environment in order to deliver multidisciplinary assessment.

INTERFACE MEDICINE, INTERFACE UNITS AND THE CRISIS PRESENTATION

Could a primary care service be developed for a defined patient group such as confused patients with needs falling uncomfortably into the gap between conventional primary and secondary care?

In the UK, general practice (the UK equivalent of primary care) has been rooted in the principles of universality of clinical coverage and, to an extent, simplicity of access to a first contact health care provider. In other words, no matter what is wrong with any patient, barring life threatening emergencies, the general practitioner located at the local practice building is the first port of call and should be able to treat, reassure or arrange ongoing assessment and care in another part of the health care system. Changing such systems needs careful assessment, as evidence from high income countries strongly suggests that robust primary care systems are associated with better population health outcomes. Population health gains should therefore not be lost in any attempt to advance primary health care for patients who may be better served by novel systems.

One can visualise traditional general practice as a vertical age generalism, as practitioners aim to be as competent with the health issues in a newborn baby as they are with those of a very elderly and frail person. However, community generalism need not be described simply in terms of age, but could be defined within an age group—particularly if that group typically had multiple co-morbidities straddling disciplinary divides. Generalist skills are particularly germane to the management of co-morbidity and to the detection of prodromes, subtly heralding the approach of a crisis. Yet primary care, as currently configured, does not make the most of the generalist skills available. Whilst describing the components of a primary care system that is separate for complex patients demonstrates considerable departure from traditional general practice, it is also clear that many features of a strong primary care system—such as those associated with greater population health outcomes—would be retained. Greater continuity in patient care would be achieved, as acute care would not be delivered by a clinical team unfamiliar with a patient's history. The system could retain the current UK model of being free from financial charges at the point of access, and pragmatic clinical management and risk stratification could still be practised.

In addition, a novel care system could be designed without the restriction of traditional working practices, which are more often inherited into current practice without critical thought. For example, the working day in general practice squeezes visiting time to see housebound patients in between surgery hours. Thus, a patient in crisis, or more typically their spouse or carer, may contact the practice at the start of the working day but not be clinically assessed until lunchtime, in between morning and afternoon surgery. Similarly, patients contacting the primary care practice at the start of afternoon surgery will not be assessed until the early evening. It is clear that this introduces an unfair 'inverse triage', as the housebound patient in crisis is likely to be the sickest person that the primary care physician will see that day, yet they may wait the longest to be seen after making contact with the practice. In other words, the ambulant and therefore more acutely well patients are de facto prioritised, even though that is not the intention of those working within this system.

A primary care system that covers these interfaces will respond in a timely manner to crises and incorporate the key skills for care. Those skills may currently exist only within separate clinical disciplines. This has implications for the training of clinicians, therapists and nurses as well as the strategic deployment of diagnostic and monitoring technologies and the utilisation of existing health care infrastructure. Novel service delivery creates novel cohorts of patients, and decision making in such settings demands a research base that addresses evidence gaps from contemporary clinical practice.

As we move further and further into an age of complexity and frailty, the health system needs as much attention as the patients it is trying to serve. Increasingly, we will fail to meet our patients' needs if we do not first treat the current primary health care system.

REFERENCES

Dasgupta M, Brymer C, 'Prognosis of delirium in hospitalized elderly: worse than we thought' 2013 Oct 3 *International Journal of Geriatric Psychiatry*. PubMed PMID: 24123329. Epub 2013/10/15. Eng.

Kringos DS, Boerma W, van der Zee J, Groenewegen P, 'Europe's strong primary care systems are linked to better population health but also to higher health spending' 2013 Apr *Health Affairs* (Project Hope);32(4):686–94. PubMed PMID: 23569048. Epub 2013/04/10. Eng.

Lugtenberg M, Burgers JS, Clancy C, Westert GP, Schneider EC, 'Current guidelines have limited applicability to patients with comorbid conditions: a systematic analysis of evidence-based guidelines' 2011 *PLoS One*;6(10):e25987. PubMed PMID: 22028802. Pubmed Central PMCID: PMC3197602. Epub 2011/10/27. Eng.

Part II

Ethical Perspectives

11

Dementia: An Ethical Overview

MICHAEL DUNN

INTRODUCTION

SLOWLY BUT SURELY, the care of people with dementia is taking more and more of the centre stage in the field of bioethics. Traditionally invoked as the protagonists in thought experiments for philosophical analyses of various kinds, people with dementia, their carers and the varied lives, needs and interests of both groups, are now taken to be topics worthy of substantive ethical enquiry in their own right. This emerging ethical landscape of dementia care is currently orientated towards a wide range of ethical issues. Such issues span from expansive questions concerning the challenges in meeting the needs of people with dementia nationally and internationally, to the subtleties of making everyday decisions about recreational activities or meal choices within paid or family care relationships. The aim of this chapter will be to outline the main ethical issues in dementia care at both the macro and micro-scale, and to briefly consider how these issues might be thought through.

Before undertaking this task, however, a few introductory remarks are useful. The ethics of dementia care can be marked out as being different from established approaches to practical ethical analysis in a number of different ways. The direct demographic challenges posed by the rapidly increasing number of people living with dementia across the world, and the changing global migratory patterns that are developing to meet the needs of these people, mean that studying the ethical landscape of dementia care is necessarily a cross-disciplinary endeavour. The ethical issues require an understanding of demographic changes and the social and transnational context of care work, according a central role to social scientists. Equally, questions of justice predominate as people move between countries for the purposes of providing and receiving care, and as resources to meet care needs become more stretched. As such, political philosophy also earns its place at the practical ethics table.

Next, whilst dementia is a progressive neurological disease associated with significant health problems, the care requirements of people with dementia are not limited to matters relating to health care (Prince et al, 2009). The cognitive impairments associated with dementia impact on people living with the condition in ways that require increasing inputs of personal and social support over time. Such care does not have as its primary aim the cure or treatment of the underlying disease, and it is now well recognised that supporting people with dementia in leading their everyday lives is best provided in community settings, often in the person's own home.

One consequence of this is that the conceptual resources, ethical frameworks and practical mechanisms specifically developed for supporting ethical analysis within health settings need to be scrutinised afresh before being translated into non-clinical care settings (Hope and Dunn, 2014). Whether a new vocabulary of principles and concepts for ethical analysis in dementia care should be devised is a question that will be returned to in the concluding remarks of this chapter.

Locating many of the ethical issues that arise in dementia care outside the domain of the health care institution also draws our attention to other differences between clinical and non-clinical care environments. Whilst medico-legal developments might provide clear boundaries for the provision of medical care to people with dementia, it is unlikely that similar regulatory clarity will extend to non-medical interventions. The governance of care standards and provision is also likely to take different forms when care is provided outside a health care system, and there may be little or no governance of the quality of care when the needs of people with dementia are met entirely by family carers within private homes.

In relation to education and support in ethical decision-making, the well-established training programmes in ethics that have proliferated in medical and nursing schools over recent years are unlikely to be paralleled in the personal and social welfare sectors. Those providing care and support to people with dementia are unlikely to be able to recognise and articulate the different ethical issues that arise in their work, and therefore struggle to recognise when they are faced with the need to make difficult decisions in their practice. Moreover, care workers or family carers are unlikely to have the requisite knowledge of ethical principles, or to be skilled in the ability to exercise practical reasoning to reflect on and analyse the issues they identify. They are also unlikely to have access to ethics support in the form of ethics committees or consultants that are often common-place features of a health care institution.

The subsequent chapters in this section take on the challenge of interrogating a range of different ethical issues in the health and social care provided to people with dementia. This chapter provides a broad introduction to what follows, with a particular emphasis on the ethics of planning and providing support to people with dementia in non-clinical care settings.

MACRO-LEVEL ISSUES

One set of ethical issues in dementia concerns the general provision of care activities; what care should be provided to people with dementia, and upon whom does the responsibility to provide it fall? These issues arise at the macro-level in the sense that they are mostly concerned with policy-orientated questions about the national and international direction of care services to people with dementia.

An Obligation to Care?

It is well recognised that informal care provided by family members represents a huge financial and human resource investment in dementia care, but it is often uncertain whether family members—and the children of a person with dementia in particular—are under a duty to support their parents in this way. Recent developments in legal and policy reform in some countries would seem to suggest so. In China, for example, a new law, 'The Protection of the Rights and Interests of the Elderly People', has been invoked to endorse the Confucian principle of filial piety, requiring children to visit or greet their parents regularly, and to provide care for them as necessary.

Does such a regulatory approach stand up to analytic scrutiny? It is important to recognise that the question of whether the children of a person with dementia have an obligation to care for their parent is a specific instance of the more general question of what adult children owe to their parents. This question has received a significant degree of attention from applied philosophers, and a distinction can be drawn between, on the one hand, arguments that seek to account for filial duties by reference to some independent duty that is taken to apply within other comparable kinds of relationships and, on the other hand, arguments that argue for special filial duties that are unique to parent–children relationships.

On the first set of arguments, Keller (2006) distinguishes between a debt theory, a gratitude theory and a friendship theory. The debt theory commands strong intuitive force, and captures something about the sense of reciprocity that is often sensed within familial relationships: that we owe our parents something for what they have done for us as children. This account of filial duties is open to critique, however, on the grounds that it is either oversensitive or under-sensitive to context—either because what we owe to our parents seems to transcend the actual degree of investment that our parents have made in us, or because what we owe to our parents must depend on what children are able to provide, given their own circumstances and life choices (English, 1992).

The gratitude theory understands filial duties in terms of children being obliged to demonstrate feelings of gratitude—tailored to the children's circumstances and those of the relationship—for the care and nurturing that parents have provided to them. Keller (2006) questions whether a duty of gratitude is the right way to account for filial duties. Displaying gratitude appropriately does not quite capture the intuition of obligation within child–parent relationships, neither does it seem correct to tailor the display of gratitude (and, therefore, the fulfilment of the duty) to the degree of sacrifice given in undertaking the parental role.

The friendship theory locates the source of filial duties in the enduring relationships between adult parents and adult children. Whether parents and their adult children would in fact characterise the connections between them as a friendship matters less than accounting for this relationship as being analogous to a friendship in terms of the mutual obligations that it gives rise to. Again, however, concerns can be raised about this account of filial duty on the grounds that the parent–child relationship is involuntary in a way that friendships cannot be (Mills, 2003), or because the kinds of mutual obligations that are taken to accompany friendships do not seem to parallel the stronger kinds of duties that we usually think that children owe to their parents (Stuifbergen and van Delden, 2011).

Alternative arguments seek to account for filial duties in terms of something that is special and/or unique to the parent–child relationship. For Keller (2006), a 'special goods theory' of filial duties concerns the goods that are intrinsic to parenting, and that can only be produced through the connections between adults and children that develop uniquely within a relationship of this kind. Such goods might include, for example, the good of having a person that you nurtured retain contact with you and the good of shared identification, understanding and unique insight obtained only from the act of bringing up children (or from being brought up by a parent). For Stuifbergen and van Delden (2011) and Mills (2003), the unique features of parent–child relationships do not centre solely on the goods that are special to them, but on the fact that such goods are capable of being produced within relationships that are unchosen by both parties.

When applied to the circumstances of dementia care, immediate issues arise regarding the implications of all these arguments. Debt and gratitude theories are—by and large—too general to be responsive to the changing level of needs of parents through the life course, and therefore unlikely to be able to generate additional obligations to meet the needs of a parent when that parent develops dementia. Equally, it is also difficult to see how the obligations that define friendships can continue if one party is unable to meet his or her mutual responsibilities, though we might hark back to the value of the friendship once experienced to ground a continuing account of what the parties owe to each other (Dixon, 1995). As Stuifbergen and van Delden (2011) contend, special goods accounts of filial obligations might ground an obligation for children to have regard for the care of their parents with dementia, but are also unlikely to be specified such that a child is additionally required to meet a person with dementia's personal and social care needs. These needs are not the kinds of needs that are derived from something special between the child and parent, and therefore could just as well be provided be another party.

The lesson to draw from this brief analysis of filial duties is that, however we best account for the existence of such duties, the claims we generate are almost certainly not going to be strong enough to generate a strong requirement for children to provide care for their parents, although they may give rise to an obligation to maintain the relationship. Any manifestation of a 'duty to care' is likely to go beyond what is agreed within friendships, the expression of gratitude, the requirements of reciprocity and the special features of unchosen parent–child relationships.

Allocating Care Resources

If family members decide to withdraw from the care role, or are otherwise unable to be involved in providing care to their loved ones, the needs of people with dementia must be met in other ways. It is well established in most countries that the state has certain moral and legal obligations to provide financial, social and medical assistance to people with long-term conditions, where necessary, and a range of different state-delivered or funded services are provided in response. Given that the obligation to provide care is unlikely to fall upon adult children, and as the predicted number of people with dementia is expected to increase across all countries, states face significant challenges in meeting needs appropriately.

In thinking about the care, support and treatment of dementia, important questions arise about how these services should be prioritised—both in terms of considering the need to provide for people with dementia alongside those with other kinds of health problems, and in terms of prioritising between people with dementia. Typically, these are questions to be answered at the national level of service delivery, though there may also be local differences in decisions about care provision if services are decentralised. In their chapter, Rand and Sheehan outline a number of ethical principles of allocating health resources, on the basis of the requirement to treat individuals fairly, and they consider how these principles ought to be applied to decisions about the distribution of treatments and health care services for people with dementia, as well as the allocation of resources to carers to support them in their roles.

As much of the care needed by people with dementia extends to personal and social support, it is important to recognise that resource allocation is not an ethical issue that is limited to health care settings. Allocating social services resources is a topic that has not enjoyed a significant amount of attention, but is likely to be just as challenging to address. Ethical frameworks that have been developed for the health care setting will be relevant to allocating these resources, not least because the principles that are endorsed within policy and practice in adult social services include the addressing of needs and the enhancement of well-being, two principles that feature strongly in most such frameworks.

Equally, however, the unique legal, practical and political contexts of social services resource allocation will shape how the relevant ethical considerations are taken into account in applying agreed principles to real-world decision-making. It will be important to consider how the aims of social services differ from those of health care. What, for example, does a good outcome in the delivery of personal and social support to a person with dementia consist of, and how can this outcome be captured in terms of considering the effectiveness and cost effectiveness of any given intervention? Recent attempts to measure social care-related quality of life (Forder and Caiels, 2011) are founded upon very different domains of well-being from approaches in health care which aim to ascertain the effect of an intervention or treatment on the length and quality of a healthy life.

Care will also be needed to ensure that ethical frameworks for allocating social services resources incorporate other values that are seen to underpin good care services. Contemporary social care policy in England, for example, stresses the importance of prevention and personalisation in the delivery of services (HM Government, 2012) alongside a requirement to improve quality of life in dementia and to respond to those with the most significant needs (Department of Health, 2009). How the requirement to meet *future* needs—and the requirement to support people with dementia in controlling how services are designed to meet their needs—should be balanced against cost-effectiveness and current needs-based considerations requires careful thought. Any conflict between competing ethical justifications within policy will also need to be addressed. The Law Commission's recent proposal for a new adult social care statute, for example, distinguishes needs-based eligibility criteria from outcome-based service provision priorities in ways that conflict with standard justifications for the cost-effective delivery of resources (Law Commission, 2011). As Rand and Sheehan argue, ensuring that a fair process for decision-making is instigated in social service settings will be important in ensuring that the decisions made in light of competing ethical considerations are legitimate, and thought will also need to be given to the way this process connects to the allocation of health resources in community-based models of care that are likely to integrate medical, social and personal support.

The Global Migration of Care Providers and Care Recipients

Issues of fairness in dementia care extend to the realms of social and transnational justice, and are not confined to concerns about distributive justice. The pool of human resources available to provide care to people with dementia differs markedly across the world as individuals move between countries, and these changes are often a direct result of changing employment opportunities in care work. A significant percentage of the dementia care workforce in the UK is made up of nationals from countries in Eastern Europe and east and south-east Asia (Hussein et al, 2010). Equally, there is evidence of an increasing trend for people with dementia, and those with other long-term conditions, to relocate to other countries for the purpose of receiving care within communities specifically designed for older people (Ono, 2008; Toyota et al, 2006).

The ethical dimensions of these trends require the negative and positive effects of the changing trends in the international distribution of care labour to be accounted for. Undertaking an ethical analysis on this topic is complex because it is difficult to correctly capture the harms and benefits associated with the migration of care providers and receivers, to isolate the impact that this particular trend has on individuals and societies and to account appropriately for the responsibilities associated with any observed injustices. In terms of the evidence, it is necessary to integrate population-level datasets with local sociological and anthropological studies, and care must be taken to handle and interpret these multiple sources of data correctly (Dunn, 2013). In terms of the relevant values, justice needs to be defined appropriately, with recent emphasis being placed on accounting for responsibility in terms of relationships between people, mediated by structural processes, rather than in light of the consequences of the intentions or actions of one person or institution towards another party (for example, Eckenwiler, 2009).

Once the relevant evidence has been obtained, it is helpful to understand the ethical dilemmas in terms of a conflict between individual freedoms and considerations of social and international justice (Dwyer, 2007). On the one hand, the choice to move between countries to undertake or receive care work looks to be the kind of choice that individuals should be permitted to make, in line with their own conception of their interests. On the other hand, these movements of people are taken to undermine just relationships between people in different countries, and between people within one country, in a range of different ways.

In particular, attention has been drawn to the ways in which changing migratory patterns in the international distribution of care labour give rise to shortages in health and care workers available to care for people with dementia and other conditions in source countries. Whilst the destination countries have an expanded workforce able to provide care to people, the health care systems of the source countries are undermined, and the funds necessary for reinvesting in training or local service development are not provided sufficiently through remittances sent home by the care workers who have relocated. As some countries (and the people with dementia living within them) benefit from these migratory patterns, other countries and individuals—who, by and large, have less economic resources to cope with the impact of these changes—are left worse off.

Considerations of social justice also need to be acknowledged. By and large, it is women who make up the greatest proportion of the care workers who move between countries. This fact has given rise to concerns about the gender injustices that result for women in source countries. It is conceivable that women will be required to take on greater responsibilities for caring activities within their own families as the professional care workforce is deplenished, preventing social advancement and undermining opportunities for advancing education or employment (Browne and Braun, 2008). In addition, both men and women in destination countries might suffer from the perception that care work is an activity associated with migrants, undervaluing this kind of employment, entrenching its low status and low pay and leading to increased stratification between individuals within a society.

If the account of justice that is endorsed is one that interprets fairness in light of the reality of complex, institutionally-mediated relationships between distant individuals, there will be significant responsibilities to act in the face of the numerous injustices associated with these migratory patterns in dementia care provision. As Eckenwiler (2009) suggests, such responsibilities will fall upon the majority of individuals who are caught up (inadvertently and non-intentionally) in perpetuating social injustices. In more practical terms, international agreements between countries that determine the scope and scale of future immigration for the purposes of care work may need to be established. Alternatively—or additionally—regulations could be introduced within destination countries that require employers, and perhaps the government itself, to provide specific benefits to source countries in light of the advantages that these employers and other institutions enjoy from the outcomes of these migratory patterns. Financial compensation could be one aspect of the attempt to redistribute benefits, as could new investments in training or educational activities in source countries that are focused on local needs in health and social service provision (Eyal and Hurst, 2008). Any such interventions would, of course, need to be tailored carefully to the unique social, gender and personal dynamics that play out in the movements of care workers or recipients in a given setting.

MICRO-LEVEL ISSUES

Shifting attention towards transnational questions of justice to the day-to-day provision of dementia care in particular localities requires the ethicist's gaze to focus on the nature of direct care relationships involving people with dementia, and the decisions that are made in practising care within these relationships. In so doing, the ethical discourse also needs to shift away from broad considerations of justice to the ethical principles that ought to govern interpersonal relationships of this kind. Again, the question of whether these principles differ in the context of the everyday care provided to people with dementia from those that are well established within hospitals or short-term, health-orientated community services needs to be considered. First, however, it is important to get a handle on the broad range of ethical issues that arise in everyday dementia care work.

Ethical Decision-Making within Dementia Care Practice

A range of ethical issues that arise in the day-to-day practice of dementia care have been identified (Baldwin et al, 2005; Hope and Dunn, 2014; Hughes and Baldwin, 2006; Kane and Caplan, 1990; Lindemann, 2007; Powers, 2003). Broadly, the form of these ethical issues differs from those relating to end-of-life care in hospitals, which have also been analysed extensively. In giving a broad illustration of the range of difficult ethical decisions that need to be made in dementia care practice, it is useful to divide these issues into two broad types.

Acting in the Interests of People with Dementia

One type of ethical issue concerns the challenges associated with acting in the interests of the person with dementia who is the recipient of care. To understand the form of these challenges, it is necessary to first consider the different ways in which the interests of people with dementia can be captured. One common way of interpreting the interests of a person with dementia is in terms of providing them with care that is personalised to that individual's own values and identity, forged over his or her life course. Despite the debate within applied philosophy about whether personhood survives the onset of dementia (for example, DeGrazia, 1999; Dresser, 1995; Hughes et al, 2006), the concepts of personalised care, advance care planning and advance directives are commonly invoked to substantiate legal obligations, policy objectives and good practice initiatives in care organisation and delivery. In so doing, we might think that care workers act to preserve the precedent autonomy of the person with dementia, when that person loses the ability to make autonomous decisions as his or her dementia advances.

In contrast, the interests of people with dementia might be interpreted in terms of these individuals' current well-being—engaging in those activities, for example, that give pleasure or that the person appears to prefer when unable to decide for himself or herself. When these two interpretations of the interests of people with dementia clash, as they might frequently do due to the identity-altering impact of dementia on individuals, it is necessary to identity which account of the person's interests ought to be endorsed when deciding on the person's behalf. Consideration also needs to be given to ascertaining whether the identity of a person with dementia has changed with the onset of the condition, or whether the person with dementia is essentially the same person as he or she was previously. The practical form of this dilemma will have a number of manifestations that concern the provision of life-sustaining treatment in health care settings, or day-to-day activities within community-based care services. Should, for example, a person who has lived his entire adult life as a conscientious objector, be removed from a social gathering in a nursing home when a number of residents in the home are watching a Remembrance Day service on television? If so, should this decision be endorsed even if the person appears to be getting significant pleasure from participating in this activity, and if removing him from the room (or changing the television channel) causes him significant distress? Determining the force of previously held values will be important, and care workers will need to decide whether particular features of a person's identity—such as those relating to religious convictions or sexual orientation—always trump a person's current preferences or sensory experiences, or if priority ought to be given to experiential considerations alone. Questions about who should be involved in the decision-making process also need to be addressed in reasoning through dilemmas such as these.

In addition to conflicts between previous values and current preferences, there may be ethical issues associated with determining precisely what the current interests of a person with dementia consist of. Sensory experiences of pleasure and pain are only one way of capturing something important about a person's interests at a given point in time. It might also be thought that there are activities or behaviours that ought to be invoked or expressed because of their objective value in living a good life, or because they are fundamental to how we should respect people—independent of consequences.

In making decisions about managing risk in the care of a person with dementia who has a tendency to walk outside and get lost, for example, there will be a tension between maintaining the person's freedom of action and protecting him or her from the harms that could occur. From a consequentalist standpoint, this tension can be analysed solely in terms of balancing the harms and benefits associated with the expected level or risk and the benefit that the person gains from being able to walk freely in his or her living environment. Alternatively, freedom of action could be understood in terms of an intrinsic moral value. Such value could be accounted for by reference to the importance of being able to be free to encounter and experience the world in which one lives, even if the person in question is not able to understand or recognise that he or she is engaged in such an activity, and gains no identifiable benefit from being accorded such freedom.

Another ethical issue concerns the use of deception in dementia care. It is not uncommon that people with dementia might forget something about aspects of their lives, or fail to understand why certain activities are being performed. For example, a person with dementia might be distressed by being offered medication that can slow the onset of cognitive decline, and a nurse might judge that it would be appropriate to hide this medication in the person's food. Alternatively, a person might forget that her spouse is deceased and become distressed every time that she is reminded that he has died. Here, a care worker might think that he should pretend that the woman's husband will visit her once he has returned from a day at work in order to reduce the distress that she is experiencing. Again, one kind of consequentialist approach would be to ascertain which action is likely to maximise expected utility. Alternatively, it might be recognised that a general principle that it is wrong to lie to, or deceive, a person with dementia should be endorsed on the grounds that such behaviour fails to show appropriate respect for the person, or that lying or deceiving the person with dementia undermines something important about the value of the care relationship within which this behaviour takes place. If the value of truth-telling is captured in these kinds of ways, determining a person's interests would require the wrongfulness of lying to be set against the harms that are likely to accrue in demonstrating appropriate respect for the person and/or in maintaining a good care relationship.

The Interests of People with Dementia and the Interests of Others

Another broad type of ethical issue in the practice of care for people with dementia arises out of the fact that people receive care in relationship with a care provider, and often in communal settings—a hospital ward, for example, or in a shared living environment such as a nursing home. However the interests of a person with dementia are ultimately determined in any given situation, there will be times when acting in line with these interests will impact on the interests of other people. Sometimes, ethical issues will arise because the decisions to support a person with dementia to act in a particular kind of way will place neighbours or members of the public more generally at physical risk. For example, it might be judged that good support requires the person to cook independently, or to retain access to a vehicle, even if these actions make it more likely that others will experience harm as a result of fire or a traffic accident.

In other situations, the clash of interests will be between the interests of one person with dementia and other people receiving care and support in the same setting. If it is judged to be in the interests of a person to listen to opera because it has always been his favourite kind of music and continues to give him pleasure when played at loud volumes, acting in his interests might go against the interests of other people who become distressed by the noise or who prefer different kinds of music. How this issue is addressed will depend on how considerations of fairness are determined when weighing up different individuals' interests.

Finally, there are likely to be issues associated with acting in the interests of the person with dementia and the interests of the person's carers. It might, for example, be judged to be right to decide that a person who is unable to make her own decision about where to reside should continue to live in her own home with additional professional input, rather than be moved to a care home, on the grounds that the person has always been fiercely independent and because she gains contentment from having contact with loved ones. This decision may, however, go against the interests of the woman's husband who provides support to his wife, and who is struggling to cope with the demands of the care role as well as experiencing his wife's cognitive decline and heightened levels of confusion. There may be situations where the interests of carers ought to accorded significant weight in determining the interests of the person with dementia. This could be because the person with dementia had expressly requested that the interests of others are taken into account in making decisions about her own care, or because the maintenance of good familial relationships is an important component of accounting for the interests of the people entwined within such relationships.

Technological Advances

One main element of recent changes in the care provided to people with dementia is the role of new technologies to support the delivery of care. These technologies can take many forms. They include devices such as fall detectors or GPS trackers that are designed to alert care workers if the person has come to harm or become lost, and also video monitoring technologies that are designed to prevent harm or observe the quality of care being delivered. Looking to the future, developments in robotics offer possibilities to supplement or replace the human being engaged in care work entirely. In a short space of time, there have been concerted efforts to introduce these new technologies into the practice of care. This technological revolution in care work can be explained partly because of the potential that such technologies are believed to offer in enhancing the well-being and independence of people with dementia, and partly because of the growing pressures in meeting people's needs effectively and in a cost-efficient way.

From an ethical perspective, two different kinds of concerns have been raised regarding the use of these new technologies in dementia care. The first kind of concern extends the practical ethical analysis that has been outlined above in relation to decision-making in dementia care practice more generally. In scrutinising tagging and tracking systems, ethicists have examined the extent to which the ways in which new technologies function reinforce the difficulties associated with balancing considerations of harm against the ethical requirement to ensure that a person with dementia can exercise maximum control over their living environment (for example, Robinson et al, 2007). Other analyses have focused on new kinds of ethical problems associated with respecting the person that can arise in how new technologies are put into practice. The use of fall detectors and video monitoring devices, for example, can involve the direct, real-time visual monitoring of a person's living environment. Even if these technologies function successfully to raise an alert if the person is exposed to harm, and the person is not aware that the technology is being used, there are likely to be residual concerns that such technologies involve an unjustified violation of a person's privacy (Ganyo et al, 2011), or increase social isolation (Sorell and Draper, 2012).

A more fundamental concern raised by the integration of new technologies into the care of people with dementia is the possibility that certain emerging technologies, particularly those relating to robotic care provision, potentially threaten the underlying value of care relationships, and even what it means to be human (for example, Baldwin, 2005; Sparrow and Sparrow, 2006). Again, care must be taken here to ascertain exactly what the effects of new technologies will be, with available empirical data suggesting that technological supports can improve the quality of social and affective relationships between care providers and recipients, at least in some settings (Pols and Moser, 2009). However, it is not unfeasible to think that, if a robotic care workforce replaces human carers entirely, something important will be stripped out of the value of care, even if the robot in question is able to replicate all the relevant human traits. Any such argument would need to ascertain why care should be understood as an intrinsically human activity, and, further, whether the rapidly increasing demands for dementia care around the world justify the use of robots regardless of the loss of human connection in the provision of care.

CONCLUSION: THE NEED FOR A NEW ETHICAL VOCABULARY?

There is likely to be much uncertainty amongst carers, practitioners and policy-makers about the nature of the ethical issues that arise in the design, provision and delivery of care for people with dementia, and how these issues ought to be addressed. This is particularly likely to be the case in the care provided to people outside hospitals, where community-based health services are closely connected to the provision of ongoing personal support within social welfare services.

Explicating the range of relevant ethical issues is only the beginning of the contribution that practical ethicists can bring to the analysis of contemporary dementia care. An orientation towards the future through a careful articulation of the values and principles that ought to guide the analysis of these issues is also important. Whether the standard account of ethical principles in medical practice is sufficient to capture the different kinds of tensions is an important question (Agich, 2003; Kuczewski, 1999) as is how any revised account of these principles can be integrated into the delivery of care itself. Such a process must garner international support if it is to be effective, partly because of the transnational nature of the macro-level issues facing the provision of dementia care within ageing societies worldwide, and partly because the dementia care workforce in any given setting is becoming increasingly international, with associated social and cultural complexities that play out in the practice of care.

International bodies and think tanks are turning their attention to examining the ethics of dementia care, with significant progress being made in addressing concerns about justice (World Health Organization, 2002), and in shaping the direction of care provision itself (Nuffield Council on Bioethics, 2009). Regarding micro-level ethical issues, the Nuffield Council has sought to develop an explicit ethical framework for dementia care that is orientated towards two principles—respect for autonomy and enhancing well-being—and that seeks to incorporate the interests of carers and professional caregivers through an account of the value of 'solidarity'. This approach chimes with the ways in which the interests of care recipients have been conceptualised within different domains of health care ethics, and is comparable to those theories of justice that have been endorsed recently to structure the transnational and social provision of long-term care services in ways that are fair to all. However, at the same time, contemporary policy in the UK emphasises different kinds of values, such as the value of respect for human dignity, and this alternative ethical orientation has itself garnered strong support from a number of commentators (Foster, 2011; McIntyre, 2003; Pullman, 1999).

Whilst there is clearly more work to be done in articulating a vocabulary of principles that can guide ethical practice in dementia care, a different way to make progress in the ethics of dementia care is to revisit the question of what it means to do good in the provision of care to people with dementia, in the broadest sense. That is to say, to examine the question of what dementia care services are *for*. Whilst it is entirely understandable that ethical analyses of dementia have been parasitical on ethical thinking in health care, the services provided to those with dementia are more akin to supporting experiments in daily living under challenging circumstances. How then ought these experiments to function? Is it the sustenance of human contact that accords value to support of this kind, or can the good life be articulated in a way that is focused entirely on the interests of the dependent partner in a care relationship?

Approaching different ethical issues by recourse to an examination of the fundamental purpose of providing support to people with a progressive condition connects dementia care to other contexts in which people living with long-term conditions are assisted in their everyday lives. It also opens the possibility of recalibrating care services in ways that are sensitive to the moral positioning of different individuals who stand in relation to those with long-term conditions, without adopting the common but myopic approach of conceiving of the various stakeholders—people with dementia, family carers, care professionals and the state—as parties with different interests that often come into conflict. Much progress has been made in the last few years in raising the profile of the ethics of dementia care. However, real challenges remain both in accounting for the direction of good care services, and in motivating policy-makers, practitioners and families to approach their support roles differently in light of any account given. Practical ethicists can, and should, remain at the forefront in making progress in addressing such challenges.

REFERENCES

Agich, GJ (2003) *Dependence and Autonomy in Old Age* (Cambridge, Cambridge University Press).

Baldwin, C (2005) 'Technology, dementia, and ethics: rethinking the issues' *Disability Studies Quarterly* 25.

Baldwin, C et al (2005) *Making Difficult Decisions: The Experience of Caring for Someone with Dementia* (London, Alzheimer's Society).

Browne, CV and Braun, KL (2008) 'Globalization, women's migration, and the long-term care workforce' 48(1) *The Gerontologist* 16–24.

DeGrazia, D (1999) 'Advance directives, dementia, and "the someone else problem"' 13(5) *Bioethics* 373–91.

Department of Health (2009) *Living Well with Dementia: A National Dementia Strategy* (London, The Stationery Office).

Dixon, N (1995) 'The friendship model of filial obligations' 12(1) *Journal of Applied Philosophy* 77–87.

Dresser, R (1995) 'Advance directives, self-determination, and personal identity' in C Hackler, R Moseley and DE Vawter (eds), *Advance Directives in Medicine* (New York, Praeger).

Dunn, M (2013) 'The concise argument: a global affair' 39(10) *Journal of Medical Ethics* 601–02.

Dwyer, J (2007) 'What's wrong with the global migration of health care professionals?' 37(5) *The Hastings Center Report* 36–43.

Eckenwiler, LA (2009) 'Care worker migration and transnational justice' 2(2) *Public Health Ethics* 171–83.

English, J (1992) 'What do grown children owe their parents?' in NS Jecker (ed), *Aging and Ethics* (Totowa, NJ, Humana Press).

Eyal, N and Hurst, SA (2008) 'Physician brain drain: can nothing be done?' 1(2) *Public Health Ethics* 180–92.

Forder, JE and Caiels, J (2011) 'Measuring the outcomes of long-term care' 73(12) *Social Science & Medicine* 1766–74.

Foster, C (2011) *Human Dignity in Bioethics and Law* (Oxford, Hart Publishing).

Ganyo, M, Dunn, M and Hope, T (2011) 'Ethical issues in the use of fall detectors' 31(8) *Ageing and Society* 1350–67.

HM Government (2012) *Caring for our Future: Reforming Care and Support* (London, The Stationery Office).

Hope, T and Dunn, M (2014) 'The ethics of long-term care practice: a global call to arms' in A Akabayashi (ed), *Towards Bioethics in 2050: International Dialogues* (Oxford, Oxford University Press).
Hughes, J and Baldwin, C (2006) *Ethical Issues in Dementia Care: Making Difficult Decisions* (London, Jessica Kingsley).
Hughes, JC, Louw, SJ and Sabat, SR (eds) (2006) *Dementia: Mind, Meaning, and the Person* (Oxford, Oxford University Press).
Hussein, S, Stevens, M and Manthorpe, J (2010) *International social care workers in England: profile, motivations, experiences and future expectations* (London, Social Care Workforce Research Unit).
Kane, RA and Caplan, AL (1990) *Everyday Ethics: Resolving Dilemmas in Nursing Home Life* (New York, Springer).
Keller, S (2006) 'Four theories of filial duty' 56 *The Philosophical Quarterly* 253–74.
Kuczewski, MG (1999) 'Ethics in long-term care: are the principles different?' 20(1) *Theoretical Medicine and Bioethics* 15–29.
Law Commission (2011) *Adult Social Care* (London, The Stationery Office).
Lindemann, H (2007) 'Care in families' in RE Ashcroft et al (eds), *Principles of Health Care Ethics*, 2nd edn (New York, John Wiley & Sons).
McIntyre, M (2003) 'Dignity in dementia: person-centred care in the community' 17(4) *Journal of Aging Studies* 473–84.
Mills, C (2003) 'Duties to aging parents' in JM Humber and RF Almeder (eds), *Care of the Aged* (Totowa, NJ, Humana Press).
Nuffield Council on Bioethics (2009) *Dementia: Ethical Issues* (London, Nuffield Council on Bioethics).
Ono, M (2008) 'Long-stay tourism and international retirement migration: Japanese retirees in Malaysia' in S Yamashita et al (eds), *Transnational Migration in East Asia: Japan in a Comparative Focus* (National Museum of Ethnology, Senri Ethnological Reports).
Pols, J and Moser, I (2009) 'Cold technologies versus warm care? On affective and social relations with and through care technologies' 3 *ALTER European Journal of Disability Research* 159–78.
Powers, B (2003) *Nursing Home Ethics: Everyday Issues Affecting Residents with Dementia* (New York, Springer).
Prince, M et al (2009) 'Packages of care for dementia in low- and middle-income countries' 6(11) *PLoS Medicine* e1000176.
Pullman, D (1999) 'The ethics of autonomy and dignity in long-term care' 18(1) *Canadian Journal of Aging* 26–46.
Robinson, L et al (2007) 'Balancing rights and risks: conflicting perspectives in the management of wandering in dementia' 9(4) *Health, Risk and Society* 389–406.
Sorell, T and Draper, H (2012) 'Telecare, surveillance, and the welfare state' 12(9) *American Journal of Bioethics* 36–44.
Sparrow, R and Sparrow, L (2006) 'In the hands of machines? The future of aged care' 16 *Minds and Machines* 141–61.
Stuifbergen, MC and van Delden, JJM (2011) 'Filial obligations to elderly parents: a duty to care?' 14 *Medicine, Health Care and Philosophy* 63–71.
Toyota, M, Bocker, A and Guild, E (2006) 'Pensioners on the move: social security and trans-border retirement migration in Asia and Europe' 40 (Spring) *Newsletter of the International Institute of Asian Studies*.
World Health Organization (2002) *Ethical Choices in Long-Term Care: What does Justice Require?* (Geneva, World Health Organization).

12

Best Interests Determinations and Substituted Judgement: Personhood and Precedent Autonomy

ANDREW McGEE

INTRODUCTION

IN THE PHILOSOPHICAL literature on patients with dementia, two issues have dominated. The first concerns the general nature of our obligations towards a patient with dementia once her dementia has reached a particularly severe state. It has been claimed that the progressive loss of cognitive capacities in dementia amounts to the progressive disintegration of the 'personhood' of these patients, and so results in a correlative reduction in our obligations towards them. I will call this the 'Personhood Problem'.

The Personhood Problem presupposes a definition of personhood exclusively in terms of the patient's cognitive capacity to reason, to be aware of herself as having a past and a future and to be able to value her ongoing existence.[1] It is the latter capacity that has been said to ground a right to life (you valuing your life generates an interest in continuing to live) and to justify our sense that we owe significant and strong obligations towards each other.

The second issue—which I will call the 'Precedent Autonomy Problem'—concerns the extent to which a patient, while competent, can legitimately have a say in the kind of care she wants to receive when no longer competent and when her dementia is particularly severe. Perhaps she has changed so much that she can no longer be considered to be the same person, and so cannot be bound by an advance decision or wishes expressed by someone who is effectively a different person (Kuhse, 1999). Alternatively—and this is where the Precedent Autonomy Problem overlaps with the Personhood Problem—perhaps she has changed so much that she can no longer be regarded as a person at all, and so, a fortiori, cannot be regarded as bound by the decision of the person that she was (Buchanan and Brock, 1990: 159).[2] This second

[1] Notoriously, different properties have been mooted, but most include some capacity to be aware of one's existence and to value it, as well as the capacity for reasoned reflection. The definition in this text is Singer's (2011) in *Practical Ethics*; but see also McMahan (2002: 6): 'throughout this book, I will use the term "person" to refer to any entity with a mental life of a certain order of complexity and sophistication. Roughly speaking, to be a person, one must have the capacity for self-consciousness'.

[2] DeGrazia, although rejecting what he calls the 'someone else problem', nonetheless accepts the Kuhse formulation of that problem, viz, that if B is not a person at all, then 'B is a fortiori not the same

issue arises when advance care planning is undertaken by the patient, either prior to the onset of dementia or prior to the resulting loss of capacity. But it can also arise when no plans have been made, and where a decision must be taken on her behalf about the care she should receive—a decision which will aim to take into account previously expressed wishes, values and beliefs in order either to give effect to them (substituted judgement), or at least to weigh them in an assessment of what is in the patient's best interests (the best interests test).

In this chapter I will take a fresh look at both the Personhood Problem and the Precedent Autonomy Problem. The Personhood Problem is important because, if the question of whether a patient at the severe stage of dementia remains a person determines our responsibilities and obligations to her, the answer we give to this question will have a significant impact on decisions taken about that patient's best interests. Yet the claim that a patient at this stage is not a person is extremely controversial. Indeed, the claim was expressly raised and rejected by the Nuffield Council on Bioethics in its 2009 report *Dementia: Ethical Issues* (hereafter, 'the Dementia Report'). Among other points emphasised by the Dementia Report is a tendency by philosophers to construe personhood exclusively in terms of cognitive abilities (Nuffield Council on Bioethics, 2009: 32). The worrying implications of that view were described at paragraph 2.51:

> The practical implications of this view might include: that the individual with severe dementia should not enjoy the protections of the law that are given to 'persons'; that the individual with dementia does not have any interests, or none beyond those of other (non-human) living creatures; that those close to the individual with dementia no longer have any interests or duties towards them; and perhaps that the views and values of the individual before the onset of dementia are no longer relevant in making decisions about their care (Nuffield Council on Bioethics, 2009: 31).

In a seminar hosted jointly in the UK by the Nuffield Council on Bioethics and the Arts and Humanities Research Council in 2011, the view that dementia patients are no longer persons after a certain stage of cognitive decline was criticised. A record of the discussion stated that '[a] shift in attitude is required, away from a "hypercognitive society"[3] where too much emphasis is placed on cognitive abilities' (Nuffield Council on Bioethics, Meeting Note, 2011). The discussion focused on the idea that an individual remains a person throughout the course of her dementia, and that this idea should form a strong basis for policy making in dementia care (Nuffield Council on Bioethics, Meeting Note, 2011).

It is with the personhood issue that I shall begin.

THE PERSONHOOD PROBLEM

We can see the relevance of the concern raised by the Dementia Report and the Meeting Note by examining some of the remarks that have been made by

person as A'. DeGrazia also accepts that severely demented patients may be what he calls 'nonpersons' (DeGrazia, 1999: 379).

[3] The term 'hypercognitive' originates with *The Moral Challenge of Alzheimer's Disease* (Post, 1995). See also 'Respectare: Moral Respect for the Lives of the Deeply Forgetful' (Post, 2006).

well-known ethicists in the dementia context. Referring to the case of an individual with severe and permanent dementia, Allen Buchanan writes:

> All that survives is a terminally ill nonperson with what we may call radically truncated interests ... The crucial point is that our obligations to such a being are at best quite limited because of the radically truncated character of its interests. In the case of those 'primitive' species of nonhuman animals who have such radically truncated interests, it is hardly controversial to conclude that our obligation is simply the negative one of not inflicting suffering (or that at most we are obligated to give them pleasure if we can do so at little cost to ourselves and without compromising the interests of other beings with more robust interests) (Buchanan, 1988: 285–86).

In a book co-written with Dan Brock, Buchanan states that:

> The right of self-determination concerning what is to happen to one's living, nonperson successor could perhaps best be conceived as something like a property right in an external object (Buchanan and Brock, 1990: 166).

It is, I think, something of an understatement to say that these passages are liable to invite resistance. They can so easily be understood as evincing an inappropriate lack of respect for a patient at her most vulnerable—at the very time when she needs the most care and concern. With their comparison to 'primitive species of non-human animals' (in an earlier passage from the same article, the mental capacities of the dementia patient are compared to those 'of a nonhuman animal such as a dog'), the claim that our obligations might be 'simply the negative one of not inflicting suffering', the claim that 'at most' we are obligated to 'give them pleasure' provided that it is 'at little cost to ourselves', and the claim that the patient is merely 'an external object' in whom their 'predecessor' might have 'property rights', these passages seem to be a blind denial of the humanity of these patients. Taken literally—and how else are we to take them?—if we accept the comparison to 'a primitive animal' and accept that our obligation 'is simply the negative one of not inflicting suffering', this seems to mean that it would be permissible to give substandard food to the patient, and that we no longer have the obligation to clothe and bathe the patient. It seems to be an instance of precisely the 'practical implications of this view' that were emphasised by the Dementia Report, viz, that ethically inappropriate views of demented patients can be encouraged by denying their personhood.

Buchanan anticipates these concerns. In a footnote to the first of the two passages cited, he immediately adds the following qualification:

> The fact that a profoundly and permanently demented Alzheimer's patient is a *human being* with radically truncated interests certainly makes a difference to most of us, psychologically speaking. Our greater sense of identification with members of our own species, unbolstered by any arguments of principle, may even be sufficient to justify behaving differently towards human beings with truncated interests simply because they are human beings, if we *choose* to do so. But none of this shows that we have robust, positive *obligations* toward them (Buchanan, 1988: 286).

This passage might at first glance seem to take the sting out of what otherwise appears to be a clearly unacceptable implication of this view. We might not consider giving our patient substandard food or leaving her naked because she is a *human being*. Our greater sense of identification with our patient might even 'justify' this reaction. But the qualification does not really succeed in mollifying the implications of Buchanan's view because, on that view, although it is justified, it is not *morally* justified but merely *psychologically* so. Our reaction responds not to the *patient's* needs (which would make it a moral reaction), but to *ours* (which makes it merely a psychological one). On this view, our inability to give the patient substandard food is akin to our feeling of fear and anxiety before a bungee jump—'feel the fear and do it anyway' becomes 'feel bad, but do it anyway'. It doesn't register as a *moral* reaction at all.

Is there a philosophically cogent way of resisting these claims? Buchanan's claims stem entirely from his acceptance of the definition of person that is prevalent in philosophy, as represented perhaps most famously by Peter Singer. Like Singer, Buchanan defines personhood in terms of the 'cognitive capacities'[4] of self-consciousness and reason (Buchanan, 1988: 284), and concludes that 'the profoundly demented patient ... is not a person' by reason of having lost those capacities (Buchanan, 1988: 284).

We might question—as others have done[5]—whether the definition of person in terms of self-consciousness and rationality is right. My main focus, however, is different. I will assume, for the sake of argument, that this definition is right, and focus instead on the assumptions Singer and Buchanan make about how those two features (self-consciousness and rationality) apply when we say, for instance, that someone is, or is not, 'a rational creature' or 'a self-conscious creature'. To approach these assumptions, I will begin by looking briefly at the following very recent discussion of the concept of personhood by Peter Hacker.

Hacker writes:

> The concept of a person is not a biological concept, but an ethical and otherwise normative one. Unlike the concept of a human being, it is not a substance concept. It is a *status concept* essential to our moral and legal thought. To be a person is to be a rational, language-using creature with powers of intellect and will, knowledge of good and evil, and possessed of free-will (Hacker, 2013: 145).

We can leave aside, here, the fact that additional properties to those mentioned above are also picked out in this passage. It suffices that the concept of rationality is mentioned, and, arguably, the other capacities mentioned (language use, the powers of intellect and possession of free will) all presuppose the capacity for self-consciousness. The significant point comes from the following claims that Hacker then goes on to add:

> That is why human beings, unlike the other anthropoid apes, qualify, *qua* species, for the status of persons. Babies are (immature, undeveloped, not yet responsible) persons, because it is part of their nature *qua* human beings to acquire those characteristics. Human beings who have lost the powers of reason through age, illness or injury are still persons precisely because they are *damaged, impaired* human beings—and must morally be treated as such. (A person in a vegetative state is not to be treated like a cabbage, but with the care due to a dreadfully injured human being.) (Hacker, 2013: 145).

[4] The phrase is Buchanan's (1988: 284).

[5] See, eg, DeGrazia (1997) and Goodenough (1997). These points are acknowledged by Buchanan (1988: 283).

Here, Hacker departs from the standard definition endorsed by Singer and Buchanan, even in respect of the capacity for rationality. Hacker makes two points. First, he makes the conceptual point that it is part of the species nature of human beings to acquire the characteristics that Singer and Buchanan pick out as definitive of persons. An immature human being will acquire those characteristics, and a human being who loses them through old age or dementia is a damaged or impaired human being. We can make Hacker's point more perspicuous here (as I shall explain in a moment) by stating that the concept of a damaged or mentally impaired *person* makes sense—it is not a contradiction in terms, ascribing to a human being a capacity while at the same time denying that the human being *has* that capacity as a consequence of her severe injury or cognitive decline. The reason for this is that the notion of impairment only makes sense if the *healthy* individual *would* possess the capacity that she, due to the impairment, now no longer possesses. By contrast, animals that *lack* the capacities of human beings are not *impaired* by doing so. Similarly, an ant is not an impaired fly merely because it has not evolved for flying; but a bluebottle with its wings removed is an impaired fly because it no longer has the capacity that natural selection evolved it to have and which is, therefore, essential to its species functioning. On the Singer and Buchanan view, by contrast, it would have to be contradictory to call a human being at a state of severe cognitive decline a person, a bluebottle without wings a fly. This is quite wrong, as we shall see. The second point Hacker makes is a moral one: a damaged human being remains a person, *and must be treated as such*. In making this claim, Hacker implies that our moral responsibilities towards these patients enter into an understanding of their very nature as persons. I will deal with each of these points in turn.

First the conceptual point. We can illustrate the point by examining in more detail how we apply terms picking out other species typical features first, and then come back to the notion of a human being as a self-conscious creature, a rational creature, a person, etc, later. Consider the concept of a 'bipedal creature'. Bipedalism is one of the many forms which a species' typical locomotion can take. On the logic of the Singer and Buchanan view, we should not say that a human infant is a bipedal creature until it stops crawling on all fours.[6] Similarly, a quadriplegic permanently paralysed and in a wheelchair would no longer be a bipedal creature on their view. Indeed, she would no longer be a walking creature at all (so, on the Singer and Buchanan logic, we should no longer regard her as a bipedal creature at all; the concept would have no application if the precondition for its applicability—the ability to walk, to locomote—has been lost). Yet there is a logical difference between claiming that a human being is not a walking creature, and claiming that a human being can no longer walk.[7] The latter claim presupposes as a condition of

[6] A chimpanzee has not evolved to become a bipedal creature, but sometimes walks bipedally—eg, when wading through water. Is it speciesist, then, to refuse to acknowledge that the chimpanzee is 'more bipedal' than an infant? Singer is, in my view, committed to saying so because he thinks it is speciesist to refuse to acknowledge the chimpanzee as 'more rational' than an infant or demented patient. But the moral irrelevance of the feature of bipedalism enables us to see more clearly that this is a mistake, for reasons I explain in the text.

[7] And, likewise, there is a logical difference between stating that a creature cannot walk and stating that it is not bipedal. The latter means that it's not the kind of creature that moves with an upright gait on two legs—but a quadriplegic still satisfies this criterion because she *is* the kind of creature who walks

its intelligibility that the being concerned is at least the kind of creature that *could* walk (it is not a stone, for example). The term 'walking creature' applies to her as a *member of the species*, whereas 'can no longer walk' applies to her *as an individual*, and the application of the latter predicate in a given case only makes sense—and is only informative—*given* the fact that she belongs to a species who are 'walking creatures' (as opposed to creatures that slither (like snakes) or crawl (like crocodiles)). If we say 'a snake cannot walk' that can only be what Wittgenstein called a 'grammatical remark', that is, it means a snake *is not the kind of thing* to which we apply the predicate 'walking', and its use would be to correct, say, a child who might have made a mistake on learning the language. It would only be informative in the sense that it tells a child what kind of creature a snake is. By contrast, to say of a human being that 'she cannot walk' is to provide a different kind of information, which only makes sense given the fact that, normally, human beings can walk. Only of a creature that *can* walk, as part of its typical species characteristic, does it make sense to say that *this individual member* of that species can no longer walk, or cannot yet walk.

Similar points apply to the concept of a carnivore, a predator, a strangler (as in a 'strangler plant') and a fly. These entities are all defined in terms of what they do, qua species, on reaching maturity. For this reason, to say that a being 'is not a bipedal creature' or, more generally, 'is not a walking creature', 'is not a predator' and the like, is to say that it is not *the kind of* being that has that predicate as its species nature.[8] If we say, of creatures that *are* bipedal, such as humans or ostriches for example, that *some* individuals are *not* bipedal creatures then what we are really saying, logically,[9] is that we have discovered that some members of the species have evolved in such a way that bipedalism has not developed in them.[10] And likewise for the capacity to walk, to fly, etc. Just as the bluebottle fly with its wings removed is still a fly, so a human being who has experienced a sufficient degree of cognitive decline remains a rational creature (and so retains the status of being a person).

with an upright gait on two legs: it's just that her condition has *disabled* her from doing what, qua species, she does. It might be thought that 'bipedal creature' differs from 'walking creature' because the former term is meant to contrast the form of locomotion that is taken by the creature (does it use two rather than four legs?) whereas the latter is more general (does it walk, or crawl?) This is true, but it does not affect the point because whether the creature walks or crawls is still a question about the form of locomotion, only a more general one.

[8] This appeal to species nature (or a species norm) has been questioned by McMahan, in my view, unsuccessfully (McMahan, 2002: 145ff). But I cannot argue that point here. For compelling criticism of McMahan, see Kittay (2005: 112ff).

[9] Ie, whether we *intend* to or not.

[10] This is confirmed by the debate following the discovery of the Ulas family in Turkey. Some members of the family walk quadrupedally, and Uner Tan claims that these members of the family exhibit atavism and are a 'throwback' to our evolutionary past. Nicholas Humphrey, by contrast, explains that the members of the family also suffer from a genuine congenital abnormality (including cerebellar ataxia) affecting balance and cognitive ability which partly explains the condition, known as Unertan syndrome. See Harrison (2006). Humphrey claims that their inability to walk bipedally was also partly due to the way they were raised—which may have been confirmed by their having learned to walk, albeit with difficulty, bipedally after scientists discovered their plight. A bipedal creature that walks quadrupedally is not a quadrupedal creature that walks quadrupedally: the former walks quadrupedally by reason of a condition (here, Unertan syndrome) which is a highly rare occurrence; the latter walks quadrupedally as part of its species nature.

The mistake of Singer and Buchanan is to cross the species characteristic with the condition of the specific individual that is a member of that species—a condition (a disabling condition) that prevents her from walking or reasoning. To repeat, it only makes sense to say a creature can't walk (say, the quadriplegic) if it is *the kind of creature* whose species characteristic (among others) is to walk. Similarly, it only makes sense to say that a human being cannot reason if the human being is a rational creature, ie, the type of creature whose species characteristic (among others) is to reason.[11] If it were otherwise, the very concepts of impairment and damage would have no application (unless we regard a species change itself as a misfortune),[12] because it would mean that the change in the individual is akin to the emergence of a new species. The idea of having suffered a misfortune would not, in that case, apply, for it depends for its sense on the relative constancy of the typical characteristics of the species to which it belongs, and the role that characteristic has in enabling it to flourish as the species that it is. If it *seems* paradoxical to say that this rational creature cannot reason, that is only because we wrongly take the term 'rational creature' to refer to her not *in her capacity as a member of the species* (as the *kind* of individual she is), but rather to her in her capacity as an *individual*. In short, it is wrong to say a dementia patient is no longer a person;[13] the correct analysis, philosophically speaking, is that disabling conditions have been realised which prevent the individual from continuing to exercise her species capacity to reason—disabling her from doing that which natural selection has enabled her to do[14] (and the same holds for the species-typical capacities of other species, including the capacity to fly, walk, eat meat or strangle host trees).[15]

The second point Hacker makes in the passage cited is equally important. In the last line of the passage quoted, Hacker states that a person in a vegetative state[16] (we can substitute 'a patient with severe dementia') is not to be treated like a cabbage, but with the care due to a dreadfully injured human being. The conceptual

[11] Compare: 'a rock is not a vehicle' and 'the car is not a vehicle'. Singer and Buchanan make the mistake of thinking that these two propositions are exactly alike if the car has irreversibly broken down. The latter, though, is the wrong way of pointing out that the car no longer functions, no longer does or can do what it was designed to do (note that this is reflected by the use of the indefinite and the definite article in the two respective sentences).

[12] An unlikely option if it is an *evolved* change, for the obvious reason that the feature would have been 'selected' because of its ability to enhance the survival of that species.

[13] This assumes, of course, that the concept of a rational creature is part of what it means to be a person (as Boethius thought and as Singer and Buchanan think to the extent they include rationality as part of their definition). But, as noted earlier, it has also been pointed out that the set of conditions included in the concept of a person 'has a slightly arbitrary air about it' (Goodenough, 1997: 146; DeGrazia, 1997).

[14] More precisely: to do what natural selection has programmed her genes to develop her to do. Note: this does not mean that the idea of *genetic* defects has no application! I can't develop this point further here.

[15] One other point is noteworthy. Above a certain minimal threshold, Singer and Buchanan conveniently revert to a species typical notion of personhood to the extent that, while those falling *below* the threshold don't on their view count as persons at all, those *above* the threshold are *not* 'more of a person' or *ultra*-persons, in comparison to those who just make it. This inconsistency is further evidence that something has gone wrong with their analysis. As soon as it is asserted that all that counts is the features the *individual* possesses *qua individual*, the convenient levelling out once we are above the threshold is untenable. Plainly, considerations about speciesism are driving them to distort their conceptual analysis. I cannot develop this point further.

[16] Note again there is no contradiction in this formulation ('a *person* in a *vegetative* state').

point here leads to the ethical point that Hacker makes; the person with PVS (or a dementia of sufficient severity to make Singer and Buchanan wrongly doubt she is still a person) is not a cabbage and so should not be treated like one. The inapplicability of the predicates of consciousness and rationality to a cabbage mean that the cabbage is not *impaired* by not being the kind of entity that typically develops such capacities. By losing the species capacity for consciousness altogether, our dementia patient becomes severely *impaired*. The ubiquitous comparison in philosophy of cognitively impaired human beings to dogs (as we saw in Buchanan's paper) is an instance of the fallacy highlighted by Hacker; it ignores the moral relevance of the impairment, of the fact that *something has gone wrong*—and all the attendant emotional, mental and ethical attitudes this stirs in us and in the patient's loved ones.[17] To fall into a state of dementia *means* something to us because of its devastating impact, both on the patient herself and on her family and friends. And the meaning of dementia—what it is to suffer from dementia—together with those emotional, mental and ethical attitudes are mutually reinforcing. These events take on their intelligibility against a background understanding of what it is to live a human life. It is against such a background that, as practically engaged agents (rather than abstract thinkers in philosophy 101), we understand our responsibilities towards each other and the general shape and extent those responsibilities take in our lives. For example, we all know that the state of the patient—her consequent vulnerability and her need for special care (which applies to a patient with dementia no less than to a PVS patient)—means that special responsibilities are enlivened, and nobody outside a philosophy classroom would ever think anything different; if anything, our ethical responsibilities *increase* or certainly intensify, rather than decreasing, as Buchanan claims. Our appreciation of just the things Hacker refers to and our understanding of what it means for a person to fall into dementia inform our sense that it is wrong to treat these patients as less than our full equals.[18] Together, these things form part of the features of our lives that shape our understanding of the human condition and hold our ordinary concept of personhood in place. As Stephen Mulhall puts it:

> We do not strive (when we do strive) to treat … the senile and the severely disabled as fully human because we mistakenly attribute capacities to them that they lack ... We do it … because they are fellow human beings, embodied creatures … who have already shared in our common life or whose inability to do so is a result of the kinds of shocks and ills to which all human flesh and blood is heir—because there but for the grace of God go I (Mulhall, 2002: 7–8).[19]

[17] McMahan is aware of this problem, but attacks, in my view unsuccessfully, the idea of misfortune and species norms. For refutation of McMahan, see Kittay (2005: 112ff) and Mulhall (2002).

[18] It is no accident that, in a related context, it has been claimed that the language used to refer to these patients—and the attitudes expressed by that language—can have a significant impact on them. This is also a consequence of a shared understanding of what it means for a person to be in this condition, both for her and her loved ones. It is not difficult to see how refusing to treat these patients as persons and adopting the language used by Buchanan of 'a successor' an 'entity' and 'an external object' is likely to have a similar impact. See the Dementia Report (Nuffield Council on Bioethics, 2009: 79). Following Tom Kitwood, Carmelo Aquilina and Julian Hughes (2006: 147) have referred to infantilisation and disempowerment as 'depriving elderly and mentally frail people of their humanity'.

[19] In what is arguably a moment of excessive literal mindedness, McMahan (2005) attempts to reject Mulhall's comment that 'there but for the grace of God go I' by trying to cite as a 'counter example' diseases from which Westerners would not suffer.

So much, then, for the Personhood Problem. I will now turn to the Precedent Autonomy Problem.

THE PRECEDENT AUTONOMY PROBLEM

The Precedent Autonomy Problem concerns the ethical justifiability of advance decisions, forms of substituted judgement and best interests determinations. As noted, these forms of decision-making all require, among other things, a consideration of the patient's past wishes, values and beliefs (that is, expressed or held while competent), as well as her current wishes, values and beliefs. A conflict might arise between the patient's past wishes—as expressed and recorded, for example, in an advance decision or as stated to a family member or a friend—and the patient's current wishes, or between past interests (generated by past values and beliefs) and current interests (which no longer reflect the past values and beliefs the patient had while competent). The Precedent Autonomy Problem is well known, and can be shortly stated. Why should we regard the decision of a competent patient, made well in advance of a future state, as binding on her once she falls into that state? For the substantial changes she anticipates mean that her interests will now be radically different from the interests she held at the time she made her advance decision or expressed any wishes that could form the basis of a substituted judgement or could inform a decision about what is in her best interests.

This problem has sometimes been expressed by claiming that the person who wrote the advance decision (or otherwise made known views prior to falling into severe dementia) 'is not the same person as' the person about whom we must now make a decision (Dresser, 1995).[20] The changes are so substantial that she is 'effectively'[21] a different person. It is neither necessary nor desirable for me to examine this version of the Precedent Autonomy Problem here. It is not desirable because the literature on the claim—and on the problematic notion of personal identity upon which it relies—is vast.[22] But it is not necessary because, even if we accept the common sense view that the changes that occur are simply drastic changes in personality (nonetheless falling short of making her 'a different person'), the Precedent Autonomy Problem is not resolved. There still remains the question

[20] Dresser herself does not necessarily endorse the view that the later patient is not the same person as the one who wrote the directive or expressed her wishes.

[21] A lot hangs on the word 'effectively' of course, as it does with Singer's 'as it were' in the following passage: 'The infant cannot be compensated for its suffering by the benefits bestowed on a potential future person. These benefits are, as it were, bestowed on someone else' (Singer and Kuhse, 2002: 242). If the patient really *were* a different person and Singer really thought that was the case, the words 'as it were' would not have been used. They are used to remove the objectionable nature of the claim—like a magician's distractive tactics.

[22] I will make only one point. If self-consciousness and rationality are capacities, they are not the kinds of things to which numerical or qualitative identity apply, for these predicates qualify *physical objects* or substances. The identity conditions for thoughts, memories, awareness and so on are either logically dependent on their content (the thought that x is not the same thought as the thought that y), or on the identity conditions of their bearers, human beings (my thoughts are mine, yours are yours). That being so, it is a mistake to look for a *psychological* criterion of personal identity. For more extensive discussion see McGee (2011).

of whether the interests of the patient in a given case have changed sufficiently to warrant a conclusion that previous wishes should be afforded less of a priority or should be discounted.

The issue of the remaining interests of the patient has been extensively discussed. Dworkin's distinction between critical and experiential interests is well known, as are the criticisms of that distinction (Dresser, 1995; Jaworska, 1999). Jaworska has argued persuasively that, while a demented patient after a certain stage may have lost capacity to make *decisions*, it does not follow that the patient has lost her autonomy *tout court*, for the patient remains capable of exercising autonomy by continuing to value, even when other aspects of the patient's mental make-up have declined. The patient, she argues, need not have the capacity, as Dworkin requires, to 'grasp what is best for his life as a whole' (Jaworska, 1999: 109).

Recently, in a further development, the emphasis has begun to shift away from autonomy altogether and towards respect for wishes, values and beliefs that may not stem from autonomy (Herring, 2009) or which may stem from attenuated autonomy—an autonomy falling short of that which applies when the patient has capacity to make decisions in the legal sense. These developments are extremely important because they confirm our recognition that these patients are persons and worthy of the utmost respect notwithstanding the loss of capacity in the legal sense. Thus, it has been argued that a decision in line with their *current* wishes—wishes they have while neither competent nor autonomous—should be respected unless there is an overwhelming reason not to do so.[23]

One point often made in the context of these developments, however, merits particular attention. When discussing the patient in her most severely demented state, it is often said that she 'no longer cares about'[24] the things that mattered to her when she was not demented. The difficulty with that view is that it implies a change of mind or of values and priorities that has been consciously and deliberately adopted—my not caring about something presupposes that I at least *could still* care about it and that, as a matter of fact, I do not. The point is not that she no longer cares, but that she is no longer *capable* of caring about that particular matter—that is, that she *neither* cares *nor does not care* about things that could only matter to her while competent and prior to the onset of severe dementia.

The consequences of this conceptual point are surprising. It might seem to support the view that the interests of the patient at the severe stage are so radically different from those she possessed prior to that point that those prior interests can have no relevance to her now.[25] But this is not so. Although not a different

[23] This ties in with the Personhood Problem in the following way: as Herring (2009: 14) points out, to 'count the wishes and desires of an incompetent person as no more than the grunts of an animal is to show a lack of respect'. Herring cites Norman Cantor (as cited in Herring, 2009: 14), who writes: 'it would be dehumanising to ignore the will and feelings of a profoundly disabled person … This would treat the prospective patient as if he or she were an inanimate object'. Note that Buchanan's reference to the 'successor' as being no more than 'an external object' confirms precisely this concern.

[24] See, eg, Jaworska (1999: 115) ('the projected future in which he will no longer care about these losses'); Dworkin (1994) speaks of their 'being ignorant of self' and again, Jaworska speaks of values and wishes 'the patient no longer espouses' (Jaworska, 1999: 108).

[25] It might also seem to express the kernel of truth in the claim made by some that the post-dementia patient is 'not the same person as' the patient prior to onset.

person, a person who can *neither* care nor *fail* to care about, for example, her prior religious beliefs, is not in the same position as a person who *no longer* cares for her prior religious beliefs. It is not as though those beliefs have been dropped or consciously impugned. This seems to suggest that those beliefs, not having been dropped, should in principle continue to carry significant weight in assessing what should count as in her best interests or should continue to represent what she would have wanted were she in a position to make a judgement for herself about the issue in question.

What implications should we draw from this? I do not believe it restores Dworkin's view that critical interests, that is, interests that give meaning and shape to one's life as a whole, should take precedence over experiential interests. The point made concerning the dehumanising impact of ignoring current wishes and desires remains untouched by these considerations. A balance must still be struck between past wishes as recorded in an advance decision or expressed to relatives or proxies, and the patient's current wishes, values and needs. Herring discusses the example of a patient of devout religious belief who, concerned she will no longer continue her religious devotions on losing capacity, writes an advance decision requiring religious services to be performed in her presence weekly (Herring, 2009: 20). It nonetheless seems wrong to follow it if she is exhibiting considerable distress or anxiety when the services take place (Herring, 2009: 20). In other cases, though, where other things are equal, perhaps the difference between no longer caring and not being capable of caring should mean that greater weight should be accorded to the prior views and wishes. For example, Tony Hope and John McMillan discuss the case of a Jewish man who, throughout his life, maintained a commitment to avoid eating pork (Hope and McMillan, 2011). In the nursing home, he now consistently demands to be given bacon and sausages like the other residents. Depending on the level of stress it causes him or the extent to which he is affected by a decision not to provide them to him, this might be a case where his prior religious commitments, not actually having been abandoned for the reasons I have stated, should take priority.[26] Answers to this question might also differ, depending on whether the decision was expressly made in an advance decision, or whether knowledge of his Jewish beliefs has simply been communicated to the carers by his family, that is, as evidence of prior values and wishes. But, in the end, each case must be decided on its own facts, taking into account the impact on him of not granting his current wishes.

It is with this last thought that I wish to conclude. This thought applies to the issues that motivated the Personhood Problem no less than to the issues that motivated the Precedent Autonomy Problem. We must be wary of our craving for generality. While we can look to general principles for guidance, in the end the dilemmas

[26] Though note another caveat pointed out by the authors: is this *really* the type of decision about which we should regard him as not having current capacity? See Hope and McMillan (2011: 2077). It seems to me that the only reason why we would regard him as not having capacity is our sense that he's not actually *abandoned* his prior beliefs; he just has no sense of them. But is this enough? If, as the law requires, we should adopt a *presumptive* attitude to capacity, arguably it is not. Again, the best approach is always: focus only on the particular decision in question and judge it on the basis of the relevant facts at the time, including the effect that holding him to his prior wishes might have on him.

just described are far too subtle, nuanced and variegated to be subsumable under a general rule that can be applied to each case. The best approach is always: let's look only at the particular case and judge it on the basis of the relevant facts at the time, including the effect that holding a patient to her prior wishes has on her.

REFERENCES

Aquilina, C and Hughes, J (2006) 'The Return of the Living Dead: Agency Lost and Found?' in JC Hughes, SJ Louw and SR Sabat (eds), *Dementia: Mind, Meaning, and the Person* (Oxford, Oxford University Press).

Buchanan, A (1988) 'Advance Directives and the Personal Identity Problem' 17(4) *Philosophy and Public Affairs* 277–302.

Buchanan, A and Brock, D (1990) *Deciding for Others* (New York, Cambridge University Press).

DeGrazia, D (1997) 'Great Apes, Dolphins and the Concept of Personhood' 35 *Southern Journal of Philosophy* 301–20.

—— (1999) 'Advance Directives, Dementia, and The Someone Else Problem' 13(5) *Bioethics* 373–91.

Dresser, R (1995) 'Dworkin on Dementia: Elegant Theory, Questionable Policy' 25(6) *Hastings Center Report* 32–38.

Dworkin, R (1994) *Life's Dominion: An Argument About Abortion, Euthanasia, and Individual Freedom* (New York, Vintage Books).

Goodenough, J (1997) 'The Achievement of Personhood' 10(2) *Ratio* 141–56.

Hacker, P (2013) 'Before the Mereological Fallacy: A Rejoinder to Rom Harré' 88(1) *Philosophy* 141–48.

Harrison, J (producer) (17 March 2006) 'The Family that Walks on All Fours' (London, BBC documentary).

Herring, J (2009) 'Losing it? Losing What? The Law and Dementia' 21(1) *Child and Family Law Quarterly* 3–29.

Hope, T and McMillan, J (2011) 'The Art of Medicine: Advance Decisions, Chronic Mental Illness and Everyday Care' 377 *The Lancet* 2076–77.

Jaworska, A (1999) 'Respecting the Margins of Agency: Alzheimer's Patients and the Capacity to Value' 28(2) *Philosophy and Public Affairs* 105–38.

Kittay, E (2005) 'At the Margins of Moral Personhood' 116 *Ethics* 100–31.

Kuhse, H (1999) 'Some Reflections on Advance Directives, Personhood, and Personal Identity' 9(4) *Kennedy Institute of Ethics Journal* 347–64.

McGee, A (2011) 'Me and My Body: The Relevance of the Distinction for the Difference between Withdrawing Life Support and Euthanasia' 39(4) *Journal of Law, Medicine and Ethics* 671–77.

McMahan, J (2002) *The Ethics of Killing* (New York, Oxford University Press).

—— (2005) 'Our Fellow Creatures' 9 *Journal of Ethics* 353–80.

Mulhall, S (2002) 'Fearful Thoughts' 24(16) *London Review of Books* 1–9.

Nuffield Council on Bioethics (2009) *Dementia: Ethical Issues*. Available at: www.nuffieldbioethics.org/sites/default/files/Nuffield%20Dementia%20report%20Oct%2009.pdf.

—— (March 2011) '"I am still the same person" – promoting respect and ethical care for people with dementia'. Note presented at the Arts and Humanities Research Council meeting. Available at: www.nuffieldbioethics.org/sites/default/files/files/AHRC_NCB_personhood_seminar_note.pdf.

Post, S (1995) *The Moral Challenge of Alzheimer's Disease*, 1st edn (London, John Hopkins University Press).
—— (2006) 'Respectare: Moral Respect for the Lives of the Deeply Forgetful' in JC Hughes, SJ Louw and SR Sabat (eds), *Dementia: Mind, Meaning, and The Person* (Oxford, Oxford University Press).
Singer, P (2011) *Practical Ethics*, 3rd edn (New York, Cambridge University Press).
Singer, P and Kuhse, H (2002) *Unsanctifying Human Life* (Oxford, Blackwell Publishing).

13

Proxy Decision-Making

JOSÉ MIOLA

INTRODUCTION

THIS CHAPTER EXAMINES the ethical issues behind proxy decision-making through the lens of UK law. It uses that legal lens in order to make practical discussions which can often be airily philosophical.

When a patient lacks the legal capacity to make her own decisions,[1] decisions need to be made for her. She may be unconscious following a road traffic accident and unable to consent to or refuse surgery, or she may have a severe learning disability and be permanently unable to make all but the most rudimentary decisions about her treatment. In such cases, either the treatment team at the hospital or clinic, or someone else, will have to act as proxy decision-makers and decide on behalf of the patient. As we shall see, such decisions involve balancing two occasionally contradictory principles: acting in the best interests of the patient and protecting her autonomy by making the decision that she would have wanted. The patient with dementia, however, provides a particular challenge for both the law and the proxy decision-maker; this is because her capacity will almost necessarily fluctuate. In general terms, the more permanent the lack of capacity, the more the patient's welfare is prioritised. While the opposite is generally true—for example, an unconscious patient's best interests almost always lie in restoring her capacity so that she can make her own decisions—the reality of dementia fits neither of these extremes comfortably. Rather, she may well inhabit the cusp of capacity and incapacity:

> It is perfectly possible to suffer from dementia and yet retain full capacity. However, the loss of cognitive faculties, difficulties with memory, communication problems and depression associated with Alzheimer's Disease and other forms of dementia can all contribute to a gradual loss of capacity. For many sufferers there will be a period of time during which their degree of competence is unknown (Herring, 2009: 4).

Moreover, it is not uncommon even for the most experienced and specialised of doctors to be unsure whether a particular patient suffering from dementia satisfies the legal test for capacity or not at a specific point in time (Herring, 2009). This is particularly the case because the legal test for capacity has as its basis not the status of the patient, nor even the content of her decision, but instead the ability of her mind to function and, in particular, to weigh information to arrive at

[1] I have referred to all patients as females in this chapter, but they could equally be male.

her own choice (Mental Capacity Act 2005, sections 2 and 3; Law Commission, 1995). This functional approach, needless to say, can be very difficult to determine in practice. Thus, the proxy decision-maker is in a difficult position. The patient's current capacity may be unclear, as might be the question of when (or indeed if) that capacity may return if it is deemed to be lacking. The correct balance between the patient's autonomy and her welfare will therefore be much more difficult to achieve. This chapter considers the legal mechanisms available to authorise and guide proxy decision-makers, concentrating on the question of balancing autonomy and welfare. Here, medical professionals are excluded, as the best interests considerations that they will use are covered in another chapter of this book.

THE MENTAL CAPACITY ACT 2005, AND A BRIEF WORD ABOUT BEST INTERESTS

The Mental Capacity Act 2005 (MCA), which came into force in 2007, replaced the old common law rules relating to adults who lack capacity. Its passing was the culmination of a long process that began in 1992 with the Law Commission being asked to look at the law relating to such adults. Critical to any examination the MCA is an acknowledgment that the legislation was conceived and passed to solve a particular problem of the time, and that was what was seen as the over-medicalisation of the law. In particular, the case of *F v West Berkshire Health Authority* (1990)[2] caused concern and provided a catalyst for change. The case concerned an adult woman with a learning disability, and the question of whether she might be sterilised despite her inability to provide legally valid consent. The House of Lords held that a sterilisation would be lawful if it was in the best interests of the patient, and defined 'best interests' in the same way as negligence was defined at the time. This meant that so long as the doctor could find some other doctors who would support sterilisation, it would be lawful to proceed.

Such an approach carries with it several disadvantages. The first, and most obvious, is that it medicalises the decision and removes the possibility of judicial oversight—it becomes one for doctors to make rather than judges (see, for example, Mason and Laurie, 2013: 329). Second, and even more importantly, this abrogation of responsibility for decision-making to the medical profession relates not to a matter of technical medical skill, but to an ethical one where the doctor has no competence greater than any other interested party, such as family members, carers or the courts (Miola, 2007). Indeed, dissatisfaction with the decision in *F* was specifically mentioned by the Law Commission (1995: paragraph 3.26) early in its report:

> The apparent conflation of the criterion for assessing complaints about professional negligence with the criterion for treating persons unable to consent has been the butt of vehement criticism. No medical professional or body ... argued in favour of retaining such a definition of 'best interests'. Many were extremely anxious to see some clear and principled guidance given as to what 'best interests' might involve. The British Medical

[2] *F v West Berkshire Health Authority* [1990] 2 AC 1.

> Association, for its part, supported our provisional proposals for statutory guidance 'without reservation'.

The answer, then, was seen as being a prioritisation of patient self-determination over the views of doctors which had produced an over-reliance on the patient's medical interests. In other words, the purpose of the Act was to realign the law so that autonomy played a much larger role in decision-making than it had previously done, while the concept of welfare was concurrently less influential. To this end, the concept of best interests became far more rooted in the patient's ascertainable desires and substituted judgement (what she would have wanted had she been competent). Alongside the new definition of best interests, various avenues for non-medical decision-making in relation to incompetent patients were outlined: advance directives were enshrined in statute; an Independent Mental Capacity Advocate service was created and Lasting Powers of Attorney could be donated in relation to medical decisions. The latter two relate to proxy decision-making and form the focus of the remainder of this chapter.

Before that, however, it is necessary to make a brief foray into the concept of best interests, considered in detail in chapters twelve and twenty-five of this book. Despite the fact that it was clearly responding to a perceived need to lessen the power of medical professionals, it would not be entirely accurate to say that the MCA prioritises autonomy over welfare (which was seen as a more objective standard mostly concentrating on medical interests) automatically. For example, the substituted judgement element of best interests, which was seen as the key to protecting autonomy, was watered down. Thus, by the time the Bill had been created and passed through Parliament, 'contrary to what was proposed by the Law Commission and accepted afterwards following consultation, the influence of substituted judgment has been downplayed, and a return to objectivity sought' (Miola, 2007: 145). Indeed, the temptation to make decisions based on welfare rather than autonomy, particularly in difficult cases, can be overwhelming. A good example of this can be found in the recent case of *Re E* (2012).[3]

The facts of the case are of little import to this chapter: it is sufficient merely to say that *E* had a history of anorexia and wished to die. On several occasions she had lost capacity due to her disease, but regained it following treatment authorised while she was incapable and restated her wish to be allowed to die. The court noted that even her parents now felt that there was little prospect of her ever recovering and reluctantly supported her wish. The court found that she lacked capacity and, in determining her best interests under the MCA, therefore had a straight choice between *E's* autonomy and her welfare. What is interesting about the case is the way in which each is dealt with by the court. After spending double the time describing the medical evidence than he did on *E's* wishes (paragraphs 71–113), the judge listed the factors involved in the balancing process between autonomy and welfare. In favour of allowing *E* to die, Jackson J identified the following:

> It reflects E's wishes.
> It respects E's personal autonomy.

[3] *Re E* [2012] EWHC 1639.

> It spares E the risks associated with treatment.
> It avoids the harrowing aspects of treatment.
> It allows E to die with dignity and close to home.
> Treatment has limited prospects of success.
> E's parents and clinicians are at best sceptical about it (paragraph 115).

In favour of forcible feeding being in her best interests, the judge identified the following:

> Without treatment, E will die.
> Without treatment, E will lose the chance to recover and lead a relatively normal life.
> There is medical opinion that E is treatable with some prospect of success.
> The longer E lives, the greater the opportunity for her to benefit from treatment and to revise her views about her future (paragraph 116).

As can be seen, the choice is a direct one between respecting her wishes and prioritising her welfare. If the MCA was merely about unquestioningly protecting autonomy, then surely the former should triumph. However, the judge found in favour of preserving life, noting that the factors were virtually at equilibrium. In such a case, he said, it was the presumption in favour of life that should prevail. I make no comment on the outcome of the case other than to say that the decision must have been agonising for all parties. Rather, I use the case to demonstrate that the MCA should not be seen merely as a vehicle for unthinking autonomy (see also Dunn et al, 2007). There is a strong current of (objectively defined) welfare that pervades it, and the right to self-determination can and should therefore only be seen as qualified. This balancing act can be seen in the other methods of proxy decision-making authorised by the Act.

PROXY DECISION-MAKING: LASTING POWERS OF ATTORNEY AND INDEPENDENT MENTAL CAPACITY ADVOCATES

A principle plank of the extra protection offered to patients in the MCA is the power to donate a lasting power of attorney (LPA) with respect to medical decisions. This is entirely new in English law, as nobody could in the past make medical decisions on behalf of an adult patient. The details and formalities of donating an LPA are not the focus of this chapter. (These can be found in sections 9–14 of the MCA and the Lasting Powers of Attorney, Enduring Powers of Attorney and Public Guardian Regulations, 2007 and DCA, 2007.) The fundamentals, however, are that a competent adult patient may choose one or more competent adults to whom she wishes to donate an LPA. The donee (or donees) may then make decisions in relation to specified matters regarding the patient's property and affairs and personal welfare—which may include decisions regarding medical treatment (MCA, 2005: section 9(1)(a) and (b)). Restrictions and conditions may be specified by the donor, which must be respected (section 9(4)(b)). The donees (if more than one has been created) may act jointly or severally, depending on the donor's expressed wishes (section 10(4)). Under section 10(5), if the donor does not specify then the donees will be assumed to be required to act jointly. Any decisions made by the donee of the LPA carry the same legal force as if they were made by the patient herself. In other words, the donee of the LPA acts as if she were the patient when the patient is not in a position to make her own decisions.

The basic principle behind this is therefore that, in accordance with the purported philosophy of the MCA, donees of LPAs will be uniquely well placed to act in the incompetent patient's best interests because they will know what the patient would have wanted (in theory a key component of the best interests calculation but, as I argue above, not all powerful). Thus, as Jo Samanta (2009: 379) notes, the patient's autonomy will be respected:

> In theory, conferment of an LPA on a self-selected and trusted person who has full knowledge of the donor's previously expressed values and opinions has potential to provide the most effective safeguard to ensure that a person's advance decisions are maximally respected in the event of her future incapacity.

To this end, then, there are several mechanisms in place that seek to maximise the patient's right to self-determination and ensure that what is decided is most likely to be what the patient herself would have wanted. Decisions made by the patient herself therefore quite reasonably take priority as an actual rather than imputed expression of her wishes. For example, donees of LPAs may only make decisions where the patient herself lacks capacity to make the decision in question (or it is reasonably believed that she lacks capacity) (MCA, 2005: section 11(2)). Also, the powers conferred on donees are subject to any advance refusal of treatment on the part of the patient (MCA, 2005: section 11(7)(b) and sections 24–26). This of course means that the decisions already made by the patient when she was competent cannot be overruled by the donees of LPAs. More controversial, however, is the stipulation that donees are restricted in that they are only permitted to make decisions that are in accordance with the MCA's principles and the patient's best interests (MCA, 2005: section 9(4)(a)). While donees' decisions being subject to the patient's advance directives can be said to be of particular use to patients with dementia as they are able to set out what treatments they do not wish to receive, the latter may—depending on how it is interpreted—lessen rather than augment the ability of the donees to make decisions that would be made by the patient if she had retained capacity.

Although not strictly authorised to make decisions themselves, Independent Mental Capacity Advocates (IMCAs) also merit some discussion here. IMCAs can be appointed when the patient lacks capacity and has nobody—such as a relative, friend or donee of an LPA—to speak for them. In such cases, under sections 35–39 of the MCA, they will represent and support the patient so that her voice is heard. Importantly, IMCAs should be appointed in relation to decisions to provide, support or withhold serious medical treatment (see section 37(1)(a)). As the name suggests, IMCAs are expected to act as advocates for the patient, and thus execute various functions under section 36(2) of the Act:

> (a) providing support to the person whom he has been instructed to represent ('P') so that P may participate as fully as possible in any relevant decision;
> (b) obtaining and evaluating relevant information;
> (c) ascertaining what P's wishes and feelings would be likely to be, and the beliefs and values that would be likely to influence P, if he had capacity;

(d) ascertaining what alternative courses of action are available in relation to P;
(e) obtaining a further medical opinion where treatment is proposed and the advocate thinks that one should be obtained.

Decision-makers are required by the Act to consider the views of the IMCAs. The idea seems to be twofold—and both are related to autonomy. First, IMCAs will strive to provide evidence of what the patient would have wanted, being a voice separate and independent from the treatment team and thus acting as a non-medical counterweight. Second, and related to the final aspect of the first idea, the IMCA's voice is important not just because of who she is, but also due to who she *is not*. It will be remembered that one of the principal concerns of the Law Commission was the over-medicalisation of the best interests definition. IMCAs seek to provide a balance to discussions and thus make it more likely that welfare considerations do not concentrate solely on medical concerns, but rather take a more holistic approach.

These two methods of proxy decision-making are designed, first and foremost, to steer the decision towards autonomy rather than welfare. That is not to say that welfare is neglected or trumped. Rather, it lurks in the background, particularly with respect to the best interests considerations. Nevertheless, LPAs and IMCAs at the very least provide a counterweight to welfare considerations, and allow the patient's voice to be heard when she is incapacitated. The patient with dementia, however, will face some specific issues in relation to these, and they are considered below.

THE PATIENT WITH DEMENTIA

While it is right that the patient's own views take precedence, it must be remembered that the Act is not just about autonomy, but rather autonomy balanced with welfare. However, all this presupposes that the patient lacks capacity, and it is not automatically the case that this is so with all dementia patients all the time. Rather, the patient with dementia may well have fluctuating capacity (in other words, be capable at some times but not others), and during significant segments of the progress of the disease at least retain some mental functioning which would render them competent and thus not allow the donees of the LPA to make the required decision. Several of the MCA's principles are particularly useful for the patient with dementia, given that they would seem to address some of these specific concerns. Thus, the very first principle states that the patient must be assumed to have capacity unless it is proved that she does not (MCA, 2005: section 1(2)). The onus is not on the patient to show that she has capacity, but whoever is alleging that she does not has to prove that. Patients cannot therefore be assumed to lack capacity merely because, for example, they are elderly, seem slightly confused or their speech is slurred. It must be shown that they lack the necessary brain function to understand, retain and weigh information to arrive at a choice before communicating it (MCA, 2005: section 3).

The second and third principles also seek to maximise the chances of the patient being able to make her own decisions: under section 1(3) '[a] person is not to be treated as unable to make a decision unless all practicable steps to help him to do so have been taken without success', while under section 1(4) '[a] person is not to be treated as unable to make a decision merely because he makes an unwise decision'. The first of these is specifically designed to protect adults with disabilities to make their own decisions, as the Code of Practice makes clear:

> People with an illness or disability affecting their ability to make a decision should receive support to help them make as many decisions as they can. This principle aims to stop people being automatically labelled as lacking capacity to make particular decisions. Because it encourages individuals to play as big a role as possible in decision-making, it also helps prevent unnecessary interventions in their lives (DCA, 2007: paragraph 2.6).

Equally, the third principle exists to protect the eccentric or contrarian patient, who may simply hold different views from doctors and carers—in the balance between autonomy and welfare, the principle makes clear that autonomy takes priority over welfare with respect to the competent patient. That said, the Code of Practice does state that while a competent person may make unwise decisions, repeatedly unwise decision-making may constitute evidence of a lack of competence. In particular, it cites the examples of repeated unwise decisions that 'put them at significant risk of harm or exploitation' or a 'particular unwise decision that is obviously irrational or out of character' (DCA, 2007: paragraph 2.11). Given the changes in personality and mood that can affect the patient with dementia, this must be seen as a potentially problematic caveat to the principle. It must be remembered that the key to capacity is not the decision itself, but whether the patient is competent to make it. Nevertheless, it must also be noted that this too seeks to respect the patient's autonomy, in the sense that the repeated unwise decisions may be seen as evidence that the patient is not themselves. In this sense, it is important not to confuse autonomy with liberty—for the former to exist the patient must not just make a decision, but make the one that they *want* to make, and if they are confused or lack understanding that will be lacking.

We shall return to the fourth principle below, but the fifth principle may serve to allay fears regarding the fourth. It states that before making a decision on behalf of an incapacitated patient, 'regard must be had to whether the purpose for which it is needed can be as effectively achieved in a way that is less restrictive of the person's rights and freedom of action' (MCA, 2005: section 1(6)). The Code of Practice (DCA, 2007: paragraph 2.14) suggests that sometimes this may mean making no decision at all at that time. This might particularly be the case for a patient with dementia whose capacity may fluctuate—the correct course of action may well be simply to delay the decision until the patient is capable and then ask her to make it herself.

We can see, then, that the vast majority of the principles appear to support and encourage the patient to make her own decision—thus minimising the role of proxy decision-makers such as donees of LPAs. Moreover, as we have seen donees of LPAs themselves are supposed to make decisions based on what the patient would have wanted—that is, fundamentally, their purpose. Nevertheless, a challenge to both the principles and the ability of donees to properly carry out their functions lies in the concept of best interests, which constitutes the fourth principle. This principle states that any 'act done, or decision made, under this Act for or on behalf of a person who lacks capacity must be done, or made, in his best interests' (MCA, 2005: section 1(5)). This includes decisions made by proxies such as donees of LPAs, and indeed section 9(4)(a) specifies that all decisions made by the donees must be in accordance with the principles of the Act and the patient's best interests. Put another way, decisions made by donees may be challenged if they do not accord with the patient's best interests. While it is easy to see why such a caveat to the power of donees was included, its inclusion cannot be said to accord with the principles behind the Act.

This is because, if the purpose of introducing LPAs was to allow those who know the patient best make decisions which would be consistent with those that would be made by the patient if she had capacity, then it is to lessen the respect for that hypothetical autonomy to then question those decisions. This is even more the case if the decisions are questioned on the basis of welfare, and unfortunately that is what is likely to be the case here, even if the best interests calculation is supposed to be more nuanced than that. Indeed, the definition of best interests in section 4 of the Act as I have argued above somewhat downplayed the substituted judgement elements and raised the profile of the objective welfare criteria. Moreover, the approach of the courts in cases such as *Re E* demonstrates that when autonomy and welfare conflict, it is not at all certain that it is autonomy that will be prioritised. One of the central planks of the Mental Capacity Act—that the definition of best interests should not be solely about best *medical* interests—therefore risks being undermined. The eccentric patient, whose views may be very accurately reflected by the decision of the donees, may find the welfare element of best interests used against that decision, and thus her autonomy compromised. This assumes a definition of autonomy that refers to the decision being the one that the patient would have made. It has been argued (Dunn and Foster, 2010) that the courts are insufficiently rigorous in defining concepts such as autonomy and welfare.

Again, given the fluctuating capacity of the patient with dementia, this should not prove too much of a problem in the early stages of the disease, but as it progresses and the time between lucidity increases, it is worth circumventing the danger posed by best interests by considering any specific requests and perhaps even creating an advance directive. Essentially, when balancing autonomy and welfare the law can be less mindful of the former than it would have us think.

That said, IMCAs provide an interesting counterpoint to this. It is easy to be critical of them—in the sense that they appear to involve someone who does not know the patient in decisions where they attempt to represent what the patient would want—but their role is, at least partially, to garner information. This does not make much sense, since if a friend or relative of the patient can be found then there should be no need for IMCA involvement. Nevertheless, as mentioned above IMCAs represent a non-medical voice, and while it may be a stretch to say that they enhance autonomy, they do at least broaden the definition of welfare as intended by the Law Commission. Perhaps most fundamental to the patient with dementia could be a tangential role of the IMCA, which is to question whether the patient lacks capacity at all. An effective advocate for the patient might well negotiate allowing the patient to make at least some of her own decisions. In other words, its most effective action as an advocate might be removing the need for a proxy. Nevertheless, the IMCA will also operate subject to the patient's best interests, and all the problems mentioned above in relation to LPAs will equally apply. Moreover, IMCAs are not proxy decision-makers but merely people involved in lobbying decision-makers, so they have little ultimate authority.

CONCLUSION

In the MCA's balance of autonomy and welfare, both LPAs and IMCAs seek to enhance the former. However, both are significantly limited by being subject to best interests, which may instinctively emphasise the latter. That is not always unreasonable, and there are times when the prioritisation of welfare is both right and necessary. Nevertheless, for the patient with dementia both LPAs and IMCAs serve useful functions. First, both allow the patient to have a voice even after she has lost capacity. Donees of LPAs will certainly be aware of the patient's wishes and feelings—particularly strongly held ones—and the progressive nature of the disease offers an opportunity for the patient to discuss matters with donees before a lack of capacity becomes an issue. IMCAs will not have this advantage, and indeed cannot even make decisions, but their role is just as important. Where the patient exists on the margins of capacity, as will be the case with many patients with dementia, an advocate who represents them and argues for their involvement in decisions can make a huge difference. Equally, they can ensure that non-medical considerations come into the best interests calculation, meaning that the substituted judgement elements of that test are not forgotten amongst the objective (medical) welfare criteria. There will never be a perfect balance between autonomy and welfare. The proxy decision-making provisions in the MCA are, in part, an attempt to recalibrate the law to enhance the former, and it must be said that it has done this while not entirely dispensing with the also important latter. For the patient with dementia, this provides useful methods for ensuring that, as much as possible, the decisions that they would have wanted made are at least considered, which can only be seen as a positive.

REFERENCES

Department for Constitutional Affairs (DCA) (2007) *Mental Capacity Act 2005 Code of Practice* (London, The Stationery Office).

Dunn, M et al (2007) 'Constructing and reconstructing "best interests": An interpretative examination of substitute decision-making under the Mental Capacity Act 2005' 29(2) *Journal of Social Welfare and Family Law* 117–32.

Dunn, M and Foster, C (2010) 'Autonomy and welfare as *Amici curiae*' 18(1) *Medical Law Review* 86–95.

Herring, J (2009) 'Losing it? Losing what? The law and dementia' 21(1) *Child and Family Law Quarterly* 3–29.

Lasting Powers of Attorney, Enduring Powers of Attorney and Public Guardian Regulations, 2007.

Law Commission (1995) *Mental Incapacity* (Law Com No 231) (London, Law Commission).

Mason, JK and Laurie, GT (2013) *Mason and McCall Smith's Law and Medical Ethics*, 9th edn (Oxford, Oxford University Press).

Mental Capacity Act, 2005.
Miola, J (2007) *Medical Ethics and Medical Law: A Symbiotic Relationship* (Oxford, Hart Publishing).
Samanta, J (2009) 'Lasting powers of attorney for healthcare under the Mental Capacity Act 2005: Enhanced prospective self-determination or a simulacrum?' 17(3) *Medical Law Review* 377–409.

14

Telling the Truth: The Ethics of Deception and White Lies in Dementia Care

MAARTJE SCHERMER

INTRODUCTION

LIES AND DECEPTION are often used in the contact with and daily care for demented elderly, often with the best intentions (James et al, 2006; Tuckett, 2012). The truth can be painful and hard to bear, and demented patients seem to have lost touch with reality anyhow. That sometimes seems to make deception less morally culpable.

The presumption should be that lies and deception are unacceptable. Kant even called deception, together with coercion, the most fundamental form of wrongdoing to others—the root of all evil (Korsgaard, 1996: 140). Kant has been criticized, however, for his 'rigorism' in his rejection of lying (Korsgaard, 1996: 133–34). In many situations lying may seem harmless, or even in the patient's best interests, and the question of whether or not to lie requires serious moral deliberation in such cases.

In this contribution[1] I will discuss two examples of deceiving demented patients for reasons of beneficence, and examine the arguments for and against such practices, as well as the relationship between well-being and truth. I will argue that even though lies and deception are prima facie wrong, they can sometimes be justified. However, even beneficent deceptive practices do not always truly enhance people's well-being, and so one should be very cautious about employing them. Methods that enhance the well-being of the patient without deception or lies should be favoured.

TWO EXAMPLES FROM PRACTICE

In the daily practice of dementia care, lies, white lies, falsehoods and deception can take different forms. Two examples will be used.

[1] This chapter is an abbreviated and revised version of my 'Nothing but the truth? On truth and deception in dementia care' (Schermer, 2007).

Simulated Presence

Simulated Presence ('SimPres®') is a device developed for Alzheimer's patients.[2] It is intended to manage behavioural problems like agitation and withdrawal that are believed to indicate personal discomfort and hence a lack of well-being. It is an audiotape that includes a caller's side of a telephone conversation. The tape is made by a family member of the patient who has been trained in special communication techniques and who has a list of cherished memories of the patient about which to talk.

The audiotape can be played through a recording device that looks like a telephone, or using a headset and auto reverse tape player enclosed in a hip pack.

Patients respond to the tape as if they were having a real telephone conversation. They smile and talk back and thus appear to believe that they are actually on the phone with their family member. Because people with Alzheimer's disease have short-term memory defects, audio taped messages can be played repeatedly and yet be perceived as fresh conversation each time (Camberg et al, 1999a). An evaluation study showed that SimPres improved agitated or withdrawn behaviours and appeared to make patients feel good. The conclusion was that: 'SimPres® appears to be a pleasurable activity when used as a complement to existing activity programs and even as a substitute for one-on-one interactions when staff must be involved with other residents' (Camberg et al, 1999b: 541).

Tricks and White Lies in Everyday Interaction

On many occasions in everyday interaction with people with dementia the question of speaking the truth or telling a 'white lie' comes up.

Imagine a woman with dementia banging on the locked door of the ward, begging everyone in the neighborhood to open the door so that she can go and collect the children from school.

Telling her that her children are long grown up and are not waiting for her only worsens her agitation and confusion. One of the nursing aides takes her arm and says: 'Come on Mrs G, the children will not be out for another hour, let's go have a cup of tea first'. Mrs G relaxes and goes with the nursing aide.

Another example: a widower keeps asking about his wife. He is inconsolable every time he is told that she has died. Why hurt such a patient by confronting him with the painful truth time and again, some of the nurses wonder. Why not just distract attention by a small lie and tell the widower his wife is out shopping?

WHAT COUNTS AS A LIE?

Are these instances of lying or deception? According to Sisela Bok (1978), in her famous *Lying*, lies are part of the broader category of deception, which includes all that we do or do not do, say or do not say, with the intention of misleading others.

[2] SimPres® is the trade mark registered name for this device.

Misleading others means making them believe something that we ourselves do not believe. Anything that is *stated*, either verbally or in writing, with the intention of making someone else believe something that the person uttering the statement believes to be false, is a lie. Anything done with the same intention, but without uttering a falsehood, is deception. Evading a question, withholding information or even certain ways of looking or gesturing can all be deceptive, according to Bok.

Jennifer Jackson, in her work on truth and trust in medicine, uses much the same definition. According to her a lie is 'the asserting of what one believes to be false in order to deceive someone' (Jackson, 2001: 48), where deceiving is understood as getting others to believe what one believes to be false.

With these definitions in mind, it is easy to classify the use of SimPres as a form of lying or deception. SimPres is clearly set up to make the patient believe he is actually on the phone, and most patients apparently do believe this since they respond to the tape talking and smiling. The device is constructed to make patients believe something that is not true, and is thus an inherently deceptive technology. Whether or not it involves *lying* to patients depends on how it is introduced to the patient. If a nurse says: 'Here's something for you to listen to', she is not lying, but if she says: 'Here's your daughter on the phone', she clearly is. As long as she does not make it absolutely clear, however, that this is merely a tape, she is deceiving the patient.

However, when we examine the daily tricks and white lies used in nursing homes, another picture emerges. Though they often include the statement of falsehoods, it is not necessarily the case that one *intends* to make the patient with dementia *believe* these falsehoods. While some tricks or 'white lies' are clearly lies—falsehoods intended to mislead—there exist other forms of dealing with truth and falsehood that do not classify as lies. Pretend play in children, jokes and jests, or exaggerations to 'spice up' a story, are all practices that border on lying but are not quite the same. In the care of patients with dementia as well, one might ask whether telling falsehoods is always properly understood as deceptive. Frequently, falsehoods are not intended to create false beliefs but to distract patients or to reach them when they have become absorbed in their own inner world. In the therapeutic approach known as 'validation' the quintessence is acceptation and confirmation of the patient's feelings and experiences regardless of their level of reality (Benjamin, 1999).

In this approach, patients are addressed on an emotional rather than a cognitive level. When a woman keeps banging the door, wanting to go to her children, a validating caregiver would not state that the children are long grown up (which is true) or that their school will be out a little later today (which is a lie). She will invite this woman to tell something more about her children and so addresses her feelings and emotions, not the cognitive content of her beliefs. Whether or not the conversation contains true statements and gives an accurate picture of reality is not the point; the point is to reach the patient and to establish a connection.

It is questionable whether such practices should be discussed in terms of truth, lying, reality and the like. First of all, at least some everyday tricks and white lies in the care for elderly people with dementia should probably not be defined as lies, because they are not intended to deceive. Put even more strongly: they should be understood as part of a completely different practice, dealing with the emotional instead of the cognitive level of interaction.

Second, in addition to the absence of an intention to mislead, the patient may be unable to form beliefs, and hence unable to form false beliefs and so be misled. If someone is living in 'his own world' this does not mean that truth does not exist any more. But as dementia progresses, the less the patient will be capable of entertaining 'beliefs', either true or false. One can often predict that although a lie will give the patient a temporary false belief, this will be forgotten very quickly—probably within moments. Perhaps only the emotional content will get through, and no real cognitive 'belief' will be formed. Once patients reach a state in which concepts such as truth and falsehood, reality and illusion or fact and fantasy do not mean anything to them any more, it becomes impossible to deceive them. Can one really lie to someone in a coma, or to a baby? Likewise, it is conceptually impossible to lie to people in the advanced states of dementia. When exactly the capacity to form beliefs and hence to be deceived is lost is a very complex question, but that it is lost at some point seems clear.

IF IT IS LYING, OR DECEPTION, IS IT WRONG?

While not all tricks, falsehoods and white lies in daily nursing home practice may constitute real instances of deception or lying, some do. Can lying to or deceiving patients with dementia ever be justified, and if so, on what grounds? To answer this question we should first consider why lying and deception are generally considered to be morally wrong, and then see how these reasons hold up where patients with dementia are concerned.

One frequently mentioned argument against lying is that it violates the autonomy of the person lied to. Lies and deception affect people's opportunities to make their own choices, because they affect the information upon which they base their choices, or because they prevent choice altogether.

This is an important argument against lying and deception in medicine, where respect for autonomy and informed consent are considered cornerstones of good practice. Deceptive practices that prevent patients from making well considered choices about their medical treatment are therefore morally wrong. Moreover, deception makes it impossible for people to relate to reality and to react to it, while it is in doing so that people can both express themselves and construct their personal narrative identity. A good example is dealing with painful truths. Once we come to know some painful truth, we can start dealing with it—mourning, accepting, struggling and 'giving it a place in our lives'. For patients in the later stages of dementia, the painful truth—for example that their spouse has died—is new every time they hear it. They cannot even start to 'deal with it' since they do not remember. New information cannot affect the identity of the patient with dementia, his outlook on life, or his plans and goals any more. This means that the truth or falsehood of this information loses much of its significance for the patient, and this weakens the argument against lying.

A second important argument against lying is connected to the autonomy argument, but goes a bit further by invoking the human dignity of the one lied to. It claims that lying to someone is a severe form of disrespect. To respect people means, in Kantian terms, to treat them always as ends in themselves, and not merely as means. This implies always treating them as free rational beings, and ascribing to them free will and rationality. Deception means withholding others the opportunity to make free and rational choices about themselves. It means manipulating them, and thus failing to treat them as ends in themselves. This means failing to respect their humanity or their human dignity. This motive is also recognized by patients with dementia themselves, as a recent study showed (Day et al, 2011). Day found that people with dementia felt that lies could be acceptable when told in the person with dementia's best interest and the person was not aware of the lie. When awareness of lies existed, however, this was considered patronizing and demeaning and impacting negatively on personhood.

Another important argument against lying and deception is that both undermine trust. Especially in the relationship between caregiver and care receiver, trust is a crucial component. Lying to or deceiving patients can severely damage trust and so undermine the care relationship. In the case of residents with dementia it may be the case that the damaging effects of lying and deception are not always a serious problem, since many people with dementia do not notice or find out subtle lies and forms of deception or quickly forget about them. On the other hand, lying can increase the confusion and disorientation that patients with dementia often suffer from.

Apart from trust within individual relationships, lying can also damage public trust in an entire practice. While the use of a technology like SimPres or white lies may not lead to a decline in trust between the patient with dementia and his caregivers, public trust in professional care might be damaged if lying and deception were known to be common practice. People might feel uncomfortable with the idea that once their faculties decline, caregivers would start deceiving them.

A final argument against lying, which gains its validity from the former arguments, concerns the effects of lying on the liar himself. Bok has argued that lying may easily become a habit, entrapping the liar in an ever more complex web of lies and falsehoods, corrupting him and damaging his integrity and credibility (Bok, 1978). According to Kant, lying destroys the human dignity of the liar himself. Even when deceptive practices and white lies in the care of patients with dementia prove to be harmless or beneficial to those patients, the effects of lying on the caregivers should be considered too. Caregivers may well be bothered by being (as they perceive it) dishonest, deceptive or untruthful. Even if they do so from good intentions, and even if they know it actually is beneficial to patients, it may still bother them and be perceived as compromising their personal integrity, or violating basic moral rules. Although there is little research in this area, there are some indications that caregivers actually find this aspect problematic (Hertogh et al, 2004; Elvish et al, 2010).

Considering these arguments against deception and lying, we can conclude that lying is prima facie wrong, but not absolutely wrong in all circumstances. In the case of patients with dementia, some arguments against lying or deceiving may not always count fully. This will depend mainly on the degree of cognitive loss. There may, for instance, be no loss of trust or infringement of autonomy. Even so, lies/deception, where used, always need to be justified. One of the possible justifications for lying or deceiving a patient is that it will prevent harm to him, or even promote his well-being. It may do so, for example, by giving the patient hope, by preventing pain or distress or by maintaining self-respect. If beneficence is invoked to justify deceptive practices, it should be clear that the well-being of the patient is indeed being protected or promoted by the deception. Is this the case with SimPres, and with everyday white lies?

CAN DECEPTION IMPROVE WELL-BEING?

Let us first consider the example of SimPres. It seems that SimPres indeed makes people with dementia feel good. It helps to resolve agitated and withdrawn behaviour, produces happy facial expressions and in general appears to be enjoyed by the patients as a pleasurable experience (Camberg et al, 1999b). From a philosophical point of view one might ask, however, what the value is of such deception-based positive feelings. Does it really add to a patient's overall well-being, evaluated as an all encompassing assessment of how well life is going for him? Does it contribute to what might be called a 'good life' (Schermer, 2003)? On this point different theories about well-being present diverging opinions. While most theories acknowledge that pleasant experiences can add to a person's well-being, there is no agreement on the question of whether pleasant experiences can enhance well-being when they are based on illusion, falsehood or deception.

In a philosophical thought experiment know as the 'Experience Machine', Robert Nozick (1974) asks his readers to imagine a machine that can be directly attached to the brain. This machine can give a person who is hooked on any kind of experience he wants. It can provide lifelike experiences of writing a book, having sex, climbing a mountain or lying in the sun—whatever one wants. Would people choose to be hooked on to such a machine for the rest of their lives, guaranteeing a life consisting of their preferred experiences? According to Nozick, people would not want this, because they do not only want to experience certain things but also to *do* things, to *be* a certain kind of person and to live in *contact with reality*.

At first sight, SimPres has some traits in common with the Experience Machine, since one is attached to it and then has an experience of something that is not real, namely a telephone conversation with a relative. However, the fact that SimPres is a temporary intervention and not a perpetual one like the Experience Machine makes, I believe, an important difference. The Experience Machine shows that there is more to the good life than merely experiences. Well-being comprises more than just 'feeling good'. But this does not necessarily show us that illusory pleasant experiences have no value at all, or that they have nothing to contribute to well-being or to a good life whatsoever. It does not tell us that 'false experiences' can never count for anything.

A slightly different problem with SimPres is that it fakes something—a conversation with a loved one—that derives its value from being real. Some things cannot be faked without losing their essential nature and thus their value. This goes, for example, for art. Imagine an art lover who succeeds in purchasing an early Van Gogh for his collection. If some years later the Van Gogh proves to be a fake, its value for the collector will reduce dramatically however much he enjoyed it before. Just like art, human relationships and conversations between loved ones appear to be the kinds of things that depend on their 'authenticity', their 'truth' or 'sincerity' for their value. In meaningful human contact mutuality, reciprocity, interaction, sincerity and trust are important—hence fake interaction loses its value *as* interaction. SimPres is faking something that derives its value from being authentic. If we agree that interacting and conversing with loved ones are things that add to a good life, things that are valuable in their own right, then it seems that fake conversations do not improve one's life in the same way that real conversations would.

Pleasant feelings could be induced in patients with dementia in other ways that are not deceptive, and such alternatives are therefore preferable. It seems perfectly possible to use some of the principles of SimPres *without* the deception. For example, one could have a familiar voice or a loved one narrating pleasant personal memories on tape. Why fake a telephone call, if a narration can do the same? And, more importantly, why not invest more time and attention in real interaction with patients with dementia? SimPres and related technologies might all too easily become substitutes for true attention.

THE VALUE OF TRUTH AND THE SOLACE OF LIES

Can lies, falsehoods and tricks be beneficial to patients with dementia? Can they, for example, spare people unnecessary distress and grief, and are they therefore justified? Many people would argue that the truth, however painful, is always important to know. Living 'in the truth' is worthwhile in itself and even a harsh reality may be preferred above blissful ignorance. The Experience Machine story can be interpreted as showing exactly that. Lying to people to protect them from grief or guilt may not actually enhance their well-being. A good life is not necessarily a life without distress, but one in which we can mourn our losses, learn to deal with our pain and find ways to show remorse.

This conclusion is relevant for dealing with truth and deception in the care of elderly dementia patients because being demented *is* in a sense like living in the Experience Machine. According to Ben Rich:

> [O]n the experience machine, and, one might also argue, in the third stage of Alzheimer's dementia, we have essentially lost touch with reality. Such a loss should concern us profoundly if what we desire is to live our lives while being in touch with reality (Rich, 1997: 143).

Many people will subscribe to this statement and agree that one of the dramatic aspects of the disease is this loss of contact with reality. Because we value contact with reality as a good thing in life, our treatment of and interaction with people with dementia is generally aimed at maintaining some contact with reality as long as possible. Truth and sincerity can help maintain a connection to reality and thus add to well-being. However, for patients who have irreversibly lost the capacity to *relate* actively to reality the value of truth changes, as discussed above. Once painful truths no longer add anything other than pain to the person's life, they lose their meaning and their value. When there is only pain, and there is no residual capacity to deal with that pain, to understand or come to grips with it, nor even to remember it for very long, the truth no longer contributes to a good life.

Outright lies to patients with dementia should be avoided if possible because they insult human dignity (even if actual capacities for freedom and rationality are lost), compromise the liar (diminishing the liar's own dignity) and threaten to undermine trust in the whole practice of care. The best solution is to find ways of getting an important yet painful truth across without hurting the person involved.

A good example of this is the case of a woman with dementia whose son had died but who could not remember this. Every time she asked how he was doing she was devastated when the staff told her that he was dead. Finally, one of the nurses dressed her in the clothes she had worn to his funeral. This made her remember and enabled her to mourn. Afterwards, she no longer asked for her son, though she still spoke about him (Yang-Lewis and Moody, 1995).

If such a solution is not possible, avoiding painful truths by circumvention and distraction are certainly legitimate options. Moreover, it should be kept in mind that it is not deceptive to refrain from telling people the truth or from correcting their false or mistaken beliefs when this is not called for. It can even be a case of 'truth-dumping' (Bok, 1978) or of overzealous candour (Jackson, 2001) to tell patients their beliefs are false and to confront them with the painful truth when they have asked nothing. Patients with dementia who 'live in their own world' should not be forced out of it with an appeal to truth and reality, if these have nothing to offer them but pain.

CONCLUSION

Assessing whether or not a (white) lie or deceptive act is justified in the care of a patient with dementia is a complex and subtle matter. Assuming that lies, deception and falsehoods in the care for demented elderly are most frequently employed with the best intentions and with an eye to the patient's well-being, the central question is how to strike the balance between well-being and truth. In general one can say that methods that enhance the well-being of the patient without deception or lies should be favoured above options that use deceit, and methods of getting the truth across without hurting the patient should be favoured above methods that hurt (see also the four step model in Wood-Mitchell et al, 2006). It demands a lot of insight into the specific patient, his capacities and his reactions as well as into the exact situation and possible alternatives, to judge fairly about individual instances of lying or deception.

As a support for those who have to make such difficult decisions on a daily basis, we can repeat three considerations that have been discussed above. First: methods relying on deception or lies to enhance patients' well-being do not always succeed because there is more to 'a good life' than just feeling good. Second: however important truth may be in many people's lives, it can lose its function and it can become a mere burden. Third: not only the patient but also the nursing and medical staff are affected by the use of lies and deception. The effects of lying and deceiving on their integrity and trustworthiness should also be taken into account.

REFERENCES

Benjamin, BJ (1999) 'Validation: A communication alternative' in L Volicer and L Bloom-Charette (eds), *Enhancing the Quality of Life in Advanced Dementia* (Philadelphia, Taylor & Francis).

Bok, S (1978) *Lying: Moral Choices in Public and Private Life* (New York, Vintage Books).

Camberg, L, Woods, P and MacIntyre, K (1999a) 'SimPres: A personalized approach to enhance well-being in persons with Alzheimer's disease' in L Volicer and L Bloom-Charette (eds), *Enhancing the Quality of Life in Advanced Dementia* (Philadelphia, Taylor & Francis).

Camberg, L, et al. (1999b) 'Evaluation of Simulated Presence: A personalized approach to enhance well-being in persons with Alzheimer's disease' 47 *Journal of the American Geriatrics Society* 446–52.

Day, AM et al (2011) 'Do people with dementia find lies and deception in dementia care acceptable?' 15(7) *Aging and Mental Health* 822–29.

Elvish, R, James, I and Milne, D (2010) 'Lying in dementia care: An example of a culture that deceives in people's best interests' 14(3) *Aging and Mental Health* 255–62.

Hertogh, CMPM et al (2004) 'Truth telling and truthfulness in the care for patients with advanced dementia: an ethnographic study in Dutch nursing homes' 59 *Social Science & Medicine* 1685–93.

Jackson, J (2001) *Truth, Trust and Medicine* (London, Routledge).

James, IA et al (2006) 'Lying to people with dementia: Developing ethical guidelines for care settings' 21 *International Journal of Geriatric Psychiatry* 800–01.

Korsgaard, CM (1996) *Creating the Kingdom of Ends* (Cambridge, Cambridge University Press).

Nozick, R (1974) *Anarchy, State and Utopia* (New York, Basic Books).

Rich, B (1997) 'Prospective autonomy and critical interests: A narrative defense of the moral authority of advance directives' 6(2) *Cambridge Quarterly of Healthcare Ethics* 138–47.

Schermer, M (2003) 'In search of "the good life" for demented elderly' 6(1) *Medicine, Health Care and Philosophy* 35–44.

—— (2007) 'Nothing but the truth? On truth and deception in dementia care' 21 *Bioethics* 13–22.

Tuckett, AG (2012) 'The experience of lying in dementia care: A qualitative study' 19(1) *Nursing Ethics* 7–20.

Wood-Mitchell, A et al (2006) 'Lying to people with dementia: Sparking the debate' 14(6) *Journal of Dementia Care* 30–31.

Yang-Lewis, T and Moody, R (1995) 'The forgetful mourner' 25(1) *Hastings Center Report* 32–33.

15

Research on Patients with Dementia

ADRIAN TRELOAR AND CLAUDIA DUNLOP

INTRODUCTION

WHILE MANY PEOPLE live well with dementia, dementia is a devastating condition for many and a serious illness whose causes, symptoms and progression may all be modified by appropriate and scientifically evidenced treatments. It is therefore essential that there is a good knowledge base around both the underpinning science of dementia as well as the practical treatment and management of dementia.

But arguably, all medical research, and certainly research on people with mental disabilities, takes place on vulnerable people who also need protection from abuse and over enthusiastic researchers. Not only that, medical research takes place against the background of the great atrocities of medical research conducted on prisoners of war, concentration camp victims and other prisoners in Germany, the Far East and elsewhere before, during and after the Second World War. It is precisely those atrocities that led to and honed the stringent international guidelines that govern medical research both on those who can consent and also on those who cannot do so.

These guidelines must protect the individual from abuse and also enable effective ethical and valid research to be carried out on people with dementia. This is necessary for the development of new dementia treatments, without denying dementia sufferers potentially significant benefits.

Achieving an appropriate balance is far from easy. In early and milder dementia it is possible to use the same rules of consent to research which pertain to all consenting adults, but in severe dementias, where understanding and memory are severely impaired, mental capacity is lost, with the result that valid consent cannot be given by an individual for participation in a research study. Yet if research cannot be undertaken on people with severe dementia, then the evidence base for innovative treatment of such patients will be lacking.

But between the time when people with early dementias can consent to relevant studies and the time when almost no one can consent to participate in research, there is an intermediate phase where some, with support, can consent but others will be unable to do so. There will always be a temptation to include the readily consented patients and exclude the others, although there is a concern that doing so may skew the study population towards the more able—thus making it unrepresentative.

HISTORICAL PERSPECTIVES

The use of concentration camp and other prisoners during the Second World War is an iconic example of the abuse of research. Many have sought to argue that the research done in such settings was not useful and lacked scientific merit; however some were eventually found to have been useful and beneficial. An example is the development of pressurised air-suits for Luftwaffe airmen. More worryingly perhaps, entirely unethical research by the Japanese in occupied China during the Second World War was used after the War by the Americans. Indeed, in Unit 731 the Americans gave immunity from prosecution to a special division of the Japanese Army which had committed crimes of experimentation on prisoners. This enabled them to continue their work (more ethically) after the War (Beevor, 2012: 722). But whatever the possible benefits of such research, there is no question that the research was unethical and the overwhelming revulsion at what was done to prisoners and others has led to the Declaration of Helsinki (see below) and, perhaps even more importantly, a recognition that whatever the possible benefits of research, there are limits on what research can be done.

INDIVIDUAL PROFESSIONAL PERSPECTIVES

One of the great challenges in medical research is the fact that researchers gain reputation and job security by publishing and producing research. Pressures come from ambition, as well as from the necessity of obtaining funding for research projects; but also, there is a danger of researchers seeing only those results which accord with their expectations. The most prominent recent example of this is that of Andrew Wakefield, who undertook research on children (who were too young to consent) into the link between autism and the measles, mumps and rubella vaccine as reported by Kmietowicz (2010). It was clear that Dr Wakefield had departed from good governance in, inter alia, interpreting his results to fit his theories from the General Medical Council hearing (2010). Fred (2008) also alludes to others too who have been found to have fixed results, and whole series of papers have been discredited. The same risks apply in research into dementia. Abbasi (2009) argues that pharmaceutical companies are renowned for selective publication of results which accord with their commercial objectives.

INDIVIDUAL PATIENT PERSPECTIVES

Patients and their relatives are vulnerable. Even in incurable conditions, when any discovery will come too late for the individual, many people wish to participate in research in the hope that others may be spared their lot. There is no doubt that faced with an incurable illness, many patients desperately hope that a new treatment may help them. When news became available of participation in a double blind study of Tacrine (a predecessor of today's anti-dementia drugs) the switchboard at the Maudsley Hospital in London was jammed for several days by people ringing up and wanting to be allowed to participate in the desperate hope of a cure of the incurable (Treloar, 2009). In such circumstances, patients require substantial protection both from themselves and from bad research.

THE DECLARATION OF HELSINKI

The Declaration of Helsinki (2008) is 'the most widely accepted guidance worldwide on research involving human subjects' (Christie, 2000: 913). Crawley and Hoet (1999) refer that it is the largely unquestioned anchor for ethical decision-making in clinical trials. The Declaration was produced in the wake of the Second World War by the World Medical Association, and first published in 1964. It was a direct response to the atrocities of the War.

The Declaration rests on the premise that medical research must ultimately involve research on human subjects (article 5). It explicitly recognises the unique dignity and rights of each individual (articles 3, 6 and 9) and the need for international regulation and standards respected by all doctors (article 10).

All research must be well designed, reviewed by research ethics committees and done by appropriately trained and qualified people. Consent is central to all research and must be formally documented and witnessed (article 24). Disadvantaged communities can only be used in research where there is a reasonable likelihood that such communities will benefit from the research (article 17).

Where an incompetent individual is able to assent but not give informed consent, the physician must seek consent from the legally authorised representative. Dissent in a potential subject must be respected (article 28).

If no one can consent, research will only be sanctioned where the condition that prevents the giving of informed consent is a necessary characteristic of the research population (article 29). In such subjects, consent must be sought from the designated proxy decision-maker, if any. The essential effect of this article is to permit appropriate and ethical research on people with dementia, provided that the research is required to further the knowledge base of people with dementia. One might therefore be able to research drugs for dementia, or do research into social care options for people with dementia, but one cannot research into treatments for conditions such as pneumonia unless the research is into a particular aspect of pneumonia which requires subjects with dementia and which will benefit those people.

Articles 17, 28 and 29 imply that study samples must be representative of the population that requires study. Therefore, to provide a robust evidence base, care must be taken to ensure that selection bias and bias from consent processes do not skew the research population, and hence the results.

UK LAW AND THE MENTAL CAPACITY ACT

The Mental Capacity Act (MCA, 2005) is the key piece of English legislation relating to decision-making by and on behalf of those who lack capacity. Enacted in 2005, the MCA defines capacity in section 5:

Box 1: Assessing mental capacity under the MCA (MCA, section 5)

A person is unable to make a decision if they cannot:

1. Understand information about the decision to be made (the Act calls this 'relevant information').
2. Retain that information in their mind.
3. Use or weigh that information as part of the decision-making process.
4. Communicate their decision (by talking, using sign language or any other means). See section 3(1).

Many dementia patients will not have the requisite capacity to consent to research. The MCA Code of Practice (Department for Constitutional Affairs, 2010) constrains research on people who lack capacity to situations where 'there are reasonable grounds for believing that the research would be less effective if only people with capacity are involved'. One can therefore include individuals who lack capacity if this research cannot be carried out on those with capacity. The inclusion of such subjects will be scrutinised closely by the Research Ethics Committee.

The ability to do research on incapacitous patients for whom the research is not directly beneficial seems (although the Act itself does not say this) to be an exception to the principle that the only lawful decision made on behalf of an incapacitous patient is one which is in their best interests.

Research is defined in the MCA 2005 as 'the attempt to derive generalizable new knowledge by addressing clearly defined questions with systematic and rigorous methods'.

Research is then allowed according to the provisions of Box 2.

Box 2: Requirements regarding potential benefit to the individual

1. The research must have some chance of benefiting the person who lacks capacity, and the benefit must be in proportion to any burden caused by taking part,

or

2. the aim of the research must be to provide knowledge about the cause of, or treatment or care of people with, the same impairing condition—or a similar condition.

> If researchers are relying on the second requirement, the Act sets out further requirements that must be met:
>
> — the risk to the person who lacks capacity must be negligible
> — there must be no significant interference with the freedom of action or privacy of the person who lacks capacity,
>
> and
>
> — nothing must be done to or in relation to the person who lacks capacity which is unduly invasive or restrictive.
>
> **(MCA Code of Practice, section 11.12)**

In addition to that, all research on the incapacitated requires a process of consultation as a further safeguard (Box 3). There is, therefore, a statutory process of consultation and other safeguards which enable those who have no advocate to enter into research studies. But of course the 'negligible risk' criterion does inhibit some research, even though that research might in the end help others.

> **Box 3: Research is allowed provided that:**
>
> The researcher must take reasonable steps to identify a person who—
>
> (a) otherwise than in a professional capacity or for remuneration, is engaged in caring for P or is interested in P's welfare, and
> (b) is prepared to be consulted by R under this section.
>
> If the researcher cannot identify such a person he must, in accordance with guidance issued by the appropriate authority, nominate a person who—
>
> (a) is prepared to be consulted by R under this section, but
> (b) has no connection with the project.

In addition all studies (as under the Declaration of Helsinki) must be approved by the 'appropriate body' and researchers are jointly responsible with the appropriate body for ensuring that the requirements of the Act are met. Helpfully the Act does accept the principle that some research will not benefit the individual, and sets out limits on that research, as above.

There is further UK legislation with regard to drug trials: see the Medicines for Human Use (Clinical Trials) Regulations 2004. Researchers are also accountable to their regulatory bodies.

RESEARCH ETHICS COMMITTEES

It is important that proposed research is reviewed before being started. Research ethics committees have the powers to prohibit research, as well as to require modifications and amendments to research protocols. One challenge for researchers has been that in multicentre trials different local committees take different views as to what is ethical and what is justified by the current research and knowledge base. As a result of this, Al-Shahi (2005) has highlighted that some multicentre trials have struggled enormously to follow a consistent methodology. Most jurisdictions have encountered similar difficulties. In response to this difficulty in the UK, Multicentre Research Ethics Committees (MRECs) were introduced to advise local research ethics committees (LRECs) on what should be approved. Where studies occur in more than four districts, an MREC will review the ethics and protocol of a study, leaving LRECs only the job of ensuring that local arrangements are satisfactory for the implementation of the MREC approved protocol.

SKEWING OF STUDIES BY RELIANCE ON CONSENT

The Declaration of Helsinki and English law, including the MCA, set out with clarity that where consent can be obtained it must be obtained prior to entry into a research study. A capacitous individual has the right to refuse consent to participate in research. As stated above, the MCA and Declaration of Helsinki provide that wherever possible those who lack capacity should not be used in research if that research can be done on people who have capacity.

But if we skew studies towards involving people with capacity, this can cause difficulties. An example of this is reported by Adamis (2005) in a study of delirium where participants had around a 50% chance of being able to give informed consent to participate in research. The researchers found that the attempt to discuss, describe and develop informed consent had two key effects. First, due to the delay and time taken to start the study some potential participants became vexed and worried about the whole study with the result that they refused to participate. But, second and more significantly, the process of this discussion effectively excluded those who lacked capacity from participating in the study. The researchers concluded that over-reliance on complex processes of consent had skewed results to the point where only those with mild delirium could be studied. This in turn, they argued, made the study unethical because the study could no longer focus on the intended study population. This study was a simple observational study which involved no specific treatments, but it would be far more complicated in intervention studies—for instance those involving the development of new treatments.

CONCLUSION

Research about dementia is essential. But people with dementia are vulnerable, especially when they are unable to consent to treatment. As well as requiring protection from unscrupulous researchers, people with dementia also require protection from the enthusiasm of committed researchers who may come to believe or hope more strongly in their hypotheses than they should. But people with dementia may also need protection from their own enthusiasm and fears, which may lead them to clutch at straws as they struggle with a devastating illness.

The Declaration of Helsinki and nationally implemented legislation are designed to protect individuals from abuse. That protection must also ensure that representative samples of patients can be recruited to important studies.

REFERENCES

Abbasi, K (2009) 'Declare all or be damned' 102(7) *Journal of the Royal Society of Medicine* 43.

Adamis, D (2005) 'Capacity, Consent, and Selection Bias in a Study of Delirium' 31(3) *Journal of Medical Ethics* 137–43.

Al-Shahi, R (2005) 'Research ethics committees in the UK – the pressure is now on research and development departments' 98(10) *Journal of the Royal Society of Medicine* 444–47.

Beevor, A (2012) *The Second World War* (London, Weidenfeld and Nicolson).

Christie, B (2000) 'Doctors revise Declaration of Helsinki' 321(7266) *British Medical Journal* 913. Available at: www.ncbi.nlm.nih.gov/pmc/articles/PMC1118720/.

Crawley, F and Hoet, F (1999) 'Ethics and law: the Declaration of Helsinki under discussion' (150) *Bulletin of Medical Ethics* 9–12 (originally published in (1998) 7 *Applied Clinical Trials* 36–40).

Department for Constitutional Affairs (2010) *Mental Capacity Act 2005 Code of Practice*. Available at: webarchive.nationalarchives.gov.uk/+/http:/www.justice.gov.uk/docs/mca-cp.pdf.

Fred, H (2008) 'Dishonesty in Medicine Revisited' 35(1) *Texas Heart Institute Journal* 6–15.

General Medical Council (2010) 'Dr Andrew Jeremy Wakefield. Determination on Serious Professional Misconduct (SPM) and sanction'. Available at: www.gmc-uk.org/Wakefield_SPM_and_SANCTION.pdf_32595267.pdf.

Kmietowicz, Z (2010) 'Wakefield is struck off for the "serious and wide-ranging findings against him"' 340 *British Medical Journal* c2803. Available at: www.bmj.com/content/340/bmj.c2803.

Treloar, A (2009) Personal communication to author.

World Medical Association (2008) *Declaration of Helsinki. Ethical Principles for Medical Research Involving Human Subjects*. Available at: www.wma.net/en/30publications/10policies/b3/ index.html.

16

Genetics and Dementia: Ethical Concerns

CAROLINE J HUANG, MICHAEL PARKER AND MATTHEW L BAUM

INTRODUCTION AND BACKGROUND

THIS CHAPTER COMPLEMENTS chapter three ('The Genetics of Dementia') by exploring the ethical issues surrounding genetic counselling and testing for dementia as they arise for health professionals, patients and families. It begins with a brief overview of genetics services before moving to a case-based discussion of ethical issues.

Genetics services in the United Kingdom are provided by regionally organised, multidisciplinary teams of clinical geneticists, genetic counsellors and laboratory scientists. Though the arrangement of genetics services may vary between countries, the work itself remains similar. Genetics professionals play a number of roles, which include but are not limited to: risk assessment, provision of genetic counselling and advice and organisation and interpretation of genetic testing. In all these roles, genetics professionals see themselves as working with both individual patients and those patients' families.

Genetic counselling aims to provide non-directive, value-neutral guidance to patients and their families. A typical counselling session might involve taking a three or four-generation family history, gathering information about the patients' knowledge and expectations of the disorder in question and options available, providing information about the disorder including risk assessment, facilitating decision-making and follow-up visits or procedures (Harper, 2010). Whilst counselling may not always lead to genetic testing, it is an important part of the consent process for any testing that does occur. If the patient ultimately pursues genetic testing, a tissue sample (for example, blood, skin, hair or amniotic fluid) may be collected and subsequently be sent to a regional or national genetics laboratory for processing. The health professional will then share the test results and their implications with the patient in person, over the phone or by letter.

This brief overview is schematic only, as the precise form and content of counselling sessions are shaped by the nature of the particular genetic condition and its corresponding test, subsequent screening or treatment options, and particular concerns, values, and beliefs of the patient. Nonetheless, it broadly contextualises the ethical and legal problems faced by genetics professionals and patients in the situations outlined below.

In the context of dementia, the kind of testing required (ie, diagnostic or predictive) particularly influences the form and content of counselling. Diagnostic testing confirms or disconfirms the presence of a genetic disorder in a symptomatic patient, whereas predictive testing assesses risk in an asymptomatic patient. Many predictive tests are predispositional, where a positive result signals an increased risk of developing the condition. A special kind of predictive testing is presymptomatic, where a positive result signals a risk so high that the patient is guaranteed to develop the condition eventually (McPherson, 2006).

Decisions about presymptomatic testing for dementia can be especially complex and emotionally difficult. Consider a healthy adult patient whose parent has Huntington's disease (HD). As chapter three explained, 50% of children of a parent with HD will inherit the mutation, and since HD is highly penetrant, those children will eventually develop HD. Given that HD is currently incurable, the results of genetic testing cannot lead to treatment that will stop or reverse the disease's course and may additionally cause serious emotional harm and deleterious implications for insurance, employment and so on. However, testing may enable the patient to make lifestyle modifications and reproductive decisions, participate in clinical research trials and begin broader discussions and long-term planning with relatives. Genetic counselling can play a useful role in helping a patient decide whether it is better to know or not to know her genetic status and how to manage her test results.

This example of HD is a useful introduction to thinking about ethical issues that might arise in counselling and testing. Genetics professionals consistently highlight three kinds of difficult situations as arising in their day-to-day work: sharing information in families, making reproductive decisions and testing in children (Parker, 2012). Unsurprisingly, these topics remain relevant in the context of genetics and dementia. Using hypothetical examples and real cases presented by clinicians, the remainder of this chapter will explore these issues in more depth, as well as three others important in the context of dementia:

- Cases where information may be shared in families.
- Cases involving reproductive decisions.
- Cases involving incidental findings.
- Cases where testing a patient with dementia may benefit others.
- Cases involving the testing of children.
- Cases involving the moral implications of prediction.

CASES WHERE INFORMATION MAY BE SHARED IN FAMILIES

Like all health professionals, those working in genetics have an ethical and legal obligation to maintain patient confidentiality except in unusual circumstances, for example, risk of death or serious harm. Confidentiality is particularly difficult for genetics professionals for two reasons. First, genetics professionals have often, especially in the context of conditions such as HD, seen several generations of members of a single family. This means that they tend to see themselves as having duties of care to entire families, not just to the patient in front of them. Second, the family and its aggregate information are key prognostic and diagnostic tools in the care of individual patients to an extent unique in medicine. This entwinement of patients and other family members can generate difficult practical ethical problems:

> [One of the main ethical issues arising] is [...] the [situation] where you have information about someone based on other family members that they don't know about and how do you convey that information without breaching confidentiality. Prime example being a [inherited condition] family, for instance, where I knew a lot about the natural history of their particular gene having seen twenty or so of their relatives but they didn't know anything about the rest of the family which made it difficult to give them [advice]. Well, I could give them information quite easily because I knew quite a lot about what the outcome was likely to be but that might have appeared to be [offering] a rather false sense of security [because] they didn't know [that I knew] about the rest of the family. So if they do a lot of reading, which of course a lot of patients do, they'll say 'well how on earth can you say all these things with such certainty?' (Parker, 2012: 21).

The problem facing the genetics professional arises from her having previously collected information from other family members that could affect the current patient's treatment and counselling, whilst simultaneously believing this information to be 'confidential'. From the clinician's description, it is not clear whether the other family members have explicitly withheld the information or just not had a chance to share it. The clinician might re-contact the other family members to ask whether they have shared the information with potentially affected family members, and to offer assistance in facilitating a conversation if they have not. Ideally, those family members will agree to speak with their relative or permit the clinician to share the information on their behalf. The patient would then be able to access the information and its implications with the clinician's help. The problem with this route, of course, is that it may reveal information about this patient to other members of the family.

An even trickier example is described below, where the affected patient has stated specifically that he does not want his information shared:

> Jim (60) has recently been diagnosed with HD, which has been confirmed molecularly. There is no reported family history of HD, but, in retrospect, several of his deceased relatives may also have had the condition. Jim himself was initially diagnosed with Alzheimer's disease (AD) in his early 50s, but the diagnosis was reviewed following brain scans and revised to HD at the age of 57 years. Jim's capacity to consent is uncertain as he has marked dementia, but he has expressed a view, strongly shared with his wife Mary, that he does not want any of their four children (aged 27–37 years) to be informed of the diagnosis or of the risk to them. Jim and Mary can only see negative consequences arising out of the sharing of such information and anticipate that they will be blamed. Mary says, 'they either have it or don't'. The couple have been advised by genetic staff that their children might in fact want to know and may want to make their own choices. They have been offered help in communicating with their children, but have declined. Recently, one of the daughters was referred to the genetics team to discuss her father's AD, the early deaths of several of his relatives and the implications this might have for her. At a staff case discussion, most health professionals in the team feel that Jim and Mary's confidentiality should be respected. Justifications for this are centred around the lack of effective interventions for HD. Nevertheless, concern is also expressed that the children have a right to know what they are actually at risk of (Lucassen and Parker, 2004: 95).

Because the health professionals believe that information about Jim and Mary is confidential, 'personal' information, their only route to inviting the four children to clinic to discuss HD is through continued communication with Jim and Mary. There are a number of ways they might go about facilitating this. The genetics team might try to schedule periodic follow-up visits with Jim and Mary to revisit the idea of telling the children, particularly as Jim's condition progresses. During the daughter's visit, the clinician may also be able to ascertain tactfully whether the daughter 'blames' her parents for the family history of dementia; if she does not and if it is possible to find a way for this to be made apparent, that information might change Jim and Mary's stance and pave the way for a broader family discussion. Furthermore, as chapter three explained, some early-onset Alzheimer's disease (AD) is associated with autosomal dominant mutations in the APP, PSEN1 and PSEN2 genes, so the daughter's referral to the genetics service is already likely to trigger questions about inherited risk of AD and the father's genetic status. A more direct option would be for the clinician to encourage the daughter to speak with Jim and Mary about her concerns, without explicitly revealing that Jim has HD.

Whatever the solution, this case highlights one of the most important clusters of ethical issues arising in genetics and dementia: how familial information is utilised in the care of family members, irrespective of whether it is explicitly 'shared'. Recently, questions have been raised about whether the 'personal account' model of confidentiality used in most of medicine is appropriate for genetics given the familial nature of genetic information. Parker and Lucassen (2004) have, for example, suggested an alternative 'joint account' model: how genetic information used in the treatment of family members should be considered analogous to how bank account information is shared equally between the holders of a 'joint account'. Here, the default is that information should be available for family members' treatment unless there is good reason *not* to do so, rather than the current 'personal' model, which assumes the reverse.

Just as ethical concerns may arise in the sharing of existing familial information in the care of individual patients, so they can arise in the decisions of individual patients to pursue genetic testing that will reveal new information about family members. Consider a patient who wants to be tested but does not want other family members to know the results or even that testing is being pursued. Such cases can present real problems for genetics professionals committed to caring for both patients and their families:

> I've got a young patient with a family history of HD who wants to have a test to see whether she is going to be affected by the disease as she gets older. She is worried because she knows that her paternal grandmother has it. During counselling my patient disclosed that she is an identical twin. She says that her twin sister is not aware of the family history and says that she does not want her sister to know because she doesn't think that she could cope with this knowledge, particularly because the disease is untreatable. When I told her that I was reluctant to do the test on her without discussing it with her sister—because the fact that they are identical twins means that the test would also be a test on her twin—she said that she didn't want her sister to be involved. To reassure me, she promised that whatever the test result she would not disclose this. The other problem I have got is that in addition to being a test on her twin the test, if positive, would also be a test on her father who, she says, also does not know that she has come in for testing. I've tried to encourage her to talk to her sister and father about the test, but she says that she's not able to do this. I feel that I have got a duty of care to my patient, but I'm also worried about her sister and father even though I have never met them (Parker, 2012: 1).

In a nutshell, the tension here is between a belief that all those who undergo a genetic test (including the sister and the father) should give their consent and have access to counselling on the one hand, and that the access of patients (including the twin attending clinic) to tests should not be subject to a veto from their relatives on the other. As with the cases previously discussed, there is no clear-cut answer on how information should be shared, though gently encouraging communication between family members often strikes a balance between maintaining confidentiality and trying to help patients to access their health information.

CASES INVOLVING REPRODUCTIVE DECISIONS

Practical ethical problems in genetics also frequently arise in the context of reproductive decision-making, when couples consider technologies such as carrier testing, pre-implantation diagnosis, prenatal diagnosis or newborn screening. One set of ethical issues here concerns when access to prenatal or pre-implantation diagnosis should be available. Views on proper availability depend not only upon assessments of the broad permissibility of termination of pregnancy, but also upon the seriousness and likelihood of the condition, availability of interventions and the respective uncertainty surrounding each. These questions can present complex and difficult ethical problems in practice (Parker, 2012: 60–87).

A second set of ethical challenges, particularly difficult in the context of early-onset dementia, is the potential for reproductive testing to raise unanticipated problems relating to the health of the potential parents. As in the following example, prospective parents may not fully understand their own genetic statuses when they begin discussing family planning:

> Family referred. First child had Down syndrome. Between the initial referral and their appointment, the family discovered that one of the husband's parents had been diagnosed with Huntington's disease. When they arrived in the clinic the woman was pregnant again. And the husband clearly had evidence of Huntington's disease. What does one do? Disclose one's concerns? I decided not to say anything—was I wrong? (Parker, 2012: 84).

The family was initially referred to discuss Down syndrome in their first child. The discovery of the husband's parent having HD, however, brings up new concerns surrounding both reproductive decisions in the new pregnancy and the husband's health. First, the couple may desire prenatal screening for Down syndrome and testing for HD in this pregnancy. Second, the husband may or may not want to find out his own genetic status. If the couple wishes to undergo prenatal testing for Huntington's, the husband's decision about his own genetic status will dictate the kind of prenatal testing that can be done: exclusionary testing if he does not want to know, and predictive testing if he does want to know (de Die-Smulders et al, 2013).

As the case is presented, however, the genetics professional worries most about whether she should discuss the husband's possible HD symptoms with him. Her concern suggests that the husband did not broach the topic. The clinician's choice not to discuss HD is in alignment with the idea of genetic counselling as non-directive and value-neutral. If the husband did not ask for the information and was there only to discuss reproductive decisions, the clinician might feel uncomfortable with suggesting that he consider genetic testing for himself—particularly given that many people in the father's position choose not to be tested. The clinician may feel a conflict between her duty of care and respect for the patient's indiscernible preference to know or not to know. Because the observed signs of HD suggest that testing would be diagnostic, not predictive, the clinician might feel that saying something would enable the couple to make a more informed reproductive decision, which was why they were originally referred. For example, if the father has HD, the couple may wish to terminate the pregnancy so the wife does not have to care for two young children and her husband, but they may equally choose to keep the pregnancy so that the father has as much time as possible with any potential children.

CASES INVOLVING INCIDENTAL FINDINGS

The case above illustrates how encounters between patients and health professionals can sometimes generate unexpected information (for example, suspected symptomatic HD), which the patient may or may not welcome. How these sorts of incidental findings ought to be managed is an important issue in the context of genetics and genomics.

Consider the following example, which illustrates how ethical difficulties surrounding incidental findings may arise as psychiatrists and neurologists utilise genetic testing:

> [Actually] this issue of psychiatrists requesting confirmatory diagnostic tests on people who don't actually have anything other than very non-specific or allegedly behavioural features is one of the biggest problem areas that we face. We have seen problems arising from that sort of request on several occasions. I think probably in that it's professionals other than geneticists who are requesting these tests without really being fully aware of the issues involved. For example, neurology putting through tests for HD to exclude the diagnosis without really thinking what they will do if the test confirms it (Parker, 2012: 97).

Suppose that the neurologist's patient tests positive for the HD mutation or a predisposing mutation for dementia. Should the clinician feed the information back? The answer might depend on which professional body is consulted. The American College of Medical Genetics suggests that certain findings be fed back regardless of patient preference (Green et al, 2013); the European Society of Human Genetics recommends that patient preference should at least inform the decision of whether to feed back results (van El et al, 2013). This discrepancy is indicative of the unresolved debate over best practices for handling incidental findings, a debate that may become more important as genomic approaches are mainstreamed, ie, used in non-genetics specialties across the whole of medicine.

Whole-genome and whole-exome sequencing can generate similarly unsolicited findings. A patient may pursue testing for one reason—for example, to diagnose a developmental disorder or guide cancer therapeutics—without understanding that information about other health risks might be uncovered. The converse case of a cancer-disposing gene found in a person undergoing testing for AD could also present challenges. Notably, whole-exome sequencing is already being offered clinically as a way of saving time and money when several individual genetic tests may otherwise be required (Yang et al, 2013); the most accurate interpretation of the results also requires the patient's parents to submit samples for exome sequencing, and therefore incidental findings may be uncovered for both patient and parents. Given the ageing population and increasing use of these technologies, incidental findings related specifically to dementia seem likely to become increasingly relevant.

CASES WHERE TESTING A PATIENT WITH DEMENTIA MAY BENEFIT OTHERS

There is evidence that many people who undertake genetic tests do so to benefit others (Hallowell, 1999). In the context of dementia, the question of whether it is legitimate to test one person for the benefit of others is especially salient when that person does not have the capacity to give consent.

The Mental Capacity Act 2005 (MCA) states that genetic testing may be carried out on adults without capacity if it is in their best interests. The Joint Committee on Medical Genetics (JCMG) report on *Consent and confidentiality in clinical genetic practice* suggests that 'broad welfare considerations' should be taken into account in determining best interests. Furthermore, benefiting relatives might qualify as a good reason to test 'if this had a positive effect on the care of the adult' (JCMG, 2011). These issues surface in the following example of a patient whose dementia precluded her capacity to consent:

> A 45-year-old woman was referred to us because her younger sister wanted testing for breast cancer. She was referred because she had been treated for breast cancer in her late 30s. It was requested that a blood sample be taken from the woman to test for a breast cancer mutation. When the referral letter came to us in clinical genetics the consent on it was signed by the woman's father who said he was the woman's guardian and was happy for the blood test to be carried out. A telephone call revealed that the woman's father was not in fact her guardian and that the woman was living in a residential care home, had had only one visit in three years and had been raised by her maternal grandparents who had subsequently died. She had had no contact with father. The woman had severe fronto-temporal dementia that began several years prior. It was felt by the carers and staff at the home that a blood test would distress her and was not appropriate. The proposed test was not going to be carried out in the patient's own best interest but for the interests of other members of her family—without the information from the test on her a test on the other family members would be less accurate (Parker, 2012: 52).

If the fronto-temporal dementia is severe enough to prevent any periods of lucidity, then legally the MCA guidelines discussed above require a best interests assessment. Given the relationships between the woman, the father and the sister, it does not seem immediately clear that testing the woman would lead to better care for her. However, testing might motivate the sister and father to visit the residential care home more frequently, which could lead to her having an enhanced familial support network. If the father and sister were to state explicitly their desire to reconnect with the woman, her carers might have the challenging task of assessing the genuineness of that desire. The woman also might be a deeply altruistic person who would have agreed to be tested prior to developing dementia, and so carrying out the test now would be in line with her previous beliefs. The JCMG report stresses the importance of not immediately assuming that a patient with dementia should not be tested to benefit others, but the evaluation of these cases is likely to remain difficult.

CASES INVOLVING THE TESTING OF CHILDREN

Young children, too, cannot give valid consent. The same JCMG report recommends that genetic testing be pursued only when in the child's best interests. Typically, this means that genetic testing would be considered appropriate if test results could lead to different clinical management *in childhood*. When testing concerns an adult-onset disease or future reproductive risks, genetics professionals usually seek to delay testing until the child can consent on her own behalf—unless there are compelling reasons to do otherwise (JCMG, 2011). In the context of adult-onset conditions with no interventions, this suggests a strong case for delaying testing. However, situations do arise in which this approach may be detrimental to the child's well-being:

> A sample from a nine-year-old boy in a residential care home was recently sent to our genetics lab by a general practitioner. The boy's mother has a neurological autosomal dominant condition and his father is schizophrenic. Several attempts have been made to adopt the boy out but all potential families have been deterred by the family history. Social workers want the boy tested because if the test results are negative he will be more easily adopted into a new family (Parker, 2012: 47).

Imagine that the 'neurological autosomal dominant condition' in question is HD. The adults involved in the child's care might be conflicted in balancing the child's right not to know and inability to consent against the possibility that testing could lead to the child having a better childhood. To the social worker, the child would be either benefited or not seriously affected by a test. If the test is negative, he will have a much better chance of being adopted. If the test is positive, he will likely remain in residential care, which he will also do if the test is not carried out. But the genetics professional, attuned to the broader implications of a positive HD test, may consider a more complicated set of tensions: the harms of living in residential care until mature enough to make his own decision about HD testing, versus the harms associated with either (a) a 50% chance of a potentially unwanted positive test and a life in care or (b) a negative test result and *possible* adoption.

If the boy's mother had a neurological condition that was not autosomal dominant, such as most forms of vascular dementia, then testing might be even more controversial. As chapter three explained, the non-autosomal dominant forms of vascular dementia are part of cardiovascular disease, so genes associated with cardiovascular disease might be relevant. Because predispositional testing does not provide a definitive answer as to the development of a disease, testing may not assuage risk-averse prospective adoptive parents, and thus improved adoption prospects would be unlikely to form a compelling reason to test.

CASES INVOLVING THE MORAL IMPLICATIONS OF PREDICTION

As the previous examples illustrated, predictive testing can be controversial when there are no effective clinical interventions. Nonetheless, testing may still be considered valuable for patients if it informs important lifestyle or reproductive decisions, improves the care of other family members or simply satisfies their preference to know. In some cases, however, testing might be sought specifically because a patient views the information as *morally useful*. Consider the following hypothetical:

> Barbara, a 60-year-old female, presented to her general practitioner with memory-related complaints and requested genetic testing for AD. Upon discussion with her clinician, Barbara explained that her mother had some kind of dementia around the same age, and now Barbara thought she might have early signs of AD too. When asked why she wanted a test, Barbara replied that she was the driver of the van for her grandchildren's playgroup and that she would stop driving the van if she knew she was at high risk of developing dementia. Years ago, Barbara's mother's profound cognitive impairment caused her to get lost when taking Barbara's toddler son to the corner store, and Barbara's family panicked for several hours until her mother and son returned. Thus, if Barbara were at high risk of developing AD, she felt it would be irresponsible of her to continue driving the playgroup van—she simply would not risk putting her family in the same situation.

For Barbara, the information from genetic testing was desired not for medical benefit, but because she viewed it as integral to her moral agency. Barbara felt an acute obligation not to risk involuntarily harming her loved ones and thus wanted to know if she had reason to take steps (for example, to stop driving) to limit the potential harmful consequences of dementia to her family. Results from the REVEAL study, which examined the communication of risk of AD based on APOE4 status, further support the perceived value of risk information to individuals whose goal is to minimise impact on others; one reason subjects wished to know their risk status surrounding the APOE4 genotype, even if it would make no clinical difference, was to help prepare family (Roberts and Tersegno, 2010).

Similarly, health professionals might consider predictive testing morally useful in certain situations. For example, a clinician might know that an airline pilot patient has a strong family history of early-onset AD. Because the patient's profession entails risk to his passengers and other aircraft if the patient develops dementia, the clinician might feel an obligation to be more vocal about suggesting genetic testing than he would be if the patient were a chef or a writer. This is not to say that the pilot should be required to have genetic testing if he were asymptomatic, or that the results of predictive genetic testing would force him to change jobs immediately if he did end up with a positive test. But it might motivate the clinician to suggest that the pilot should have frequent follow-up visits to monitor for possible signs of dementia, and to encourage the pilot to think about contingency plans should the dementia develop. If the pilot were to become symptomatic and refuse to tell his company, however, his clinical team would be in the difficult position of deciding whether to breach confidentiality to prevent serious risk of harm to the pilot and others (General Medical Council, 2009).

CONCLUSION

In this chapter, we have sought to illustrate some of the most important ways in which ethical issues can arise for health professionals, patients and families in relation to genetics and dementia. We have done so by drawing on the experience of the Genethics Club—a national ethics forum for genetics professionals in the United Kingdom—and the evidence that practical ethical issues most commonly emerge in cases involving sharing information in families, testing children and reproductive decision-making (Parker, 2012). Additionally, we have explored three other kinds of cases that seem particularly relevant to genetics and dementia: situations involving 'incidental findings', situations where patients with dementia might be tested to benefit other family members, and situations where patients feel they should undergo testing for moral reasons. Table 1 below summarises reasons why testing may or may not be appropriate in these cases.

Table 1: Summary of cases where ethical issues may arise in relation to genetics and dementia

Type of case	Reasons testing may be appropriate	Reasons testing may be inappropriate
Sharing familial information	'Joint account' model—family members all should have access to shared information	'Personal account' model—individual decides whether to share information
	Family members have discussed genetic condition and agreed to have information shared	Family members have explicitly said they do not want their information to be shared
	Patient could suffer serious emotional consequences if testing denied ('right to know' not respected)	Testing patient would directly test other family members who have not been consulted ('right not to know' not respected)
	Family members are unreasonably difficult to contact (eg, due to estrangement or location) or do not care to be involved	Clinician thinks patient may notify family members of their statuses without their consent or proper counselling
Reproductive decisions	Family wishes to use genetic status to inform reproductive decision/preparations for child	Family does not think genetic status would alter reproductive decision/ preparations for child
	(Type of testing determined by knowledge of/desire to know familial genetic status)	
Incidental findings	Patient knows of family history of condition	Patient does not know of family history of condition
	(In general: if medical management could address condition)	(In general: if medical management could not address condition)
Testing a patient with dementia to benefit others	Testing could have a positive effect on patient's care	Testing only done to benefit others
	Altruism consistent with patient's personality/previous wishes	Altruism inconsistent with patient's personality/previous wishes

(*Continued*)

Table 1: (*Continued*)

Type of case	Reasons testing may be appropriate	Reasons testing may be inappropriate
Testing of children	In the child's best interests (In general: when medical management could be changed in childhood)	For carers' benefit only (In general: when medical management could not be changed in childhood)
Moral implications of prediction	Asymptomatic patient freely pursues testing in order to modify lifestyle to protect others	Asymptomatic patient feels coerced into being tested in order to modify lifestyle to protect others

REFERENCES

de Die-Smulders, CE et al (2013) 'Reproductive options for prospective parents in families with Huntington's disease: clinical, psychological and ethical reflections' 19(3) *Human Reproduction Update* 304–15: dx.doi.org/10.1093/humupd/dms058.

General Medical Council (GMC) (2009) *Confidentiality.* Available at: www.gmc-uk.org/static/documents/content/Confidentiality_0910.pdf.

Green, RC et al (2013) 'ACMG recommendations for reporting of incidental findings in clinical exome and genome sequencing' 15(7) *Genetic Medicine* 565–74: dx.doi.org/10.1038/gim.2013.73.

Hallowell, N (1999) 'Doing the right thing: genetic risk and responsibility' 21(5) *Sociology of Health & Illness* 597–621: dx.doi.org/10.1111/1467-9566.00175.

Harper, P (2010) *Practical Genetic Counselling*, 7th edn (London, Edward Arnold).

Joint Committee on Medical Genetics (JCMG) (2011) *Consent and confidentiality in genetic practice: guidance on genetic testing and sharing genetic information.* Available at: www.bsgm.org.uk/media/678746/consent_and_confidentiality_2011.pdf.

Lucassen, A and Parker, M (2004) 'Confidentiality and "serious harm" in genetics – preserving the confidentiality of one patient and preventing harms to relatives' 12(2) *European Journal of Human Genetics* 93–97.

McPherson, E (2006) 'Genetic diagnosis and testing in clinical practice' 4(2) *Clinical Medicine and Research* 123–29.

Parker, M (2012) *Ethical Problems and Genetics Practice* (Cambridge, Cambridge University Press).

Parker, M and Lucassen, AM (2004) 'Genetic information: a joint account?' 329(7458) *British Medical Journal* 165–67: dx.doi.org/10.1136/bmj.329.7458.165.

Roberts, JS and Tersegno, SM (2010) 'Estimating and disclosing the risk of developing Alzheimer's disease: challenges, controversies and future directions' 5(4) *Future Neurology* 501–17.

van El, CG et al (2013) 'Whole-genome sequencing in health care: recommendations of the European Society of Human Genetics' 21(6) *European Journal of Human Genetics* 580–84: dx.doi.org/10.1038/ejhg.2013.46.

Yang, Y et al (2013) 'Clinical whole-exome sequencing for the diagnosis of Mendelian disorders' 369(16) *New England Journal of Medicine* 1502–11: dx.dox.org/10.1056/NEJMoa1306555.

17

Common Perceptions of Dementia

PERLA WERNER

INTRODUCTION

'IN SOME WAYS disease does not exist until we agree it does—by perceiving, naming, and responding to it'. This sentence, taken from *The Emperor of all Maladies: A Biography of Cancer* by Dr Siddhartha Mukherjee—an Indian-born American physician—reflects the importance of perceptions in the understanding and experience of disease (Mukherjee, 2010).

The perception of disease, both by patients and others, has been discussed in the psychological and socio-medical literature for many decades (Conrad and Barker, 2010; Downey and Chang, 2013). In the context of mental disorders, the concept of 'mental health literacy' has been introduced and extensively studied. Defined as 'knowledge and beliefs about mental disorders which aid their recognition, management or prevention' (Jorm et al, 1997: 182), this concept stresses the importance of the individual affected by the disorder and of those in contact with the individual (ie, the lay public) in managing the disorder's symptoms (Jorm et al, 2000). Studies assessing mental health literacy have shown that the lay public's beliefs can have important consequences for help-seeking patterns, the kind of treatments used for the specific disorder and the stereotyping of people with mental disorders. Despite their importance, for many years these studies have focused almost exclusively on assessing lay beliefs regarding depression and schizophrenia, ignoring one of the main mental disorders of old age—Alzheimer's disease (AD) (Werner, 2005). This situation has changed over the last 15 years, and we are currently witnessing an increasing body of research assessing lay persons' beliefs and knowledge regarding AD.

Most of this research has been conceptualized in three ways. First, in accordance with the assumptions of several cognitive models, such as the 'Common Sense Model' (CSM) (Leventhal et al, 1980) and the 'Health Belief Model' (HBM) (Janz et al, 2002), several of the studies stress the importance of examining lay beliefs and knowledge of AD and its effects on help-seeking behaviour and prevention. Second, a more culturally-oriented line of research, examining lay perceptions regarding AD, has evolved over the last years. Studies in this body of knowledge are based on the assumption that cultural differences in ageing perceptions exist across different cultures, as well as among members of different subcultures (Cavallini et al, 2013; Sayegh and Knight, 2013). And third, another line of research in the area of perceptions about AD has examined the consequences of knowledge and perceptions regarding AD, concentrating mainly on stigmatic beliefs (for a review, see Werner, 2014).

Thus the burgeoning literature assessing lay perceptions of AD shows that the studies are based on cognitive, social and cultural frameworks. However, to the best of our knowledge, this body of research has not been examined using an ethical framework, and its ethical corollaries have not been discussed. This is the aim of the present chapter. It is not intended to present here the many ethical questions affecting individuals with dementia, their caregivers and society, but rather to discuss how lay perceptions of the disease affect these questions. I will first present a short description of the ethical framework constituting the basis for this chapter, followed by a presentation about how research on lay perceptions in the area of AD affects these principles. The chapter will conclude with theoretical and practical implications and suggestions for future research.

AN ETHICAL FRAMEWORK FOR ASSESSING THE IMPACT OF COMMON PERCEPTIONS OF ALZHEIMER'S DISEASE

The ethical framework suggested in this chapter adopts three of the six components comprising the dementia ethical framework proposed by the Nuffield Council on Bioethics (2009):

1. *A belief about the nature of dementia*: This component states that dementia arises as a result of a brain disorder, and is harmful to the individual.
2. *The importance of promoting the interests of the person with dementia*: People with dementia have interests, both in their autonomy and their well-being. Promoting autonomy involves enabling and fostering relationships that are important to the person, and supporting them in maintaining their sense of self and expressing their values. Autonomy is not simply to be equated with the ability to make rational decisions. A person's well-being includes both their moment-to-moment experiences of contentment or pleasure.
3. *Recognizing personhood, identity and value*: The person with dementia remains the same, equally valued, person throughout the course of their illness, regardless of the extent of the changes in their cognitive and other functions (Nuffield Council on Bioethics, 2009: XVIII).

In the next section, I will elaborate on how studies in the area of lay perceptions about AD support these ethical components.

Component 1: A Belief about the Nature of Dementia

Most studies adhering to the first line of research described above—ie, based on the assumptions of cognitive models—provide information for supporting this component. Indeed, research reveals that despite high levels of awareness about the disease (most participants in all the reviewed studies reported hearing about AD), the public has poor-to-moderate objective knowledge about the disease and its causes and treatments (Anderson et al, 2009; Arai et al, 2008; Ayalon and Arean, 2004; Sahin et al, 2006; Blay et al, 2008; Hudson et al, 2012; Tan et al, 2012; Werner, 2004; Wortmann et al, 2010).

Studies adhering to the second line of research described above (ie, those based on cultural assumptions) corroborated these findings in cross-national studies (Bond et al, 2005; Rimer et al, 2005; Wortmann et al, 2010). However, studies assessing knowledge and perceptions in ethnically, racially and culturally-diverse populations showed a more complex picture. On the one hand, several studies, mainly based on structured quantitative surveys, demonstrated lower levels of adequate knowledge and beliefs in minority groups (Low et al, 2010; Ayalon and Arean, 2004; Purandare et al, 2007; Roberts et al, 2003). On the other hand, studies based on qualitative methods stressed the similarities, rather than the differences, between culturally-diverse groups (Mahoney et al, 2005), as well as the unique beliefs guiding minorities' awareness and understanding of dementia (La Fontaine et al, 2007; Lanting et al, 2012; Lee, Lee and Diwan, 2010; Schelp et al, 2008; Siddiqui et al, 2011).

Furthermore, in providing empirical data for the first ethical component, studies showed that increased knowledge and appropriate beliefs were associated with a more adequate intention of seeking help and treating the disease (Anderson, McCaul and Langley, 2011; Blay et al, 2008; Hamilton-West et al, 2010; Werner, 2002; Werner, 2003a; Werner, 2003b; Werner, 2004).

Finally, regarding the factors associated with knowledge about AD, studies showed that female gender and exposure to the disease are associated with increased knowledge (Arai et al, 2008, Lee, Lee and Diwan, 2010; Cheng et al, 2011).

Based on these empirical findings, several ethical corollaries can be derived from the first component of our ethical framework.

Corollary 1: Dealing with and providing support in regard to the ethical issues arising within the AD framework require knowledge and appropriate beliefs about the disease. Thus, increasing appropriate knowledge and beliefs about the causes, symptoms and treatments of AD is required to deal with the complex and difficult circumstances related to the prevention, diagnosis and treatment of the disease.

Corollary 2: Efforts to increase knowledge and appropriate beliefs about AD should be attuned to the needs of specific groups, such as ethnically and culturally-diverse populations.

Corollary 3: Efforts should be made to increase the exposure and familiarity of lay persons with individuals suffering from AD.

Component 2: The Importance of Promoting the Interests of the Person with Dementia

This component deals with the reinforcement and promotion of autonomy and well-being in persons with AD. Although these ethical issues have been, and continue to be, at the forefront of the discourse in the area of cognitive deterioration, in general, and AD in particular (Gauthier et al, 2013), empirical studies assessing lay perceptions about these issues is unexpectedly scant. This is surprising, especially since there are many autonomy and capacity issues associated with cognitive deterioration and encompass a wide range of areas such as managing financial affairs, driving, making health-related decisions, participating in research and more. Moreover, as the number of individuals with AD increases worldwide (Alzheimer's Association Report, 2013), an increasing number of lay persons will come into contact with individuals who have the disease; their behaviour towards these people might be affected by their perceptions about their decision-making capacity.

Indeed, we are aware of only one study assessing lay perceptions about the competence of a person with AD in a variety of areas—driving, health-related decision-making, financial decisions and the performance of daily activities. In a survey of 206 adults aged 49 and over, Werner (2006) showed that lay persons are able to differentiate between different types of competence. More study participants thought that patients with AD would be unable to drive and to make financial decisions than thought that AD patients would be unable to ride on a bus or make a cup of tea. Interestingly, only two-fifths of the participants considered a person with AD as being incapable of making health care decisions. More interestingly, this survey's findings showed that lay persons' perceptions about competence affected their discriminatory behaviour towards a person with AD.

Based on these empirical findings (or lack thereof), a main ethical corollary can be derived from the second component of our ethical framework.

Corollary 4: The autonomy and independent decision-making ability of persons with AD should be kept and respected. Thus, research assessing lay perceptions regarding autonomy and decision-making capacities of individuals with AD should be increased and expanded.

Component 3: Recognizing Personhood, Identity and Value

This component is empirically based in particular on the studies adhering to the third line of research described above—ie, research assessing the consequences of lay knowledge and perceptions regarding AD, concentrating mainly on stigmatic beliefs.

Stigma has been defined as some form of mark or sign that denotes disgrace or discredit (Goffman, 1963), and has recently been conceptualized as including three aspects, namely: stereotypes, prejudice and discrimination (Werner, 2014). *Stereotypes* describe collective judgements about groups of people—for example, people with dementia; *prejudice* refers to emotional reactions to a stereotyped person; and *discrimination* refers to behavioural reactions associated with prejudice, including avoidance, coercion and segregation (Werner, 2014).

Although an examination of the published literature on the topic of stigma and AD presents us with a picture in which stigma is perceived as pervasive and associated with negative consequences at the individual level (low self-esteem, feelings of shame and humiliation and social isolation); the family level (feelings of shame, social isolation, moral failure as a family, increased burden and depression, as well as concealment and decreased use of services); the professional level (differential and/or delayed diagnosis and treatment); and the societal level (differential access and use of services, increased institutionalization), only a few of the studies are based on an empirical examination of the concept of lay persons' stigmatic beliefs within the framework of AD (Werner, 2014). This is surprising, especially since over the last years reducing stigma associated with AD has been one of the main initiatives promoted by Alzheimer's associations around the world (Alzheimer's Association Report, 2013; Alzheimer's Disease International, 2012; Department of Health, 2009; Hughes, 2010).

In this area, studies based on labelling theory (Link et al, 1989) deal with the impact of labelling on the loss of personhood and on the dehumanization of persons with AD (Behuniak, 2011; Miyamoto et al, 2011). Two additional studies, assessing lay persons' perceptions and using experimental designs, showed that being exposed to a label of dementia increases stigma (Cheng et al, 2011; Wadley and Haley, 2001).

Another group of studies, based on assumptions of 'Attribution Theory' (Corrigan, 2000), showed that although lay persons' stigmatic beliefs towards a person with AD (expressed particularly as stereotypes, prejudice and social distance) are moderate, they increase if levels of familiarity with the disease are low, and if the person with AD is perceived as being dangerous or in the advanced stages of the disease (Blay and Peluso, 2010; Bourkel et al, 2012; Crisp et al, 2000; Devlin et al, 2007; Werner, 2005; Werner, 2008). Emotional reactions to persons with AD are reported to be higher than behavioural reactions (Cartz Piver et al, 2013; Werner and Davidson, 2004).

Based on these empirical findings, a main ethical corollary can be derived for the third component of our ethical framework.

Corollary 5: The understanding of stigma associated with AD should be improved and addressed.

THEORETICAL AND PRACTICAL IMPLICATIONS

The literature reviewed in this chapter shows that although the number of studies assessing common beliefs about AD is increasing (Cahill, 2012), their meaning and significance for the development of an ethical framework from which ethical corollaries may be derived is still lacking. This is surprising, especially since the importance of public opinion to informed policy-making has been long and continuously recognized (Gutmann and Thompson, 1997; Kim et al, 2011; Smith Iltis, 2004). In order to advance this body of research, several theoretical and practical developments are needed.

Theoretically, if, as stated in the introduction to this chapter, we intend to expand the area of mental health literacy and to include AD in this area of study, we will benefit if the studies aimed at understanding lay perceptions and beliefs about AD are built on an understanding of the mores and social and moral values guiding the public's understanding of the disease.

Such a framework will also allow us to more structurally develop and evaluate interventions aimed at increasing the knowledge and motivating beliefs that more adequately fit the ethical principles and values of the society. Integrating a theoretically-based ethical framework into the study of common perceptions about AD might facilitate professionals interested in developing intervention programmes to make ethically sound choices regarding target groups, determinants, techniques for an increase in knowledge and changes in beliefs and the choice of design and evaluation of the intervention.

FUTURE RESEARCH

As we are currently seeing an increasing number of studies assessing common perceptions of dementia, this warrants an examination of the associations between these perceptions and the public's moral and ethical values related to dementia, such as decision-making and autonomy.

REFERENCES

Alzheimer's Disease International (2012) *World Alzheimer Report: Overcoming the stigma of dementia* (London, Alzheimer's Disease International).

Alzheimer's Association (2013) 'Alzheimer's Association report 2013: Alzheimer's disease facts and figures' 9(2) *Alzheimer's and Dementia* 1–68.

Anderson, LA et al (2009) 'The public's perceptions about cognitive health and Alzheimer's disease among the US population: A national review' 49 *The Gerontologist* S3–S11.

Anderson, LN, McCaul, K and Langley, LK (2011) 'Common-sense beliefs about the prevention of Alzheimer's disease' 17(7) *Aging & Mental Health* 922–31.

Arai, Y et al (2008) 'What do we know about dementia?: A survey on knowledge about dementia in the general public of Japan' 23(4) *International Journal of Geriatric Psychiatry* 433–38.

Ayalon, L and Arean, AP (2004) 'Knowledge of Alzheimer's disease in four ethnic groups of older adults' 19 *International Journal of Geriatric Psychiatry* 51–57.

Behuniak, SM (2011) 'Death with "dignity": The wedge that divides the disability rights movement from the right to die movement' 30(1) *Politics and the Life Sciences* 17–32.

Blay, SL, Furtado, A and Peluso, ET (2008) 'Knowledge and beliefs about help-seeking behavior and helpfulness of interventions for Alzheimer's disease' 12(5) *Aging and Mental Health* 577–86.

Blay, SL, and Toledo Pisa Peluso, E (2011) 'Public stigma: the community's tolerance of Alzheimer disease' 18(2) *American Journal of Geriatric Psychiatry* 163–71.

Bond, J, et al (2005) 'Inequalities in dementia care across Europe: Key findings of the Facing Dementia Survey' 146 *International Journal of Clinical Practice* 8–14.

Bourkel, E, Ferring, D and Weber, G (2012) 'Perceived rights of and social distance to people with Alzheimer's disease' 25(1) *The Journal of Gerontopschology and Geriatric Psychiatry* 25–32.

Cahill, S (2012) 'What do we know about understandings and attitudes to dementia?' paper presented at the Alzheimer's Disease international conference, Vienna. Available at: www.alzheimer-europe.org/Conferences/Previous-conferences/2012-Vienna/Detailed-Programme-abstracts-and-presentations.

Cartz Piver, L et al (2013) 'Describing perceived stigma against Alzheimer's disease in a general population in France: The STIG-MA survey' 28(9) *International Journal of Geriatric Psychiatry* 933–38. doi: 10.1002/gps.3903.

Cavallini, E et al (2013) 'Age and subcultural differences on personal and general beliefs about memory' 27(1) *Journal of Aging Studies* 71–81.

Cheng, ST et al (2011) 'The effects of exposure to scenarios about dementia on stigma and attitudes toward dementia care in a Chinese community' 23(9) *International Psychogeriatrics* 1433–41.

Conrad, P and Barker, KK (2010) 'The social construction of illness: Key insights and policy implications' 51 *Journal of Health and Social Behavior* S67–S79.

Corrigan, PW (2000) 'Mental health stigma as social attribution: Implications for research methods and attitude change' 7(1) *Clinical Psychology: Science and Practice* 48–67.

Crisp, A et al (2000) 'Stigmatisation of people with mental illnesses' 177 *British Journal of Psychiatry* 4–7.

Department of Health (2009) *Living well with dementia: A National Dementia Strategy* (London, COI and the Department of Health).

Devlin, E, MacAskill, S and Stead, M (2007) '"We're still the same people": Developing a mass media campaign to raise awareness and challenge the stigma of dementia' 12 *International Journal of Nonprofit and Voluntary Sector Marketing* 47–58.

Downey, CA and Chang, EC (2013) 'Assessment of everyday beliefs about health: The Lay Concepts of Health Inventory, college student version' 28(7) *Psychology & Health* 818–32. doi: 10.1080/08870446.2012.762099.

Gauthier, S et al (2013) 'Diagnosis and management of Alzheimer's disease: Past, present and future ethical issues' 110 *Progress in Neurobiology* 102–13.

Goffman, E (1963) *Stigma: Notes on the Management of Spoiled Identity* (New York, Simon & Schuster).

Gutmann, A and Thompson, D (1997) 'Deliberating about bioethics' 27 *Hastings Center Report* 38–41.

Hamilton-West, KE et al (2010) 'Help-seeking in relation to signs of dementia: A pilot study to evaluate the utility of the common-sense model of illness representations' 15(5) *Psychology and Health Medicine* 540–49.

Hudson, et al (2012) 'Beliefs about Alzheimer's disease in Britain' 16(7) *Aging and Mental Health* 828–35.

Hughes, J (2010) *Ethical Issues and Decision-Making in Dementia Care* (Canberra, Alzheimer's Australia).

Janz, NK, Champion, VL and Strecher, VJ (2002) 'The Health Belief Model' in K Glanz, BK Rimer and FM Lewis (eds), *Health Behaviour and Health Education: Theory, Research and Practice* (San Francisco, Jossey-Bass).

Jorm, AF et al (1997) '"Mental health literacy": A survey of the public's ability to recognise mental disorders and their beliefs about the effectiveness of treatment' 166 *Medical Journal of Australia* 182–86.

—— (2000) 'Public belief systems about the helpfulness of interventions for depression: associations with history of depression and professional helpseeking' 35 *Social Psychiatry and Psychiatric Epidemiology* 211–19.

Kim, SY et al (2011) 'Effect of public deliberation on attitudes toward surrogate consent for dementia research' 77(24) *Neurology* 2097–104.

La Fontaine, J et al (2007) 'Understanding dementia amongst people in minority ethnic and cultural groups' 60(6) *Journal of Advanced Nursing* 605–14.

Lanting, S et al (2012) 'Aboriginal experiences of aging and dementia in a context of sociocultural change: Qualitative analysis of key informant group interviews with aboriginal seniors' 26 *Journal of Cross Cultural Gerontology* 103–17.

Lee, SE, Lee, HY and Diwan, S (2010) 'What do Korean American immigrants know about Alzheimer's disease (AD)? The impact of acculturation and exposure to the disease on AD knowledge' 25(1) *International Journal of Geriatric Psychiatry* 66–73.

Leventhal, H, Meyer, D and Nerenz, D (1980) 'The common sense representation of illness danger' in S Rachman (ed), *Contributions to Medical Psychology* (New York, Pergamon Press).

Link, BG et al (1989) 'A modified labelling theory approach to mental disorders: An empirical assessment' 89(54) *American Sociological Review* 400–23.

Low, LF et al (2010) 'Recognition, attitudes and causal beliefs regarding dementia in Italian, Greek and Chinese Australians' 30(6) *Dementia and Geriatric Cognitive Disorders* 499–508.

Mahoney, DF et al (2005) 'African American, Chinese, and Latino family caregivers' impressions of the onset and diagnosis of dementia: Cross-cultural similarities and differences' 45(6) *The Gerontologist* 783–92.

Miyamoto, M, George, DR and Whitehouse, PJ (2011) 'Government, professional and public efforts in Japan to change the designation of dementia (chiho)' 10(4) *Dementia* 475–86.
Mukherjee, S (2010) *The Emperor of all Maladies: A Biography of Cancer* (New York, Scribner).
Nuffield Council on Bioethics (2009) *Dementia: Ethical issues* (London, Cambridge Publishers).
Purandare, N et al (2007) 'Knowledge of dementia among South Asian (Indian) older people in Manchester, UK' 22(8) *International Journal of Geriatric Psychiatry* 777–81.
Rimmer, E et al (2005) 'Implications of the Facing Dementia Survey for the general population, patients and caregivers across Europe' 146 *International Journal of Clinical Practice* 17–24.
Roberts, JS et al (2003) 'Differences between African Americans and whites in their perceptions of Alzheimer disease' 17(1) *Alzheimer Disease and Associated Disorders* 19–26.
Rovner, BW et al (2013) 'Cultural diversity and views on Alzheimer disease in older African Americans' 27 *Alzheimer's Disease & Related Disorders* 133–37.
Sahin, HA et al (2006) 'The attitude of elderly lay people towards the symptoms of dementia' 18(2) *International Psychogeriatrics* 251–58.
Sayegh, P and Knight, BG (2013) 'Cross-cultural differences in dementia: The Sociocultural Health Belief Model' 25(4) *International Psychogeriatrics* 517–30.
Schelp, AO et al (2008) 'Public awareness of dementia: A study in Botucatu a medium-sized city in the state of Sao Paulo, Brazil' 2(3) *Dementia and Neuropsychologia* 192–96.
Siddiqui, M et al (2011) 'Awareness of dementia among general population of Islamabad/Rawalpindi' 6(3) *Pakistan Journal of Nerologycal Sciences* 1–4.
Smith Iltis, A (2004) 'Bioethics: The intersection of private and public decisions' 29(4) *Journal of Medicine and Philosophy* 381–88.
Tan, WJ et al (2012) 'The lay public's understanding and perception of dementia in a developed Asian nation' 2 *Dementia and other Geriatric Cognitive Disorders* 433–44.
Wadley, VG and Haley, WE (2001) 'Diagnostic attributions versus labeling: Impact of Alzheimer's disease and major depression diagnoses on emotions, beliefs, and helping intentions of family members' 56(4) *Journals of Gerontology* 244–52.
Werner, P (2002) 'Assessing correlates of concern about developing Alzheimer's disease among adults with no family history of the disease' 17(6) *American Journal of Alzheimer's Disease & Other Dementias* 331–337.
—— (2003a) 'Knowledge about symptoms of Alzheimer's disease: Correlates and relationship to help-seeking behavior' 18 *International Journal of Geriatric Psychiatry* 1029–36.
—— (2003b) 'Factors influencing intentions to perform a cognitive examination: A study based on the Health Belief Model' 18(9) *International Journal of Geriatric Psychiatry* 787–94.
—— (2004) 'Perceptions about memory problems and help seeking in elderly persons: A qualitative analysis' 27(4) *Clinical Gerontologist* 19–30.
—— (2005) 'Social distance towards a person with Alzheimer's disease' 20(2) *International Journal of Geriatric Psychiatry* 182–88.
—— (2006) 'Lay perceptions regarding the competence of persons with Alzheimer's disease' 21 *International Journal of Geriatric Psychiatry* 674–80.
—— (2008) 'Discrimination towards a person with Alzheimer's disease: Examining the effects of being in a nursing home' 12(6) *Aging and Mental Health* 786–94.
—— (2014) 'Stigma and Alzheimer's disease: A systematic review of evidence, theory and methods' in PW Corrigan (ed), *The Stigma of Disease and Disability: Empirical Models and Implications for Change* (Washington DC, American Psychological Association).
—— and Davidson, M (2004) 'Emotional reactions to individuals suffering from Alzheimer's disease: Examining their patterns and correlates' 19(4) *International Journal of Geriatric Psychiatry* 391–97.
Wortmann, M et al (2010) 'Evolving attitudes to Alzheimer's disease among the general public and caregivers in Europe: Findings for the IMPACT survey' 14(7) *Journal of Nutrition, Health and Aging* 531–36.

18

Ethical Perspectives on End-of-Life Care: Euthanasia, Assisted Suicide and the Refusal of or Withdrawal of Life-Sustaining Treatments in those Living with Dementia

MICHAEL GORDON

INTRODUCTION

EVEN IN A context of marvellous advances in medical science there are a number of challenges that have yet to be met. Among these challenges is the medical condition usually called dementia, which of course includes many sub-categories. Alzheimer's disease is the most common cause of dementia, according to our current medical knowledge, and with the efforts of the Alzheimer's Societies worldwide, most people recognize the condition and its major clinical and psychosocial manifestations (Alzheimer's Society, 2011; World Health Organization, 2012). In Western societies, many efforts have gone into the development of clinical programmes to detect and medically treat this condition and all the other causes of dementia. Social programmes have also been devised to assist individuals and their families living with dementia to cope with the years of progressive decline that usually occurs with this condition.

It is inadequately understood that, like many other chronic diseases, many dementias have a terminal phase. End of life care in dementias is correspondingly under-discussed and implemented. This means that, for many living with this condition and the families that have devoted much life and energy to support them during the final period of their disease with its associated decline, the necessary supports for the end-of-life and terminal phase of the disease are not addressed to the psychological and humanistic satisfaction of all concerned, including families and health care professionals.

THE CONCEPT OF THE TERMINAL PHASE OF DISEASE, EUTHANASIA AND PHYSICIAN ASSISTED SUICIDE (PAS): A FOCUS ON DEMENTIA

Inadequate discussion of the terminal nature of some dementias, and the palliative care available, have led to the belief by some that euthanasia or Physician Assisted

Suicide (PAS) might be necessary to avoid the sufferings and indignities of late stage dementia.

The historical progress of the legalization of PAS and euthanasia in some Western jurisdictions stems from a number of evolutionary legal achievements, the most significant of which was the removal of suicide as a criminal act which occurred in a parallel manner in many Western countries. One of the first milestones in this journey was the Suicide Act 1961 in the United Kingdom. It decriminalized the act of suicide so that those who failed in the attempt would no longer be prosecuted. This was followed in short course by a similar law in Northern Ireland and some years later in Canada. The various States in the United States followed suit in a gradual process so that by the early 1990s two States still listed suicide as a crime but these subsequently removed that classification (*Wackwitz v Roy* 1992). However, even though in Canada and most of the US the act itself was decriminalized, assisting suicide was often criminalized. Thus, for instance, in Canada:

> [S]omeone who now attempts suicide is not liable to sanction under the Criminal Code, anyone found guilty of counselling another to take his or her own life or of aiding a suicide is liable to imprisonment of up to 14 years, whether or not the suicide attempt is successful. A peace officer or a physician may order involuntary detention of any person judged to be a danger to him or herself (Litman, 1966–67; Simon et al, 2005).

THE ETHICS OF EUTHANASIA: PHYSICIAN ASSISTED SUICIDE IN CASES OF THOSE LIVING WITH DEMENTIA

Once suicide itself was decriminalized, the next logical step was to explore—and in some situations lobby for—legalization of assisted suicide, with some advocates promoting the legalization of euthanasia as well. One can postulate that it was the introduction of the foundational ethical concept of *personal autonomy* in medical decision-making as espoused by Beauchamp and Childress (Beauchamp and Childress, 2012) and discussed at length by Pellegrino (1993) that promoted the discussion of this conceptual framework within reputable medical ethics, legal and health care policy forums (Dryden, 2010). Beauchamp and Childress, in their classic book *Principles of Biomedical Ethics*, as they defend four principles for ethical decision-making (of which 'respect for autonomy' is the first, even though it is not intended to override other moral considerations) 'The negative obligation for health care professionals is that patients' autonomous decisions should not be constrained by others. The positive obligation calls for "respectful treatment in disclosing information and fostering autonomous decision-making"' (Beauchamp and Childress, 2012: 64).

This concept had a profound impact on all the deliberations that occur in those in the process of considering or needing end-of-life care. For centuries there had been a long medical tradition of focusing on the principles of beneficence and non-maleficence. Now a new ethical principle, autonomy, became paramount as health care related decisions were being made and laws and policies were being developed. According to Jane Dryden of Mount Allison University,

> Beauchamp and Childress accept that a patient can autonomously choose to be guided by religious, traditional, or community norms and values. While they acknowledge that it

> can be difficult to negotiate diverse values and beliefs in sharing information necessary for decision-making, this does not excuse a failure to respect a patient's autonomous decision: 'respect for autonomy is not a mere *ideal* in health care; it is a professional *obligation*. Autonomous choice is a *right*, not a *duty* of patients' (Dryden, 2010).

If one examines the various jurisdictions in which this evolutionary process has taken place it is clear that in each jurisdiction the deliberations between the public, religious leaders, ethicists and philosophers, social scientists, the legal establishment and lawmakers have followed a very similar course, even taking into account the different systems of law that exist in the different jurisdictions. For those countries that work within the common law legal framework the processes are very similar and the legal precedents often refer to each other as new laws come into being.

In the quest for the legalization of assisted suicide and the more extreme case of euthanasia, the Netherlands was in many ways the world leader (Ezekiel, 2001; Buiting et al, 2009; Onwuteaka-Philipsen et al, 2012; Griffiths et al, 1998). As other jurisdictions followed, often limiting their legal framework to PAS because euthanasia appeared to many legislators and ethicists to be an extreme situation and one fraught with dangers of abuse, the culture of the public in these jurisdictions became more accepting and supportive of such efforts even in the face of vociferous opposition by many religious leaders who find a common ground in the theistic opposition to PAS. The ethical principles of Beauchamp and Childress were used by both sides of the confrontational spectrum to support their contrary positions—ie, autonomy versus beneficence and non-maleficence in particular.

THE ETHICAL PRINCIPLES UNDERLYING EUTHANASIA AND PAS IN THE NETHERLANDS

Euthanasia and PAS are regulated by the Termination of Life on Request and Assisted Suicide (Review Procedures) Act first enacted in 2002 (Buiting et al, 2009; Griffiths et al, 1998). The basis of the Act is that euthanasia and PAS will not be punishable if the attending physician acts in accordance with criteria of due care. Each of the criteria which buttressed the conceptualization of the Act drew heavily from the ethical principle of autonomy and therefore the law reflects that ethical principle and how it is translated into the legal concept of consent to treatment. The important point is that the acts are still illegal, but are not punishable if the criteria are followed. These criteria concern the patient's request; the patient's suffering (the terms used are 'unbearable' and 'hopeless' as expressed by the patient and accepted by the physician); the information provided to the patient which would have to include the presence of reasonable alternatives; consultation with another physician and the options as to how the life would be ended. As a safeguard to ensure compliance, the law requires physicians to report their involvement and actions to a review committee that is responsible for assuring that all the necessary steps have been taken and the criteria for non-prosecution fulfilled (Griffiths et al, 1998).

The 2002 Act legalized euthanasia and PAS in very specific cases, under very specific circumstances (Griffiths et al, 1998; Lo, 2012). The procedures codified in this law had already been a practice of the Dutch medical community for over twenty years with a legal framework which was now in place with the passage of the Act (Griffiths et al, 1998; Lo, 2012). In relation to dementia, the issue of whether or not a person living with dementia can actually manifest the ethical principle of autonomy through the process of consent which allows for euthanasia and PAS being provided is of great interest. The law in the Netherlands 'allows a medical review board to suspend prosecution of doctors who performed euthanasia when each of the following conditions is fulfilled:

1. "The patient's suffering is unbearable with no prospect of improvement.
2. The patient's request for euthanasia must be voluntary and persist over time (the request cannot be granted when under the influence of others, psychological illness or drugs).
3. The patient must be fully aware of his or her condition, prospects and options.
4. There must be consultation with at least one other independent doctor who needs to confirm the conditions mentioned above.
5. The death must be carried out in a medically appropriate fashion by the doctor or patient, in which case the doctor must be present.
6. The patient is at least 12 years old (patients between 12 and 16 years of age require the consent of their parents)."'

Based on these specific legal criteria it is hard to imagine which patients living with a diagnosis of dementia of virtually any type would come close to fulfilling any of the first three of these criteria, without which one could not comply with the law. Depending on the stage of progress of the dementia, either the person would have as their main symptom some degree of cognitive impairment which could be very variable across the spectrum of the disease and if there is an measure of 'unbearable suffering' (criterion 1) it could only be of a psychological nature, presumably resulting from knowledge of the prognosis. If the disease has progressed further, it would be difficult to establish criterion 3. Many would argue that the ethical principles of beneficence and non-maleficence would be violated if one acted in a way contrary to the patient's autonomy.

The other safeguards in the Act have to do with reporting mechanisms which are quite stringent and the existence of a review committee. Importantly, when dealing with the issue of dementia, there is also the ability for a patient to undertake an advance directive outlining the criteria and wish for euthanasia should they be in a 'coma' or otherwise not be able to state if they wish to undergo euthanasia. That advance directive has to be executed by the person when they are competent to do so. There have been media reports of individuals with mild dementia requesting and undergoing euthanasia and in 2011 there was a major media buzz about the 'first' patient with advanced dementia being euthanized. According to one newspaper report,

> [a] woman with advanced Alzheimer's disease has been euthanized in the Netherlands, a first in a country that requires patients to be fully mentally alert to request to die, activists said. The 64-year-old woman died in March after being sick 'for a very long time', said a spokesman for the Right to Die-NL (NVVE) group. She had insisted 'for several years' that she wanted to be euthanized, added spokesman Walburg de Jong. 'It is really a very

> important step—before, patients dying by euthanasia were at really very early stages of dementia, which was not the case with this woman' (Agence France-Press, 2009; Sheldon, 2011).

There are few other documented cases of euthanasia of dementia patients in Dutch nursing homes resulting from compliance with an advanced directive. The conclusion of a review published in 2011 states that,

> [a]dvance directives for euthanasia are never adhered to in the Netherlands in the case of people with advanced dementia, and their role in advance care planning and end-of-life care of people with advanced dementia is limited. Communication with the patient is essential for elderly care physicians to consider adherence to an advance directive for euthanasia of a person with dementia (de Boer et al, 2011).

If this proves to be the case then there is little to be concerned about in terms of the 'slippery slope' of providing euthanasia to those who at the time of the proposed actual act would not be in a position to act autonomously and therefore verify their wishes. It will be a matter of time before it becomes clear whether the case reported in the media is an anomaly or the beginning of a trend that repositions the issue of what constitutes autonomy when an act that ends life is performed. The spectre of those acting with less than beneficent motivations providing permission for a life-ending act based on discussions and documents from a distant past may become a real concern to those who oversee the Termination of Life Act. For those whose only concern is a 'strict' interpretation of autonomy, an advance directive indicating a wish for someone in the future to interpret the expressed wish for euthanasia rather than limiting such advance directive decisions for treatment decisions which might include the withdrawal or withholding of treatments is likely to be interpreted by some as overstepping the meaning of autonomy in decision making. It could also potentially lead to less than beneficent actions on the parts of substitute decision-makers who may have ulterior motives in enacting such decisions when the person cannot participate in 'real time' (Foster, 2010; Gessert, 2008; Gillon, 2003; Tauber, 2001).

The kinds of treatments and decisions that do not come under the Act because in essence they are part of good medical and palliative care include the following:

1. Stopping or not starting a medically useless (futile) treatment.
2. Stopping or not starting a treatment at the patient's request.
3. Speeding up death as a side-effect of treatment necessary for alleviating serious suffering.

PRACTICE

The issue for much of the world where there are legislative initiatives to introduce some measure of PAS is judging the result of such legislation in the Netherlands, which is the longest standing natural experiment that exists. For those predicting that such practices would lead to the 'slippery slope' of involuntary euthanasia and a cavalier view of the aged, the experience in the Netherlands is worth noting. There appeared to be very few breaches of the protocol. When a breach occurred the reason was usually deemed to be ignorance of the regulatory requirements.

In 2010, 4050 persons died from euthanasia or from assisted suicide on request. According to research by the Vrije Universiteit (Amsterdam), University Medical Center Utrecht and Statistics Netherlands, published in *The Lancet*, this is not more than before the introduction of the Termination of Life on Request and Assisted Suicide (Review Procedures) Act in 2002. According to the *Lancet* article, 'Ending of life without an explicit patient request in 2010 occurred less often than in 2005, 2001, 1995, and 1990'. In an accompanying editorial some concerns were raised about the current practice in the Netherlands, even with the commendable data gathering and reporting mechanism that is in place and the apparent accuracy and transparency of the practice. The editorial, instead of being critical of the practice, outlined some of the concerns that must be addressed in order for the practice to avoid leading to a level of interaction that contradicts the initial intent of the legislation which was, for the most part, a combined respect for individual autonomy and the avoidance of unremitting suffering (ethical principle of non-maleficence) (Agence France-Press, 2009).

Of special interest—and worth mentioning within the context of the concern of some critics of the erosive impact on society of legalizing euthanasia and PAS—was the February 2010 citizens' initiative called *Out of Free Will* which in essence demanded that Dutch people over 70 *who feel tired of life* should have the right to professional help in ending it. The question for those who care for individuals living with dementia is whether there might be a special attraction for them of such a programme if they perceive their future as dismal. The organization started collecting signatures and lobbying in support of this proposed change in Dutch legislation. Some prominent Dutch citizens supported the initiative, including former government ministers, artists, legal scholars and physicians. This law has not been implemented and has enormous implications conceptually for all those involved in elder care and geriatric medical care and the care of those living with dementia (Folkert, 2010).

It is well recognized that older individuals are prone to a number of medical conditions that may result in them having feelings of despondency and of being 'tired of life'. If properly addressed through a combination of proper medical assessment and care with well formulated psycho-social interventions, such feelings of 'hopelessness' that might lead an older person to wish for his or her life to end can be reversed, only for them to be happy that such a step was not undertaken (Hunkeler et al, 2006). In the meantime, under current Dutch law, euthanasia and PAS by doctors is only legal in cases of 'hopeless and unbearable' suffering—in short according to the original criteria which includes suffering from serious medical conditions and being in considerable pain. Dementia is clearly not part of that list of reasons, but that does not mean it could not be so in the future. The arguments that might be brought against the inclusion of dementia as part of the euthanasia criteria is that at this point, for example, there is no concrete test to guarantee that the diagnosis is 'correct' as it is primarily a clinical assessment; the course of the illness can be very variable; the medications available may improve the symptoms and progress of the condition significantly; and many people living with dementia appear to be able to participate in a wide range of activities and apparently 'enjoy' many aspects of life. The implications for the moral fabric of society, including the medical profession, rather than just the decision of the patient cannot be easily ignored. In any event, at this point, to help somebody to commit suicide without meeting the qualifications of the current Dutch euthanasia criteria remains illegal (Griffiths et al, 1998; Agence France-Press, 2009; Arias, 2013).

THE STIMULUS TO THE AMERICAN DEBATE: DR JACK KEVORKIAN

The person who may have stimulated the discourse on legalizing euthanasia and/or PAS in North America is someone who at the time was considered by many as a renegade, by others as a heroic visionary who brought the subject to public awareness through the use of and effect on the popular media, and by the legal authorities as a criminal. Dr Jack Kevorkian, often known as 'Dr Death', employed unconventional methods and in the end paid a high price for his campaign to legalize euthanasia and PAS in the United States (Kevorkian, 2012). The impact that he had on the public and the media is likely to have been instrumental in paving the way for the legalization of PAS, first in Oregon, then Washington State, then Montana, and then, in May 2013, the State of Vermont.

In 1990, Kevorkian assisted in the suicide of Janet Adkins, a 45-year-old Alzheimer's patient from Michigan. Adkins, a member of the Hemlock Society—an organization that advocates voluntary euthanasia for terminally ill patients—wanted to die before she developed the late stages of the disease. Adkins sought the aid of someone to end her life prior to the degenerative disease taking full effect. She contacted Kevorkian, who had already made his name in the media by using the so-called 'suicide machine'. Kevorkian helped Adkins to kill herself inside his Volkswagen van and filmed the event, in Adkins self-administered her own painkiller and then a lethal substance which killed her within five minutes. Many in the field of dementia care felt that Adkins was not given the benefit of a proper and knowledgeable medical assessment or had explained to her the options for various interventions and support, and some suggest that had she been advised otherwise, she may have altered her decision to end her life. At the early stage of her apparent cognitive impairment (45 is very early for such a diagnosis and other options would normally be pursued before such a diagnostic label is applied) Kevorkian was unlikely to be medically knowledgeable in the field of dementia to be in a position to make such a determination.

Eventually, after much publicity and a number of high profile cases, Kevorkian challenged the courts to pursue him legally. This resulted in a second-degree murder conviction. On 1 June 2007, after serving about eight years of his sentence, Kevorkian was released from prison for good behaviour and with his agreement that he would not assist in any more suicides. He died four years later at the age of 83 from a combination of kidney and heart problems.

The legacy of Dr Kevorkian depends on one's perspective of euthanasia and PAS. Some see him as a fearless pioneer who fought for the rights of individuals (and therefore ultimate respect for the ethical principle of autonomy) to end their own lives. For others he was a murderer who, despite being a physician, abandoned all the principles of contemporary medical practice and ethics and assisted individuals (many of whom may have responded to medical intervention, whether therapeutic or palliative) who were suffering from various medical conditions to die.

OREGON, WASHINGTON, MONTANA AND VERMONT

It may be possible to make a connection between what happened in the Netherlands, the actions of Dr Kevorkian and the legal processes by which the State of Oregon became the first State in the United States to legalize PAS. The measure was approved in the 1994 general election by a slim but favourable margin (627,980 votes (51.3%) for and 596,018 votes (48.7%) against). There were a number of legal challenges, which ultimately resulted in the law being upheld by the Supreme Court of the United States in *Gonzales v Oregon* in 2006 (Enouen, 2012; O'Reilly, 2008). Washington State and Montana (O'Reilly, 2010; Johnson, 2010; *Baxter v Montana*, 2009) followed suit in 2008 and 2009 respectively. In these three States with congruent laws and regulations the focus is primarily on individuals who are competent to choose PAS. Those with significant cognitive impairment or dementia would not have the capacity to make such a decision; it is also likely that most physicians would be opposed to someone in such a state of cognitive impairment undertaking such a decision.

Thus far it has not seemed possible to include those living with dementia in a category that would come within the PAS laws of Oregon, Washington State, Montana or Vermont, and thus the concerns about a 'slippery slope' resulting in the premature death of those living with dementia are probably, for the moment, misplaced (Mitchell, 2009). One can surmise that the reason that these States chose to allow only PAS—and not PAS and euthanasia like the Netherlands—is that they are willing to address only the wishes of clearly competent persons who can, as far as possible, truly express their own ethical status of autonomy. Any hesitation about a person's ability to participate in such a deliberation (with their physician, family and often a second physician) would eliminate that person from the life-ending equation. Although one could argue that it was an act of ethical reluctance that led to such a construct and limitations on the law, it appears to have satisfied the wishes and needs of the majority of those who voted for and in all other ways supported the structure of this particular framework of life-ending legislation. Might this change in the future? It is hard to predict, but considering the history thus far in Oregon, the State with the longest history of PAS, there has not been a loud demand.

LEGAL THINKING AROUND THE ISSUE: THE US PERSPECTIVES

A review of the case law of the United States' Supreme Court decisions on PAS (euthanasia itself has been regarded as unarguably beyond the pale) must start with the landmark case of *Washington v Glucksberg* in 1997, which was soon followed by *Vacco v Quill*, also in 1997. In both of these cases, the Supreme Court ruled that 'prohibiting assisted suicide was constitutional as applied to the terminally ill, *mentally competent adults*'.

The Court unanimously decided that Washington's assisted suicide ban was '*not* unconstitutional'. The Court observed that in 'almost every State—indeed, in almost every western democracy—it is a crime to assist a suicide'. The Court concluded that 'we are confronted with a consistent and almost universal tradition that has long rejected the asserted right, and continues explicitly to reject it today, even for terminally ill, mentally competent adults'. 'Because assisted suicide has been consistently rejected in the history and tradition of our nation', the Court wrote, 'the asserted "right" to assistance in committing suicide is not a fundamental liberty interest protected by the Due Process Clause'. The Court's ruling was 9–0 in the *Glucksberg* case.

Of special interest in *Vacco v Quill* was the acknowledgement and mention of the role of palliative care as a potential viable alternative to the act of PAS. As part of the introduction to their promotion of palliative care the Court made a very specific point of promoting the concept that competent individuals or their proxies are allowed to refuse medical treatments even if potentially lifesaving. '*Everyone*, regardless of physical condition, is entitled, if competent, to refuse unwanted life-saving medical treatment; *no one* is permitted to assist a suicide'. Thus, in both seminal rulings, the Court determined that there was no federal *constitutional right* to PAS, but in essence turned the *decision back to the States* for deliberation at the State level which can craft laws that are not operative in any other jurisdiction. This resulted in the three States (with the fourth—Vermont—in May 2013) approving PAS laws. All the laws focus on the competent adult, utilizing as the basic argument the ethical principle of autonomy as the overriding ethical principle when compared to beneficence, non-maleficence and justice, the three other foundational ethical principles that generally guide such deliberations. Since many dementia patients lack autonomy, they tend to be excluded from the existing PAS provision in the US.

OTHER IMPORTANT CLINICAL DECISIONS BY THOSE LIVING WITH DEMENTIA FOR WHICH ETHICS MIGHT HOLD THE KEY TO DECISION MAKING

A major problem for those who care for those living with dementia, for whom there may be varying degrees of physical and psychological suffering at the end of life, is how to bridge the clinical and conceptual gap which results in legal, policy and professional unfamiliarity with the late and often terminal phase. Individuals in this phase pose many clinical challenges that have their own peculiar components of suffering. The clinical difficulty which often translates into ethical issues is how to help families confronted with such situations from having to follow what are often inappropriate approaches to medical interventions that add little if anything to comfort or care during the late and terminal stages of dementia-related conditions (Byock, 1993; Gordon and Baker, 2011; Mitchell et al, 2010). Therefore, discussions and expressed wishes or the substitute decision-maker's (SDM) interpretation of wishes and values related to important end-of-life potential medical interventions are very important.

The issues that are generally of most concern in the later stages of dementia are artificial nutrition and hydration (ANH), Cardio-Pulmonary Resuscitation (CPR) and limitations on modern medical treatments in the downward spiral of the living trajectory which cannot be ignored in focusing on euthanasia and PAS (Gordon and Baker, 2011). Such issues are more likely to be relevant than the more dramatic issues of physician induced cessation of life (Mitchell et al, 2010). In order to avoid the introduction of ANH, it is most important that if the person cannot participate in the discussion at the time of proposed treatment, the SDM should make the decision based on their understanding of the expressed wishes of the person, although there has often been no such expression. Many family members do not know how to broach such a subject and often it is during a time of medical crises that the decision is made to undertake ANH. There are also misconceptions by family members and sometimes by health care professionals about the benefits of ANH and its role in preventing such problems such as aspiration—which may not be prevented by the insertion of a feeding tube. When ANH is raised as a possibility, family members often say that they cannot bear the idea of 'starving their parent to death'. Thus, it is best to undertake any discussion on the matter not when there is a crisis, but beforehand, and for health care providers to assure loved ones that all steps will be taken to avoid 'suffering', thus adhering to the principle of non-maleficence (Brody et al, 2011).

Evidence strongly suggests that the results of performing CPR in the later stages of age-related decline are dismal. This is especially true in relation to the frail elderly, including those living with late stage dementia. CPR can often be harmful (for instance causing broken ribs), and may thus add to the distress of the end of life process (Gordon and Baker, 2011; Gordon, 2007).

'Salvage' interventions in people at the later stages of their life, especially with late-stage dementia, are often pursued because it can be difficult to decide not to treat what is often interpreted as a 'treatable' condition such as a pulmonary tract or urinary tract infection. Yet the results are often of only temporary benefit and one infection is often followed by another with the ultimate result being a more prolonged dying period. Discussions about such 'terminal' active interventions are best undertaken prior to such events rather than in the middle of a crisis, where careful thought and consideration are more difficult (Mitchell et al, 2009; Millar, 2012; Niederman and Berger, 2010; Chang and Walter, 2010).

THE CANADIAN PICTURE OF PAS: ETHICS AND LAW

In Canada, the public interest in this topic has become so large that major newspapers are publishing articles on the subject in great numbers, and the *Toronto Star* has recently launched an *Atkinson Series* on issues of life and death. In many ways, the articles written for the lay public summarize the whole range of issues involved, ranging from the law, ethics, religious beliefs and practices and experience worldwide (Cribb, 2012a; 2012b).

The recent case of *Carter v Canada* (2012) brought the issue of PAS into unprecedented public focus in Canada. The same type of case had been brought to the courts about a decade earlier in the case of Sue Rodriguez, also from British Columbia. In the *Rodriguez* case (1993) the Supreme Court of Canada maintained the previous position—namely that physician-assisted suicide was a criminal offence. This created a great deal of controversy in the media and in legal circles (Smith, 1993; Tiedemann et al, 2011).

In *Canada v Carter,* the British Columbia Supreme Court struck down Canada's ban on doctor-assisted suicide as unconstitutional, but the judge suspended her ruling for one year to give the federal government time to craft legislation to comply with the Constitution. She said:

> The claimed infringement of s 7 rights differs as among the plaintiffs. With respect to Ms Taylor, the legislation affects her rights to liberty and security of the person, as was found in Rodriguez. In addition, the legislation affects her right to life because it may shorten her life. Ms Taylor's reduced lifespan would occur if she concludes that she needs to take her own life while she is still physically able to do so, at an earlier date than she would find necessary if she could be assisted. With respect to Ms Carter and Mr Johnson, the legislation affects their rights to liberty because they are at risk of incarceration, at least in theory, for having helped a loved one who obtained assisted death in Switzerland (*Carter v Canada*, 2012: paragraph 17).

> The legislation deprives the plaintiffs of their s 7 rights inconsistently with the principles of fundamental justice. First, the legislation is overbroad. Second, the legislative response—an absolute prohibition—is grossly disproportionate to the objectives it is meant to accomplish. As with the s 15 infringement, the s 7 infringement would not be justified under s 1 (*Carter v Canada*, 2012: paragraph 18).

The federal government appealed the decision, arguing that the Criminal Code provisions against anyone counselling or assisting an individual in a suicide are constitutional.

The British Columbia Court of Appeal (2013) struck down the decision of the court of first instance, restoring the status quo ante. The case has been appealed to the Supreme Court of Canada, and will be heard in 2014 (Stueck, 2013). Public debate in doctor-assisted suicide has also been sparked by a video featuring Donald Low, a well-known Canadian microbiologist who, shortly before he died of a brain tumour in September 2013, made an impassioned plea to allow physician-assisted suicide for some people who are in pain and terminally ill. The final decision of the BC Court of Appeal surprised many who felt public and legal sentiment had changed since the previous Rodriguez case Supreme Court ruling in1993. According to the *Globe and Mail* newspaper report:

> In a split decision, two BC Appeal Court judges said while the law relating to the Canadian Charter of Rights and Freedoms has evolved since 1993—when the Supreme Court turned down Ms. Rodriguez's bid to overturn the law—it has not changed enough to set aside the ruling in that case and that no change sufficient to undermine Rodriguez as a binding authority has occurred (Stueck, 2013).

WHAT MAKES DEMENTIA SO DIFFERENT?

It would be a welcome change if the efforts to deal with end-of-life issues in dementia were driven primarily by the ethical principle of beneficence. Yet financial considerations (translated ethically into the idea of distributive justice), often seem to be the main drivers (Hurd et al, 2013).

Pain is rarely the main force driving people to consider the PAS option attractive. Yet most of the jurisdictions that have accepted legislation to allow for PAS or euthanasia focus on 'suffering' and 'pain' as the main reasons for providing such an *outlet* to the concept of suffering. One might question in the current era of very effective modalities of symptom management, including the common symptoms so often addressed by people and in the legislation, whether pain is really the culprit. For the most part, in those living with dementia but also those living with other illnesses in the terminal phase of their trajectory, fear of the continuous decline and apparent 'loss of self' which many people associate with chronic late-stage debilitating illnesses drives many to consider. Some who have experienced a loved one living with the disease for a prolonged period, accept the decline and the care needed as part of life that has to be endured and dealt with in the most compassionate manner possible; others may view it as a hopeless illness, not so much in the sense of possible cure or amelioration, but because many aspects that they associate with self are lost; for them without those aspects life no longer has an existential meaning (World Health Organization, 2012). In the clinical setting it is common to hear comments that relate to the person who 'used to be' when referring to a loved one in very late-stage dementia. This is often very hard for families to experience and they need a great deal of psychosocial support to recognize that their loved one is still important even with all the apparent losses (Alzheimer's Society of British Columbia, 2009; Georges et al, 2008; Woodman, 2005).

The contrast between those family members who accept the responsibility as a 'blessing' and 'privilege' and those who consider it a 'burden' is great and probably has to do with the nature of human beings, relationships, value systems, moral and religious beliefs and the nature of the relationship between the afflicted loved one and their care givers that existed long before the disease became manifest. All those factors play out in the world of policymaking with the goal of trying to meet everyone's needs and wishes one way or the other within some defined acceptable civil, ethical, legal and most of all, humane context. The development of protocols for palliative sedation within the palliative care lexicon allows physicians and SDMs to decide on methods of symptom management when usual symptom control measures are unsuccessful. The controversy about whether palliative sedation is just euthanasia in another form is an issue that often leads to heated debate and harsh differences of opinion (Swart, 2012). It is clear that, depending on one's social, cultural, ethnic and religious background and education, there may be significant negative stereotypes and stigma associated with dementia, whether with the diagnosis, cognitive or behavioural effects (Batsch and Mittelman, 2012).

The great and understandable concern about the potential risk to the older person living with dementia, especially those residing in long-term care facilities, cannot be ignored. Even though the current legislation in those jurisdictions that allow for PAS or euthanasia for *competent* individuals under carefully prescribed situations, there is a worry about the erosion of an intrinsic 'respect for life'. This potentially may lead health care professionals to act in a more cavalier or even callous manner towards frail, older residents of long-term care facilities, who are living with late-stage dementia. This might occur in particular when someone develops an otherwise potentially treatable condition, but 'allowed to die' is which by definition not PAS or euthanasia, but on many occasions is very close to the line. There might even be some subconscious collusion on the part of SDMs who no longer value the person or may see them as a burden. This is an ethical conundrum that has to be addressed so that SDMs, acting on behalf of these frail and very vulnerable individuals, do so in a way that reflects the previously expressed wishes and values of the person and when necessary meets a more difficult to define best interests standard. Most importantly, SDMs should address issues of unnecessary suffering and provide compassionate concern and care (Hesselink et al, 2012).

In the Canadian context, there has, unsurprisingly, been intense interest in the *Carter v Canada* litigation. Legislative amendments are on hold until the judgment of the Supreme Court of Canada in that case. But euthanasia and PAS are on the public agenda as never before. According to newspaper reports:

> The euthanasia debate has jumped onto the political agenda, with the country's health ministers calling for discussion on allowing physicians to help patients end their lives. Even the federal government, which has steadfastly refused to change the Criminal Code to allow assisted suicide nationally, is ready to join the conversation (Morrow, 2013).

LESSONS TO BE LEARNED

Although several societies have allowed PAS and euthanasia, there is very strong opposition to such laws in many jurisdictions. This is the case even when many in the public sphere, including large numbers of the electorate, support laws similar to those in those European countries where PAS and even euthanasia are legalized, or at least those states in the United States where PAS is allowed. The media, press, editorials in many Western countries where the controversy exists are full of opinions from reputable physicians, ethicists, legal experts and religious leaders, either espousing or condemning the practice. There is one silver lining to the controversy. There has been, as an outcome of the focus on end-of-life issues and the duty to try to avoid and adequately treat the symptoms and suffering associated with dying, a greater emphasis on palliative care. This has achieved a greater legitimacy and focus with the general acknowledgement that, with proper palliative care, many of the concerns for which people look to the option of PAS or euthanasia can be avoided without compromising the quality of life while in the process of dying.

What is often overlooked in the heated arguments for and against PAS and euthanasia, is that the most common clinical events that occur in those living with late-stage dementia which often lead to ethical challenges are three major and common clinical scenarios: (1) whether or not to provide artificial nutrition and hydration to those who can no longer take adequate oral intake to maintain themselves; (2) whether or not to provide CPR (Gordon, 2007; Gordon and Baker, 2011) as the last *heroic* attempt to keep someone alive, who by all accounts is really in the process of dying; and (3) to decide on what limitations on typical late-life treatments make clinical, professional and ethical sense. The most common occurrence is whether—in the face of a likely life-ending infection in someone who is on the downward trajectory of life—the introduction of antibiotics and often more extreme interventions such as intensive care modalities fulfil our expectations of sound and ethical late-life care.

CONCLUSION

Law and ethics are not always congruent. It is generally hoped that the laws of a jurisdiction will be based on the best of ethical principles. There is a long history demonstrating that there is often a lag between the evolution of laws which make them more congruent with generally agreed-to ethical principles. There is much written about the relationship. One example of a simplified version of the relationship comes from the American Medical Association:

> The Relation of Law and Ethics—The following statements are intended to clarify the relationship between law and ethics. Ethical values and legal principles are usually closely related, but ethical obligations typically exceed legal duties. In some cases, the law mandates unethical conduct. In general, when physicians believe a law is unjust, they should work to change the law. In exceptional circumstances of unjust laws, ethical responsibilities should supersede legal obligations. The fact that a physician charged with allegedly illegal conduct is acquitted or exonerated in civil or criminal proceedings does not necessarily mean that the physician acted ethically (American Medical Association Code of Ethics, 1994: updated June 1994).

But even ethical principles have a wide range of interpretation and acceptance. The quest for some universally acceptable basis for ethical concepts and practice in societies goes back to ancient times and is often congruent or in conflict with the range of religious belief systems. Thus, a robust agreement on the ethics and law in any jurisdiction is a project always in process.

When it comes to end-of-life care and the values and belief systems that go into the practical implementation of the requirements to achieve a quality end to the lives of those approaching their last period of life is a laudable goal. The focus in particular on those individuals living with dementia presents special nuances in the process that exists during the terminal phases of all medical conditions because in many cases the person with dementia can no longer express in real time their wishes as their medical condition changes. This is the enormous challenge of substitute decision-makers trying to fulfil their filial, ethical and legal duties and obligations. Into this mix has been thrown the controversial tension between optimal palliative care as the best ethical, legal and clinical approach to avoid or treat end-of-life suffering, in contrast to PAS or euthanasia which eliminates the presumed or observed individual suffering, by eliminating the life period for which palliative care would otherwise have been provided.

The answers to all these conundrums are not absolutely clear. We do however have an enormous collective experience that encompasses all the variable factors and the processes by which each society, and as a consequence each person and family and health care professional, can deal with the very human and daunting challenge of providing the best end-of-life care that is possible with the humanity and sensitivity towards suffering that is required.

REFERENCES

Agence France-Presse (2009) 'Euthanasia in Netherlands of severe Alzheimer's patient performed'. More from Agence France-Presse: news.nationalpost.com/2011/11/09/first-euthanasia-in-netherlands-of-severe-alzheimers-patient/.

Alzheimer's Society (2011) *The Rising Tide*. Available at: www.alzheimer.ca/en/on/Get-involved/Raise-your-voice/Rising-Tide/Rising-tide-summary).

Alzheimer's Society of British Columbia (2009) 'Caring for people with dementia at the end of life: A review of the literature'. Available at: www.alzheimerbc.org/getdoc/b8841ffc-4336-46bb-abf1-5156d0a91db0/End-of-Life-Care---Lierature-Review.aspx.

American Medical Association (1994) Code of Medical Ethics: Opinion 1.02 – The Relation of Law and Ethics. Available at: www.ama-assn.org/ama/pub/physician-resources/medical-ethics/code-medical-ethics/opinion102.page.

Arias, JJ (2013) 'A time to step in: Legal mechanisms for protecting those with declining capacity' 39(1) *American Journal of Law & Medicine* 134–59. Available at: litigation-essentials.lexisnexis.com/webcd/app?action=DocumentDisplay&crawlid=1&doctype=cite&docid=39+Am.+J.+L.+and+Med.+134&srctype=smi&srcid=3B15&key=b7447b1ccc984a52c92bd2ca7a10f8e8.

Batsch, NL and Mittelman, MS (2012) 'Alzheimer's Disease International: World Alzheimer Report 2012: Overcoming the Stigma of Dementia'. Available at: www.alz.org/documents_custom/world_report_2012_final.pdf.

Beauchamp, TL and Childress, JF (2012) *Principles of Biomedical Ethics*, 7th edn (US, Oxford University Press). Available at: www.amazon.com/Principles-Biomedical-Ethics-Tom-Beauchamp/dp/0199924589/ref=dp_ob_title_bk.

Brody, H et al (2011) 'Artificial Nutrition and Hydration: The Evolution of Ethics, Evidence, and Policy' 26(9) *Journal of General Internal Medicine* 1053–58. Available at: www.ncbi.nlm.nih.gov/pmc/articles/PMC3157529/.

Buiting, H et al (2009) 'A Reporting of euthanasia and physician-assisted suicide in the Netherlands: descriptive study' 10 *BMC Medical Ethics* 18. Available at: www.biomedcentral.com/1472-6939/10/18.

Byock, IR (1993) 'Consciously Walking the Fine Line: Thoughts on a Hospice Response to Assisted Suicide and Euthanasia' 9 *Journal of Palliative Care* 25–28. Available at: www.dyingwell.org/fineline.htm.

Chang, A and Walter, LC (2010) 'Recognizing dementia as a terminal illness in nursing home residents: Comment on "Survival and comfort after treatment of pneumonia in advanced dementia"' 170(13) *Archives of Internal Medicine* 1107–09. Available at: www.ncbi.nlm.nih.gov/pubmed/20625014.

Cribb, R (2012a) Atkinson Series: Life or Death. Available at: www.thestar.com/topic/atkinson2012.

—— (2012b) 'Physician-assisted suicide remains illegal in Canada' *Toronto Star* (26 October). Available at: www.thestar.com/news/insight/article/1277923-physician-assisted-suicide-remains-illegal-in-Canada.

de Boer, ME et al (2011) 'Advance directives for euthanasia in dementia: How do they affect resident care in Dutch nursing homes? Experiences of physicians and relatives' 59 *Journal of the American Geriatrics Society* 989–96. Available at: www.ncbi.nlm.nih.gov/pubmed/21649621.

Dryden, J (2010) 'Autonomy: Overview' (21 November) *Internet Encyclopaedia of Philosophy*. Available at: www.iep.utm.edu/autonomy/.

Ebrahimi, N (2012) 'The ethics of euthanasia' 3(1) *Australian Medical Student Journal* 73–75. Available at: www.amsj.org/archives/2066.

Enouen, SW (2012) Oregon's Euthanasia Law: Life Issues Institute. Available at: www.lifeissues.org/euthanasia/oregons_law.htm.

Ezekiel, JE (2001) 'Euthanasia: Where the Netherlands leads will the world follow? Legalisation is a diversion from improving care for the dying' 322(7299) *British Medical Journal* 1376–77. Available at: www.ncbi.nlm.nih.gov/pmc/articles/PMC1120458/.

Folkert, J (2010) 'A citizens action group wants to legalise assisted suicide for all people over 70' (9 February 2010-NRC International). Available at: www.rnw.nl/english/article/right-die-elderly-back-centre-dutch-debate.

Foster, C (2010) 'Autonomy should chair, not rule' 375(9712) *Lancet* 368–69. Available at: www.thelancet.com/journals/lancet/article/PIIS0140673610601560/fulltext?rss=yes.

Gessert, CE (2008) 'The Problem with Autonomy: An overemphasis on patient autonomy results in patients feeling abandoned and physicians feeling frustrated' (April) *Minnesotamedicine*. Available at: www.minnesotamedicine.com/PastIssues/PastIssues2008/April2008/CommentaryApril2008.aspx.

Georges, J et al (2008) 'Alzheimer's disease in real life – the dementia carer's survey' 23(5) *International Journal of Geriatric Psychiatry* 546–51. Available at: www.ncbi.nlm.nih.gov/pubmed/18232054.

Gillon, R (2003) 'Ethics needs principles – four can encompass the rest – and respect for autonomy should be "first among equals"' 29 *Journal of Medical Ethics* 307–12. Available at: jme.bmj.com/content/29/5/307.full.

Gordon, M (2007) 'Cardiopulmonary Resuscitation in the Frail Elderly: Clinical, Ethical and Halakhic Issues' 9(3) *Israel Medical Association Journal* 177–79. Available at: www.ima.org.il/imaj/ViewArticle.aspx?aId=1072.

—— (2011) 'Assault as Treatment: Mythology of CPR in End-of-Life Dementia Care' 19(5) *Annals of Long-Term Care: Clinical Care and Aging* 31–32. Available at: www.annalsoflongtermcare.com/article/assault-treatment-mythology-cpr-end-life-dementia-care?page=0,1.

Gordon, M and Baker, N (2011) *Late-stage Dementia: Promoting Comfort, Compassion and Care* (Bloomington, IND, IUniverse Press).

Griffiths J, Bood, A and Weyers, H (1998) *Euthanasia and Law in the Netherlands* (Amsterdam, Amsterdam University Press).

Hemlock Society: Final Exit Network^{TM}: www.finalexitnetwork.org/new/advisory-board/.

Hesselink, BA et al (2012) 'Do guidelines on euthanasia and physician-assisted suicide in Dutch hospitals and nursing homes reflect the law? A content analysis' 38(1) *Journal of Medical Ethics* 35–42. Available at: www.ncbi.nlm.nih.gov/pubmed/?term=Do+guidelines+on+euthanasia+and+physician-assisted+suicide+in+Dutch+hospitals+and+nursing+homes+reflect+the+law%3F+A+content+analysis.

Hunkeler, EM et al (2006) 'Long term outcomes from the IMPACT randomized trial for depressed elderly patients in primary care' 332(7536) *British Medical Journal* 259–62.

Hurd, MD et al (2013) 'Monetary Costs of Dementia in the United States' 368(14) *New England Journal of Medicine* 1326–34. Available at: www.nejm.org/doi/full/10.1056/NEJMsa1204629.

Johnson, K (2010) 'Montana Ruling Bolsters Doctor-Assisted Suicide' *New York Times* (1 January). Available at: www.nytimes.com/2010/01/01/us/01suicide.html?_r=0.

Kevorkian, J (2012) 'Biography.com'. Available at: www.biography.com/people/jack-kevorkian-9364141.

Litman, RE (1966–67) 'Medical-Legal Aspects of Suicide' 6 *Washburn Law Journal* 395–401. Available at: heinonlinebackup.com/hol-cgi-bin/get_pdf.cgi?handle=hein.journals/wasbur6§ion=41.

Lo, B (2012) Editorial: 'Euthanasia in the Netherlands: What lessons for elsewhere?' 380(9845) *Lancet* 869–70.

Millar, M (2012) 'Constraining the use of antibiotics: Applying Scanlon's contractualism' 38(8) *Journal of Medical Ethics* 465–69. Available at: www.ncbi.nlm.nih.gov/pubmed/22431559.

Mitchell, JB (2009) 'Physician-Assisted Suicide and Dementia: The Impossibility of a Workable Regulatory Regime' 88(4) *Oregon Law Review* 1085–137. Available at: litigation-essentials.lexisnexis.com/webcd/app?action=DocumentDisplay&crawlid=1&doctype=cite&docid=88+Or.+L.+Rev.+1085&srctype=smi&srcid=3B15&key=29db08bd37bc28fa04236a68ea40606a.

Mitchell, SL et al (2009) 'The Clinical Course of Advanced Dementia' 361(16) *New England Journal of Medicine* 1529–38. Available at: www.ncbi.nlm.nih.gov/pmc/articles/PMC2778850/.

—— (2010) 'The Advanced Dementia Prognostic Tool (ADEPT): A Risk Score to Estimate Survival in Nursing Home Residents with Advanced Dementia' 40(5) *Journal of Pain and Symptom Management* 639–51. Available at: www.ncbi.nlm.nih.gov/pmc/articles/PMC2981683/.

Morrow, A (2013) 'Quebec's euthanasia law reopens national right-to-die debate' *The Globe and Mail* (3 October).

Niederman, MS and Berger, JT (2010) 'The delivery of futile care is harmful to other patients' 38(10 Suppl) *Critical Care Medicine* S518–22. Available at: www.ncbi.nlm.nih.gov/pubmed/21164391.

Onwuteaka-Philipsen, BD et al (2012) 'Trends in end-of-life practices before and after the enactment of the euthanasia law in the Netherlands from 1990 to 2010: A repeated cross-sectional survey' 380(9845) *Lancet* 908–15. Available at: www.ncbi.nlm.nih.gov/pubmed/22789501.

O'Reilly, KB (2008) 'Oregon still stands alone: Ten years of physician-assisted suicide' *amednews* (12 May). Available at www.amednews.com/article/20080512/profession/305129970/4/.

—— (2010) 'Assisted suicide laws cited in 95 deaths in Washington, Oregon' *amednews* (25 March). Available at: www.ama-assn.org/amednews/2010/03/22/prse0325.htm.

Pellegrino, ED (1993) 'The Metamorphosis of Medical Ethics A 30-Year Retrospective' 269(9) *Journal of the American Medical Association* 1158–62.

Sheldon, T (2011) 'Dementia patient's euthanasia was lawful, say Dutch authorities' 343 *British Medical Journal*. Available at: www.ncbi.nlm.nih.gov/pubmed/22106373.

Simon, RI, Levenson, JL and Shuman, DW (2005) 'On sound and unsound mind: The role of suicide in tort and insurance litigation' 33(2) *Journal of the American Academy of Psychiatry and the Law* 176–82. Available at: www.ncbi.nlm.nih.gov/pubmed/15985659.

Smith, M (Law and Government Division, Government of Canada, October 1993) *The Rodriguez* Case: *A Review of the Supreme Court of Canada Decision on Assisted Suicide*. Available at: publications.gc.ca/Collection-R/LoPBdP/BP/bp349-e.htm.

Stueck, W (2013) 'BC court upholds ban on assisted suicide as public debate heats up' *The Globe and Mail* (10 October). Available at: www.theglobeandmail.com/news/british-columbia/bc-appeals-court-upholds-law-against-assisted-suicide/article14796425/.

Suicide: The Canadian Encyclopaedia: www.thecanadianencyclopedia.com/articles/suicide.

Suicide in the United States: en.wikipedia.org/wiki/Suicide_legislation#United_States.

Swart, SJ et al (2012) 'Considerations of physicians about the depth of palliative sedation at the end of life' 184(7) *Canadian Medical Association Journal* E360–E366.

Tauber, AI (2001) 'Historical and Philosophical Reflections on Patient Autonomy' 9(3) *Health Care Analysis* 299–319. Available at: blogs.bu.edu/ait/files/2012/08/Tauber-Hist-and-Phil-Reflections-on-Pat-Aut.pdf.

Tiedemann, M (Social Affairs Division), Nicol, J and Valiquet, D (Legal and Legislative Affairs Division) (*revised 8 April 2011)* 'Euthanasia and Assisted Suicide: International Experiences' Library of Parliament Research Publications (Canada). Available at: www.parl.gc.ca/Content/LOP/ResearchPublications/2011-67-e.htm.

UK Suicide Act 1961: en.wikipedia.org/wiki/Suicide_Act_1961.

Woodman, CE (2005) 'Seeking meaning in late stage dementia' 59(4) *Journal of Pastoral Care & Counseling* 335–43. Available at: www.ncbi.nlm.nih.gov/pubmed/16392644.

World Health Organization (2012) *Dementia*. Available at: www.alzheimer.ca/en/sk/Get-involved/Raise-your-voice/WHO-report-dementia-2012.

World Health Organization and Alzheimer's Disease International (2012) *Dementia: A public health priority* (Geneva, WHO Press).

CASES

Baxter v Montana P 3d 2009 WL 5155363 (Mont 2009). Available at: www.americanbar.org/content/dam/aba/migrated/aging/PublicDocuments/baxtr_v_mont_sum.authcheckdam.pdf.
Carter v Canada (Attorney General, British Columbia Supreme Court, 2012: 886). Available at: www.courts.gov.bc.ca/jdb-txt/SC/12/08/2012BCSC0886cor1.htm.
Carter v Canada (2013) BCCA 435.
Gonzales v Oregon (04-623) 546 US 243 (2006) 368 F 3d 1118, affirmed. Cornell University Law School: www.law.cornell.edu/supct/html/04-623.ZS.html.
Vacco, Attorney General of New York, et al v Quill et al (1997). Available at: caselaw.lp.findlaw.com/scripts/getcase.pl?court=US&vol=000&invol=95-1858.
Wackwitz v Roy 418 SE 2d 861 (1992); *Marie Wackwitz, Administrator of the Estate of Bryon Henry Wackwitz, Deceased v Gaston Roy, MD, et al.* Record No 911384. Supreme Court of Virginia. 5 June 1992. Available at: www.leagle.com/xmlResult.aspx?page=1&xmldoc=19921279418SE2d861_11268.xml&docbase=CSLWAR2-1986-2006&SizeDisp=7.
Washington v Glucksberg: Supreme Court of the United States: 521 US 702: – Certiorari to the United States Court of Appeals for the Ninth Circuit: 96–110. Argued: 8 January 1997 – Decided: 26 June1997. Available at: www.law.cornell.edu/supct/html/historics/USSC_CR_0521_0702_ZC4.html.

19

Resource Allocation Issues in Dementia

LEAH RAND AND MARK SHEEHAN

INTRODUCTION

DEMENTIA POSES AN unusual challenge for resource allocation since, in addition to being a widespread condition it raises distinct and difficult questions about how we assess the benefits of treatment and care. Any account of resource allocation for dementia will have to consider that it is a resource-consuming condition that affects many people. In Europe, there are ten million people with dementia with a prevalence of 6.2% (Wimo et al, 2013). In the UK alone, there are 800,000 people with dementia, and it is estimated that by 2021 there will be one million people living with dementia in the UK (Kane and Cook, 2013). The increasing prevalence of dementia will place new strains on the resources available for health care and social care and how these are distributed.

Dementia treatment currently relies on drugs, hospitalization, in-patient residential care and social care. Social care covers all types of support a person might need to live independently, such as care homes, short-break care, day services, home care and provision of meals (National Collaborating Centre for Mental Health, 2007). Dementia is the most expensive mental health condition with the highest cost per person, but a large amount of this cost is borne by informal carers, such as family and friends (McCrone et al, 2008). Dementia costs the British National Health Service (NHS) and related local services about £23 billion per year, which is projected to rise to £27 billion in 2018 and £34.8 billion by 2026 (Kane and Cook, 2013; McCrone et al, 2008). In comparison, the annual NHS budget is about £108.9 billion in 2012/2013 for a population of 63.2 million people (The NHS in England, 2013). The direct costs of Alzheimer's disease alone are greater than the total costs for stroke, cancer and heart disease (NICE, 2006). Dementia care requires a large financial commitment, but it also requires a human commitment from carers. However, working in residential care tends to have a low status, so it is understaffed and may be led by people without the full range of professional qualifications (National Collaborating Centre for Mental Health, 2007). This points to a larger problem that dementia faces as a mental health problem: as a society, we are often uncomfortable facing mental health conditions and as a result, in addition to the difficulties of the close interactions between medical and social care that are necessary for treatment, it is easy for a condition like dementia to receive less attention than other medical conditions.

The resources available for health care are limited, so resource allocation is inevitable in any health care system. Health care costs keep rising with the discovery of new technologies, and since our societal expectations of medicine have grown it is not possible for the health care resources to meet the demand for them (Daniels and Sabin, 2008). A health care system without resource allocation, where individuals have to pay for their own treatment, excludes much of the population from access to health care and effectively rations it by distributing health care based on economic means or status. Instead, ethical principles, like need and equality, will suggest different ways of allocating health care.

In this chapter, we examine the principles that guide resource allocation decisions in health care and how those principles are adopted in the case of dementia. In the first part, we will discuss principles that are at play in resource allocation decisions—particularly the tension between cost-effectiveness and need. Then, we will look at how those two principles are specified in dementia. In the conclusion, we will suggest future routes for meeting the challenges of resources and allocation that dementia poses. Overall, two themes will guide the discussion. The first is the role of cost-effectiveness and how we ought to count the gains of dementia treatment since they do not easily fit into the usual models for measuring effectiveness. The second is to question whether the benefits to carers rather than to patients ought to be relevant to resource allocation.

ETHICAL PRINCIPLES OF RESOURCE ALLOCATION

In this section, we examine some of the main ethical principles that could provide practical reasons for allocation decisions, starting with general ethical considerations. We understand 'principle' to mean a prima facie consideration that will determine a range of ethical and practical distributions; it is not used to mean a rule that should be followed in every case.

The background condition constraining a health care system is that there is only a finite amount of resources. Distributive justice addresses this problem (Broome, 1988; 1990). The principles we will discuss could each be used to distribute resources.

It is important to observe that it is justice, rather than respect for autonomy, that is the relevant consideration for deciding how to allocate resources. Respect for autonomy is important in health care, but it is a mistake to think it has a place in resource allocation; allocation decisions are decisions made about how to distribute between autonomous individuals. This does not mean that patients should be coerced or their views treated as invalid. However, the purpose of resource allocation is to distribute a resource that is in limited supply and cannot satisfy the claims of the patients who have autonomously decided to use it.

The basic principle here that ought to guide allocations is formal justice (or 'formal fairness'). The principle of formal justice is that we ought to treat like cases alike, but it does not specify in which ways we should determine likeness or what the treatment of the cases should be. Formal justice is a content-neutral principle in that it tells us how to apply other principles (Daniels and Sabin, 2008; Lyons, 1985). It does not tell us the relevant respects in which people are equal or unequal, or alike and not alike. In order to make distinctions between people for the purposes of distributive justice, we will look at different principles for distribution and mainly two forms of equality that are in tension with each other: equality of outcome and equality of opportunity for health.

Cost

Cost matters, since it determines how much resource someone will need, and it could be used to determine the distributive principle. If cost (or the overall share of the budget) were ignored, resources would effectively be distributed on a first-come, first-served basis until they were exhausted. This looks to be an unjust system: there is nothing morally significant about falling ill or having been diagnosed earlier in the financial year and therefore able to receive treatment as compared with someone else who is diagnosed later in the year (Sheehan and Hope, 2012; Sheehan and Newdick, 2013). To use cost as a distributive principle, we could decide, for example, to fund only those treatments that are least expensive, so as to fund as many as possible. Alternatively, we could decide to fund only those that are most expensive, or decide on any trade-off between these two distributions based on cost.

Relatedly, any system will have to take into account opportunity cost. This is the idea that if money is spent on intervention A, it is not available to be spent on something else. The opportunity costs are the costs associated with opportunities for spending that are lost as a result of using money for intervention A. So, if A is funded it may mean not funding B, C, or D. This is a particularly salient issue in the setting of a fixed budget when there will be direct trade-offs made between ways to spend money.

Appealing to cost alone ignores what we have spent resources on and in particular what we have gained from the spent resources. In order to make a more nuanced distribution, we next look to effectiveness.

Effectiveness

Effectiveness is the extent, probability and duration of the effect of any treatment. Effectiveness matters because it describes what effect is achieved by spending resources. A system of health care resource allocation should take effectiveness into account since the system's central aim is to affect the health of those it cares for. One implication is that resources should not be used for treatments that do not work. A distribution based solely on effectiveness would prioritize treatments from most to least effective. However, there may be reasons why we decide that a less effective treatment should be funded instead of a more effective one: it may be that the effective one is significantly more expensive (particularly in the light of the effectiveness gains) or it may be that the effective treatment addresses a less significant health care need than the less effective one.

Cost-Effectiveness

When we focus on equality of outcome we suggest that what counts as equal treatment is determined by those outcomes: if two treatments, A and B, have the same outcome, they ought to be funded to an equal extent, but if A has a better outcome compared with B, then it will be given priority over B.

Equality of outcome is perhaps most easily understood in terms of cost-effectiveness, which is the idea of maximizing the outcome per unit of resource. The option that is the best value for the resources—ie, highest level of effectiveness for the resources used—is the one that ought to be chosen. As a sole principle of distributive justice, cost-effectiveness claims that it is fair if the resources available are used to bring about the most overall benefit to the relevant population. An advantage of cost-effectiveness is that it is impartial between people and types of condition. If two peoples' treatments are equally cost-effective, we should fund them equally.[1] A disadvantage of cost-effectiveness is that it disregards patient needs.

Need

An alternative approach to distributive justice in health care is to consider people's needs and a principle of equal opportunity at health. The principle of equal opportunity at health is realized in using need as a distributive principle: if people with the same level of need are given the same resources, then they are given equal opportunities to achieve their best possible health state.

The three main problems with using need as the only principle of allocation are: (1) how to define and rank needs; (2) what to do when what is required to meet needs is greater than the resources available; and (3) how to respond to the likelihood that a large proportion of resources will be spent on marginally effective interventions for the most needy. With regard to the first issue, we can make some basic distinctions between needs. For example, a patient with end-stage renal failure has a greater need for dialysis than a patient with a healed burn scar has for cosmetic surgery although both patients will benefit (Scanlon, 1975; Lockwood, 1988). If needs are needs for something—we need F in order to G—all the work is being done in the way in which we assess the value and importance of that something, 'G'. One suggestion for how to discriminate and rank between needs is with reference to our capacity to flourish as human beings (Wiggins, 1998). This may be a good account of needs, but until we determine what it means to flourish as a human being, we cannot use it as a practical solution.

The second difficulty with need is the concern that the available resources will not be able to meet all the needs that we would be able to meet were resources not limited. We could allocate more resources to the more pressing needs, for example, funding coronary artery bypass surgeries instead of hip replacements. However, the problem is that once we have dealt with the most pressing needs, the 'lesser' needs may not have the resources necessary to meet them. It might be right not to

[1] There are various ways to measure cost-effectiveness in health care. One of the most prominent is the quality-adjusted life year (QALY). The QALY takes a healthy year of life expectancy to be worth 1, and a year of unhealthy life expectancy is worth less than 1, adjusted for health related quality of life (NICE, 2004; Williams, 1988). The idea of using QALYs is that health care activity that generates a positive number of QALYs is beneficial, and it is efficient when the cost per QALY is as low as possible. Fitting this back into equality of outcome, treatments with low costs per QALY would be prioritized over those with high costs per QALY.

fund lesser needs if we do not have sufficient resources for saving lives. If we can satisfactorily rank the needs, then we will be closer to satisfying the ethical claims of needs. The second problem leads us to the third problem, which is how we ought to rank interventions for pressing needs that are very expensive but have a low probability of extending life against other needs, like some end-stage cancer treatments against hip replacements. It seems that cost and effectiveness must both be taken into account alongside need in order to create a system in which health care is available to people other than the very sickest.

Tensions Between Principles

Choosing between distributions based on equality of outcome or of opportunity at health, realized as cost-effectiveness or need is, we suggest, the primary ethical tension in resource allocation. We can see this played out as the conflict between the obligation of the health system to provide care for the population as a whole and the obligation of the same system to care for each individual. The intuition that we have about what is just in particular cases shows that neither obligation can consistently be prioritized over the other. Indeed, individuals differ in the ways in which they would make these judgements; that is, about how they balance and judge the competing obligations.

Fair Process

Putting in place a fair process is the important step in enabling practical decision-making and allowing for the tension between principles to be resolved in a legitimate way. A fair process treats all people equally by enabling the full and equal consideration of reasons that are relevant to the allocation decision. In this approach, distributive justice can only be achieved using something like the 'accountability for reasonableness' process (Daniels and Sabin, 1997; 2008). In practice, 'accountability for reasonableness' provides a structure for decision-making, and to varying extents commissioning bodies in the UK have adopted it for their procedures (NICE, 2008). When following a fair procedure, like accountability for reasonableness, the system strives to be publicly accountable both in the decisions it makes and also, crucially, in the reasons for making the decisions.

An advantage of a fair process is that it governs the way in which decisions are made rather than deciding the content of decisions. Because the fair process does not proscribe substantive content, the resulting decisions can be based on each of the principles. As a result, the principles of cost-effectiveness and need can be appropriate, in addition to others in each case. In practice, decision-makers will have to direct part of their efforts towards the functioning and regulation of the process and the decision-making rather than the decisions themselves.

In the next section, we turn to the specific challenge that dementia presents for resource allocation. We assume that any decision-making follows a fair process. The tension between cost-effectiveness and need remains important and will continue to challenge how we decide to allocate resources.

RESOURCE ALLOCATION AND DEMENTIA: ETHICAL DILEMMAS

In this section, we consider the principles discussed above in the specific context of dementia and dementia treatment. The discussion will focus on cost-effectiveness and need. The normal measures for cost-effectiveness fail to accurately reflect the effects of dementia treatment or the need they meet. The main question we will raise and discuss is what should be counted among the costs and benefits of dementia care. How we answer the question could lead us to privilege dementia over other conditions.

Dementia is characterized by a progressive deterioration of cognitive function for which there is no curative treatment. The deterioration in cognition (thinking and reasoning) is also marked by a decline in the ability to carry out activities of daily life, such as bathing, dressing and using money, as well as behavioural and non-cognitive symptoms like aggression, depression, delusion and hallucination. In the later stages of the disease, physical and cognitive symptoms increase to include memory loss, fear, confusion, apathy, incontinence, unsettling behaviour and difficulty swallowing. As dementia progresses, treatments include complementary and alternative therapies, drugs to treat the mental symptoms, such as antidepressants and anti-psychotics, personal care and care in residential care homes (Alzheimer's Society, 2011b; NICE, 2011). For Alzheimer's disease and dementia with Lewy bodies there are also four drugs, three acetylcholinesterase (AChE) inhibitors and memantine, that improve the symptoms of dementia but do not stop its progression (NICE, 2011). Dementia is a long-term condition, and on average people live eight to ten years with it, though this varies with age at diagnosis (Alzheimer's Society, 2011b). The aim of treatment for dementia is to maximize the time people with dementia are autonomous and independent. In addition to pharmaceutical treatments, people with dementia require increasing assistance in daily functioning. Personal attention and interaction are very important and can improve the symptoms of dementia by decreasing aggressive or unsettling behaviour and calming the person with dementia (National Collaborating Centre for Mental Health, 2007). Treating dementia brings together medical care, social care and personal care, often delivered by informal carers who are family members or friends. A person with dementia has to use all three of these systems in order to receive the care and support they need.

Need

Dementia is a demanding condition to treat because it requires financial resources and many human hours of work. In addition to its resource requirements, dementia faces problems because of what seems to be a social discomfort around mental health problems and dementia. Society's reactions might often be described as a mix between not caring and feeling awkward about the mental decline of others. Residential care for people with dementia is understaffed because it is a job with low status and not enough training (National Collaborating Centre for Mental Health, 2007).

Need is also relevant when considering the carers of people with dementia. Among all carer groups, carers of people with dementia are some of the most vulnerable, and the ill health they experience, both mental and physical, is another health need arising from dementia (National Collaborating Centre for Mental Health, 2007; NICE, 2006). Being a carer is especially disruptive for young carers who often give up jobs and have to restructure their lives in order to care for someone with dementia, a parent for example.

The cognitive decline of dementia and its related symptoms are a health need that proper care can assuage to some extent. The deterioration of quality of life is the most pressing need for dementia sufferers given its effect on day-to-day life. If we were to adopt a needs-based principle for resource allocation, we would have to consider how to weigh dementia against other needs that we might consider more pressing or acute, such as coronary bypass surgery or appendectomies. The second part of need that we could take into account is the carer's need and how treatment of dementia reduces their burden. However, as we will discuss in the next section, if we count the carer's need, then we may discriminate against other conditions where carers do not play such a large role and are not counted.

Cost-Effectiveness

Dementia presents special challenges when we attempt to assess the cost-effectiveness of treatments. In the discussion of dementia and cost-effectiveness in the section below, we consider both carers' drug treatments and how the NHS funds them.

The drug treatments for Alzheimer's, AChE inhibitors and memantine (Ebixa), are not effective for all people with Alzheimer's. They improve cognitive symptoms, like motivation and memory, temporarily for 6–12 months. Memantine also improves behavioural symptoms (Alzheimer's Society, 2011a). Drug treatments for Alzheimer's disease produce temporary gains, which are weighed against their costs and side effects.

The usual way of measuring QALYs fails to capture the extent of gains made by treatment for Alzheimer's disease. Because the drugs do not prevent the progression of the disease, cure it or prolong life, they do not fit into the usual rubric of effectiveness. The QALY measure has difficulty reflecting the full value of the benefits to quality of life patients and carers gain.

The National Institute for Health and Care Excellence (NICE)[2] advises the NHS on particular decisions about allocations at a system-wide level. NICE is guided by values, such as need, but also gives considerable weight to economic considerations in the form of cost-effectiveness. NICE cites average monthly prices for AChE inhibitors that range from £72.00 to £97.00, and memantine's average monthly price is £71.00 (NICE, 2011). However, the assessment group for NICE cites QALYs for AChE inhibitors of between £55,000 and £58,000 per QALY for mild Alzheimer's, £31,550 per QALY for moderate Alzheimer's and above £53,000 per QALY for memantine for severe Alzheimer's (PenTAG, 2010). The difference between the monthly price and QALY reflects adjustments made for patient disability, the effectiveness of the treatment and effect on quality of life among other weightings.

[2] Known as the National Institute for Health and Clinical Excellence, prior to 1 April 2013.

NICE recommends that the AChE inhibitors are cost-effective for mild to moderate dementia and that memantine is cost-effective for severe dementia and patients with moderate dementia who are intolerant of AChE inhibitors (NICE, 2011). In reaching this decision, the NICE advisory committee considered that the drugs delay the time to institutionalization, which has a mean monthly cost of £2941, and that the drugs are more cost-effective than best supportive care (NICE, 2011). There are several cost elements at play and increasing support in one area of care can have beneficial repercussions in another area of care.

The carers of people with dementia play an important role and take on many of the burdens, including financial, of dementia care. If the NHS were to decrease their funding of the drugs, the costs would be incurred elsewhere (Clegg et al, 2000). It is estimated that there are 670,000 informal carers, mostly family members, acting as the primary caregivers for people with dementia, and that they save the state £8 billion each year in care costs (Kane and Cook, 2013). One conservative estimate is that informal care alone accounts for 40% of the cost of dementia (National Collaborating Centre for Mental Health, 2007). However, informal carers suffer from high rates of psychological problems including stress, guilt and depression, and these effects also increase costs for the NHS (National Collaborating Centre for Mental Health, 2007; PenTAG, 2010). Informal carers also often have to give up work in order to care for the person with dementia, resulting in lost economic productivity especially since many informal carers are young. When calculating the costs of dementia and QALYs, the carers could be a considerable influence on the results.

In its most recent guidelines, NICE took into account this range of issues surrounding treatment for dementia. NICE extended the guidance on Alzheimer's drugs to include people with mild and moderate dementia. When the NICE advisory committee considered whether AChE inhibitors or memantine ought to be funded, it accepted evidence from patient experts about quality of life improvements, like prolonged independence, stable mood and maintained social interest and ability, in order to understand the benefits not reflected in the QALY. The committee also took into account the trade-off in cost between drugs and institutionalization and to some—unquantified—extent the benefit to the carer's quality of life (NICE, 2011).

The problem, here, of how to account for the gains from dementia treatment and the failure of the QALY to reflect them, requires that we reconsider the scope of what counts as a health care benefit. Dementia care is provided across a range of services including health care, social care and informal carers. Treating dementia with drugs, which is a cost to the health care system, results in benefits in social care and for informal carers. There is a problem with simply counting up all the benefits and ways of spending resources to produce benefit, for example increasing the number of carers or creating a better environment to reduce behavioural symptoms (Waller, Masterson and Finn, 2013). When deciding how to allocate a budget for health care, how should the benefits of dementia care in different sectors be weighed up against their costs to the health care budget? The problem with including all the benefits outside the health care system is that we may unfairly privilege dementia over other conditions where the costs and benefits are contained within the health care system. This might be redressed if we begin to consider the same broader conception of benefits for other treatments. The danger with taking this route—aside from the added difficulties in assessing these broader social benefits—is that the health care system begins to focus less on health care and more on the general social benefits to be achieved through various kinds of health provisions.

Related to this problem is the problem of how we count carers and what weight they should be given in determining the benefits of dementia care. Considering carers recognizes their need, but in doing so the calculation of cost-effectiveness is changed in a way that may unfairly disadvantage other conditions. Since drug treatments for dementia benefit carers, should their improved quality of life be counted in the QALY? Carers of people with dementia take on a great burden that the health care system is thereby relieved of, and it is possible that we might think the health care system has a duty to them as carers rather than as patients and users of it. Though carers provide the majority of care, it is hard to assess and measure their contribution and losses. The biggest concern with counting the benefits to the carers is that these will double the effect of dementia care (assuming one carer per person). Counting carers could be discriminatory against other conditions where there are no carers or the quality of life of carers is not counted in assessing the benefits of a treatment.

CONCLUSION

This chapter has provided a general outline of the principles and processes for resource allocation and their application in the case of dementia. We have focused on the tension that arises between considering the need that people with dementia and those who care for them have and the cost-effectiveness of providing resources to them. The picture of care that has emerged is one where the costs are not easily traceable since they are mixed between medical care, system supported social care and informal care. Since April 2013, social care has come under the purview of NICE, so we hope that by joining health and care under the same body, a better balance will be struck between them. Making sense of the trade-offs between health and social care is important for understanding the true costs of dementia, and the development of better measures would assist in resource allocation decision-making.

Moving forward, clear pathways of care for people with dementia will ensure consistency across a health care system and help move it towards being as fair as possible. Care pathways and guidelines need to be flexible to adapt to new technologies and treatments, constraints on resources and revisions. Recognizing the value of social care and increasing its status will also help ensure that there are the skilled people available to provide much of the care that is needed.

A particular problem that must continue to be examined and monitored in practice is what effect counting carers has on distributions. While NICE has considered the benefits to them in formulating its guidance on dementia drugs, close scrutiny will reveal whether this practice and giving more weight to carers is or becomes discriminatory.

Throughout these considerations, a publicly accountable fair process will remain important as new evidence is gathered and the care pathways are revised. By following a fair process in decision-making, the fairest result for patients and carers can be achieved and balanced against the other demands on the health care and social care systems. Articulating and clarifying the principles and their practical application will help the health care system deliver decisions that are just and meet future constraints. Dementia is one case that shows how examining the problems in allocation and making improvements to the procedure will help the system to be flexible enough to handle future trends.

REFERENCES

Alzheimer's Society (2011a) *Drug treatments for Alzheimer's disease*. Available at: www.alzheimers.org.uk/site/scripts/download_info.php?fileID=1760.

—— (2011b) *The progression of Alzheimer's disease and other dementias*. Available at: www.alzheimers.org.uk/site/scripts/download_info.php?downloadID=1110.

Broome, J (1988) 'Good, fairness, and QALYs' in JM Bell and S Mendus (eds), *Philosophy and Medical Welfare* (Cambridge, Cambridge University Press).

—— (1990) 'Fairness' 91 *Proceedings of the Aristotelian Society* 87–102.

Clegg, A et al (2000) *Clinical and Cost Effectiveness of Donepezil, Rivastigmine and Galantamine for Alzheimer's Disease* (National Institute for Clinical Excellence). Available at: www.nice.org.uk/nicemedia/live/11413/32138/32138.pdf.

Daniels, N and Sabin, J (1997) 'Limits to health care: fair procedures, democratic deliberation, and the legitimacy problem for insurers' 26(4) *Philosophy & Public Affairs* 303–50.

—— (2008) *Setting Limits Fairly: Learning to Share Resources for Health*, 2nd edn (Oxford, Oxford University Press).

Kane, M and Cook, L (2013) *Dementia 2013: The hidden voice of loneliness* (Alzeheimer's Society). Available at: www.alzheimers.org.uk/site/scripts/download_info.php?fileID=1677.

Lockwood, M (1988) 'Quality of Life and resource allocation' in JM Bell and S Mendus (eds), *Philosophy and Medical Welfare* (Cambridge, Cambridge University Press).

Lyons, D (1985) 'Formal Justice and Judicial Precedent' 38 *Vanderbilt Law Review* 495–512.

McCrone, P et al (2008) *Paying the Price* (London, The King's Fund). Available at: www.kingsfund.org.uk/publications/paying-price.

National Collaborating Centre for Mental Health (2007) *Dementia. A NICE–SCIE Guideline on supporting people with dementia and their carers in health and social care*, rev edn (London, British Psychological Society and the Royal College of Psychiatrists). Available at: www.nice.org.uk/nicemedia/live/10998/30320/30320.pdf.

National Institute for Health and Clinical Excellence (NICE) (2004) *Guide to the Methods of Technology Appraisal*. Available at: www.nice.org.uk/niceMedia/pdf/TAP_Methods.pdf.

—— (2006) *Costing report: Implementing NICE SCIE guidance in England*. Available at: www.nice.org.uk/nicemedia/live/10998/30324/30324.pdf.

—— (2008) *Social Value Judgements: Principles for the Development of NICE guidance*, 2nd edn. Available at: www.nice.org.uk/media/C18/30/SVJ2PUBLICATION2008.pdf.

—— (2011) *NICE technology appraisal guidance 217: Donepezil, galantamine, rivastigmine and memantine for the treatment of Alzheimer's disease*. Available at: www.nice.org.uk/nicemedia/live/13419/53619/53619.pdf.

Peninsula Technology Assessment Group (PenTAG), University of Exeter (2010) *The effectiveness and cost-effectiveness of donepezil, galantamine, rivastigmine and memantine for the treatment of Alzheimer's disease (review of TA111): a systematic review and economic model*.

Scanlon, TM (1975) 'Preference and urgency' 72 *Journal of Philosophy* 655–69.

Sheehan, M and Hope, T (2012) 'Allocating Health Care Resources in the UK: Putting Principles into Practice' in R Rhodes, MP Battin and A Silvers (eds), *Medicine and Social Justice: Essays on the Distribution of Health Care*, 2nd edn (New York, Oxford University Press).

Sheehan, M and Newdick, C (2013) 'Commissioning ethically and legally: the more things change, the more they stay the same' 63(614) *British Journal of General Practice* 496–97. doi:10.3399/bjgp13X671812.

The NHS in England (2013) *The NHS in England*. Available at: www.nhs.uk/NHSEngland/thenhs/about/Pages/overview.aspx.

Waller, S, Masterson, A and Finn, H (2013) *Improving the patient experience: Developing Supportive Design for People with Dementia* (London, The King's Fund). Available at: www.kingsfund.org.uk/publications/developing-supportive-design-people-dementia.

Wiggins, D (1998) *Needs, Values, Truth*, 3rd edn (Oxford, Clarendon Press).

Williams, A (1988) 'Ethics and Efficiency in the Provision of Health Care' 23 *Royal Institute of Philosophy Lecture Series* 111–26. doi:10.1017/S0957042X00003904.

Wimo, A et al (2013) 'The GERAS Study: A Prospective Observational Study of Costs and Resource Use in Community Dwellers with Alzheimer's Disease in Three European Countries – Study Design and Baseline Findings' 36(2)*Journal of Alzheimer's Disease* 385–99. doi:10.3233/JAD-122392.

20

Sexuality in Dementia

JULIAN C HUGHES, AILEEN BEATTY AND JEANETTE SHIPPEN

INTRODUCTION

SEXUALITY IS OFTEN the subject of mirth. Part of the humour around sex and sexuality stems from its status as a taboo. Humour often arises in the context of incongruity. Sexuality is an ever-present aspect of our lives, but one which, for the most part, we keep private. When sex does, then, intrude into our public lives it can make us laugh; but, by the same token, it can be shocking. Sexual humour is readily apparent in connection with age, but so too is the tendency to be shocked when the private becomes public. If we move into the arena of dementia, sexuality becomes more shocking than funny: there is a tendency for it not to be tolerated.

In a nursing home for people with dementia, staff were often physically assaulted. They took this in their stride: it came with the job; it was usually no worse than scratches, slaps and squeezes of the arm during personal interventions with residents. But when Jim started squeezing the breasts of the nursing assistants and tried to put his hand on a nurse's crotch, which was accompanied by an overtly lewd suggestion, it was difficult for the home to tolerate the behaviour. It was also difficult for the staff even to describe, because it was too rude to speak of it.

Attitudes, both to physical and sexual aggression in care homes, are changing. In order fully to understand ethical issues around sexuality and dementia we would need to understand attitudes to sexuality in older people generally. We should also be clear about our own views around sexuality at any age, in particular in connection with older age and dementia. Even the short account of Jim's apparent sexual disinhibition in the nursing home helps to highlight a key feature, which is that these issues tend to elicit quite different reactions or intuitions, reflecting different values.

The approach to ethical issues around sexuality in dementia which we wish to commend is that of values-based practice. We shall start by setting the scene in the context of the literature around sexuality in older age generally and in connection with dementia in particular. We shall then give an (albeit adumbrative) account of values-based practice and show how it might be used to approach fictitious cases, which are nonetheless based on reality.

SETTING THE SCENE

It is by now well established that sexual activity does not cease with ageing (Bouman, 2008; Stratford and Warner, 2010). It is true that the proportion of people engaged in regular sexual activity decreases with age; and it may become increasingly appropriate to talk of 'intimacy' rather than 'sexuality' (Benbow and Beeston, 2012). Nonetheless, there is a cohort effect because sexual activity has seemingly become more important to older people over time. In a Swedish study, which included questions on sexual intercourse in 70-year-olds, in 1971–72 the study found that 52% of married men and 38% of married women had had intercourse in the previous year; but by 2000–01the figures were 68% and 56% (Beckman et al, 2008).

Sexuality in care homes has been called 'the last taboo' in a publication that provides a rich source of advice and discussion of attitudes, policies and approaches (ILC-UK, 2011). Holmes et al (1997), in a postal survey of care homes in the US, found generally positive attitudes amongst staff towards sexuality and sexual expression in residents. Respondents to the survey agreed that more staff training was required. Nevertheless, attitudes and values amongst staff and residents and their families can act as barriers to sexuality and intimacy in older people, especially in nursing and residential homes. With reference to residents of care homes, Rheaume and Mitty comment:

> Some of the barriers to sexuality and intimacy in this age group are likely to be rooted in notions of body image, beliefs, and values regarding sexual expression (eg, outside marriage), and lack of knowledge about or, especially for women, comfort with their sexuality (Rheaume and Mitty, 2008: 344).

One such barrier in care homes is the loss of privacy—loss of physical privacy and loss of privacy of information—both of which undermine the person's autonomy (Rheaume and Mitty, 2008: 345).

Undoubtedly, another barrier to a fulfilled sexual life in old age is illness. A variety of age-related changes can affect our expressions of sexuality, from loss of libido, to erectile dysfunction, to any form of pain, as well as depression and a host of chronic diseases (Rheaume and Mitty, 2008: 346–47; Bouman, 2008: 696). Dementia itself can affect sexuality. It often reduces sexual interest; but concerns are usually raised when sexual activity is heightened. This sort of hypersexuality may have an organic basis: for instance, it may reflect the disinhibiting effects of frontotemporal dementias. So-called 'sexual disinhibition' is said to have a prevalence rate of anywhere between 2% and 25% (Stratford and Warner, 2010: 261). It is the management of such disinhibited sexual behaviour that leads to most ethical discussion.

SEXUALITY IN DEMENTIA AND ETHICAL ISSUES

Pace the rather positive attitudes found in Holmes et al (1997), staff in institutions for older people with dementia in Israel admitted to 'difficulties, confusion, embarrassment and helplessness' when they encountered erotic sexual situations involving patients (Ehrenfeld et al, 1997). The same team reported that 'Behaviour at the level of eroticism aroused anger and objections. Staff reactions were particularly strong: rejection, disgust and anger' (Ehrenfeld, et al, 1999). The central ethical dilemma for staff was the conflict between the need to protect and maintain the dignity of their patients and 'the patients' desire to fulfil their sexual needs' (Ehrenfeld et al, 1997).

The study team used case histories to try to define the problems, to reflect on the beliefs of staff and to choose a desirable course of action.

There are a number of specific ethical issues that arise in connection with dementia and sexuality. We shall briefly mention just three. First, tensions often arise in connection with families. If, in a care home, a sexual liaison has formed and one or other of the people involved is still married, but has either forgotten this fact or is misidentifying the person in the home as his or her spouse, it can be difficult for staff to know whether or how to tell the family of what is occurring. Although many families can be supportive and accepting, some may object even if the spouse has died. A new relationship may be seen as disrespectful to the memory of the deceased parent; or, if the relationship were to involve another resident who was still married, it might be considered out of keeping with the parent's previously held beliefs about the sanctity of marriage. A variety of views can be found depending on the gender, marital status and relationship involved.

Bauer et al (2013) found that families, on the whole, were supportive of kissing, touching, hand-holding and hugging amongst people with dementia, but reacted less favourably to sexual intercourse. The families tended to think that they needed to know what was going on, partly so that they could offer some sort of protection if necessary. As the authors commented, 'There is a fine line, however, between needing to *know* what's going on and needing to *control* what's going on, particularly when it is couched as being in the resident's "best interests"' (Bauer et al, 2013: 9).

Second, it is increasingly recognized that there are particular issues in connection with gay and lesbian carers of people with dementia. Lesbian, gay, bisexual and transgender (LGBT) carers can meet a variety of reactions from acceptance to a disregard of their particular needs. Lesbian, gay and bisexual carers may have to accept that the dementia in their partner will lead to their sexual orientation being revealed in ways over which they have little control (Price, 2010). In an intolerant environment it can become even more difficult for any form of sexual expression to be revealed (Johnson et al, 2005). In a recent UK report, one care home manager described how, when staff found a female resident who was felt to prefer women to men trying to touch another women, this 'either provoked complete outrage or extreme amusement amongst the staff' (ILC-UK, 2011). Any form of discrimination is, of course, an ethical matter; but, for the LGBT community, discrimination in connection with their specific sexuality is superadded to the negative attitudes in relation to sexuality, older people and dementia in general (Peate, 2011).

Third, there is what Benbow and Beeston (2012) have called the 'elephants in the room': capacity and consent. The overwhelming concern here is that sexual intercourse without consent is rape. For our purposes, however, it is of note that so much of the literature on sexuality in institutionalized older people is concerned with the principle of autonomy and, therefore, with issues of consent and capacity (Mahieu and Gastmans, 2012). Of course, other issues also appear in the literature, such as the importance of privacy. But Mahieu and Gastmans found that arguments related to principles, not just respect for autonomy, but also the principles of beneficence, non-maleficence and justice, 'seem to play a prominent role in ethically evaluating the sexual behaviour of institutionalized elderly' (Mahieu and Gastmans, 2012: 353). They went on to comment that: 'Complex situations caused by having dementia seem to warrant different ethical concepts such as care and dignity' (2012: 353). We shall return to their arguments later.

In their discussion of capacity and consent, Tarzia et al (2012) suggest that risks are inherent to any relationship and the person with dementia should not be protected from risks in a manner that is essentially paternalistic and undermining of the person's standing as someone in need of and able to benefit from intimacy and happiness. Thus:

> A person-centred approach ... would take at face value the assumption that residents with dementia should have the freedom and indeed have the right to enjoy sexual expression, and from there, examine strategies and guidelines that would support resident autonomy and manage risk (Tarzia et al, 2012: 612).

They argue that the onus should not be on people with dementia to 'prove' they have capacity to decide on sexual relationships, but on professionals to prove 'incontrovertibly' that they do not (Tarzia et al, 2012: 611). They went on to suggest:

> The only justification for interfering in a sexual relationship between two residents who appear happy ... is if one or both residents are not aware of the identity of the other person and believes the person to be someone else (2012: 612).

This argument is predicated on the worry that in an emotional moment old recollections might be stirred up which would induce shame at the recognition that their sexual behaviour was with someone who was essentially a stranger. This obviously is a concern, but it raises further problems. First, how do we know (incontrovertibly) that the relationship is based on misidentification? If a man with dementia refers to a woman as his wife when she is not, it could be that he is simply signalling, within the bounds of his language impairment, the closeness of their relationship. Second, it may seem harsh to intervene just in case a harm arises when we have no real idea how often this happens. Third, the suggestion (which comes from Mahieu and Gastmans, 2012) that the other person in the relationship will be 'a total stranger' will not always be true, if for instance they have been living together in the care home for some while. The realization that this is not the person you thought it was may be shocking, but it may not be a catastrophe!

Having made these points, it is not our intention to argue that the justification given by Tarzia et al (2012) for interfering is totally without foundation. Rather, our aim is simply to point to the difficulty in this area of setting down any hard and fast rules in anticipation of considering individual cases. The importance of casuistry—looking at things case by case—is, therefore, something we wish to emphasize (Murray, 1994).

CHEMICAL CASTRATION

The ethics of treatment seems worthy of specific mention. The management approach we would encourage for any form of behaviour in dementia which might be found challenging would be psychosocial and person-centred (Hughes and Beatty, 2013). This does not preclude the possibility of pharmacological management. We do not intend to review the management of sexually disinhibited behaviour, which is very adequately covered elsewhere (Series and Dégano, 2005; Bouman, 2008; Stratford and Warner, 2010; Tucker, 2010; Benbow and Beeston, 2012). Various different types of medication have been used with varying degrees of success: there is no definitive drug treatment. Nevertheless, case reports on the use of both hormonal and non-hormonal anti-androgens, usually as a last resort, have often shown improvement of 'inappropriate sexual behaviors' (Tucker, 2010). This type of treatment is sometimes referred to as 'chemical castration' (Stratford and Warner, 2010).

This is an emotive term, for the idea of castration is repugnant. But why does it seem repugnant and might there be ethical grounds to justify such hormonal manipulation? After all, we might use an antidepressant with similar intentions (knowing that the selective serotonin re-uptake inhibitors can cause sexual dysfunction) and we do not feel so squeamish about manipulating chemicals in the body to try to change other behaviours.

An answer comes from the parallel case of someone with mania. If a person were just happy, we would not even entertain the diagnosis of mania and no medical intervention is justified. So, too, there would seem to be no grounds on which to intervene when a person is enjoying a perfectly normal and harmless relationship, even a sexual one. Where the person is in real danger of harm to self or others and the use of alternative interventions is either unlikely to be, or has not been, effective, then more draconian measures (for example, injecting antipsychotic medication in the case of mania and using hormonal manipulation in the case of someone with dementia and sexual disinhibition) become justifiable. The inclination neither to interfere with nor to stop (to castrate) a normal biological function (the sexual urge) is strong. But just as certain levels of exuberance become unacceptable, so too with sexual relations; and just as the manic woman may not recognize the risks she faces, so too the man with dementia who is sexually disinhibited.

In these sorts of cases it will always be a matter of judgement as to whether the more extreme type of behaviour has yet been reached. Even the distinction between normal and abnormal involves a value judgement. Hence, the real focus has to be on the evaluative nature of the judgements being made.

VALUES-BASED PRACTICE

Over the last ten years there has been growing interest in values-based practice (VBP) (Woodbridge and Fulford, 2004), which can be regarded as complementary to evidenced-based practice. Hence, just as the facts of each case must be carefully considered, so too do values; and the first step is to recognize that values are critically relevant. Thus, values-based practice has been defined as 'the theory and practice of effective healthcare decision-making for situations in which legitimately different (and hence potentially conflicting) value perspectives are in play' (Fulford, 2004: 205).

Recognizing facts and values can also be regarded as a necessary feature of clinical judgement: making judgements without knowledge of the facts is foolhardy; but even when the facts are known an evaluative judgement is usually required. Such judgements will often involve a framework of shared but nonetheless conflicting values, which will have to be worked out and balanced in a given context (Fulford et al, 2012). This process requires mutual respect for different values, even if some values, such as racism and ageism, are excluded. Fulford (2004) sets out ten key elements for the process of VBP, as shown in Table 1.

Table 1: The 10 key elements of values-based practice (adapted from Fulford, 2004)

Element	Description
1. The 'two-feet' principle	All clinical decisions require attention to both facts and values
2. The 'squeaky wheel' principle	We tend to notice diverse or conflicting values because they are problematic
3. The 'science-driven' principle	Progress in science increases complexity and choices and makes values more numerous and apparent
4. The 'patient-perspective' principle	For any given decision, the perspective of the patient should be centre-stage
5. The 'multi-perspective' principle	Where values conflict, the right outcome will generally follow from the right process which supports the legitimately held views of others
6. The 'values-blindness' principle	Awareness of values is encouraged by careful attention to language
7. The 'values-myopia' principle	We tend not to see the values of others, or to think they are the same as our own
8. The 'space of values' principle	Ethical reasoning explores differences in value judgements, recognizing their legitimacy
9. The 'how's it done' principle	Good communication, which will include skills in negotiation and compromise, must form part of the process of reaching decisions
10. The 'who decides' principle	The right decision is made in partnerships involving all concerned

In the cases that follow, we shall demonstrate how elements of VBP might be used in a way that supports decision-making in complex situations. In fact, elements of this process featured in the discussion of difficult cases described in Ehrenfeld et al (1997); and attention to values also featured in the ILC-UK (2011) document. The case-by-case approach (casuistry) is one that encourages reflection on the important values that emerge in any particular case and was commended in the Nuffield Council's report on ethical issues in dementia (Nuffield Council on Bioethics, 2009).

CASES

Vignette 1: Patrick and Faye

Patrick is 79 years old and lives in a nursing home. He has moderately severe Alzheimer's disease. He has been devotedly married to Maggie for 51 years. They have rarely been apart. Although Patrick still recognizes Maggie as family, he is not sure about the nature of their relationship and often refers to her as his sister or mother.

Having moved into the home about six months ago, Patrick was initially reluctant to leave his room and was frequently irritable. However, he met another resident called Faye and they appeared instantly to be mutually attracted. They would stroll hand in hand, enjoying each other's company.

Faye's husband was recently admitted to hospital, which was one of the reasons for her admission to care. He had been her main carer. They, too, had been happily married for many years. Faye does not always remember that he is in hospital, sometimes forgets she is married, but still occasionally asks for him.

Staff in the home have been increasingly concerned about the closeness of the relationship. They feel Faye is very vulnerable, as she has been found in a bedroom with Patrick who had his hand down her blouse. She did not appear to be distressed by the incident at all. Staff do not, however, perceive Patrick as vulnerable; instead he is portrayed as the perpetrator.

Prior to this, Faye's family had asked the home staff to keep them apart as they were spending too much time together. They didn't feel it was appropriate, especially with their father being in hospital. They believed that Faye would be horrified if she had a better understanding of her situation. The current incident has left them angry and upset. They demand that Patrick is moved away from their mother. Patrick's wife, Maggie, was less upset—although still saddened and preoccupied—by their 'friendship' as she felt he was coming out of his room to socialize more and appeared generally more settled and content.

Discussion

It is quite clear in this case that there are both facts and values to be considered (element 1 from Table 1, hereafter VBP1). Awareness of values involves awareness of different values. In discussing this case the professionals must seek to encourage all those involved to express their views in order to understand the different values that underpin them. Key here, however, are the values of the protagonists (VBP4). Patrick and Faye can no longer give a coherent account of their prior values, which would undoubtedly have been offended by any form of adultery, but they are still valuers (Jaworska, 1999). As such, we should pay attention to their current actions, which demonstrate what is of value to them. Mutual understanding between all those involved must develop, which will require careful navigation and negotiation on the part of the professionals (VBP9). But they might start by exploring how it could be that Patrick and Faye still cherish their previous values despite their current relationship (VBP8). The value judgements of both families are legitimate, but they can perhaps be brought closer by a greater understanding of dementia and the effects it is having (for example, in terms of misidentification). There are undoubtedly issues of dignity and safety, so a plan needs to be established to maintain some boundaries. But it may be agreed, after appropriate meetings and consultation (VBP10), that this will not involve separating Patrick and Faye.

Vignette 2: Jack and Martin

Jack has been admitted to a long-stay ward because of moderate dementia and behavioural disturbance. He is 88 years old and has lived with Martin for many years. Martin visits Jack regularly and describes himself as his best friend. Staff suspect that Jack and Martin are partners, although Martin is conservative, from a generation less open about such matters. On account of his dementia, Jack is quite openly affectionate and sometimes overtly disinhibited in a sexual manner towards Martin, who can appear embarrassed by this. Martin occasionally reprimands Jack for his behaviour and can appear irritated, although staff sense this is mainly caused by embarrassment. Staff have observed them holding hands when they sit alone in the conservatory and try to give them privacy at this time. Some staff, however, are uncomfortable with the situation and have aired concerns about what they should do if Martin wants to take Jack to his room or out of the ward.

Discussion

We tend to notice conflicting values when they are problematic (VBP2). The possibility of latent homophobia might be an issue here: would staff feel similarly uncomfortable if the couple were heterosexual? The fact that staff give Jack and Martin privacy in the conservatory shows they recognize this as important, as something of value (VBP6). This needs to be squared with the objection to greater privacy (VBP8). All of this should be discussed in the multidisciplinary team and it will need to be acknowledged that the relationship of Jack and Martin may simply be more difficult for some staff than for others because of different values systems (VBP7). But through a transparent process of discussion (VBP5) and by recognizing the saliency of the values of Jack and Martin (VBP4) it should be possible to agree an appropriate plan amongst the team (VBP9).

Vignette 3: Hussain and Mahbubah

Mahbubah has been in an NHS assessment ward for three months. She has a diagnosis of young-onset Alzheimer's disease, which is now quite advanced. Prior to her admission, Mahbubah was cared for at home by her husband Hussain. As her condition deteriorated Hussain felt he could no longer cope and reluctantly agreed to the admission with a view to assessment for permanent care. Hussain visits Mahbubah every day. Although there are days when she doesn't seem to recognize him—times when she can rail against him—she generally seems most content when he is with her. The couple have been in a long and happy marriage and Hussain remains very loving towards Mahbubah: kissing, hugging and holding her hand. Recently, Hussain has asked to take Mahbubah home for overnight leave. Staff are reasonably sure that this is to facilitate intimate sexual activity but they are concerned that because of her advanced dementia Mahbubah no longer recognizes the nature of her relationship with Hussain and she lacks capacity to consent to sexual contact. Staff raised their concerns at a multidisciplinary team care review meeting and suggested that Hussain's request for overnight leave should be refused.

Discussion

It seems important in this case not just to recognize facts and values (VBP1), but to establish them. One fact that has not been questioned is that Hussain loves Mahbubah. But the reasons for Hussain's wish to take his wife home have not been established—staff are only 'reasonably sure'; so it may be important to go further than this and discuss concerns overtly with Hussain (VBP6). In doing so, staff need to be open to the values of Hussain (VBP7), but might also wish to explore with him the differences in terms of the value judgements being made (VBP8). There will, after all, be practical matters to be considered, but it may be that in part the possibility of going home is made more realistic by advances in assistive technologies (VBP3). Nevertheless, the perspective of Mahbubah must be considered: whether, for instance, the change of environment will do her good or be confusing and upsetting (VBP4).

In moving forwards, staff might also wish to consider the values that underpin their own concerns about lack of capacity (VBP8). In their review of the literature, Mahieu and Gastmans commented:

> By referring to the concept of informed consent ..., the choice to engage in a sexual relationship is made within a framework of personal capabilities. Within this framework, mental and physical conditions are attached to human lovingness and sexual intimacy. Because elderly people suffering from mental and physical deterioration do not meet these pre-conditions, their need and desire for sexual fulfilment and human intimacy is being denied (2012: 355).

They are critical of an approach, seen in the literature, which reduces discussion of ethical issues around sexuality to standard principles (autonomy, beneficence, non-maleficence and justice) as if these issues can be discussed in a standardized way. They comment: 'The danger of standardization, however, is that ethicists will tend not to reflect on the fundamental values that underlie these basic principles' (Mahieu and Gastmans, 2012: 355). Their own inclination, therefore, is to enrich the discussion by using notions from the ethics of care, 'empathy, responsibility, respect, and vulnerability might provide us with a new orientation for dealing with the sexual needs and desires of institutionalized residents with dementia' (Mahieu and Gastmans, 2012: 355). The underlying values attached to the undisputed love of Hussain for Mahbubah need to be brought into play rather than allowing a prohibition on overnight leave to hold sway on the basis of concerns about legal concepts, which may have limited applicability in the context of love and intimacy.

Vignette 4: Hugo

Hugo is 74 years old and has lived in a care home for the past two years. He has a probable diagnosis of frontotemporal dementia. Hugo's family report that the condition has affected his personality—he has become increasingly inconsiderate and obstinate—but his memory and functioning abilities remain reasonably intact. On two occasions staff have found Hugo masturbating in the bedroom of a more vulnerable female resident whose outer clothing he had removed. It is also a daily occurrence that staff find Hugo masturbating in his own room. Whilst acknowledging that in the privacy of his bedroom he is at liberty to do as he wishes, staff get upset that he continues to masturbate after they have entered his room, having always knocked and been invited in by him beforehand. The incidents involving the vulnerable female resident raised a safeguarding alert and in preparation for the strategy meeting Hugo was approached by the home's deputy manager to discuss the safeguarding process and the potential outcomes, which include the possibility that he will be moved to an all-male environment. During the discussion Hugo appeared totally unconcerned about his behaviour, but he was worried about the possibility of having to move. He said he was happy living in the home.

At the strategy meeting it was agreed to implement a number of measures to try and contain Hugo's behaviour and minimize the risks posed to others. However, it was also agreed that should these measures fail the only option would be to move Hugo to an all-male environment. Towards the end of the meeting Hugo was invited in to hear the outcomes. At this point Hugo revealed he could only achieve complete sexual satisfaction if he masturbated into women's underwear. He said that not having the garments readily accessible meant he needed to masturbate more often to try and achieve satisfaction. He also gave this as the reason for removing the outer clothing of the female resident.

Discussion

Again, in this case, there may well be some conflicting values at play (VBP2). There may, after all, be slightly different views about masturbation under any circumstances. Different perspectives will need to be acknowledged and accepted (VBP5). Perhaps some staff will regard Hugo as no worse than a young boy, whilst others will see him as a 'dirty old man' (VBP6 and VBP7). The possibility that he could be given medication to decrease his libido should also be considered (VBP3), along with the underpinning values of such an approach. In the end, part of the concern was lessened by the knowledge that Hugo enjoyed women's underwear (VBP4), which provided a controlled strategy for the home to adopt. By providing him with the means to his sexual satisfaction, they were more able to set other boundaries to his behaviour (VBP9 and VBP10).

CONCLUSION

Ethical issues around sexuality in the context of dementia are difficult because of the conflicting values that emerge. Our own attitudes towards sexuality and to sexual relations are often at issue and, given that these are frequently intensely private, confronting conflicting values in an overt manner presents problems. Nevertheless, it seems important that sex and sexuality should be regarded and dealt with at the level of underpinning values given the centrality of these issues to our lives. Little is said here or in the literature about ethical issues in connection with sexual relationships in the privacy of the person's own home. The literature focuses on institutional care. This should be a cause of concern for two possible reasons: either it suggests that there is the possiblity of unethical practices in the privacy of people's own homes on a scale that is undetermined; or it suggests that sexual intimacy only becomes routinely ethically problematic once a person with dementia is institutionalized. The latter seems to us more likely and more disturbing. It suggests, for instance, that deep friendships are problematic in care homes, despite the benefits of social interaction for people with dementia (Sabat and Lee, 2011). A values-based practice approach is a way to bring into the open the values that support or inhibit intimacy. Sexual intimacy may be unwanted or inappropriate for a variety of reasons, but it shoud not be regarded as routinely problematic when it otherwise provides the possibility of authentic human flourishing.

REFERENCES

Bauer, M et al (2013) "'We need to know what's going on": Views of family members toward the sexual expression of people with dementia in residential aged care' *Dementia*, published online 13 March 2013. doi: 10.1177/1471301213479785. Available at: http://dem.sagepub.com/content/early/2013/03/13/1471301213479785.

Beckman, N et al (2008) 'Secular trends in self reported sexual activity and satisfaction in Swedish 70 year olds: cross sectional survey of four populations', 1971–2001' 337 *British Medical Journal* a279. doi: dx.doi.org/10.1136/bmj.a279.

Benbow, SM and Beeston, D (2012) 'Sexuality, aging, and dementia' 24(7) International Psychogeriatrics 1026–33. doi: 10.1017/S1041610212000257.

Bouman, WP (2008) 'Sexuality in later life' in R Jacoby et al (eds), *Oxford Textbook of Old Age Psychiatry* (Oxford, Oxford University Press).

Ehrenfeld, M et al (1997) 'Ethical dilemmas concerning sexuality of elderly patients suffering from dementia' 3 *International Journal of Nursing Practice* 255–59. doi: 10.1111/j.1440-172X.1997.tb00110.x.

—— (1999) 'Sexuality among institutionalized elderly patients with dementia' 6(2) *Nursing Ethics* 144–49. doi: 10.1177/096973309900600207.

Fulford, KWM (2004) 'Ten principles of values-based medicine' in J Radden (ed), *The Philosophy of Psychiatry: A Companion* (New York, Oxford University Press).

Fulford, KWM, Peile, E and Carroll, H (2012) *Essential Values-Based Practice: Clinical Stories Linking Science with People* (Cambridge, Cambridge University Press).

Holmes, D et al (1997) 'Sexual expression and dementia' 12(7) *International Journal of Geriatric Psychiatry* 695–701. doi:10.1002/(SICI)1099-1166(199707)12:7<695::AID-GPS546>3.0.CO;2-C.

Hughes, JC and Beatty, A (2013) 'Understanding the person with dementia: a clinicophilosophical case discussion' 19 *Advances in Psychiatric Treatment* 337–43. doi: 10.1192/apt.bp.112.011098.

International Longevity Centre-UK (ILC-UK) (2011) *The Last Taboo: A Guide to Dementia, Sexuality, Intimacy and Sexual Behaviour in Care Homes* (London, ILC-UK). Available at: www.ilcuk.org.uk.

Jaworska, A (1999) 'Respecting the margins of agency: Alzheimer's patients and the capacity to value' 28(2) *Philosophy and Public Affairs* 105–38. doi: 10.1111/j.1088-4963.1999.00105.x.

Johnson, MJ et al (2005) 'Gay and lesbian perceptions of discrimination in retirement care facilities' 49(2) *Journal of Homosexuality* 83–102. doi: 10.1300/J082v49n02_04.

Mahieu, L and Gastmans, C (2012) 'Sexuality in institutionalized elderly persons: a systematic review of argument-based ethics literature' 24(3) *International Psychogeriatrics* 346–57. doi: 10.1017/S1041610211001542.

Murray, TH (1994) 'Medical ethics, moral philosophy and moral tradition' in KWM Fulford, GR Gillett and JM Soskice (eds), *Medicine and Moral Reasoning* (Cambridge, Cambridge University Press).

Nuffield Council on Bioethics (2009) *Dementia: ethical issues* (London, Nuffield Council on Bioethics). Available at: www.nuffieldbioethics.org/dementia.

Peate, I (2011) 'Sexuality, non-traditional relationships and mental health in older people' in MT Abou-Saleh, CLE Katona and A Kumar (eds), *Principles and Practice of Geriatric Psychiatry*, 3rd edn (Chichester, Wiley-Blackwell).

Price, E (2010) 'Coming out to care: gay and lesbian carers' experiences of dementia services' 18(2) *Health and Social Care in the Community* 160–68. doi: 10.1111/j.1365-2524.2009.00884.x.

Rheaume, C and Mitty, E (2008) 'Sexuality and intimacy in older adults' 29(5) *Geriatric Nursing* 342–49.

Sabat, SR and Lee, JM (2011) 'Relatedness among people diagnosed with dementia: social cognition and the possibility of friendship' 11(3) *Dementia* 315–27. doi: 10.117/1471301211421069.

Series, H and Dégano, P (2005) 'Hypersexuality in dementia' 11 *Advances in Psychiatric Treatment* 424–31. doi: 10.1192/apt.11.6.424Ŭ.

Stratford, J and Warner, J (2010) 'Sexuality and dementia' in D Ames, D Burns and J O'Brien (eds), *Dementia*, 4th edn (London, Arnold Health Sciences).

Tarzia, L, Fetherstonhaugh, D and Bauer, M (2012) 'Dementia, sexuality and consent in residential aged care facilities' 38 *Journal of Medical Ethics* 609–13. doi:10.1136/medethics-2011-100453.

Tucker, I (2010) 'Management of inappropriate sexual behaviors in dementia: a literature review' 22(5) *International Psychogeriatrics* 683–92. doi: 10.1017/S104161020000189.

Woodbridge, K and Fulford, KWM (2004) *Whose Values? A Workbook for Values-Based Practice in Mental Health Care* (London, Sainsbury Centre for Mental Health).

21

The Use of New Technologies in Managing Dementia Patients

JULIAN C HUGHES

INTRODUCTION

OVER-ENTHUSIASM, SO FAR as assistive technology in connection with dementia goes, is prone to be greeted by a Luddite reflex. There is an intuitive inclination towards scepticism. Yet there is a strong intuition in the other direction too, since it would be prudent to grasp the promise of technology. As Aristotle might have said, the good life navigates between the excesses of enthusiasm and scepticism: 'virtue is a mean'!

Nonetheless, this should not be taken to suggest that the answer is simple, as if it were just a matter of using technology in a proportionate way. In dementia, where our standing *as selves* is under threat (Sabat, 2001), the issues run deep. The egregious belief is that our very selves can be bolstered or preserved by technology. Thomas Carlyle (1795–1881), writing of the 'Genius of Mechanism', not long after the Luddite disturbances, was similarly struck by the depth of the issue:

> These things, which we state lightly enough here, are yet of deep import, and indicate a mighty change in our whole manner of existence. For the same habit regulates not our modes of action alone, but our modes of thought and feeling. Men are grown mechanical in head and in heart, as well as in hand. They have lost faith in individual endeavor' (Carlyle, 2010).

A recent film, 'Robot and Frank', tells the tale of a man with mild dementia whose son buys him a robot to care for him. Frank turns out to have been a jewellery thief. He hits upon the idea of enlisting the robot's help in further escapades. The sceptic can plausibly view this as being most unlikely. The enthusiast can retort that, nevertheless, the idea that a robot might help someone to pursue old hobbies is not so far-fetched. But the film has a deeper piquancy, namely that it is also about loneliness, isolation, ageing and the inability of modern families or society to compensate. The robot occupies a personal vacuum—one affecting the head and heart—it doesn't just do technical things. The problem is the lack of individual human endeavour—and the robot fills the gap.

Assistive technology has been defined by the Royal Commission on Long Term Care (1999) as 'any device or system that allows an individual to perform a task that they would otherwise be unable to do, or increases the ease and safety with which the task can be performed' (quoted by Siotia and Simpson, 2008). Thus, it includes a huge array of equipment, from feeding cups to walking frames, even though our attention in this chapter will primarily be on the newer electronic technologies which are perceived to raise ethical issues of a particular nature.

I shall start by outlining an ethical framework to consider the issues around the use of new technologies to help with dementia. I shall then look at some of the literature in this area. The ethical framework points to deeper concerns to do with personhood, with which I shall conclude.

THE NUFFIELD COUNCIL'S REPORT

The Nuffield Council report, *Dementia: Ethical Issues*, specifically considers assistive technologies, but it starts by setting out an ethical framework (Nuffield Council on Bioethics (hereafter 'NCoB'), 2009: 20–33). The framework has six components.

The first component is a case-based, or casuistic, approach to ethical dilemmas and involves 'identifying the relevant facts; interpreting and applying appropriate ethical values to those facts; and comparing the situation with other similar situations to find ethically relevant similarities or differences' (NCoB, 2009: 21, Box 2.1). The second and third components emphasize that, although it is a harmful brain disease, with the right support it is possible to live well with dementia. The fourth component considers the importance of promoting the interests of both the person with dementia and of his or her carers. People with dementia will have interests in autonomy and in well-being. But this component gives these notions an important spin. First, it says that autonomy is better thought of as 'relational' autonomy. So we have to consider the person in the context of, for instance, family carers. In addition, well-being—especially for someone in the severer stages of the disease—is often a matter of moment-to-moment well-being. What counts is what is happening now. The fifth component of the framework encourages us to consider dementia from the societal perspective of solidarity, the idea being that we are all in this together. The final component, to which I shall return, highlights the notion of personhood.

The report pinpointed the potential for dilemmas by quoting from two of the respondents to the consultation that helped to inform it. The first said of assistive technology that 'It makes for a better, fuller life all round for carer and sufferer', whereas the second said, 'How would a confused person react to a disembodied voice from the wall asking why they are opening the door?!' (NCoB, 2009: 98). In order to deal with the ethical issues around assistive technology, the report drew upon its ethical framework. How technology is used determines its rightness or wrongness. In other words, in casuistic mode, we must look at the particularities of the case; but we must also consider the person's interests in both autonomy and well-being.

> A monitoring device which alerts care workers that a person with dementia is moving out of a safe area of a care home may trigger very different responses. On the one hand, the person might be firmly taken back to their chair and encouraged to keep still. On the other, the care worker might respond by seeking to find out what the person wishes to do, and doing their best to assist them in achieving it. In the first case, the device may be keeping a person safe, but only by prompting restrictive action. In the second case, the device has not only kept the person safe but has also prompted support to enable the person to carry out their

> autonomous wishes. Even in this second, 'benign' scenario, it should be emphasised that the technological device is not a substitute for good care: rather it has the potential to enhance the care which the care worker is able to offer (NCoB, 2009: 99, paragraph 6.9).

With this ethical framework in mind, I shall now turn to consider some of the relevant literature.

THE LITERATURE

Cash (2003) provided a useful overview of the research around different types of assistive technology. Smart homes, for instance, incorporate sensors and alarms that would deal with a variety of different circumstances, from gas being left on, to the use of medicines and so on. Telecare enables monitoring from a distance and will increasingly allow the possibility of interaction between carers and people with dementia. At the end of the paper there are two significant ethical claims. First, Cash states that, 'In an ethical sense technology is neutral' (2003: 318). Second, she says that the central issue is informed consent.

Now, of course, the first claim is mundanely true: the sensor itself is neither good nor bad. This seems irrelevant given that the question is never about the device itself, but about its use. Second, it is true that informed consent is an important issue. It may not be the main issue, however, which is perhaps the concern Carlyle highlighted about the loss of human 'individual endeavor' (Carlyle, 2010).

Topo (2009) suggested that assistive technology is helpful, but in relation to ethics only emphasized safety and carer well-being. In Robinson et al (2009) a number of people with dementia voiced concerns about the risk of stigma and the feeling of a loss of liberty. For instance, one woman with dementia said 'Because it makes you feel like your freedom is taken away from you, and if somebody sees you have a card or something, they think well, I'm stupid you know' (Robinson et al, 2009: 497). Bjørneby et al (2004) reflected on the ethical issues that arose in the course of an international project (ENABLE), which used various technological means to empower and support the person with dementia (Bjørneby et al, 1999). To a large extent they were concerned with research ethics and they stuck to well-known principles of medical ethics. Respect for autonomy mostly involved considerations around consent. Beneficence involved monitoring the trial closely in case the devices being used had any undesired effects. Under the heading of justice, the researchers considered the right of people with dementia to have access to assistive technologies.

The same principles have been used in a paper looking at the ethical issues around assistive technology and telecare in connection with intellectual disabilities (Perry et al, 2009). Although some of the issues are different, for instance because of the tendency to use small group homes for people with intellectual disabilities, many are the same. These authors drew from the notion of autonomy concerns about information-giving (albeit mainly in connection with research), the possibility of coercion (because the device may be more valued by the carer than by the person wearing or using it) and the right to privacy. The clear intention of these technologies is to do good (beneficence) and to avoid harm (non-maleficence), but in considering these principles the authors highlighted the issues of stigma (which might be increased), risk (which might be decreased) and social contact (which might be enhanced). The principle of justice encourages discussion of resources and the worry that assistive technology is being used to reduce costs associated with care provided by human contact.

Zwijsen et al (2011) provide the most thorough review of the relevant ethics literature to date. They found 46 papers specifically looking at ethical issues in connection with assistive technology and older people living in the community. They made the point that ethical reflection in the literature seemed to be lagging behind technical developments. From the literature, they developed three central themes and eight sub-themes as shown in Table 21.1.

They regarded the notion of 'obtrusiveness' as problematic, because it seemed to lump together a number of ethical concerns around how noticeable or prominent (physically or psychologically) a device might be and could involve various ethical values such as privacy, stigma and affordability. This stresses the importance of assessment against the individual's needs. One of their recommendations is that a risk–benefit analysis must be performed to establish that assistive technology is warranted.

In their discussion, Zwijsen et al (2011) acknowledge that some authors see assistive technology as being the least restrictive method of safeguarding people. But they go on to point out that just because frail older people accept this technology as an 'adaptive preference' it does not mean this is an 'informed preference', which would depend on other realistic options having been presented and considered. Finally, they challenge the idea that the notion of autonomy, developed to describe the political rights of robust citizens exercising self-rule, is being used appropriately in connection with frail, dependent, older people. This would take us back to the idea, commended for similar reasons by the Nuffield Council's (2009) report, of 'relational' autonomy.

If the principles of beneficence and non-maleficence are subsumed by the notion of safety and the principle of justice by the idea of an individual approach and affordability, Table 21.1 sets out the main ethical issues which arise in connection

Table 21.1: Ethical themes and sub-themes arising from the literature on assistive technology from Zwijsen et al (2011)

Central theme	Sub-theme
The personal living environment	Privacy
	Autonomy
	Obtrusiveness
The outside world	Stigma
	Human contact
Design and application of the device	Individual approach
	Affordability
	Safety

with assistive technology and dementia. In the sections that follow we shall see how these themes and issues play out in connection with some particular types of technology.

Wandering and Tracking

Even if in general the ethics literature has not kept pace with the advances in technology, devices purporting to deal with wandering received some ethical attention even when the devices were in their infancy (McShane et al, 1994). The concerns have mainly focused on the tension between safety and liberty, with some arguing that a slight loss of liberty is a price worth paying for the sake of safety and that concerns about privacy are only relevant if the person is trying to hide (McShane et al, 1994). Nevertheless, it can still be argued that the libertarian flag should be kept flying for the sake of the individual, even if there is evidence that electronic tagging might improve quality of life (Hughes and Louw, 2002). These tensions were demonstrated in a survey which showed that 79% of those who strongly agreed with the statement that electronic tagging would mean less worry for carers were themselves carers; whereas those who disagreed or strongly disagreed with this view were, in 75% of cases, psychiatric nurses (Hughes et al, 2008). This takes us back to the framework of the Nuffield Council on Bioethics (2009). Clearly the interests of family carers must be given considerable weight because it is not just the autonomy of the person with dementia that is an issue. There is the stress and anxiety associated with people with dementia becoming lost. A focus on well-being brings in both the person's safety and her moment-to-moment enjoyment, which might stem from the freedom to 'wander'.

The very use of the term 'wandering' in connection with dementia, however, itself raises issues. It may be taken to suggest that the person's walking is *without* purpose. But, in fact, it has been increasingly recognized that people with dementia may have different purposes in mind when they 'wander'. It may be to find a person or some place, but it may simply be for exercise. It may represent a perfectly rational response to other events. So there has to be a good deal of balancing between the real well-being of the person with dementia with the justifiable concerns and wishes of those who love and care for them.

The tensions involved in these issues were revealed in a project looking at the management of wandering in people with dementia, where one family carer said,

> I think one of the main dilemmas about caring for people with dementia is always bringing up the safety aspects and yet giving them some sort of freedom ... walking might be the only thing they can do independently when they have lost nearly everything else (Robinson et al, 2007).

In the same project a person with dementia said, 'Sometimes we just go out ... haven't any idea where I am going ... just enjoy the fresh air' and someone else with dementia said, 'I want to feel as if I've got a bit of independence and while I can I just go out'. These quotes illustrate the importance of looking at individuals. Clearly, the person with more severe dementia who becomes lost may well be at risk. But people with mild dementia may be at no particularly increased risk. It would be an unethical infringement of liberty to prevent people from getting out. This argues in favour of a case-by-case assessment of risks and benefits in order to balance safety and the person's human rights.

Landau and Werner (2012) have made a number of recommendations for the ethical use of Global Positioning Systems (GPS) to track people with dementia. They suggest:

1. That it is crucial to maintain a balance between the needs of the person with dementia for protection and safety and the need for the person to have autonomy and privacy.
2. That decisions about the use of GPS should be made jointly between the person with dementia and the family carers.
3. If possible, the person with dementia should give informed consent and should certainly not be coerced.
4. It may be that advance care plans, using attorneys or proxy decisions, would be useful, especially if based on the prior attitudes and values of the person with dementia.
5. The current best interests of the person with dementia, as well as the interests of family carers must be taken into consideration.
6. The views of professional carers must also be taken into account.
7. That appropriate advance care planning for end-of-life decisions takes place, which might include the use of GPS tracking.
8. That any tracking devices used should be light-weight, small and comfortable.

Telecare and Electronic Surveillance

Although ethical issues appear early in the literature on wandering in dementia, elsewhere this is not the case. Many studies make little mention of any concern about ethical issues. Boekhorst et al (2013) compared surveillance technology with physical restraint. They noted the presupposition that surveillance technology would give the person with dementia greater freedom of movement. But surveillance technology may only help those who are less dependent and freer to move themselves. Although this paper does not specifically comment on ethical issues, it reinforces the point that we must look at *actual* benefit in particular cases.

In Smith et al (2007) there is, again, little overt comment about ethics; but nonetheless the paper demonstrates ways in which a two-way interactive video to monitor medication compliance in people with mild dementia might be helpful. Not only did the technology appear to reassure carers, but there also seemed to be some beneficial social aspects to the use of the technology. For instance, the son of one patient said that, 'She enjoyed it. She is a very social person, and she felt like she made a new friend' (Smith et al, 2007). Furthermore, there was a strong feeling that the intervention had prevented the need for a move into a higher level of care. Such results argue in favour of the technology being beneficent, doing some good, but do not offer a critique of the evaluative decisions that would have to be made around its use.

In a useful paper by Siotia and Simpson (2008) the ethical issues around the use of telecare are discussed in terms of the four principles of medical ethics. The authors suggest that respect for autonomy is played out in terms of privacy, ensuring confidentiality and obtaining informed consent. Regarding beneficence and non-maleficence, they suggest that technology should not cause the person to lose their skills and should not be 'an inappropriate substitute for human care'. Again, this is Carlyle's (2010) lack of human 'individual endeavor'. Justice suggests that there must be clear benefit, comprehensive assessment and regular monitoring.

The literature shows an increasing awareness of the issue of human contact. Engström et al (2009) interviewed 14 staff working with people with dementia before, during and after the installation of information and communication technology (ICT). They were able to show some adaptation amongst the staff to the technology, but the staff voiced ambivalence and concerns that the residents might 'miss out on human contact'. The discussions of the staff sometimes specifically focused on ethical issues around the quality or type of care that people would receive.

The most sustained and thoughtful discussion of telecare and surveillance is found in Sorell and Draper (2012). They consider the analogies that are sometimes made between the use of telecare and other means of surveillance in care settings and the use of surveillance by police in a possibly Orwellian fashion. Although telecare can sometimes invade privacy, so too can other forms of health care that do not involve technology. Rather than the spectre of a police state or Orwell's 'big brother' they suggest, on the contrary that,

> [t]he most pressing objections against telecare lie well away from the ethics of surveillance. They are to do with depersonalizing care, increasing the isolation of patients, and adopting technology in order to achieve cost-savings rather than health gains' (Sorell and Draper, 2012: 37).

Later they make the point that sensors used in assistive technology 'Are not a vehicle for all-out surveillance'. Their arguments are detailed and trenchant. For instance,

> [i]t is hard to see how telecare can promote independent living without keeping carers (informal or otherwise) out of the homes of users. And if carers are typically important members of an elderly person's social network, the conclusion that telecare is isolating is unavoidable' (Sorell and Draper, 2012: 42).

As an example of their detailed handling of issues, which is necessary if we are to consider the ethics of assistive technology on an individual basis, Sorell and Draper (2012) provide a nice discussion of enuresis sensors. Bed-wetting is clearly embarrassing. Some people might wish to deal with this problem privately and not have the fact of their bed-wetting broadcast to carers whose interventions may then draw attention to the problem. Privacy in institutional settings is, in any case, always under threat. So, enuresis sensors may be wrongly used in as much as they compromise a person's privacy. But, of course, there are also circumstances under which the swift and discrete changing of wet sheets would be an ethical necessity, for instance where the person was willing to receive help or where there was a risk of falling. So these issues need to be dealt with on an individual, case-by-case, basis and in detail, taking into account what the Nuffield Council (2009) called 'actual benefit' as well as the person's own views and concerns, both past and present.

Robots

It turns out that 'Robot and Frank' is not as far-fetched as some would suggest. There is increasing interest in and enthusiasm for the use of robots of various different types in dementia care. Some of these robots have human forms, but some are in the shape of animals. Martín et al (2013) used a humanoid robot to stimulate cognitive function. Patients showed a fairly positive attitude towards the use of the robot in connection with cognitive therapy, including music, activities and language sessions, as well as physiotherapy sessions. The suggestion, albeit in the absence of ethical deliberation, is clearly that robots may well be beneficial.

One of the most popular robots has been Paro, which looks like a baby seal and was designed in 1993 in Japan by Takanori Shibata. There have been various studies which have shown that interaction with Paro improves mood and communication and is also acceptable as well as having beneficial effects (for example, Moyle et al, 2013). Wada et al (2008) noted that some people seem to treat Paro as if it were a real seal, whereas others recognize it is not. Again, individual responses seem to be important in assessing whether the use of such a robot is a good or bad thing.

In general, people can see that robots might be useful for various aspects of care. The issue is to do with drawing lines around the reasonable and unreasonable. Broadbent et al (2012) found that there was considerable agreement amongst residents, managers and carers that robots would be useful in connection with falls, lifting and the like; but there was concern that carers might lose their jobs and personal care would be affected. On the other hand, some felt that if robots took away tasks from carers, this would allow staff more 'quality time with residents'. There was certainly the perception that some tasks were just 'too personal' to be taken over by robots; an example would be showering (Broadbent et al, 2012).

Misselhorn et al (2013) provide a nuanced discussion of the ethical issues around the use of robots, particularly thinking about the use of Paro. They suggest that what is required is 'a more differentiated ethical evaluation'. This would have to look at particular contexts in order to assess the good and bad points associated with using robotic technology. They note the studies that show that Paro can contribute to well-being in terms of improving a person's general affect. This is because Paro's eyes respond to people. It thus helps social interaction, but these authors note the accusation that the apparent reciprocity is only 'pretend'. They comment, however, that it would be possible to regard human–robot interactions as *just different* from human–human social interactions. Arguably, there is nothing ethically problematic in having human–robot interactions as long as those interactions do not replace human–human interactions. They argue that the robot could also encourage autonomy. The issue of dignity was slightly more complicated in that they felt that Paro could be regarded as disrespectful because 'it involves a kind of fraud'. The user is being 'tricked or fooled into ascribing emotional states to the robot seal which do not pertain to it' (Misselhorn et al, 2013). They go on to argue, however, that there is a type of imaginative perception which is perfectly acceptable and does not have to involve the false belief that the social robot really has feelings. They quote a resident saying, 'I don't care if he is real or not. I love him!' but then they move on to consider the case of someone with more severe cognitive impairment, unable to hold in mind both the imaginative and real perception of Paro, so that its use would be a type of fraud. But, argue Misselhorn et al (2013), in someone with severe dementia it could be argued that the issue of fraud becomes less ethically important. Even so, it could still be regarded as lacking in dignity if an old person is seen to be playing with a toy as if it were human.

In an interesting discussion Misselhorn et al (2013) go on to consider the possibility that the issue is not to do with a person's individual rational autonomy being violated:

> Rather, the violation of the dignity of humanity as a whole takes place on a symbolic level in the experience of the observer. Although playing with Paro may not violate the individual autonomy of the involved subject, it does—vicariously—offend the dignity of the whole species, because what is symbolically represented is the manipulation of an autonomous rational being (Misselhorn et al 2013: 130).

Despite this rather strong argument, they then set out some counter-arguments. First, they point out that this could lead to an overly moralistic perspective because there are numerous instances of irrational behaviour which could be said to 'violate the dignity of humanity'. Second, they note that this mere symbolic violation of humanity should not outweigh the affective well-being of the person with dementia. This calls to mind once more talk about moment-to-moment well-being, which may be more significant than anything merely symbolic. In a similar way, Misselhorn et al (2013) also discuss self-respect. Of course, for someone whose intelligence forms part of their self-identity, playing with a pretend animal may seem demeaning. But in advanced dementia it may be that this play instils moment-to-moment well-being, which can then be thought of as in itself a good. Overall, therefore, Misselhorn et al (2013) conclude that the ethical issue is really to do with how best to implement the use of this sort of new technology. They offer the 'important caveat' that 'social robots should not *replace* other forms of care and therapy' (Misselhorn et al, 2013: 131).

CONCLUSION: TECHNOLOGY AND PERSONHOOD

The Nuffield Council's report (2009) ended its discussion of assistive technology with this recommendation:

> Where a person with dementia lacks the capacity to decide for themselves whether to make use of a particular technology, the relative strength of a number of factors should be considered on a case-by-case basis, including:
>
> — the person's own views and concerns, past and present, for example about privacy;
> — the actual benefit which is likely to be achieved through using the device;
> — the extent to which carers' interests may be affected; and
> — the dangers of loss of human contact (NCoB, 2009: 100, paragraph 6.12).

These considerations do, indeed, seem to capture the main ethical concerns around the use of assistive technology in connection with dementia. In particular there is the tug-of-war between concerns about the person's autonomy and privacy on the one hand and, on the other, worries about safety and beneficence. This tension can be settled by taking an appropriately broad view of well-being. A judgement will be required. But it should be clear that if the infringement of privacy is so great as to outweigh the well-being associated with safety, it should be questioned; contrariwise, if respect for autonomy entails allowing the person to do themselves great harm, it should cause real concern.

If the notion of well-being is important as a unifying concept, the emphasis in the final component of the Nuffield Council's (2009) framework on personhood is fundamental. We need a rich notion of personhood, which situates the individual in his or her real multifarious context as an embodied agent with a unique narrative, a raft of personal values and singular concerns (Hughes, 2011). We cannot avoid, then, the difficulty that we shall have to make evaluative decisions in connection with the use of any particular type of assistive technology. There is still, however, the lurking worry from two hundred years ago about deficits in human 'individual endeavor' created by our propensity to look for technological solutions (Carlyle, 2010). In a study involving healthy couples over the age of 70 years in Sweden, the worry about relationships was real:

> Technical devices, regardless of the form in which they are used, are still only devices and cannot replace human relationships ... There was a fear that the person would be reduced to *a thing*, with relational coldness, detachment and instrumentality ... elders regard human encounters as fundamental in care (Harrefors et al, 2010: 1530–31).

Assistive technology of any sort has the potential to enhance our standing as persons; but it can also undermine personhood, especially if it detracts from the value associated with 'real human encounters, where embodied subjects meet in the raw' (Hughes, 2011: 208).

REFERENCES

Bjørneby, S, Topo, P and Holthe, T (eds), (1999) *TED. Technology, ethics and dementia. A guidebook on how to apply technology in dementia care* (Oslo, Norwegian Centre for Dementia Care, INFO-banken).

Bjørneby, S et al (2004) 'Ethical considerations in the ENABLE project' 3(3) *Dementia* 297–312. doi: 10.1177/1471301204045162.

Boekhorst, ST et al (2013) 'Quality of life of nursing-home residents with dementia subject to surveillance technology versus physical restraints: an explorative study' 28(4) *International Journal of Geriatric Psychiatry* 356–63. doi: 10.1002/gps.3831.

Broadbent, E et al (2012) 'Attitudes towards health-care robots in a retirement village' 31(2) *Australasian Journal on Ageing* 115–20.

Carlyle, T (2010) 'Signs of the times' in HD Traill (ed), *The Works of Thomas Carlyle. Volume 27: Critical and Miscellaneous Essays II* (Cambridge, Cambridge University Press). ('Signs of the times' first published in 1829 and also available from The Victorian Web at: www.victorianweb.org/authors/carlyle/signs1.html).

Cash, M (2003) 'Assistive technology and people with dementia' 13 *Reviews in Clinical Gerontology* 313–19. doi: 10.1017/S0959259804001169.

Engström, M et al (2009) 'Staff members' perceptions of a ICT support package in dementia care during the process of implementation' 17(7) *Journal of Nursing Management* 781–89.

Harrefors, C, Axelsson, K and Sävenstedt, S (2010) 'Using assistive technology services at differing levels of care: healthy older couples' perceptions' 66(7) *Journal of Advanced Nursing* 1523–32. doi: 10.1111/j.1365-2648.2010.05335.x.

Hughes, JC (2011) *Thinking Through Dementia* (Oxford, Oxford University Press).

Hughes, JC and Louw, SJ (2002) 'Electronic tagging of people with dementia who wander' 325(7369) *British Medical Journal* 847–48.

Hughes, JC et al (2008) 'Ethical issues and tagging in dementia: a survey' 3(1) *Journal of Ethics in Mental Health* 1–6.

Landau, R and Werner, S (2012) 'Ethical aspects of using GPS for tracking people with dementia: recommendations for practice' 24(3) *International Psychogeriatrics* 358–66. doi: 10.1017/S1041610211001888.

Martín, F et al (2013) 'Robots in therapy for dementia patients' 7(1) *Journal of Physical Agents* 48–55.

McShane, R, Hope, T and Wilkinson, J (1994) 'Tracking patients who wander: ethics and technology' 343(8908) *Lancet* 1274. doi: 10.1016/S0140-6736(94)92159-8.

Misselhorn, C, Pompe, U and Stapleton, M (2013) 'Ethical considerations regarding the use of social robots in the fourth age' 26(2) *Journal of Gerontopsychology and Geriatric Psychiatry* 121–33. doi: 10.1024/1662-9647/a000088.

Moyle, W et al (2013) 'Exploring the effect of companion robots on emotional expression in older adults with dementia: a pilot randomized controlled trial' 39(5) *Journal of Gerontological Nursing* 46–53. doi: 10.3928/00989134-20130313-03.

Nuffield Council on Bioethics (2009) *Dementia: Ethical Issues* (London, Nuffield Council on Bioethics). Available at: www.nuffieldbioethics.org/dementia.

Perry, J, Beyer, S and Holm, S (2009) 'Assistive technology, telecare and people with intellectual disabilities: ethical considerations' 35 *Journal of Medical Ethics* 81–86. doi: 10.1136/jme.2008.024588.

Robinson, L et al (2007) 'Balancing rights and risks: conflicting perspectives in the management of wandering in dementia' 9(4) *Health, Risk and Society* 389–406. doi: 10.1080/13698570701612774.

—— (2009) 'Keeping In Touch Everyday (KITE) project: developing assistive technologies with people with dementia and their carers to promote independence' 21(3) *International Psychogeriatrics* 494–502. doi: 10.1017/S1041610209008448.

Royal Commission on Long Term Care (1999) *With respect to old age: long term care – rights and responsibilities* (London, The Stationery Office).

Sabat, SR (2001) *The Experience of Alzheimer's Disease: Life through a Tangled Veil* (Oxford, Blackwell).

Siotia, R and Simpson, C (2008) 'Applying telecare in dementia: what psychiatrists need to know' 14 *Advances in Psychiatric Treatment* 382–88. doi:10.1192/apt.bp.107.003566.

Smith, GE et al (2007) 'Telehealth home monitoring of solitary persons with mild dementia' 22(1) *American Journal of Alzheimer's Disease & Other Dementias* 20–26. doi: 10.1177/1533317506295888.

Sorell, T and Draper, H (2012) 'Telecare, surveillance, and the welfare state' 12(9) *American Journal of Bioethics* 36–44.

Topo, P (2009) 'Technology studies to meet the needs of people with dementia and their caregivers: A literature review' 28(1) *Journal of Applied Gerontology* 5–37. doi: 10.1177/0733464808324019.

Wada, K et al (2008) 'Robot therapy for elders affected by dementia' 27(4) *IEEE Engineering in Medicine and Biology Magazine* 53–60. doi: 10.1109/MEMB.2008.919496.

Zwijsen, SA, Niemeijer, AR and Hertogh, CMP (2011) 'Ethics of using assistive technology in the care for community-dwelling elderly people: An overview of the literature' 15(4) *Aging & Mental Health* 419–27. doi: 10.1080/13607863.2010.543662.

22

Abuse, Safeguarding and Dementia

BRIDGET PENHALE

INTRODUCTION

IN THE LAST three decades, there has been a gradual increase in concern about the abuse and neglect of elderly people throughout the world. This concern has principally focused on abuse of elders by their caregivers in the domestic setting, although in recent decades there has been a much needed move towards consideration of abuse occurring within institutional settings (Stanley et al, 1999).

The phenomenon of elder abuse is not new (Stearns, 1986), but it has effectively only been since 1988 that the problem has really begun to be explored in the United Kingdom (UK) and responses developed to try and deal with such situations when they occur. However, in a number of respects—particularly on a more global level—it is still relatively early in the stages of problem identification and the development of positive action(s) to combat elder abuse and neglect is only just beginning to happen in a number of countries.

WHAT IS KNOWN ABOUT ELDER ABUSE?

The area of elder abuse and neglect is complex and wide-ranging and it is apparent that this is a difficult area to investigate adequately. For instance, comparative and developmental norms are much more difficult to establish for older people than with children who have been abused (Bennett et al, 1997). Additionally, there have been real difficulties in trying to determine a sound theoretical base to the phenomenon. This is in part because there has been a lack of agreement concerning a standard definition, but also because there have been assumptions that theories developed in relation to other forms of violence could be applied to elder abuse, without these being fully tested to ascertain the extent of fit. Furthermore, there have been significant problems in researching the topic (see, for example, Ogg and Munn-Giddings 1993; Penhale, 1999). As an example of this, many of the research studies that have been carried out consist of very small-scale samples and have tended to concentrate on cases already known to professionals.

Although English doctors identified the phenomenon in the mid-1970s, it was not until the mid-1980s that the issue was really picked up on in the UK. By contrast, in the United States (US) the issue was identified from the early 1970s and was researched from that time in attempts to clarify the problem and to provide solutions to it. Whilst research results from the US originally suggested that somewhere between 4% and 10% of the elderly population were either at risk of, or were experiencing, abuse from their caregivers (Gioglio and Blakemore, 1985; Pillemer and Finkelhor, 1988; US House of Representatives, 1981), more recent research indicates that somewhere in the region of between 4% and 5% of the US population of older people are potentially affected by abuse or neglect (Lachs and Pillemer, 1995) and this is accepted as the likely community prevalence rate. However, in the UK the community prevalence study that reported in 2007 indicated an overall prevalence rate of between 2.6% and 4%, depending on the breadth of definition that was used in relation to the research (O'Keeffe et al, 2007).

A Taboo Topic

Elder abuse is perhaps the most recent form of interpersonal violence to have been recognised as a problem in need of resolution. It is also, however, an area that has been hidden from public concern and has been predominantly regarded as a 'taboo topic'. Much of the abuse that happens takes place behind closed doors and is not open to public scrutiny, even within institutional settings (Bennett et al, 1997). Identifying what happens in private as a matter for public concern is not necessarily straightforward. This is at least partly due to the effects of societal ageism, and ambivalence about the care of older people. However, in addition, this is not a pleasant area to focus on, perhaps particularly as it challenges some of the deeply held beliefs that have been constructed over time within many societies, our own included. Examples of such beliefs are that society provides care for vulnerable individuals when this is needed, and that institutions are safe and nurturing places for older people to live in.

It has not been easy to challenge this taboo and such beliefs, nor to encourage people to discuss situations, let alone to disclose them. As an example, the sexual abuse of older women is an area that has proved extremely difficult to consider fully; this is related to the fact that it is difficult for many people to consider older people as sexual beings. Since the mid-1990s we have seen issues concerning violence towards older people being raised, and the silence produced by the taboo has been challenged and has diminished.

Definitions

Although there have been difficulties in relation to defining abuse, a number of definitions of elder abuse have emerged. Initially, the most usual types of abuse included in the majority of definitions were: physical, psychological, financial and neglect and financial abuse (this also refers to misappropriation and exploitation of an individual's property and possessions). To this list sexual abuse—as distinct from physical abuse—and in a number of definitions, social abuse have been added. Violations of rights may also appear in some definitions. Categories such as enforced isolation and deprivation of necessary items for daily living (warmth, food or other aspects, such as hearing aids or teeth) are often captured within constructions of neglect. And within institutions, abuse also encompasses situations that arise because of the regime or system that may exist in the unit as well as individual acts of mistreatment that happen. There may also be abusive situations that arise between a resident and a member of care staff, initiated by the older person as protagonist, so there may be dual directionality of abuse, or uni-directional abuse from resident towards staff member (McCreadie, 1996a).

It is also possible to list indicators of abuse, although it is difficult to diagnose mistreatment using these indicators in isolation. For instance, to link a bruise to mistreatment would require much more evidence than just the presence of an injury (in this case the bruising). In general terms, indicators should be used to identify the need for further exploration of the situation and a raised index of suspicion about the situation.

In addition to different types of abuse and different settings in which mistreatment may occur, we need to be aware that there may be a range of different participants involved in situations, including as witnesses to situations that occur, perhaps particularly in care settings. We should also recognise that a change of setting (from home to care setting, perhaps) does not necessarily mean that any pre-existing abuse will automatically cease; rather, this may mean that a different type of abuse then occurs or that the nature of the abuse becomes somewhat transformed. And differing responses and interventions to relieve or prevent the differing forms of abuse may be necessary, depending on the type of abuse that is happening as well as the setting in which the abuse occurs.

As stated elsewhere, it is possible that different groups may require different definitions to suit their own purposes (Penhale and Kingston, 1995). Researchers, politicians and practitioners may all need their own working definition of what constitutes abuse (Bennett and Kingston, 1993). Rather than lose time in searching for the ideal definition, covering all situations, it is probably better to accept and work with the different definitions that are currently in use or being developed. What seems to be important, however, is that those different definitions should be explicit and acknowledged as different, in order to avoid unhelpful assumptions being made that definitions are the same across different organisations and professional groups.

The Dynamics of Abuse

Reports of which type of abuse is most common vary across the surveys that have been undertaken. Early research from the US suggested that most instances of elder abuse are recurrent and part of a pattern, rather than a single incident (O'Malley et al, 1981). This tallies with the situation for other forms of violence. Other researchers in the US found that neglect is the most commonly found type (Valentine and Cash, 1986), whilst yet other research from the US suggested that psychological abuse (Block and Sinott, 1979) or physical abuse (Lau and Kosberg, 1979) are the most common. These early studies were, however, small-scale samples using different definitions and it is thus difficult to generalise from them. The UK prevalence study established that neglect and financial abuse appear to be the most frequently reported phenomena (O'Keeffe et al, 2007). In the Abuse and Violence against Older Women (AVOW) study, a prevalence study undertaken in five European countries, psychological abuse was the most frequently reported form of abuse, followed by financial abuse in all countries except Austria, where neglect was reported as occurring more often than financial abuse (Luoma et al, 2011).

In trying to determine the dynamics of elder abuse, much early research concentrated on attempts to establish a profile of victims of abuse. A number of studies, unfortunately, settled on the 'typical victim' as being a frail, dependent female of 75 years or older, who is impaired (either physically, mentally or both) and living with an adult child (O'Malley et al 1981; Lau and Kosberg 1979). The levels of dependency of the older person due to the degree of impairments experienced were viewed as being a source of extreme stress for the caregiver. In addition, it was considered that the degree of frailty of the victim put them at higher risk and increased their susceptibility to abuse.

However, such a view of elderly people as being dependent and vulnerable may add to widely held negative views and attitudes about older people that appear particularly prevalent throughout Western society. Indeed, one US commentator suggested that one of the reasons that elder abuse gained currency in the US (and the status of a legitimate social problem) was strongly connected with the fact that it accorded with the predominant focus of research on ageing in the US: a focus on problems associated with ageing (Baumann, 1989).

From further research in the US, it would appear that victims have different characteristics, depending on the type of abuse that is present. To develop this slightly, after considering the US research over the past two decades, Wolf (1989) suggested that older people who are subject to neglect appear to fit the characteristics of the stereotypical victim (as presented above), and are a source of extreme stress to their caregiver. However, those elders who are physically or psychologically abused are less likely to be physically dependent, but may have high levels of emotional difficulties. This group of older people may often live with their abuser who is dependent on them, especially financially. Elders who experience financial abuse would appear to be less dependent on physical care from relatives, and are more likely to be unmarried and live alone, although in comparatively isolated situations (Wolf, 1989, cited in Bennett and Kingston, 1993).

The research that followed some of the early US studies has tended to focus on the characteristics of abusers. These studies should be considered to be empirically more informative, because of their case control methodology. The assumptions outlined above about the stress of caring have generally not been upheld. Rather, individuals involved in abusive situations as abusers appear to be more likely (when compared with non-abusive caregivers) to have substance-misuse related problems and mental health/psychological problems (Pillemer, 1986; Bristowe and Collins, 1989; Wolf, 1986; Homer and Gilleard, 1990; Grafstrom et al, 1992; Anetzberger et al, 1994).

These particular patterns seem to be especially salient in those situations that involve physical or psychological abuse. There may also, within such situations, be a history of long-term difficulties in the relationship between the parties (Homer and Gilleard, 1990; Grafstrom et al, 1992). In the debate concerning dependency, some investigators have indicated that abusers may be very dependent on their victims. The principal areas of dependence that have been identified are finance (Hwalek et al, 1986) and also housing and transportation (Pillemer, 1986), as well as for emotional support. In relation to the characteristics of those who abuse, in general research tends to suggest that physical and financial abuse are linked with the dependency of the abuser on the abused, whilst psychological abuse and neglect may perhaps be more associated with caregiver stress.

Although in many countries, or even globally, there is still uncertainty regarding the rates of elder abuse either as an overall figure, or with regard to the various subtypes, it can be stated with some certainty that abuse within the domestic setting occurs across all ethnic and socioeconomic groups and in both urban and rural areas (Steuer and Austin, 1980).

Whilst both men and women are abused, the majority of victims of elder abuse are female, even when this is corrected for by the fact that there are more older women in the population. Rates of abuse and neglect do not appear to be higher for elders from ethnic minority populations than for white elders; nor are the rates higher for people over 75 years rather than those between 64 and 74 years of age. In the AVOW study, rates of abuse were higher for women aged between 60 and 69 years (Luoma et al, 2011). Additionally, specific religious, cultural and economic backgrounds of individual elders do not appear to be of particular significance within the development of abusive situations (Pillemer and Finkelhor, 1988).

Those who abuse may be male or female partners, adult children or other relatives. They may also be non-relatives, perhaps especially considering abuse within institutional settings. However, it seems that as with other forms of interpersonal violence—specifically situations of child abuse and violence towards younger women—the majority of those who abuse are men. Finkelhor (1983) proposed that when the probability of abuse is corrected for by the amount of time that the abuser spends with the victim, men are much more likely to be involved in abusive acts, particularly physically violent acts and those with more severe consequences.

Elder Abuse in Institutional Settings

Abuse in care settings and environments is also an important area in its own right that is difficult to resolve. Although the main focus of concern has been on abuse of older people by their caregivers and relatives in the domestic setting, the development of work in the area of elder abuse has seen a much needed move towards attention to abuse occurring within institutional settings (Glendenning and Kingston, 1999; Stanley et al, 1999). The abuse of older people seems to be part of the experience of many people in a number of different settings and such abuse appears to be both widespread and systematic (Glendenning, 1999a). As Glendenning (1999b) observed, there has been a lengthy tradition in the UK of scandals in institutional care relating to older people and, in the US, detailed research concerning this aspect stretches back to the early 1970s. However, many of these scandals tend to have been investigated and treated as separate enquiries into standards of care rather than as directly concerned with abuse. In addition, unfortunately, interest following such reports tends to be short-lived and rather superficial—including at a political level—although the recent report of the Francis Inquiry (2013) into conditions and care of patients at Mid-Staffordshire Hospital appears to have resulted in rather more sustained interest.

Abuse in institutions may take place at an individual level, between staff member and resident, relative to resident, or resident to resident, or it may take place at a structural level concerning the fabric of the establishment and how it is run. It appears that often in such circumstances, systems that are in place are largely for the benefit of the organisation and the needs of the workforce and management rather than for the older people who live in the setting. There are many reasons for institutional abuse, but the nature and impact of ageism and ambivalence concerning the care offered to older people in institutions may be important factors. Within care settings, systems for detection of abuse need to be in place, together with associated guidance and protocols for professionals to follow when abuse or neglect are identified. This should include some protection for 'whistleblowers', who are members of the staff workforce who report abuse within an institution. In recent years, some steps have been taken to strengthen the position of whistleblowers through the Public Interest Disclosure Act, 1998 and the extension of the NHS Whistleblowing helpline to include social care professionals from January 2012.

Licensing and registration of care homes (for residential and nursing home care) and regular inspections of care facilities by an independent organisation are likely to be valuable in preventing abuse from developing in such environments. It is also likely to assist in the development of a culture of openness in the setting (more links with local communities, open visiting times) and recognised systems for complaints to be made and acted upon. Processes for staff support and development, together with the maintenance of the morale of the workforce in order to prevent 'staff burn-out' may also assist. If there is very serious abuse or gross neglect of a substantial number of older residents in a care facility, then the closure of that establishment and transfer of residents may be necessary. In general terms, action to improve standards in the home and to prevent abuse and/or neglect from recurring may be the preferred approaches taken in order to minimise trauma and distress for the older residents of the home, which would be likely to result from the closure of a home.

Causation and Management of Elder Abuse

In terms of possible causative factors it appears unlikely that any one factor causes abuse, but rather that there is a complex interplay between a number of different factors. There are numerous possible reasons why abuse may occur. Factors such as the following may be associated with the development of abuse:

— A history of long-standing poor relationships within the family.
— The dependency of the abuser for finance, accommodation or emotional support from the victim.
— The abuser having a history of mental health or substance misuse problems.
— A pre-existing history and pattern of family violence (intergenerational transmission of violence).
— The social isolation of the victim and the abuser.

A number of additional risk factors have also been identified: the inability of a caregiver to care for the older person; other stressors within the family system (for example, unemployment, finance, overcrowding); and inadequate support systems for individuals may all be implicated.

Although it has been established that there does not appear to be any simple or linear causal relationship between caregiver stress and abuse, it is evident that some caregivers eventually find the task of caring for a frail, dependent older person (often a close relative) too stressful and difficult, and that abuse may follow. It is apparent that there are some caregivers who are not suited to providing care, either physically or psychologically, but who are expected to take on the caregiving role for their relative. Such individuals may also have their own difficulties in terms of relationships, personality or mental health related problems or issues relating to substance misuse, finance or accommodation. In the absence of sufficient support to enable caregivers to provide care, or if their own difficulties are not recognised and assistance offered when necessary, a difficult and stressful set of circumstances may deteriorate into an abusive situation.

The development of conceptual frameworks concerning the possible causes of family violence so far comprises a number of distinct theories drawn from the disciplines of sociology, psychology and feminism. Common themes which appear in all forms of family violence, albeit in differing degrees, include gender relations, power, stress, isolation and diminished resources (either emotional or physical, or both) with which to deal with such difficulties.

Awareness and recognition of the phenomena of abuse and neglect have been developing in a number of countries across the world in recent decades. However, the identification of abuse by professionals has, at times, proved problematic. In an increasing number of countries, policies, protocols and guidance have been developed to assist in this area. Such documents generally provide definitions of abuse, together with the types of abuse, information on possible indicators of abuse and neglect and detail concerning frameworks for responding to such situations (see Department of Health (DOH), 2000, for an example of this type of guidance). Education and training for professionals has also been developing, with a primary aim of preparing professionals to recognise abusive situations (as an initial part of the process) and providing knowledge and information concerning when and how to intervene (when situations have been identified or referred). In some countries, screening tools for the detection of abuse are in development (see World Health Organization (WHO), 2006 for detail relating to this area).

Interventions for abusive situations have also begun to be developed in a number of countries. Many such strategies have focused on the provision of practical support and assistance (DOH, 1993) in order to relieve stress from situations. The provision of respite care services, alternative accommodation away from the abusive environment either temporarily or permanently, counselling for individuals or the family unit, telephone helplines or even legal remedies to resolve situations are essential strategies to be developed further. In addition, systems of family therapy and/or relationship therapy to assist in the resolution of fractured relations between family members also need to be devised. Furthermore, a variety of interventions with those who abuse—such as treatment for substance abuse, or techniques to enhance anger management—are also likely to be needed (Penhale, 1993).

In order for interventions to be effective, it is important that the primary or main cause of the abuse is identified, so that interventions may be appropriately targeted.

For example, if the abuse is principally due to the stress of caregiving, then the provision of community services may be appropriate to support and relieve the situation. If however, the abuse results from some form of psychopathology of the abuser, then an approach that provides for treatment of the abuser, together with any necessary protection of the older person, is more likely to be indicated.

Good practice in elder abuse should include such elements as a distinction between initial referral (or report) and subsequent investigation; the careful coordination of the investigation and assessment; separate, sensitive and suitable arrangements for interviews. The use of case conferences in order to determine a protection or safety plan for an individual, where necessary, and as an effective means of promoting shared decision-making, is also suggested as indicative of good practice. Clearly a balance between the likely needs of the older person for support and protection and the possible need for sanction of the abuser is necessary here. The protection plan is likely to include attention to the needs of the elder for safety, support and service provision (or treatment), together with issues relating to the ongoing management of risk. Multidisciplinary working between the different agencies involved with individuals and with abusers, and involvement of the elder, is an essential part of the process here.

Having briefly outlined the more general aspects of elder abuse it seems appropriate to move to a consideration of elder abuse in relation to issues surrounding mental health of both the individual who experiences the abuse and those who abuse.

ELDER ABUSE AND MENTAL HEALTH

Dementia and Elder Abuse

The first area to consider is the situation of older people with cognitive impairments, in particular those with dementia. As seen earlier in this chapter, some of the early research in the area of elder abuse suggested that the dependence of the victim was a risk factor associated with abuse. Therefore, it is necessary to consider whether people with dementia and associated mental health difficulties are more likely to be victims of elder abuse than unimpaired individuals. However, it is perhaps not surprising, given the previous comments made about lack of research generally in elder abuse, to find that there is rather limited research into this situation and no definitive answer concerning this question. There may also be a related question as to whether an abusive situation, particularly one that is of a long-standing nature, may result in a mental health problem for the individual.

In the elder abuse literature there are a number of examples that include dementia as a component factor (Homer and Gilleard, 1990; Grafstrom et al, 1992; Social Services Inspectorate (SSI), 1992). Although there have been few prevalence studies relating to this area, there have been several studies which have begun to explore the extent of the relationship between dementia and abuse and it is worth reviewing these, albeit briefly. Two UK based articles have suggested that rates of abuse among older people with mental health problems, in particular those relating to dementia, are higher than in the general population of older people (Wilson, 1994; Cooney and Howard, 1995). The first of these studies looked at levels of elder abuse among older people using a psychogeriatric service, but living in the community. Although this was a survey of staff of the service and did not just consider dementia, the findings are of some relevance in this context (Wilson, 1994). The second article consists of a review of existing knowledge (at that point) concerning elder abuse and dementia (Cooney and Howard, 1995). Several of the studies reviewed by these researchers will be outlined in the following sections.

The first such study from the US to be considered is that by Coyne and colleagues who sent out questionnaires to caregivers who had contacted a free dementia helpline (Coyne et al, 1993). Of the one-third of caregivers, mostly women, who responded (342), some 33.1% (92 caregivers) stated that their relative with dementia had physically abused them. The survey also found that 11.9% of respondents (33 caregivers) indicated that they had physically abused the person they cared for through a number of different acts (biting, kicking and hitting, for example).

In this study, there appeared to be a relationship between those caregivers who had been abusive towards their relatives and those who had themselves been the subject of abuse by the relatives that they were caring for. There also seemed to be a strong relationship between high physical and psychological demands of caregiving and physical abuse. Just over a quarter of those caregivers who reported being abused (26%) stated that they had been abusive to their relative. By contrast, only 4.8% (10 caregivers) who had not been abused reported that they had been abusive towards their relative (Coyne et al, 1993). It is perhaps probable that aggressive or violent behaviour by the 'patient' or care recipient might provoke a similar response by the caregiver, that in effect the abuse is mutual and dual directional in certain situations. In addition, those caregivers who reported abusive behaviour had been providing care for longer periods of time overall and were caring for longer periods during the day than those caregivers who did not report abuse.

Certainly, this finding relates to earlier research by Levin and colleagues, in the UK. This research did not specifically consider elder abuse but instead explored the situation of families caring for 'confused older people' (Levin et al, 1989). One of the main findings, however, was the high risk to caregivers of both verbal and physical abuse by the person receiving care (the care recipient). A later Australian study by Cahill and Shapiro asked a group of female caregivers of people with dementia about their experiences of physical and verbal abuse and sexual violence by the care recipient (Cahill and Shapiro, 1993). Of the 39 respondents, 44% said that pushing and shoving had occurred, whilst 25% stated that hitting and pinching had happened to them. With regard to verbal abuse, 61% of the caregivers indicated that shouting had occurred, whilst 48% reported verbal threats and swearing.

Similarly, a US study by Pillemer and Suitor, concerning caregivers of people with Alzheimer's disease, indicated that those caregivers who were caring for relatives who were violent on occasion were themselves fearful of becoming violent and reported that they had violent feelings. Although the fear of becoming violent was not significantly different between groups of married and non-married caregivers, spouses were much more likely to be violent in response to violence by the care recipient (in this case their partner) and to act on violent feelings than other caregivers (Pillemer and Suitor, 1992).

In this study, violence seemed to be related to disruptive or provocative behaviour by the care recipient and also to the caregiver and the care-recipient living together. Caregiver distress generally concerning caring for people with dementia appears to be greatest when the two parties live together; this is perhaps because stressors, tensions and conflicts are more difficult to avoid in such situations (George and Gwyther, 1986; Long, 1981). In addition, in the Pillemer and Suitor study, both higher levels of stress and greater degrees of opportunity from more frequent, perhaps even unavoidable, contact seemed to contribute to the positive association between co-residence and caregiver fear of becoming violent (Pillemer and Suitor, 1992).

Suitor and Pillemer conducted a further study the following year examining the effects of network factors on the support of caregivers (Suitor and Pillemer, 1993); however, this did not consider the possible effects of support networks on violence by caregivers. This aspect was therefore the subject of a subsequent study by Kilburn, which used the same dataset but slightly different analyses (Kilburn, 1996). This latter study confirmed many of the earlier findings—for example, that violence and disruptive behaviour by the care recipient was significantly related to the fear of caregivers of hurting the person with dementia. However, being married was not significantly related to violent feelings. Additionally, the study suggested that the characteristics of networks may well be of significance in the development and maintenance of violent feelings of caregivers. The exact nature of these relationships appears somewhat unclear at present: for instance, the relationship of a number of people in close contact with the caregiver did not appear to be significant (ie, contact with close relatives), whilst contact with a number of others with caregiving experience did appear to give the caregiver significant support. However, this was also often linked with raised stress levels for the caregiver. This survey did not consider attitudes of caregivers or the degrees of support given to the caregiver or even the experience of the caregiver. Further examination of the nature of caregivers' support systems might well assist in relation to such aspects.

There have been a number of other studies concerning the possible links between dementia and elder abuse and it is worth mentioning several of these. One study in the Netherlands found high levels of verbal aggression (30.2% of caregivers stated they had been verbally aggressive) whilst 10.7% of respondent caregivers reported that they had been physically aggressive towards the person they cared for (Pot et al, 1996). Both types of aggression appeared to be related to living in the same household as the person they were caring for, caring for a male and caring for a person with high levels of cognitive impairment and physical dependence (Pot et al, 1996). Australian research by Kurrle and colleagues found that in their sample, 46% of those who were abused had significant dementia, whilst almost two-thirds (65%) had major disabilities (Kurrle et al, 1992).

A further Australian study reported on 54 cases of abuse and 100 people with dementia who had not been abused, all of whom were clients of a specific Rehabilitation and Aged Care Service (Sadler et al, 1995). This study seems to confirm the existence of a strong link between dementia and elder abuse. When dementia was present with other pre-disposing factors such as a psychiatric illness, substance abuse on the part of the caregiver, or some form of pre-existing family conflict, then there was a significant risk of abuse happening. The mere presence of dementia, even with the existence of disturbed and aggressive behaviour on the part of the person with dementia, did not appear to result in a higher risk of either psychological or physical abuse for the person with dementia. However, caregivers did appear to be at risk of physical and/or psychological abuse occurring (Sadler et al, 1995).

In their UK study of older people receiving respite care on a regular basis, of whom approximately two-fifths had a diagnosis of dementia, Homer and Gilleard found that 45% of caregivers reported that they had abused their relative. However, they found that there was no apparent association between a diagnosis of dementia, or the degree of impairment and abuse, but they did find that violence (or threat of violence) by the person with dementia appeared to result in a violent response by the caregiver (Homer and Gilleard, 1990). This finding lead the researchers to suggest that it was disturbed and disruptive behaviour by the care recipient which was likely to result in abuse by the caregiver, rather than merely the presence of cognitive impairment such as dementia.

A small-scale study of 38 caregivers in Northern Ireland seems to echo this finding as the factors of apparent significance within abusive situations were poor pre-morbid relationships; abuse (physical or verbal) or problem behaviours by the person being cared for and the poor health of the caregiver (Compton et al, 1997). Within this study, 34% (13) of the caregivers admitted to verbal abuse and 10% of caregivers admitted to physical abuse. A UK study by Cooney and Mortimer focused on asking caregivers of people with dementia about the possible occurrence of physical and verbal abuse and neglect of the person they were caring for. This was achieved by way of an anonymous survey completed by caregivers, which was distributed by a voluntary organisation for caregivers of individuals with dementia (Cooney and Mortimer, 1995).

Although there was a relatively low response rate (33.5%), of those who replied, 55% admitted to being involved in at least one type of abuse, with verbal abuse being the most common type. Verbal abuse appeared to be associated with the degree of social isolation of the caregiver and with an existing poor relationship; it also appeared to be a risk factor for physical abuse. Those caregivers who scored highly on the General Health Questionnaire (measuring psychological health of caregivers: ie, caregivers in poorer psychological health) and who had been caring for longer periods, appeared to be most at risk of abusing the person they were caring for. Within this study, other variables such as levels of satisfaction with services provided and amounts of both informal and formal support did not appear to be related to abuse (Cooney and Mortimer, 1995).

There seemed to be some evidence supporting reciprocity of abuse in that caregivers who admitted to either physical or verbal abuse were also more likely to report concurrent abusive behaviour of a similar type by the care recipient as being problematic. Caution should be exercised in relation to his latter finding, however, as these reports by caregivers were not substantiated at all in any objective sense and the overall response rate was low. Those 'patient' variables such as levels of physical dependency or behaviour and mood disorder did not appear to be of significance as no difference was found between individuals who had been abused and those who had not. This suggests some discrepancy between the perceptions of the caregivers and the actual behaviour of the individual(s), which the researchers were aware of from the findings (Cooney and Mortimer, 1995).

However, the finding that those caregivers who reported being abusive to the person they cared for were more likely to report abuse (of themselves) by that person, has been duplicated in studies already mentioned from the US (Coyne et al, 1993) and Australia (Sadler et al, 1995). This suggests a degree of consistency despite cultural variability and differing populations studied. One possible interpretation here is that the presence of abusive or challenging behaviour by the impaired person is a risk factor for the development and perpetuation of abusive situations. Further research would help to determine if this finding holds for other cultures (for instance in developing countries, or in southeast Asia) and could establish if there are any other significant variables that need to be taken into account.

Abuse and Mental Health

Much of the research attention in this area appears to have examined the possible relationship between the psychological and emotional ill-health of caregivers, and elder abuse. Some of the most well known research in this field is that of US researchers Wolf and Pillemer, who discovered from their sample that 38% of the abusers had a history of mental ill-health and that 46% of abusers reported a recent decline in their mental health (Wolf and Pillemer, 1989). In this study, psychological and physical abuse seemed to be most related to the deterioration in health of the caregiver (both mental and physical ill-health). In a further related study, some 41% of abusers had a reported history of mental health problems (Godkin et al, 1989).

This finding appears consistent on an international basis: from the UK, Clarke and Ogg found in their small sample of 11 cases of abuse that three of the abusive caregivers had a problem of mental ill-health (Clarke and Ogg, 1994) whilst Cooney and Mortimer established in their sample that caregivers who admitted being physically abusive had significantly higher rates of poor psychological health than non-abusive caregivers (Cooney and Mortimer, 1995). Research by Saveman and Norberg in Sweden indicated that some 15% of abusers had mental health problems (Saveman and Norberg, 1993), whilst a study from the Netherlands also suggests that physical aggression by caregivers of care-recipients who had dementia appeared to be associated with a higher degree of psychological disturbance of the caregiver as well as caring for a spouse (Pot et al, 1996).

Canadian research also supports the evidence concerning the mental distress of abusive caregivers. In this study, Podnieks found that within her sample, 56% of spouses who were physically abusive reported psychiatric or emotional problems as contrasted with 3% of spouses who did not act abusively. Those partners who were abusive were also far more likely to report major and serious problems with their physical health: 70% as compared with 33% of non-abusers (Podnieks, 1990). Further Canadian research by Penning indicated that 27% of abusers had 'psychiatric problems' (Penning, 1992).

The study by Homer and Gilleard also reported a notable finding in relation to this aspect. Those caregivers who reported physical and verbal abuse were significantly more likely to be depressed than those caregivers who were not involved in abusive situations (Homer and Gilleard, 1990). This finding has also been determined in several other studies (Paveza et al, 1992; Coyne et al, 1993). As McCreadie shrewdly recognised, 'Mental and emotional problems may be both a cause and an effect of elder abuse. It would hardly be surprising if people living with abuse, some of which may be long term, displayed psychological effects' (McCreadie, 1996a: 43). This may apply to individuals who act abusively, as well as to those who experience abuse. In addition to this, there is a great deal of information available, collated over the past three decades (at least), concerning the stressful effects of caregiving, especially in relation to caring for people with dementia. A useful review of the psychiatric and physical effects of caregiving in situations of dementia (albeit without a specific focus on elder abuse), was provided by Schulz and colleagues in 1995 (Schulz et al, 1995). What is still not yet clear, however, is the exact nature of the relationship between caregiving and stress, let alone abuse, stress and caregiving.

When considering the stress of caregiving and the possible relationship of this to the development (and maintenance) of abusive situations, there appear to be several relevant factors. First, in spite of an early and possibly lasting perception of much elder abuse being caused by the stress of caregiving, it is clear that there are many dependent older people who receive care and who are not abused, even when the experience of providing care is stressful. It therefore seems necessary to establish an explanation that encompasses the differences between abusive and non-abusive situations. Second, there has been a tendency to equate stress with high levels of physical dependence. This appears to have failed to adequately explore the possible importance of factors such as psychological and emotional dependence in abusive situations (Nolan, 1993). Third, research undertaken by Steinmetz indicates that it is the perception of the situation by the caregiver as stressful which seems to correlate with the presence of abusive situations rather than stress per se (Steinmetz, 1990). Although stress may certainly contribute to the development and continuation of abusive situations, it does not appear sufficient, in isolation from other factors, to provide a satisfactory explanation for elder abuse and neglect.

As seen earlier, a large amount of the early research in the field set out to establish the 'typical characteristics' of victims of abuse, resulting in some unfortunate stereotypes (see Penhale, 1992 in relation to this). And as indicated, subsequent research focused on establishing profiles of those individuals who abuse. Although similar suggestions may be made concerning stereotypes, this research has value in that it has provided useful information in relation to the psychopathology of at least a proportion of those individuals who act abusively. Further, this research has indicated that there are likely to be a number of individuals who take on caring roles (no doubt for a variety of reasons, some willing, some unwilling) who are wholly unsuitable for these tasks. Such individuals may well be physically, practically, emotionally or psychologically unsuited to caring. For those people who have existing or historical mental health or psychological problems, personality or relationship difficulties, the tasks associated with caring may prove too difficult and problematic. If some deterioration occurs in their own health or that of the person they care for, an abusive relationship may develop (or possibly continue at a more severe level). Additionally, if there are reductions in the availability and extent of welfare assistance to help such situations, this will not help in the resolution of such problems.

Finally, there is a further group of individuals who have been identified as producing some possible concern in the arena of abuse and mental health. These are adults with severe and enduring mental illnesses who are living with and being cared for by their ageing parents. McCreadie perceptively described many of these individuals as being the legacy of UK community care policies of the latter part of the last century. These individuals were discharged as young adults from large psychiatric hospitals back into the community on the closure of those institutions. It is likely that a number of those individuals were not able to live independently in the community and therefore returned to live with their parents who provided care for them. As these parents become older, however, some of those adults with mental health problems may have to provide care for their parents (McCreadie, 1996b). Yet, as suggested above, these individuals may not be able to provide care at the level at which it is required and abuse and/or neglect may ensue. A study in the US of over 200 confirmed cases of abuse involving older parents and their adult children revealed that in some 16% of situations, the adult children had some form of mental illness and quite a number of them were also receiving care from their parent (Greenberg et al, 1990). Such results corroborate earlier reported work concerning the difficulties that older parents have in providing care for a severely mentally ill individual (Lefley, 1987). And as established earlier, it is likely that difficult, provocative or even aggressive behaviour by the care-recipient may be contributory factors within the development of abusive situations by the caregiver. These mechanisms may be similar whether the care-recipient has a severe mental illness, a severe learning disability or is significantly cognitively impaired due to an illness such as dementia.

Furthermore, taking into account the potential for aggressive or violent behaviour by disturbed individuals, it is evidently possible that a mutually abusive relationship may exist or develop in such situations. However, the findings by Sadler and colleagues indicate that it may be more likely that the existence of other pre-disposing factors, such as a history of family conflict, or psychopathology on the part of the abuser, is of fundamental importance in the development of abuse (Sadler et al, 1995). Discrepancies such as these in the findings from different studies to an extent amplify some of the complexities of the field in general. They also strongly suggest that no one factor provides adequate explanation but that in many situations, a number of interrelated factors are likely to coexist and interact.

CONCLUSION

There is no categorical evidence that dementia necessarily results in elder abuse. Nevertheless, it is clearly an important factor in the development and perpetuation of a number of abusive situations. As is clear from other aspects of elder abuse and neglect, research has been rather limited in this area. A number of studies rely on reports by caregivers, or professionals, are somewhat non-specific regarding mental health difficulties or cover limited types of abuse. Yet others are not methodologically sound. As a whole, such studies can hardly be considered to be conclusive. However, they do present findings which need to be followed up with further research, which should help to establish their validity.

Whilst the exact nature of the link between dementia and abuse and the degree of importance of dementia are not yet clear-cut, nonetheless it seems that those individuals with dementia who become violent, or develop behaviour that challenges, may be at increased risk of abuse. And as seen in this chapter, this may well be in the context of a mutually abusive relationship. The presence of other pre-disposing factors may mean that the risk of abuse for individuals with dementia appears to be particularly high. A history of problematic relationship(s), of substance misuse or psychiatric illness on the part of the caregiver, or of some type of increased vulnerability of the individual, appears to be of importance within this multifactorial context. The research evidence showing that those individuals who perpetrate abuse are more likely to have substance abuse or mental health problems, including personality disorders, is rather more convincing at present.

Not enough is known yet about elder abuse and neglect. Recognition and identification of such situations and some of the causes need to improve; further research will undoubtedly help in this matter. For those practitioners dealing with such situations, professional and personal standards need to be acknowledged, explored and developed. Work to establish full and effective systems of public accountability, including the development of well-defined lines of individual support and clear expectations of what is required, needs to continue. When developing individual care plans with the person and other parties, practitioners need to consider the nature and extent of any cognitive impairment. Additionally, they must take into account aspects relating to safety or protection planning that might be needed. This should also include determining the benefits and costs, financial and otherwise, of particular interventions to improve situations.

As far as possible, the interventions that are developed need to be both suitable and sensitively tailored to meet individuals' needs. Awareness and knowledge of the problem need to increase, through the provision of appropriate education and training. This will then act as the basis for the development of relevant responses. However, in order to do this effectively there needs to be more research in this whole area to improve both knowledge and understanding of abuse and neglect, and fundamentally understanding the extent of the link between these and dementia (and cognitive impairments in a more general sense). Much work will be required in coming years in this area in order to address this most persistent of problems.

REFERENCES

Anetzberger, GJ, Korbin, JE and Austin, C (1994) 'Alcoholism and Elder Abuse' 9(2) *Journal of Interpersonal Violence* 184–93.

Baumann, E (1989) 'Research rhetoric and the social construction of elder abuse' in J Best (ed), *Images of Issues: Typifying Contemporary Problems* (New York, Aldine de Gruyter).

Bennett, GC and Kingston, PA (1993) *Elder Abuse: Theories, Concepts and Interventions* (London, Chapman & Hall).

Bennett, GC, Kingston, PA and Penhale, B (1997) *The Dimensions of Elder Abuse: Perspectives for Practitioners* (Basingstoke, Macmillan).

Block, MR and Sinott, JD (1979) *The Battered Elder Syndrome: An exploratory study* (College Park, University of Maryland Center on Aging).

Bristowe, E and Collins, J (1989) 'Family mediated abuse of non-institutionalised frail elderly men and women in British Columbia' 1(1) *Journal of Elder Abuse and Neglect* 45–64.

Cahill, S and Shapiro, M (1993) '"I think he might have hit me once": aggression towards caregivers in dementia' 12(4) *Australian Journal on Ageing* 10–15.

Clarke, M and Ogg, J (1994) 'Recognition and prevention of elder abuse' 8(2) *Journal of Community Nursing* 4–6.

Cloke, C (1983) *Old Age Abuse in the Domestic Setting – A Review* (Portsmouth, Age Concern).

Compton, SA, Flanagan, P and Gregg, W (1997) 'Elder abuse in people with dementia in Northern Ireland: Prevalence and predictors in cases referred to a psychiatry of old age service' 12 *International Journal of Geriatric Psychiatry* 632–35.

Cooney, C and Howard, R (1995) 'Abuse of patients with dementia by their carers: out of sight but not out of mind' 10 *International Journal of Geriatric Psychiatry* 735–41.

Cooney, C and Mortimer, A (1995) 'Elder Abuse and Dementia: A Pilot Study' 41(4) *International Journal of Social Psychiatry* 276–83.

Coyne, AC, Reichman, WE and Berbig, LJ (1993) 'The relationship between dementia and elder abuse' 150(4) *American Journal of Psychiatry* 643–46.

Department of Health (DOH) (1993) *No Longer Afraid: the safeguard of older people in domestic settings* (London, HMSO).

Department of Health (DOH) (2000) *No Secrets: the protection of vulnerable adults-guidance on the development and implementation of multi-agency policies and procedures* (London, HMSO).

Finkelhor, D (1983) 'Common Features of Family Abuse' in D Finkelhor et al (eds) (1983) *The Dark Side of Families: Current Family Violence Research* (Newbury Park, Sage).

Francis, R (2013) *Report of the Mid-Staffordshire NHS Foundation Public Inquiry* (HC 947) (London, The Stationery Office).

George, LK and Gwyther, LP (1986) 'Caregiver well-being: A multidimensional examination of family caregivers of demented adults' 26(3) *Gerontologist* 253–59.

Gioglio, GR and Blakemore, P (1985) 'Elder abuse in New Jersey: The knowledge and experience of abuse among older New Jerseyians' (Trenton, New Jersey Division of Youth and Family Services, Bureau of Research and New Jersey Department of Community Affairs, New Jersey Division of Aging).

Glendenning, F (1999a) 'The abuse of older people in institutional settings: An overview' in N Stanley, J Manthorpe and B Penhale (eds), *Institutional Abuse: Perspectives Across the Life Course* (London, Routledge).

—— (1999b) 'Elder abuse and neglect in residential settings: The need for inclusiveness in elder abuse' in F Glenndenning and P Kingston (eds), *Elder Abuse and Neglect in Residential Settings: Different National Backgrounds and Similar Responses* (New York, Haworth Press).

Glendenning, F and Kingston, P (eds) (1999) *Elder Abuse and Neglect in Residential Settings: Different National Backgrounds and Similar Responses* (New York, Haworth Press).

Godkin, MA, Wolf, RS and Pillemer, KA (1989) 'A case comparison analysis of elder abuse and neglect' 288(3) *International Journal of Aging and Human Development* 207–25.

Grafstrom, M, Norberg, A and Wimblad, B (1992) 'Abuse is in the eye of the beholder. Reports by family members about abuse of demented persons in home care. A total population-based study' 21(4) *Scandinavian Journal of Social Medicine* 247–55.

Greenberg, J, McKibben, M and Raymond, J (1990) 'Dependent adult children and elder abuse' 2(1/2) *Journal of Elder Abuse and Neglect* 73–86.

Homer, AC and Gilleard, C (1990) 'Abuse of elderly people by their carers' 301(6765) *British Medical Journal* 1359–62.

Hwalek, M, Sengstock, M and Lawrence, R (1986) 'Assessing the probability of abuse of the elderly' 5 *Journal of Applied Gerontology* 153–73.

Kilburn, JC (1996) 'Network effects in Caregiver to Care Recipient Violence: A study of caregivers to those diagnosed with Alzheimer's disease' 8(1) *Journal of Elder Abuse and Neglect* 69–81.

Kurrle, SE, Sadler, PM and Cameron, ID (1992) 'Patterns of Elder Abuse' 157(10) *Medical Journal of Australia* 673–76.

Lachs, M and Pillemer, K (1995) 'Abuse and Neglect of Elderly Persons' 332(7) *New England Journal of Medicine* 437–43.

Lau, EE and Kosberg, JI (1979) 'Abuse of the elderly by informal care providers' 299 *Aging* 10–15.

Lefley, HP (1987) 'Aging parents as caregivers of mentally ill adult children: an emerging social problem' 38(10) *Hospital Community Psychiatry* 1063–70.

Levin, E, Sinclair, I and Gorbach, P (1989) *Families, Services and Confusion in Old Age* (Aldershot, Avebury).

Long, C (1981) 'Geriatric Abuse' 3 *Issues in Mental Health Nursing* 123–35.

Luoma, ML et al (2011) *Prevalence study of abuse and violence against older women: results of a multi-cultural survey in Austria, Belgium, Finland, Lithuania, and Portugal (European Report of the AVOW Project)* (Finland, National Institute of Health and Welfare).

McCreadie, C (1996a) *Elder Abuse: an update on research* (London, Age Concern Institute of Gerontology).

—— (1996b) Personal communication to the author.

Nolan, M (1993) 'Carer–dependent relationships and the prevention of elder abuse' in P Decalmer and F Glendenning (eds), *The Mistreatment of Older People* (London, Sage).

Ogg, J and Munn-Giddings, C (1993) 'Researching elder abuse' 13(3) *Ageing and Society* 389–414.

O'Keeffe, M et al (2007) *UK Study of Abuse and Neglect of Older People: Prevalence Survey Report* (Department of Health, London).

O'Malley, H, Segars, H and Perez, R (1981) 'Elder Abuse in Massachusetts: A Survey of Professionals and Paraprofessionals' (Boston, MA, Legal Research and Services for the Elderly).

Paveza, GJ et al (1992) 'Severe family violence and Alzheimer's disease: Prevalence and risk factors' 32(4) *Gerontologist* 493–97.

Penhale, B (1992) 'Elder Abuse: an overview' 1(3) *Elders* 36–48.

—— (1993) 'The Abuse of Elderly People: Considerations for Practice' 23(2) *British Journal of Social Work* 95–112.

—— (1999) 'Research on elder abuse: lessons for practice' in M Eastman and P Slater (eds) *Elder Abuse: Critical Issues in Policy and Practice* (London, Age Concern Books).

Penhale, B and Kingston, P (1995) 'Social perspectives on elder abuse' in P Kingston and B Penhale (eds), *Family Violence and the Caring Professions* (Basingstoke, Macmillan).

Penning, MJ (1992) *Elder Abuse resource centre: Research component-final report* (Winnipeg, University of Manitoba Centre on Aging).

Pillemer, KA (1986) 'Risk factors in elder abuse: Results from a case-control study' in KA Pillemer and RS Wolf (eds), *Elder Abuse: Conflict in the Family* (Dover, MA, Auburn House).

Pillemer, KA and Finkelhor, D (1988) 'The prevalence of elder abuse: A random sample survey' 28(1) *Gerontologist* 51–57.

Pillemer, KA and Suitor, JJ (1992) 'Violence and violent feelings: What causes them among family caregivers?' 47(4) *Journal of Gerontology* 165–72.

Podnieks, E (1990) *National Survey on abuse of the elderly in Canada: The Ryerson Study* (Toronto, Ryerson Polytechnical Institute).

Pot, AM et al (1996) 'Verbal and Physical Aggression against Demented Elderly by Informal Caregivers in the Netherlands' 31(3–4) *Social Psychiatry and Psychiatric Epidemiology,* 156–62.

Sadler, P, Kurrle, S and Cameron, I (1995) 'Dementia and Elder Abuse' 14(1) *Australian Journal on Ageing* 36–40.

Saveman, BI and Norberg, A (1993) 'Cases of elder abuse, intervention and hopes for the future, as reported by home service personnel' 7(1) *Scandinavian Journal of Caring Sciences* 21–28.

Schulz, R et al (1995) 'Psychiatric and Physical Morbidity Effects of Dementia Caregiving: Prevalence, Correlates and Causes' 35(6) *Gerontologist* 771–91.

Social Services Inspectorate (SSI) (1992) *Confronting Elder Abuse* (London, HMSO).

Stanley, N, Manthorpe, J and Penhale, B (eds) (1999) *Institutional Abuse: Perspectives Across the Life Course* (London, Routledge).

Stearns, P (1986) 'Old age family conflict: The perspective of the past' in KA Pillemer and RS Wolf (eds), *Elder Abuse: Conflict in the Family* (Dover, MA, Auburn House).

Steinmetz, SK (1990) 'Elder Abuse: Myth and Reality' in TH Brubaker (ed), *Family Relationships in Later Life*, 2nd edn (Newbury Park, CA, Sage).

Steuer, J and Austin, E (1980) 'Family Abuse of the Elderly' 28 *Journal of the American Geriatrics Society* 372–76.

Suitor, JJ and Pillemer, KA (1993) 'Support and interpersonal stress in the social networks of married daughters caring for parents with dementia' 48(1) *Journal of Gerontology* S1–S8.

United States House of Representatives, Select Committee on Aging (1981) *Elder Abuse: The Hidden Problem* (Washington, DC, US Government Printing Office).

Valentine, D and Cash, T (1986) 'A definitional discussion of elder mistreatment' 9 *Journal of Gerontological Social Work* 17–28.

Wilson, G (1994) 'Abuse of elderly men and women among clients of a community psychogeriatric service' 24(4) *British Journal of Social Work* 681–700.

Wolf, RS (1986) 'Major findings from three model projects on elder abuse' in KA Pillemer and RS Wolf (eds), *Elder Abuse: Conflict in the Family* (Dover, MA, Auburn House).

—— (1989) 'Testimony before the Subcommittee of Human Services: Select Committee on Aging; US House of Representatives Hearings on Elder Abuse' in G Bennett and P Kingston (1993) *Elder Abuse: Theories, Concepts and Interventions* (London, Chapman & Hall).

Wolf, RS, Godkin, M and Pillemer, KA (1984) *Elder Abuse and Neglect: Final report from three model projects* (Worcester, MA, University Center on Aging, University of Massachusetts Medical Center).

Wolf, RS and Pillemer, KA (1989) *Helping Elderly Victims: The reality of elder abuse* (New York, Columbia University Press).

World Health Organization (WHO) (2006) *A Global Response to Elder Abuse and Neglect: Building PHC Capacity to Deal with the Problem Worldwide* (Geneva, World Health Organization).

Part III

Legal Perspectives

23

A Legal Overview

MARY DONNELLY

INTRODUCTION

WHEN THE LAW views dementia, it does so primarily through the prism of capacity. Although recent years have seen a movement away from the automatic conclusion that a designation of incapacity allows the wholesale overriding of an individual's views, it remains the case that important legal consequences follow from a designation that a person lacks the capacity to make a decision. In providing an overview of the law's response to the issues to which dementia gives rise, this chapter reflects the law's approach by identifying the central role of capacity; it also problematises this central role. There are several reasons why thinking about dementia solely in terms of capacity is flawed. First, any approach based on incapacity draws together a group of people from disparate situations, defining them solely on the basis of a characteristic which they lack. In a legal world still largely centred on the autonomous, capacitous individual, these people are designated as exceptional or 'other'. Yet, clearly not all people with diminished mental capacity are the same. The family context, life experiences and future potential of a person with dementia may be very different from those of a person with acquired brain injuries or with intellectual or psychosocial disabilities. Failing to recognise these differences results in an overly simplified framework within which the complexity of disparate needs can be obscured. Second, when used as a point for legal distinction, capacity can constitute a rather blunt instrument, leaving limited space within which to recognise the personality of the individual or to address the complexities of decision-making processes or the unique pressures to which a person with dementia may be subjected (Herring, 2009a). The growing jurisprudence around 'vulnerability' provides one way of addressing this, although a great deal more work needs to be done to establish an appropriate legal framework in this regard (Dunn et al, 2008; Herring, 2009b).

In providing a legal overview, this chapter begins by outlining in brief the applicable legislative frameworks in England and Wales, as contained in the Mental Health Act 1983 (MHA) and the Mental Capacity Act 2005 (MCA). It then identifies a changing legal landscape which, among other aspects, includes an increased role for human rights and greater recognition of the will and preferences of people with impaired capacity. The chapter then identifies particular legal challenges which arise in applying a capacity-based approach in respect of dementia. It outlines difficulties faced by clinicians in making determinations of capacity in the context of dementia and recognises the inability of capacity-based differentiation to deal with broader issues of personhood, agency and control. The chapter concludes with the argument that the issues arising in respect of dementia must be engaged with on their own terms and not simply as a sub-category of a broader capacity/incapacity debate but acknowledges that there are also valuable insights to be gained from this debate.

ADDRESSING DEMENTIA: LEGISLATIVE FRAMEWORKS

In England and Wales, a person with dementia may fall within one of two distinct legislative frameworks. The MHA provides for formal admission and treatment for a mental disorder, which includes dementia (MHA, section 1), provided that the statutory requirements (MHA, sections 2 and 3) are met.[1] A 'patient' who has been formally admitted under the MHA encounters significant limitations in respect of liberty and treatment choices (MHA, sections 26 and 63). However, they are also afforded protections in the form of tribunal review (MHA, sections 66 and 68) and independent oversight of some treatment decisions (MHA, sections 57, 58 and 58A). Although open to criticism on a number of grounds, these protections constitute important safeguards not least because, for the most part, they arise automatically rather than requiring action on the part of the patient (Richardson, 2002). For patients with dementia, the benefits of automatic, rather than self-starting, review are considerable, and ensure a degree of protection regardless of the ability of the patient to initiate the necessary steps. The protective framework can be further enhanced by the statutory role afforded to the 'nearest relative', although the effectiveness of this aspect of the MHA protection is wholly reliant on the attitude and abilities of the person who fills this role (Keywood, 2003). The MHA also provides for admission to guardianship of persons who meet the statutory criteria (MHA, section 7). A guardian appointed under the MHA may decide where the patient lives; can require the patient to attend specified places for medical treatment, occupation, education or training and may require that access be given to the patient by a medical practitioner or approved mental health professional (MHA, section 8). The MHA guardianship mechanism is used relatively rarely; the most recent statistics indicate that, in 2012–13, there were only 271 new guardianship cases in England and Wales (NHS Information Centre, 2013), and the modern preference is to deal with issues of adult incapacity though the MCA framework.

The MCA outlines the legislative framework for decision-making where a person lacks capacity. The legislation provides for a functional, task-specific assessment of capacity (MCA, sections 2 and 3) and allows acts in connection with the care and treatment of a person lacking capacity to be performed without incurring legal liability, provided that the person doing the act takes reasonable steps to ascertain whether the person lacks capacity and reasonably believes that it is in the best interests of the person that the act be done (MCA, section 5). Several aspects of the MCA promote the provision of decision-making supports (MCA, sections 1(3) and 3(2))

[1] In brief, the person must be suffering from a mental disorder of a nature or degree that warrants his or her admission for assessment or treatment and admission is necessary for the health and safety of the patient or for the protection of other persons.

and the participation of the person lacking capacity in the decision-making process (MCA, sections 4(4) and 4(6)). However, the MCA is weak on enforcement and on the actual delivery of these supports (Donnelly, 2010: 208–09). Following amendments made by the Mental Health Act 2007, the MCA now also includes provisions in respect of deprivations of liberty. The Deprivation of Liberty Safeguards (DoLS) (MCA, Schedule A1) outline procedures to be observed where a person lacking capacity is admitted to a hospital or care home in circumstances in which the admission amounts to a deprivation of liberty while, if the deprivation of liberty does not involve admission (for example, if it occurs in the person's own home), an application for authorisation may be made to the Court of Protection (MCA, section 4A).

A CHANGING LEGAL LANDSCAPE

In order to understand how the law responds to dementia, it is necessary to begin with the law's approach to autonomy. The traditional liberal view that '[o]ver himself, over his own body and mind, the individual is sovereign' (Mill, 1859: 14) is deeply ingrained in the common law tradition, where it is given effect through recognition of the individual's right of autonomy or self-determination.[2] Within this traditional formulation of autonomy, capacity serves as the critical dividing point. As described by Buchanan and Brock (1989: 27), capacity is used

> to sort persons into two classes: (1) those whose voluntary decisions ... must be respected by others and accepted as binding, and (2) those whose decisions, even if uncoerced, will be set aside and for whom others will act as surrogate decision-makers.

Once a determination was made that a person lacked capacity, traditional liberalism largely lost interest, resulting in impoverished conceptual and legal frameworks (Donnelly, 2010: 176). The person lacking capacity became, in effect, a 'non-person' for whom others acted, typically on the basis of an objective (though largely unmonitored) assessment of his or her best interests.

The kind of simplistic distinction drawn by the common law is, in theory at any rate, no longer legally acceptable. This shift in the law's approach has derived from two rather different sources and these differences can create potential for conflict, especially in the context of dementia. The first source of change, which began to have a significant impact from the 1980s, has been the recognition of the conception of precedent (or prior) autonomy, through which a person with capacity is facilitated in directing, to varying degrees, the fate of his or her subsequently incapacitated self. This conception has been given effect through legislation allowing a person to make an advance directive, usually employed in the health care context, or to grant a lasting (or enduring) power of attorney, authorising a designated person to make decisions on his or her behalf in the event of a loss of capacity. Both measures are legislatively provided for across the common law world. In England and Wales, sections 24–26 of the MCA provide for advance refusals of treatment and sections 9–14 provide for the grant of lasting powers of attorney, although the

[2] *S v McC (orse S) and M (DS Intervener); W v W* [1972] AC 24, 43; *St George's Healthcare NHS Trust v S* [1998] 3 WLR 936.

effectiveness of both sets of measures in protecting precedent autonomy has been questioned (MacLean, 2008; Samanta, 2009). A less formal means of recognising precedent autonomy is through a recognition of the past views and preferences of the person who now lacks capacity in making present-day determinations of his or her best interests. This mechanism is also utilised by the MCA where the statutory test for best interests requires that account be taken of the past (as well as the present) wishes and feelings of the person lacking capacity and of the beliefs and values that would be likely to influence his or her decision if he or she had capacity (MCA, section 4(6)). This approach to decision-making is clearly of particular relevance to people with dementia, presupposing the existence of previously capable views and the opportunity (and the foresight) to put in place the necessary steps to ensure that these are respected post-incapacity. Conceptually, the model, especially in its more formalised iteration, remains clearly aligned with the traditional liberal approach centred on respect for autonomy (Dworkin, 1993). Thus, it remains focused on the views of the person with capacity; it is simply that the temporal context is expanded.

The second impetus for change derives from the growing role played by human rights instruments in the construction of capacity, in particular, the European Convention on Human Rights (ECHR) and, increasingly, the United Nations Convention on the Rights of Persons with Disabilities (CRPD).[3] These instruments affirm that an absence of capacity does not mean an absence of rights and the focus of the measures is on the individual's current position rather than on his or her past preferences. In respect of the ECHR, the European Court of Human Rights (ECtHR) has affirmed the importance of the right to liberty (under Article 5) and the right to physical and psychological integrity (under Article 8), regardless of capacity.[4] In this respect, the ECtHR has afforded increasing levels of respect and recognition to the individual's (current) will, notwithstanding his or her lack of capacity.[5]

The equal rights of all persons with disabilities, regardless of capacity, are also central to the CRPD.[6] The principles underpinning the CRPD include respect for the inherent dignity and individual autonomy—including the freedom to make one's own choices—of persons with disabilities (Article 3). From the perspective of people with dementia, important rights protected by the CRPD include the right to liberty and security of the person (Article 14); the right to freedom from exploitation, violence and abuse (Article 15); the right to respect for physical and mental integrity (Article 17); and the right to live independently and be included in the community (Article 19). Article 12 is of particular significance for people who suffer from cognitive impairment because of dementia. This Article requires States Parties to recognise that 'persons with disabilities enjoy a right to legal capacity on an equal

[3] The CRPD entered into force on 2 May 2008 on receipt of its twentieth ratification. As of May 2014, the CRPD had been signed by 158 states and ratified by 145, including Australia, Canada, the United Kingdom and most members of the European Union.

[4] *HL v United Kingdom* (2005) 40 EHRR 32; *Glass v United Kingdom* (2004) 29 EHRR 341.

[5] *Storck v Germany* (2005) 43 EHRR 96, para 143; *Stanev v Bulgaria* (2012) ECHR 46, para 153.

[6] Persons with dementia clearly fall within the ambit of 'persons with disabilities' as defined in Art 1 of the CRPD to include 'those who have long-term physical, mental, intellectual or sensory impairments which in interaction with various barriers may hinder their full and effective participation in society on an equal basis with others'.

basis with others in all aspects of life'. It also requires that all measures relating to the exercise of legal capacity provide for appropriate and effective safeguards to prevent abuse in accordance with international human rights law. These safeguards must ensure that

> measures relating to the exercise of legal capacity respect the rights, will and preferences of the person, are free of conflict of interest and undue influence, are proportional and tailored to the person's circumstances, apply for the shortest time possible and are subject to regular review by a competent, independent and impartial authority or judicial body.

Article 12 also imposes a positive duty on States Parties to ensure that persons with disabilities have access to the support they require in exercising their legal capacity.

Many commentators regard Article 12 as constituting a 'paradigm shift' in the law's approach to capacity (Bach and Kerzner, 2010; Bartlett, 2012). As described by Bach and Kerzner (2010: 30), the language used in Article 12 'represents a shift from the traditional dualist model of [mental] capacity versus [mental] incapacity' and instead Article 12 establishes a 'philosophical foundation on which to ground the positive duty of the state to maximize autonomy for people with significant intellectual, cognitive and psychosocial disabilities' (2010: 72). There is ongoing debate regarding the scope of the obligations imposed by Article 12 and in particular whether the concept of incapacity can still be used as a relevant concept in the law without breaching the CRPD (Bartlett, 2012: 762). There are also important practical questions regarding how to deliver the support mechanisms required under Article 12, while at the same time ensuring protection from abuse (Bach and Kerzner, 2010: 37). Nonetheless, the CRPD framework offers important benchmarks for the developing legal response to people with impaired capacity, including people with dementia, not least because of the CRPD's focus on both negative and positive rights and on the establishment of support structures to facilitate the exercise of rights (Bartlett, 2012).

Aspects of the more rights-centred approach are reflected in the MCA, in particular in the requirement that 'so far as reasonably practicable', a person lacking capacity should be permitted and encouraged to participate 'as fully as possible in any act done and any decision affecting him' (MCA, section 4(4)) and that his or her wishes and feelings must be taken into account (MCA, section 4(6)). The significance of support is recognised in the MCA's underlying principles, which require that a person is 'not to be treated as unable to make a decision unless all practicable steps to help him to do so have been taken without success' (MCA, section 1(3)). While the current legislative position certainly constitutes progress on the common law position, it falls short of providing effective protection for the rights of persons lacking capacity. Bartlett (2012: 767) points out that the MCA is clearly lacking in the necessary degree of procedural safeguards to be compliant with the CRPD while the DoLS are widely regarded as bureaucratic measures which strive to deliver technical ECHR compliance but provide limited actual protection for persons lacking capacity (Gostin et al, 2010: 391–410). At the same time, local authorities have been increasingly active in seeking deprivation of liberty authorisations in respect of people living in their own homes, the effect of which has been to formalise and bureaucratise existing care arrangements and, in some situations, this has had substantial negative effects on the quality of life of people with dementia

(Fennell, 2012). Judicial responses to the more participative decision-making model required under the MCA have also been patchy (Donnelly, 2011; Harding, 2012). Thus, while the legal landscape may be changing, its common law, capacity-centred, underpinnings remain strong and there is still some way to go in developing a legal framework which respects the rights and takes account of the needs of persons lacking capacity. Bearing this in mind, it now falls to examine difficulties which arise in applying a capacity-focused approach in the context of dementia.

CHALLENGES IN APPLYING A CAPACITY-BASED APPROACH TO DEMENTIA

Any approach to law which uses capacity as a dividing point for the recognition of rights is problematic. The problems vary, however, depending on the nature of the capacity impairment and it is essential that the specifics of individual conditions are engaged with. In the context of dementia, three challenges merit more detailed discussion. The first relates to the determination of decision-making capacity; the second relates to the tensions between an individual's past wishes/values and his or her current preferences; and the third relates to the tensions around vulnerability in the absence of a legal determination of lack of capacity. Recognising these problems with a capacity-based approach serves two functions. First, it is a reminder of the limitations of such an approach to dementia and of the need for fundamental changes in the law's approach and second, it allows for the consideration of more immediate practical steps to alleviate the individual difficulties.

Determining Capacity

Although the law (and traditional liberal theory) has tended to treat the matter of capacity determination as a question of fact, in reality, a decision about capacity 'necessarily reflects a balancing of two important, sometimes competing objectives: to enhance the patient's well-being and to respect the person as a self-determining individual' (President's Commission, 1982: 57). This decision has two aspects. The first, more obviously normative, element is the establishment of the standard for capacity; the second is the application of this standard in practice. Under the MCA, as at common law, capacity is determined on a functional and decision-specific basis. While this approach has undeniable advantages in minimising interference with decision-making autonomy (within the traditional liberal legal meaning at any rate), it is clearly best suited to the situation of one-off, significant decisions, such as consent to surgical intervention. The approach is less closely aligned with the myriad of less dramatic, everyday, choices which, for a patient with dementia, can constitute the difference between maximal and minimal autonomy as well as enhanced or diminished quality of life (Lidz et al, 1992).

The MCA standard for capacity, which is, again, largely in line with that which applied at common law, requires that the individual must be able to understand and retain information relevant to the decision to be made; to use and weigh that information in reaching the decision and to communicate the decision (MCA, section 3(1)). This relatively high standard can be criticised as 'cognitivistic and rationalistic' and as failing to take account of considerations such as emotion, identity and narrative (Herring, 2009a: 26). It is, however, tempered by a number of factors; first, there is a presumption of capacity; second, before this standard is applied, the incapacity must arise from an impairment or disturbance in the functioning of the mind or brain (MCA, section 2(1)); and third, a person may not be regarded as unable to understand if he or she is able to understand an explanation given in an appropriate way in his or her circumstances (MCA, section 3(2)). These requirements, together with other measures confirming that capacity may not be determined merely on the basis of age, appearance or a condition of the person (MCA, section 2(3)) or merely because he or she makes an unwise decision (MCA, section 1(4)), are designed to protect people from inappropriate designations of incapacity. Their effectiveness in this is, however, questionable, not least because of the lack of any meaningful enforcement mechanisms (Donnelly, 2010: 169).

While the statutory standard provides the legal basis for capacity determinations, delivery on the legal standard is largely dependent on the people who are providing care on the ground. In the context of dementia, at its most formal, this may involve assessment by a geriatric specialist; at its least, it will involve assessment by a carer, whether family or friend or a paid carer (MCA Code of Practice, 2007: paragraph 4.38). The assumption underpinning section 5 of the MCA, which is that every act in connection with the care or treatment of a person is preceded by an evaluation of capacity and best interests, is clearly in the realm of a legal fiction. The reality is much less structured and, although efforts are made through the Code of Practice to provide information to carers and other relevant parties, there is very limited evidence regarding whether, and to what extent, the statutory scheme has actually permeated practice.

Although it is easier to monitor the more formal, professional, assessments of capacity, the data in this context is still relatively limited. Such data as is available suggests that professionals are not particularly effective in carrying out the task, whether because of a lack of legal knowledge (Jackson and Warner, 2002) or because of their application of the legal standard in practice (Marson et al, 1997; Raymont, 2004). In the words of one geriatrician 'while one may have reasonable high confidence in, say, a liver specialist's judgement that a patient has cirrhosis, the same is not true for even an expert and conscientious judgement of a patient's capacity' (O'Keeffe, 2008: 44). These difficulties are, of course, not unique to the geriatric context; however, given that the demographic variable most associated with findings of incapacity is age (Okai et al, 2007), difficulties in determining capacity are especially worrying in this context. Capacity determinations in dementia are also made more difficult because of structural factors, such as conditions of passivity in nursing homes (Lidz et al, 1992) as well as, sometimes, by the grief and dislocation that accompanies the loss of a long-term life partner.

These difficulties with determining capacity in dementia can, to a degree, be countered through better empirical research into the assessment process actually employed and more informed practitioners (Moye and Marson, 2007). However, even if an improvement does take place, the core difficulty remains that individualised assessments of capacity are not reliable determinants of individual rights.

Balancing Past and Current Interests

As discussed earlier, the shift towards a more inclusive approach to people with capacity impairments has two foundations: increased recognition of precedent autonomy and greater respect for human rights. These conceptual underpinnings push the law in different directions; the former emphasises the past (capable) self while the latter is primarily concerned with the current self. While in many cases involving impaired capacity, this is unproblematic, in the context of dementia, there can be tensions. Even in the absence of the kind of direct conflict between past views and present interests explored (from opposing perspectives) by Dworkin (1993) and Dresser (1995), it is clearly the case that the role of a person's past life and of how he or she will be remembered is much more likely to be ethically significant in the context of dementia than in most other contexts of impaired capacity (Matthews, 2006). The MCA offers little help in the task of balancing past and present selves, simply requiring that account be taken of both sets of views. This is not the place to explore in detail how tensions between past views and present interests should be resolved in respect of people with dementia; indeed, it is probable that any kind of neat resolution is unachievable (and undesirable). It is clear, however, that the task gives rise to unique challenges in the dementia context and that these must be engaged with in their own terms.

Bright-Line Divisions and Vulnerability

Within the traditional capacity-based approach, the law's protective function was engaged by a lack of capacity. Once a person met the standard for capacity, his or her decisions were, for the most part, beyond the purview of the law. In the classic Millian tradition, the person's 'own good, either physical or moral, [was] not a sufficient warrant' for interference (Mill, 1859: 14). With some limited exceptions (for example, the equitable doctrine of unconscionability), this bright-line, capacity-based division continues to dominate. As a consequence, the law has tended to avoid engaging with broader questions of decision-making agency, preferring instead to shoehorn questions of agency into the test for capacity (Donnelly, 2010: 59–65). Yet, many of the issues arising in the context of dementia can more accurately be defined as matters of agency rather than capacity. A person with dementia forced to choose between continuing to live at home with an abusive adult child or life in a nursing home, can hardly be described as an autonomous agent, notwithstanding whether or not he or she meets a legal standard for capacity.

To date, the main way in which the law has engaged with agency questions is through the developing jurisprudence on vulnerability as an aspect of the court's inherent jurisdiction (Dunn et al, 2008; Herring, 2009b). In the leading judicial statement in this respect, Munby J identified the 'vulnerable adult' as

> someone who, whether or not mentally incapacitated, and whether or not suffering from any mental illness or mental disorder, is or may be unable to take care of him or herself, or unable to protect him or herself against significant harm or exploitation.[7]

[7] *Re SA (Vulnerable Adult with Capacity: Marriage* [2005] EWHC 2942 (Fam), [82].

Clearly, as stated in these broad terms, this would permit very wide-ranging use of the court's inherent jurisdiction to intervene in decision-making and, as such, the development of the vulnerability-based inherent jurisdiction gives rise to legitimate cause for concern (Dunn et al, 2008: 241). However, the decision to extend the inherent jurisdiction in this way also responds to an important need which is clearly not addressed within the capacity-based approach. Our agency, or decision-making freedom, is dependent to varying degrees on our social context, including a range of structural factors, and, this dependence is poorly reflected in the use of individualist, capacity-based, mechanisms.

Focusing on vulnerability as a basis for overriding people's decisions may be missing the potential of a vulnerabilities-based approach. Fineman (2008; 2012) has argued that vulnerability can be seen as inherent in the human condition and 'while sometimes, and perhaps even ultimately, our vulnerability results in weakness, or physical or emotional decline', vulnerability is also generative, presenting opportunities for 'innovation and growth, creativity, and fulfilment' (2012: 126). Fineman argues that the way in which each subject's vulnerability is managed depends on the quality and quantity of resources which he or she can command. Thus, recognising vulnerability can lead to 'a discussion of the nature of a responsive state and draws connections between the vulnerable subject and the state and its institutions' (Fineman, 2012: 128). Viewed in this way, a focus on vulnerability offers the potential for an approach to law which seeks to address underlying impediments to agency rather than designating vulnerable subjects as 'other' in the way in which the traditional capacity-based approach responded to people lacking capacity. Thus, recognition of vulnerability may be linked to broader conceptions of capabilities-building, and to the goal of developing the skills and the environment within which individual autonomy can flourish (Nussbaum, 2000). In practical terms, this requires legal engagement not just with individuals but with surrounding practices, asking whether these enhance or erode autonomy capabilities. In this way, the legal lens is expanded beyond the individualist focus which still remains central in the law's dealing with dementia.

CONCLUSION

A core argument developed in this chapter is that the law must address issues raised by dementia on their own terms and not simply as a subset of a broader capacity/incapacity agenda. However, this is not to underplay the potential contribution of advancements in the law relating to capacity in developing the legal framework in respect of people with dementia. The CRPD offers new ways of thinking about capacity and its emphasis on the provision of support provides the foundations for a more integrated approach to decision-making. In this, the CRPD has a good deal in common with the capabilities approach which broadens the lens of engagement and recognises that external factors can impede or enhance individual agency and that this is ethically and legally significant. The conceptual underpinnings for the law in respect of dementia have moved a good distance in the past two decades; it is now time for the law to catch up.

REFERENCES

Bach, M and Kerzner, L (2010) *A New Paradigm for Protecting Autonomy and the Right to Legal Capacity* (Toronto, Law Commission of Ontario).

Bartlett, P (2012) 'The United Nations Convention on the Rights of Persons with Disabilities and Mental Health Law' 75(5) *Modern Law Review* 752–78.

Buchanan, A and Brock, D (1989) *Deciding for Others: The Ethics of Surrogate Decision-Making* (Cambridge, Cambridge University Press).

Donnelly, M (2010) *Healthcare Decision-making and the Law: Autonomy, Capacity and the Limits of Liberalism* (Cambridge, Cambridge University Press).

—— (2011) 'Determining Best Interests under the Mental Capacity Act 2005' 19(2) *Medical Law Review* 304–13.

Dresser, R (1995) 'Dworkin on Dementia: Elegant Theory, Questionable Policy' 25(6) *Hastings Center Report* 32–38.

Dunn, M, Clare, I and Holland, A (2008) 'To Empower or to Protect? Constructing the "Vulnerable Adult" in English Law and Public Policy' 28(2) *Legal Studies* 234–53.

Dworkin, R (1993) *Life's Dominion: An Argument About Abortion, Euthanasia, and Individual Freedom* (New York, Alfred A Knopf).

Fennell, P (2012) 'Co-Ordinating Deprivation of Liberty: Human Rights Turned Upside Down' 2(1) *Elder Law Journal* 82–87.

Fineman, MA (2008) 'The Vulnerable Subject: Anchoring Equality in the Human Condition' 20(1) *Yale Journal of Law and Feminism* 1–23.

—— (2012) '"Elderly" as Vulnerable: Rethinking the Nature of Individual and Societal Responsibility' 20(1) *Elder Law Journal* 71–112.

Gostin, L et al (eds) (2010) *Principles of Mental Health Law* (Oxford, Oxford University Press).

Harding, R (2012) 'Legal Constructions of Dementia: Discourses of Autonomy at the Margins of Capacity' 34(4) *Journal of Social Welfare and Family Law* 425–42.

Herring, J (2009a) 'Losing It? Losing What? The Law and Dementia' 21(1) *Child and Family Law Quarterly* 3–29.

—— (2009b) 'Protecting Vulnerable Adults: A Critical Review of Recent Case Law' 21(4) *Child and Family Law Quarterly* 498–512.

Jackson, E and Warner, J (2002) 'How Much do Doctors Know about Consent and Capacity?' 95(12) *Journal of the Royal Society of Medicine* 601–03.

Keywood, K (2003) 'Gatekeepers, Proxies, Advocates? The Evolving Role of Carers under Mental Health and Mental Incapacity Law Reforms' 25(4) *Journal of Social Welfare and Family Law* 355–68.

Lidz, C, Fischer, L and Arnold, R (1992) *The Erosion of Autonomy in Long-Term Care* (New York, Oxford University Press).

MacLean, A (2008) 'Advance Directives and the Rocky Waters of Anticipatory Decision-Making' 16(1) *Medical Law Review* 1–22.

Marson, D et al (1997) 'Consistency of Physicians' Judgments of Capacity to Consent to Mild Alzheimer's Disease' 45(4) *Journal of the American Geriatrics Society* 453–57.

Matthews, E (2006) 'Dementia and the Identity of the Person' in JC Hughes, SJ Louw and SR Sabat (eds), *Dementia: Mind, Meaning, and the Person* (Oxford, Oxford University Press).

Mental Capacity Act 2005: Code of Practice (2007) (London, The Stationery Office).

Mill, JS (1859) *On Liberty* in J Grey (ed) (1991) *On Liberty and Other Essays* (Oxford, Oxford University Press).

Moye, J and Marson, D (2007) 'Assessment of Decision-making Capacity in Older Adults: An Emerging Area of Practice and Research' 62B *Journal of Gerontology B Psychological Sciences and Social Sciences* 3–11.

National Health Service Information (NHS) (2013) *Guardianship under the Mental Health Act 2013*.

Nussbaum, M (2000) *Women and Human Development: The Capabilities Approach* (Cambridge, Cambridge University Press).

Okai, D et al (2007) 'Mental Capacity in Psychiatric Inpatients: Systematic Review' 191(4) *British Journal of Psychiatry* 291–97.

O'Keeffe, S (2008) 'A Clinician's Perspective: Issues of Capacity in Care' 14(5) *Medico-Legal Journal of Ireland* 41–46.

President's Commission for the Study of Ethical Problems in Medicine and Biomedical and Behavioral Research (1982) *Making Health Care Decisions: A Report on the Ethical and Legal Implications of Informed Consent in the Patient-Practitioner Relationship* (Washington, DC, United States Superintendent of Documents).

Raymont, V et al (2004) 'Prevalence of Mental Incapacity in Medical Inpatients and Associated Risk Factors: Cross-Sectional Study' 364(9443) *Lancet* 1421–27.

Richardson, G (2002) 'Autonomy, Guardianship and Mental Disorder: One Problem, Two Solutions' 65(5) *Modern Law Review* 702–23.

Samanta, J (2009) 'Lasting Powers of Attorney for Healthcare under the Mental Capacity Act 2005: Enhanced Prospective Self-Determination for Future Incapacity or a Simulacrum?' 17(3) *Medical Law Review* 377–409.

United Nations General Assembly *Convention on the Rights of Persons with Disabilities*, 13 December 2006, A/RES/61/106, Annex I.

24

Assessing Capacity

LESLEY KING AND HUGH SERIES

ASSESSING CAPACITY: LEGAL ASPECTS

Legal Aspects of Capacity

This chapter focuses on the position in England and Wales.

There is no one legal test of capacity. It is issue and time specific. A person may have the capacity to make one decision but lack the capacity to make another. So, for example, in *A v X*[1] the Court of Protection had to determine whether an elderly man had capacity for all or any of the following: (i) to marry; (ii) to make a will; (iii) to grant an enduring power of attorney; (iv) to manage his affairs; (v) to conduct litigation. Each issue had to be approached separately and the Court decided the issues differently

The Relationship between the Mental Capacity Act 2005 and Common Law Tests

The Mental Capacity Act 2005 ('MCA') introduced[2] a change in the way the Court of Protection approached its role. Under the former regime, the Court of Protection made a decision to act based on a general finding under Part VII of the Mental Health Act 1983 that the patient lacked capacity to manage his affairs. It then retained jurisdiction in respect of all transactions carried out during the period of incapacity. Under the MCA, the Court of Protection takes decisions where a person lacks capacity in respect of that particular decision at that particular time.

The MCA does not regulate the conduct of any other court. In the definitions section of the MCA,[3] 'court' is defined as 'Court of Protection' and so, for example, the Act is not relevant when the High Court considers the question of whether a person has capacity to carry out a particular function such as the capacity to make a will or lifetime gift, enter into a contract for land or enter into marriage for which there are existing common law tests. The Act would not apply to capacity to litigate were it not for the fact that Part 21 of the Civil Procedure Rules states that 'lacks capacity'

[1] *A v X* [2012] EWHC 2400 (COP).
[2] For most purposes from 1 October 2007. See SI 2007/1897.
[3] MCA 2005, s 64.

means lacks capacity within the meaning of the MCA thereby importing the test of capacity set out in section 2.[4]

However, the various common law tests of capacity are essentially the same as the definition contained in section 3 of the MCA (see below). As Munby J said in *Local Authority X v MM*[5] the general rule of English law, whatever the context, is that the test of capacity is the ability (whether or not one chooses to exercise it) to understand the nature and quality of the relevant transaction.

The Code of Practice which accompanies the MCA refers[6] to the existing common law tests of capacity. Paragraph 4.33 of the Code is as follows:

> The Act's new definition of capacity is in line with the existing common law tests, and the Act does not replace them. When cases come before the court on the above issues, judges can adopt the new definition if they think it is appropriate. The Act will apply to all other cases relating to financial, healthcare or welfare decisions.

Munby J clarified the meaning of 'if they think it is appropriate' in *Local Authority X v MM*[7] saying that, while judges sitting in the Court of Protection and exercising the statutory jurisdiction under the MCA are obviously bound to apply the statutory principles contained in that Act, judges sitting elsewhere and deciding cases for which there is an existing test can adopt the formulation from the MCA if it corresponds to the existing common law test, having regard to the existing principles of the common law.

Capacity under the Mental Capacity Act 2005

Section 1 sets out the principles that govern the Act.

1. The principles
(1) The following principles apply for the purposes of this Act.
(2) A person must be assumed to have capacity unless it is established that he lacks capacity.
(3) A person is not to be treated as unable to make a decision unless all practicable steps to help him to do so have been taken without success.
(4) A person is not to be treated as unable to make a decision merely because he makes an unwise decision.
(5) An act done, or decision made, under this Act for or on behalf of a person who lacks capacity must be done, or made, in his best interests.
(6) Before the act is done, or the decision is made, regard must be had to whether the purpose for which it is needed can be as effectively achieved in a way that is less restrictive of the person's rights and freedom of action.

[4] See discussion in *Saulle v Nouvet* [2007] EWHC 2902 (QB).

[5] In *Local Authority X v MM (by her litigation friend, the Official Solicitor), KM* [2007] EWHC 2003 (Fam), [67].

[6] At para 4.3279.

[7] In *Local Authority X v MM (by her litigation friend, the Official Solicitor), KM* [2007] EWHC 2003 (Fam) at para 79.

The Philosophy of the Act is Empowerment.

A person must be assumed to have capacity until it is proved otherwise and must be supported to make his own decision, as far it is practicable to do so. The Act requires 'all practicable steps' to be taken to help the person. This could include, for example, making sure that the person is in an environment in which he is comfortable or involving an expert to help him express his views. It is expressly provided that a person is not to be treated as lacking capacity to make a decision simply because he makes an unwise decision. This means that a person who has the necessary ability to make the decision has the right to make irrational or eccentric decisions that others may not judge to be in his best interests.

Section 2 sets out the test for determining capacity for the purposes of the Act.

2. People who lack capacity

(1) For the purposes of this Act, a person lacks capacity in relation to a matter if at the material time he is unable to make a decision for himself in relation to the matter because of an impairment of, or a disturbance in the functioning of, the mind or brain.

(2) It does not matter whether the impairment or disturbance is permanent or temporary.

(3) A lack of capacity cannot be established merely by reference to—
   (a) a person's age or appearance, or
   (b) a condition of his, or an aspect of his behaviour, which might lead others to make unjustified assumptions about his capacity.

(4) In proceedings under this Act or any other enactment, any question whether a person lacks capacity within the meaning of this Act must be decided on the balance of probabilities.

(5) No power which a person ('D') may exercise under this Act—
   (a) in relation to a person who lacks capacity, or
   (b) where D reasonably thinks that a person lacks capacity,
   is exercisable in relation to a person under 16.

(6) Subsection (5) is subject to section 18(3).

The section focuses on the particular time when a decision has to be made and on the particular matter to which the decision relates, not on any theoretical ability to make decisions generally. It follows that a person can lack capacity for the purposes of the Act even if the loss of capacity is partial or temporary[8] or if his capacity fluctuates and a person may lack capacity in relation to one matter but not in relation to another.

The inability to make a decision must be caused by an impairment of or disturbance in the functioning of the mind or brain. This can cover a range of problems, such as psychiatric illness, learning disability, dementia, brain damage or even a

[8] Eg, in *Re M, N v O & P (unreported)* 28 January 2013, a lawyer and businessman suffered a serious heart attack and stroke while on a business trip abroad. He was likely to regain capacity although it was difficult to say when that would be. A deputy had to be appointed to deal with his property and financial affairs until that date.

toxic confusional state, as long as it has the necessary effect on the functioning of the mind or brain, causing the person to be unable to make the decision.

Nothing in the MCA makes express provision with respect to individuals who may lack capacity for a reason other than an impairment of, or disturbance in the functioning of, the mind or brain. However, the High Court retains an inherent jurisdiction to intervene where the facts justify it. For example, the Court exercised this jurisdiction to protect an elderly couple from their coercive son where capacity to make balanced and considered decisions was compromised by their vulnerability.[9]

Section 3 sets out the test for determining when a person lacks capacity for the purposes of the Act.

3. Inability to make decisions

(1) For the purposes of section 2, a person is unable to make a decision for himself if he is unable
  (a) to understand the information relevant to the decision,
  (b) to retain that information,
  (c) to use or weigh that information as part of the process of making the decision, or
  (d) to communicate his decision (whether by talking, using sign language or any other means).

(2) A person is not to be regarded as unable to understand the information relevant to a decision if he is able to understand an explanation of it given to him in a way that is appropriate to his circumstances (using simple language, visual aids or any other means).

(3) The fact that a person is able to retain the information relevant to a decision for a short period only does not prevent him from being regarded as able to make the decision.

(4) The information relevant to a decision includes information about the reasonably foreseeable consequences of—
  (a) deciding one way or another, or
  (b) failing to make the decision.

It is a 'functional' test involving four elements. The first three (subsections (1)(a)–(c)) will cover the vast majority of cases. If the person cannot undertake one of these three aspects of the decision-making process, then he is unable to make the decision.

Section 3(1)(d) provides for those who are unable to communicate a decision in any way. This clearly covers people with physical disorders of the brain, for example, head injuries or strokes, which prevent them communicating as well as people with disorders of the mind which have the same effect.[10] People suffering from such conditions may, in fact, still understand, retain and use information so would not be regarded as lacking capacity under section 3(1)(a)–(c).

[9] *A Local Authority v DL* [2012] EWCA Civ 253.

[10] See *R v C* [2009] UKHL 42, [35].

Any residual ability to communicate (such as blinking an eye to indicate 'yes' or 'no' in answer to a question) means that the person is not within section 3(1)(d).

Where a person lacks capacity to make their own decisions, with the result that someone has to make that decision on their behalf, the decision must be made in their best interests. The factors to be considered when determining best interests are set out in section 4. They include 'the person's past and present wishes and feelings'. However, the wishes and feelings are just one element to be considered.

The Role of Case Law

All decisions made under the MCA have to be evaluated by reference to sections 1–3 which McFarlane LJ described as clear and straightforward, saying that there is neither need nor justification for the plain words of the statute to be embellished.[11]

Both in relation to decisions under the MCA and other decisions, the court has to decide on the particular person's capacity to make that particular decision. Case law gives guidance on what is involved in a particular decision. However, decisions made in previous cases cannot be of any assistance in establishing whether the test is satisfied in the case it is considering.

The Standard and Burden of Proof

The standard of proof whether under the MCA[12] or at common law is the civil standard of the balance of probabilities.

Section 1 of the MCA includes a presumption of capacity. Introducing the Second Reading of the Bill for this Act in the House of Commons the then Parliamentary Under-Secretary of State for Constitutional Affairs (David Lammy) said as follows:

> The Bill is about empowering and protecting people who lack mental capacity. That is its starting point. People have told us that they feel as though they have been 'written off' as unable to do anything for themselves. That is why the principle of an assumption of mental capacity is set out in the very first clause of the Bill.

This presumption applies for the purposes of the MCA and does not necessarily apply in other contexts.[13]

Suggestibility and Undue Influence

A person may have the capacity to make a decision but be prevented from exercising a free choice because of the coercion of another. The High Court retains inherent jurisdiction to intervene in such cases to protect the vulnerable.[14]

[11] *PC (by her litigation friend the Official Solicitor), NC v City of York Council* [2013] EWCA Civ 478, [35].

[12] See MCA 2005, s 2(4).

[13] See *Scammell v Farmer* [2008] EWHC 1100 (Ch) [25]–[30] discussed below in relation to testamentary capacity.

[14] See *A Local Authority v DL* [2012] EWCA Civ 253 and *PC (by her litigation friend the Official Solicitor), NC v City of York Council* [2013] EWCA Civ 478.

Where a person enters into a transaction—typically a lifetime gift—as a result of undue influence, the court can set aside the transaction. Where the donor reposes trust and confidence in the donee and the gift is one which requires an explanation, there is a presumption of undue influence which the donee will have to rebut.[15] The presumption is helpful for those alleging undue influence. No presumption exists in relation to gifts by will. The person alleging undue influence in relation to a will has to prove it and this is often difficult.

Evidence

Professionals who take instructions to carry out a transaction on behalf of another should consider whether the client has the necessary capacity as the validity of the transaction may subsequently be challenged.

Wills are particularly likely to be challenged on the basis of lack of capacity as many testators are elderly or very unwell. It is most important that there is a record of the questions asked to establish capacity and the responses of the client.

Specific Capacities

The statutory test of capacity contained in the MCA, section 2 is prefaced by the words 'for the purposes of this Act'. Accordingly, it should not affect the existing common law definitions of capacity, such as that for making a will.

We saw above that Munby J said in *Local Authority X v MM*[16] the general rule of English law, whatever the context, is that the test of capacity is the ability (whether or not one chooses to exercise it) to understand the nature and quality of the relevant transaction. Later,[17] he identified the elements necessary for a person to have sufficient understanding of any problem in order to have capacity to decide what to do about it, namely the ability to: (i) recognise the problem; (ii) obtain, take in, comprehend and retain information about it; (iii) believe that information; and (iv) evaluate that information so as to arrive at a solution.

Of course, a different level of capacity may be required depending upon the nature of the decision being taken, for example, there is a difference between deciding to go to a foreign country for a short holiday or deciding to emigrate. Despite these differences, stripped of the factors that distinguish one decision from another, the test for capacity in all domains of decision-making is fundamentally the same.

This section of the chapter considers the tests for a representative selection of decisions.

[15] The leading case is the House of Lords decision in *Royal Bank of Scotland v Etridge (No 2) and other appeals* [2001] UKHL 44.

[16] In *Local Authority X v MM (by her litigation friend, the Official Solicitor), KM* [2007] EWHC 2003 (Fam) [67].

[17] At paras 134 and 135.

Testamentary Capacity

The Test

The common law test of testamentary capacity is set out in *Banks v Goodfellow*:[18]

> It is essential to the exercise of such a power that a testator shall understand the nature of the act and its effects; shall understand the extent of the property of which he is disposing; shall be able to comprehend and appreciate the claims to which he ought to give effect; and, with a view to the latter object, that no disorder of the mind shall poison his affections, pervert his sense of right, or prevent the exercise of his natural faculties—that no insane delusion shall influence his will in disposing of his property and bring about a disposal of it which, if the mind had been sound, would not have been made.

Usually people say that there are four elements to the test. The testator must understand:

1. The nature of the act.
2. The extent of the property he has to dispose of.
3. The claims he ought to consider.

In addition the testator must:

4. Not be subject to any disorder of the mind as shall '*poison his affections, pervert his sense of right or prevent the exercise of his natural faculties*', ie, must not be suffering from an insane delusion which affects the dispositions made in the will.

There have been some judicial comments suggesting that the statutory test contained in the MCA has replaced the common law test for testamentary capacity but it is difficult to see that this is correct. As explained at the start of this Chapter, the MCA regulates the Court of Protection not other courts. As the question has so far not been in issue in any case, this Chapter proceeds on the basis that the common law test continues to apply.

In *Banks v Goodfellow* the testator suffered from extreme delusions (that he was pursued and molested by a dead man). However, the delusion did not affect the will he made which left everything to the niece who had cared for him with the result that the will was declared valid.

Of course it is frequently difficult for a court to decide whether or not the dispositions made in a will have been affected by an illness from which the testator was suffering. In *Sharp v Adams*[19] Mr Adams made a will when he was paralysed and unable to speak as a result of advanced multiple sclerosis. Instructions were taken in the form of closed questions from his solicitor. The will was executed in the presence of his doctor and signed by another solicitor who had been asked to attend.

The will excluded Mr Adam's adult daughters, the main beneficiaries being two employees of the testator, with a legacy for a carer. This was contrary to the testator's earlier wills. However, his employees were loyal and hardworking and an earlier will left legacies to them.

[18] *Banks v Goodfellow* (1869–70) LR 5 QB 549.
[19] *Sharp v Adams* [2006] WTLR 1059.

The Court of Appeal hesitantly agreed with the trial judge that the will was invalid.

May LJ made the following points. Mr Adams was in the final stages of a severely debilitating progressive disease, the agreed effect of which was to have impaired his cognitive functions. The question was whether at the time of execution he had crossed an imprecise divide. The first three elements of the *Banks v Goodfellow* test were satisfied. The fourth (no poisoning of the affections) was not.

The trial judge was correct in saying that the justice or otherwise of the exclusion of the daughters must have a bearing on the validity of the decision although such an enquiry must be directed to the testator's soundness of mind and not to general questions of perceived morality. Leaving the residuary estate to the employees was understandable. Leaving nothing at all to his daughters was not.

The case of *Key v Key*,[20] introduced a further development in the application of the *Banks v Goodfellow* test. The case concerned the validity of the will of Mr Key, who died in July 2008. Mr Key made the will at the age of 89, just over a week after the sudden death of his wife.

Mr Key's two daughters discovered that the pre-2006 will left virtually the whole estate to his two sons. They regarded this as unfair and arranged for their father to see a solicitor about a new will. The solicitor did not obtain medical evidence as to testamentary capacity.

Mr Key's sons successfully challenged the new will on the grounds of lack of testamentary capacity and lack of knowledge and approval.

The medical evidence of the experts was that in some cases the effects of bereavement can be almost identical to that associated with severe depression. An effect of this may be increased suggestibility, whereby a person simply assents to suggestions from others. Such an effect could be particularly severe where a person was already suffering some age-related cognitive decline, as was the case with Mr Key.

In the judge's view, while Mr Key had not conspicuously failed to satisfy the test in *Banks v Goodfellow*, psychiatric medicine had come a long way since 1870. The test therefore had to be developed so as to accommodate a wider range of circumstances now regarded as sufficient to give rise to a risk of mental disorder, sufficient to deprive a patient of the power of rational decision-making. A person might have the capacity to understand what his property was, and even who his relatives and dependants were, without having the mental energy to make any decisions of his own about whom to benefit. Briggs J held that Mr Key had been devastated by his wife's death and that during the week following his wife's death he had been 'incompetent to the exertion required' in respect of the decision-making powers of a testator. He therefore did not have testamentary capacity.

The Burden of Proof

The person putting forward a will has to prove that the will is valid. This includes showing that the testator has capacity.

[20] *Key and another v Key and others* [2010] EWHC 408 (Ch).

At common law if the will is rational on its face and the testator is normally capable there is a presumption of mental capacity. However, where there is evidence casting doubt on the testator's capacity, the presumption is rebutted and the person alleging that the will is valid must prove that the testator fulfilled the *Banks v Goodfellow* test. The importance of the burden of proof is illustrated in *Vaughan v Vaughan*[21] where the evidence was equivocal. The will was found invalid on the basis that capacity had not been proved.

Under the MCA the presumption of capacity means that the onus of proof of incapacity is always on the complainant. In *Scammell v Farmer*[22] Stephen Smith QC, sitting as a deputy judge declined to find that the Act applied to the case he was considering for two reasons:

1. The death and commencement of proceedings predated the MCA and it, therefore, could not apply.
2. In any event issues of testamentary capacity were not within the purposes of the MCA.

When Must the Testator have Capacity?

If a testator lacks testamentary capacity at the time the will is executed the will is normally invalid.

The only exception is the rule in *Parker v Felgate*.[23] Under this rule, a will may be valid even though the condition of a testator has deteriorated after giving instructions to such an extent that testamentary capacity is absent at the time the will is executed. The will may still be valid provided when the will was executed the deceased:

— Remembered and understood the instructions he or she had given to the will-maker.
— Understood that he or she was engaged in executing the will for which he or she had given instructions.

If these conditions are satisfied, it does not matter that the testator was not capable of understanding each clause if it had been put to him or her.

Capacity to Make a Gift

In *Re Beaney (Deceased)*[24] Martin Nourse QC, sitting as a deputy judge of the High Court, considered the capacity required to make a gift. A mother who was suffering

21 *Vaughan v Vaughan* [2002] EWHC 699 (Ch) [105].

22 *Scammell v Farmer* [2008] EWHC 1100 (Ch) [25]–[30].

23 *Parker v Felgate and Tilley* (1883) 8 PD 171 applied by the Privy Council in *Perera v Perera* [1901] AC 354 and *Perrins v Holland* [2010] EWCA Civ 840.

24 *Re Beaney (Deceased)* [1978] 2 All ER 595. *Re Beaney* was considered and approved in *Special Trustees for Great Ormond Street Hospital for Children v Pauline Rushin, Caroline Michelle Billinge & others sub nom In the Estate of Lily Louisa Morris (Deceased)* [2001] WTLR 1137. This was a shocking case of 'carer abuse' where a number of substantial gifts made by an elderly lady before her death were held to be invalid. See also *Pesticcio v Huet* [2003] All ER 237 and *Williams v Williams and Another* [2003] EWHC 742 (Ch) where the *Re Beaney* test was applied.

from dementia gave her house (her only substantial asset) to one of her three children. The rival contentions as to the test of capacity were:

i. a narrow view which was that it was only necessary for Mrs Beaney to understand, (1) that she was making a gift, (2) that the subject-matter of the gift was the house, and (3) that the person to whom she was giving it was her daughter, or
ii. a wider view that Mrs Beaney must also understand that she was giving away her only asset of value, and was thus depriving her other two children of any real interest in her estate.

The wider view was essentially an argument that the degree of understanding required for a lifetime gift is the same as that required for the making of a valid will, where it is necessary to show an understanding of the claims of all potential beneficiaries and the extent of the property to be disposed of. Martin Nourse QC accepted that in a case where the gift was of the donor's 'only asset of value' 'the degree of understanding required is as high as that required for a will, and a donor must understand the claims of all potential donees and the extent of the property to be disposed of'.

Where the subject-matter and value of a gift is trivial in relation to the donor's other assets, a lower degree of understanding would suffice.

Capacity to Make an LPA

The capacity to create an enduring power of attorney was considered in *Re K; Re F (Enduring Powers of Attorney)*[25] by Hoffman J who gave the following summary:

> Plainly one cannot expect that the donor should have been able to pass an examination on the provisions of the 1985 Act. At the other extreme, I do not think that it would be sufficient if he realised only that it gave cousin William power to look after his property. Counsel as amicus curiae helpfully summarised the matters which the donor should have understood in order that he can be said to have the nature and effect of the power: first, if such be the terms of the power, that the attorney will be able to assume complete authority over the donor's affairs; second, if such be the terms of the power, that the attorney will in general be able to do anything with the donor's property which the donor could have done; third, that the authority will continue if the donor should be or become mentally incapable; fourth, that if he should be or become mentally incapable, the power will be irrevocable without confirmation by the court (p 316).

The criteria relevant to testing capacity to create a lasting power of attorney will differ somewhat because of the significant differences between EPAs and LPAs. Senior Judge Denzil Lush of the Court of Protection suggests[26] that the donor must be aware of the foreseeable consequences of not executing an LPA,[27]and understand that:

- The LPA cannot be used until it is registered by the Public Guardian.
- In the case of a Health and Welfare LPA the attorney can only make decisions that the donor is contemporaneously incapable of making for himself.

[25] *Re K; Re F (Enduring Powers of Attorney)* [1988] Ch 310.
[26] D Lush (2009) *Cretney & Lush on Lasting and Enduring Powers of Attorney* (UK, Jordan Publishing Ltd) 35.
[27] This is required by the statutory definition of capacity contained in the MCA 2005, s 3(4).

— The donor can revoke an LPA at any time he has capacity to do so without the confirmation of the court.
— The authority conferred by an LPA is subject to the provisions of the MCA and, in particular, section 1 (the principles) and section 4 (best interests).

Capacity to Litigate

Masterman-Lister v Jewell[28] is the leading decision. The Court of Appeal emphasized that, given the issue-specific nature of the test of capacity, it was necessary to consider the nature and complexity of the particular transaction.

Claimants in personal injury actions may well have capacity to deal with all matters and take all 'lay client' decisions related to their actions up to and including a decision whether or not to settle, but may lack capacity to decide (even with advice) how to administer a large award.

The question to be decided is whether the party has the mental capacity, with the assistance of such proper explanation from legal advisers and experts in other disciplines as the case might require, the issues on which his consent or decision was likely to be necessary in the course of those proceedings.

On 1 October 2007 a new Part 21 of the Civil Procedure Rules ('CPR') came into force which provides that for the purposes of the CPR 'lacks capacity' means lacks capacity within the meaning of the MCA. In *Saulle v Nouvet*[29] Andrew Edis QC held that, although Part 21 requires any court considering capacity to litigate to apply the principles of the MCA, the common law test and the MCA are coextensive.

Capacity to Manage One's Affairs

On 23 March 1962 Wilberforce J in *In re CAF* (unreported) held that, when considering a person's capacity to manage and administer his property and affairs, it is necessary to have regard to the complexity and importance of that person's property and affairs. This has been a matter of some debate in Australia, where there has been a suggestion that the test might be that of ability to deal in a reasonably competent fashion with the ordinary affairs of man, but on 12 November 1987 in *White v Fell* (unreported) Boreham J confirmed that the whole test was related to the individual plaintiff and her immediate problems.

In *A v X*,[30] where the Court of Protection had to determine the capacity of an elderly man (X) in relation to a variety of decisions, the medical evidence suggested that X's mental abilities were declining but that there might be some fluctuations. Hedley J said that the management of affairs involves a continuous state of affairs whose demands might be unpredictable and occasionally urgent. X's business affairs were complex and X did not have capacity to manage them. While much of the detail of his affairs was delegated to professional advisers, they were precisely that, advisers and not decision-makers. Decisions on principle, decisions relating to

[28] *Masterman-Lister v Jewell* [2002] EWCA Civ 1889.
[29] *Saulle v Nouvet* [2007] EWHC 2902 (QB) [22].
[30] *A v X* [2012] EWHC 2400 (COP).

the discharge or avoidance of tax liabilities and those kinds of matters had to be taken by X himself, even if the decision was no more than an informed decision as to whether to rely on advice, but he could not escape personal responsibility for a number of decisions that related to his own affairs.

Capacity to Marry

In *Sheffield City Council v E*,[31] a case prior to the MCA, Munby J held that it was not enough for a person to appreciate that she was taking part in a marriage ceremony or understand its words; rather she had to understand the nature of the marriage contract and be mentally capable of understanding the duties and responsibilities that normally attached to marriage. However, 'The contract of marriage is in essence a simple one, which does not require a high degree of intelligence to comprehend'.[32] Munby J added in a later passage that 'There are many people in our society who may be of limited or borderline capacity but whose lives are immensely enriched by marriage. We must be careful not to set the test of capacity to marry too high, lest it operate as an unfair, unnecessary and indeed discriminatory bar against the mentally disabled'.[33]

Having reviewed all the authorities he concluded that the test was capacity to understand the nature of the contract of marriage and not capacity to understand the implications of a *particular* marriage. This is an important distinction as the issue causing concern is often the suitability of the other party. *Sheffield*, is an example of exactly this. E was a 21-year-old girl who functioned at the level of a 13-year-old and planned to marry the second defendant, a man with a substantial history of sexually violent crimes.

The subsequent implementation of the MCA 2005 does not establish any basis for questioning the continued applicability of a general and non-specific approach to capacity to marry in proceedings under the Act[34] and indeed the decision has been followed at first instance after the MCA.[35] Note, however, that the Court of Appeal in *PC and NC v City of York Council* said that while it was clear that capacity to marry is to be assessed in general and as a matter of principle, and not by reference to any particular prospective marriage, it was permissible for the court to personalise the question of whether there is capacity to decide whether or not to have contact with, or reside with, a particular spouse. Because questions of capacity are issue specific, capacity to marry is not the same as capacity to look after oneself. Someone may have the capacity to marry whilst lacking capacity to take care of her own person.

[31] *Sheffield City Council v E* [2005] Fam 326, applying *In the Estate of Park* [1954] P 112.

[32] *Sheffield City Council v E* [2005] Fam 326 [68].

[33] Ibid, [144].

[34] *PC (by her litigation friend the Official Solicitor), NC v City of York Council* [2013] EWCA Civ 478 [23].

[35] In *M v B, A and S (by the Official Solicitor)* [2005] EWHC 1681 (Fam); [2006] 1 FLR 117 and *A, B and C v X and Z* [2012] EWHC 2400 (COP).

Capacity to Consent to Sexual Relations

In Local Authority *X v MM*[36] Munby J applied the same approach, for the same reasons, to the capacity to consent to sexual relations. At paragraph 86 he said:

> The question [capacity to consent to sexual relations] is issue specific, both in the general sense and, as I have already pointed out, in the sense that capacity has to be assessed in relation to the particular kind of sexual activity in question. But capacity to consent to sexual relations is, in my judgment, a question directed to the nature of the activity rather than to the identity of the sexual partner.

Munby J's approach in *MM* was doubted by Baroness Hale in the context of a criminal prosecution for an offence of 'sexual activity with a person with a mental disorder impeding choice' contrary to Sexual Offences Act 2003, section 30. Baroness Hale stated:[37]

> My Lords, it is difficult to think of an activity which is more person and situation specific than sexual relations. One does not consent to sex in general. One consents to this act of sex with this person at this time and in this place. Autonomy entails the freedom and the capacity to make a choice of whether or not to do so.

Subsequently Mostyn J held that the House of Lords decision in *R v Cooper* is limited to the application of the test in section 30 of the 2003 Act and is not inconsistent with the approach of Munby J in *X v MM*. Mostyn J therefore held that in proceedings under the MCA capacity to consent to sexual relations is act-specific and not partner-specific. This was confirmed by the Court of Appeal in *IM v LM and others [2014] EWCA Civ 37*. The Court of Appeal found that, when determining consent to sexual relations, the Court of Protection's focus was necessarily forward-looking whereas the focus of the criminal courts was on a particular past event, with the issue of consent being evaluated retrospectively. The appeal judges also found that it would be totally impractical for the Court of Protection or a local authority to assess capacity to consent in respect of every prospective partner.

As is the case with capacity to marry, the test raises difficult issues. In *Local Authority X v M*[38] Munby J referred to this passage from *Rook & Ward* on Sexual Offences—*Law and Practice*.[39] At paragraph 7.03 the learned authors observe that:

> Although there is a clear need to protect the mentally disordered from sexual abuse, it is important that the law is not drawn so restrictively that it denies the mentally disordered their right to engage in sexual relationships ... There is in this area an inherent potential conflict between legislative paternalism and sexual freedom; what is clear is that there is a delicate balance to be struck between undue state interference in an individual's sexual life and the state's responsibility to protect an individual from exploitation and abuse.

[36] *X v MM* [2007] EWHC 2003 (Fam) at [38].
[37] *R v Cooper* [2009] UKHL 42 [27].
[38] *Local Authority X v M* [2007] EWHC 2003.
[39] *Rook & Ward on Sexual Offences—Law and Practice*, 3rd edn (London, Sweet & Maxwell, 2004).

ASSESSING CAPACITY: MEDICAL ASPECTS

Assessing Capacity in Life

Capacity as a Cognitive Process

In England and Wales, the term 'capacity' has come to refer to both the clinical and legal concept of the ability to make particular decisions. The passage of the Mental Capacity Act 2005 ('MCA') has reinforced this usage. In the US, there has been a tendency to use the term 'competency' for a person's legal status in terms of decision-making power, and 'capacity' to refer to the clinical status as judged by a health care professional. A judge might therefore use a clinical assessment of capacity to come a legally binding decision as to whether or not a particular person is competent to carry out a specific act. In practice, even in the US the two terms have tended to become conflated.

Capacity can fluctuate. Some types of dementia such as dementia with Lewy bodies or Parkinson's disease dementia are more likely than others to fluctuate, often quite markedly. This can make it difficult to reach a conclusion following assessment that a person lacks capacity since it is possible that on another occasion, the person might have capacity. Similarly a person may experience a temporary worsening in mental state, and hence in capacity, because of a temporary physical illness such as an infection of the urinary tract or chest (this may be referred to as delirium or acute confusional state). Repeated interviews on different occasions can help to make clear these kinds of variations. Under previous English legislation it was necessary to register an Enduring Power of Attorney at the specific moment when the donor of the power was considered to have lost capacity to manage his or her affairs. From that point on, the donor was no longer considered able to make any financial decisions. Under the MCA, the matter is treated more flexibly, and for each decision, if the donor has capacity to make the decision he may do so, but if not, the attorney under a Lasting Power of Attorney should make it for him. This accords much more closely with the reality that capacity is not an all or nothing affair: it may vary with the occasion and with the task to be decided.

Diagnosis and capacity are not the same thing. The MCA states at section 2(3)(b) that a decision about a person's capacity should not be made on the basis of 'a condition of his … which might lead others to make unjustified assumptions about his capacity'. Clearly, there are many diagnoses which may affect capacity—these included not only the various forms of dementia, but also depression, anxiety, psychotic illnesses and intellectual disability—but one is not entitled to conclude without further assessment that a person with any of these diagnoses necessarily lacks capacity for any given matter.

In general terms, as discussed above, in order to have the capacity to make a particular decision the decision-maker needs to understand the nature and quality of that decision. This requires a cognitive process of understanding to occur. A number of researchers have developed the assessment of capacity by defining more clearly exactly what the underlying cognitive requirements for capacity are, and then developing test scales which examine these underlying elements more closely. This approach has been developed most fully for capacity to make treatment decisions (Appelbaum and Grisso, 1995; Marson et al, 2012). Typically, the assessor presents a series of vignettes and asks a number of questions about each, designed to bring out the elements underlying the treatment decision. Marson and colleagues used their Capacity to Consent to Treatment Instrument (CCTI) (Marson et al, 1995) to assess the capacity of a group of older controls (healthy people without mental disorder) and people with mild or moderate Alzheimer's disease to consent to medical treatment. They found no differences between the groups for the simplest levels of understanding, but limitations in the dementia groups for the more complex understanding required for competency. As might be expected, these limitations were greater the more severe the dementia. It is helpful to have clear empirical evidence that people with dementia may still have capacity to make decisions, particularly in the early stages.

Setting up the Interview to Enhance Capacity

The MCA Code of Practice makes clear that everything possible should be done to enhance capacity. Thought should be given to carrying out the assessment at a place and time where the person concerned will be likely to feel most comfortable and at ease. It may be helpful to have a trusted friend or family member available (but care must be taken to ensure that any additional person cannot influence the capacity assessment inappropriately). Where necessary, an interpreter, or simple aids and reminders may be useful. It is a moot point how far one can go in providing reminders. For example, the case law tests of testamentary capacity require the testator to understand the extent of his estate and the claims of those who might be considered in the will. Is it reasonable to provide reminders of these things at the time of the assessment, or should the testator be able to remember them without assistance? Is it sufficient for the testator to be able to explain a written summary of these matters which has been prepared as a reminder for him and to retain it in his mind for long enough to give his instructions? Case law is not clear on these points, but it is suggested that as the MCA and its Code require that everything possible is done to promote capacity, including the provision of information (Code, paragraph 3.7), that this approach of providing written reminders may be reasonable. They can certainly be helpful in enabling a discussion with the testator as to what his wishes are and why he has come to that position.

Asking Questions and Establishing Understanding

In evaluating a person's understanding, it is not sufficient for the assessor simply to state the details of the matter to be understood, and then ask if the subject understands it. Many people, even with quite severe mental disorders, may understand that they are being asked a question to which it would be polite to answer, 'yes', and will do so. It is necessary to hear the subject explain back the meaning of the matter in question. A useful scheme, having explained the purpose of the interview, is to ask the subject to explain his understanding of the matter. If he is unable to do so, the assessor may give an explanation in terms which are simple enough to have an expectation that the subject should understand (the Code of Practice encourages the use of simple, clear language), and then invite the subject to explain it back in his own words. The requirement of the MCA is that the subject should retain this understanding for long enough to use or weigh the information in order to make the decision in question, and so it may be necessary to ask again at the end of the interview to check that the understanding has been retained.

The Place of Rating Scales

In a study of 74 patients with varying degrees of cognitive impairment, 25 of those with mild impairment were considered to have testamentary capacity while two did not, 14 of those with moderate cognitive impairment had testamentary capacity while 13 did not, and only one of those with severe cognitive impairment had testamentary capacity, while 19 did not (Roked and Patel, 2008). Clearly and unsurprisingly, cognitive impairment often but not always impairs capacity to make decisions, and the more severe it is the more likely it is that capacity is undermined. In a subject where there is a suspicion of impaired capacity, and an expert assessment of capacity has been requested, it is suggested that it is good practice to assess the level of cognitive function. This is not a requirement, since the MCA requirement is only to determine whether or not the subject is capable of managing the four-stage test of capacity, to understand, retain, use or weigh and communicate a decision. However, if one is making an expert assessment of capacity on an important matter such as any of those discussed in the first part of this chapter, it is important to show that the underlying cognitive abilities have been considered.

Assessment of cognitive function can vary enormously in complexity from the simple and quick ten item Hodkinson mental test score to a neuropsychological assessment lasting many hours spread across several test sessions. Not every case requires detailed assessment, and it is reasonable to have a sense of proportion in relation to the significance of the matter to be determined, and the doubtfulness of capacity in that subject. It may be very obvious that the person lacks capacity, in which case the assessment might be quite short. Borderline capacity normally takes longer to assess. Relevant cognitive skills include not only the understanding of language and memory, but also include judgement and the ability to weigh things up in a reasonable way. Some disorders, characteristically fronto-temporal dementias, may affect judgement quite subtly, and may require specific kinds of assessment to diagnose. Knowledge of a person's history and decision-making over recent years may be relevant: in order to determine this will often require an interview with an informant or consulting relevant medical or other records. A person who starts to make rash or unwise decisions later in life could be suffering from one or another form of dementia, even though memory changes are not obvious. Formal neuropsychological tests and brain imaging can help to disclose such disorders.

Keeping Records

Clearly, any professional who makes a formal assessment of capacity needs to keep appropriate records in the event of a later challenge. A doctor who acts as a witness to a will should assume that a court will expect him to have satisfied himself as to the capacity of the testator before witnessing it.

Assessing Capacity Retrospectively

Obtaining Records

In making a retrospective assessment of capacity the assessment is clearly greatly hindered by the lack of interviewee. Nevertheless, courts may need such an assessment to be carried out on the basis of whatever evidence may be obtained. This usually arises in the context of a claim against a disputed will, contract or gift. The first step therefore is to consider what sources may be available. Medical records are needed. These are likely to include GP records, but may also include hospital records. There may be social services records. Where there has been a contemporaneous assessment of capacity this can be extremely helpful. Where a person has been cared for at home, there may be records of the daily carer visits. Solicitors will usually make an attendance note. Those who knew the testator may be able to make depositions about their knowledge of him or her at the material time.

Establishing a Chronology

A chronology is an extremely helpful way of organizing what is often a diverse and possibly extensive mass of material. It is useful to set this out as a table giving the date and source of each piece of information. It is important to distinguish the date of the record from the date of the event to which it refers. Records are very often written in an imprecise or casual way, and it is often important to refer to the exact wording used in the record.

Reaching a Conclusion

Although the question of capacity to carry out a particular act is the focus of the enquiry, there are key related questions. In the UK, a lack of capacity must be due to 'an impairment of, or a disturbance in the functioning of, the mind or the brain' (MCA 2005, section 2(1)). To this extent, diagnosis is important. It is not enough simply that the person made an unwise decision. There must be evidence of impairment or disturbance in mind or brain function. For older clients this will most commonly be in the form of a diagnosis of dementia or cognitive impairment, though other diagnoses can and often do affect capacity. The leading case of *Banks v Goodfellow* concerned a psychotic illness, not dementia.

A second question is whether the doubt is over capacity or undue influence. In the UK, it is generally very difficult to demonstrate undue influence at a level that meets the legal test of the will being overborne, and so most case law concerns capacity. In the US, undue influence is more often argued than in the UK. Frolik (2001) summarizes the essential elements of undue influence as:

1. A confidential relationship existed between the testator and the influencer.
2. The influencer used that relationship to secure a change in how the testator distributed his estate.
3. The change in the estate plan was unconscionable or did not reflect the true desires of the testator.
4. The testator was susceptible to being influenced.

Points 1–3 are external to the testator, but point 4 can be affected by his mental state and/or diagnosis. As with capacity, the mere fact of a diagnosis does not establish susceptibility, but it may be highly relevant.

Once the issue is defined, and the material assembled, the task of the assessor is then to take what information there is and reach a conclusion on the balance of probability. The task is to reach the best opinion possible on the evidence available, and this will rarely be as confident an opinion as one might reach on the basis of an interview during life.

REFERENCES

Appelbaum, PS and Grisso, T (1995) 'The MacArthur Treatment Competence Study' 19(2) *Law & Human Behavior (Springer Science & Business Media BV)* 105–74. doi: 10.1007/BF01499321.

Frolik, LA (2001) 'The strange interplay of testamentary capacity and the doctrine of undue influence: are we protecting older testators or overriding individual preferences?' 24(2–3) *International Journal of Law and Psychiatry* 253–66. doi: dx.doi.org/10.1016/S0160-2527(00)00081-9.

Marson, DC et al (1995) 'Assessing the competency of patients with Alzheimer's disease under different legal standards: A prototype instrument' 52(10) *Archives of Neurology* 949–54. doi: 10.1001/archneur.1995.00540340029010.

—— (2012) 'Assessing civil competencies in older adults with dementia' in GJ Larrabee (ed), *Forensic Neuropsychology: a scientific approach*, 2nd edn (New York, Oxford University Press).

Roked, F and Patel, A (2008) 'Which aspects of cognitive function are best associated with testamentary capacity in patients with Alzheimer's disease?' 23(5) *International Journal of Geriatric Psychiatry* 552–53. doi: 10.1002/gps.1947.

25

Best Interests and Dementia

JONATHAN HERRING

THIS CHAPTER CONSIDERS the law that applies in England and Wales when a person with dementia is found to lack capacity. Of course, it does not follow that because a person has dementia they therefore lack capacity. Plenty of people with dementia will have the capacity to make some decisions. The test for capacity under the Mental Capacity Act 2005 (MCA) is decision-specific, meaning that a person may have sufficient understanding to make some decisions, but not others. So, in *Cardiff County Council v Ross* (2011) it was held that an 82-year-old woman with dementia had sufficient capacity to decide to go on a cruise with a friend, even though she lacked the capacity to make other decisions. Where a person lacks capacity their treatment is covered by the MCA and decisions can be made on their behalf based on their 'best interests'. This chapter will primarily focus on what 'best interests' means in this context.

WHICH DECISIONS ARE SUBJECT TO THE BEST INTERESTS TEST?

Before exploring the meaning of best interests it is worth noting that there are some things that it is not possible to authorize on behalf of a person lacking capacity. These include:

- Consenting to marriage or a civil partnership.
- Consenting to have sexual relations.
- Consenting to a decree of divorce on the basis of two years' separation.
- Consenting to the dissolution of a civil partnership.
- Consenting to a child being placed for adoption or the making of an adoption order.
- Discharging parental responsibility for a child in matters not relating to the child's property.
- Giving consent under the Human Fertilisation and Embryology Act 1990.
- Voting in an election.

(MCA, 2005: sections 27–28)

On those issues—even though someone thought it would be in someone's best interests—a decision could not be made on their behalf. So, even if a close relative thought it would be in the best interests of a person with dementia to marry, they could not provide consent for that; only if the person with dementia had capacity to decide to marry, and decided they wished to marry, could they do so.

WHO MAKES THE DECISION?

If the patient has made an advance decision which is valid and applicable, it must be complied with. These are discussed in chapters eight and twenty-six, and will not be discussed further here, save to recall that they can only be used to refuse treatment and cannot be used to insist on treatment.

If there is no valid and applicable advance decision, a decision must be made in the best interests of the person lacking capacity (P). The assessment will be made by the holder of a lasting power of attorney or a deputy appointed by the court, if there is one. Most commonly, the best interests assessment is to be made by those who care for P. If there is a dispute, the court will need to determine what is to be done based on what is in P's best interests.

ASSESSING BEST INTERESTS: THE GENERAL APPROACH

The MCA, section 4, states that, in deciding what is in a patient's best interests, the decision maker (D) must consider all the relevant circumstances. This involves consideration of a wide range of factors. It is important to realize that D is not trying to work out what P would have decided, nor are they deciding what decision they would make for themselves. The decision is about what is best for P. The Mental Capacity Act *Code of Practice* states:

> When working out what is in the best interests of the person who lacks capacity to make a decision or act for themselves, decision makers must take into account all relevant factors that it would be reasonable to consider, not just those that they think are important. They must not act or make a decision based on what they would want to do if they were the person who lacked capacity (DCA, 2007: paragraph 5.7).

Munby J (as he then was) in *Re MM* (2007) summarized well the approach that should be adopted in determining a person's best interests:

> MM's welfare is the paramount consideration. The focus must be on MM's best interests, and this involves a welfare appraisal in the widest sense, taking into account, where appropriate, a wide range of ethical, social, moral, emotional and welfare considerations. Where, as will often be the case, the various factors engaged pull in opposite directions, the task of ascertaining where the individual's best interests truly lie will be assisted by preparation of a 'balance sheet' of the kind suggested by Thorpe LJ in *Re A (Male Sterilisation)* [2000] 1 FLR 549 at page 560. This will enable the judge, at the end of the day, to strike what Thorpe LJ referred to as 'a balance between the sum of the certain and possible gains against the sum of the certain and possible losses (paragraph 99).

We will now explore some particular aspects of the best interests test.

A PERSON'S POTENTIAL CAPACITY

Section 4(3) of the MCA states that the decision maker must consider '(a) whether it is likely that the person will at some time have capacity in relation to the matter in question, and (b) if it appears likely that he will, when that is likely to be'. This is an important provision. If P lacks capacity, but is likely to regain it soon and the decision can be put off until then, it should be. So if P is having a bad day and is particularly confused and so lacks capacity to make a decision about non-urgent medication, there should be a delay until they are able to make the decision. In *CC v KK* (2012) where it was held that although a woman with dementia did not currently understand the issues about residence, she would do if given more information; she should be enabled to make the decision, rather than the best interests test being used. This reflects the principle that wherever possible it is best if a person makes a decision for themselves.

CURRENT VIEWS

Section 4(4) of the MCA states that the decision maker must 'so far as reasonably practicable, permit and encourage the person to participate, or to improve his ability to participate, as fully as possible in any act done for him and any decision affecting him'. Further, the decision maker must consider, so far as is reasonably ascertainable that, '(a) the person's past and present wishes and feelings (and, in particular, any relevant written statement made by him when he had capacity)' (MCA, 2005: section 4(6)).

These provisions make it clear that even though P may lack capacity that does not mean P's views and feelings count for nothing. Indeed, there is recognition in section 4 that even if it is not possible for P to make a decision, they should still be involved to a reasonable extent in the decision-making process and their views should be listened to.

Of course there are some people with very advanced dementia where it will be impossible to ascertain their views. In other cases care must be taken to ensure P's views are understood. In *IIBCC v LG* (2010), involving an elderly woman with dementia, there was considerable discussion over when she said she wanted to 'go home' that referred to her childhood home or to live with her daughter.

There are two primary ways that P's views may be relevant for a best interests assessment. The first is a practical one. If P resists the proposed course of action, force may be required or distress may be caused. Therefore, when considering whether giving treatment against P's wishes is in their best interests, the medical benefits of the treatment must be weighed against the emotional distress and force which may be required. It has been suggested by Mary Donnelly (2009) that where a patient is actively resisting the course of action it should only be performed if there is evidence that the procedure is very much in their best interests.

In *A Local Authority v Mrs A and Mr A* (2010) it was held that Mrs A lacked capacity to make a decision about whether to receive a contraceptive injection because her husband dominated her will. The court determined that it would be in her best interests to receive the injection. However, despite that conclusion, the court went on to hold that it would not order her to be given the contraception without her consent because that would cause her too much harm and indignity. The decision has proved controversial. It has been criticized for downplaying the dangers of not receiving contraception (Herring, 2010). Although compelling her to receive the contraceptive injection would have interfered with her bodily integrity, would it have done so any less than an unwanted pregnancy?

Second, even if P's views are not entirely rational they are deserving of respect. Even people with capacity act on the basis of emotional responses. It is important to listen to P and respect P's dignity, by taking their feelings into account, even if P has lost capacity (Herring, 2009). As Norman Cantor has argued, 'It would be dehumanizing to ignore the will and feelings of a profoundly disabled person and to simply impose a surrogate's will. This would treat the prospective patient as if he or she were an inanimate object' (2005: 206). This argument may be particularly strong where P is on the borderlines of incapacity.

As Munby J stated in *Re MM (An Adult)*:

> The nearer to the borderline the particular adult, even if she falls on the wrong side of the line, the more weight must in principle be attached to her wishes and feelings, because the greater the distress, the humiliation and indeed it may even be the anger she is likely to feel (2007: paragraph 121).

There appears to be some judicial disagreement over the weight to be attached to P's views.

In *Re S and S (Protected Persons) (2008)* Judge Marshall QC stated that P's views and wishes should carry 'great weight' (paragraph 55) in a best interests assessment, but are not paramount (paragraph 56). She added:

> What, after all, is the point of taking great trouble to ascertain or deduce P's views, and to encourage P to be involved in the decision making process, unless the objective is to try to achieve the outcome which P wants or prefers, even if he does not have the capacity to achieve it for himself? . . . Given the policy of the Act to empower people to make their own decisions wherever possible, justification for overruling P and 'saving him from himself' must, in my judgment, be strong and cogent (paragraphs 57–58).

Judge Lewison in *Re P (2009)* thought that Judge Marshall may have 'slightly overstated' the importance of P's wishes. In his view the wishes of the individual were a part of the 'balance sheet' to be used to determine best interests; but only a part. Eleanor King J more recently in *IIBCC v LG* (2010) has emphasized that P's views are 'an important part' of the best interests assessment.

In perhaps the most helpful guidance, Munby J in *Re MM* (2007) warned against having a precise formula for the weight to attach to a person's wishes and feelings, saying it was 'case-specific and fact-specific'. He went on to list the factors to be considered when determining the weight that should be attached to them: the degree of the person's incapacity; the strength and consistency of the views being expressed by the person; the possible impact on the person of knowledge that her wishes and feelings are not being given effect; the extent to which the person's wishes and feelings are, or are not, 'rational, sensible, responsible and pragmatically capable of sensible implementation in the particular circumstances'; and, 'crucially, the extent to which P's wishes and feelings, if given effect to, can properly be accommodated within the court's overall assessment of what is in her best interests' (paragraph 35).

Whatever weight is given to P's current wishes, it is clear that it may ultimately be decided that P's wishes do not coincide with their best interests. The Code of Practice (DCA, 2007: 81) provides an example:

> Andre, a young man with severe learning disabilities who does not use any formal system of communication, cuts his leg while outdoors. There is some earth in the wound. A doctor

> wants to give him a tetanus jab, but Andre appears scared of the needle and pushes it away. Assessments have shown that he is unable to understand the risk of infection following his injury, or the consequences of rejecting the injection. The doctor decides that it is in Andre's best interests to give the vaccination. She asks a nurse to comfort Andre, and if necessary, restrain him while she gives the injection. She has objective reasons for believing she is acting in Andre's best interests, and for believing that Andre lacks capacity to make the decision for himself. So she should be protected from liability under section 5 of the Act.

A PERSON'S PAST VIEWS

Section 4(6) of the Mental Capacity Act states that when determining a person's best interests D must consider, so far as is reasonably ascertainable: '(a) the person's past and present wishes and feelings (and, in particular, any relevant written statement made by him when he had capacity), (b) the beliefs and values that would be likely to influence his decision if he had capacity, and (c) the other factors that he would be likely to consider if he were able to do so'.

It is clear that the best interests test is different from the substituted judgement test (*M v A NHS Trust* (2011) and see chapter 12). Under that approach, D must seek to guess what decision P would have made had P had capacity. Under the best interests test it is perfectly possible for D to decide that something is in P's best interests, even while accepting it is not the decision P would have made had P got capacity. Nevertheless, an assessment of what decision P would have made if competent can be taken into account in deciding what are in P's best interests. In particular, one could imagine a case where there are a range of options which could plausibly be in P's interests, but P's past wishes clearly indicate which would be best for them. For example, in *Ahsan v University Hospitals Leicester NHS Trust* (2006) a dispute arose in the context of a tort case over the care of a Muslim woman who had been seriously injured and was unaware of what was happening to her. Her family wanted her to be cared for in accordance with Muslim tradition, but this would be more expensive than other care. The defendant argued that, as she had no awareness of what was happening to her, it was not in her best interests to receive Muslim care. This was firmly rejected by Hegarty J:

> I do not think for one moment that a reasonable member of the public would consider that the religious beliefs of an individual and her family should simply be disregarded in deciding how she should be cared for in the unhappy event of supervening mental incapacity. On the contrary, I would have thought that most reasonable people would expect, in the event of some catastrophe of that kind, that they would be cared for, as far as practicable, in such a way as to ensure that they were treated with due regard for their personal dignity and with proper respect for their religious beliefs.

Ahsan was an easy case in that was clear what P's views were. In other cases that may be debatable. In *M v A NHS Trust* (2011) Baker J refused to place substantial weight on general remarks P made several years before she became ill about not wanting to be dependent on others in deciding whether to continue life-sustaining treatment. It seems that only clear expressions of opinion on issues that directly relate to P's condition will carry significant weight.

THE VIEWS OF P'S RELATIVES AND CARERS

Another aspect to be taken into account in assessing best interests are the views of: '(a) anyone named by the person as someone to be consulted on the matter in question or on matters of that kind, (b) anyone engaged in caring for the person or interested in his welfare, (c) any donee of a lasting power of attorney granted by the person, and (d) any deputy appointed for the person by the court, as to what would be in the patient's best interests'. The decision maker should consult with these people and may consult with others who know P well (DCA, 2007: paragraph 4.23). However, the views of family members are to be taken into account only in so far as they assist in determining P's best interests (*Re MM (An Adult)* (2007): paragraph 108). They can never be used to justify making an order which would be against P's best interests (*A Primary Care Trust v P, AH, A Local Authority* (2008)). Where a family member has abused P their views are likely to carry little weight (*IIBCC v LG* (2010)). What might or might not be more convenient for the relatives or in accordance with their religious beliefs is not to be taken into account: only their views about what will be best for P can be. In *A Local Authority v K* (2013) the views of P's parents about what was best for them were taken into account, but were not determinative.

As already mentioned, care must be taken to ensure that, when taking the views of carers and relatives into account, the focus is on what is best for P, rather than what is best for their relatives. However, it is not always easy to separate out the interests of P and those who care for P.

This is demonstrated in the case *Re Y (Mental Patient: Bone Marrow Donation)* (1997). Y (aged 25) was severely mentally and physically handicapped. She lived in a community home but was regularly visited by her mother. Y's sister suffered from a bone disorder and her only real prospect of recovery was a bone marrow donation. Y was in medical terms a suitable donor but due to her disabilities was unable to consent. The sister sought a declaration authorizing the harvesting of bone marrow.

Connell J granted the declaration. The basis of the reasoning was that by making the donation to her sister this would benefit Y's mother who was very important to Y's well-being. Y's mother was in ill health, partly due to anxiety concerning the sister's state of health. There was some evidence that if the sister were to die this would be fatal to the mother. If she were to die this would severely distress Y. Also, it was held that Y would receive an emotional, psychological and social benefit from the operation. Connell J indicated that the fact that the operation required Y to suffer only a 'minimal detriment' was an important aspect of the decision to authorize the harvesting.

It has been argued that it is not in a patient's interests to live in a relationship in which no account is taken of the interests of their carer, especially where that carer is a member of their family. Few people would be happy with the idea that if they were to fall incompetent, a decision would have to be made if it benefited them a little bit, even if that caused grave harm to the person caring for them (Herring, 2008). Indeed, no carer could take every decision for a person who had lost capacity based solely on what is in that person's best interests. This argument might suggest that the interests of P's carers are relevant as part of P's best interests.

This raises a broader issue about whether the interests of others are relevant in assessing the interests of P. In *Re G (TJ)* (2010) a woman had lost capacity. The question arose whether payments she had been making to her adult daughter, of whom she was fond and who was in financial need, should continue. Morgan J held:

> [T]he word 'interest' in the best interests test does not confine the court to considering the self-interest of P. The actual wishes of P, which are altruistic and not in any way, directly or indirectly self-interested, can be a relevant factor. Further, the wishes which P would have formed, if P had capacity, which may be altruistic wishes, can be a relevant factor (paragraph 56).

As this case demonstrates 'best interests' need not be interpreted in a selfish way (Herring and Foster, 2012). It can include acting altruistically to one's friends and family.

REMOVING P FROM THEIR HOME

A particularly difficult issue that can arise in some cases involving those with dementia concerns moving P from their home and their family. This is dealt with on the basis of the best interests test. In *A Local Authority v E (2007)* it was held that although there is no presumption that a person lacking capacity is better off cared for by their family than in an institution, 'nevertheless the normal assumption [is] that mentally incapacitated adults who have been looked after within their family will be better off if they continue to be looked after within the family rather than by the state' (paragrah 66). In *K v LBX* (2012) the Court of Appeal emphasized that there was no presumption that a person was better off living with their family. Nevertheless, removing someone from their family could interfere with their rights under Article 8 of the European Convention on Human Rights and so the court must be sure that interference is justified.

In these cases the courts will take into account the quality of care offered by the family. So where there is evidence that family members cannot cope with P's needs, then a decision is likely to be made to move them to a care home (*SCC v LM* (2013)). Nevertheless, in *Re P* (2011) there was judicial acknowledgement of the desire to allow people, if at all possible, to spend their end time within the family rather than in an institution, even if there would be shortcomings in terms of care.

FACTORS NOT TO BE CONSIDERED

There are two factors which the decision maker should not take into account in determining a person's best interests:

1. A decision as to what is in a person's best interests should not be made merely on the basis of: '(a) the person's age or appearance, or (b) a condition of his, or an aspect of his behaviour, which might lead others to make unjustified assumptions about what might be in his best interests'. (MCA, 2005: section 4(1)). This might be most relevant in combating assumptions about older people and what is best for them.

2. Section 4(5) states: 'Where the determination relates to life-sustaining treatment [the decision maker] must not, in considering whether the treatment is in the best interests of the person concerned, be motivated by a desire to bring about his death'. Life-sustaining treatment is defined as 'treatment which in the view of the person providing the health care for the person concerned is necessary to sustain life'.

USE OF FORCE

The Mental Capacity Act 2005, section 1(6) emphasizes that:

> Before the act is done, or decision is made, regard must be had to whether the purpose for which it is needed can be effectively achieved in a way that is less restrictive of the person's rights and freedom of action.

There are special rules which apply where force or restraint is to be used against P. A Code of Practice (*The Deprivation of Liberty Code of Practice*) has indicated the kinds of people for whom these special rules apply:

> The safeguards apply to people in England and Wales who have a mental disorder and lack capacity to consent to the arrangements made for their care or treatment, but for whom receiving care or treatment in circumstances that amount to a deprivation of liberty may be necessary to protect them from harm and appears to be in their best interests. A large number of these people will be those with significant learning disabilities, or older people who have dementia or some similar disability, but they can also include those who have certain other neurological conditions (for example as a result of a brain injury) (Ministry of Justice 2009: paragraph 1.7).

The Code produced the following non-exhaustive list of factors which would indicate whether someone is deprived of their liberty (see *J v GU* (2012) for further discussion on these):

- Restraint is used, including sedation, to admit a person to an institution where that person is resisting admission.
- Staff exercise complete and affective control over the care and movement of a person for a significant period.
- Staff exercise control over assessments, treatment, contacts and residence.
- A decision has been taken by the institution that the person will not be released into the care of others, or permitted to live elsewhere, unless the staff in the institution consider it appropriate.
- A request by carers for a person to be discharged to their care is refused.
- The person is unable to maintain social contacts because of restrictions placed on their access to other people.
- The person loses autonomy because they are under continuous supervision and control. (Ministry of Justice, 2009: paragraph 2.5)

The Deprivation of Liberty Code of Practice adds:

> Depriving someone who lacks the capacity to consent to the arrangements made for their care or treatment of their liberty is a serious matter, and the decision to do so should not

be taken lightly. The deprivation of liberty safeguards make it clear that a person may only be deprived of their liberty:

— in their own best interests to protect them from harm
— if it is a proportionate response to the likelihood and seriousness of the harm, and
— if there is no less restrictive alternative
(Ministry of Justice, 2009: paragraph 1.13).

These provisions recognize that, where a person is having force used against them or is being deprived of their liberty, their human rights are being infringed and so an especially strong justification is required.

CONCLUSION

Where a person lacks capacity and a decision is to be made on their behalf then the best interests test is to be used. The notion of best interests has been interpreted broadly: it includes not just medical issues, but also questions of a person's social, family and moral best interests too. This is a welcome acknowledgement of the complexity of human life and that there are many facets to human nature. The courts have also, correctly, avoided creating any presumptions about best interests and encouraged decision makers to look at all the different factor and consider the particular person at the heart of the decision-making process to decide what is best for them.

REFERENCES

Cantor, N (2005) *Making Medical Decisions for the Profoundly Mentally Disabled* (New York, MIT Press).

Department for Constitutional Affairs (DCA) (2007) *Mental Capacity Act 2005: Code of Practice.*

Donnelly, M (2009) 'Best interests, patient participation and the Mental Capacity Act 2005' 17(1) *Medical Law Review* 1–31.

Herring, J (2008) 'Caregivers in medical law and ethics' 25(1) *Journal of Contemporary Health Law and Policy* 1–37.

—— (2009) 'Losing it? Losing what? The law and dementia' 21(1) *Child and Family Law Quarterly* 3–29.

—— (2010) 'The right to choose' 160 *New Law Journal* 1066–68.

Herring, J and Foster, C (2012) 'Welfare means rationality, virtue and altruism' 32 *Legal Studies* 480–99.

Mental Capacity Act 2005.

Ministry of Justice (2009) *Deprivation of Liberty Safeguards* (London, The Stationery Office).

CASES

A Local Authority v E [2007] EWHC 2396 (Fam).
A Local Authority v K [2013] EWHC 242 (COP).
A Local Authority v Mrs A and Mr A [2010] EWHC 1549 (Fam).
A Primary Care Trust v P, AH, A Local Authority [2008] EWHC 1403 (Fam).

Ahsan v University Hospitals Leicester NHS Trust [2006] EWHC 2624 (QB).
Cardiff County Council v Ross (2011) COP 12063905.
CC v KK [2012] EWHC 2136 (COP).
HBCC v LG [2010] EWHC 1527 (Fam).
J v GU [2012] EWHC 3531 (COP).
K v LBX [2012] EWCA Civ 7.
M v A NHS Trust [2011] EWHC 2443 (Fam).
Re MM (An Adult) [2007] EWHC 2003 (Fam).
Re G (TJ) [2010] EWHC 3005 (COP).
Re P [2009] EWHC 163 (Ch).
Re P [2011] EWHC 2778 (Fam).
Re S and S (Protected Persons) Cases 11475121 and 11475138 (COP) (25 November 2008).
Re Y (Mental Patient: Bone Marrow Donation) [1997] 2 FCR 172.
SCC v LM [2013] EWHC 1137 (COP).

26

Proxy Decision-Making: A Legal Perspective

WINSOR C SCHMIDT

INTRODUCTION

> Last summer, Frederick C Hayes was admitted to the advanced-dementia unit at Jewish Home Lifecare, on West 106th Street. It was not an easy arrival. Hayes, a veteran of the Korean War, had been a trial lawyer for five decades. He was tall, and, though he was in his early eighties, he remained physically imposing, and he had a forceful disposition that had served him well in the courtroom. One of his closest friends liked to say that if things were peaceful Hayes would start a war, but in war he'd be the best friend you could have.
>
> Hayes practiced law until 2010, when he went to hospital for a knee operation. While there, he was given a diagnosis of Alzheimer's disease. His combative tendencies had become markedly pronounced, and before arriving at Jewish Home he was shuttled among several institutions. Nobody could manage his behavior, even after Haldol, a powerful antipsychotic drug, was prescribed. In the advanced-dementia unit, he appeared to be in considerable discomfort, but when doctors there asked him to characterize his pain on a scale of one to ten, he insisted that he was not in pain at all. Still, something was clearly wrong: he lashed out at the nurses' aides, pushing them away and even kicking them. It took three aides to get him changed. (Mead, 2013: 92).

THIS NARRATIVE ABOUT an attorney with Alzheimer's disease provides a poignant reminder that a legal perspective on proxy decision-making in dementia is personal for many readers of this chapter. The law regarding proxy decision-making and dementia should do unto others what it would have done to its own practitioners.

A 'proxy' is '[o]ne who is authorized to act as a substitute for another', '[t]he grant of authority by which a person is so authorized' or, '[t]he document granting this authority' (Garner, 2009). 'Proxy decision-making' in dementia refers to (a) decisions made by an individual or entity authorized to act for a person with dementia, (b) the granting of authority by which the proxy is authorized to act, or (c) a document granting authority of a proxy to act for a person with dementia.

This chapter addresses major problems and questions about proxy decision-making in dementia from a legal perspective focusing on: proxy decision-making as a constitutional right; advance directives; family consent statutes; guardianship; and supported decision-making under the Convention on the Rights of Persons with Disabilities (CRPD). The chapter begins with proxy decision-making as a constitutional right.

PROXY DECISION-MAKING AS A CONSTITUTIONAL RIGHT

Proxy decision-making is arguably a constitutional right in American law. In *Cruzan v Director, Missouri Department of Health* (1990), the US Supreme Court recognized (a) the common law doctrine of informed consent generally encompassing 'the right of a competent individual to refuse medical treatment' (at 277) and (b) the 'principle that a competent person has a constitutionally protected interest in refusing unwanted medical treatment' (at 278). For an incompetent person, the Court concluded 'that a State may apply a clear and convincing evidence standard in proceedings where a guardian seeks to discontinue nutrition and hydration of a person diagnosed to be in a persistent vegetative state' (at 284). Chief Justice Rehnquist's majority opinion noted that the Court was not faced with the question of whether a state is 'required to defer to the decision of a surrogate if competent and probative evidence established that the patient herself had expressed a desire that the decision to terminate life-sustaining treatment be made for her by that individual' (at 287: fn 12). However, Justice O'Connor's concurring opinion providing the majority's decisive fifth vote specifically emphasized that while the Court was not deciding whether a state must 'give effect to the decisions of a surrogate decisionmaker' (at 289), in her view 'such a duty may well be constitutionally required to protect the patient's liberty interest in refusing medical treatment' (at 289).

Dissenting Justices Brennan, Marshall and Blackmun asserted that Nancy Cruzan 'has a fundamental right to be free of unwanted artificial nutrition and hydration' (at 302) and that Missouri's 'improperly biased procedural obstacles ... impermissibly burden that right' (at 302). They agreed with the New Jersey Supreme Court in *In re Jobes* that

> 'Family members are best qualified to make substituted judgments for incompetent patients not only because of their peculiar grasp of the patient's approach to life, but also because of their special bonds with him or her ... It is ... they who treat the patient as a person, rather than a symbol of a cause' (at 327–28).

The three dissenting justices observed that 'A fifth of all adults surviving to age 80 will suffer a progressive dementing disorder prior to death' (at 329). Regarding proxies, the dissenting justices prescribed:

> A State may ensure that the person who makes the decision on the patient's behalf is the one whom the patient himself would have selected to make that choice for him. And a State may exclude from consideration anyone having improper motives. But a State generally must either repose the choice with the person whom the patient himself would most likely have chosen as proxy or leave the decision to the patient's family (at 328).

In closing, the dissenting justices quoted the famous warning by Justice Brandeis about good intentions: 'Experience should teach us to be most on our guard to protect liberty when the government's purposes are beneficent ... The greatest dangers to liberty lurk in insidious encroachment by men of zeal, well meaning but without understanding' (at 330).

ADVANCE DIRECTIVES

In the aftermath of *Cruzan*, every state has statutory provision for advance directives including health care powers of attorney and living wills (ABA Commission on Law and Aging, 2013). At the federal level, Congress enacted the federal Patient Self-Determination Act (PSDA) (1990). The PSDA requires American hospitals, skilled nursing facilities, home health agencies, hospice programmes and health maintenance organizations receiving Medicare and Medicaid to provide each patient with information about rights to accept or refuse treatment, to formulate advance directives, to document whether an advance directive is signed, to assure related state law is followed and to provide for education of staff and public about advance directives. A minority of countries in Europe have legislation permitting the nomination of a substitute decision-maker (World Health Organization and Alzheimer's Disease International, 2012).

Advance Directive Document Completion and Compliance

Despite state statutes and the federal Patient Self-Determination Act, the prevalence of advance directives has declined from 40% in the early 1990s after the PSDA (Aitken, 1999) to a range more recently of from only 28% (Moorman and Inoue, 2013) to about 33% (Morhaim and Pollack, 2013; Sharma and Dy, 2011). When patients have formal written advance directives, only 36% of the medical records included any mention of the subject, and the relevant document was filed in the medical records of only two of 618 patients (Teno et al, 1994). Teno and colleagues concluded: '[q]uite simply, as far as we could tell, advance directives were irrelevant to decision making' (1994: 27) by medical providers. Subsequent studies have reached the same conclusion that patient preferences do not impact treatment ultimately received (Danis et al, 1996). Advance directives are still physically unavailable to providers, and care remains inconsistent with patient instructions half the time (Collins et al, 2006).

Legal Remedies for Advance Directive Non-Compliance

In response to advance directive non-compliance, legal commentators advocate such remedies as wrongful living lawsuits (Lynch et al, 2008), declaratory actions or injunctions to enforce the advance directives and wrongful prolongation of life lawsuits (Saitta and Hodge, 2011). Government regulators and private litigants are resorting to the imposition of a range of sanctions ["'one of the next frontiers in healthcare litigation'" (Parker, 2006)] that are increasingly frequent and severe, including: (a) civil liability in battery, negligence and breach of contract through health care decisions statutes and POLST (Physician Orders for Life Sustaining Treatment) statutes, to section 1983 and the False Claims Act; (b) administrative sanctions from medical board discipline, health care facility inspections and Medicare conditions of participation; and (c) criminal sanctions from criminal penalties protecting advance directives integrity through clinician non-compliance with advance directives, to criminal false claims for unwanted treatment (Pope, 2013).

The related proxy decision-making mechanism of a power of attorney concerning the principal's property and finances has a significant problem with power of attorney abuse (Stiegel and Klem, 2008). The broad decision-making authority of the agent, lack of court oversight, accounting and monitoring and unclear agent conduct standards make financial exploitation of a person with incapacity relatively easy. In addition to 21 recommended provisions in the Uniform Power of Attorney Act to protect against power of attorney abuse and promote autonomy (Stiegel and Klem, 2008), the common law extensively defines the agent's fiduciary responsibility and offers many remedies and causes of action for the 57% of principals who are competent when the financial power of attorney abuse occurs (Hughes, 2000). Solace for financially abused principals with incompetence seems more limited.

FAMILY CONSENT STATUTES

Where an individual has not completed an advance directive, proxy decision-making for health care may occur on the legal authority of family consent statutes. At least 44 states have family consent statutes (ABA Commission on Law and Aging, 2009). Family consent statutes generally authorize designated close family members in a prescribed hierarchy to provide health care decisions when a patient is incompetent and without an advance directive (Furrow et al, 2000). The typical family consent statutory hierarchy is: (1) guardian of the person; (2) spouse; (3) adult child; (4) either parent; (5) adult sibling; (6) adult grandchild (Furrow et al, 2000). Although conceptually similar to intestate succession, no state has the same hierarchy for family consent and for intestacy because in intestacy grandchildren take precedence over parents and siblings. Twenty-three states include a close friend in the hierarchy usually at the lowest level (ABA Commission on Law and Aging, 2009).

At least nine states authorize a physician in the surrogate consent hierarchy (ABA Commission on Law and Aging, 2009) despite significant ethical and other problems with surrogate decision-making for patients by physicians (Schmidt, 2011; White et al, 2007). Surrogate decision-making by physicians: (a) does not impart 'adequate safeguards to [assure] that decisions for these patients [critically ill patients lacking decision-making capacity and surrogates] are fair and consistent' (White et al, 2006: 2058); (b) is based subjectively and erroneously on such criteria as 'the patients' anticipated quality of life, [the physician's] own perception of what was in the patients' best interest, and concerns about appropriate resource allocation' (White et al, 2006: 2057); (c) judges patient quality of life systematically lower than patients themselves judge quality of life (Pearlman and Uhlmann, 1988); (d) chooses less assertive treatment for marginally housed or homeless patents than the patients choose (Norris et al, 2005); (e) presents physician conflict of interest and absence of due process for the patient (White et al, 2006); and (f) 'may result in similarly situated patients receiving different levels of treatment' (White et al, 2006: 2058) because of significant variations in physician beliefs about limiting life-sustaining treatment.

Designating a physician as a patient's surrogate decision-maker seems almost as wrong as the discredited US practice of naming a psychiatric or other institution as a patient's guardian, a practice often still occurring in many other nations (Perlin, 2013). Such practice is not only 'a conflict of interest *per se* and terribly wrong', but 'If the patient's guardian is the institution wishing to medicate the person over the person's wishes, it becomes an absurdity to consider this a fair or equitable process' (Perlin, 2013: 1165, 1167).

Medical literature documents conflicts of interest when physicians provide a proxy consent decision for their own patients, a colleague's patients or a patient of the physician's hospital (White et al, 2012; White et al, 2006). There is also concern that 'depending on the reimbursement structure of the ... hospital, there may be a systematic bias in favor of either overtreatment or undertreatment of these patients [incapacitated patients without surrogates]' (Meier, 1997; White et al, 2006: 2057). Such conflicts of interest, over-treatments and under-treatments suggest a risk of 'false claims' for Medicare and Medicaid reimbursement under federal and state 'fraud and abuse' statutes (Furrow et al, 2000; Furrow et al, 2012; Schmidt, 2011). Physician surrogate financial benefit from these conflicts of interest and self-referrals seems highly problematic.

Physicians rarely receive sufficient training in capacity evaluations to know when a proxy decision is appropriate (Dudley and Goins, 2003). Since only 15 states train or examine professional guardians through professional guardian licensing, certification or registration (Schmidt et al, 2011), physicians also rarely receive any or any adequate training or certification in guardianship and legal proxy decision-making.

GUARDIANSHIP

Guardianship is discussed in detail in chapter twenty-eight.

A legal guardian through a judicial guardianship proceeding is the proxy mechanism available for individuals with dementia and incompetence who do not have either an advance directive or a willing and responsible family member making health care decisions by the authority of a family consent statute. Guardianship is a product of the *parens patriae* authority and responsibility of the state as sovereign to serve as general guardian or 'super guardian' for such people with legal disabilities as children and persons with mental illness or with intellectual disabilities.

Incidence of Guardianship

The reported incidence of guardianship ranged from one in every 1785 (.056%) for Florida in 1977, to one in every 1706 (.059%) for six states (Delaware, Minnesota, North Carolina, Ohio, Washington and Wisconsin) in 1979 (Schmidt, 1981). In 1995, the total number of people under guardianship in the United States was half a million (Schmidt, 1995). By 2008, the median annual incidence of incoming adult guardianship cases was 87 per 100,000 (.087%) for 14 reporting states (Uekert and Van Duizend, 2011). The total number of people under guardianship from four reporting states (Arkansas, District of Columbia, Ohio, Vermont) in 2008 was an average of 664 per 100,000 (0.6%), or 1.5 million adults under guardianship nationally (Uekert and Van Duizend, 2011). Compared with .087% of the US adult population under guardianship in 2008, the percentages of international populations adjudicated with guardianship and trusteeship orders ranged from 0.444% in Alberta, Canada in 2003, to 0.459% for Israel, 0.625% for Austria, 0.721% for Ontario, Canada, 0.850% for Switzerland and 1.345% in Germany (Kroch, 2009).

There are approximately 80,000 people under guardianship in Hungary and 300,000 people under guardianship in Russia (Perlin, 2013).

Unmet Need for Guardianship

One of the biggest social problems with guardianship as a proxy decision-making device is the extent of unmet need for legal guardians. A 1983 survey in Florida discovered 11,147 identifiable persons reportedly in need of a public guardianship, defined as 'the judicial appointment and responsibility of a public official ... to serve a legal incompetent, the "ward", who does not have willing or responsible family members or friends to serve as guardian' or resources to employ a professional guardian (Schmidt and Peters, 1987: 70). A 1988 study of elderly nursing home residents in Tennessee identified 364 nursing home residents in need of plenary guardianship of person and property (Hightower et al, 1990). A 2002 survey estimated a need for 1425 public guardianships in Virginia (Teaster and Roberto, 2002). A Bar Association task force report calculated 4265 Washington state residents in need of public guardianship services in 2005 (Public Guardianship Task Force, 2005). A multi-year, multi-method follow-up study confirmed between 4000 and 5000 Washington residents qualified for a public guardian in 2009 and 2011 (Burley, 2011a). Most recently, there are 305 individuals in need of plenary public guardian services in North Dakota (Schmidt, 2013).

The consequences for individuals with incompetency without guardians are substantial. Of foremost importance, without a guardian, individuals with incompetency lack a proxy to provide protection and individual decision-making. Economically, 'Without sufficient appropriate guardianship services, significant health care costs are incurred through inappropriate institutionalization, insufficient deinstitutionalization, excessive emergency care, and lack of timely health care' (Schmidt, 2012: 15–16).

Cost-Effectiveness of Guardianship

If a public guardian was available, half of Florida's legally incapacitated public mental patients without a guardian would be immediately dischargeable (Schmidt and Peters, 1987). Four hundred un-discharged patients awaiting appointment of guardians cost the Greater New York Hospital Association $13 million (Schmidt, 1996). Appropriate public guardian services for 85 patients in Virginia saved $5.6 million in health care costs in one year (Teaster and Roberto, 2003). Patients without capacity and without a surrogate have a median intensive care unit (ICU) length of stay that is twice as long as other ICU patients (White et al, 2006). Appropriate public guardian services saved Florida $3.9 million in health care costs in one year (Teaster et al, 2009). Appropriate public guardian services in Washington state resulted in: (a) a decrease in residential settings' average costs that exceeded the cost of providing a guardian within 30 months in 2008–2011; (b) a decrease of an average of 29 hours in personal care hours needed each month for public guardian clients, compared with an increase in care hours for similar clients without a guardian; and (c) 21% of clients with a public guardian improved in self-sufficiency in the previous three months (Burley, 2011b). The Vera Institute of Justice Guardianship Project in New York City saved a $2,500,026 in net Medicaid cost-savings for 111 guardianship clients in 2010 (Guardianship Project, 2010).

Guardianship Outcomes

Although there are calls for evaluation of legal intervention strategies such as guardianship and adult protective services for persons with dementia (Kapp, 2001), systematic outcomes studies of guardianship and other adult protective services are generally lacking (Wilber, 1997). For example, the authoritative National Research Council report on elder mistreatment research concluded that, 'no efforts have yet been made to develop, implement, and evaluate interventions based on scientifically grounded hypotheses about the causes of elder mistreatment, and no systematic research has been conducted to measure and evaluate the effects of existing interventions' (Bonnie and Wallace, 2003: 121). A more recent review determined 'Little evidence is available that supports any intervention to prevent elder abuse' (Daly et al, 2011: 362).

Nonetheless, the few systematic outcomes studies of guardianship are important and instructive. The first such study, a quasi-experimental design conducted by Blenkner and colleagues through the service, research and advocacy leading Benjamin Rose Institute in Cleveland, discovered that the experimental group receiving enriched protective services including guardianship had a higher rate of institutionalization and mortality than the control group, as well as failing to have deterioration or mortality forestalled (Blenkner et al, 1971; Bloom et al, 1974). The Blenkner study design and conclusions were questioned (Dunkle et al, 1983), and a reanalysis by other researchers suggested that the mortality findings came from initial group differences not controlled by the random sampling, but the reanalysis confirmed the institutionalization tendency (Berger and Piliavin, 1976).

The results of the 'landmark' Blenkner study were not 'revisited in an epidemiologically rigorous fashion' until 30 years later by Lachs and colleagues (Lachs et al, 2002: 734). The research question for the Lachs study was 'whether APS [adult protective services] use for abuse and self-neglect is an independent predictor of NHP [nursing home placement] after adjusting for other factors known to predict institutionalization (eg, medical illness, functional disability, and poor social support)' (2002: 735). The research discovered that

> the relative contribution of elder protective referral [including 'pursuit of guardianship'] to NHP is enormous ['4- to 5-fold risk conferred by elder mistreatment and self-neglect, respectively'] and far exceeds the variance explained by other variables such as dementia, functional disability, and poor social networks (Lachs et al, 2002: 736–38).

The clinicians and APS clients acknowledged that dramatic quality of life improvements often resulted from nursing home placement but thought it 'remarkable that controlled studies of differential outcomes of APS have not yet been conducted' (Lachs et al, 2002: 738). The literature review showed 'no systematic attempt to evaluate program outcomes or to examine unintended consequences of APS intervention. Given the findings of the present study, APS should be subjected to rigorous evaluation research' (Lachs et al, 2002: 738). While the need for adult protective services may seem as self-evident as child protective services, 'the positive benefits of APS intervention must be scientifically documented, to justify the possible risk of negative outcomes such as institutionalization' (Lachs et al, 2002: 738).

Contrary to recommendations (Kapp, 2001), systematic evaluation of guardianship and adult protective services outcomes for people with dementia are generally lacking. The few available studies (Blenkner et al, 1971; Lachs et al, 2002) show that such legal interventions contribute very much more to the likelihood of institutionalization than dementia itself. Nursing home admission is expected by age 80 for 75% of people with Alzheimer's compared with 4% of the general population (Arrighi, et al, 2010), with two-thirds of people dying with dementia doing so in nursing homes compared with 20% of cancer patients and 28% from all other conditions (Mitchell et al, 2005). Alternative approaches to guardianship for people with dementia seem imperative.

Procedural and Accountability Issues

In addition to the risk of negative outcomes with guardianship, there are myriad well-documented procedural issues beyond the scope of this chapter, such as: mandatory abuse and neglect reporting; petitioner conflicts of interest; right to counsel and legal counsel for indigents; right to jury trial; right of cross-examination; standard of proof; right to appeal; clinical evidence quality; preservation of civil liberties; emergency guardianship with too little due process (Schmidt, 1995; Schmidt, 2012; Teaster et al, 2010). Some of the biggest concerns about guardianship as a proxy decision-making tool most recently include: lack of oversight and active monitoring of guardians and guardian annual reports; lack of criminal background checks and credit checks of guardians; lack of guardian licensing, certification or registration; too high guardianship staff–client ratios; and non-compliance with guardian visitation-of-ward standards (Government Accountability Office (GAO), 2010; Schmidt, 2012; Schmidt et al, 2011).

Legally incompetent dementia patients who do not have either an advance directive or a willing and responsible family member making health care decisions by the authority of a family consent statute are dependent upon the kindness and fiduciary duties of a guardian. Procedural laxity and nominal accountability are intolerable in the context of guardianship (Schmidt, 1995).

CONVENTION ON THE RIGHTS OF PERSONS WITH DISABILITIES

The problems with proxy decision-making mechanisms like advance directives, family consent statutes and guardianship have generated the need for 'a dramatic paradigm shift from the medical or social welfare model of disability that focuses on diagnosis and inability to the human rights model that focuses on capability and inclusion' (Kanter, 2009: 572). The paradigm shift and human rights model are represented in the Convention on the Rights of Persons with Disabilities (CRPD, 2006).

For the purposes of proxy-decision-making and expansion of the rights of people with dementia under international law, Article 12(2) regarding equal recognition before law provides that 'States Parties shall recognize that persons with disabilities enjoy legal capacity on an equal basis with others in all aspects of life'. Article 12(3) addresses the overarching problem of how to deal with the circumstances of individuals with disabilities who cannot exercise legal capacity without assistance: 'States Parties shall take appropriate measures to provide access by persons with disabilities to the support they may require in exercising their legal capacity'. Paragraph (j) of the Preamble records the States Parties 'Recognizing the need to promote and protect the human rights of all persons with disabilities, including those who require more intensive support'. Article 19 recognizes the 'equal right of all persons with disabilities to live in the community' with assurance in paragraph (b) that 'Persons with disabilities have access to a range of in-home, residential and other community support services, including personal assistance necessary to support living and inclusion in the community, and to prevent isolation or segregation from the community'.

The CRPD forces abandonment of substituted decision-making paradigms that treat persons with disabilities as objects of protection and take away rights, and replaces them with supported decision-making paradigms that treat persons with disabilities as persons with autonomy, independence and dignity and which add a profusion of rights (Kanter, 2009; Perlin, 2013). The CRPD is consistent with arguments that substituted decision-making in American guardianship constitutes illegal discrimination under the American with Disabilities Act (Salzman, 2010) and violates the Supreme Court's integration mandate in *Olmstead v LC* (1999): 'Unjustified [institutional] isolation ... is properly regarded as discrimination based on disability' (at 598).

Supported decision-making is defined as 'a series of relationships, practices, arrangements, and agreements, of more or less formality and intensity, designed to assist an individual with a disability to make and communicate to others decisions about the individual's life' (Dinerstein, 2012: 10). Salzman (2011) advocates the study of existing supported decision-making models to determine best practices that:

> (1) maximize the individual's responsibility for and involvement in decisions affecting his or her life; (2) ensure that the individual's wishes and preferences are respected; (3) ensure legal recognition of decisions made with support or by the individual's appointed agent; (4) provide the most appropriate qualifications and training for support persons, and standards for carrying out support responsibilities; (5) create the most efficient and effective mechanisms for funding support programs (including the possibility of volunteer support services); (6) have the most effective mechanisms for oversight and monitoring to ensure that the support relationship does not result in harm to the individual and protects against conflicts of interest, undue influence, or coercion of the individual needing support; (7) create standards for appointment of a substitute decision-maker that ensure that an individual is divested of decision-making rights only to the extent and for the time period that is absolutely necessary (2011: 328–29).

The key elements of a supported decision-making system adopted at the General Assembly are:

1. Promotion and support of self-advocacy.
2. Using mainstreaming mechanisms for the protection of the best interests of a person.

3. Replacing traditional guardianship by a system of [gradually implemented] supported decision-making.
4. Supporting decision-making.
5. Selection and registration of support persons [including 'obligatory and regular training'].
6. Overcoming communication barriers.
7. Preventing and resolving conflicts between supporter and supported person [including addressing 'the question of the liability and insurance of the supporter'].
8. Implementing safeguards.
(Inclusion Europe, 2008: 3–5)

Article 12(4) of the CRPD is quite specific about safeguards relating to enjoying legal capacity on an equal basis through supported decision-making:

> State Parties shall ensure that all measures that relate to the exercise of legal capacity provide for appropriate and effective safeguards to prevent abuse in accordance with international human rights law. Such safeguards shall ensure that measures relating to the exercise of legal capacity respect the rights, will and preferences of the person, are free of conflict of interest and undue influence, are proportional and tailored to the person's circumstances, apply for the shortest time possible and are subject to regular review by a competent, independent and impartial authority or judicial body. The safeguards shall be proportional to the degree to which such measures affect the person's rights and interests.

Examples of supported decision-making configurations including legislation exist in Canada, Germany, Norway and Sweden (Dinerstein, 2012). The Canadian provinces of Alberta, British Columbia (Representation Agreements, Enduring Powers of Attorney, registration), Manitoba, Quebec, Saskatchewan (Surtees, 2010) and Yukon Territory have legislation recognizing a form of supported decision-making. Common elements in Canada include: (1) emphasis on 'the person with disability's autonomy, presumption of capacity, and right to make decisions on an equal basis with others'; (2) the person with disability's intent can serve as a basis of a decision-making process that does not involve removal of the person's decision-making rights; and (3) individuals with disabilities often need decision-making assistance 'through such means as interpreter assistance, facilitated communication, assistive technologies and plain language' (Dinerstein, 2012: 10–11).

In the United States, the court in *Matter of Mark CH* (2010) ruled that state interventions like guardianship are subject to annual reporting by the guardian and review (monitoring) by the court as a matter of fundamental due process and international human rights law through the Supremacy Clause and Article 12 of the CRPD. In *Matter of Dameris L* (2012), the court held that, as a matter of substantive due process and international human rights through Article 12(3) of the CRPD, substituted decision-making by guardianship cannot be imposed until supported decision-making by 'family, friends and professionals' (at 579) is 'explored and exhausted' (at 580).

In addition to the challenge of heeding the call for research and evaluation of such strategies as supported decision-making for persons with dementia (Kapp, 2001; Then, 2013) formalized in Article 31 of the CRPD, the need for legal counsel is a significant 'red flag' of concern (Perlin, 2013). A national Associated Press investigation of 2200 randomly selected guardianships found that the proposed ward had no representation by an attorney in 44% of cases (Bayles and McCartney, 1987). The number of states with a statutory right to counsel in guardianship proceedings has grown slightly from 22 states in 1981 to 25 states in 2005 (Teaster, et al, 2010). The Second National Guardianship Conference recommended:

> 28. Counsel always [is] appointed for the respondent and act as an advocate rather than as guardian *ad litem*.
> 29. The Wingspread Recommendation regarding the role of counsel as zealous advocate be amended and affirmed as follows: Zealous Advocacy—In order to assume the proper advocacy role, counsel for the respondent and the petitioner shall: (a) advise the client of all the options as well as the practical and legal consequences of those options and the probability of success in pursuing any one of these options; (b) give that advice in the language, mode of communication and terms that the client is most likely to understand; and (c) zealously advocate the course of actions chosen by the client (Wingspan, 2002: 601).

The Model Public Guardianship Act recommends further specification of the duties of counsel:

> The duties of counsel representing an [alleged incapacitated person] at the hearing shall include at least: a personal interview with the person; counseling the person with respect to his or her rights; and arranging for an independent medical and/or psychological examination (Teaster et al, 2010: 167).

Counsel for all guardianship respondents would facilitate negotiation, settlement and achievement of the least restrictive supported decision-making for the alleged incapacitated person (Schmidt, 2012). In any event, the key to meaningful if not 'emancipatory' CRPD enforcement is the 'right to adequate and dedicated counsel', 'vigorous, advocacy-focused counsel', that is 'free … and regularized and organized' leavened with sufficient 'cause lawyers' to accomplish the rights paradigm shift (Perlin, 2013: 1175, 1179, 1180).

In the dementia context, the human rights based model of decision-making is sometimes problematic. For example, assisted decision-making arrangements may not be suitable: guardianship is preferred in Alberta when adults with dementia cannot communicate or make decisions (Then, 2013). An attorney ethically shall otherwise maintain a normal client–lawyer relationship 'as far as reasonably possible' (Flowers and Morgan, 2013: 127) in the event of client diminished capacity while retaining the ability to take protective action like seeking appointment of a guardian when the attorney believes the client 'is at risk of substantial physical, financial or other harm unless action is taken' (Flowers and Morgan, 2013: 147; Law and Peck, 2013). If the right to a zealous, advocacy-focused counsel is not realized, then who remains to facilitate and achieve proxy decision-making and proxy decision-making procedure?

CONCLUSION

This chapter has provided a legal perspective on proxy decision-making. It began with the narrative about trial lawyer Frederick C Hayes, 'the best friend you could have' in a legal war, his admission to the advanced-dementia unit at Jewish Home Lifecare, his unmanageable behaviour despite a Haldol prescription, and his considerable discomfort. Despite knowledge that a person like Frederick C Hayes with Alzheimer's is likely to spend 40% of their total disease years in the most severe stage (Arrighi et al, 2010), there is more to Mr Hayes' story.

An experienced 'support' person named Tena Alonzo stopped by to find Mr Hayes (a person who had 'trouble thinking', in her parlance) with his face

> contorted in a grimace, writhing and moaning. She crouched next to him, asked him 'in a quiet, intimate tone' if he hurt anywhere, and moved her hand gently over his chest, abdomen, arms and legs: 'Do you hurt *here*?' His moaning stopped when her hand reached his stomach and he said, 'I hurt so bad'. She said, 'I promise you, we are going to fix this'. Ms Alonzo explained that it is hard for people with dementia to identify the source and experience of pain: 'All behavior is communication' (Mead, 2013: 92, 94).

The newer holistic approach articulated in this chapter focuses more on the way one feels rather than the way one thinks. In this model, medical care is less intrusive: there is more attention to a comfortable decline and less dependence on psychotropic medication. Supported decision-making is preferred to substituted decision-making.

Mr Hayes was placed on a higher dose of pain medication. He became more verbal, and he stopped making threatening gestures. The narrative about Mr Hayes concludes:

> Frederick Hayes was unrecognizable from the man who had arrived at the unit, kicking and screaming, several months earlier. By observing his behavior carefully, nurses' aides had learned that he liked to watch television as a distraction while he was being changed or washed, and that it was important not to block his view of the set. Now that Hayes was receiving enough pain medication, he enjoyed it when the aides talked to him, and even responded to their jokes. His son told me, 'They understand how to get along with him. They know not to push too much'. Hayes particularly enjoyed being complimented; aides tell him he is a handsome man, which, in spite of everything, he still is (Mead, 2013: 101).

The approach taken in Mr Hayes' case seems to result in the maintenance of body weight, reduction in drug costs (Long and Alonzo, 2008) and reduction in pain (Long et al, 2010).

One would like to think that the care of Mr Hayes shows a kind of supported decision-making to which proxy decision-making in advance directives, family consent statutes, guardianship and the Convention on the Rights of Persons with Disabilities aspire.

REFERENCES

ABA Commission on Law and Aging (2009) 'Default surrogate consent statutes'. Available at: www.americanbar.org/groups/law_aging/resources/health_care_decision_making.html.

—— (2013) 'State health care power of attorney statutes: Selected characteristics'. Available at: www.americanbar.org/groups/law_aging/resources/health_care_decision_making.html.

Aitken, P (1999) 'Incorporating advance care planning into family practice' 59(3) *American Family Physician* 605–12.

Arrighi, HM et al (2010) 'Lethality of Alzheimer disease and its impact on nursing home placement' 24(1) *Alzheimer Disease & Associated Disorders* 90–95.

Bayles, F and McCartney, S (1987) *Guardians of the elderly: An ailing system part I: Declared legally dead by a troubled system* (Associated Press) Available at: www.apnewsarchive.

com/1987/Guardians-of-the-Elderly-An-Ailing-System-Part-I-Declared-Legally-Dead-by-a-Troubled-System/id-1198f64bb05d9c1ec690035983c02f9f.

Berger, R and Piliavin, I (1976) 'The effect of casework: A research note' 21(3) *Social Work* 205–08.

Blenkner, M, Bloom, M and Nielsen, M (1971) 'A research and demonstration project of protective services' 52(8) *Social Casework* 483–99.

Bloom et al (1974) *Protective services for older people: Final report. Findings from the Benjamin Rose Institute study* (Cleveland, OH, Benjamin Rose Institute).

Bonnie, RJ and Wallace, RB (eds) (2003) *Elder mistreatment: Abuse, neglect, and exploitation in an aging America* (Washington DC, National Academies Press).

Burley, M (2011a) *Assessing the potential need for public guardianship services in Washington state* (Olympia, WA, Washington State Institute for Public Policy).

—— (2011b) *Public guardianship in Washington state: Cost and benefits* (Olympia, WA, Washington State Institute for Public Policy).

Collins, LG, Parks, SM and Winter, L (2006) 'The state of advance care planning: One decade after SUPPORT' 23(5) *American Journal of Hospice and Palliative Medicine* 378–84.

Convention on the Rights of Persons with Disabilities (CRPD) (2006) (New York, NY, United Nations). Available at: www.un.org/disabilities/convention/conventionfull.shtml.

Daly, JM, Merchant, ML and Jogerst, GJ (2011) 'Elder abuse research: A systematic review' *23(4) Journal of Elder Abuse & Neglect* 348–65.

Danis, M et al (1996) 'A prospective study of the impact of patient preferences on life-sustaining treatment and hospital cost' 24(11) *Critical Care Medicine* 1811–17.

Dinerstein, RD (2012) 'Implementing legal capacity under article 12 of the UN Convention on the Rights of Persons with Disabilities: The difficult road from guardianship to supported decision-making' 19(2) *Human Rights Brief* 8–12.

Dudley, KC and Goins, RT (2003) 'Guardianship capacity evaluations of older adults: Comparing current practice to legal standards in two states' 15(1) *Journal of Aging & Social Policy* 97–115.

Dunkle, R et al (1983) 'Protective services reanalyzed: Does casework help or harm?' 64(4) *Social Casework* 195–99.

Flowers, R and Morgan, R (2013) *Ethics in the Practice of Elder Law* (Chicago, ABA).

Furrow, B et al (2000) *Health Law*, 2nd edn (St Paul, MN, West Group).

—— (2012) *Health Care Reform: Supplementary Materials* (St Paul, MN, Thomson Reuters).

Garner, B (2009) *Black's Law Dictionary*, 9th edn (US, West Group).

Government Accountability Office (GAO) (2010) *Guardianships: Cases of financial exploitation, neglect, and abuse of seniors*. Available at: www.gao.gov/products/GAO-10-1046.

The Guardianship Project (2010) *Summary of Medicaid cost-savings* (New York, Vera Institute of Justice, Inc).

Hightower, D, Heckert, A and Schmidt, W (1990) 'Elderly nursing home residents' need for public guardianship services in Tennessee' 2(3–4) *Journal of Elder Abuse & Neglect* 105–22.

Hughes, MM (2000) 'Remedying financial abuse by agents under a power of attorney for finances' 2 *Marquette Elder's Advisor* 39–48.

Hurd, MD et al (2013) 'Monetary costs of Dementia in the United States' 368(14) *New England Journal of Medicine* 1326–34.

Inclusion Europe (2008) *Key elements of a system for supported decision-making*. Available at: inclusioneurope.org/images/stories/documents/PositionPapers/Position_Supported_Decision_Making_EN.pdf.

Kanter, AS (2009) 'The United Nations Convention on the Rights of Persons with Disabilities and its implications for the rights of elderly people under international law' 25(3) *Georgia State University Law Review* 527–73.

Kapp, MB (2001) 'Legal interventions for persons with dementia in the USA: Ethical, policy and practical aspects' 5(4) *Aging & Mental Health* 312–15.

Kroch, U (2009) 'The experience of being a dependent adult (ward) – A hermeneutic phenomenological study' (unpublished doctoral dissertation, University of Calgary).

Lachs, MS et al (2002) 'Adult protective service use and nursing home placement' 42(6) *Gerontologist* 734–39.

Law, R and Peck, K (2013) *Alzheimer's and the Law: Counseling Clients with Dementia and their Families* (Chicago, ABA).

Long, CO and Alonzo, T (2008) 'Palliative care for advanced dementia: A model teaching unit – Practical approaches and results' 13(2) *Arizona Geriatrics Society Journal* 14–17.

Long, CO et al (2010) 'Improving pain management in long-term care: The campaign against pain' 12(3) *Journal of Hospice & Palliative Nursing* 148–55.

Lynch, HF, Mathes, M and Sawicki, NN (2008) 'Compliance with advance directives: Wrongful living and tort law incentives' 29(2) *Journal of Legal Medicine* 133–78.

Mead, R (20 May 2013) 'The sense of an ending: An Arizona nursing home offers new ways to care for people with dementia' *New Yorker* 92–103.

Meier, DE (1997) 'Voiceless and vulnerable: Dementia patients without surrogates in an era of capitation' 45(3) *Journal of the American Geriatrics Society* 375–77.

Mitchell, SL et al (2005) 'A national study of the location of death for older persons with dementia' 53(2) *Journal of the American Geriatrics Society* 299–305.

Moorman, SM and Inoue, M (2013) 'Persistent problems in end-of-life planning among young-and middle-aged American couples' 68(1) *The Journals of Gerontology Series B: Psychological Sciences and Social Sciences* 97–106.

Morhaim, DK and Pollack, KM (2013) 'End-of-life care issues: A personal, economic, public policy, and public health crisis' 103(6) *American Journal of Public Health* e8–e10.

Norris, WM et al (2005) 'Treatment preferences for resuscitation and critical care among homeless persons' 127(6) *CHEST Journal* 2180–87.

Parker, L (2006, December 19) 'In a crisis, do-not-revive requests don't always work' *USA Today*. Available at: http://usatoday30.usatoday.com/news/health/2006-12-19-do-not-revive-cover_x.htm.

Patient Self-Determination Act 1990, 42 USC sections 1395 *et seq.*

Pearlman, RA and Uhlmann, RF (1988) 'Quality of life in chronic diseases: Perceptions of elderly patients' 43(2) *Journal of Gerontology* M25–M30.

Perlin, ML (2013) '"Striking for the guardians and protectors of the mind": The Convention on the Rights of Persons with Mental Disabilities and the future of guardianship law' 117(4) *Penn State Law Review* 1159–337.

Pope, T (2013) 'Clinicians may not administer life-sustaining treatment without consent: Civil, criminal, and disciplinary sanctions' 9(2) *Journal of Health & Biomedical Law* 213–96.

Public Guardianship Task Force (2005) *Report of the public guardianship task force to the WSBA elder law section executive committee*. Available at: www.wsba.org/Legal-Community/Sections/Elder-Law-Section/Guardianship-Committee.

Saitta, NM and Hodge, SD (2011) 'Wrongful prolongation of life – A cause of action that has not gained traction even though a physician has disregarded a do not resuscitate order' 30 *Temple Journal of Science, Technology & Environmental Law* 221–38.

Salzman, L (2010) 'Rethinking guardianship (again): Substituted decision making as a violation of the integration mandate of title II of the Americans with Disabilities Act' 81 *University of Colorado Law Review* 157–245.

—— (2011) 'Guardianship for persons with mental illness – A legal and appropriate alternative?' 4 *Saint Louis University Journal of Health Law & Policy* 279–329.

Schmidt, W (1981) 'Guardianship of the elderly in Florida: Social bankruptcy and the need for reform' 55 *Florida Bar Journal* 189–195.

—— (ed) (1995) *Guardianship: Court of last resort for the elderly and disabled* (Durham, NC, Carolina Academic Press).

—— (1996) 'Public guardianship issues for New York: Insights from research' 6 *Elder Law Attorney, New York State Bar Association* 31–37.

—— (2011) 'Medicalization of aging: The upside and the downside' 13 *Marquette Elder's Adviser* 55–88.

—— (2012) *Final report: A study of guardianship services for vulnerable adults in North Dakota* (Bismarck, ND, Human Services Committee, North Dakota Legislature).

—— (2013) 'Guardianship for vulnerable adults in North Dakota: Recommendations regarding unmet needs, statutory efficacy, and cost effectiveness' 89(1) *North Dakota Law Review* 77–142.

Schmidt, W, Akinci, F and Magill, S (2011) 'Study finds certified guardians with legal work experience are at greater risk for elder abuse than certified guardians with other work experience' 7(2) *NAELA Journal* 171–97.

Schmidt, W and Peters, R (1987) 'Legal incompetents' need for guardians in Florida' 15(1) *Journal of the American Academy of Psychiatry and the Law* 69–83.

Sharma, RK and Dy, SM (2011) 'Documentation of information and care planning for patients with advanced cancer: Associations with patient characteristics and utilization of hospital care' 28(8) *American Journal of Hospice and Palliative Medicine* 543–49.

Stiegel, L and Klem, E (2008) *Power of attorney abuse: What states can do about it. A comparison of current state laws with the new Uniform Power of Attorney Act* (Washington DC, American Association of Retired Persons).

Surtees, D (2010) 'The evolution of co-decision-making in Saskatchewan' 73(1) *Saskatchewan Law Review* 75–92.

Teaster, P and Roberto, K (2002) 'Living the life of another: The need for public guardians of last resort' 21(2) *Journal of Applied Gerontology* 176–87.

—— (2003) *Virginia public guardian and conservator programs: Evaluation of program status and outcomes* (Blacksburg, VA, The Center for Gerontology, Virginia Polytechnic Institute and State University).

Teaster, P et al (2009). *The Florida public guardian programs: An evaluation of program status and outcomes* (Lexington, KY, University of Kentucky Graduate Center for Gerontology).

—— (2010) *Public guardianship: In the best interests of incapacitated people?* (Santa Barbara, CA, Praeger Publishers).

Teno, JM et al (1994) 'Do formal advance directives affect resuscitation decisions and the use of resources for seriously ill patients?' 5(1) *Journal of Clinical Ethics* 23–30.

Then, SN (2013) 'Evolution and innovation in guardianship laws: Assisted decision-making' 35 *Sydney Law Review* 133–66.

Uekert, BK and Van Duizend, R (2011) *Adult guardianships: A 'best guess' national estimate and the momentum for reform* (Williamsburg, VA, National Center for State Courts).

White, DB et al (2006) 'Decisions to limit life-sustaining treatment for critically ill patients who lack both decision-making capacity and surrogate decision-makers' 34(8) *Critical Care Medicine* 2053–59.

—— (2007) 'Life support for patients without a surrogate decision maker: Who decides?' 147(1) *Annals of Internal Medicine* 34–40.

White, DB, Jonsen, A and Lo, B (2012) 'Ethical challenge: When clinicians act as surrogates for unrepresented patients' 21(3) *American Journal of Critical Care* 202–07.

Wilber, KH (1997) 'Choice, courts, and competency: The coming of age of protective services research' 37(2) *Gerontologist* 272–74.

Wingspan – The Second National Guardianship Conference (2002) 'Recommendations' 31 *Stetson Law Review* 595–609.

World Health Organization and Alzheimer's Disease International (2012) *Dementia: A public health priority* (Geneva, WHO Press).

CASES

Cruzan v Director, Missouri Department of Health, 497 US 261 (1990).

In re Jobes, 108 NJ 394, 529 A.2d 434 (1987).

Matter of Dameris L, 38 Misc.3d 570, 956 NYS.2d 848 (Surr Ct NY Cnty 2012).

Matter of Mark CH, 28 Misc.3d 765, 906 NYS.2d 419 (Surr Ct NY Cnty 2010).

Olmstead v LC, 527 US 581 (1999).

27

Being and Being Lost: Personal Identity and Dementia

JESSE WALL

THE PURPOSE OF this chapter is to sketch some of the philosophical work on personal identity and connect these theoretical accounts of personhood with how the law approaches the treatment of patients with dementia. Our grasp of personal identity is pertinent to our understanding of dementia. It is not only a philosophical concept that can help clarify the duties we owe one another; our experience with patients with dementia also leaves us with the sense that aspects of a patient's identity have been lost. I will begin by briefly clarifying the focus of my philosophical enquiry. I will then explain the differences in philosophical views of personal identity. I suggest that there are two main planes or axes of disagreement. The first concerns how our *experience* of the world constructs our personal identity. The second plane or axis of disagreement concerns how it is we *unify* our experiences of the world to construct our personal identity. I will then discuss the implications of these theoretical views, focusing on the relationship between personal identity and mental capacity and the relationship between prior and current decisions as to treatment.

QUALITATIVE PERSONAL IDENTITY

Philosophical accounts of personal identity, personhood or selfhood (terms used interchangeably here) may be concerned with subtly different philosophical questions. I will be primarily concerned with identifying the qualities or features of our existence that construct our personal identity (qualitative identity: see McMillan, 2006). This main enquiry is related to other philosophical enquiries into personal identity. For instance, we may also be interested in the question of personal identity *over time* (numerical identity: McMillan, 2006), which asks whether someone is the same person as they once were. Moreover, even if we identify the qualities that we consider to be constitutive of personal identity, it does not necessarily follow that these qualities solicit a set of moral attitudes about that person. There is an additional enquiry—often assumed into the qualitative enquiry—into the moral relevance of personal identity (the moral content of personal identity).

Here, I will be concerned with the question of qualitative identity as it is, in my opinion, a prior question to questions of numerical and moral identity. This is because it is difficult to assess whether a person's identity or selfhood has changed over time, or assess the moral relevance of personal identity, without a sense of the features or qualities that are relevant to the person's identity or selfhood to begin with. In terms of our philosophical interest in the personal identity of patients with dementia, we ought to first identity which qualities of our existence constitute our personal identity. Hence, this discussion will focus on this qualitative question. It may then be possible to address a series of subsequent questions, such as whether patients with dementia lose their personal identity when their cognitive ability is impaired; whether the loss of personal identity changes their moral status; and the relationship between a patient with dementia and the person he or she was at an earlier point in time.

THEORIES OF PERSONAL IDENTITY

As I will explain in this section, theories of personal identity concern two aspects of our existence or 'being'. The first is how we experience the world. The second is how we connect or unify the series of experiences of the world. Both aspects of our existence are necessary for a theory of personal identity. Consider Locke's definition of the person in *Essays Concerning Human Understanding*, according to which a person is a 'thinking intelligent Being, that has reason and reflection, and can consider it self as it self, the same thinking thing in different times and places' (1975: 335). This definition of the person provides us with two initial observations. First, a person is a thinking-thing. According to the Lockean definition, thinking and reasoning (about the things around them) is how a person is a person. Second, personhood requires the thinking-thing be able to attribute their thinking-and-reasoning from different times and places to themselves. Although we may find this definition of the person to be lacking, it nonetheless engages in the two-fold task of explaining how a person connects with (or experiences) the world and how a person is also able to connect (or unify) their connections with the world.

Consider the experience of finding your way in an unfamiliar city. You may be able to find your way home because you know of the streets and lanes that you need to walk down, and also know how these streets and lanes connect with each other. When we become lost in an unfamiliar city, it is because we are either unable to recall the streets or lanes to walk down or we are unable to recall how the streets and lanes fit together to provide a coherent path from where we are, to where we were. If our ability to connect with the world, or our ability to connect our connections with the world together, were to be somehow impaired, we would lose our personal identity; we would be metaphysically lost.

As we shall see, the simple Lockean definition of the person is contestable. Philosophical accounts of personal identity differ, both in terms of how we experience the world and how we unify (or connect together) these experiences. The remainder of this section will explore the main theoretical positions along these two planes or axes of disagreement.

How We Experience the World

The Lockean definition explains how we connect or engage with the world in terms of reasoning and thinking. The contemporary equivalent of the Lockean definition is

Parfit's psychological criterion of personal identity, which defines personal identity in terms of overlapping chains of psychological connectedness. The psychological connectedness is made up of memories, intentions, beliefs, goals, desires and similarity of character (Parfit, 1984: 207). Like the Lockean definition, the component parts of Parfit's psychological theory (memories, intentions, beliefs etc) are cognitive abilities. As mental processes, these components of how we experience the world are components that are located *in* the person (ie, in the mind). My ability to find my way home this evening can be explained by a set of memories of High Street, Magpie Lane and Merton Street which I can connect together. So too, according to psychological theories, my personal identity can also be explained by a set of memories, intentions and beliefs that are also connected together. This is a 'cognitivist' or 'internalist' view of how we experience, or connect with, the world around us.

Opponents of the cognitivist view of the person aim to show that the *connection* between the person and the world is not located *in* the person. Even if we start with the simple act of perceiving an object (the cobblestones on Merton Street), we can say that I have a representation of the object (the cobblestones) *in* my mind, but there is nonetheless a sense that my thought about the object is unavoidably *about or directed towards* the 'external' world. All thoughts are 'external' in this sense. Opponents of the cognitivist view therefore offer a competing view—'externalism'—which is

> a thesis about the relationship between the mind and the world: it says that the world enters constitutively into the individualisation of states of mind; mind and world are not, according to externalism, metaphysically independent categories, sliding smoothly past each other (McGin, 1989: 9).

Externalism may not have far reaching implications for how we perceive mere objects. Yet, when we consider the use of language, our interaction with other people and our embodiment, externalism can provide a very different explanation of how we connect with the world. As a result, it also provides a number of theories of personal identity that rival the psychological criterion or the general cognitivist view by identifying a wide range of qualities that can be used to construct a person's identity beyond a person's cognitive ability. Put simply, the contrast is between a cognitivist view that explains our being or existence in terms of psychological states that correspond to the things in the world, and externalist views that explain our being in terms of the relationship between ourselves and the things in the world.

Communication

Our being in the world is more than just the perception of objects; our being is (amongst other things) a discursive being. Even if we were to accept that our thoughts are *internal* to the person, externalists contend that the communication of thoughts cannot be internal to the person. As Harré and Gillet explain (1994: 43):

> [T]he things that fix the meanings of words cannot be hidden inside the respective heads of different people or else we would each be uncertain all the time what anybody else was talking about ... the problem runs very deep because others cannot get outside their veils of perception.

The suggestion here is that the act of communication (through words, gestures or actions) is an act that externalises thought. The purpose of the communication is to place our thoughts (that may be internal to us) in an external or public place. By placing thought in a public space, we invite others to direct themselves (their minds) to our (now externalised) thought. We may communicate (externalise thought) as a means of transferring information to other persons (such as the words on a street sign) or we may also communicate merely to include others in our experience of the world (such as a sigh in frustration). As Taylor (1985: 260) explains: 'To express something, to formulate it, can be not only to get it in articulate focus, but also to place it in public space, and thus bring us together *qua* participants in a common act of focussing'. The purpose of communicating is to externalise thoughts and engage other minds. Yet, in order to share thoughts and experiences, there is a need for some shared interpretative assumptions. Just as there is a need for some shared linguistic assumptions about the meaning of the word '*lane*', there is also a need for shared assumptions about the meaning of a person *reaching for the hand of another* or the meaning conveyed by someone *wincing*. It follows for McCulloch that our consciousness is 'interpretational', and that 'when we are communicating with others, the shared contents are as much a part of the scene of which we are conscious as are the colours of nearby objects' (McCulloch, 2003: 30). If we consider communication to be a critical aspect of how we engage in the world around us, then communicative acts (as interpretational or social acts) ought to feature in our account of personal identity. Such communicative acts are social acts in public space.

Others

We are confronted with a world populated by other people. Like our perception of objects, we form thoughts and attitudes (fear, confusion, affection, indifference) towards other people. Yet, unlike our interaction with objects, other people are (like us) also attitude-bearing-things. This enables us to share thoughts and experiences with other people—to be jointly attentive towards the same object (Eilan, 2007)—in a way in which the experience of the object is a social experience.

Moreover, the interaction with others (as attitude-bearing-things) also means that we can become *the subject* or content of the thoughts or attitudes of the people we interact with. When two people form thoughts or attitudes towards each other, there is 'mutual recognition between two people' (Oppenheimer, 2006: 199). Simply put, these instances of joint attentiveness and mutual recognition become the basis of our relationships with others. When we recall our prior experiences—especially those to which we attribute value and use to build a sense of our selfhood—such experiences will often be experiences with others. Once we start locating our sense of selfhood in our relationships with others, it becomes possible to formulate a *relational* view of personal identity (see, for instance, Herring and Foster, 2012).

As we have seen, communicative acts invite others into our set of thoughts and the communicative acts of others invite us into their thoughts. The suggestion here is that we are also pulled together through shared or jointly attentive experiences and the mutual recognition between two attitude-bearing things. Crucially, we cannot sensibly locate these experiences inside a particular person. These meaningful experiences, that provide some of the building blocks of our personal identity, are externalised experiences.

The Body

The experience of my walk home this evening is only possible through the perceptual apparatus of my body: to view (and then reflection upon) the cobblestones, to read (and take directions from) street signs and to feel (and become discontent with) the rain in June, requires my body. The suggestion is that, although we are thinking and reflective things, this 'subjectivity' is only possible through the integration of thought with the body. Matthews argues that we are 'body-subjects' that are 'neither simply a piece of biological machinery, nor a pure consciousness, but a unity of the two: a consciousness that expresses itself through the bodily activity (2006: 173). An implication of this view of the person as the body-subject is that we undertake pre-reflective bodily action. In other words, we perform intentional bodily activity without conscious thought or reflection. For instance, I am currently typing without thinking about the location of each key that correlates to each letter. I may acquire a habit through conscious or reflective activity, but I may perform the habit without necessarily 'thinking' about it. The retention of habits or skills is possible through the unity of the body-subject. The suggestion here is that whether a person loses or retains pre-reflective skill (such as typing or playing the piano) will depend on the integration of the body-subject and not merely on the preservation of a cognitive process.

Moreover, my communicative acts and the interaction of others with me also require my body as the 'medium of social experience' (Carman, 2008: 137). As Carman argues: 'Others are present to us, just as we are present to ourselves, in a bodily way *before* we are able to conceive of either them or ourselves as minds standing in relations of mutual distrust, suspicion, or uncertainty' (2008, 136).

In sum, since we are attempting to isolate the qualities that are constitutive of personal identity, we can isolate these features by examining how we experience and connect with the world. Psychological or cognitive theories explain our engagement with the world in terms of the mental processes of obtaining, retaining and using information. Externalism attempts to broaden the enquiry beyond our cognitive qualities by explaining our being as a discursive, social and embodied being.

How We Unify Our Experiences

Recall that the Lockean definition of the person requires that the 'thinking intelligent Being ... can consider it self as it self, the same thinking thing in different times and places'. Personal identity, according to the definition, requires a unity between the thoughts in different times and places. As I will explain here, theories of personal identity also diverge in terms of how thoughts or experiences are unified to form the basis of personal identity. Here I will sketch two general views: the broadly Lockean requirement of 'unity of experiences' and the broadly Kantian requirement of 'unity of narration'.

According to Hume in the *Treatise of Human Nature*, a person is 'nothing but a bundle or collection of different perceptions' (1978: 252). Locke, like Hume, defines the self as the collection or bundling of ideas (thoughts and perceptions). On my walk into college this morning, I experienced a set series of thoughts and perceptions, and I will know my way home this evening because I can bundle those thoughts and perceptions together into a unified path. Similarly, my personal identity is made up of bundling my prior thoughts and experiences together. My memory of these thoughts and experiences serves as the main bundling tool. As Luntley explains: 'The Lockean model has a collection of Ideas, which, taken together make up a self: Ideas are items with an identity and selves are defined over some function for collecting Ideas together into collections' (2006, 107). Hence, personal identity under the Lockean model is provided through the (mere) unity of experiences. For Kant, the definition of personal identity as the mere bundling of experiences overlooks how *the activity of* bundling experiences constructs our personhood. Since all thoughts and perceptions are experienced by someone, it follows for Kant that 'it must be possible for the "I think" to accompany all my representations' (1929: 152). When we connect or bundle our experiences together, every connection we make with the world is always a connection that 'I' am making. Moreover, when we connect or bundle our experiences together, it is the same 'I' making the connections or undertaking the activity of bundling. Following this Kantian model, theorists such as Gillett (2004: 29–30) explain personal identity in terms a unity of narration: 'In making sense of the world, we apply discursive skills and norms of judgment to what is going on in that [neurophysicological] stream to produce the narratives of our lives according to the framework we have made our own'. To make sense of how I walked to college this morning I must be able to apprehend the experiences of crossing High Street or turning left onto Merton Street as experiences that are not just connected together but connected together through the common point of reference: the 'I' that experienced these things. To find my way home is to rehearse *my* narrative. Personal identity, according to the Kantian model, requires the capacity to *self-reference* our experience of the world. The unity of ideas required for personal identity must be more than the ability to connect together experiences (in some kind of order); personal identity includes the ability to appreciate our self-authorship over the series of experiences.

The metaphysical question then becomes whether there is anything more to our personal identity than the mere collection or bundle of experiences. Note how the 'I' or 'self-author' that the Kantian model introduces is elusive. Consider this very moment of reading this paragraph on this page. As Murdoch (2003: 257) muses, 'this present moment is the whole of one's reality'.

When the moment passes and we try and recall what the previous moment 'was like' we normally forget 'what it was like' to be in-that-moment-just-past, in a way 'as if we have to forget [the moment just past]'. Murdoch suggests that this 'natural lostness' of past moments 'may suggest its general nearly-non-existence and so its irrelevance'. The suggestion is that *all* that can be said about the moment-just-gone is that it was an experience that we had, and our attempts to self-reference the moment may be irrelevant.

Alternatively, the impasse that we reach between the unity of experiences and the unity of narration can be explained as reflecting an underlying moral disagreement. If the moral assumption is that *having experiences* is the basis of value, then nothing (of value) is obscured in viewing personal identity as a (mere) bundle of experiences. Alternatively, if the moral assumption is that our *agency over experiences* is the basis of value, in order for our conception of personal identity to capture the value of personal identity, then personal identity needs to be understood in terms of the unity of a narrative (Korsgaard, 1989: 29). In either case, a theory of personal identity requires an explanation of how it is we connect together our connections with the world.

IMPLICATIONS FOR LAW AND PRACTICE

Against the backdrop of this pencil-sketch of the philosophical landscape, we can now explore the two main implications for the treatment of patients with dementia. The first concerns the relationship between mental incapacity and personal identity, and the second concerns the relevance of a patient's (competent and) prior decisions as to their current treatment.

Personal Identity and Mental Incapacity

When we enquired into *how it is we experience the world* we encountered two clusters of views. The 'cognitivist view' explained our personal identity with the use of psychological or cognitive criteria. 'Externalists', in contrast, explained our personal identity in terms of our interaction with the world, drawing upon observations about our use of language, the use of our body and the relationships we form with others. An important implication of externalism is that there are a number of qualities to *who we are*, or our *being-in-the-world*, beyond our cognitive abilities.

Under the Mental Capacity Act 2005, sections 2 and 3, a person lacks the capacity to make a decision if, because of an impairment or disturbance of the mind, the person is unable to understand, retain or weigh the information relevant to the decision. From an externalist point of view a patient who lacks the capacity to make a decision (or a series of decisions) because of their dementia, is a patient who nonetheless retains a set of qualities that are constitutive of their personhood. The patient may retain the ability to express themselves, communicate with others, sustain or form relationships with others and retain pre-reflective skills or habits, all of which are qualities that are constitutive of someone's identity or personhood.

There is, for externalists, a conceptual gulf between personal identity and mental capacity. In contrast, if we view our connections with the world as internal mental representations or thoughts (cognitivism), then few qualities of personhood remain after the loss of cognitive abilities. There is, for cognitivists, substantial conceptual overlap between personal identity and mental capacity.

It is worth noting that it is open for cognitivists to find that a patient with dementia has lost their personhood (because of their loss of cognitive ability) but still attribute the patient a moral status. For instance, a cognitivist may hold that we owe duties of benevolence and dignity to the patient but no, or a lessened, duty to respect the autonomy of the patient (see, for instance, Luntley, 2006: 120). As mentioned earlier, not all theories of personhood attempt also to be complete moral theories of the person.

If a person is deemed to lack capacity to make a decision under the MCA, the decision can be made on their behalf based upon their 'best interests'. The views, wishes and feelings of the patient who lacks capacity will be taken into account, *insofar as* the views of the patient can help determine or ascertain the patient's best interests (section 4(6), MCA).

In approaching the question of the 'best interests' of the patient, the externalist view prompts us to consider the patient's (non-cognitive) qualities of personhood; their expressive use of communicative acts, the value of relationships and interaction with others and their unity with their body. This has implication for how patients with dementia should be cared for. In terms of communicative acts, Williams (2005) has suggested that, 'where communication is broken, disfunctional, turned back on itself, persons are trapped; care for persons is care for their language, listening to the worlds they inhabit'. In terms of relationships and interaction with others, Oppenheimer (2006: 321) reports that

> patients, for all their impaired autonomy, play an immensely significant part in the lives of the people who are connected to them ... it is the emotional context of these relationships (or their absence) that determine how much each person flourishes or withers, how much his potential for affection, enjoyment, humour, and the vivid communication of feeling, are stifled or expressed.

Kontos (2005: 565) suggests that, for the treatment of patients with dementia,

> embracing embodied selfhood in dementia care would sensitize care providers to how self resides in the pre-reflective body: the way that persons with dementia unthinkingly carry and project their bodies with coherence ... acknowledgment of embodied selfhood would also foster awareness of deeper understanding of the ways in which persons with dementia use non-verbal behaviour within the context of social interactions.

Philosophical assumptions as to *how it is we experience the world* inform our views on whether a patient has a personal identity beyond the impairment of their cognitive ability. If we consider our existence to be shaped by our thoughts about the world, then dementia is the loss of self. However, if we consider our existence to be shaped by our engagement with the world, then we may retain our personhood even when we lack legal capacity. Respect for the personhood of the patient may require that we give weight to the wishes and feelings of the patient as a value 'in and of itself' and not just as means of ascertaining the patient's best interests (Herring, 2009). At minimum, it requires that we acknowledge when ascertaining the patient's best interests that the patient benefits from being listened to, benefits from the emotional content of relationships and benefits from expressing themselves through embodied activity.

Past and Future Selves

We have also canvassed the difference between personal identity that is pulled together by the unity of experiences and personal identity that requires unity of narrative. These two philosophical views underpin the disagreement as to whether the treatment of an incompetent patient with dementia ought to be guided solely by their best interests or in accordance with an earlier (and competent) decision by the patient about their treatment. The law provides for the latter (insofar as section 26 of the MCA gives legal force to 'advance decisions to refuse treatment'). In support of this approach, Dworkin (1994: 228) contends that 'A competent person's right to autonomy requires that his past decisions about how he is to be treated if he becomes demented be respected even if they contradict the desires he has at a later point'. To explain this view, Dworkin draws a distinction between critical interests (values that construct meaning and coherence in life) and experiential interests (the quality of experiences in life). The contention is that, although incompetent patients will continue to have experiential interests, they lack the capacity to formulate critical interests. Their prior and competent decisions as to their treatment represent their critical interests, and furthermore, these critical interests ought to have priority over their experiential interests.

In other words, where a person is able to view the bundle of past, present and future experiences as part of a narrative (that has meaning and coherence), Dworkin is suggesting that decisions made in reference to this narrative ought to be respected over and above decisions that are only made in reference to present experience. Dworkin, therefore, adopts the Kantian model of personal identity (the unity of narrative). This view, however, is built upon a metaphysical premise and a moral premise, and we need not accept either.

Just as Murdoch doubted whether we ever achieve a unity of narrative, we can also doubt whether we have critical interests. Although it is true that we have goals and values, and we plan our lives according to these goals and values, these goals and values are directed towards current or future *experiences in life*. We may view our past or future experiences as fitting into a grand narrative, but *this view*—after all—is only a feature of our current experience. It follows that we can resist Dworkin's contention on a metaphysical basis: that the 'present moment is the whole of one's reality' and earlier decisions about our current reality has a 'general nearly-non-existence'.

In addition, we can also refuse the moral premise in Dworkin's argument. The agency, or autonomy, in formulating goals and coherence in life, is only relevant if we proceed from the moral assumptions that *agency over experiences* is the basis of value (rather than *having experiences*). Moreover, even if we accept that there is value in the agency over our experiences, it does not follow that we ought to prioritise the earlier agency regarding treatment, over the current experience of non-treatment. As Dresser explains, 'The goal of establishing a coherent narrative may be a less common life theme than the simple effort to accept and adjust to the changing natural and social circumstances that characterize a person's life' (Dresser, 1995: 36). Why should, for instance, a person's preconceived notion of dignified old-age trump the pain and suffering that can be avoided through medical treatment that the patient (who is experiencing the pain and suffering) consents to? Part of our response to this question will depend on whether we conceive of personal identity as a simple bundle of experiences or as a grandiose narrative of meaning and coherence.

SUMMARY

I have attempted here to sketch out theories of personal identity along two planes or axes by asking two philosophical questions: how it is we experience the world and how it is we unify these experiences. In identifying which qualities constitute a personal identity, we will need to consider whether there are aspects of our being or existence beyond our cognitive ability to obtain, retain and use information about the world (the first axis). If not, then deterioration of cognitive abilities will amount to the deterioration of a patient's personhood. If there are other, non-cognitive, aspects to our existence then a patient's personhood may survive the onset of dementia, and these qualities are relevant to the duties that we owe a patient who lacks capacity under the MCA.

We will also need to consider whether a patient has capacity to pull their past experiences into a self-authored narrative, or merely the ability to bundle together past experiences (the second axis). The unity of narrative model sets out a more demanding standard for personal identity as it requires the capacity to view past experiences and judgements of value through the single focal point of the transcendental 'I'. The unity of narrative model is able to explain the view that a dementia patient's prior decisions as to their current treatment ought to be given priority over their current desires. According to the narrative model, when the patient has lost the capacity to *self-reference* experience of the world into a framework of judgment and value, the patient has lost (all of an aspect of) their personhood. I have suggested here that it is possible to doubt the metaphysical and moral assumptions that underlie this explanation.

REFERENCES

Carman, T (2008) *Merleau-Ponty* (London, Routledge).

Dresser, R (1995) 'Dworkin on Dementia: Elegant Theory, Questionable Policy' 25(6) *Hastings Center Report* 32–38.

Dworkin, R (1994) *Life's Dominion* (New York, Vintage).

Eilan, N (2007) 'Consciousness, Self-Consciousness and Communication in Merleau-Ponty' in T Baldin (ed), *Reading Merleau-Ponty* (London, Routledge).

Gillett, G (2004) 'Cognition: brain pain: psychotic cognition, hallucinations, and delusions' in J Radden (ed), *The Philosophy of Psychiatry: A Companion* (New York, Oxford University Press).

Harré, R and Gillett, G (1994) *The Discursive Mind* (London, Sage).

Herring, J (2009) 'Losing it ? Losing what? The law and dementia' 21(1) *Child and Family Law Quarterly* 3–29.

Herring, J and Foster, C (2012) 'Welfare means relationality, virtue and altruism' 32(3) *Legal Studies* 480–98.

Hume, D (1978) *A Treatise of Human Nature* (eds L Selby-Bigge and P Nidditch) (Oxford, Clarendon Press).

Kant, I (1929) *Critique of Pure Reason* (trans N Kemp Smith) (London, Macmillan).

Kontos, P (2005) 'Embodied Selfhood in Alzhiemer's Disease: Rethinking Person Centred Care' 4(4) *Dementia* 553–70.

Korsgaard, C (1989) 'Personal Identity and the Unity of Agency: A Kantian Response to Parfit' 18(2) *Philosophy and Public Affairs* 101–32.

Locke, J (1975) *Essays Concerning Human Understanding* (Oxford, Clarendon Press).

Luntley, M (2006) 'Keeping track, Autobiography, and the Conditions for Self-erosion' in JC Hughes, SJ Louw and SR Sabat (eds), *Dementia: Mind, Meaning and the Person* (Oxford, Oxford University Press).

Matthews, E (2006) 'Dementia and the Identity of the Person' in JC Hughes, SJ Louw and SR Sabat (eds), *Dementia: Mind, Meaning and the Person* (Oxford, Oxford University Press).
McCulloch, G (2003) *The Life of the Mind. An Essay on Phenomenological Externalism* (London, Routledge).
McGin, C (1989) *Mental Content* (Oxford, Blackwell).
McMillan, J (2006) 'Identity, self, and dementia' in JC Hughes, SJ Louw and SR Sabat (eds), *Dementia: Mind, Meaning and the Person* (Oxford University Press).
Murdoch, I (2003) *Metaphysics as a Guide to Morals* (UK, Vintage).
Oppenheimer, C (2006) 'I Am, Thou Art: Personal Identity in Dementia' in JC Hughes, SJ Louw and SR Sabat (eds), *Dementia: Mind, Meaning and the Person* (Oxford, Oxford University Press).
Parfit, D (1984) *Reasons and Persons* (Oxford, Oxford University Press).
Taylor, C (1985) 'Theories of Meaning' in *Human Agency and Language. Philosophical Papers 1* (Cambridge, Cambridge University Press).
Williams, R (2005) 'The Care of Souls' 11 *Advances in Psychiatric Treatment* 4–5.

28

Dementia, Autonomy and Guardianship for the Old

MARGARET ISABEL HALL

INTRODUCTION

GUARDIANSHIP FOR THE old is most usefully understood as a *complex*, in which three ideational mechanisms fit together in a particular way, for the purpose of effecting a particular social outcome. The legal mechanism of guardianship, and the discourse which surrounds it, is one of these constituent elements. The liberal ideal of personhood as, fundamentally, a condition of autonomy, is another. The disease model of cognitive ageing as a pathological phenomenon—dementia—is the essential third piece, resolving the apparent tension between the guardianship mechanism and autonomy for the old. The idea of decision making connects all three: autonomy arises from and is exercised through decision making; the cognitive effects of ageing are legally relevant only to the extent that decision-making (and therefore autonomy) is impaired; guardianship works as, formally, a response to impaired decision-making/autonomy (through appointment of a 'substitute decision-maker'). Modern-era guardianship reforms seek to maximise individual autonomy through the crafting of guardianship mechanisms that enable individual decision making, either through supported decision making mechanisms or through the appointment of a substitute (as opposed to replacement) decision maker.

As described above, the complex of guardianship for the old tells a story in which guardianship does not interfere with individual autonomy but in fact protects it. In this story, autonomy is the defining characteristic of personhood. Because autonomy is defined in terms of independent decision making, the person whose cognitive ability to make decisions has been eroded by dementia is not, fully, autonomous. A person who is not capable of making decisions about X or Y can make (mere) *choices*, but because the individual does not have the capacity to engage in the underlying process of deliberation that gives rise to genuine decisions, those choices are disconnected from his or her autonomous self. Giving the fullest possible effect to such an individual's autonomy in these circumstances requires giving effect to the decisions that the individual *would have made* if capable of making decisions about X or Y; guardianship provides the legal mechanism through which this is effected, either through supported or substitute decision making, depending on the level of impairment. 'Co' or 'supported' decision-making models modify the substitute decision-making narrative without altering its fundamental terms, in which A and her guardian and together enact a version of A's previously autonomous self, through some combination of A's direct input and what is known of her former decision-capable self.

The bio-mechanical characterisation of cognitive decision making capacity is essential to this story. The kind of value judgement required for substantive evaluation of an individual's decisions or behaviour ('X's decision to give the house to Y is foolish and self-destructive') would unjustly undermine X's autonomy, which includes (and in some respects is defined by) the right to make foolish decisions. If X *could have* made a different decision, the decision he or she in fact made is not a proper concern of the State (or anyone else). Evaluating an individual's mental or cognitive capacity to make decisions while avoiding value-based judgements regarding the substantive content of those decisions is therefore a difficult but essential precondition for guardianship. That task is assigned primarily to members of the medical profession, as experts in this kind of objective bio-mechanical knowledge, with the court providing a supervisory role in certain circumstances (the courts play virtually no role where statutory guardianship mechanisms are used, for example).

This chapter suggests that the guardianship complex described above, while it succeeds as an abstract ideological narrative about autonomy and ageing, is inadequate as an embodied social response to the vulnerabilities experienced by individuals as a result of cognitive ageing. The complex of guardianship for the old and the quest for its autonomy-maximising perfection dominate the legal discourse about cognitive ageing and social response, however, leaving little space in which to imagine other, possible responses. Taking apart the theoretical complex of guardianship for the old—dementia, mental/decision making capacity, autonomy and guardianship—creates a space in which a different response to the embodied vulnerability of old age becomes imaginable; *not* a further finer reification (such as an abstract and therefore objectively measurable 'vulnerability' standard), but a social response that is guided by embodied need, efficacy of response and a civic ethics that is not limited to or by the mandate to promote and preserve the liberal autonomy ideal.

MENTAL CAPACITY AND DECISION MAKING: THE LEGAL CONSTRUCT

Mental capacity as a theoretical or conceptual construct in both law and medicine refers to a person's cognitive ability to understand the nature of a particular kind of *decision*, including the reasonably foreseeable consequences of making or not making that decision in a particular way. 'Decision' for this purpose refers to a special kind of choice, defined in the *Oxford English Dictionary* as a 'conclusion or resolution reached after consideration'. A person who is 'mentally incapable' of making a certain kind of decision is a person who is incapable of engaging in the necessary underlying process of consideration (equivalent to the capacity for rationality, the ability to think sensibly or logically) that is productive of such decisions. Such a person is considered not to possess the 'cognitive requisites necessary for individuals to be recognised as able to exercise legal capacity' (Bach and Kerzner, 2010).

Mental capacity may become a legal issue in several civil (as opposed to criminal) contexts: adult guardianship interventions are distinct because they require the evaluation of an individual's capacity to make *future* decisions (unlike the legal enquiry into whether an individual *had* sufficient capacity to make a will or to transfer property, for example), the complete nature and extent of which are not precisely knowable at the time the evaluation is made (unlike the legal/medical enquiry into whether an individual presently *has* sufficient capacity to consent to health treatment that is imminent, discrete and therefore knowable). The predictive nature of the capacity enquiry in this context necessarily flows from its purpose or objective: to provide for the consequences of ongoing and projected incapacity in situations where requiring a determination of capacity preceding each discrete decision point would prove hopelessly unwieldy. Indeed, the decision-making model of mental capacity is less coherent generally in the guardianship context, in contrast to the punctuate decisions/choices involved in property or health care decision-making (selling a house or consenting to medication) (Kukla, 2005; Chia, 1994). Arguably, the kind of ongoing and fluid care and assistance that is triggered and made possible by guardianship interventions cannot usefully be described in terms of 'decision making' at all. This conclusion is consistent with Lorraine Landry's definition of guardianship as, de facto, a 'legal device whereby the diverse needs of the elderly may be met' (Landry, 1999).

The legal idea of mental capacity as a measure of decision-making ability was first developed in the common law as a theoretical mechanism for establishing the validity (or otherwise) of property or relationship-related transactions (wills and marriage, for example). The idea of mental capacity as decision-specific also developed in this context, with different 'degrees' of mental capacity being required for the purposes of certain decisions. Some kinds of decisions require a relatively complex, underlying process of consideration and so require a higher 'degree' of mental capacity.[1] The distribution of benefits under a will is one such decision, as described in the classic and still authoritative case of *Banks v Goodfellow*:

> It is essential to the exercise of such [testamentary] power that a testator shall understand the nature of the act and its effects; shall understand the extent of the property of which he is disposing; shall be able to comprehend and appreciate the claims to which he ought to give effect; and with a view to the latter object, that no disorder of the mind shall poison his affections, pervert his sense of right, or prevent the exercise of his natural faculties—that no insane delusion shall influence his will in disposing of his property and bring about a disposal of it which, if the mind had been sound, would not have been made.[2]

Other kinds of decisions are considered by the law to require a less multifaceted and sophisticated kind of reasoning process. The decision to marry is this kind of decision, requiring only the ability to understand the nature of the marriage relationship (and not the significant financial implications of that relationship), and so a person who is found to be incapable of managing his or her person or property or both may nevertheless be considered capable of making the decision to marry.[3]

[1] *Countess of Portsmouth v Earl of Portsmouth* (1828) 1 Hagg Ecc 355, 362–63, 162 ER 611 (Arches Ct); see also, *Park v Park* [1953] 2 All ER 1411, 1434, [1954] P 112 (CA).

[2] *Banks v Goodfellow* (1870) LR 5 QB 549, 567.

[3] See *Feng v Sung Estate* (2003) 37 RFL (5th) 441 (OSC); *Banton v Banton* 1998 (Ont SC) CanLii 14926; *Stanton v Stanton Estate* 2008 BCCA 32; *Barrett Estate v Dexter* 2000 ABQB 530.

Individuals do make *choices* about matters that they are 'incapable' of making a decision about. Such choices may be understood as arbitrary, or as the manifestation of disordered thinking. They may be conceptualised as merely mechanical responses to physical or emotional needs or desires, or as directed by the will of another person (for whom the incapable 'chooser' acts as mere amanuensis). Whatever the origin or animus of these choices, they are not decisions. In this way and for this reason, insufficient mental capacity only appears to create one of a limited number of exceptions to the general legal rule of non-interference with personal decision-making, however foolish, as a structural guarantor of personal liberty or autonomy: '[t]he right knowingly to be foolish is not unimportant; the right to voluntarily assume risks is to be respected. The State has no business meddling with either. The dignity of the individual is at stake'.[4] Non-recognition in this instance *protects* the autonomy of the individual by refusing to legally enforce or recognise choices that are not, truly, the decisions of that person.

The core common law idea of mental capacity as a human quality measurable by degree (as opposed to an all or nothing approach) has been incorporated within modern health care consent and adult guardianship legislation, replacing the status-based enquiry/outcome (is this person mentally capable?) with a decision-making model (is this person capable of making decision X)? The focus on decision-making capacity is conceptualised as least intrusive and autonomy-impairing, carving out a more precise and limited scope of permitted interference; B may be capable of making simple decisions while incapable of other, more complex decisions. Mental disorder per se is not conclusive of impaired decision-making abilities (a mentally disordered person may nevertheless be capable of making decision X if not Y), but the cognitive nature of the decision-making enquiry means the medically established existence of mental disorder is always important, providing an bio-mechanical explanation for B's impaired decision making that avoids the need for value judgment. This explanation is particularly important given the behavioural nature of the evidence involved; the problem with B's large financial gift to a young woman he met in the supermarket last week can be explained in terms of B's cognitive failure, as opposed to a subjective evaluation of his behaviour. So explained Y's gift becomes a problem justifying social response, while his autonomy to make foolish decisions remains intact.

MENTAL CAPACITY AND DECISION MAKING IN THE ADULT GUARDIANSHIP CONTEXT

The modernising movement in both guardianship and health care consent legislation, from the 1980s and 1990s to the present, has sought to codify this decision-based common law concept of mental capacity in each respective area. This generic *idea* of mental capacity functions very differently, however, depending on the purpose of the enquiry. The construct works well enough in the context of property-related decisions (and indeed this is the purpose for which it was developed). The construct also

[4] *Re Koch*, 1997 CanLII 12265 (Ont SC) (Quinn J).

works well for the purpose of determining whether a person *has* sufficient mental capacity to make a discrete decision about a particular heath care procedure, as it does to determine whether a person *had* the capacity to make discrete a decision in the past (who to benefit in a will, for example) (Hall, 2012).

'Decision-making' in the health care context really refers to consent, and the common law origins of the legal requirement lie in the law of tort, specifically, battery. A battery is committed where one person invades or interferes with the body of another without that person's consent (a trespass to the person analogous to trespass to land), and medical 'interference' is tortious without consent, regardless of purpose or intent. A problem arises where the person is not 'capable' of giving or withholding that consent, and the body of case law which has developed around this issue has aligned that question (the kind of capacity required to give or withhold consent) with the decision-making model developed in the property context. The question of B's mental capacity to make a decision relating to pending medical treatment refers to a present decision (unlike the past decisions at issue in the property context) and, accordingly, B's current cognitive condition (his or her ability to engage in the kind of cognitive reasoning process essential to decision making) is all that matters. This enquiry (*preceding* treatment) will be carried out and controlled by medical actors with reference to (solely) medical evidence; the medical finding of capacity may subsequently be challenged, but retrospective legal review will be very much the exception to the rule. Even where that finding is legally challenged, its basis—the medical assessment of capacity to consent preceding treatment—ensures a continuing level of medical evidentiary control. If treatment has (or has not) taken place, no retrospective evaluation can set aside that action and rearrange the outcome accordingly, unlike in the property cases discussed above. The remedy, if any, will be damages.

The origins of the law of guardianship lie elsewhere, in the Crown's interest in the stewardship of property belonging to 'idiots' (those never having capacity) and 'lunatics' (those losing capacity as adults, who may yet regain it) (Surtees, 2012). The modern decision-making based model of adult guardianship theoretically works (and is intended) to bring the mental capacity issue in the guardianship context into alignment with the evaluation of decision-making capacity in the property and health contexts. The decision-making model is significantly less coherent in this context, however, despite the apparent resolution it provides to the ethical and ideological/theoretical problem of autonomy (no real decisions without mental capacity; no autonomy without decisions; no impairment of autonomy where the individual lacks decision-making capacity). *Unlike* (current) medical decision-making and (past) property transactions, both of which involve discrete or punctuate decisions, the evaluation of decision-making capacity in the guardianship context requires the evaluator to determine today whether this person, now and for an indeterminate future period, has the cognitive ability to make non-discrete *kinds* of decisions in unknowable (future) factual circumstances.

Ironically, however, the ongoing and open-ended interference with autonomy that guardianship entails makes the need for such a resolution especially acute. Indeed, in the property context, the donor is most likely to be deceased and any 'interference' with her autonomy will be symbolic only. The *loss* of autonomy involved where the subject of the enquiry is old—a person whose autonomy (and capacity) has hitherto been unquestioned, as opposed to one who never had it (and who, unlike the mentally ill, cannot be expected to regain it)—works to magnify this interference. The guardianship complex resolves this dilemma: the substitute or supporting decision-maker effects the decision that the individual would have made if decision-competent, thereby preserving autonomy where giving effect to the individual's mere choice would violate that person's 'true' or genuine autonomous self.

GUARDIANSHIP FOR THE OLD: SITUATING DEMENTIA

'Decision-making capacity' has (formally) replaced the diagnosis-based status of incapacity ('X has dementia = X is mentally incapable') in modern adult guardianship legislation (Surtees, 2012; Booth Glen, 2012), but the dementia diagnosis remains crucially important, providing both an (objective–scientific) *explanation* for the loss of decision-making ability in the old and a *prognosis* that the required cognitive functions will never be regained but will instead progressively degenerate (thereby justifying appointment of a continuing substitute/supporting decision-maker or guardian).

Guardianship is not, of course, specific to the old. Guardians may be appointed for (non-old) mentally disabled adults whose lack of mental capacity carries through from childhood, and for (non-old) adults who have 'lost' mental capacity through disease or accident. Adults of all ages diagnosed with mental illness may also have guardians appointed for them. Guardianship interventions involving the old are conceptually distinct, however, because of the difficult but ideologically imperative task of maintaining the liberal *ideal* of autonomous personhood throughout the *embodied* process of ageing. That ideal was described by Lorraine Code through the metonym of 'autonomous man':

> [S]elf-sufficient, independent, and self-reliant, a self-realizing individual who directs his efforts toward maximizing his personal gains. His independence is under constant threat from other (equally self-serving) individuals: hence he devises rules to protect himself from intrusion [and accordingly] ... talk of rights, rational self-interest, expediency, and efficiency permeates his moral, social, and political discourse (Code, 1991).

Few of us will suffer acquired brain injury, and the cognitive changes associated with it, and none of us expect to. Virtually all of us, in contrast, expect to grow old (unless we expect premature death). If dementia, and the diminished mental capacity it gives rise to, are (as Jonathan Herring has suggested) a 'natural part' of the ageing process and not a 'horrific, terrifying and widely feared' disease (Herring, 2008: 1645) growing old *entails* the loss of autonomy and the sequelae of that loss within the liberal legal paradigm: loss of dignity, personhood and human/legal rights. The disease model of dementia, in which dementia is more like acquired brain injury—exceptional, pathological, avoidable—in the absence of which cognition functions unchanged unto death, resolves this problem. The disease characterisation works to hive off something called 'dementia' from an imagined norm of 'healthy ageing' in which 'autonomous man' (as described by Code, above) remains unchanged: the perpetually 'vigorous citizen, who—with a smile on his lips—realises his life, while he runs unto death' (Tornstam, 1992). The disease characterisation of dementia provides an explanation for how and when 'interference' with the old will be justified as not infringing the autonomy of the old; the 'healthy' old do not require interference, and the 'sick' old have no current autonomy to interfere with.

The embodied nature of dementia problematizes this story, however. If dementia is a disease it is a special kind of disease, a *description* of behaviours that may (or may not) be linked one of several possible physiological sources: Alzheimer's plaques (diagnosable after death); vascular events ('small strokes'); cognitive ageing (the manifestation of which, like other physical ageing processes, will not be uniformly experienced). Unlike the cancerous cell on the slide, the diagnosis of dementia is a conclusion arrived at through observation of a person's speech, actions and behaviours. 'At the heart of the diagnosis of dementia' Hughes, Louw and Sabat have noted 'lurks some sort of evaluative judgement':

> At the most objective end of 'mental' illness (that is, in the field of 'organic' dementias) it turns out there is no hard scientific boundary between disease and normality. Lines can be drawn, but their exact location is a matter of evaluative judgement based on correlations between neuro-pathology and symptoms and signs. But which symptoms and signs? How much forgetfulness is pathological? What counts as normal aging? (Hughes et al, 2006).

'Dementia' is an interpretation of behavioural indicia when read as indicating something specific about the internal workings of the brain, a medical construct that gathers together and contains these indicia within a discursive boundary that, through the language of diagnosis, provides for some future action to take place (admittance to a care facility, for example, or the appointment of a guardian). The scientific–objective language of the diagnosis—the disease model—works to position dementia as *something like* the cell on the slide, *something like* ALS or acquired brain injury. Cognitive testing 'tools' such as the mini-mental status examination (MMSE) and the MacArthur competence assessment tool-treatment (MacCAT-T) work to a similar effect by providing apparently objective rateable scores that (like diagnosis) obscure the evaluative processes behind them. Kapp and Mossman have, evocatively, described the power and allure of these tools, which they describe as 'capacimeters':

> The idea of a capacimeter ... resonates powerfully with relevant scientific findings and with modern society's sometimes uncritical faith that human problems can be mastered through quantification. A measure that produced a definitive, objective, numerical readout addressing the ultimate capacity question in any ... setting would carry understandable (if illusory) appeal (Kapp and Mossman, 1996).

The recasting of the evaluative dementia diagnosis as 'hard' and quantifiable is troubled, however, by the unstable and often fluctuating nature of its 'symptoms' and 'signs' (so *unlike* the cell on the slide). This feature of dementia is most problematic in the context of the projected enquiry required for guardianship (unlike the point in time 'snapshot' which suffices to establish a person's current ability to make a known, discrete and immediate health care decision). The individual diagnosed with dementia at a particular point in time may be 'found' to possess decision-making capacity on Day A, in Context B and according to tool C, but perform quite differently where these factors are configured differently (Day X, Context Y, Tool Z). One response to this challenge has been the call for a still more perfect capacimeter capable of more accurately measuring the mutable effects of dementia on decision-making capacity. A more prosaic and de facto effect, however, may be to encourage the use of plenary guardianship orders, despite the availability of limited or partial guardianship orders, to take account of and prepare for the fluctuating (but inevitably declining) effect of dementia without the need for further applications.

Traditional guardianship legislation accommodated both the *ambiguity* of dementia and the projected nature of the mental capacity enquiry through the theoretical mechanism of 'mental disorder' (as opposed to 'decision making'), and the ability of the traditional model to accommodate dementia is no doubt the reason for its stubborn de facto persistence in the face of legislative reform, a phenomenon noted by several authors (Wright, 2010; Frolik, 1998; 2002; Surtees, 2012). The instrument provided is a blunt one, however: the very accommodating capaciousness of the traditional guardianship model is inappropriately and unnecessarily intrusive where dementia presents as *less than* severe, consistently obvious and consistently impairing.

What to do? One conclusion is that, from the law's perspective, in cases of 'dementia' (where cognitive changes are associated with the ageing process), social response is possible and permissible only where dementia *is* persistently severe and obvious. Outside of this category, if decision making is the measure and decision making maximisation of some kind (through support or substitution) the response on offer, decision making capacities are too much a moving target, and too ambiguous, for response to be practicable. Co or supported decision-making models, created to respond to the needs of young adults with developmental and intellectual disabilities, are not compatible with the embodied nature of dementia. Another conclusion is that the problems of dementia are not, essentially, problems of 'decision making' at all; that decision-making ability is the wrong ruler to use here, and that both substitute and supported decision-making are the wrong response. The inability of the law to respond in a meaningful, de facto sense to the embodied challenges posed by cognitive ageing/dementia is the inevitable consequence of this conceptual mistake.

UNRAVELLING THE COMPLEX: IMPLICATIONS

At the beginning of this chapter, I suggested that guardianship for the old was most usefully understood as a complex, in which a particular set of ideas and mechanisms worked together in a particular, iterative relationship. No one piece can work here in the absence of the others; the coherent whole is dependent on the theoretical integrity of each piece, individually and in relation to each other. The challenge dementia poses for the decision-making model of mental capacity is a challenge to the theoretical coherence of the guardianship complex.

Imagining another paradigm, a truly *different* response to cognitive ageing (inclusive of but not confined to the category of dementia), must start with the question of *why* guardianship for the incapable old exists in the modern law. Why not just leave such people to their own devices? Why, given the central significance of the autonomy value, and the inevitable tension between that value and guardianship intervention, the persistent attempt to mediate between the two? Why not let the chips fall where they may? Why do we care? What is the social objective served by the guardianship response in this context, and what options other than substitute decision-making might more effectively meet that objective?

Of course, there are many, many individuals experiencing private need who *are* left to their own devices; guardianship protects a special class or classes of people in relation to whom the protective response is considered justified. The old (meaning those evincing the effects of ageing, including cognitive ageing, and not the merely chronologically old) are one such class (Hall, 2014). Guardianship for the old in modern Western societies exists as a function and expression of social compassion or empathy for individuals whose well-being is negatively impacted by cognitive ageing; guardianship operationalises that social value through a privatising mechanism in which the 'substitute decision-maker' assumes responsibility with no more diffuse social response required.

If we accept that guardianship is a response to vulnerability in old age (as opposed to failed decision-making), it is clear that the premise of guardianship as a mechanism for substitute *or* supported decision-making is both inadequate and inappropriate. I have argued, moreover, that the decision-making model in this context (where dementia will virtually always be implicated) cannot be effected coherently, despite its theoretical appeal. The reification of vulnerability as a more accurate but equally abstract category/measurable quality, must be resisted, however; 'vulnerability' most usefully refers to the need for assistance from others that arises out of our human embodiment. Martha Fineman has described this quality of vulnerability as the 'universal' human condition (as opposed to the 'vulnerable populations' approach which would separate out from the non-vulnerable norm, stigmatising those deemed 'vulnerable' and therefore abnormal), experienced most intensely (but not exclusively) at the two 'pillars' 'anchoring' human embodiment: childhood, and old age. The precise measurement of decision-making capacity and/or dementia through 'capacimeters' or other pseudo-objective measurements is irrelevant to the social question of how to effectively *respond* to vulnerability in this sense. The question becomes more practical in nature: what is the nature of the vulnerability experienced and how (if at all) can it best be responded to? And, as a matter of social policy, does the political will exist to provide that response?

This understanding and approach is *implicit* in Article 12 of the UN Convention on the Rights of Persons with Disabilities (the CRPD), in particular subsections 1–4:

1. States Parties reaffirm that persons with disabilities have the right to recognition everywhere as persons before the law.
2. States Parties shall recognize that persons with disabilities enjoy legal capacity on an equal basis with others in all aspects of life.
3. States Parties shall take appropriate measures to provide access by persons with disabilities to the support they may require in exercising their legal capacity.
4. States Parties shall ensure that all measures that relate to the exercise of legal capacity provide for appropriate and effective safeguards to prevent abuse in accordance with international human rights law. Such safeguards shall ensure that measures relating to the exercise of legal capacity respect the rights, will and preferences of the person, are free of conflict of interest and undue influence, are proportional and tailored to the person's circumstances, apply for the shortest time possible and are subject to regular review by a competent, independent and impartial authority or judicial body. The safeguards shall be proportional to the degree to which such measures affect the person's rights and interests.

Kayess and French have criticised Article 12 as 'border[ing] on a complete denial of the instrumental limitations associated with cognitive impairments' (Kayess and French, 2008) Indeed, the UN model is incoherent, and difficult to imagine as realisable, if we continue to conceptualise 'legal capacity' as fundamentally concerned with the mental capacity to make decisions; of course, no amount of support will render every individual capable of making his or her 'own' decisions. If we conceptualise individual 'instrumental limitations' without reference to the theoretical device of mental capacity/decision making, however, that denial is irrelevant.

Why do we, as a society, care about the 'instrumental limitations associated with cognitive impairments'? Not because the individual so affected cannot make his or her own decisions, but because of a desire to support and protect those who are unable to provide and protect for their own well-being. The kinds of 'supports' and safeguards' referred to in the UN document are more appropriate as a means of achieving that objective than the mechanism of substitute decision-making; these alternate approaches have yet to be fully explored (and thereby defined) in part because they cannot fully be imagined from inside the capacity/substitute decision-making paradigm. I suggest here that the special nature of dementia and its ambiguous relationship to 'normal' cognitive ageing, as it problematises the theoretical mechanism of mental capacity and guardianship for the old, compels this kind of reimagining.

CONCLUSION

Western societies such as Canada have made a collective, ethical decision to respond to the needy old differently from the way we respond to other individuals (the chronically poor, for example, or the addicted) who are equally needy. One function of the disease characterisation of dementia is to disguise this response, which becomes not to the old per se but to the 'sick'. That categorisation is deeply problematic, however, on several levels, perversely pathologising the embodied process of ageing and inadequately limiting social response through the theoretical and legal model of 'substitute decision-making'. The disease model also works to preclude what should be the core policy question here: *why* respond differently to the old? Why not respond to the needs of other, equally (but differently) vulnerable adults, if a helpful social response is possible? Rethinking the social response to (not inevitable, not uniform) vulnerability arising from cognitive ageing as one particular aspect of the (not inevitable, not uniform) vulnerability arising from the embodied ageing process will enable—will *require*—rethinking possibilities for response to other vulnerabilities, and other members of the social collective. Rethinking the kind and scope of that response will, in turn, require a reimagining of autonomy beyond the liberal autonomy ideal (as embodied in Lorraine Code's 'autonomous man'), incorporating a 'relational' idea of autonomy as a quality to be developed—and not lost—through context and relationship with others.

REFERENCES

Areheart, BA (2011) 'Disability Trouble' 29(2) *Yale Law & Policy Review* 347–88.

Bach, M and Kerzner, L (2010) *A New Paradigm for Protecting Autonomy and the Right to Legal Capacity* (Toronto, Law Commission of Ontario). Available at: www.lco-cdo.org/disabilities/bach-kerzner.pdf.

Bartlett, P (2012) 'The United Nations Convention on the Rights of Persons with Disabilities and Mental Health Law' 75(5) *Modern Law Review* 752–78.

Booth Glen, K (2012) 'Changing Paradigms: Mental Capacity, Legal Capacity, Guardianship and Beyond' 44 *Columbia Human Rights Law Review* 93–169.

Brown, P (1995) 'Naming and Framing: The Social Construction of Diagnosis and Illness' 36 *Journal of Health and Social Behavior* 34–52.

Buchanan, A (2004) 'Mental Capacity, Legal Competence and Consent to Treatment' 97(9) *Journal of the Royal Society of Medicine* 415–20.

Chia, R (1994) 'The Concept of Decision: A Deconstructive Analysis' 31(6) *Journal of Management Studies* 781–806.

Code, L (1991) *What Can She Know? Feminist Theory and the Construction of Knowledge* (Ithaca, NY, Cornell University Press).

Frolik, LA (1998) 'Guardianship Reform: Where the Best is the Enemy of the Good' 9 *Stanford Law & Policy Review* 347–55.

—— (2002) 'Promoting Judicial Acceptance and Use of Limited Guardianship' 31(3) *Stetson Law Review* 735–55.

Hall, MI (2012) 'Mental Capacity in the (Civil) Law: Capacity, Autonomy, and Vulnerability' 58(1) *McGill Law Journal* 61–94.

Hall, MI (2014) '"Old age" or, do we need a critical theory of law and ageing?' 35 *Windsor Review of Legal and Social Issues*

Harding, N and Palfrey, C (1997) *The Social Construction of Dementia: Confused Professionals?* (London, Jessica Kingsley).

Herring, J (2008) 'Entering the Fog: On the Borderlines of Mental Capacity' 83(4) *Indiana Law Journal* 1619–49.

Hughes, JC, Louw, SJ and Sabat, SR (eds) (2006) *Dementia: Mind, Meaning, and the Person* (Oxford, Oxford University Press).

Kapp, MB and Mossman, D (1996) 'Measuring Decisional Capacity: Cautions on the Construction of a Capacimeter' 2(1) *Psychology, Public Policy, and Law* 73–95.

Kayess, R and French, P (2008) 'Out of Darkness and into Light? Introducing the Convention on the Rights of Persons with Disabilities' 8(1) *Human Rights Law Review* 1–34.

Kukla, R (2005) 'Conscientious Autonomy: Displacing Decisions in Health Care' 35(2) *Hastings Center Report* 34–44.

Landry, LL (1999) 'Normativity, Guardianship and the Elderly: Some Lessons from Canadian Legislation' 20 *Theoretical Medicine* 69–84.

Surtees, D (2012) 'How Goes the Battle? An Exploration of Guardianship Reform' 50(1) *Alberta Law Review* 115–27.

Tornstam, L (1992) 'The Quo Vadis of Gerontology: On the Scientific Paradigm of Gerontology' 32(3) *Gerontologist* 318–26.

Whitehouse, P (2001) 'The End of Alzheimer Disease?' 15(3) *Alzheimer Disease & Associated Disorders* 59–62.

Wright, JL (2010) 'Guardianship for your own good: Improving the well-being of respondents and wards in the USA' 33(5–6) *International Journal of Law and Psychiatry* 350–68.

29

Restriction of Liberty

MICHAEL SCHINDLER AND YAEL WAKSMAN

INTRODUCTION

IN THE LEGAL context, the right to liberty is clearly expressed in people's right to autonomy. The right to autonomy is the individuals' ability to make their own decisions and to channel their own activities (Dworkin, 1988: 13). This is based on the recognition that human beings are autonomous, intelligent creatures, who are responsible for their lives. Hence, one should refrain from external intervention with a person's reasoning, wishes and life plan (Beauchamp and Childress, 2000: 99). According to various scholars, the right to realize one's autonomy requires certain capabilities, such as the ability to understand and evaluate relevant information, and to conduct a logical thinking process, which considers the different aspects of decisions and their outcomes (Dworkin, 1988: 13, 14; Raz, 1986: 154–56).

According to liberal thinking, a person's liberty is a natural right and the intention to restrict this right requires justification. When the right to liberty is regularized in a legislative system, then the threshold for justifying its restriction is raised (Kohn, 2012: 22). Indeed, the individual's right to liberty and autonomy is entrenched in many judicial systems, embedded in many constitutions, as well as being part of international human rights declarations and conventions.[1]

In these judicial systems, justification to intervene and restrict a person's liberty is relevant in regard to individuals whose fundamental capability of autonomous action is limited or defective. In such cases, the intervention exists for their benefit and to protect them from potential harm from both themselves and others. It is from here that the accepted legal perception (or, at least, the perception that was accepted in the past) is derived, which makes a clear, dichotomous distinction between those with and without legal capacity, and grants only the former the liberty to perform legal actions (Herring, 2009: 5).

Even though restricting the liberty and legal capacity of persons with dementia can be expressed in different juridical fields such as inheritance law and contract law, in the present chapter, we focus on the legal context that allows the restriction of personal liberty, but whose purpose is to provide a broad, comprehensive response for individuals with dementia who have difficulty caring for their own

[1] See, eg: European Convention on Human Rights 1950; US Constitution Amendment XIV, s 1; Israel Basic Law: Human Dignity and Liberty 1992 (Israel) §5; British Columbia Adult Guardianship Act, RSBC 1996, c 6; Alberta: Adult Guardianship and Trusteeship Act, SA 2008, c A-4.2.

needs. First, we will address the legal institution of guardianship and its alternative models: alternative decision-making and supported decision-making. We will then focus on Adult Protective Services. Even though these arrangements refer to any adults who are incapable of dealing with their affairs because of mental incapacity, in this chapter, we will discuss these legal schemes in the context of persons with dementia.

Before elaborating on the various legal arrangements, we will briefly expand on the concept of legal capacity.

LEGAL CAPACITY

In Western and developed judicial systems, the presumption is that adults have legal capacity (Sabatino and Wood, 2012: 35). Although legal capacity is a controversial concept (Qualls and Smyer, 2007: 7), in this chapter, we use one of its accepted definitions: legal capacity means individuals' capability to make legal decisions and to perform legal actions based on their ability to exercise rational judgement to evaluate the relevant facts and the different alternatives at their disposal (Gorman, 1996: 225). The significance of this presumption is that unless it is refuted, adults have the capacity to make decisions and to perform legal actions pertaining to their lives.

Unequivocal assessment of legal capacity, including that of persons with dementia, is no simple matter. A mental capacity diagnosis cannot lead to a clear conclusion about a person's legal capacity to perform one action or another. Hence, the legal capacity will not always be equivalent to the mental capacity or the capacity to make decisions from a medical or psychiatric perspective (Spiegle and Crona, 2003: 65). For example, even if the clinical diagnosis indicates dementia that is manifested in partial impairment to time, place and judgement-related capabilities, from a legal point of view the person might still have the capacity to perform legal actions that bear no relation to this impairment. The person might have retained the ability to perform certain legal actions but not others, for example, having the capacity to draw up a will but not to make property transactions (Arias, 2013: 140). In addition, the person's legal capacity might change due to various parameters, such as the influence of medication, alcohol,[2] tiredness and emotional stress.

PERSONS WITH DEMENTIA AND NOMINATING A GUARDIAN

The prevalent legal framework for restricting an individual's legal capacity in the Western world and other developed countries is the nomination of a guardian.[3] This is a legal procedure in which the state nominates a guardian, via the judicial authority, to deal with affairs relating to the person's property, health and other issues. The origins of this institution can be found in legislation from the Roman Empire and in early English law (Carney, 1982: 205; Doron, 1998: 100).

[2] See, eg, the law in Nova Scotia (Canada): Inebriates' Guardianship Act, RSNS 1989, c 227.

[3] In this chapter, we use 'guardian', although additional terms, such as 'conservator', are used in various states.

The nomination of a guardian for persons with dementia is based on the paternalistic perception that grants the state the right and the obligation to protect those who are incapable of dealing with their own affairs, even when this results in an infringement of their liberty. The nomination is based also on the view that dementia is a disease with which the loss of the capacity to make legal decisions is inherent.

In some judicial systems, there is no formal declaration of the restriction of the individual's capacity as an inseparable part of the guardian nomination procedure, such as in the State of Maryland in the US, Japan, Germany and Sweden (Doron, 2002: 373, 376, 378, 384). However, in reality, the nomination of a guardian infringes on their wards' autonomy and denies their capability to perform certain legal actions, because it is the guardian who makes the personal, medical and economic decisions on their behalf.

The paternalistic perception that it is appropriate, in certain cases, to restrict the liberty of individuals and to act on their behalf through restricting their legal capacity and/or nominating a guardian originates in the *parens patriae* doctrine (Sabatino and Wood, 2012: 36; Salzman, 2010: 164). Nevertheless, the doctrine does not indicate a specific point in time for its implementation or for intervening in the individual's affairs (Sabatino and Wood, 2012: 35). The difficulty of determining this point in time is reinforced in cases of dementia, as this is not a binary condition, but a disease that develops slowly and consistently over many years. Moreover, as already mentioned, a dementia diagnosis does not necessarily mean that the person has lost all of his or her autonomous and cognitive capabilities.

Acknowledgment that the nomination of a guardian can constitute a serious infringement of a person's liberty (Andrews, 1997: 76) led to the recognition that only minimal use of the institution of guardianship should be made, if at all, using the appropriate procedural protection (Doron, 2002: 390) and clearer tests and criteria (Sabatino and Wood, 2012: 37, 38). Indeed, starting in the 1960s, judicial systems began to design different types of legal arrangements pertaining to legal capacity, which place greater emphasis on the values of liberty and autonomy and reduce the scope of paternalistic intervention (Carney, 2012: 1, 2). In this context, it is possible to identify three important developments that have significant implications for persons with dementia. The first is the use of guardianship on a partial and temporary basis ('tailored guardianship'), the second is the creation of an additional model of alternative decision-making and the third is the creation of a model of supported decision-making.

Partial, Temporary and Tailored Guardianship

The first essential change introduced mainly in the second half of the twentieth century and assimilated into many judicial systems is the use of partial and temporary guardianship, which offers 'tailored guardianship' in accordance with the ward's autonomous capabilities (Sabatino and Wood, 2012: 39; Salzman, 2010: 171). This change was made out of the recognition: (a) that if persons with cognitive disorders such as dementia retain some of their autonomous capabilities, then partial guardianship is appropriate, and (b) that people's lack of legal capacity and competence to deal with their own affairs can be temporary, when it is the outcome of different factors such as the nature of the disease and medication. In such cases, the guardian will be nominated for a temporary period only. One place where this perception can be found is in section 12(4) of the Convention on the Rights of Persons with Disabilities (2006), which asserts that 'States Parties shall ensure that all measures that relate to the exercise of legal capacity provide ... are proportional and tailored to the person's circumstances, apply for the shortest time possible', as well as in the Yokohama Declaration from the World Congress on Adult Guardianship (2010), which states that 'Capacity is both "issue specific" and " time specific" and ... measures of protection should not be all-embracing'.

Despite this important development, its implementation in practice is lacking. Studies indicate that in many states, a significant discrepancy exists between the law in books, which allows for partial and temporary guardianship, and the law in action, in the nomination of plenary and permanent guardianship (Kohn et al, 2013: 1118; Frolik, 1998: 347). Moreover, even partial and temporary guardianship is criticized because it still constitutes an infringement of the person's right to liberty in contrast to less detrimental alternatives such as the supported decision-making model, and because of its negative therapeutic implications for the ward: less interaction with the surrounding society, low self-image, etc. Furthermore, the stigma of requiring a guardian can damage the ward's self-esteem and their perception of their ability to cope with daily life (Salzman, 2010: 169).

Alternative Decision-Making Model

The second development is the alternative decision-making model, which is different from guardianship. The principal legal arrangement of this model is based on prevention and advanced legal planning. As the issue is covered in other chapters of this book, we will address the model only briefly. These tools offer persons with dementia the opportunity to prepare in advance for a situation in which they will not have the capacity to make decisions about their own affairs. This is generally performed through durable/continuing power of attorney or giving advance directives/instructions that authorize others to make decisions on their behalf according to past instructions and preferences. These tools are available for personal, financial and medical issues. This model emphasizes decision making on behalf of persons with dementia in accordance with their wishes and instructions, and unlike the nomination of a guardian, prevents an infringement of their liberty. This model exists in a considerable number of judicial systems in the Western and developed world (Doron, 2002: 390).

Despite the importance of this model, it is not a sufficient alternative to guardianship because granting this authority to others is subject to advanced planning, in which most older adults are not engaged (Salzman, 2010: 177).

Another type of alternative decision-making model is the Representation Agreement, which exists in British Columbia in Canada. Entering into this agreement permits another party to act on behalf of the person with dementia when making personal and property-related decisions. Furthermore, this legal framework allows for such agreements to be made even when the person in question does not have the capacity to perform certain actions, subject to having the ability to express choices and preferences.[4] Finally, these instruments can be misused as in many cases there are no supervision mechanisms for them, neither in law nor in practice.

The Supported/Shared Decision-Making Model

The third development is the supported/shared decision-making model. This model undermines the incapacity paradigm. The model is based on the perception that all people have legal capacity and that it is therefore appropriate to assist and support those who have difficulty making decisions and performing legal actions, in lieu of nominating an alternative decision-maker such as a guardian. This model aims to empower individuals to help them make their own decisions according to their needs and outlooks, thereby preventing an infringement of their liberty. This model exists in different forms in several states and can be helpful for some persons with dementia. For example, in Alberta, Canada[5] it is expressed in two forms: the first aids adults who are capable of making decisions but who require assistance in doing so; the second form, sometimes referred to as the co-decision-making model, is designed for adults whose capability of making decisions is significantly diminished. In a case such as this, decisions are made jointly by the 'supporter' and the adult and are implemented subject to both parties' agreement. Sweden offers the model of the 'god man' ('good man' in English), whose role is to help people arrange their affairs, while consulting with them and obtaining their consent (Herr, 1995: 216).

The use of this type of support is also in line with what is stated in section 12(2) of the UN Convention on the Rights of Persons with Disabilities (2006): 'States Parties shall recognize that persons with disabilities enjoy legal capacity on an equal basis with others in all aspects of life'. In section 12(3) it is written that 'States Parties shall take appropriate measures to provide access by persons with disabilities to the support they may require in exercising their legal capacity'.

Different scholars, such as Kanter, are of the opinion that the Convention seeks to abolish the institution of guardianship, and to replace it with a supported decision-making model (Kanter, 2009: 563). This model raises substantial questions regarding its proper implementation. Thus, for example, Kohn et al pointed to the risk that in lieu of providing support for people who are mentally incompetent, supporters might exercise inappropriate influence over their decisions, thereby infringing upon their civil rights. In light of this, they recommend further research that will examine the practical implementation of the model and what is required for its proper realization (Kohn et al, 2013: 1157).

In light of all the above, it appears that in recent decades a significant change has occurred in the legal frameworks, whose goal, among other things, is to assist persons with dementia to manage their affairs and to make legal decisions. This change has occurred partly due to the fact that human rights, including the rights of people with disabilities, have become an integral part of Western, developed and international judicial systems. As clarified above, the 'traditional' legal framework

[4] Representation Agreement Act, RSBC 1996, Ch 405.

[5] Adult Guardianship and Trusteeship Act (AGTA).

that was historically acceptable for managing the affairs and making decisions on behalf of persons with dementia was the institution of guardianship, of which the restriction of liberty is a fundamental part. In recent years, this legal system has undergone changes and reforms, and the restriction of the liberty of persons with dementia, if at all, has been reduced to the necessary minimum, both by tailored guardianship and by the adoption of alternative, supported or co-decision-making models. As mentioned earlier, despite these changes, a significant gap still exists between the written law and its practical implementation.

Following this review of guardianship and its various alternatives, in the next section, we will address another legal arrangement: Adult Protective Services.

ADULT PROTECTIVE SERVICES

The legal institution of guardianship and its various alternatives professes to provide a legal solution for adults who are incapable of making decisions and managing their affairs. In contrast, the legal framework of Adult Protective Services[6] focuses on specific treatment responses for adults, including persons with dementia, who, because of intellectual or physical disabilities, are unable to deal with their own needs and who are exposed, among other things, to abuse, neglect or self-neglect. These interventions are implemented mainly subject to the individual's wishes. Nevertheless, under certain conditions, these services can be enforced, in most cases, via the law courts.

Adult Protective Services exist in a considerable number of Western and developed judicial systems and they vary from state to state, subject to policy and resources. Some of them include only personal and medical interventions and others also address the financial aspect. Despite the broad differences between the various judicial systems, most of them include enforceable medical and nursing services, including the transfer to institutional frameworks.

The possibility of enforcing such interventions, even without the consent of the person with dementia, is subject to certain conditions and principles. The following principles are common to most judicial systems: (a) intervention will be enforced only in cases of adults' diminished cognitive ability, which impairs their ability to understand that they require these services. In different countries, it is explicitly stated that the person does not have legal capacity;[7] (b) no other party is authorized to give consent on their behalf; (c) such intervention is necessary for the adult's well-being; (d) In certain judicial systems, such as in most North American states, the adult's situation must pose direct risk to his or her well-being (Duke, 1997: 52); and (e) instructions should be given for persons with dementia to receive the least restrictive intervention, with the least possible infringement of their liberty.

The difficulty noted above regarding unequivocal assessment of the capacity of persons with dementia is relevant also in regard to Adult Protective Services,

[6] This legal arrangement is called Adult Protective Services only in some countries, such as North America. Nevertheless, this is the term we will use in the context of this chapter.

[7] See, eg: Protection of Personal and Property Rights Act 1988 in New Zealand.

specifically in regard to whether to respect their refusal to receive specific services that they require, or whether to force these services upon them in light of their incapacity.

There are those who see Adult Protective Services as an additional arrangement which, in certain circumstances, can serve as a suitable alternative to guardianship. This is because the responses are mainly specific to and focused on the needs of the adult, and hence, any infringement of the individual's autonomy is minimal (Gordon, 2001: 24).

Nevertheless, for Adult Protective Services to constitute an appropriate alternative to guardianship, and especially to provide a comprehensive response for the needs of persons with dementia while minimizing and even preventing the infringement of their liberty, this legal arrangement should incorporate a 'basket of services'. These should include support and assistance in the social and medical fields, which will be clearly enshrined in the legislation, determining the state's responsibility to provide these services. The broader and more varied this basket of services, the greater will be the likelihood of finding services to which the individual will give consent. Indeed, in different judicial systems, we find judicial arrangements that include such a basket of services, for example, in the Canadian province of Prince Edward Island.[8] The legislation dealing with adult protection includes personal services such as diagnosis and consultation, speech and hearing therapy, occupational therapy and psychotherapy, day centres, nursing and supportive therapy, social activities and professional training, housing and housing adaptation, nutrition and more.

In the presence of certain aforementioned conditions, this legal arrangement also allows for authority and coercion-based intervention. This notwithstanding, a broad basket of services will decrease the need for this type of intervention and even in the event that coercive intervention is necessary, a wider variety of services will enable the enforcement of less detrimental intervention.

A clear example of the claim that a broader basket of services will prevent the need for coercive intervention with persons with dementia can be found in a plea to the Supreme Court of Israel. The plea was filed on behalf of a senior citizen with physical and mental disabilities, who claimed that her enforced removal from home to an institutional framework was unjustified. This was because she had an appropriate alternative that did not infringe on her liberty, in the form of ongoing in-home care, which should be funded by the state. The judicial procedure led to a specific individual solution for this woman, but did not constitute a judicial precedent that would oblige the state to fund 24-hour in-home care.[9]

To sum up, legal arrangements that include a basket of services are a broadening trend in many judicial systems and create a practical transition from paternalistic Adult Protective Services, based on coercive authoritative intervention, to protection services used primarily on a voluntary basis. Being voluntary, these services empower the persons with dementia, and can be adapted to their natural home environment,

[8] The Adult Protection Act, RSPEI 1988, c A-5.

[9] HCJ 1192/12: *Krakow and others versus the Municipality of Haifa, Ministry of Social Affairs and Social Services, Ministry of Health, and others*—the judicial arrangement in Israel enables 24-hour in-home medical and nursing assistance only to those who are in a position to pay, whereas care in institutional frameworks is funded by the state, even though the costs are higher than for in-home care.

while maintaining respect for their liberty and right to personal autonomy. They are also consistent with section 19(b) of the Convention on the Rights of Persons with Disabilities (2006), which states that 'Persons with disabilities have access to a range of in-home, residential and other community support services, including personal assistance necessary to support living and inclusion in the community, and to prevent isolation or segregation from the community'.

Nevertheless, to provide an appropriate response, these protection services should include a wide variety of services.

CONCLUSION

The right to liberty for persons with dementia is a broad and complex legal issue and can certainly not be covered in one short chapter. In light of this, we focused on several legal institutions and frameworks that attempt to provide a general judicial response for persons with dementia, while addressing the tension between the need to act for their protection on the one hand, while maintaining their right to liberty on the other. We started with the issue of legal capacity and the difficulty of assessing the legal capacity or incapacity of persons with dementia. We then presented the change that has occurred in recent decades, from an all-embracing, 'global' paternalistic attitude towards persons with dementia through nomination of an overall, permanent guardian, to emphasis on their right to liberty through partial and temporary tailored guardianship, an alternative decision-making model as well as a supported decision-making model. We clarified the fact that, despite these changes, a significant gap still exists between the written law and its practical implementation (use of a general, permanent guardian is still all-embracing; use of legal planning and prevention tools in many countries is rare) and there is room to examine the practical implementation of the supported decision-making model. Following this, we expanded on the legal arrangement of Adult Protective Services, where an apparent trend can also be seen towards a preference to create social services that prevent the need for lawful intervention, over lawful intervention that coercively restricts the liberty of persons with dementia.

The various models were developed as a result of progress in the medical sciences and because of changes in the ethical perceptions of people with disabilities, including persons with dementia. This is manifest in the emphasis placed on their rights in general and their right to liberty in particular. Designing judicial models for the benefit of these populations is no simple task and they will continue to be developed (Sabatino and Wood, 2012: 56). We hope that all legislators will continue to develop models and to introduce legislative changes, which will minimize the need to negate or restrict the personal freedom of persons with dementia, by empowering them and realizing their capabilities.

REFERENCES

Andrews, MD (1997) 'The Elderly in Guardianship: A crisis of constitutional proportions' 5 *Elder Law Journal* 75–116.

Arias, JJ (2013) 'A time to step in: Legal mechanisms for protecting those with declining capacity' 39(1) *American Journal of Law & Medicine* 134–59.

Beauchamp, TL and Childress, JF (2009) *Principles of Biomedical Ethics*, 6th edn (Oxford, Oxford University Press).

Carney, T (1982) 'Civil and Social Guardianship for Intellectually Handicapped People' 8(4) *Monash University Law Review* 199–232.

—— (2012) 'Guardianship, "social" citizenship and theorizing substitute decision-making law' in I Doron and AM Soden (eds), *Beyond Elder Law* (New York, Springer Press).

Doron, I (1998) 'From lunacy to incapacity and beyond: Guardianship of the elderly and the Ontario experience in defining "Legal incompetence"' 19(4) *Health Law in Canada* 97–114.

—— (2002) 'Elder Guardianship Kaleidoscope: A comparative perspective' 16(3) *International Journal of Law, Policy and the Family* 368–98.

Duke, J (1997) 'A national study of involuntary protective services to adult protective services clients' 9(1) *Journal of Elder Abuse & Neglect* 51–68.

Dworkin, G (1988) *The Theory and Practice of Autonomy* (Cambridge, Cambridge University Press).

Frolik, LA (1998) 'Guardianship reform: When the best is the enemy of the good' 9 *Stanford Law & Policy Review* 347–55.

Gordon, RM (2001) 'Adult protection legislation in Canada, models issues, and problems' 24(2–3) *International Journal of Law and Psychiatry* 117–34.

Gorman, F (1996) 'Testamentary Capacity in Alzheimers's Disease' 4 *Elder Law Journal* 225–46.

Herr, SS (1995) 'Maximizing Autonomy: Reforming Personal Support Laws in Sweden and the United States' 20(3) *Journal of the Association for Persons with Severe Handicaps* 213–23.

Herring, J (2009) 'Losing it? Losing what? The law and dementia' 21(1) *Child and Family Law Quarterly* 3–29.

Kanter, AS (2009) 'The United Nations Convention on the Rights of Person with Disabilities and its implication for the Rights of Elderly People under International Law' 25(3) *Georgia State University Law Review* 527–73.

Kohn, AK (2012) 'A civil rights approach to elder law' in I Doron and AM Soden (eds), *Beyond Elder Law* (New York, Springer Press).

Kohn, NA, Blumenthal, JA and Campbell, AT (2013) 'Supported Decision-Making: A viable alternative to guardianship' 117(4) *Penn State Law Review* 1111–57.

Qualls, SH and Smyer, MA (2007) *Changes in Decision-making Capacity in Older Adults: Assessment and Intervention* (Hoboken, NJ, John Wiley & Sons).

Raz, J (1986) *The Morality of Freedom* (Oxford, Oxford University Press).

Sabatino, CP and Wood, E (2012) 'The conceptualization of legal capacity of older persons in western law' in I Doron and AM Soden (eds), *Beyond Elder Law* (New York, Springer Press).

Salzman, L (2010) 'Rethinking Guardianship (Again): Substituted Decision Making as a Violation of the Integration Mandate of Title II of the Americans with Disabilities Act' 81 *University of Colorado Law Review* 157–245.

Spiegle, RF and Crona, SJ (2003) 'Legal Guidelines and Methods for Evaluating Capacity' 32(6) *Colorado Lawyer* 65–72.

30

Research on Patients with Dementia

PHIL BIELBY

INTRODUCTION

THE REGULATION OF biomedical research involving people with dementia is an important but under-explored area of medical law and ethics. In an era of increasing scientific progress in dementia research, as well as the growing societal priority attached to it, this under-exploration is surprising. Yet, at the same time, regulatory approaches to dementia research encounter similar ethical and legal controversies to those found elsewhere in law relating to research involving adults with questionable decisional competence. In this chapter, I will discuss the legal regulation of medical research involving people with dementia, including clinical trials, by paying particular attention to three areas of controversy which confront it. All these are in some way connected to the potential participant's decisional (in)competence. These are, first, problems of assessing decisional competence to consent to research where decisional competence is questionable but not necessarily absent; second, the role of proxy consent by a legally authorised representative where the potential participant lacks decisional competence; and, third, the possibilities offered by anticipatory decision-making via advance directives for use in dementia research. Despite significant developments over the last decade in the evolution of the present regulatory framework, I will highlight areas where scope for further development exists. I will approach these issues within the context of English law and the professional ethics guidance that applies within the UK, though the implications of these issues for medical and mental capacity law, as well as for biomedical ethics, resonate beyond any one jurisdiction.[1]

WHAT NEEDS TO BE REGULATED? IDENTIFYING THE IMPERATIVES FOR MEDICAL RESEARCH INTO DEMENTIA

Demographic, economic and scientific factors (also highlighted elsewhere in this book) are driving the development of medical research into dementia. Responding to the health care, social and economic challenges posed by dementia via medical research is an increasing priority, recognised by charities and, more recently, the British Government. In the Alzheimer's Society report, *Dementia UK* (2007), it

[1] The legal and professional ethics regulatory position discussed is current as of June 2013.

was estimated that there are almost 700,000 people in the UK living with dementia (Alzheimer's Society, 2007: 23), a figure put at over 800,000 in the more recent Alzheimer's Research Trust *Dementia 2010* report (Luengo-Fernandez et al, 2010: 7). In the former, the Alzheimer's Society urged that funding for research 'into the causes, prevention, cure and care of dementia' should be increased (Alzheimer's Society, 2007: 82), echoed in the UK Department of Health's *National Dementia Strategy*, which affirmed the importance of adequate funding and identifying unmet need in dementia research (UK Department of Health, 2009: 69). The *Dementia 2010* report found that the investment in dementia research was disproportionately low compared with the economic impact of the disease (Luengo-Fernandez et al, 2010: 7) and that of government funding into cancer, heart disease, stroke and dementia in the late 2000s, only 9% of these funds were spent on dementia research (Luengo-Fernandez et al, 2010: 7). This figure was even lower for research funding from charities (Luengo-Fernandez et al, 2010: 7).

Following this, as well as calls from Alzheimer's Research UK in 2012, a major charitable organisation funding dementia research, for government funding to improve capacity for such research (Alzheimer's Research UK, 2012), and the recognition of the imperative to enhance dementia research in *The Ministerial Advisory Group On Dementia Research* (UK Department of Health, 2011) and the *Prime Minister's Challenge on Dementia* (UK Department of Health, 2012a), the UK's NHS National Institute for Health Research announced a funding commitment of £22 million in late 2012 for dementia research projects (UK Department of Health, 2012b), including research involving drugs and new technologies. A research network, the Dementia and Neurodegenerative Diseases Research Network (DeNDRoN), created under the auspices of the National Institute for Health Research Clinical Research Network to facilitate research into dementia along with other neurodegenerative diseases states on its website that:

> For 2012 and beyond, DeNDRoN has ambitious plans ... to optimise the significant opportunities presented by the Government's prioritisation of dementia research. The challenge ahead is to enable 10% of people with dementia and neurodegenerative diseases to participate in clinical research (DeNDRoN, undated).

In May 2013, the Government also published an annual update on progress in responding to the *Prime Minister's Challenge on Dementia*, which included a dedicated chapter on research (UK Department of Health, 2013). After a period of being eclipsed by research on other major health issues, the value and significance of dementia research is now beginning to be reflected at the level of public policy. Given the wider social impact of dementia, it is also unsurprising that dementia research is increasingly headline news (for example, Kollewe, 2012).

At a scientific level, the nature of medical research into dementia has gained considerable momentum in recent years, in parallel with other developments elsewhere in neuroscientific and psychiatric research (for a comprehensive summary of the field see, for example, Merkel et al, 2007). Advances in genetics, neuroscience and psychiatry in particular have yielded insights into dementia and related neurodegenerative conditions (see, for example, Andreasen, 2001; Rosenberg, 2005 and the summary of research projects funded by the Alzheimer's Society in Alzheimer's Society, 2012). Specifically, in recent years, studies have pointed to the rise in pharmacological treatments for dementia (Issa and Keyserlingk, 2000: 1231–35), including drugs to enhance cognition (Simard and van Reekum, 1999) and even the emerging possibility of neuro-regenerative treatment such as the replacement of neural cells (Glannon, 2011: 202). New frontiers in dementia research that hold out the promise of enhancing the lived experience of people with dementia, but which involve different degrees of risks and benefits for research participants, are therefore continuously arising. Many of these research projects will require the participation of people with dementia in order to generate meaningful results.

It is plainly beyond doubt that medical research into dementia now represents a significant imperative for society as well as groundbreaking opportunities for science. With this in mind, our attention now turns to the regulatory framework itself to establish how well equipped it is to deal with the ethical and legal challenges that dementia research faces.

THE CURRENT REGULATORY FRAMEWORK IN ENGLAND AND WALES

This section offers an overview of the regulatory framework—comprising law and professional ethics perspectives—that relates to medical research involving people with dementia. I will pay particular attention to the provisions that apply to decisionally incapacitated adults, a legal category highly relevant to people with dementia due to either already lacking decisional competence or expecting to lose it in the future due to the neurodegenerative progression of the disease. Three particular controversies relevant both to this framework in particular, and the regulation of dementia research more generally, will be discussed in the following section.

Legal Framework

I will focus upon two legislative frameworks which currently regulate medical research involving people with dementia in England and Wales: the Mental Capacity Act 2005 (hereafter MCA 2005) and The Medicines for Human Use (Clinical Trials) Regulations 2004 (hereafter the Clinical Trials Regulations (CTR)). (Other legislation applies to the specific contexts of research with human tissue and in the safeguarding of data obtained from participants in the course of medical research—namely the Human Tissue Act 2004 and the Data Protection Act 1998—although these will not be discussed here.) This framework is relatively new: at the time of writing, both the MCA 2005 and the Clinical Trials Regulations have been in existence for less than a decade. The former applies to 'intrusive research' on adults who lack capacity that does not constitute a clinical trial (DCA, 2007: 204–05, paragraph 11.6). 'Intrusive research' is defined under section 30(2) of the MCA 2005 as 'of a kind that would be unlawful if it was carried out—(a) on or in relation to a person who had capacity to consent to it, but (b) without his consent'. The Clinical Trials Regulations, by contrast, regulate medical research that involves clinical trials with 'investigational medicinal products'. In dementia research, examples of the former could range from the taking of a blood sample to a novel neurosurgical procedure, whereas an example of the latter might include a clinical trial of cognition-enhancing drugs. In 2012, the European Commission confirmed that they plan to replace the parent EU Directive (Directive 2001/20/EC) that the Clinical Trials Regulations implemented in the UK, though these changes pertain largely to research ethics oversight and will not affect the position on consent (Waligora, 2013: 408). The replacement EU legislation is anticipated to be introduced in 2016 (European Commission, 2012).

The provisions of the MCA 2005 which regulate research with adults who lack decisional capacity are found in sections 30–34, and those that pertain to the conditions for approval specifically in section 31(1)–(6). (The legal definition of lacking decisional capacity itself, discussed elsewhere in this book, can be found in sections 2 and 3.) These provide that a research ethics committee (referred to in the Act as an 'appropriate body') will only be able to approve research to be undertaken with a decisionally incompetent adult if it relates to an 'impairing condition' which affects the person or the treatment of this condition (section 31(2)(a)–(b)); research would not be as effective if it were undertaken with persons who have decisional competence to consent (section 31(1)–(4)); it must offer potential benefits to the person concerned whilst not creating disproportionate burdens (section 31(5)(a)) or, it must aim to offer benefit to individuals who suffer from 'the same or a similar condition' as the incapacitated person (section 31(5)(b)) provided it only poses a negligible risk (section 31(6)(a)), it does not affect the person's 'freedom of action or privacy in a significant way' (section 31(6)(b)(i)) and is not 'unduly invasive or restrictive' (section 31(6)(b)(ii)).

There is also a requirement for those conducting research to approach the potential participant's informal carer or someone otherwise with an interest in her welfare, including any Lasting Power of Attorney made under the provisions of the MCA, for a view (or if such a person does not exist, nominate someone else willing to be consulted) as to whether the decisionally incapacitated adult should be involved and the 'wishes and feelings' she may have had in relation to the research if she had capacity to decide (section 32(1)–(4) and 32(7)).[2] Any reservations in this regard expressed by the individual consulted must lead to the decisionally incapacitated adult not taking part or being withdrawn from the research if it has already commenced, unless this would pose 'a significant risk' to that person's health (section 32(5)–6)). Additionally, signs of unwillingness to continue with participation in the research by the incapacitated adult herself should lead to her being 'withdrawn without delay' unless, again, this would pose 'a significant risk' to her health (section 33(2)(a); 33(4) and 33(6)). It is also possible for a decisionally incompetent adult to refuse research participation prospectively via an advance directive (section 33(2)(b)(i)).

In relation to clinical trials undertaken with decisionally incapacitated adults, the most relevant provisions for dementia research are found in Schedule 1, Part 5 of the Clinical Trials Regulations (which applies only if there has been no prior consent or refusal offered prior to the loss of decisional competence, in which case Schedule 1, Part 3 applies, discussed below). This provides for the potential participant's legal

[2] For stylistic simplicity, in this chapter I will refer to the person with dementia by the female pronoun 'she'/'her'.

representative—in other words, a proxy decision-maker—to offer their consent to the participation of a decisionally incompetent adult in a clinical trial (CTR, Schedule 1, Part 5). It requires that the legal representative herself is properly informed as to 'objectives, risks and inconveniences of the trial and the conditions under which it is to be conducted' (CTR, Schedule 1, Part 5, paragraph 1), and that her consent is given for the incapacitated adult to be included in the trial (CTR, Schedule 1, Part 5, paragraph 4), which can be revoked at any point subsequently (CTR, Schedule 1, Part 5, paragraph 5). Despite the decisional incompetence of the potential participant, there is still a requirement that she or he is provided with 'information according to his capacity of understanding regarding the trial, its risks and its benefits' (CTR, Schedule 1, Part 5, paragraph 6) and that the 'explicit wish' of the participant not to or no longer to take part in the trial 'is considered by the investigator' (CTR, Schedule 1, Part 5, paragraph 7). The consent which the legal representative provides in relation to the decisionally incompetent adult taking part in the clinical trial 'shall represent that adult's presumed will' (CTR, Schedule 1, Part 5, paragraph 12).

The trial itself must satisfy one of either two conditions: either that its benefits for the participant are anticipated to be greater than the risks involved—or that the research involves no risk (CTR, Schedule 1, Part 5, paragraph 9). In either case, it must pertain to 'a life-threatening or debilitating clinical condition from which the subject suffers', such as dementia (CTR, Schedule 1, Part 5, paragraph 11) and the minimisation of 'pain, discomfort, fear and any other foreseeable risk in relation to the disease and the cognitive abilities of the patient' must feature within the design of the clinical trial (CTR, Schedule 1, Part 5, paragraph 13). Schedule 1, Part 5 of the Clinical Trial Regulations are governed by the principles set out in Schedule 1, Part 2—which for the present purposes, include the now familiar general research ethics prescription that 'The rights, safety and well-being of the trial subjects shall prevail over the interests of science and society' (CTR, Schedule 1, Part 2, paragraph 1) and stipulate compliance with the Declaration of Helsinki (CTR, Schedule 1, Part 2, paragraph 6). The Declaration of Helsinki offers a seminal (though non-legally binding) international code of professional ethics, which itself identifies participants who are decisionally incompetent as requiring 'special protection' (World Medical Association, 1964, rev 2008, paragraph 9—though, as Pattinson notes (2011: 402), the CTR make reference to the earlier 1996 version which has been superseded by subsequent versions).[3]

Notwithstanding the relevance of decisional incapacity regarding research participation, it should not be overlooked that research participants with early stage dementia may well retain decisional competence to make a decision on their own behalf. The legal position here, though, is less comprehensive. Schedule 1, Part 3 provides requirements for participation in clinical trials by decisionally competent adults or adults who have such competence at the time the decision to participate is

[3] Since this chapter was completed, the Declaration of Helsinki has been revised again (World Medical Association, 1964, rev 2013). A consequence of this is the removal of examples of potential participants who require (in the revised phrasing) "specifically considered protection" (World Medical Association, 1964, rev 2013, paragraph. 19). Rather, this requirement now relates to "All vulnerable groups and individuals" (World Medical Association, 1964, rev 2013, paragraph 19).

made. Consent in relation to participation in a clinical trial is governed by Schedule 1, Part 1 and Part 3 of the Clinical Trials Regulations, which defines consent as involving a decision 'given freely after that person is informed of the nature, significance, implications and risks of the trial' (CTR, Schedule 1(1), paragraph 3). Moreover, Schedule 1, Part 3, paragraph 1 expands upon this information disclosure requirement, specifying that the participant must be 'given the opportunity to understand the objectives, risks and inconveniences of the trial and the conditions under which it is to be conducted'. This standard displays some affinities with, though is arguably more rigorous than, the English common law position on information disclosure regarding medical treatment (developed in cases such as *Sidaway v Board of Governors of the Bethlem Royal Hospital*; *Pearce v United Bristol Healthcare NHS Trust* and *Chester v Afshar*)[4], which would form the basis of the information disclosure standard for other types of research not covered by the Clinical Trials Regulations. This is because, as Biggs acknowledges, there are no cases in English law which relate to consent to research (Biggs, 2010: 80). We will return to consider the question of decisional competence as a specific issue raised by dementia research in the next section.

Professional Ethics Perspectives

In addition to the legal framework, professional ethics guidance exists which relates to the regulation of research with adults with questionable or no decisional competence to consent to participation, such as may typically be encountered in dementia research. Influentially, the World Medical Association Declaration of Helsinki recognises vulnerable research participants (WMA, 1964, rev 2008, paragraph 9), which include (but are not limited to) decisionally incompetent participants with a neurodegenerative condition such as dementia as well as those with the condition when they still retain decisional competence. The Helsinki Declaration requires that their inclusion in this research is justified only if it is concerned with their 'health needs and priorities' and provided as well that there exists 'a reasonable likelihood that this population or community stands to benefit from the results of the research' (WMA, 1964, rev 2008, paragraph 17).[5] These principles are, as we have seen, reflected in the MCA and Clinical Trials Regulations, though without use of vulnerability as a signifying category.

In the UK, the principal examples of professional ethics guidance relevant to dementia research are the General Medical Council's (GMC) *Good practice in research and Consent to research* (2010) and the Medical Research Council's (MRC) *Medical research involving adults who cannot consent* (2007). To be clear, neither explicitly discusses dementia research, and much of this guidance seeks to summarise the existing legal position for the benefit of researchers. Nonetheless, both raise points which are salient to this research. In the former, the GMC

[4] *Sidaway v Board of Governors of the Bethlem Royal Hospital* [1985] 1 AC 871; *Pearce v United Bristol Healthcare NHS Trust* [1999] 48 BMLR 118; *Chester v Afshar* [2004] 4 All ER 587.

[5] These provisions are broadly retained in the 2013 revisions to the Declaration of Helsinki, adopted once this chapter was completed (WMA, 1964, rev 2013, paragraphs 19 and 20).

specifically directs attention to the risks associated with undertaking research with vulnerable adults, emphasising the importance of ensuring understanding that may involve additional support (GMC, 2010: 10, paragraph 21). In relation to adults who have lost decisional competence, there is a specific requirement that doctors 'take all reasonable steps' to establish any wishes the individual may have had about consenting to or refusing research participation (GMC, 2010: 11, paragraph 29). This position reflects the obligation on researchers present in section 32(1)–(5) of the MCA 2005 and in Schedule 1, Part 5, paragraph 12 of the Clinical Trials Regulations (when reading the wording of the relevant provision in the CTR that 'Informed consent given by a legal representative to an incapacitated adult in a clinical trial *shall* represent that adult's presumed will' (emphasis added) (CTR, Schedule 1, Part 5, paragraph 12) in terms of the more prescriptive language of the parent Directive that this 'consent *must* represent the subject's presumed will' (emphasis added).[6] (See further, Pattinson, 2011: 418, fn 180.)

The MRC guidance primarily summarises the legal provisions of the MCA and the Clinical Trials Regulations for medical researchers. However, it explicitly affirms the benefits in terms of health care developments of the pursuit of medical research with decisionally incompetent adults, emphasising that such research

> can substantially improve their health and quality of life and that of others with similar conditions ... [t]o exclude them from any research would be discriminatory and would diminish their ability to participate as fully as possible in society (MRC, 2007: 4).

This understanding of exclusion from medical research as being contrary to the interests of decisionally incompetent adults can be seen as a move away from the traditional approach whereby exclusion of vulnerable groups (including vulnerable decisionally competent adults) was perceived as a measure of their protection to a position whereby protection is understood in terms of empowerment (Bielby, 2008: 51). Indeed, the MRC is not alone in adopting this approach. At a global level, there are parallels with the position taken by the Council for International Organizations of Medical Sciences (CIOMS) in their most recent guidance, *International Ethical Guidelines for Biomedical Research Involving Human Subjects* (CIOMS, 2002). In this, they recommend that 'Members of vulnerable groups also have the same entitlement to access to the benefits of investigational interventions that show promise of therapeutic benefit as persons not considered vulnerable' (CIOMS, 2002: 61). In the specific context of dementia research, Alzheimer Europe, an organisation which consists of the national Alzheimer associations of over 30 European countries, has also affirmed the importance of research participation by people with dementia (2009a). In their discussion paper, they claim that 'People with dementia have a right to participate in research, should they so desire' and go on to state that 'Research is extremely important if the care and treatment of people with dementia is to be improved' (2009a). However, Alzheimer Europe is careful to only

[6] Art 5a, Directive 2001/20/EC of the European Parliament and of the Council on the approximation of the laws, regulations and administrative provisions of the Member States relating to the implementation of good clinical practice in the conduct of clinical trials on medicinal products for human use. OJ 01/05/01, L121/34. Available at: eur-lex.europa.eu/LexUriServ/LexUriServ.do?uri=OJ:L:2001:121:0034:0044:en:PDF.

endorse—at least for now—participation in medical research and clinical trials that offer a benefit to the potential participant, unless consent to participation in research or a clinical trial that does not offer such benefit has been given in advance of losing decisional competence via an advance directive (Alzheimer Europe, 2009a; 2009b).

Returning to the UK context, the Nuffield Council on Bioethics—an independent organisation which considers topical questions in bioethics and provides policy recommendations—considered dementia research as part of a wider recent study into the ethical questions that arise in dementia, *Dementia: ethical issues* (Nuffield Council on Bioethics, 2009). In this report they expressed broad support for the current English regulatory position relevant to dementia research, but pointed to the possibility of developing this to allow both for 'non-binding' anticipatory expressions of consent to research participation that would take effect following loss of decisional competence (Nuffield Council on Bioethics, 2009: 142) and to allow for personal welfare Lasting Power of Attorneys (LPAs) created under the MCA 2005 to make decisions in respect of research participation under the MCA and the Clinical Trials Regulations (Nuffield Council on Bioethics, 2009: 142). At the time of writing, however, neither of these recommendations have been addressed by UK government departments (such as the Department of Health) or by the Law Commission. They do, however, raise two further ethico-legal controversies in dementia research—the role of proxies and advance directives—which will be addressed in addition to decisional competence in the next section.

THREE CONTROVERSIAL ISSUES IN THE REGULATION OF RESEARCH INVOLVING PEOPLE WITH DEMENTIA

Decisional Competence in Dementia Research

As Harding puts it, 'People with dementia inhabit a position at the intersections of capacity and incapacity' (Harding, 2012: 440). In terms of decision making in research and health care, some people with dementia—even if only a minority—in the early stages of the illness may still retain decisional competence (Kim et al, 2001) even if the cognitive abilities associated with competence are likely to become considerably impaired after two years following the initial stage (Huthwaite et al, 2006). We also encounter an important ethical question about whether we should err on the side of judging decisional competence to be present or absent in cases where it is called into question (see Bielby, 2008). In light of this, it is no surprise that decisional capacity, or decisional competence (for the purposes of this chapter, decisional competence is used to denote the same concept as decisional or mental capacity) to consent to or refuse participation in dementia research is increasingly studied (see, for example Kim et al, 2001; Buckles et al, 2003; Warner et al, 2008). What is surprising, perhaps, is the relative lack of attention this has received in legal scholarship. In English law, decisional (in)competence to consent to research that falls within the ambit of the MCA 2005 is governed by the general test of lacking mental capacity set out in section 2 and section 3 of the MCA 2005. By contrast, as I (Bielby, 2008: 173) and subsequently Biggs (2010: 137) have noted, the Clinical Trials Regulations do not address competence assessment, and neither is mental capacity defined within it, so one must look to the MCA 2005 to flesh out the meaning of decisional capacity in the context of the Regulations.

It is worth stressing that procedures to assess competence need to be particularly supportive given the prevalence of incompetence to make decisions about research participation amongst people with dementia. Based on discussion of a research study, Warner et al highlight that only a minority of people with 'mild–moderate' dementia in research may actually have decisional competence to participate in medical research on a standard consistent with the MCA 2005 (Warner et al, 2008: 168). In their research, Warner et al found that just under a quarter of the participants were decisionally competent to give consent to the trial in question (Warner et al, 2008: 168). The authors emphasise the need to move beyond mere cognitive functioning in reaching competence judgements, which may not capture more complex traits such as appreciation (Warner et al, 2008: 169). Rather, they argue that information must be capable of being comprehended, with enough time set aside for it to be understood and retained, and for a potential participant's capacity to retain, believe and evaluate ('weigh') information to be tested (Warner et al, 2008: 170). This is consistent with the subsequent observation made by the Nuffield Council on Bioethics, which recommended:

> The ability of people with dementia to give, or withhold, valid consent to research should not be underestimated. The information provided both in written and verbal form, however, may need to be provided in a different form for people with some cognitive impairment compared with people without such impairment. Both researchers and ethics committees should adapt the informing process in a way to enable, rather than to exclude, people with dementia in making a valid decision as to whether or not to participate in research (2009: 142).

On a technical level, this endorsement of an approach towards supporting and preserving decisional competence is in keeping with the requirements of the MCA 2005, especially section 1(3): 'A person is not to be treated as unable to make a decision unless all practicable steps to help him to do so have been taken without success' and section 3(2): 'A person is not to be regarded as unable to understand the information relevant to a decision if he is able to understand an explanation of it given to him in a way that is appropriate to his circumstances (using simple language, visual aids or any other means)'. Yet, as Donnelly (2009) has argued, these requirements may encounter practical challenges in the context of competence assessment. This highlights the continuing scope for closing the gap between the legal requirements and actual health care practice.

One possible response to this is to consider the opportunities presented by what Norman et al (2006) propose as a 'cyclical consent model'. The authors state that the objective behind this proposal is

> to ensure that the standards … set by the MCA 2005 for assumed capacity, the decision specific nature of capacity judgements and the principles of best interest and least restrictive practice can be met alongside the promotion of self-determination for those whose capacity may be under question (Norman et al, 2006: 230).

Such a model exhibits affinities with participant-centred discussions of empowerment and supported discussion making elsewhere in the literature (such as Feenan, 1997; Bielby, 2009). Further research would be valuable, however, to test the strengths and limitations of this model in the context of various types of medical research involving people with dementia, including clinical trials. An alternative possibility is presented by 'a dual consent procedure', involving a proxy decision-maker alongside that of decisionally competent person with dementia (Vorm and Olde Rikkert 2008: 89). Without a doubt, there are compelling arguments, particularly those informed by relational autonomy, that can justify why and how proxy decision-making can coexist whilst the patient still retains decisional competence (Bielby, 2012) although currently such models of decision making are not available in the legal framework that regulates research with persons with dementia in England and Wales. The closest example is of a property and affairs Lasting Power of Attorney (LPA) which offers the possibility of the proxy decision-making power taking effect before the donor loses decisional competence (DCA, 2007: 115; 116, paragraph 7.5; 124–25, paragraphs 7.32, 7.34).

Taken together, an ethical and legal imperative emerges for pursuing measures intended not only to carefully assess, but to support and enhance the decisional competence of people with dementia when their participation in research is at issue. This requires a more imaginative and thoroughgoing approach than simply focusing upon narrower measures of short-term information recall that fails to capture the depth to which a person with dementia may in reality be able to understand (Kim et al, 2002: 160). As such, it is important for professionals involved in assessing the decisional competence of people with dementia to engage with a range of supportive interventions available to elicit latent decisional abilities, especially one-to-one discussion (Flory and Emanuel, 2004: 1599; see further, Bielby, 2008: 142). By the same token, the possibility—and, in many cases, probability—of incompetence to decide about research participation amongst the wider population of people with dementia also requires an ethically and legally satisfactory response. It is decisional incompetence which provides the basis for the next two controversies that regulating research on people with dementia confronts.

Proxy Decision-Making in Dementia Research

Consent to dementia research may still be ethically and legally valid when obtained from a proxy. Proxy consent might be accompanied by participation from the potential research participant in the decision-making making process to the extent that this is possible (ie, consent from the proxy and assent from the participant). The ethical and legal controversy about proxy consent in research participation typically turns on the nature and extent of the proxy's role as well as the legal authority she possesses.

In English law, there is no provision for personal welfare LPAs to consent to research that falls within the scope of the MCA 2005. Rather, as noted above, an LPA (or someone else, such as a family carer), may act in an advisory role in relation to reaching a decision on the research participation of the person with dementia and be asked to give a view on the incompetent person's 'wishes and feelings' about research participation if she were to have decisional competence at the present time (MCA, 2005, section 32(1)–(5) and (7)). This clearly distinguishes the consultative role in research participation from the decisive role a personal welfare LPA occupies in relation to giving consent to and refusing medical treatment on behalf of a now decisionally incompetent person who appointed the LPA prior to the onset of incompetence (see MCA, 2005, section 9–11). By contrast, the position of the legal representative—in other words, the proxy decision-maker—under Schedule 1, Part 5 of the Clinical Trials Regulations involves a more clearly defined role and attaches decisive significance to her decision, rather than merely constituting an advisory opinion.

In recognition of this, the Nuffield Council on Bioethics recommended in their *Dementia: ethical issues* report 'that serious consideration be given to enable the role of the welfare attorney in England and Wales to be explicitly extended to include decisions over research, both within the Mental Capacity Act and the Clinical Trials Regulations'. This is because in the view of the Council, 'in nominating a welfare attorney, the person is trusting the nominated individual to make a decision on their behalf in the context of that trusting relationship' (Nuffield Council on Bioethics, 2009: 137). The Council also recommended 'that the Mental Capacity Act Code of Practice should provide guidance on the role of the welfare attorney in decisions about participation in research governed by the Mental Capacity Act' (2009: 142). A possible explanation for why at the time of writing neither recommendation has been taken forward might be that, whereas personal welfare LPAs are required to make decisions in the 'best interests' of the decisionally incompetent person under the MCA 2005 (section 9(4)(a) and section 4), 'best interests' are not applicable in the context of research undertaken under the MCA 2005 (DCA, 2007: 67–68, paragraph 5.4), and the Clinical Trials Regulations do not utilise a legal concept of best interests to determine the permissibility of research participation.

Such a positive view of the role of proxies as a 'trusted other' can be supported by arguments from relational autonomy (for example, Bielby, 2012). This is consistent with a wider movement in ethico-legal scholarship that refocuses attention on the value of care and the importance of caring practices (Held, 2006; Herring, 2013). Karlawish and Casarett have sought to highlight the relational traits of proxy decision-making in dementia research, offering proposals to enhance the ethical soundness of clinical trials involving people with dementia, including 'caregiver informed consent' (Karlawish and Casarett, 2001: 222). They point to 'the intimate and critical role' (at 226) that the carer occupies in the life of the decisionally incompetent person as the basis for the justification of their acting as proxy (at 225–26). However, they observe that 'In many instances, a caregiver may not be able to provide a substituted judgment of the patient's decision' but nonetheless claim 'the caregiver can certainly make a decision that is in the patient's best interests' (at 225–26). Although what is meant by best interests here is not explained, what the idea of 'caregiver informed consent' does suggest is the potential contribution a legal representative can make who is known well and trusted by the person with dementia to more sensitively discharging her functions in accordance with the legal framework. This both further supports the recommendations of the Nuffield Council on Bioethics and may also lead to a greater likelihood of the person with dementia being able to participate in decisions made concerning her, recognised in Schedule 1, Part 5, paragraph 7 of the Clinical Trials Regulations.

However, this positive view of the role of proxies has been questioned by Wrigley, who in the context of medical treatment, has argued in favour of the advisory approach currently embodied in the MCA 2005 concerning research, claiming that the proxy's role can only be that of 'a useful advisor to the professional team' because the concept of proxy consent involves ethically and legally overreaching what the proxy can accomplish, thus frustrating rather than advancing the patient's autonomy (Wrigley, 2007: 530–31). In the context of research, a vivid example of Wrigley's scepticism about proxy consent can be found in Schedule 1, Part 5, paragraph 12 of the Clinical Trials Regulations, which posits an equivalence between the consent of the proxy and the 'presumed will' of the decisionally incompetent adult. Pattinson describes this provision as being grounded in the idea of 'fictionalised consent' (Pattinson, 2011: 418), remarking that 'The legal representative's consent cannot, in fact, be based on the participant's will where ... the legal representative has no evidence of the participant's will' (2011: 418). This may well be the case in dementia research where the potential participant has never proffered views that explicitly or even implicitly could be seen as inclining her to participate in medical research following the loss of decisional competence.

Even if the patient's 'presumed will' can be more firmly established through looking to her values and wishes prior to the loss of decisional competence—what Dworkin would refer to as 'critical interests' (Dworkin, 1993: 201–06)—this may risk ascribing to the potential participant certain evaluative commitments which she may no longer hold. For example, the present unease and confusion of a person with dementia at being in a clinical environment may stand at odds with views she held whilst decisionally competent about the importance of medical research and altruism. Such concerns can be raised irrespective of whether one believes that personal identity (in a philosophical sense) is sustained following the onset of dementia (on this, see further McMillan, 2006). This highlights that no matter how wide the scope of proxy decision-making in research may be in law, the proxy's receptiveness to the contemporaneous concerns of the decisionally incompetent person is always crucial.

Advance Decision-Making in Dementia Research

A further regulatory challenge in research involving people with dementia surrounds the role of advance directives (alternatively known as 'advance decisions' in the MCA 2005 and common law and often referred to in public debate as 'living wills'). Anticipatory statements of this kind allow an individual—typically someone who has been diagnosed with dementia and expects to lose decisional competence at some point in the future—to express in advance their consent to certain types of dementia research, or alternatively their refusal to participate in some or all of these. The idea of being able to specify one's wishes regarding research participation in advance of losing decisional competence has received support from Alzheimer Europe, which states they 'would like to encourage newly diagnosed people with dementia to consider drafting advance directives in which they set out their wishes regarding future participation in research' (Alzheimer Europe, 2009a). As noted above, Schedule 1, Part 3 of the Clinical Trials Regulations allow for consent to participation in a clinical trial prior to the loss of decisional competence, although as will be considered below, the position regarding advance consent is highly circumscribed (Lötjönen, 2006: 259). The MCA 2005, as we have seen, recognises that a valid and applicable advance decision (which pertains to anticipatory refusal and not consent) can also extend to research covered by the MCA 2005 (section 33(2)(b)(i)). Research participation may also be refused in advance by 'any other form of statement made by him and not subsequently withdrawn' which the researcher knows to exist (section 33(2)(b)(ii)).

In recognising the absence of a position in current English law on statements of positive wishes about future research participation, the Nuffield Council on Bioethics recommended 'that the UK Departments [*sic*] of Health should commission research on the feasibility of developing some form of (non-binding) advance statement on research participation which could influence decisions on research participation after loss of capacity' (Nuffield Council on Bioethics 2009: 142). The Council stated this was based in part on the 'significant support' in the responses to the Council's consultation exercise for a move towards expressing positive wishes about research participation in advance of the loss of decisional competence (at 136), whilst accepting that prior consent should not allow that research to go ahead without any further consideration at the relevant time, given the possibility for 'unforeseen distress' (at 136). This is consistent with the point expressed in the previous section about the centrality of the present wishes of the decisionally incompetent person in the decision-making process.

Within the academic literature on the use of advance directives in dementia research, some misgivings about their use emerge. Berghmans expresses scepticism about the use of advance directives for clinical research with dementia patients that lack any therapeutic potential accruing to her involving 'more than minimal risk' (which also extends to surrogate decision-making in these contexts) (Berghmans, 1998: 33). Amongst other reservations, Berghmans suggests that relatively few individuals not suffering from dementia are likely to choose to complete a research advance directive, so a consequent need arises to initiate dementia testing at an earlier stage, when even then the sophisticated level of decisional competence required to make this decision may already be in decline (Berghmans, 1998: 35–36). There may also be difficulties with framing the advance directive so as to relate sufficiently clearly to particular types of research whilst maintaining enough flexibility to accommodate future types of dementia research which at the time of drawing up the advance decision cannot be anticipated (Berghmans, 1998: 36). In one sense, Berghmans's criticisms would seem to have less force when considered in terms of the Clinical Trials Regulations, given the requirement that the benefits of the research to the participant are anticipated to be greater than the risks involved or that the research involves no risk (CTR, Schedule 1, Part 5, paragraph 11), as well as when considered in terms of the negligible research risks which the MCA 2005 permits in research that lacks direct benefit to the participant (the MCA Code of Practice uses minimal risk as a synonym for negligible risk—see DCA, 2007: 209, paragraph 11.18). Yet, whether in the context of the Clinical Trials Regulations or the MCA 2005, concerns may be raised about certainty and clarity of wording in research advance directives, even if we are prepared to accept that their uptake may well be low.

Lötjönen (2006) observes that advance decision-making under the EU Clinical Trials Directive (which the Clinical Trials Regulations implement in the UK) is more apparent than real (Lötjönen, 2006: 259), unless the wishes set out in an advance directive are to constitute 'the presumed will' of the potential participant to which the legal representative is required to give effect (in the UK under CTR, Schedule 1(5), paragraph 12) (Lötjönen, 2006: 259). Echoing Berghmans, Lötjönen observes that it is unlikely an advance directive would meet the informed consent requirements in relation to a given trial (2006: 259) and if these were satisfied, they would have the undesirable consequence of denying the protections for decisionally incompetent adults set out in CTR, Schedule 1, Part 5 (2006: 259). Despite the lack of clarity on this, Lötjönen nonetheless takes a broadly supportive view of the regulatory position on research advance directives in the EU Clinical Trials Directive, and by implication, the Clinical Trials Regulations (Lötjönen, 2006: 260).

A possible response to this, as Berghmans appears to acknowledge (Berghmans, 1998: 36), is a fusion of proxy and advance decision-making. In a fusion model, neither the previously expressed wishes contained in the advance directive nor the views of proxy alone would be determinative of whether the potential participant actually takes part in research. Rather, both would inform the final decision, and the weight given to each would depend on the individual circumstances. The use of proxy as well as advance decision-making may also allay concerns raised by Berghmans and Lötjönen about the lack of specificity in research advance directives. Guinn offers one such proposal which combines proxy and advance decision making specifically in dementia research in order to promote collaboration between the proxy and the potential participant as well as with additional carers and those undertaking the research (Guinn, 2002: 239, 241). In any such model, however, it would be crucial that the advance directive and proxy authorisation are created in partnership by the potential participant and her proxy, in order to minimise the risk of her proxy wrongly deciding as to the potential participant's wishes about participation (Stocking et al, 2006: 1361).

Berghmans claims that this role occupied by the proxy may conflict with what are the participant's best interests (Berghmans, 2008: 36), at least in the context of research involving more than a minimal risk. However, giving effect to the potential participant's best interests need not necessarily amount to exclusion from participation. Rather, best interests understood in a wider psychological and social sense could be understood as attentiveness to the wishes expressed in the advance directive, mediated by the participant's feelings about possible participation now she is incompetent—even if research participation is seldom in the participant's best interests on a narrower medical understanding of the term (Lötjönen, 2006: 256). This also seems to chime with the stance expressed by the Nuffield Council on Bioethics concerning positive wishes about future research participation. Interestingly, there is evidence to suggest that where both advance and proxy decision-making coexist in planning for future dementia research participation, many potential participants are content to bestow final decision-making authority on the proxy (Stocking et al, 2006: 1364).

CONCLUSION

Because dementia strikes at the heart of decisional competence, many of the key regulatory challenges are underpinned by ethical and legal debates about what mechanisms might support a person with dementia in deciding—or being involved in a decision—about research participation. In this chapter, I have considered three key issues that follow from this: the challenge of judging decisional competence itself when this is questionable, along with opportunities for proxy decision-making and advance directives applicable when the person with dementia lacks decisional competence. Although each present independent challenges, a consistent theme surrounds the responsiveness of the regulatory framework to the needs and interests of the individual potential participant. The major developments in English law that have occurred within the last decade regarding medical research, especially those involving decisionally incompetent participants, represented by the MCA 2005 and the Clinical Trials Regulations, have left it better equipped to respond to these challenges, and the framework which they provide offers a detailed foundation on which to build. However, I have identified areas for further regulatory development. A promising future direction for this would be to explore the potential offered by combining proxy and advance decision-making, as well as taking further the recommendations proposed by the Nuffield Council on Bioethics on anticipatory expressions of consent to research participation and expanding the role of personal welfare LPAs to make research participation decisions. There is a reason to hope that the increasing attention and priority being devoted to dementia research by society, as well as in science, may create the momentum needed for this to happen.

REFERENCES

Alzheimer Europe (2009a) 'Research with people with dementia' (Luxembourg, Alzheimer Europe). Available at: www.alzheimer-europe.org/Y%20EN/Policy-in-Practice2/Our-opinion-on/Participation-of-people-with-dementia-in-research#fragment-1.

—— (2009b) 'Clinical Trials' (Luxembourg, Alzheimer Europe). Available at: http://www.alzheimer-europe.org/Policy-in-Practice2/Our-opinion-on/Participation-of-people-with-dementia-in-clinical-trials#fragment-1.

Alzheimer's Research UK (2012) *Defeating Dementia: Building capacity to capitalise on the UK's research strengths* (Cambridge, Alzheimer's Research UK). Available at: http://www.alzheimersresearchuk.org/siteFiles/resources/documents/reports/ARUK_Defeating_Dementia_-_Building_capacity_to_capitalise_on_the_UKs_research_strengths.pdf.

Alzheimer's Society (2007) *Dementia UK: The Full Report* (London, Alzheimer's Society). Available at: www.alzheimers.org.uk/site/scripts/download_info.php?fileID=2.

—— (2012) *Cause, cure, care and prevention: Impact of Alzheimer's Society's dementia research programme 1990–2012* (London, Alzheimer's Society). Available at: www.alzheimers.org.uk/site/scripts/download_info.php?fileID=1546.

Andreasen, NC (2001) *Brave New Brain: Conquering Mental Illness in the Era of the Genome* (New York, Oxford University Press).

Berghmans, RL (1998) 'Advance directives for non-therapeutic dementia research: Some ethical and policy considerations' 24(1) *Journal of Medical Ethics* 32–37.

Bielby, P (2008) *Competence and Vulnerability in Biomedical Research* (Dordrecht, Springer).

—— (2009) 'Towards supported decision-making in biomedical research with cognitively vulnerable adults' in O Corrigan et al (eds), *The Limits of Consent: A Socio-Ethical Approach to Human Subject Research in Medicine* (Oxford, Oxford University Press).

—— (2012) 'Ulysses Arrangements in Psychiatric Treatment: Towards Proposals for their Use Based on "Sharing" Legal Capacity' *Health Care Analysis*. Online first publication: doi: 10.1007/s10728-012-0215-2.

Biggs, H (2010) *Healthcare Research Ethics and Law: Regulation, Review and Responsibility* (London, Routledge-Cavendish).

Buckles, VD et al (2003) 'Understanding of Informed Consent by Demented Individuals' 61(2) *Neurology* 1662–66.

Council for International Organizations of Medical Sciences (2002) *International Ethical Guidelines for Biomedical Research Involving Human Subjects*, 2002 revision (Geneva, Council for International Organizations of Medical Sciences (CIOMS) and the World Health Organization (WHO). Available at: www.cioms.ch/publications/layout_guide2002.pdf.

Dementias and Neurodegenerative Diseases Research Network (undated) 'Our Objectives and Performance' (Dementias and Neurodegenerative Diseases Research Network and the NHS National Institute for Health Research). Online. Available at: www.dendron.nihr.ac.uk/dendron/our-goals-and-performance/.

Department for Constitutional Affairs (DCA) (2007) *Mental Capacity Act Code of Practice* (London, The Stationery Office). Available at: www.justice.gov.uk/downloads/protecting-the-vulnerable/mca/mca-code-practice-0509.pdf.

Donnelly, M (2009) 'Capacity assessment under the Mental Capacity Act 2005: Delivering on the functional approach?' 29(3) *Legal Studies* 464–91.

Dworkin, R (1994) *Life's Dominion: An Argument About Abortion, Euthanasia, and Individual Freedom* (reissued with a new preface) (New York, Vintage Books).

European Commission (2012) 'Fostering EU's attractiveness in clinical research: Commission proposes to revamp rules on trials with medicines' (press release) (Brussels, European Commission). Available at: ec.europa.eu/health/files/clinicaltrials/2012_07/press-releases/ip-12-795_en.pdf.

Feenan, D (1997) 'Capable People: Empowering the Patient in the Assessment of Capacity' 5(3) *Health Care Analysis* 227–36.

Flory, J and Emanuel, E (2004) 'Interventions to Improve Research Participants' Understanding in Informed Consent for Research: A Systematic Review' 292(13) *Journal of the American Medical Association* 1593–1601.

General Medical Council (2010) *Good practice in research and Consent to research* (London, GMC). Available at: www.gmc-uk.org/static/documents/content/Research_guidance_FINAL.pdf.

Glannon, W (2011) *Brain, Body, and Mind: Neuroethics with a Human Face* (New York, Oxford University Press).

Guinn, DE (2002) 'Mental Competence, Caregivers and the Process of Consent: Research Involving Alzheimer's Patients and Others with Decreasing Mental Capacity' 11(3) *Cambridge Quarterly of Healthcare Ethics* 230–45.

Harding, R (2012) 'Legal constructions of dementia: discourses of autonomy at the margins of capacity' 34(4) *Journal of Social Welfare and Family Law* 425–42.

Held, V (2006) *The Ethics of Care: Personal, Political and Global* (New York, Oxford University Press).

Herring, J (2013) *Caring and the Law* (Oxford, Hart Publishing).

Huthwaite, JS et al (2006) 'Declining Medical Decision-Making Capacity in Mild AD: A Two-Year Longitudinal Study' 24(4) *Behavioral Sciences and the Law* 453–63.

Issa, AM and Keyserlingk, EW (2000) 'Current and Future Clinical Trials for Alzheimer's Disease: Evolving Ethical Concerns' 24(8) *Progress in Neuro-Psychopharmacology and Biological Psychiatry* 1229–49.

Karlawish, JHT and Casarett, D (2001) 'Addressing the Ethical Challenges of Clinical Trials that Involve Patients with Dementia' 14(4) *Journal of Geriatric Psychiatry & Neurology* 222–28.

Kim, SYH et al (2001) 'Assessing the Competence of Persons with Alzheimer's Disease in Providing Informed Consent for Participation in Research' 158(5) *American Journal of Psychiatry* 712–17.

Kim, SYH, Karlawish, JHT and Caine, ED (2002) 'Current State of Research on Decision-Making Competence of Cognitively Impaired Elderly Persons' 10(2) *American Journal of Geriatric Psychiatry* 151–65.

Kollewe, J (2012) 'AstraZeneca focuses on Alzheimer's hunt' *The Guardian* (15 October 2012). Available at: www.guardian.co.uk/business/2012/oct/15/hunt-alzheimer-cure-hots-up.

Lötjönen, S (2006) 'Medical Research on Patients with Dementia – the Role of Advance Directives in European Legal Instruments' 13(3) *European Journal of Health Law* 235–61.

Luengo-Fernandez, R, Leal, J and Gray, A (2010) *Dementia 2010: The economic burden of dementia and associated research funding in the United Kingdom* (Cambridge, Alzheimer's Research Trust). Available at: www.dementia2010.org/reports/Dementia2010Full.pdf.

McMillan, J (2006) 'Identity: Self and Dementia' in JC Hughes, SJ Louw and SR Sabat (eds), *Dementia: Mind, Meaning, and the Person* (Oxford: Oxford University Press).

Medical Research Council (MRC) (2007) *MRC Ethics Guide 2007: Medical research involving adults who cannot consent* (London, Medical Research Council). Available at: www.mrc.ac.uk/Utilities/Documentrecord/index.htm?d=MRC004446.

The Medicines for Human Use (Clinical Trials) Regulations (2004) SI 2004/1031. Available at: www.legislation.gov.uk/uksi/2004/1031/pdfs/uksi_20041031_en.pdf.

Mental Capacity Act 2005 (c 9). Available at: www.legislation.gov.uk/ukpga/2005/9/pdfs/ukpga_20050009_en.pdf.

Merkel, R et al (2007) *Intervening in the Brain: Changing Psyche and Society* (Berlin, Springer).

Norman, R, Sellman, D and Warner, C (2006) 'Mental capacity, good practice and the cyclical consent process in research involving vulnerable people' 1(4) *Clinical Ethics* 228–33.

Nuffield Council on Bioethics (2009) *Dementia: ethical issues* (London, Nuffield Council on Bioethics). Available at: www.nuffieldbioethics.org/sites/default/files/Nuffield%20Dementia%20report%20Oct%2009.pdf.

Pattinson, SD (2011) *Medical Law and Ethics*, 3rd edn (London, Sweet & Maxwell).

Rosenberg, RN (2005) 'Translational research on the way to effective therapy for Alzheimer's disease' 62(11) *Archives of General Psychiatry* 1186–92.

Simard, M and van Reekum, R (1999) 'Memory Assessment in Studies of Cognition-Enhancing Drugs for Alzheimer's Disease' 14(3) *Drugs & Aging* 197–230.

Stocking, CB et al (2006) 'Speaking of research advance directives: Planning for future research participation' 66(9) *Neurology* 1361–66.

UK Department of Health (2009) *Living well with dementia: A National Dementia Strategy* (London, Department of Health) Available at: www.gov.uk/government/uploads/system/uploads/attachment_data/file/168220/dh_094051.pdf.

—— (2011) *The Ministerial Advisory Group on Dementia Research: Headline report* (London, Department of Health). Available at: www.gov.uk/government/publications/the-ministerial-group-on-dementia-research-headline-report.

—— (2012a) *The Prime Minister's Challenge on Dementia: Delivering major improvements in dementia care and research by 2015* (London, Department of Health). Available at: www.gov.uk/government/uploads/system/uploads/attachment_data/file/146773/dh_133176Advisory.pdf.pdf.

—— (2012b) 'Funding made available for dementia research projects' (London, Department of Health). Available at: www.gov.uk/government/news/funding-made-available-for-dementia-research-projects.

—— (2013) *The Prime Minister's Challenge on Dementia: Annual report of progress* (London, Department of Health). Available at: https://www.gov.uk/government/publications/the-prime-ministers-challenge-on-dementia-annual-report-of-progress.

Vorm, AVD and Olde Rikkert, MGM (2008) 'Informed consent in dementia research' in G Stoppe (ed) (on behalf of the European Dementia Consensus Network) *Competence Assessment in Dementia* (Vienna, Springer).
Waligora, M (2013) 'A European consistency for functioning of RECs? We just lost our chance' 39(6) *Journal of Medical Ethics* 408–09.
Warner, J et al (2008) 'Participation in dementia research: rates and correlates of capacity to give informed consent' 34(3) *Journal of Medical Ethics* 167–70.
World Medical Association (1964, rev 2008) *Declaration of Helsinki. Ethical Principles for Medical Research Involving Human Subjects*, revised by the 59th WMA General Assembly in 2008. Available at: www.wma.net/en/30publications/10policies/b3/index.html.
World Medical Association (1964 rev 2013). *Declaration of Helsinki. Ethical Principles for Medical Research Involving Human Subjects*, revised by the 64th WMA General Assembly in 2013. Available at: http://www.wma.net/en/30publications/10policies/b3/.
Wrigley, A (2007) 'Proxy Consent: Moral Authority Misconceived' 33(9) *Journal of Medical Ethics* 527–31.

31

Dementia and Carers: Relationality and Informal Carers' Experiences

ROSIE HARDING

IN THE 2011 census, just over one-tenth of the UK population (some 5.8 million people) identified themselves as providing some unpaid care to a family member, friend or neighbour on a regular basis. The care of people living with dementia is a growing social and economic challenge, and the so-called 'dementia burden' is increasingly prominent in political and public discourse (for example, Peel, forthcoming). The Alzheimer's Society estimates that over 670,000 people in the UK act as a primary carer to a person living with dementia, saving the UK economy over £8 billion per year (Alzheimer's Society, 2012). Many more people provide some regular unpaid care and support to a person living with dementia, but do not define themselves as being that person's 'primary carer'. Given the value of unpaid dementia care to the UK economy, and the number of individuals who undertake unpaid care, it is important to be alert to the social and legal issues that unpaid dementia care and support gives rise to. In this chapter, I explore carers' subjective understandings of how attentive professional care providers are to their needs through responses to a recent survey about caring for people living with dementia. The conceptual lens of relationality is used to explore this layered and multidimensional context of dementia care.

Providing high quality care for people living with dementia often requires the negotiation and navigation of a wide range of different services, from social activities and day centres through to personal care services and health care provision (Peel and Harding, 2013). Yet, previous research with carers of people with dementia has identified unmet service needs (Stirling et al, 2010) alongside an under-utilisation of available services. For example, 58% of respondents to one survey (Innes et al, 2005) had refused services offered to them because the offered services were not suitable for their needs. Participants gave a range of complex and layered reasons for their refusal of services, including distress to the service users, feelings of guilt, a desire to remain at home, feeling able to cope and wanting to protect privacy. Similarly, Brodaty et al (2005) identified four categories of service non-use in their research with dementia carers in Tasmania: perceived lack of need for services; unsuitable service characteristics; lack of knowledge of available services; and reluctance to use services. However, this lack of support service use appears to increase the burden on carers of people with dementia, and can result in higher levels of emotional and physical distress for carers (Gaugler et al, 2004) which is, in turn, predictive of nursing home placement, and even death, for people with dementia (Gaugler et al, 2005).

One explanation for this seeming paradox between carers' need for, yet refusal of, formal support services has been put forward by Lloyd and Stirling (2011) who developed the concept of 'ambiguous gain' to interrogate the potential negative impacts that contact with formal dementia services can have on informal carer identities. They argued that 'when experienced by dementia carers, ambiguous gain can be understood as a product of a mismatch between the operational logics of bureaucratic "systems" and domestic "lifeworlds"' (Lloyd and Stirling, 2011: 900). Another explanation is that because of the complexity of dementia care systems, carers find navigating formal care provision time-consuming, unpredictable and often more difficult than the caring work they undertake (Peel and Harding, 2013). As such, they struggle to see how they or the person with dementia would benefit from support offered, because it does not fit with their relational context or care patterns.

RELATIONALITY

These research findings and the associated explanations for why familial dementia carers sometimes have a low uptake of formal care services draw attention to the complex and layered relationships that form the basis of care and caring in dementia contexts. One way to more deeply interrogate these relationships is with a conceptual understanding of care that is focused on relationality. Broadly speaking, there are three approaches to relationality evident in the contemporary academic literature: relationality as care ethics (see, for example, Drakopoulou 2000; Sevenhuijsen, 2003; Tronto, 1993); relationality as constraint (see, for example, Mackenzie and Stoljar, 2000a; Priaulx, 2007) and relationality as interpersonal context (for example, Herring, 1999; 2013; Herring and Foster, 2012). A fourth approach has recently begun to emerge: relationality as a lens, focused on interwoven dynamics of everyday life (for example, Nedelsky, 2012).

The approach to relationality that stems from care ethics draws on the idea that relationality and relational approaches are a gendered attribute (most often read as feminine). This approach is most evident in work that takes forward the insights from Carol Gilligan's classic book *In a Different Voice*, where she argued that this different voice was marked by 'a mode of thinking that is contextual and narrative ... this conception of morality as concerned with the activity of care centers moral development around the understanding of responsibility and relationships' (Gilligan 1982: 19). Gilligan's work is widely cited as the starting point for the wealth of scholarship in the 'ethic of care' tradition (for example, Tronto, 1993; Sevenhuijsen, 2003), much of which seeks to differentiate the ethics of care from an ethics of justice (see further Held, 2006; Slote, 2007). The key critique that the ethics of care literature seeks to make is to undermine the idea that 'individuals basically make rational decisions to act in their best interests, and that they do this from a position in which they see themselves as (and are) disconnected from others and able to act not only rationally but autonomously' (Barnes, 2012: 12). Rather, an ethics of care approach seeks to embed an understanding of relationality into legal and political theory. A more recent version of these arguments has been taken up by Fineman (2008; 2010; 2012) arguing for a refocusing of political thought on the inevitability of human vulnerability. There is not space here to do justice to all the rich and thought provoking scholarship in this area, but the central insight from the care ethics approach to relationality, and from Fineman's vulnerability thesis, appears to be that a moral focus on care and human interdependence offers a different, and arguably better, understanding of how people live and interact than a focus on the liberal autonomous individual.

The second approach to relationality, 'relationality as constraint', has developed as an extension of the ethics of care approach, but is more specifically concerned with providing a critique of autonomy through relational analysis. In their introduction to the most cited collection of essays on the topic of relational autonomy, Mackenzie and Stoljar (2000b: 5) outline five feminist critiques of autonomy: first, the symbolic critique, which focuses on the fallacy of the abstract, self-sufficient, independent individual; second, a metaphysical critique, which aims to expose the impossibility of the atomistic individual; third, care critiques, which attack substantive independence along the lines outlined above; fourth, postmodern critiques, which draw on a range of critical and conceptual approaches to demonstrate that 'autonomy is a kind of conceit or illusion of the Enlightenment conception of the subject' (Mackenzie and Stoljar 2000b: 11); and fifth, diversity critiques, that draw attention to the multiplicity of perspectives on any given issue and the problematic of intersectionality. These different critiques, whilst being nuanced in their own ways, all seek to highlight the asymmetry between *autonomy* and the *individual*, leading to arguments for the reorientation of autonomy as a relational value. Where these relational approaches to autonomy have developed through practical application, however, these authors seem more interested in understanding that choices are made within constraints, than refocusing on the inherent relationality of the human experience (Harding, 2012). Priaulx's (2007) exploration of the concept of wrongful conception and wrongful birth is most useful in demonstrating the 'choices within constraints' model of relationality:

> A relational perspective challenges such narrow approaches to humanity: renders visible the broad spectrum of concerns that motivate human decision making; makes understandable what law sees as contradiction and can explain those instances where individuals are caught between yes/no, black/white and choice/no choice (Priaulx 2007: 170).

A third approach to relationality apparent in the literature moves away from the simple focus on autonomy and seeks to understand relationality as an inevitable aspect of human life, such that legal actors should consider the relational context of decisions. One such approach has been Herring's (1999) suggestion that some of the limitations of the welfare principle in child law could be addressed by taking a relational approach to decision making in the best interests of children, in order to better balance children's welfare with parental rights. Herring (1999: 233) argues that: 'The child's welfare is promoted when he or she lives in a fair and just relationship with each parent, preserving the rights of each, but with the child's welfare at the forefront of the family's concern'. Similarly, he has more recently argued, alongside Foster, that:

> We are such quintessentially relational creatures that we should (and for all practical purposes do) abandon the legal fiction of a person who is an island unto herself. A judge who

> seeks to assess the best interests of X by taking her out of her social context and examining her in isolation in a forensic petri dish will come to a wrong conclusion. Essentially this is because it is meaningless to continue to talk about 'X' once she has been removed from her context. She will have ceased to exist. The judge will be determining the best interests of a non-entity (Herring and Foster 2012: 499).

These arguments work together to demonstrate that an understanding of interpersonal and relational context is fundamental to all legal subjects, which is an important insight, but nonetheless one that requires further interrogation. A key problem that comes up when thinking through the implications of a relational approach based on context, is how to deal with situations where a person's relational context is, de facto, deleterious of her autonomy and/or best interests. This leads us to the final conceptualisation of the value of relationality: as a lens focused on dynamics of everyday life.

Where a person lives within structures of oppression, a relational view allows us to be attentive to the effects of these structures on her life. It allows us to understand the ways that broader, macro norms impact on everyday life. As Nedelsky (2012) has argued:

> Intimate relations, such as spousal relationships, are shaped by societal structures of relationship such as those formally shaped by family law as well as powerful norms of gender roles. These structures will be shaped by patterns of economic relationships, such as employers' preference for hiring men in high paying jobs, expectations that authority should be exercised by men over women, and governmental policies that ensure the availability of (overwhelmingly female) child care workers from abroad who will accept low pay. The availability of such workers arises from long-standing relations of global economic inequality. Each set of relations is nested in the next, and all interact with each other. Relational selves shape and are shaped by all interactions (Nedelsky 2012: 31).

This emerging fourth dimension of relationality is the most conceptually rich, and potentially the most empirically powerful. It provides the theoretical tools required to unpack the different influences that interact to create lived experience. It allows a focus on the embodied individual, whilst being mindful of the interpersonal and structural contexts that shape lives. In the next part, I draw on this conceptual understanding of relationality to explore quantitative findings from empirical research with carers of people with dementia.

FINDINGS: WHO CARES?

The Duties to Care project (Harding and Peel, 2010; 2013; Peel and Harding, 2013) sought: to explore the everyday experiences of carers of people living with dementia of the regulation of care services; to gain a greater understanding of the effectiveness of legal frameworks surrounding dementia care; and to identify key issues and concerns that carers of people living with dementia have in relation to accessing health and social care support services. Following university ethical approval, data were generated through a mixed-method (quantitative and qualitative) questionnaire (n = 185) and four focus groups (n = 15) with carers of people with dementia. Data collection was carried out between February and December 2011. Questionnaire respondents were recruited through strategic opportunistic and snowball sampling via charitable and third sector organisations with an interest in dementia care. Paper recruitment packs were posted to a total of 461 dementia and/or care-focused support groups run by the Alzheimer's Society and the Princess Royal Trust for Carers.[1] Postal recruitment packs were followed up a fortnight later with email reminders. Electronic recruitment emails were sent to an additional 13 dementia-focused organisations, and questionnaire details were posted on four online discussion forums. Respondents could either complete the questionnaire online (n = 154) or by post (n = 31). Response rate to the survey is estimated at approximately 20%. Focus group participants were primarily recruited from within the questionnaire respondents. A total of 190 individual carers participated in this research. Only the questionnaire data is presented here.

Table 1 provides a breakdown of the demographic characteristics of the respondents and the person with dementia for whom they provide care. The majority of respondents were women (n = 128, 69.2%) caring for slightly more women (97, 52.5%) than men (87, 47%). Respondents were overwhelmingly white (97.2%) and heterosexual (97.3%), with a mean age of 62.2 years. A majority identified their religion as Christian (n = 139, 75.1%). Most carers (n = 143, 77.3%) reported no disability, though just under a quarter (n = 42, 22.7%) reported having a disability, including arthritis, cancer, diabetes and mobility impairment. Most carers (n = 116, 63%) were caring for a spouse or partner, with a further third (n = 66, 33%) providing care to a parent and the remaining 7 respondents caring for a grandparent (n = 3), sibling (n = 2), aunt (n = 1) and friend (n = 1). Over half these respondent carers lived with the person with dementia (n = 110, 62.1%), and a minority of people with dementia (n = 39, 22%) lived in a formal care setting.

Most participants (78.5%, 142) were 'under strain' as indicated by their responses to the Caregiver Strain Index (Robinson, 1983), which was embedded in the questionnaire. No significant associations were found in chi-square analyses on demographic variables, dementia diagnosis, severity of dementia, medications prescribed or where the person with dementia lives which would account for these high levels of carer strain. In spite of these high levels of identified carer strain, just half (51%, 92) of these respondents reported ever having been offered a carer's assessment of their own needs. Of those who answered both questions about whether or not they live with the person with dementia, and whether they had been offered a carer's assessment, 55.5% (61) of those who live with the person they care for, and just 40% (25) of those who do not live with the person they care for had been offered an assessment. Yet, of these respondents, three-quarters (75.3%, 137) reported doing at least 'some' care on a day-to-day basis. Importantly, all carers who provide 'regular' and 'substantial' care are entitled to a carer's assessment, as provided for by the Carers (Recognition and Services) Act 1995 (as amended by the Carers (Equal Opportunities) Act 2004). Under the legislation, local authorities are also under a duty to inform them of their right to an assessment. Current legislation does not, however, provide a duty on local authorities to meet any support needs that are identified through such an assessment. It is with this regulatory context that the statistical results must be understood.

[1] The PRTC is now known as the Carers Trust.

Table 1: Questionnaire Demographics (n = 185)

	Carers			People with dementia		
Age range	Min	Max	Mean	Min	Max	Mean
Years	26	87	62.6	44	97	76.2
	N	**%**		**N**	**%**	
Gender						
Female	128	69.2		97	52.5	
Male	56	30.3		87	47	
Total[1]	184	99.5		184	99.5	
Race						
White British	161	87		157	84.9	
White Irish	6	3.2		7	3.8	
White other	13	7		16	8.6	
Mixed (white and Asian)	1	0.5		2	1.1	
Black African	1	0.5		0	0	
Asian other	1	0.5		0	0	
Mixed (other)	0	0		1	0.5	
Total	183	98.9		183	98.9	
Disability						
Reported disability	42	22.7		140	75.7	
No disability	143	77.3		45	24.3	
Total	185	100		185	100	
Sexual orientation						
Heterosexual	180	97.3		180	97.3	
Bisexual	2	1.1		0	0	
Total	182	98.4		180	97.3	
Religion						
No religion	37	20		30	16.2	
Christian	139	75.1		149	80.5	
Buddhist	2	1.1		0	0	
Jewish	2	1.1		0	0	
Muslim	1	0.5		3	1.6	
Other	3	1.6		2	1.1	
Total	185	100		185	100	
Self-defined social class						
Middle class	109	58.9		100	54.1	
Working class	73	39.5		77	41.6	
Other	1	0.5				
Total	183	98.9		177	95.7	

[1] Where totals do not add to n = 185/100% this is due to missing responses.

Respondents were asked to rate 26 statements, covering a range of issues about service provision (11 statements) and rights and responsibilities (15 statements), on a 5-point Likert scale (1 = 'strongly agree'; 2 = 'agree'; 3 = 'neither agree nor disagree'; 4 = 'disagree'; 5 = 'strongly disagree'). These statements covered a range of different topics, including best interests, decision making, care home regulation and training levels of professional caregivers. A range of descriptive statistical analyses and t-tests[2] were run on the questionnaire data using IBM® SPSS 20. These statistics were used to determine whether there were any statistically significant differences relating to the types of caring relationships that respondents were in. In addition to demographic characteristics (gender, class and whether the person with dementia lives in a formal care setting or the community), three substantive layers of difference were interrogated: (1) the relationship between the carer and the person with dementia (spouse/partner n = 116 or parent/other n = 68); (2) whether or not the carer lives with the person with dementia (lives with = 110; does not live with = 65); and (3) whether or not the carer's answers to questions drawn from the Caregiver Strain Index suggested that they were 'under strain' (under strain = 142, not under strain = 43). A wide range of statistically significant differences were found, particularly in relation to whether or not the respondent lived with the person with dementia. There is not space here to discuss all the statistically significant results (for discussion of other findings, see: Harding and Peel, 2013; Peel and Harding, 2013). Rather, three of the statements will be explored in more detail (see Table 2).

These three statements are closely related in that they are all concerned with carers' subjective experience of how they are treated and consulted by professional care providers. The majority of respondents were either neutral about (22.7%, 42) or disagreed (43.2%, 80) that 'Professionals involved with the person I care for are not sensitive to my needs' (SPL4). Yet respondents who cared for a parent or other family member or friend (M = 2.88; SD = 1.191) were significantly more likely ($p = 0.048$) to agree with this statement than those caring for a spouse or partner (M = 3.23; SD = 1.115). Female carers (M = 2.95; SD = 1.179) were more likely to agree ($p = 0.010$) with that statement than male carers (M = 3.43; SD = 1.042). There were no statistically significant differences here on the basis of carer strain or whether or not the carer lived with the person with dementia. This finding suggests that care professionals are more sensitive to the needs of spousal carers and to male carers than to women or those who care for parents or in different relational contexts. Interestingly, these two statistically significant differences in views about this statement combine to reflect the difference in gender of carers depending on the relationship they have with the person they care for: whereas 43 (37%) of those caring for a spouse/partner were men, just 12 (17.6%) of those caring for a parent or other were men, as compared with 73 (63%) women caring for a spouse/partner and 56 (82.3%) women caring for a parent or other.

Nearly half of respondents agreed (48.3%, 85) that 'Health care professionals take my needs into account when considering what is in the best interests of the

[2] T-tests are statistical calculations designed to test equality of means for two groups to see if the variance between the groups is statistically significant. The threshold for statistical significance used here was $p < 0.05$, which means the likelihood of the variance being a chance finding is less than 1 in 20.

Table 2: Statistically significant results

Likert ID	Statement	Variable	Mean	SD	$p =$ [2]	t-value[3]	df[4]
SPL4	Professionals involved with the person I care for are not sensitive to my needs	Spouse/partner	3.23	1.115	0.048	–1.989	178
		Parent/other	2.88	1.191			
		Lives with PWD	3.19	1.125	0.200 (ns)	1.288	169
		Does not live with PWD	2.95	1.188			
		Under strain	3.36	1.063	0.113 (ns)	–1.591	178
		Not under strain	3.03	1.171			
		Male carer	3.43	1.042	0.010	2.601	177
		Female carer	2.95	1.179			
RRL10	Health care professionals take my needs into account when considering what is in the best interests of the person I care for	Spouse/partner	2.54	1.172	0.000	3.673	174
		Parent/other	3.19	1.200			
		Lives with PWD	2.50	1.128	0.000	–3.682	166
		Does not live with PWD	3.18	1.223			
		Under strain[5]	2.89	1.263	0.008	2.727	67.845
		Not under strain	2.37	0.942			
RRL15	I am always consulted about significant medical decisions regarding the person I care for	Spouse/partner[6]	2.00	1.027	0.010	2.623	111.771
		Parent/other	2.51	1.364			
		Lives with PWD	1.99	0.995	0.027	–2.249	103.057
		Does not live with PWD	2.43	1.341			
		Under strain	2.14	1.167	0.781 (ns)	0.279	174
		Not under strain	2.21	1.198			

[2] Significance. Where $p \leq 0.05$, this suggests a less than 1 in 20 chance that the difference between the groups is down to chance (ns) signifies a non-significant result.

[3] Probability.

[4] Degrees of freedom.

[5] Because the variances for the two groups were unequal ($F = 8.175$, $p = 0.005$) a t-test for unequal variances was used.

[6] Because the variances for the two groups were unequal ($F = 14.223$, $p = 0.000$) a t-test for unequal variances was used.

person I care for' (RRL10). Respondents caring for a parent/other (M = 3.19; SD = 1.223) were, however, significantly more likely to disagree (p = 0.000) than carers of spouses or partners (M = 2.54; SD = 1.172). Perhaps unsurprisingly, a similar statistically significant difference (p = 0.000) was observed between those who live with the person with dementia (M = 2.50; SD = 1.128) and those who do not (M = 3.18; SD = 1.223). Importantly, carer strain also appears to be linked to this issue, with those who reported being 'under strain' (M = 2.89; SD = 1.263) in their responses to the Caregiver Strain Index being statistically less likely (p = 0.008) to agree with the statement than those who were not 'under strain' (M = 2.37; SD = 0.942). These findings again suggest that the normative, cohabiting spousal relationship was the care context that was most readily considered important to the best interests of a person with dementia. Worryingly, it appears that carers who are under significant strain may not have their needs considered as relevant to the best interests of the person with dementia, in spite of robust evidence that suggests that carer strain can lead to early institutionalisation of people with dementia and other negative outcomes, including death (Gaugler et al, 2005).

Finally, under section 4(7)(b) of the Mental Capacity Act 2005 (MCA), anyone making a determination about what is in the best interests of a person lacking capacity 'must take into account, if it is practical and appropriate to consult them, the views of ... anyone engaged in caring for the person or interested in his welfare'. In this research, the majority of respondents agreed (73.3%, 129) that 'I am always consulted about significant medical decisions regarding the person I care for' (RRL15). Again, however, spousal carers (M = 2.00; SD = 1.027) were significantly more likely to agree (p = 0.010) than those caring for a parent/other (M = 2.51; SD = 1.364) and carers who live with the person with dementia (M = 1.99; SD = 2.43) were also more likely to agree (p = 0.027) than those living apart from the person with dementia (M = 2.43; SD = 1.364). Whilst these differences relate to quite small numbers—just one-tenth (10%, 12) of those caring for a spouse/partner and a quarter (25%, 17) of respondents caring for a parent or other family member or friend disagreed that they were always consulted—the implications of this finding are not insignificant. At the very least, this points towards unevenness in the application of section 4 of the MCA 2005, but it also highlights again the disparities between how different forms of caring relationships are treated.

CARING ABOUT RELATIONALITY

The findings outlined above suggest that different relational contexts between carers and people with dementia have an impact on whether health and social care service providers are sensitive to the needs of the carer; take carers' needs into consideration when assessing service or health care needs of a person living with dementia; or consult carers about significant health care decisions. Cohabiting and spousal care relationships appear much more readily understood, more consistently recognised by health and social care professionals and therefore are better supported than other types of caring relationship. There are a number of key problems that these findings highlight about carers of people with dementia and the regulatory context that surrounds them. First, the relative invisibility of non-cohabiting and/or non-spousal care may serve to undermine or reinforce potentially negative understandings of care for people with dementia and what that involves. Second, the lack of recognition of non-cohabiting care and also the intergenerational nature of much dementia care reinforces assumptions that care is 'women's work'. Finally, these findings point to a certain level of unevenness in the application of the MCA in dementia care contexts.

Negative connotations of care for people living with dementia include the assumption that caring only happens within the domestic private sphere and that it only 'counts' as care if it happens in that context and involves assistance with the activities of daily living (for example, getting washed, dressed, feeding and so on). This type of care is often assumed to involve only one caregiver and one receiver who live in the same house and that care is unidirectional and provided by the caregiver to the care receiver, without any recognition of the interdependency of everyday relational lives. Indeed, some literature on carer strain in dementia care focuses exclusively on co-resident spousal couples (for example, Schneider et al, 1999). These sorts of negative connotations of care and carers potentially serve to reinforce discriminatory ideas about who 'does care' in society, as well as constructing people with dementia as passive receivers of care, rather than active members of a relational and interdependent caring relationship (Herring, 2013). As such, there is potential for the erasure of the agency of people with dementia and a flattening of the complexities of lived relationships and interdependencies into a one-directional flow of support from carer to dementia patient.

Third, the findings outlined above demonstrate, perhaps unsurprisingly, that gender retains a significant role in how care is understood. Relational contexts where the carer is male appear to have greater access to support, and report higher levels of sensitivity to the carer's needs. This is not to suggest that it is inappropriate for professionals involved in dementia care to be sensitive to the needs of male carers, but simply that they should also be equally sensitive to the needs of female carers. The fact that care remains predominantly undertaken by women (57.7% in the 2011 UK Census), serves to normalise and potentially make invisible the very real strain that carers of people with dementia experience irrespective of their relational configuration or gender. Policy documents are beginning to recognise the added complexities in care for the 'sandwich generation', referring to those with contemporaneous caring responsibilities for both elderly parents and for young children. In recent research from Carers UK (2012), 84% of those undertaking this dual care role were women, reflecting findings from the British Household Survey (Agree et al, 2003). Nearly a quarter (24%) of these 'sandwich carers' were providing care to a person with dementia, and 43% to someone with 'needs that arise from being older'. Carers UK found that sandwich carers were often struggling to cope, experienced negative impacts on both family and working lives and many had been forced to give up work to care. Such complex relational dynamics of care in society may go some way to explain the significant proportion of our respondents reporting high levels of carer strain. Taken together, these findings and those from other research on the consequences of carer strain on people living with dementia, suggest that professionals involved with dementia care should be alert to the possibility that more, rather than less, support may be required where the carer is not in a cohabiting or spousal relationship with the person living with dementia. This is particularly important given research that suggests that having a co-resident informal carer can be protective against institutionalisation for people with dementia (Banerjee et al, 2003).

Finally, the three statements that were analysed above all intersect with different aspects of the aims of the MCA, alongside legislation providing for assessments and services for carers. Whilst living with dementia undoubtedly raises questions of capacity and best interests, it does not necessarily and/or immediately follow a dementia diagnosis that a person with dementia would lack capacity to make health and welfare decisions. Yet when issues of capacity and best interests do arise, it is vital that the effects on carers of any decisions about formal health and social care provision are appropriately considered. It is good that most carers who responded to this study reported that they were consulted about significant medical decisions, but again, being attentive to the relationality and caring contexts of people living with dementia is vital if carers are to be supported and enabled to continue caring. A key aim of the MCA was to put in place an assumption of capacity and a set of frameworks to be followed where capacity was in question. By focusing on the decision-making capabilities of the individual, however, the importance of relationality to our everyday experience of life can be erased. As such, being mindful of the relationality and interdependency of caring is one way to ensure that more people with dementia are supported to live as well as possible for as long as possible.

In conclusion, this chapter has explored one dimension of the relationship between carers and dementia: carers' subjective understandings of the ways that professionals engage with and value their role as carers of a person with dementia. Understanding carers' perspectives enables professional care service providers the opportunity to address some of the issues that may account for previous findings of service non-use by carers of people with dementia. By being attentive to relationality, we can interrogate the multidimensional layers of interpersonal and structural context that shape the lives of people with dementia and explain different patterns of service engagement. Approaching carer support services and services for people with dementia with attentiveness to the relationality of care, could facilitate the development of services that better meet the interrelated needs of people living with dementia and their informal carers.

REFERENCES

Agree, E, Bissett, B and Rendall, M (2003) 'Simultaneous care for parents and care for children among midlife British women and men' 112 (Summer) *Population Trends* 29–35.

Alzheimer's Society (2012) *Dementia 2012: A national challenge*. Available at: www.alzheimers.org.uk/site/scripts/download_info.php?fileID=1389.

Banerjee, S et al (2003) 'Predictors of institutionalisation in people with dementia' 74(9) *Journal of Neurology, Neurosurgery & Psychiatry* 1315–16.

Barnes, M (2012) *Care in Everyday Life: An ethic of care in practice* (Bristol, The Policy Press).

Brodaty, H et al (2005) 'Why caregivers of people with dementia and memory loss don't use services' 20(6) *International Journal of Geriatric Psychiatry* 537–46.

Carers UK (2012) 'Sandwich Caring: Combining childcare with caring for older or disabled relatives' (London, Carers UK).

Drakopoulou, M (2000) 'The ethic of care, female subjectivity and feminist legal scholarship' 8(2) *Feminist Legal Studies* 199–226.

Fineman, MA (2008) 'The Vulnerable Subject: Anchoring equality in the Human Condition' 20(1) *Yale Journal of Law and Feminism* 1–23.

—— (2010) 'The Vulnerable Subject and the Responsive State' 60(2) *Emory Law Journal* 251–75.

—— (2012) '"Elderly" as Vulnerable: Rethinking the Nature of Individual and Societal Responsibility' 20(1) *Elder Law Journal* 71–112.

Gaugler JE et al (2004) 'The emotional ramifications of unmet need in dementia caregiving' 19(6) *American Journal of Alzheimer's Disease & Other Dementias* 369–80.

—— (2005) 'Unmet Care Needs and Key Outcomes in Dementia' 53(12) *Journal of the American Geriatrics Society* 2098–105.

Gilligan, C (1982) *In a Different Voice: Psychological Theory and Women's Development* (Cambridge, MA, Harvard University Press).

Harding, R (2012) 'Legal constructions of dementia: discourses of autonomy at the margins of capacity' 34(4) *Journal of Social Welfare and Family Law* 425–42.

Harding, R and Peel, E (2010) 'Duties to Care: A socio-Legal Exploration of Caring for People with Dementia' funded by the British Academy (grant no: SG1000017).

—— (2013) '"He was like a zombie": Off-label prescription of antipsychotic drugs in dementia' 21(2) *Medical Law Review* 243–77.

Held, V (2006) *The Ethics of Care: Personal, Political and Global* (New York, Oxford University Press).

Herring, J (1999) 'The Human Rights Act and the Welfare Principle in Family Law – Conflicting or Complementary?' 11(3) *Child and Family Law Quarterly* 223–43.

—— (2013) *Caring and the Law* (Oxford, Hart Publishing).

Herring, J and Foster, C (2012) 'Welfare means relationality, virtue and altruism' 32(3) *Legal Studies* 480–98.

Innes, A et al (2005) 'Dementia care provision in rural Scotland: Service users' and carers' experiences' 13(4) *Health and Social Care in the Community* 354–65.

Lloyd, BT and Stirling, C (2011) 'Ambiguous gain: Uncertain benefits of service use for dementia carers' 33(6) *Sociology of Health & Illness* 899–913.

MacKenzie, C and Stoljar, N (eds) (2000a) *Relational Autonomy: Feminist Perspectives on Autonomy, Agency and the Social Self* (Oxford, Oxford University Press).

—— (2000b) 'Introduction: Autonomy Refigured' in C MacKenzie and N Stoljar (eds), *Relational Autonomy: Feminist Perspectives on Autonomy, Agency and the Social Self* (Oxford, Oxford University Press).

Nedelsky, J (2012) *Law's Relations: A Relational Theory of Self, Autonomy and Law* (Oxford, Oxford University Press).

Peel, E (forthcoming) '"The living death of Alzheimer's" versus "Take a walk to keep dementia at bay": Representation of dementia in print media and carer discourse' *Sociology of Health & Illness*.

Peel, E and Harding, R (2013) '"It's a huge maze, the system, it's a terrible maze": Dementia carers' constructions of navigating health and social care services' *Dementia: The International Journal of Social Research and Practice*. Advance access. doi: 10.1177/1471301213480514.

Priaulx, N (2007) *The Harm Paradox: Tort law and the Unwanted Child in an Era of Choice* (Abingdon, Routledge).

Robinson, BC (1983) 'Validation of a Caregiver Strain Index' 38(3) *Journal of Gerontology* 344–48.

Schneider J et al (1999) 'EUROCARE: A cross-national study of co-resident spouse carers for people with Alzheimer's Disease: I factors associated with carer burden' 14(8) *International Journal of Geriatric Psychiatry* 651–61.

Sevenhuijsen, S (2003) 'The place of care: The relevance of the feminist ethic of care for social policy' 4(2) *Feminist Theory* 179–97.

Stirling, C et al (2010) 'Measuring dementia carers' unmet need for services – An exploratory mixed method study' 10 *BMC Health Services Research* 122. Available at: www.biomedcentral.com/1472-6963/10/122.

Slote, M (2007) *The Ethics of Care and Empathy* (Abingdon, Routledge).

Tronto, JC (1993) *Moral Boundaries: A Political Argument for an Ethic of Care* (London, Routledge).

32

End-of-Life Care

OFRA G GOLAN

INTRODUCTION

DEMENTIA IS ASSOCIATED with end-of-life (EOL) care decisions since it is a terminal condition that affects mainly old people. Moreover, many find dementia more frightening than death. As described by The President's Council on Bioethics (2005):

> Besides the normal fear of senescence and death, many people are horrified at the thought of ending their lives only after a long period not just of physical frailty and disability but also of mental incapacitation, impaired memory, diminished awareness, loss of modesty and self-control, distortion of personality and temperament, inability to recognize friends and loved ones, and general dullness and enfeeblement of inner life.

Thus, the unique characteristics of this condition encourage people to search for legitimate options to decrease the period of dementia, even if this involves shortening the patient's life.

Very few jurisdictions allow active practices to hasten the death of any patient—in the form of euthanasia or assisted suicide (AS), and legal euthanasia of demented patients is extremely unusual. On the other hand, the withdrawal of life sustaining treatment (LST) is relatively common, and often lawful. The case of dementia is very peculiar in this respect, since the patient involved will commonly lack legal capacity and (at least at the advanced stages of the condition) will be unable to express his or her will to live or to die. In these circumstances there are, practically, two options for any form of voluntary euthanasia (including AS): either the patient's life should be ended while still sufficiently competent to ask for it (ie, when the patient hasn't yet reached the situation which they appreciate as life not worth living), or at a more advanced stage of dementia, according to their former wishes as made while still in possession of their mental faculties. Both options raise heavy ethical concerns that are well reflected in the law.

Terminology

Euthanasia, AS and withdrawal of life sustaining treatment (LST) are medical practices which inevitably hasten the patient's death. The latter is sometimes referred to as 'passive euthanasia'. However, while the intention to terminate the life of the patient is encompassed in the definition of the former terms, withdrawal of LST is quite commonly presented as intended to relieve the patient from the burdens of an inappropriate treatment. This practice, per se, does not hasten death, which is a natural result of the patient's condition; however, unless LST is withdrawn, the patient would continue living.

The term 'euthanasia' is 'a multi-faceted and culture laden term' (Blank, 2011). In certain cultures it covers all life-ending practices. Others (see the definitions in the Dutch and the Belgian Acts) use it in a narrower sense, for any form of 'deliberate termination of another's life at his request' (Gevers, 1992), while many jurisdictions draw a clear differentiation between euthanasia and AS (Table 1).

The terms 'AS' or 'physician AS' (PAS) also have various definitions. According to the wide definition: 'AS should be understood as the fact that a doctor intentionally assists another person to commit suicide or provides another person with the means to that end, on the express and voluntary request of that person' (Luxembourg Law, 2009). In contrast, the Oregon Act from 1997 relates just to the 'prescription of medication for the purpose of ending [the patient's] life in a humane and dignified manner'. According to the American Public Health Association (2006) the life-ending practice as in the narrow definition in the Oregon Act should not be referred to as AS or PAS, but should rather be described by 'accurate, value-neutral terms such as "aid in dying" or "patient directed dying"'.

In light of the above, in this chapter the prescription of lethal medication by a physician for self-administering by the patient will be referred to as 'aid in dying'. The term 'AS' will be used for the wider description of acts taken by physicians to assist patients in terminating their life, and the term 'euthanasia' should be understood as relating to any other practice performed by a physician with the intention of ending the life of a patient upon his or her request. All these three practices will be referred to as physician-assisted death (PAD).

THE LEGAL STATUS OF PAD AROUND THE WORLD

Most countries do not permit any form of planned life-ending practices. However, in three European countries (the Netherlands, Belgium and Luxembourg), euthanasia is not illegal and can be practised without prosecution under certain conditions. AS is permitted under legislation in Switzerland, Oregon and Washington, as well as in Vermont (McLure, 2013). It should be noted, though, that the Oregon Death with Dignity Act of 1997, which is the first and probably the most famous AS legislation, actually permits only aid in dying. The Act permits physicians to write prescriptions for a lethal dose of medication to people with a terminal illness, and expressly rules out any form of euthanasia (section 3.14). The Washington Death with Dignity Act of 2008 is based on the Oregon Act and is substantially similar to it, but expressly states that the patient must self-administer the medication.

Aid in dying is protected to a certain extent by case law in the state of Montana. In *Baxter v Montana* (2009) the state Supreme Court has recognized that the consent of a terminally ill patient can constitute a statutory defence to a charge of homicide against an aiding physician. In reviewing the relevant state's legislation and jurisprudence, the Court concluded that there was 'no indication in Montana law that physician aid in dying provided to terminally ill, mentally competent adult patients is against public policy'.

Similarly, in Colombia, as a result of the Constitutional Court's decision of May 1997, assisted death is permitted so long as it is performed by a medical professional with the consent of a patient who is experiencing intense suffering as a consequence of a terminal illness. The Court also urged legislative action in this area in accordance with the principles developed in its decision, but the legislative efforts have not been successful (*Carter v Canada*, § 618–20).

The most recent precedent in this issue is the decision of the British Columbia Supreme Court in *Carter v Canada* (2012). In her remarkably comprehensive judgment, Lynn Smith J concluded that the absolute prohibition on AS contained in section 241(b) of the Canadian Criminal Code, falls outside the bounds of constitutionality as disproportionate. The British Columbia Court of Appeal subsequently reversed the decision of Lynn Smith J (*Carter v Canada*, 2013). The case is being appealed to the Supreme Court of Canada and will be heard in 2014. Subsequent references to *Carter v Canada* in this chapter are to the first instance decision.

Tucker (2012) argues that provision of aid in dying does not constitute AS or euthanasia and that it is a practice with growing support in the public and medical and health policy communities. In the US, Idaho and Arkansas prohibit the practice, while apart from the states that allow it

> [t]he status in other states is unclear; certainly, some empower their citizens with broad autonomy over medical and EOL decision-making, and absent a prohibition, the practice in these states can proceed subject to best practices and an emerging standard of care (Tucker, 2012).

Indeed, there are a growing number of societies that endorse aid in dying and promote legislation towards this end.

PAD IN RELATION TO PATIENTS WITH DEMENTIA

In recent years there has been a growing tendency to influence the euthanasia debate through media representation and public understanding in relation to patients with dementia. A very recent book that explores this phenomenon, named it 'the "Alzheimerisation" of the euthanasia debate' (Johnstone, 2013). This trend seems to have caused a shift in public attitudes towards the desirability and moral permissibility of euthanasia as an EOL 'solution' for people living with the disease—not just at its end stage, but also at earlier stages. Henk ten Have's review of the book summarizes the issue as follows:

> This book demonstrates how perceptions of dementia have changed. Alzheimer's disease in particular is presented as a terrifying calamity with pre-emptive euthanasia as ultimate remedy. Portraying this disease as worse than death fuels an ideological crusade to promote ending life as a treatment option.

Bearing this in mind, we should now turn to examine the truth about this alleged connection between euthanasia and dementia.

The Law

In all jurisdictions that allow euthanasia, AS or aid in dying, the patient's voluntary and well informed request is essential (Table 1). Thus, by definition, these practices cannot be applied to dementia patients, unless the patient is at an early stage of

Table 1: Current Legal Status of Euthanasia and AS in Various Jurisdictions

Country	Euthanasia	Assisted suicide (AS)	Withdrawal of LST	Advance directives (AD)
Australia[5]	Illegal in all states and territories. On January 2013 Australia21 recommended that State governments should develop legislation to permit voluntary euthanasia and AS in defined and limited circumstances	Illegal in all states and territories.	Recognized by common law and statute law if: (a) voluntary choice of competent adult patient; (b) direction contained in a valid AD executed by a competent person; (c) valid decision by an agent appointed by the patient through enduring power of attorney	AD Legislation exists in South Australia, Queensland, Victoria, the ACT and the Northern Territory
Austria[3]	Illegal	Illegal	Not illegal if: illness is irreversible or involves damage which will inevitably lead to death	Covered by legislation. Can be laid down in binding or non-binding form
Belgium[1,2]	Legal if: voluntary, well-considered and repeated written patient's request; medically futile condition of constant and unbearable physical or mental suffering that cannot be alleviated	The definition of euthanasia encompasses physician-AS	The patient has the right to refuse a particular treatment or to withdraw his prior consent at any time. Such a refusal may be made in AD	The patient's written instructions to refuse a certain treatment must be respected. A physician is under no legal obligation to comply with a patient's AD concerning euthanasia
Brazil[3]	Illegal		Unsettled, new concept	Limited use
Bulgaria[1]	Illegal	Illegal	According to the Penal Code, non-assistance to a person in danger is a criminal action	AD do not have legal status

Canada[2]	Illegal	Illegal. In British Columbia Supreme Court decision that allows physician AS provided there are safeguards for the protection of vulnerable patients	Physicians are allowed to follow patients' or substitute decision-makers' instructions to withhold or withdraw life-sustaining treatment from patients. It is unclear whether a patient's substituted decision-maker can require the maintenance of LST against medical advice	AD are legally binding
China[3,5]	Illegal. However, the government authorises hospitals to practice euthanasia in the terminal phase of an illness if patients formally request it		No clear standards	
Colombia[2]	The Constitutional Court found that a doctor could not be prosecuted after committing voluntary euthanasia for a terminally ill patient	The Constitutional Court held that physician AS is permitted for a consenting terminally ill patient		

(*Continued*)

Table 1: (*Continued*)

Country	Euthanasia	Assisted suicide (AS)	Withdrawal of LST	Advance directives (AD)
Cyprus[1]	No legislation. Doctors who carry out euthanasia may face disciplinary proceedings	Prohibited by law	The patient's appointed agent may refuse treatment if not in the patient's best interests. Where the patient is incompetent, his/her consent to urgent treatment may be presumed, unless it is obvious, from previously expressed wishes that s/he would have refused	In any case where proper consent is impossible to be obtained any previously expressed wishes of the patient concerning health care shall be taken into consideration
Czech Republic[1]	Unacceptable according to Ethical Code of The Czech Medical Chamber	Unacceptable according to Ethical Code of The Czech Medical Chamber	An appointed curator's refusal of consent to LST is not binding, and depends on the doctor's decision	There is no legislative framework for AD
Denmark[1]	Illegal	Illegal	Legal	Legally binding if the testator were facing unavoidable death, and advisory in situations that cause such a severe invalidity that the testator would be permanently unable to take care of him/herself physically and mentally

Estonia[1]		Not punishable	Patients have the right to withdraw consent within a reasonable period of time after having given it, and doctors are obliged to discontinue treatment if the patient's AD so direct	Legally binding
Finland[1]	Not permitted	Not considered a criminal act under the Penal Code	Health care professionals who respect the patient's wishes given while competent, to forgo LST—would not be prosecuted	Recognized. Health care proxies cannot forbid treatment which is necessary to ward off a threat to the life or health of the person
France[1]	Illegal. In December 2012 the French government announced that it will introduce legislation allowing AS and some forms of euthanasia	Illegal. In December 2012 the French government announced that it will introduce legislation allowing AS	The doctor may withhold or end treatment that appears pointless and disproportionate, or have no other purpose except the artificial maintenance of life	AD drafted less than three years before the person became incompetent, should be taken in account in all decisions concerning investigation, medical procedure or treatment
Germany[3]	Illegal	Not punishable as long as the death does not occur in the physician's presence	Allowed by the courts if the will of the patient is known	Legally binding
Greece[1]	Prohibited by law	Prohibited by law	Non-assistance to a person in danger is a criminal action under the Penal Code	Previously expressed wishes must be taken into account

(*Continued*)

Table 1: (*Continued*)

Country	Euthanasia	Assisted suicide (AS)	Withdrawal of LST	Advance directives (AD)
Hungary[1]	Illegal	Illegal	Legal, but in the absence of a previously made declaration, the patient's consent to LST must be assumed	Refusal of LST in the context of an AD should normally be respected
Iceland[1]	Prohibited by law	Prohibited by law	Legal. The express wish of a dying patient to decline further life-prolonging treatment must be respected. If the patient is incompetent, the decision is made by the doctor after consulting his/her colleagues and the patient's relatives	Making AD is recommended, though its legal status is not clear
India[3]	Against the law	Against the law	Against the law	Not recognized by law
Ireland[1,4]	Prohibited by law	Prohibited by law	The foregoing or withholding of LST for terminally ill patients does not involve a crime and is compatible with the Constitution	In July 2008, the Law Reform Commission published a Consultation Paper on Bioethics: Advance Care Directives recommending legislation to cater for people who make AD

Israel[4]	Prohibited by law	Prohibited by law. Private Bills to allow physician's aid in dying had been submitted	Only termination of intermittent or cyclic treatment related to the incurable conditon may be permitted, for a terminally ill patient who is suffering significantly, if this was their wish. Withholding or withdrawal of nutrition and ancillary treatment may be permitted only in end stage patients. Forgoing hydration is forbidden unless contra-indicated. The status of withdrawal or withholding of LST for non-terminally ill patients following the enactment of the Dying Patient Law 2005, is disputed.	Recognized by law for incompetent terminally ill patients if made voluntarily by the patient while competent. Can be done as medical directives or by appointing a representative. Recognition of AD of non-terminally ill patients following the enactment of The Dying Patient's Law 2005, is disputed.
Italy[1]	Prohibited by law	Prohibited by law	Withholding of LST is illegal and could be considered as 'incitement or assisted suicide'	
Japan[3]	Illegal	Illegal, but the courts have shown leniency, especially for family members who do so	Legal	Recognized by law
Kenya[3]	Illegal	Illegal	Against the law	Rarely used, seen by some African cultures as inviting death

(*Continued*)

Table 1: (*Continued*)

Country	Euthanasia	Assisted suicide (AS)	Withdrawal of LST	Advance directives (AD)
Latvia[1]	Illegal	Not clear. The Criminal Code relates only to AS with cruel treatment or systematic demeaning of the other person	The patient, and if not competent his relatives or lawful representative, have a right to refuse treatment	
Lithuania[1]	Illegal	Illegal	Patients have the right to withdraw consent. In cases of disagreement between the treating physician and the patient's legal representative who refuses treatment, the medical commission of the health care institution or the Committee for Medical Ethics of Lithuania, has the right to give consent for such treatment	According to the Law on Human Death and Critical Care, a person should not be resuscitated if s/he has expressed a wish to this effect and provided that there is approval from a doctors' committee

Luxembourg[1,2]	Legal if: voluntary, considered, repeated written request by a terminally ill adult capable patient, conscious at the time of the request, who is experiencing constant and unbearable physical or psychological suffering with no hope of improvement	Same as euthanasia	AD might include the conditions, limits and withdrawal of treatment. In the event of incurable or terminal illness, the treating hospital doctor should avoid 'acharnement thérapeutique' (ie, the relentless pursuit of treatment even when there is no hope of recovery, cure or improvement)	The doctor must take into consideration the patient's AD. If a patient in a state of irreversible unconsciousness and suffering from a serious and incurable condition has drafted and registered an 'end of life provision' with the National Control and Assessment Commission ('NCAC'), a physician may provide euthanasia to the person
Netherlands[1,4]	Legal if: voluntary, well informed and carefully considered patient's request; unbearable suffering with no prospect of improvement	Same as euthanasia	Recognized by law. The withholding/withdrawal of food and drink when a patient is not asking for it spontaneously is not illegal	AD binding, but care providers may deviate from it if there are good reasons for so doing. AD should not be confused with statements requesting euthanasia, which are also recognized by the law
New Zealand[5]	Illegal. Two attempts at passing legislation on legalised euthanasia failed to get through Parliament	Illegal	Patients are able to withhold treatment if it may shorten their life	Recognized by law
Norway[1]	Prohibited by law	Prohibited by law	Allowed if requested by the patient's next of kin, as long as it corresponds to the patient's wishes	Not legally binding but people write them. Guidelines for decisions regarding prolonging treatment for seriously ill and dying persons were supposed to be issued in 2009

(*Continued*)

Table 1: (*Continued*)

Country	Euthanasia	Assisted suicide (AS)	Withdrawal of LST	Advance directives (AD)
Poland[1]	Euthanasia is prohibited by the Penal Code. In some extraordinary circumstances the court may apply an extraordinary mitigation of the penalty or even renounce its imposition	Prohibited by law	Non-assistance to a person in danger is an offence under the Penal Code	There is no legal framework in Poland for the use of AD in health care and for end-of-life decision-making
Slovania[1]	Prohibited by law	Prohibited by law	The court can overrule a legal representative's refusal of treatment if the doctors are of the opinion that such treatment is in the patient's best interests	The Act on Patients Rights permits a person with full disposing capacity to state in writing his/her AD
Spain[1]	Illegal	Illegal	The doctor shall not undertake or pursue diagnostic or therapeutic treatment that is without hope, useless or futile. The doctor shall take into consideration and assess the previously expressed wishes of the incompetent patient and the opinion of other relevant people	Allowed by law, but are not binding and often ignored

Sweden[1]	No legislation	Prohibited by law, but if done as a result of a great compassion towards the victim, a lighter sentence can be given		
Switzerland[1,2]	Illegal	Not a criminal offence when the assistance is not 'for selfish reasons' (but not permitted explicitly in law either)	People who are allowed to decide on behalf of the patient also have the right to refuse treatment on his/her behalf	In a few cantons AD are covered by legislation. Can direct consent or refusal of LST. Not binding if there are grounds to believe that the document no longer corresponds to the patient's wishes
Taiwan[3]	Illegal	Illegal	Recognized by law (the Natural death Act 2002)	The Natural Death Act 2002 recognizes the right of terminally ill patients to make AD or appoint a durable power of attorney that can be executed after certification that the patient is terminally ill
Turkey[1,3]	Prohibited by law		Against the law	There are no legal regulations governing the use of AD in Turkey

(*Continued*)

Table 1: (*Continued*)

Country	Euthanasia	Assisted suicide (AS)	Withdrawal of LST	Advance directives (AD)
UK[4]	Illegal. Failed experience to legalize it (in 2004)	Illegal. Failed experience to legalize it (in 2004). A Bill seeking to legalize AS is to be tabled in Parliament by Lord Falconer of Thoroton, a former Lord Chancellor	The mere prolongation of the life of a PVS patient is not necessarily in his best interests and LST may be discontinued. A declaration as that withdrawal of treatment would be lawful is not required as a matter of law. A lasting power of attorney does not authorize decisions on LST, without express provision to that effect	The Mental Capacity Act 2005 provides for an AD which is valid and applicable to the treatment in question to have effect as if it had been made by someone with capacity to make it at the time when the questions arose

United States[2,4]	Illegal	Aid in Dying is legal only in **Oregon**, **Washington** State and **Vermont** if: voluntary written request by an adult capable patient, suffering from a terminal disease. In **Montana** doctors may use a consent defence if charged for AS. Since January 2013, bills in favour of physician-assisted death have been introduced on ballots and in state legislatures in Connecticut, Hawaii, Kansas, Massachusetts, Montana, New Jersey and New Hampshire	Recognized by common law and statute law. Twenty-three states impose explicit limitations on substituted consent to forgo life-sustaining treatments via their AD or default surrogate laws	Recognized by law

[1] Alzheimer Europe (2011).
[2] *Carter v Canada*.
[3] Blank (2011).
[4] Local laws and precedents.
[5] Local reports: Griffith, 2001; Douglas et al (2013); Voluntary Euthanasia and New Zealand (2003).

the disease and still able to make such a grave decision, or upon a prior request, stated in the patient's advance directive (AD). However, another condition must be fulfilled before any action to terminate a patient's life is taken: the patient should be experiencing unbearable suffering. Mental or psychological suffering is recognized in this regard no less than physical suffering (for example, Luxembourg Law, 2009; the Dutch Supreme Court's decision in the *Chabot* case (1994)). Yet, according to the scholar Raphael Cohen-Almagor (2009b), who studied the subject in both the Netherlands and Belgium, dementia does not qualify as unbearable suffering. Furthermore, the Dutch Alzheimer Foundation warned that dementia itself could never be a reason for AS because the patient is incapable of making an informed request. Nevertheless, according to the official publication of The Netherlands Ministry of Foreign Affairs regarding Dutch law on euthanasia (2010: 15), in the case of patients at the early stage of dementia:

> The unbearable nature of the patient's suffering consists in his awareness that he is already beginning to lose his personality, skills and ability to function, and that this will only worsen, resulting in profound dependence and total loss of self.

So, apparently, a patient who has been diagnosed with dementia, who experiences unbearable psychological suffering thereof, could use a physician's aid in dying, as long as he or she is competent enough to make a valid request for it.

In the Netherlands, in principle, doctors are not allowed to comply with a request for euthanasia made by a person suffering from dementia; however, in exceptional circumstances, such a request may be granted. This might happen if the patient is in the early stages of dementia and able to understand his or her illness and its symptoms as well as the consequences of a request for their life to be terminated. In such circumstances, the patient can be considered competent to make a reasonable appraisal of his or her own interests. But, in such situations the doctor's assessment needs to be conducted with particular care, and it is advisable for the doctor to consult more specialists. 'Extremely careful deliberation is required in assessing whether the request is voluntary and well-considered and in determining that there is no prospect of improvement and, in particular, that suffering is unbearable' (The Netherlands Ministry of Foreign Affairs, 2010: 15). Regarding advanced dementia, several Dutch expert committees arrived at the conclusion that this condition does not meet the criteria for lawful euthanasia (Hertogha et al, 2007). Though the law states that doctors can act on an earlier AD once a patient becomes incompetent, it turns out that to date there are differences of opinion in the Netherlands over whether an AD can replace the verbal confirmation of a euthanasia request. This issue is under revision now by a joint working group of senior figures in Dutch medicine and politics which has been launched to provide clarity under the present law on the validity of AD for patients with dementia (Sheldon, 2013).

In some other countries, the relevant laws set further limitations which make such patients unqualified for the procedure. For instance, certain laws require that the patient should have a 'terminal disease', which is defined, for example, by the Oregon Death with Dignity Act (section 101), as 'an incurable and irreversible disease that has been medically confirmed and will, within reasonable medical judgment, produce death within six months'. In Belgium, when the patient is not considered 'terminally ill', at least one month must elapse between the written request and the mercy killing (*Carter v Canada*, 2012, § 511).

At the other end of the spectrum, even in jurisdictions which count a written directive as a well-considered request for euthanasia (ie, the Netherlands, Belgium and Luxembourg), the request of an incompetent dementia patient, who had written a valid advance euthanasia directive while still competent, might not be respected. This is due to the legal requirement that the request must have been expressed continuously and steadfastly by the patient over a long period of time (as in the Dutch law of 2002).

In Belgium, euthanasia for patients with dementia is illegal (Cohen-Almagor, 2009a), though the law on euthanasia of 2002 allows doctors to perform euthanasia on patients who are unconscious or cannot express their will, if the patient made the advance directive for euthanasia within five years of having lost capacity and this fact has been added to his or her medical file (Belgian Act 2002: Chapter III Section 4). A proposal for a Bill to allow euthanasia for patients with dementia as well as minors has been recently submitted to the Belgian Parliament (Cook, 2012).

In Luxembourg, if a patient in a state of irreversible unconsciousness and suffering from a serious and incurable condition has drafted and registered an 'EOL provision' with the National Control and Assessment Commission, a physician may provide euthanasia to that person (*Carter v Canada*, § 609).

The Reality

In fact, studies carried out in the Netherlands show that Dutch physicians are reluctant to perform euthanasia on patients with dementia, even when this may be done lawfully, because they feel that honouring such a request betrays their obligation to help these patients (Cohen-Almagor, 2009b).

The first reported case of a doctor complying with a request for AS from a patient with Alzheimer's disease in the Netherlands was in 2004. The patient was 65 years old, and had had Alzheimer's disease for three years. Since his diagnosis he had said that he did not wish to endure the full course of his illness and had in the previous year repeatedly asked for help to commit suicide. The doctor judged him to be suffering unbearably. He was conscious that he could no longer function independently and faced the future prospect of increasing dementia (Sheldon, 2005). The first case of euthanasia in a 'heavily demented' patient was reported in 2011. Since she had been diagnosed with Alzheimer's disease, the woman had regularly discussed her wish for euthanasia with her doctor and her family, and while she was still considered competent she made a living will. She repeated her wish to die until the very end (Sheldon, 2011). According to Sheldon (2013), the acceptance of requests from patients in the early stages of dementia has increased and grown from 25 in 2010 to 49 in 2011.

In Belgium, one case of AS for a dementia patient was publicly reported in February 2006, by the doctor who had carried it out. Marc Cosyns, a GP and a lecturer in EOL care at the University of Ghent, gave an 87-year-old dementia patient named Roegiest a lethal drink and she drank from the cup herself and died shortly afterwards. Cosyns argued that he had given Mrs Roegiest a drink containing barbiturates, after she had asked in a 'lucid' moment to be allowed to die. The case came before the public prosecution office which decided that Cosyns did not break the law (Cohen-Almagor, 2009b). Moreover, the Chambaere et al (2010) population study revealed that in 21.1% of the LAWER ['legally assisted dying without explicit request'] cases in Flanders, Belgium, the decision was not discussed with the patient because of his or her dementia (*Carter v Canada*, § 568). More recent data show that since the implementation of the Belgian Act in 2002, out of 355 patients who requested euthanasia, four had a diagnosis of (early) dementia (*Carter v Canada*, § 520).

In Oregon, the 'Insights into Hastened Death' study, which contained multiple qualitative, indepth, semi-structured interviews with 35 families of patients who had sought AS, revealed a few cases of dementia. One patient, who had openly communicated an enduring interest in physician AS to her spouse and family over many years prior to the onset of dementia, was decisionally incapacitated during the planning phase, due to advanced vascular dementia. Three patients (9%) who had actively sought and planned their physician AS over many months were decisionally incapacitated on the day of death due to advanced dementia and/or superimposed delirium (*Carter v Canada*, § 440–42).

In Switzerland, according to the Federal Statistical Office (FSO), dementia was reported in one out of 300 AS deaths during 2009 among persons residing in Switzerland (FSO, 2012: 14). In March 2013, the English media reported that a British 83-year-old professional man who suffered from early-stage dementia planned to die at the Dignitas AS clinic in Switzerland, and that he would be the first Briton to end his life at the Swiss clinic purely because of dementia. The man had obtained a psychiatric report that stated that he was 'mentally competent' to decide to end his life (Templeton, 2013), and therefore may be qualified for AS under Swiss law, which requires only that the individual wanting help to commit suicide must have decisional capacity (*Carter v Canada*, § 592). It should be noted, though, that in a very recent decision of the European Court of Human Rights, the Court concluded that the Swiss authorities should issue comprehensive and clear guidelines on whether and under what circumstances someone not suffering from a terminal illness should be granted the ability to acquire a lethal dose of medication allowing them to end their life (*Gross v Switzerland*, 2013, § 69).

The Relation between Dementia and PAD in the Legal Discourse

Following the above, it seems that euthanasia and AS are almost non-existent as legitimate practical options for dementia patients. Very interestingly, though, the reason for the almost absolute prohibition against euthanasia and AS in all jurisdictions is the need to protect the demented, among other vulnerable persons. On top of the risk that PAD might be practised on such patients without their explicit request, another concern has been raised:

> It might well send out a subliminal message to particular vulnerable groups—such as the disabled and the elderly—that in order to avoid consuming scarce resources in an era of shrinking public funds for health care, physician assisted suicide is a 'normal' option which any rational patient faced with terminal or degenerative illness should seriously consider (*Fleming v Ireland*, 2013, § 68).

The leading court cases on PAD are concerned with motions of 'grievously and irremediably ill adult persons, who are competent, fully-informed, non-ambivalent and free from coercion or duress—to access physician-assisted death' (*Carter v Canada*, *§16*). The courts deal with the question of whether the purpose to efficiently protect those who are vulnerable in society justifies the very severe adverse effects of the blanket prohibition on PAD on patients like the claimants. Therefore, courts look into the impact of legally permitted PAD on vulnerable populations in order to consider whether the risks to the latter can be avoided by setting appropriate safeguards. The relevant data have been thoroughly examined recently by both the British Columbia Supreme Court in the case of *Carter v Canada* (2012) and the High Court of Ireland in the case of *Fleming v Ireland* (2013). According to the evidence in those cases, studies in Belgium found that 'the use of life-ending drugs without explicit patient request occurred predominantly in hospital and among patients 80 years or older who were mostly in a coma or had dementia'. 'Family burden and the consideration that life should not be needlessly prolonged were more often cited as reasons for LAWER (*Carter v Canada*, *§* 572 and 569).

On the other hand, the evidence shows that in both the Netherlands and Belgium, after the legalization of PAD, the number of LAWER deaths has significantly declined (*Carter v Canada*, *§* 1241). Even though, according to the latest data from jurisdictions which have liberalized their law on AS, the number of LAWER cases ranged from 0.4% of all deaths in the Netherlands to 1% in Switzerland and 1.9% in Belgium. Very interestingly, while the Canadian judge Lynn Smith J reviewed the available evidence from the jurisdictions with liberalized legislation and concluded that there was no evidence of abuse, Judge Kearns, in Ireland, drew exactly the opposite conclusion from the same evidence. In the latter's words: 'contrary to the views of the Canadian court, there is evidence from this literature that certain groups (such as disabled neonates and disabled or demented elderly persons) are vulnerable to abuse' (*Fleming v Ireland*, *§* 104). This opinion is compatible with the decision of the European Court of Human Rights in the case of *Pretty v United Kingdom* (2002), which stated that 'Clear risks of abuse do exist, notwithstanding arguments as to the possibility of safeguards and protective procedures'. Consequently, the Strasbourg Court took the view that the ban on AS in English law was justifiable, since it 'was designed to safeguard life by protecting the weak and vulnerable and especially those who are not in a condition to take informed decisions against acts intended to end life or to assist in ending life'. The Court did not consider that the blanket nature of the ban on AS was disproportionate, taking into account that 'The more serious the harm involved the more heavily will weigh in the balance considerations of public health and safety against the countervailing principle of personal autonomy'.

WITHDRAWAL OF LIFE SUSTAINING TREATMENT (LST)

The withdrawal of LST involves steps that would inevitably be followed by the patient's death. The very same risks that prevent legalizing euthanasia and AS apparently exist with respect to the withdrawal of LST. As such, it is quite surprising that many jurisdictions treat this practice in a much more permissive manner than other PAD practices. This phenomenon can be explained by the fact that, unlike the latter, decisions to withhold or withdraw treatment are not and should not be made with the intention of causing the death of the patient. In fact, such decisions are part of the regular practice of medicine. It happens either when the patient refuses to undergo or continue the discussed treatment, or when the treatment is not appropriate, according to the doctor's clinical judgement. When withdrawal of an essential treatment is being considered in the case of a capacitous patient, this should entail a discussion between the caring team and the patient (and whoever he or she would involve) resulting in a conclusion, that the burden of the treatment outweighs its expected benefits. However, the core issues of the legal and ethical discourse on withdrawal of LST concern incapacitous patients.

A review of the legal status of withdrawal of LST by jurisdiction (Table 1) reveals that in most countries withdrawal of LST at the EOL is allowed in certain circumstances. Yet, such practice is illegal in four out of the 40 reviewed jurisdictions: India, Kenya and Turkey—in which the prohibition is practically theoretical, due to the lack of life-support facilities at the EOL in these countries (Blank, 2011)—and Italy. In two other countries (Bulgaria and Greece) the only information relevant to this issue that had been published by Alzheimer Europe, was that non-assistance to a person in danger is a criminal action under the Penal Code of these countries. At the other end of the spectrum, there are jurisdictions in which doctors are required to avoid pursuit of treatment when there is no hope of recovery, cure or improvement in the patient's state (Luxembourg and Spain). Others allow doctors to withdraw treatment if it has no other purpose except the artificial maintenance of life (France, Austria—if the illness is irreversible or involves damage which will inevitably lead to death, and Ireland—for terminally ill patients). A more personalized version of this attitude is that LST may be withdrawn where the health care providers are of the opinion that artificially prolonging the patient's life is not in his or her best interests (UK and US). Nevertheless, in most countries a decision to forgo treatment depends on the wishes of the patient, as previously expressed by her (Australia, Belgium, Canada, Estonia, Finland, Germany, Hungary, Iceland, Israel, New Zealand, Norway and Spain). In some jurisdictions, in the absence of a previously made declaration or expressed wishes to the contrary, the patient is presumed to have wished to continue living and would have consented to LST (Cyprus, Hungary and Israel).

Limitations on Decisions to Withdraw LST

Where it is legally possible to withdraw life-sustaining treatment, this capacity is not always uninhibited; as will be further elaborated, legal limitations have a direct effect on the feasibility of the withdrawal of LST from demented patients.

Limitations Regarding Diagnostic Preconditions

Some jurisdictions allow withdrawal of LST from a person who has 'an advanced or end stage of a serious and incurable condition' (for example, Luxembourg) or 'an advanced progressive fatal illness' (for example, Oregon), while many others allow it only for patients who are in 'terminal condition', 'end-stage condition', 'the final stages of a terminal illness', 'permanent unconsciousness' or in 'a persistent vegetative state' (PVS) (some states in Australia and the US, and in Ireland and Israel). Definitions of these preconditions vary. The narrow and most common definition of terminal disease is as defined in the Oregon Death with Dignity Act as 'an incurable and irreversible disease that has been medically confirmed and will, within reasonable medical judgment, produce death within six months'. In Queensland, the law relates to a disease of the same kind, but when death is expected within one year (Griffith, 2001). In some jurisdictions, the prognosis relates to the patient's life expectancy, 'even if receiving medical treatment' (for example, Israel), while in others (for example, Illinois) a patient may be defined as terminally ill 'in the sense that his illness would have been terminal if current means of keeping him alive were unavailable' (*In re Estate of Sidney Greenspan*, 1990).

Dementia patients, even at the last stage of the disease, do not necessarily qualify for withdrawal of life sustaining treatment according to the limits of those narrow definitions.

Limitations Regarding the Nature of the Treatment

Though withdrawal of LST is, by definition, expected to result in the patient's death, some jurisdictions that allow it treat different life supporting measures differently. Thus, in relation to artificial nutrition and hydration (ANH) some US states restrict the authority of substitute decision-makers to forgo ANH for an incompetent patient, while in others such a decision can be made if directed specifically by the patient in his or her AD. Yet others (Oklahoma) allow withdrawal of ANH even without a specific AD in this regard, when the 'Patient is in final stage of terminal illness or injury', unless forgoing ANH 'would result in death from dehydration or starvation rather than from the underlying terminal condition' (Hickman et al, 2008: 136). In Israel, the law allows for withdrawal of ANH as well as other kinds of 'ancillary treatment'—defined as medical treatment 'that is totally unrelated to the patient's incurable condition, including routine treatments necessary for the treatment of simultaneous or background illnesses and palliative care'—only when the patient is 'an end-stage patient', defined by the law as 'in a medical condition in which a number of vital systems in his body have failed and his life expectancy, even if receiving medical treatment, does not exceed two weeks' (the Dying Patient Law, 2005, § 8(b), 16(b) and 17). The Israeli law further differentiates between 'Cyclical medical treatment'—defined as 'Medical treatment administered cyclically and with interruptions, regarding which it is possible to clearly and practically distinguish between the end of one cycle of treatment and the beginning of the next cycle'—and 'Continuous medical treatment'. The former may be withdrawn under the predefined conditions for withdrawal of treatment, while the latter may never be withdrawn unless it 'was planned in advance, using appropriate technological means, for being administered cyclically, even though in its essence it was administered in a continuous and non-interrupted manner' (the Dying Patient Law, 2005, § 3 and 21).[1] Before 2005, few Israeli court cases had recognized non-terminal patients' wishes to forego LST, either

[1] See also Steinberg A, Sprung CL (2007) 'The dying patient act, 2005: Israeli innovative legislation' 9(7) *Israel Medical Association Journal* 550–52.

when cognitively competent or through AD. One case even confirmed the validity of a dementia patient's AD not to be artificially fed at the advanced stages of her disease. The legal status of withdrawal or withholding of LST for non-terminally ill patients following the enactment of the Dying Patient Law in 2005 is disputed (Doron and Shalev, 2011).

The case law relating to the withdrawal of LST from incompetent patients typically relates to patients in PVS. The landmark case in the US relating to the withdrawal of life-sustaining treatment from a patient in PVS was that of Karen Quinlan in 1976. In this case, the Supreme Court of New Jersey ruled that the father of the patient could be appointed her guardian *ad litem* and could order withdrawal of her ventilation. Only more than a decade later, in the case of *Nancy Cruzan* (1990), did the US Supreme Court indicate that the court itself could approve withdrawal of ANH from a vegetative patient. According to Jennett's (2005) review of the following case law, 'Several different types of treatment withdrawal were subsequently authorized by State courts in the US, most for acutely ill patients with terminal conditions, some of whom were competent to refuse treatment'. The author adds that:

> By the time the vegetative case of Cruzan came to US Supreme Court in 1990, there had been 27 vegetative cases through various State courts. Since the Bland case in 1992, when all 9 English judges (including 5 in the House of Lords) agreed to withdrawal of ANH (Airedale NHS Trust v Bland, 1993), there have been more than 25 cases in the English High Court (none of them refused). Single cases have been approved by courts in Ireland, Scotland, South Africa, New Zealand, Germany, and the Netherlands (Jennett, 2005, 542).[2]

Limitations Regarding the Authority to Make the Decision

In the case of an incapacitous patient who has no AD, a substitute decision-maker does not always have the authority to forgo LST. For example, 23 states in the US impose such explicit limitations (Hickman et al, 2008). In several other jurisdictions, a substituted refusal of a treatment which the doctor believes to be in the patient's best interests may be overruled by the court or by an ethics committee or similar authority (Cyprus, Lithuania, Slovenia) or by the doctor (Czech Republic). The American courts, following the Quinlan decision, held the view that decisions about withdrawal should be made by the family and physician alone, unless there was a dispute between them. As Jennett (2005: 543) notes, this approach 'depends largely on most hospitals in that country having in-house ethics committees always available to advise on difficult clinical decisions and to mediate where there are conflicting views'. This might explain why in England a court review had been required before withdrawal of ANH from a vegetative patient. However, in 2005 the Court of Appeal clarified the law in this regard saying that 'Good practice might require doctors to seek a court declaration where the legality of a proposed treatment was in doubt, but that was not required as a matter of law' (*Regina (Burke) v General Medical Council*, 2005).

[2] See also 'Euthanasia at patient's request deemed legal in Germany'. Published on 25 June 2010, RNW Radio Netherlands Worldwide. Available at: www.rnw.nl/english/article/euthanasia-patients-request-deemed-legal-germany.

Limitations Regarding the Standards for the Decision to Forgo LST

The provision of LST may raise an ethical and/or legal dilemma when there are grounds to assume that the burden of the treatment for the patient might outweigh its benefits. This can happen either when the intervention itself is burdensome, or when the patient appreciates his or her life to be so miserable that death is preferable. When the patient is incompetent to decide or to express his or her wishes, treatment decisions may (depending on the law in the relevant jurisdiction) be made according to the patient's presumed will as far as this can be determined, based on his or her prospectively stated preferences, if there were any. When the patient's subjective views are unknown or inadequately evidenced, some jurisdictions allow withdrawal of LST based on a determination that the treatment is not in the patient's best interests. In the US, following the landmark case of *In Re Conroy* (1989) the legal standard of 'best interests' is 'defined by the courts in terms of what a "reasonable person" would decide in the same situation' (the President's Council, 2005: 231). Yet, as the President's Council on Bioethics observed (at 66): 'So far, neither the courts nor policymakers have adequately investigated what patient welfare really means—a task that properly begins in ethical reflection, not legal decision-making'.

In England and Wales, in determining what is in a person's best interests, the decision-maker must consider the patient's past and present wishes and feelings, the beliefs and values that would be likely to influence his decision if he had capacity, and the other factors that he would be likely to consider if he were able to do so (Mental Capacity Act, 2005, § 4(1)). However, in the key case of *Airedale NHS Trust v Bland* (1993), the House of Lords dealt with the meaning of the 'best interests' test in the case of a PVS patient. They said that in such a case, the patient, by being permanently insensate, *has no best interests of any kind*. Therefore, since the patient has no interest in treatment being continued, there is no longer a duty to provide LST, and a failure to do so cannot be a criminal offence. It should be noted, though, that 'if these last two principles were to be uncritically applied to Alzheimer's disease during the greater part of its course, harm could be done on a vast scale' (Roth, 1996: 275).

WITHDRAWAL OF LST IN RELATION TO PATIENTS WITH DEMENTIA

Dementia differs from other EOL states in quite a few respects which should be taken into account when considering withdrawal of LST. These unique features of dementia include:

a. Slow degenerative and irreversible decline in the cognitive capacities of the patient—which differentiate it from the sudden occurrence of loss of consciousness that turns a previously competent person to a permanently incompetent patient (for example, PVS).
b. During the deterioration in the patient's cognition, there may be some fluctuations thereof—which might influence the patient' ability to communicate their wishes regarding treatment.
c. The cognitive impairment does not necessarily involve the patient's emotional capacities—in the sense that he or she might still have interest in the continuation of life.

d. A long process of personality changes—which may affect the validity of the patient's prior wishes and advanced directives.
e. Medically, dementia is a terminal condition, but it does not fit the narrow legal definition of terminal as having an expected life span of less than six months.
f. At the final stage of the disease, patients have difficulties in swallowing, which results in their dependence on artificial nutrition and hydration (ANH).

Indeed, some of these concerns, which are discussed in the medical and ethical literature, turn out to be the core issues in the case law regarding withdrawal of care from demented patients.

The main problem is to determine the patient's will: when patients express their wishes while already suffering from dementia, they are often regarded legally as having no sufficient mental capacity to make such decisions; whereas AD made while still competent may not accord with their current will. However, some courts deal with this problem in ways that support decisions to withdraw treatment. For example, in *In re Gordy* (1994) the Delaware Court of Chancery held that, in spite of her Alzheimer's disease, the patient was not suffering from 'mental incapacity' and that she made a rational choice not to be fed by a gastric feeding tube; yet, with the foresight that at some point she would no longer have sufficient residual mental capacity to make decisions concerning her care, the Court appointed her son as guardian and stated that he was authorized to follow his mother's expressed direction to decline the proposed treatment. In the *Matter of Roche* (1996), the plaintiff, who was diagnosed with senile dementia with delusions, executed an AD after being adjudicated incompetent. The Court held that an AD executed by incompetent persons can have no binding effect on health care providers, but if the incompetent patient clearly understood the nature and effect of the AD at the time it was executed, this document may be considered as evidence of her subjective intent (subject to the guardian's duty to carefully consider and weigh all other probative evidence in making such a determination).

Most of the cases that deal with the withdrawal of LST from patients with dementia involve withholding or withdrawal of ANH, where this option is legal. Occasionally it takes some legal sophistry to authorize withdrawal of ANH from a demented patient. One such decision is that of the Supreme Court of Illinois in *In re Estate of Sidney Greenspan* (1990). In this case, the Court held that when, as a result of an incurable illness, a patient cannot chew or swallow and a 'death-delaying feeding tube is withdrawn in scrupulous accordance with law, the ultimate agent of death is the illness and not the withdrawal'. Rejecting the trial judge's decision that 'Death in this case would be imminent from the withdraw[a]l of the food and the hydration', the Supreme Court further held that Mr Greenspan was 'terminally ill in the sense that his illness would have been terminal if current means of keeping him alive were unavailable', and that 'Imminence must be judged as if the death-delaying procedures were absent'.

In the Australian case of *BWV* (2003), the Supreme Court of Victoria discussed the status of ANH for a woman who was in the advanced stages of dementia, in relation to the Medical Treatment Act 1988, which effectively allows a guardian, on behalf of a patient, to refuse medical treatment, but not to refuse palliative care. The Court held that:

> The administration of ANH via a PEG cannot be regarded as palliative care, where that expression is used in its natural sense. Such a procedure is, in essence, a procedure to sustain life; it is not a procedure to manage the dying process, so that it results in as little pain and suffering as possible.

Moreover, the Court stated that in the circumstances of *BWV* the further provision of ANH was not reasonable.

> In forming this view I would rely upon the evidence of the medical witnesses who observed BWV: the view of her guardian that it would be contrary to her wishes to continue to receive nutrition and hydration through the PEG; her existing condition; the period for which she had been in her existing condition; her prognosis, and the fact that continued feeding was doing no more than merely postponing the natural dying process.

CONCLUSIONS

This review of the legal status of PAD practices demonstrates that, to date, almost all jurisdictions prohibit these practices in relation to dementia. The only exception to this approach relates to ANH at the end stage of the disease, which is both medically and ethically controversial. It seems as if the law in all countries corresponds to a certain extent with the Dutch physicians' ethical insight: 'The "treatment" of demented patients is not to kill them, but rather investing in them, caring for them, providing them with compassion and attention' (Cohen-Almagor, 2009b).

REFERENCES

Alzheimer Europe (2011) 'Healthcare and decision-making in dementia (country comparison)'. Available at: www.alzheimer-europe.org/EN/Policy-in-Practice2/Country-comparisons/Healthcare-and-decision-making-in-dementia.

American Public Health Association (APHA) policy (2006) 'Supporting Appropriate Language Used to Discuss End of Life Choices, LB-06-02'. Available at: community.compassionandchoices.org/document.doc?id=268.

Blank, RH (2011) 'End-of-Life Decision Making across Cultures' 39(2) *Journal of Law, Medicine & Ethics* 201–14. doi: 10.1111/j.1748-720X.2011.00589.x.

Chambaere, K et al (2010) 'Physician-assisted deaths under the euthanasia law in Belgium: A population-based survey' 182(9) *Canadian Medical Association Journal* 895–901. doi: 10.1503/cmaj.091876.

Cohen-Almagor, R (2009a) 'Belgian euthanasia law: A critical analysis' 35(7) *Journal of Medical Ethics* 436–39. doi: 10.1136/jme.2008.026799.

—— (2009b) 'Euthanasia policy and practice in Belgium: Critical observations and suggestions for improvement' 24(3) *Issues in Law & Medicine* 187–218.

Cook, M (December 2012) 'Belgium debates euthanasia for minors and demented' *BioEdge*. Available at: www.bioedge.org/index.php/bioethics/bioethics_article/10353.

Doron, I and Shalev, C (2011) 'From the Patients' Rights Act 1996 to The Dying Paient Act 2005: Moving forward or backwards' 43 *Journal of Medicine and Law* 25–39 (Hebrew).

Douglas, B, Willmott, L and White, B (2013) 'The right to choose an assisted death: Time for legislation?' report following a Roundtable in Brisbane, January 2013: 'How should Australia regulate voluntary euthanasia and assisted suicide?' (Australia 21 Ltd).

Federal Statistical Office (FSO) (2012) *Cause of Death Statistics 2009: Assisted suicide and suicide in Switzerland*. Available at: www.bfs.admin.ch/bfs/portal/en/index/themen/14/22/publ.html?publicationID=4732.

Gevers, JKM (1992) 'Legislation on euthanasia: Recent developments in the Netherlands' 18(3) Journal of Medical Ethics 138–41.

Griffith, G (2001) *Briefing Paper No 3/2001 – Euthanasia: An Update* (New South Wales Parliamentary Library Research Service).

Hertogha, CMPM et al (2007) 'Would We Rather Lose Our Life Than Lose Our Self? Lessons from the Dutch Debate on Euthanasia for Patients with Dementia' 7(4*) American Journal of Bioethics* 48–56.

Hickman, SE et al (2008) 'The POLST (Physician Orders for Life-Sustaining Treatment) Paradigm to Improve End-of-Life Care: Potential State Legal Barriers to Implementation' 36(1) *Journal of Law, Medicine & Ethics* 119–140. doi: 10.1111/j.1748-720X.2008.00242.x.

Jennett, B (2005) 'Thirty years of the vegetative state: Clinical, ethical and legal problems' 150 *Progress in Brain Research* 537–43.

Johnstone, MJ (2013) *Alzheimer's Disease, Media Representations and the Politics of Euthanasia – Constructing Risk and Selling Death in an Ageing Society* (Farnham, Ashgate Publishing).

McLure, J (2013) 'Vermont passes law allowing doctor-assisted suicide' *Reuters* (21 May). Available at: joemiller.us/2013/05/vermont-passes-law-allowing-doctor-assisted-suicide/.

Parliamentary Support Research papers (2003) *Voluntary Euthanasia and New Zealand*. Available at: www.parliament.nz/en-NZ/ParlSupport/ResearchPapers/7/2/9/729250622d0244a9b43774f6270ddbcb.htm.

Roth, M (1996) 'Euthanasia and related ethical issues in dementias of later life with special reference to Alzheimer's disease' 52(2) *British Medical Bulletin* 263–79.

Sheldon, T (2005) 'Dutch Approve Euthanasia for a Patient with Alzheimer's Disease' 330(7499) *British Medical Journal* 1041.

—— (2011) 'Dementia patient's euthanasia was lawful, say Dutch authorities' *British Medical Journal 343*:d7510. doi: 10.1136/bmj.d7510.

—— (2013) 'Dutch doctors to receive more clarity over use of advance euthanasia directives for patients with dementia' *British Medical Journal* 346:f3545. doi: 10.1136/bmj.f3545.

Templeton, SK (2013) 'Dementia sufferer prepares for Dignitas suicide' *The Sunday Times* (17 March). Available at: www.thesundaytimes.co.uk/sto/news/uk_news/Society/article1231010.ece.

The Netherlands Ministry of Foreign Affairs, FAQ. EUTHANASIA (2010) *The Termination of Life on Request and Assisted Suicide (Review Procedures) Act in Practice*. Available at: www.patientsrightscouncil.org/site/wp-content/uploads/2012/03/Netherlands_Ministry_of_Justice_FAQ_Euthanasia_2010.pdf.

The President's Council on Bioethics (2005) *Taking Care: Ethical Caregiving in Our Aging Society* (Washington, DC). Available at: bioethics.georgetown.edu/pcbe/reports/taking_care/.

Tucker, KL (2012) 'Aid in Dying – Guidance for an Emerging End-of-Life Practice' 142(1) *Chest* 218–24. doi: 10.1378/chest.12-0046.

STATUTES

[Belgian Act on Euthanasia of May 28th 2002] Kidd D, trans. Translation in *Ethical Perspectives* 9 (2002)2–3, p 182. Available at: www.ethical-perspectives.be/viewpic.php?LAN=E&TABLE=EP&ID=59 (accessed 10 March 10 2014).

The Dying Patient Law 2005 (Israel) (trans V Ravitsky and M Prawer). Available at: 98.131.138.124/articles/JME/JMEM12/JMEM.12.2.asp.

Luxembourg Law of 16 March 2009 on Euthanasia and Assisted Suicide, Mémorial A-No 46, 16 March 2009. Available at: www.sante.public.lu/publications/sante-fil-vie/fin-vie/euthanasie-assistance-suicide-25-questions-reponses/euthanasie-assistance-suicide-25-questions-reponses-en.pdf.

Mental Capacity Act 2005 (UK). Available at: www.legislation.gov.uk/ukpga/2005/9/contents.

The Oregon Death with Dignity Act, Oregon Revised Statutes (2011 edition), §127.800–§127.995. Available at: www.leg.state.or.us/ors/127.html.

Termination of Life on Request and Assisted Suicide (Review Procedures) Act, 2002 (Netherlands). Available at: www.schreeuwomleven.nl/abortus/text_of_dutch_euthanasia_law.doc.

The Washington Death with Dignity Act. Washington State Legislature. Chapter 70, 245 RCW. Available at: apps.leg.wa.gov/RCW/default.aspx?cite=70.245.

CASE LAW

Airedale NHS Trust v Bland [1993] 1 All ER 821 (HL).

Baxter v State of Montana, 354 Mont 234 (2009).

Carter v Canada (Attorney General), 2012 BCSC 886 (CanLII). Available at: canlii.ca/t/frpws.

Carter v Canada [2013] BCCA 435.

Chabot, NJ 1994, no 656.

Cruzan v Director, Missouri Dept of Health, 497 US 261, 289, 110 S Ct 2841, 2857 (1990).

Fleming v Ireland and others [2013] IEHC 2 (10 January 2013).

Gardner; re BWV [2003] VSC 173.

Gross v Switzerland (Application no 67810/10) of the European Court of Human Rights, Judgment of 14 May 2013. Available at: hudoc.echr.coe.int/sites/fra/pages/search.aspx?i=001-119703#{'itemid':['001-119703']}.

In re Estate of Sidney Greenspan, a Disabled Person. No 67903 Supreme Court of Illinois, 137 Ill 2d 1; 558 NE2d 1194; 1990 Ill.

In re Gordy, No CM 7428, 658 A 2d 613; 1994 Del Ch.

In re Quinlan, 70 NJ 10, 355 A 2d 647 (1976).

Matter of Clementine Roche, 296 NJ Super 583; 687 A 2d 349; 1996 NJ Super.

Matter of Conroy, 486 A 2d 1209 (NJ 1989).

Pretty v United Kingdom (2002) 35 EHRR 1.

Regina (Burke) v General Medical Council (Official Solicitor and Others intervening) (2005), (CA) QB 424.

33

Health Care Resource Allocation Issues in Dementia

KEITH SYRETT

DEMENTIA PLACES A significant—and growing—pressure upon the finite resources which are available to fund health care facilities, services and treatments. The United Kingdom (UK) presently has more than 820,000 persons living with dementia, a figure which is expected to increase to 1.7 million by 2050. The current direct cost to the Treasury is £10.2 billion, of which £9 billion is spent on social care and £1.2 billion on health care; this figure is projected to rise to £16.7 billion by 2031. Up to 25% of all hospital beds in the UK are occupied by older patients with dementia, and such patients tend to remain longer in hospital than patients with other conditions: each bed in the National Health Service (NHS) costs an average of £260 a day (Age UK, 2013). Of course, high levels of expenditure are not confined to the UK. The total worldwide costs, direct and indirect, of dementia have been estimated at $604 billion in 2010, or approximately 1% of the world's gross domestic product, with an increase of 85% projected by 2030. Direct medical costs account for a smaller proportion (16%) of this total cost than the costs of social care (42.3%) and informal care (ie, that provided by family, friends and others) (41.7%), but the amounts are still significant, standing at $96.41 billion in 2010 (Alzheimer's Disease International, 2010). The overall societal costs of the condition appear to be considerably greater than those for other chronic diseases, almost matching those of cancer, heart disease and stroke combined (Luengo-Fernandez et al, 2010).

The high levels of expenditure disbursed upon the condition render it an obvious target for strategies or individual instances of rationing, a term which may be defined as the deprivation of care, usually for financial reasons, which is of benefit to, and which is desired by, a patient (Maynard, 1999). This is especially so in an era in which policymakers are seeking to make significant savings in the cost of health services in light of a global economic crisis. The objective of this chapter is to explore the legal framework governing the allocation of scarce resources for the provision of care for, and treatment of, dementia. While instances in which treatment for sufferers of dementia is denied or restricted have yet to form a major component of the growing jurisprudence surrounding health care rationing, it seems certain that the increasing incidence of the condition, and the associated strain which it places upon health systems, will render this an area of considerable activity in the short to medium term. It is therefore important to identify the contours of the relevant areas of law which may be applicable in this context. Accordingly, the first task will be to outline how courts have responded to the problem of health care rationing in a general sense, before the discussion turns to the specific context of dementia.

IS RATIONING LAWFUL?

Prior to the 1980s, challenges to the *legality*—as distinct from the political acceptability—of allocative decisions in health care were unheard of. This was not because rationing did not exist: famously, the chief architect of the NHS, Aneurin Bevan, resigned from government three years after the establishment of the Service in protest at a decision to introduce charges for prescriptions, spectacles and dental care in light of spiralling expenditure. However, the manner in which the majority of allocative choices took place was such as to render them relatively invisible to the public in so far as they were concealed behind a veil of clinical judgement, which disguised the resource dimensions of decisions not to treat. The exception to this trend was rationing by delay, in the form of waiting times for treatment, but while this formed the basis of the first notable (unsuccessful) legal challenge in the English courts, the case of *R v Secretary of State for Social Services, West Midlands Regional Health Authority and Birmingham Area Health Authority (Teaching), ex parte Hincks* (1980) 1 BMLR 93, the phenomenon did not tend to provoke widespread resistance, seemingly being regarded by most as an inevitable fact of life.

This pattern began to change as modes of resource allocation altered, most notably as more explicit forms of rationing were adopted by policymakers who sought to exercise greater central control over managerial and clinical decisions at local level. Mechanisms such as health technology assessment, clinical guidelines and limitations to the 'menu' of treatments and services represented more visible resource-driven means through which care was rationed, and such decisions tended to stimulate resistance, this sometimes taking the form of litigation. Courts were consequently obliged to determine their stance upon the legality of the denial or restriction of health care to individuals. The position taken is, to a large extent, contingent upon the manner in which the legal claim is formulated. Three possibilities may be identified from the general case law relating to health care rationing: the principles which are articulated here, while developed in other contexts, are equally applicable to the specific case of treatment for dementia, as will presently be discussed.

First, where the challenge is to the *substantive lawfulness* of the decision to deny or restrict access to facilities, services and treatments, the starting point for the courts is to view rationing of resources as prima facie lawful, and to permit decision-makers to engage in the setting of priorities which will establish which individuals, groups or conditions have first claim on the limited resources which are available for the provision of health care. This is perhaps best illustrated by a *dictum* of Auld LJ from the leading English Court of Appeal case of *R v North West Lancashire Health Authority, ex parte A, D and G* [1999] EWCA Civ 2022:

> It is an unhappy but unavoidable feature of state funded healthcare that Regional Health Authorities have to establish certain priorities in funding different treatments from their finite resources. It is natural that each Authority, in establishing its own priorities, will

> give greater priority to life-threatening and other grave illnesses than to others obviously less demanding of medical intervention. The precise allocation and weighting of priorities is clearly a matter of judgement for each Authority, keeping well in mind its statutory obligations to meet the reasonable requirements of all those within its area for which it is responsible. It makes sense to have a policy for the purpose—indeed, it might well be irrational not to have one.

As this statement indicates, courts will usually defer to choices made by the allocative decision-maker as to how scarce resources should best be prioritised. There are only limited exceptions to this position. One was articulated in this case: a failure to consider the circumstances which may render the individual's claim exceptional, and which should therefore demand a reordering of the priorities to address such particular circumstances. The other was stated in the earlier case of *R v Central Birmingham Health Authority, ex parte Collier* (unreported, 6 January 1988) and represents the guiding principle of judicial intervention in cases of this type, at least in common law jurisdictions:

> The courts of this country cannot arrange the lists in the hospital, and, if there is not evidence that they are not being arranged properly due to some unreasonableness in the *Wednesbury* sense on the part of the authority, the courts cannot, and should not, be asked to intervene (Stephen Brown LJ).

That is, unless a rationing choice crosses a very high threshold of egregiousness (a decision which is '*Wednesbury* unreasonable' that is, 'so unreasonable that no reasonable authority could ever have come to it': see *Associated Provincial Picture Houses Ltd v Wednesbury Corporation* [1947] EWCA Civ 1), the courts will not interfere. This enables them to avoid 'second-guessing' decisions which necessitate the application of clinical and/or health managerial expertise and intruding upon decision making which has been properly entrusted to executive agencies (such as health authorities), which would represent an undemocratic breach of the principle of the separation of powers.

Second, this stance of judicial restraint is, however, subject to modification where the challenge is to the *procedure* by which a rationing decision has been reached. Here, the courts have demonstrated much greater willingness to intervene to declare allocative decisions unlawful, exhibiting a particular concern that decision making should meet standards of transparency so that those who lose out may, at least, understand on what basis the rationing choice was reached. This is especially true in situations where the decision-maker has departed from a body of respected medical opinion, from national policy guidance, or from evidence-based clinical guidelines, as seen respectively in the English cases of *ex parte A, D and G* (above), *R v North Derbyshire Health Authority, ex parte Fisher* [1997] EWHC 675 (Admin) and *R (Otley) v Barking and Dagenham NHS Primary Care Trust* [2007] EWHC 1927 (Admin). It is important to note that a determination that a decision-maker has acted unlawfully in this manner will not necessarily result in a revisiting of priorities in favour of the affected individual. Rather, the decision is remitted to the responsible agency, to which it is open to reach the same choice again, provided that there is compliance with the procedural requirements specified by the court on this subsequent occasion.

Third, where the claim to access health care resources is formulated as a matter of *legal right*, courts evince greater willingness to intrude upon the outcome of the rationing choice than is the case where the challenge is one to the lawfulness of the exercise of administrative discretion (as in the first category outlined above). However, the extent to which they will do so is contingent both upon the degree of protection afforded to the right to health, or the right of access to health care, in the jurisdiction in question and upon precedent case law. Three scenarios may be identified.

In some instances, litigation based upon constitutionally protected rights has had a significant, and arguably disruptive, impact upon priority-setting choices made within health systems: this is particularly so in South America (Yamin and Gloppen, 2011). In other cases, courts have regarded constitutionally entrenched socioeconomic rights such as the right to access health care services as susceptible to judicial scrutiny but have signalled their reluctance radically to disturb the separation of powers by regarding their function as one of stimulating *dialogue* upon the proper allocation of scarce resources with other branches of government (Syrett, 2007). This is best exemplified by the well known case brought by the Treatment Action Campaign to secure access to anti-retroviral drugs in South Africa, *Minister of Health v Treatment Action Campaign (No 2)* [2002] ZACC 15, in which the court conceived of its role as one of partnership with executive and legislature in addressing the major social problem of HIV/AIDS in the country; a more reticent stance which may, in part, have been informed by earlier case law which exhibited the type of judicial restraint apparent in the first category of cases identified above (see *Soobramoney v Minister of Health, Kwazulu-Natal* [1997] ZACC 17). Finally, where no constitutional status is accorded to health or health care, courts may nonetheless afford some protection to disappointed patients by placing a justificatory obligation upon the decision-maker to explain why their interests and claims have been deemed insufficiently weighty to necessitate expenditure of resources upon their health. Thus, in the UK, arguments based upon alleged violations of the Human Rights Act 1998 (which gives further effect to the European Convention on Human Rights, an instrument which contains no provision *directly* guaranteeing a right to health or to access health care) have routinely failed to date (see, for example, *R (Condliff) v North Staffordshire Primary Care Trust* [2011] EWCA Civ 910). However, courts have been willing to require 'substantial objective justification' to be offered to 'rights-holders' in such cases, in the absence of the provision of which they are prepared to consider a decision to be unlawful (see the decision of Laws J in the High Court in *R v Cambridge Health Authority, ex parte B* [1995] 1 FLR 1055); and further *R (Rogers) v Swindon NHS Primary Care Trust* [2006] EWCA Civ 392, paragraph 56; *R (Ross) v West Sussex Primary Care Trust* [2008] EWHC 2252 (Admin), paragraph 38).

COURTS, RESOURCES AND DEMENTIA

As previously noted, notwithstanding that there are significant and increasing numbers of sufferers of dementia across the globe, instances of litigation concerning restriction or denial of treatment on resource grounds for such sufferers are very rare. Analysis of why this might be the case is beyond the scope of this chapter, but it is surely plausible to suppose that those who are affected by the various forms of the condition are amongst the individuals in society least likely to be in a position to undertake a legal challenge. Consequently, litigation is only likely to eventuate in circumstances where others—whether family or friends, or a patient organisation or other stakeholder—are sufficiently motivated and resourced to go to court on behalf of the affected individual/s. It is notable that this was the case in both of the instances of litigation examined in this section.

New Zealand

In *Shortland v Northland Health Ltd*, HC (Auckland) M.75/97 (20 September 1997)/HC (Whangerei) M.75/97 (6 November 1997)/(1997) 50 BMLR 255 (CA) the treatment which was denied was dialysis for end-stage renal failure. However, the patient in question, Rau Williams, suffered from moderate dementia and it was the presence of this condition which was decisive in triggering the limit-setting decision.

Following an interim assessment of the patient's suitability which established that, as a consequence of his mental state, Mr Williams was unable to learn the basic concepts of his dialysis treatment despite intensive and repeated attempts to teach him, physicians at Whangarei Hospital withdrew haemodialysis. They did so in accordance with clinical guidelines, which stated that incidence of moderate to severe dementia was likely to determine that an individual was unsuited to treatment of end-stage renal failure on the basis that a patient's mental capacity was such as to make it unlikely that she or he would cooperate with the dialysis therapy. It seems clear—notwithstanding the judicial opinions which will be analysed below—that both the guidelines and the decision which rested upon them contained a significant allocative component. The aim of the guidelines was expressed to be 'to ensure that, so far as possible *within the available resources*, all patients are offered access to the treatment modality which is most suitable clinically and socially and which offers the greatest opportunity to benefit' (quoted in Paterson, 1998: 578, emphasis added) and, as Paterson (1998: 574) notes:

> In a world of unlimited resources, it would be possible to provide 24-hour care to ensure that such a patient does not disconnect his continuous ambulatory peritoneal dialysis. In the real world, it would seem reasonable for a hospital to say, 'Yes, we accept that this patient is being denied treatment because of his disability, but in order to provide services, we would have to do so in a special manner and we cannot reasonably be expected to do so'.

Nonetheless, when the matter reached the High Court, Salmon J viewed the decision as one dependent primarily upon the *exercise of clinical judgement*, with which a court should not intervene. Notably, however, the judge expressed himself to be 'not clear' as to whether the decision had been based upon the patient's best interests or upon resources, and expressed 'no doubt' that the hospital authority 'will want to ensure that there is absolute clarity as to the reasons for refusing the treatment' (HC (Auckland) M.75/97 (20 September 1997), 13). However, in a further hearing of the application, the judge took the view that the decision comprised no substantial administrative component which might render it, in principle, reviewable by a court on the basis of a deficiency in the process of allocative decision-making (HC (Whangerei) M.75/97 (6 November 1997), 15–16). This was a conclusion with which the Court of Appeal concurred, going even further in holding that 'there was no resource dimension in the present case' ((1997) 50 BMLR 255, 266) and accordingly construing the decision as 'one par excellence of clinical and professional judgement' which was not susceptible to review by a court ((1997) 50 BMLR 255, 265).

The decision was also challenged by way of a complaint of disability discrimination to the Human Rights Commission. It was argued that the decision not to provide dialysis was taken primarily as a consequence of the patient's dementia and that this contravened section 44(1)(b) of the Human Rights Act 1993, which provides that there should be no discrimination in the provision of public services, including on grounds of 'intellectual or psychological disability or impairment'. Following conciliation between the patient, his family and the health authority, the complaint was withdrawn. This meant that the question of whether the guideline itself was discriminatory in treating dementia as a factor determining access to treatment was not tested in court. A further investigation undertaken by the Health and Disability Commissioner on her own initiative did, however, result in a partial finding of breach of the Code of Health and Disability Services Consumers' Rights upon procedural grounds; namely, that there had been insufficient discussion of the basis for and implications of the decision with the patient in a manner which was culturally sensitive to his Maori heritage (Health and Disability Commissioner, 1999).

England and Wales

R (Eisai Limited) v National Institute for Health and Clinical Excellence [2007] EWHC 1941 (Admin)/[2008] EWCA Civ 438 was a challenge, launched by a pharmaceutical company and with the Alzheimer's Society joining as an interested party, to guidance issued by the National Institute for Health and Clinical (now Care) Excellence (NICE), which performs health technology appraisal functions in the NHS in England and Wales. NICE had recommended that the drug donepezil, together with other acetylcholinesterase inhibitors used for palliative treatment of Alzheimer's disease, should not routinely be made available on the NHS for those newly diagnosed as suffering from a mild form of the disease, on the basis that it was not sufficiently cost-effective. Although providers of health care are not obliged to follow a negative recommendation by NICE (as distinct from a positive recommendation, for which they are statutorily obliged to provide funding), any such determination is likely in practice to result in denial of access to the treatment in question, given the scarcity of resources available to spend on treatments. Accordingly, the NICE guidance in effect functioned to ration this drug, a decision which was estimated to exclude access for 60% of the Alzheimer's patient population (Maynard, 2007).

With the exception of a point relating to the ambiguity and discriminatory nature of the guidance in relation to those with learning disabilities or for whom English was not a first language, the grounds of challenge which related to the substantive lawfulness of the NICE decision proved unsuccessful in court. These included arguments that the benefits to carers which would follow from provision of the drug had been insufficiently accounted for, and that evidence of cumulative benefits to patients had been ignored. The judge at first instance, Dobbs J, reiterated the standard judicial stance of non-intervention in such matters, stating that 'the Court has no part to play in adjudicating between the rival merits of the arguments of the experts, of whom there are many who take a view different from the Claimant's experts' ([2007] EWHC 1941 (Admin), paragraph 111). Indeed, she was at pains to conceptualise the challenge as not being about resources at all in order to emphasise that the court had no place in adjudicating upon the *merits* of the decision to limit availability of treatment:

> This is not, as has been suggested in some of the media, a challenge to a decision by NICE or the NHS not to fund treatment for certain Alzheimer's Disease sufferers ... It is also not about the court having to decide whether an Alzheimer's Disease sufferer is worth £2.50 a day, a figure which is said to be the cost of treatment with the drug ([2007] EWHC 1941 (Admin), paragraph 3).

By contrast, claims based upon the alleged unfairness of the NICE decision-making process were accorded more weight in the litigation. The claimant company argued that the failure to provide a fully-executable version of the economic model which had been developed to illustrate the cost-effectiveness of the inhibitors, and which formed the basis of NICE's recommendation, had deprived it of the opportunity to check its accuracy and to test alternative assumptions. This was alleged to be unfair as it meant that the company had been provided with insufficient information to understand the case which it had to meet, and to enable it to provide alternative submissions, in order to demonstrate that the drug was cost-effective. These arguments were rejected at first instance but succeeded on appeal, the court stating that failure to disclose a fully-executable model limited the 'ability [for drug companies and other consultees] to make an intelligent response on something that is central to the appraisal process' ([2008] EWCA Civ 438, paragraph 66). In light of the court's judgment, NICE agreed to release the fully-executable model, on the basis of which the company made further submissions. Initially, NICE confirmed its original recommendation; however, this guidance was reviewed following the emergence of new evidence. New guidance was subsequently issued which additionally recommended use of the drug for those with mild forms of Alzheimer's disease, although not for other forms of dementia.

Conclusion

These two instances of litigation concerning dementia map quite conveniently onto the threefold typology of judicial approaches to resource questions which was identified above. In neither *Shortland* nor *Eisai* was the court prepared to substantively 'second-guess' a decision which determined access to a treatment on the basis that the decision-maker's understanding or application of clinical or health economic evidence was flawed. The courts in these cases regarded intervention as being beyond their competence and sought to downplay the allocative dimension of the decision so as to justify adoption of a stance deferential to clinical expertise. Contrastingly, arguments of unfair procedure proved to have greater purchase. This was especially so in *Eisai*, where the Court of Appeal decision can be seen as an illustration of a broad judicial commitment to requiring decisions with an allocative component to be transparent, with a view to stimulating both stakeholder participation in decisions and public understanding of the criteria on which they are based (Syrett, 2007; 2011). However, such arguments were also evident—albeit less decisive—in *Shortland*, notably in the first instance judge's call for clear reasons to be given for the allocative choice, which appears to echo Laws J's injunction to the decision-maker in *R v Cambridge Health Authority, ex parte B* to 'do more than toll the bell of tight resources' ([1995] 1 FLR 1055, 1065).

Perhaps the least clear-cut picture which emerges from these cases relates to the potency of the third category of legal argument deployed in rationing cases, that which is based upon alleged violation of rights. The only instance in which a court explicitly adverted to right-based analysis came in *Shortland*, where a claim that there had been a violation of the right not to be deprived of life under section 8 of the New Zealand Bill of Rights Act 1990 was dismissed on the basis that the decision was one, instead, 'to let life take its natural course' (HC (Whangerei) M.75/97 (6 November 1997), 19). Given that neither of the jurisdictions concerned recognises a positive right of access to health or health care, the paucity of argument from this perspective is scarcely surprising.

However, both challenges did raise issues of *equality* which, alongside autonomy, represents an underlying value of human rights, as recognised by Article 1 of the Universal Declaration of Human Rights. In *Eisai*, such an argument succeeded. The High Court found that the guidance was formulated in such a way that it was not made sufficiently clear that certain atypical groups should not be assessed in accordance with the standard test for measurement of the severity of Alzheimer's disease; nevertheless, it rejected the claim that this amounted to a violation of the Human Rights Act 1998, resting its decision instead on breach of obligations prescribed by anti-discrimination legislation. It is uncertain whether a claim based upon equality would have prevailed in *Shortland* as it was not presented to the court, although Paterson (1998: 574) considers that it 'seems to offer more scope' than that based on section 8 of the Bill of Rights Act, querying whether denial of dialysis to a blind patient—who, like Rau Williams, would also have experienced difficulties in cooperating with the therapeutic regime—would have been lawful. Accordingly, he expresses regret that 'an opportunity was missed for judicial clarification of an issue that goes to the heart of human rights and health care' (1998: 575).

FUTURE PROSPECTS

Denial or restriction of access to existing or new treatments for dementia amounts to a 'tragic choice' (Calabresi and Bobbitt, 1978) in that it exposes deeply held and incommensurable moral positions within society and, as such, is liable to constitute a site of profound ethical contestation. The preceding discussion suggests that there are limitations to the capacity of the courtroom to function as an arena for this purpose, since judges are reluctant to question the substance of a rationing choice. For example, in *Eisai*, the pharmaceutical company used NICE's internal appeal process to challenge both the specific restriction on access to Alzheimer's drugs and, more broadly, the appropriateness of the methodology upon which the Institute conducts its appraisals, formulating its arguments in ethical rather than legal terms:

> Any assessment based on QALYs (Quality Adjusted Life Years) discriminates against older people and those with shorter life expectancies because greater QALY benefits can be

> gained by treating younger people with longer life expectancies ... To allow discrimination on these grounds would seem analogous to determining treatment on the basis of deservedness (Eisai Limited, 2006: paragraph 3.1).

It chose not to pursue these potent ethical arguments in court, a strategy which appears to have been sensible given Dobbs J's deference to NICE's expertise on matters of health technology appraisal. It might be concluded from this instance that courts will eschew intervention in cases where the basis of challenge amounts, in essence, to a political or moral claim: for example, that the fundamental objective of health systems is to maximise the aggregate population health gain and that resources should be allocated accordingly (the QALY being one means through which such an objective may be pursued).

However, the scope for judicial involvement is inevitably broadened if such arguments are (re)conceptualised as claims to equal treatment and rights in law. Formulation of a challenge in such a manner makes it constitutionally improper for a court wholly to abdicate responsibility for adjudicating upon the case on the basis that it more properly falls within the province of the legislature or a specialised agency: the matter sits within the competence of the judiciary as a consequence of its framing as a question of law. It does not follow, of course, that the aggrieved patient or other stakeholder will always prevail in such circumstances; indeed, judges frequently demonstrate considerable deference to decision making in situations of allocation of scarce resources. Nonetheless, as noted previously, this form of framing puts the decision-maker to proof and, absent provision of adequate justification for the allocative choice which has been reached, a court may choose to deem the decision to be unlawful.

The two cases discussed in the preceding section demonstrate that arguments rooted in equality and rights can play a part in this area, albeit that this role is, as yet, somewhat embryonic in character. However, recent developments point to such claims being accorded greater weight in future litigation. The enactment of broad-ranging equalities laws, such as the UK's Equality Act 2010, serves to proscribe discrimination against persons with dementia not only on grounds of disability, but also on grounds of age, and extends well beyond the employment protection sphere covered by earlier legislation, such as Directive 2000/78/EC, to encompass provision of services. Denial of access to dementia care and treatment *solely* on grounds of age (or disability) will clearly be unlawful; the lawfulness of the use of metrics such as the QALY to determine access to treatment appears questionable and is accordingly being kept 'under review' (Department of Health, 2010: 29), although NICE has defended its use of the methodology (Stevens et al, 2012). Nonetheless, at the least, objective justification which demonstrates that the allocative policy or decision is a proportionate means of achieving a legitimate aim of management of scarce resources is likely to be required under legislation of this type (Department of Health, 2012). This reinforces the explanatory trend previously identified as emergent when rights claims have been advanced in the courtroom.

Beyond laws which seek to proscribe unequal treatment, arguments that rest on alleged violation of international human rights norms appear germane in this context. Article 12 of the International Covenant on Economic, Social and Cultural Rights requires that, in pursuit of the right of everyone to enjoyment of the highest attainable standard of mental health, health facilities, goods and services should be available to everyone without discrimination on any of the prohibited grounds, which include mental disability and health status. While the Covenant acknowledges the existence of constraints due to limited resources, non-discriminatory access is an obligation of immediate effect. The protection which this provision offers has recently been reinforced by obligations flowing from the Convention on the Rights of Persons with Disabilities, which was adopted by the UN General Assembly in 2006. Article 25 of this Convention stipulates that states shall provide health services needed by persons with disabilities specifically because of those disabilities, and that they shall prevent discriminatory denial of health care or services on the basis of disability. Once again, the obligations are subject to the constraints imposed by availability of resources, but non-discriminatory access should be accorded immediate effect.

In theory, these requirements should render it harder for governments to lawfully justify denial of access to treatments or services for sufferers of dementia on cost grounds. In practice, their value is likely to be more indirect. Given weak mechanisms for enforcement of such rights, ongoing doubts as to justiciability (especially in circumstances where expenditure is necessary for their realisation) and the dualist nature of many state jurisdictions which renders international law separate from domestic law, the principles seem likely primarily to lend normative and discursive weight to other claims advanced in litigation on rationing—such as those based upon violation of specific provisions in domestic equality laws—rather than being decisive in themselves.

CONCLUSION

Notwithstanding such limitations, the developments traced in the preceding section appear to have expanded the range of arguments which are available to litigants who wish to contest the rationing of dementia care. While it may overstate the case to suggest that the balance has tilted against those who make limit-setting choices in this area, it seems apparent that those charged with allocation of scarce health care resources cannot now simply assume that judges will dismiss challenges to decisions of this type absent some evidence of procedural unfairness. Given the continuing financial pressures which dementia places on health systems, further litigation appears inevitable. It will be intriguing to observe the manner in which the courts choose to respond to such cases as and when they arise in the future.

REFERENCES

Age UK (2013) *Later life in the United Kingdom*. Factsheet. Available at: www.ageuk.org.uk/.

Alzheimer's Disease International (2010) *World Alzheimer Report 2010: the global economic impact of dementia* (London, Alzheimer's Disease International).

Calabresi, G and Bobbitt, P (1978) *Tragic Choices* (New York, WW Norton & Co).

Department of Health (2010) *Age equality in health and social care: A report on the consultation* (London, Department of Health).

—— (2012) *Implementing a ban on age discrimination in the NHS – making effective, appropriate decisions* (London, Department of Health).

Eisai Limited (2006) 'Appeal against the Final Appraisal Determination by the National Institute of Health and Clinical Excellence for donepezil, galantamine, rivastigmine (review) and memantine for the treatment of Alzheimer's Disease'. Available at: www.nice.org.uk.

Health and Disability Commissioner (1999) *Northland Health: Report on Opinion – Case 97HDC8872*.

Luengo-Fernandez, R, Leal, J and Gray, A (2010) *Dementia 2010: The economic burden of dementia and associated research funding in the United Kingdom* (Cambridge, Alzheimer's Research Trust).

Maynard, A (1999) 'Rationing health care: An exploration' 49(1–2) *Health Policy* 5–11.

—— (2007) 'Transparency in health technology assessments' 334(7594) *British Medical Journal* 595–96.

Paterson, R (1998) 'Rationing health care and human rights: The *Northland Health* case' *New Zealand Law Review* 571–84.

Stevens, A et al (2012) 'National Institute for Health and Clinical Excellence appraisal and ageism' 38(5) *Journal of Medical Ethics* 258–62.

Syrett, K (2007) *Law, Legitimacy and the Rationing of Health Care: A Contextual and Comparative Perspective* (Cambridge, Cambridge University Press).

—— (2011) 'Health technology appraisal and the courts: Accountability for reasonableness and the judicial model of procedural justice' 6(4) *Health Economics, Policy, and Law* 469–88.

Yamin, AE and Gloppen, S (eds) (2011) *Litigating Health Rights: Can Courts Bring More Justice to Health?* (Cambridge, MA, Harvard University Press).

34

The Use of New Technologies in the Management of Dementia Patients

KAREN ELTIS

> Technology has the potential to disable a person with dementia as well as enable them.[1]
>
> What is heralded as an opportunity for increased liberty must not degenerate into the denial of basic human rights and dignity.[2]

THERE HAS BEEN a steady movement towards the recognition of human rights protection mechanisms for vulnerable populations, particularly older adults and dementia patients more broadly. While the most obvious forms of abuse of the vulnerable have increasingly been the object of greater scrutiny, the focus has nevertheless been rather narrow, addressing only the most apparent manners of domestic or institutional maltreatment. A far more subtle form of potential disregard for basic rights relates to new technologies, and their application to the vulnerable.

Too often, it appears, we take the limitations imposed on the liberties and dignity of those with dementia for granted, as a presumed natural consequence of their degenerating health and our well-intentioned but paternalistic desire to ensure their medical well-being. Not surprisingly, perhaps, this is all the more true in relation to assistive technologies, which, as their name suggests, tend to be judged innocuous. The use of Global Positioning System (GPS) technology to tag and track typically elderly, typically female,[3] dementia patients raises more than a few key human rights concerns and the issue of plural constructions of harm, thus far overlooked by the relevant legal literature.

New assistive technologies create some new and interesting legal difficulties. Some of those difficulties force us to confront problems in the interpretation of the 'best interests' test which are exacerbated by the law's inability to grasp fully the nuances of dementia.[4] Caregivers, both institutional and familial, are left with very little guidance when much direction is needed.

[1] Guidelines. Available at: www.alzheimers.org.uk/site/scripts/documents_info.php?documentID=579.

[2] Welsh, S et al (2003) 'Big brother is watching you—the ethical implications of electronic surveillance measures in the elderly with dementia and in adults with learning difficulties' 7(5) *Aging & Mental Health* 372–75.

[3] Because Alzheimer's disease is more common in women: see, eg, Vina, J and Lloret, A (2010) 'Why women have more Alzheimer's disease than men: gender and mitochondrial toxicity of amyloid-beta peptide' 20 (Suppl 2) *Journal of Alzheimer's Disease* S527–33. doi: 10.3233/JAD-2010-100501.

[4] Herring, J (2008) 'Caregivers in Medical Law and Ethics' 25(1) *Journal of Contemporary Health Law and Policy* 1–37.

At first glance, recent technological advances can serve to protect dementia patients from misadventure and in some cases allow them to maintain a much-valued degree of autonomy. They can also potentially relieve some of the anxiety and financial hardship generally experienced by their families and caregivers.[5] Thus, GPS tracking in some instances may allow dementia patients to retain or prolong cherished independence, live at home longer and go on certain errands unaccompanied, as the technology enables their caregivers to locate them should they wander or are otherwise in need of assistance. Aside from enhancing quality of life for patient and caregiver, assistive technologies such as GPS presumably yield additional *social* benefits such as reducing the cost of care.[6] The latter factor is particularly desirable in publicly funded systems such as Canada's, for example, which has a rapidly ageing population, if not the fastest growing population of aged people in the developed world. It can of course also serve to reduce private insurance costs.

New technologies may be said to bring into question the individualistic paradigm of medical law, as we consider the intersection or 'intermingling' of interests—and potential conflict—between the 'best interests' of the dementia patient and those of their caregivers, which may not always align.

How then can the law properly account for dementia patients' interests (at the time of diagnosis and later on) and those of caregivers and society more generally? How are (presumably) non-medical rights such as dignity and privacy weighed and balanced against what are arguably more obvious needs such as security and mobility?[7] What are the relevant distinctions between various forms of dementia tracking, and are some forms more palatable than others? Can the law incorporate such differences, and guard against abuses, by introducing norms aimed at better regulating assistive technologies? These are the questions policymakers and courts must tackle if they are to weigh equitably the rights and interests in the digital age.

[5] Hirst, M (2005) 'Carer Distress: A Prospective, Population-Based Study' 61(3) *Social Science & Medicine* 697–708. Caregiver burden is defined as 'the subjective assessment of stress and anxiety, which may result from the perception that external caregiving demands exceed available resources' Chumbler, N et al (2003) 'Gender, kinship and caregiver burden: the case of community-dwelling memory impaired seniors' *International Journal of Geriatric Psychiatry*, 18: 722–32; Bruce, JM et al (2008) 'Burden among Spousal and Child Caregivers of Patients with Mild Cognitive Impairment' *Dementia and Geriatric Cognitive Disorders* 385–90.

[6] Thus, for instance, '[T]he graying of the world population poses formidable socioeconomic challenges to the provision of acute and long-term healthcare. Approximately 28 million persons worldwide suffer from dementia and account for 156 billion dollars in direct care costs annually. In the United States alone, the population aged 65 and older will double in size to 72 million within the next 25 years, with the segment over age 85 years growing at the fastest rate. Alzheimer disease (AD) is the leading cause of dementia in this elderly cohort and afflicts nearly 4.5 million Americans. If current population trends continue, an estimated 13 million Americans will have the disease by 2050. Currently, the national direct and indirect costs of caring for AD exceed $100 billion a year, with long-term institutional care accounting for majority of the expenditure. More recently, a study commissioned by the Alzheimer's Association predicts that the total Medicare spending on AD will triple to $189 billion by 2015, and around mid-century, the Medicare and Medicaid combined cost of caring for AD will exceed $1 trillion annually'. Full quotation available at: www.ncbi.nlm.nih.gov/pmc/articles/PMC2768007/. See Bharucha, AJ et al (2009) 'Intelligent Assistive Technology Applications to Dementia Care: Current Capabilities, Limitations, and Future Challenges' 17(2) *American Journal of Geriatric Psychiatry* 88–104.

[7] On mobility see Landau, R et al (2012) 'Caregiving burden and out-of-home mobility of cognitively impaired care-recipients based on GPS tracking' 24(11) *International Psychogeriatrics* 1836–45.

Mindful of modern 'interdependencies' between patient, caregiver and society, this chapter raises and considers the issues involved in striking a fair balance between the *rights* (or non-physical concerns) and physical *needs* of dementia patients (often part of the broader cohort of elderly people), in a way that proportionately heeds the interests of their caregivers and society. This is with an eye towards developing parameters that employ the least restrictive means that technology offers in order to reconcile risk management with, in Richards' words, 'the promotion of a person-centred approach in dementia care'.[8]

This chapter proceeds in three parts. Part one will briefly examine the thorny matter of consent and the challenges that new technologies, particularly GPS tracking of dementia patients, present for normativity. Part two will explore the distinction between more invasive and less stigmatizing tracking technologies as a starting point for developing much-needed protocols, thus preserving pragmatism while revisiting the 'safety first' (or safety only) narrative to account for other interests (primarily constitutional rights). Part three further examines potential regulation of this emerging phenomenon, with special emphasis on preventing the more foreseeable abuses associated with geo-location devices. This is an area that is truly susceptible to misuse, a fortiori when situated within the general context of maltreatment and exploitation of vulnerable populations.

PART 1

REVISITING LEGAL STANDARDS: A NEW SET OF CHALLENGES

Negotiated Consent at Time of Diagnosis and Other Interdependencies

The attraction of managing risk and scare resources in a drained system said to be 'saddled' with an ageing, dementia-prone population is certainly not surprising. As previously noted, to insurers, governments and caregivers alike, GPS tracking of dementia patients seems to offer a most tempting solution. For not only can assistive technologies help to relieve some of the anxiety and emotional burdens related to caring, but can at times even justify 'the withdrawal of staff and financial resources from the care of people with complex needs'.[9] That, in turn, provides opportunity for reassessing the delicate issue of consent and appropriateness of the 'best interests' test in the dementia setting.

No less pertinent is the question of intra-familial conflicts and, on a broader scale, conflicts of interests between the patient, caregivers and broader societal economic interests, as regards the use of assistive technologies. Thus, although it is naturally presumed that patients and caregivers share common interests, that is not always the case; perceptions of 'best interests' tend to differ in the health milieu. Accounting for many constructions of harm, extending beyond (perceived) medical needs, is therefore of the essence.

[8] See, eg, the American Society on Aging's position online: www.asaging.org/blog/person-centered-dementia-care-should-be-new-norm; see also http://www.ccal.org/national-dementia-initiative/.

[9] See Welsh et al, above (n 2).

Dementia challenges the law's often over-tight distinction between those deemed 'competent' and their 'incompetent' counterparts.[10] A detailed discussion of the law and ethics of consent is beyond the scope of this chapter, but it should be noted that this general challenge is further compounded by the advent of new technologies. Most studies assessing the value of assistive technologies have surprisingly failed to account for the views of dementia patients themselves, leaving policymakers and courts in an unenviable position.[11]

A Word on Consent

> No right is held more sacred, or is more carefully guarded ... than the right of every individual to the possession and control of his own person, free from restraint or interference of others, unless by clear and unquestionable authority (*Union Pacific Railway Company R v Botsford*).[12]

Although dementia patients often have difficulty making lucid choices with regard to their treatment, decisions respecting assistive technologies can and should be made at the time of diagnosis,[13] when patients generally possess the requisite mental capacity.[14] While this approach is by no means foolproof, it does appear to palliate some of the difficulties involved, particularly if decisions are made together with family, structured by professional guidance.

In effect, George Smith's notion of 'negotiated consent',[15] whereby caregivers are involved in the decision-making process (to varying degrees) provides some helpful direction with respect to assistive technologies.

[10] See generally, Herring, J (2008) 'Entering the Fog: On the Borderlines of Mental Capacity' 83(4) *Indiana Law Journal* 1619–49. See also Klein, DW (2012) 'When Coercion Lacks Care: Competency to make medical treatment decisions and *parens patriae* civil commitments' 45(3) *University of Michigan Journal of Law Reform* 561–93: 'Generally, tests for determining competency to make medical treatment decisions require only that someone possess the capacity to understand the potential advantages and disadvantages of a proposed treatment'.

[11] Robinson, L et al (2007) 'Balancing rights and risks: Conflicting perspectives in the management of wandering in dementia' 9(4) *Health, Risk and Society* 389–406. According to Robinson et al: 'Studies on interventions have neglected users' views. It is important to establish the views of people with dementia on the acceptability of new interventions prior to evaluating their effectiveness through complex and expensive trials'.

[12] *Union Pacific Railway Company R v Botsford* 141 US 250 (1891).

[13] Landau, R et al (2010) 'What do cognitively intact older people think about the use of electronic tracking devices for people with dementia? A preliminary analysis' 22(8) *International Psychogeriatrics* 1301–109. According to Laudau and colleagues: 'To facilitate family decision-making on the use of tracking devices, structured meetings guided by professionals and including persons with dementia and their family caregivers are suggested'.

[14] Consonant with the Alzheimer's Society UK position: The Alzheimer's Society suggests that a person with dementia makes an advance decision on the use of technology for a time in the future when they may lack capacity'.'The use of technology is less likely to be appropriate in the later stages when consent may be more difficult to gain and risk harder for an individual with dementia to assess. People with dementia in the later stages may also be more vulnerable and at more immediate risk, and may require different interventions that provide a more immediate solution'. Available at: www.alzheimers.org.uk/site/scripts/documents_info.php?documentID=579.

[15] See Herring, 'Caregivers in Medical Law and Ethics', above (n 4).

Even if the matter of lucidity is addressed collaboratively, the issue of coerced decisions persists. Patients may be unduly influenced by a desire not to 'burden' family members or caregivers, or by a fear of being seen as 'unreasonably' refusing the fruits of progress in a digital age (where technology is often blindly embraced). This is particularly problematic when caregiver and patient interests—or respective constructions of harm—diverge. For instance, caregivers (particularly institutional) are generally said to value non-malfeasance over what are perceived to be more abstract rights.[16] That perception might overshadow the dementia patient's non-medical considerations (including but not limited to personal dignity), that may be conveniently dismissed as capricious or unimportant compared with physical safety and the fear of litigation and caregiver anxiety that dementia inevitably instills.[17]

As John Eekelaar observes:

> [T]o exercise care is also to exercise power. True, it is to be hoped that it is a beneficent exercise of power, but it is power nonetheless. The key element, overlooked in some communitarian accounts, is the role of force or coercion. There are many examples where the role of caregiver, even if applied with good intentions, has adverse consequences.[18]

This is all the more so when new technologies (commonly equated with 'progress') are involved.

Thus, for the purpose of consent to the use of technology, the law must account for the probability of concerns about efficiency overshadowing a patient's wishes, even when lucidity is not yet a concern.[19]

[16] See, eg, Kitwood, TM (1997) *Dementia Reconsidered: The Person Comes First* (Buckingham, Open University Press) 27 (revisiting the psychological needs of people with dementia: ie, love and dignity, which are not simply physical). Tom Kitwood, a leading Alzheimer's medical researcher, once cautioned that personhood and the inalienable rights intrinsic to it are not supplanted by age-related illness and the pragmatic health care considerations that accompany it, despite the tragic loss of autonomy from dementia (fn 86). As he so eloquently stated, '[t]he unifying theme is the personhood of men and women who have dementia—an issue that was grossly neglected for many years both in psychiatry and care practice'.

[17] Thereby amplifying the complexity of obtaining consent since most benefits accruing from assistive technologies appears to be to caregiver. ('The main benefits of using such devices were felt to be increased confidence and peace of mind for family carers' (Melillo, KD and Futrell, M (1998) 'Wandering and technology devices: Helping caregivers ensure the safety of confused older adults' *Journal of Gerontological Nursing* 24(8) 32–38; *Altus, DE*, et al (2000) 'Evaluating an electronic monitoring system for people who wander' *American Journal of Alzheimer's Disease and Other Dementias* 15(2) 121–25; Miskelly, F (2004) 'A novel system of electronic tagging in patients with dementia and wandering' *Age Ageing* 33(3) 304–06) and a reduction in stress and release of time for other duties for nursing home staff (Nicolle, C (1998) 'Issues in the use of tagging for people who wander: a European perspective' Proceedings of the Conference Working with Vulnerable Adults: Innovative Practice and Technology in Risk Management, Belfast, 10–22.

[18] 'One of the most powerful criticisms of an ethic of care is that care relationships, despite their cozy sounding image, are in fact about power. John Eekelaar wrote: ...'. Herring cites Ecklaar in Herring, 'Caregivers in Medical Law and Ethics', above (n 4).

[19] See, eg, the discussion of 'pragmatic' concerns trumping others in Robinson et al, above (n 11) 400: 'Family carers exhibited greater tolerance of risk, with professional carers favouring patient safety over autonomy due to a fear of litigation; this appeared to affect the provision of person-centred care'.

The 'Best Interests Test' Revisited

Currently, the little guidance that the law does generically offer in most common law jurisdictions is the following: simply put, caregivers must demonstrate that assistive technologies are in the 'best interests' of the dementia patient in order to use them (in the absence of uncontested advance directives).

While the best interests test serves as a default 'go to' in the most delicate of settings (such as family, health), whether it lends itself to GPS monitoring of dementia patients is debatable. Lyria Bennet Moses explains in her paper on the merits of revisiting norms in light of technological change, generally: '[E]xisting rules were not formulated with new technologies in mind. Thus, some rules in their current form inappropriately include or exclude new forms of conduct'.[20] For the purposes of our discussion, the 'best interests' test appears not to fully capture the complexity of assistive technologies in dementia given the multiplicity of delicate and possibly conflicting interests.

With this in mind, it bears repeating that the general difficulty of obtaining true (or even negotiated) consent is exacerbated by new technologies such as GPS, which are sometimes seen as primarily benefiting caregivers rather than the patient. Studies indicate that 5% of wandering dementia patients will sustain significant injuries from that wandering.[21] Wandering is now more commonly referred to as 'walking' in order to do away with the unpleasant connotations and emphasize the related benefits such as exercise and fresh air. This is notwithstanding the terrible anxiety that 'wandering' or 'walking' demonstrably causes caregivers, who in the family setting are themselves often female, and often elderly.[22]

Accordingly, as one critic of GPS monitoring put it:

> In dementia we need to move beyond quick fix practical solutions such as electronic tagging, which so often serve the needs of formal caregivers while eroding the rights of those with a cognitive impairment. For people with dementia wandering may well be pottering with a purpose—a desire to use up excess energy, to check out an unusual aspect of the local environment, or simply to seek fresh air. Let us not stigmatise and dehumanise this vulnerable group any further; rather, let us rise to the challenge of attempting to understand the meaning behind these behaviours and develop person centred and creative ways of addressing the issue.[23]

If we acquiesce to the psychological and economic concerns of caregivers any balance ultimately struck must account for another problem—the 'concern that

[20] Discussing the scope of rules, see Bennett Moses, L (2007) 'Why have a Theory of Law and Technological Change?' 8(2) *Minnesota Journal of Law, Science & Technology* 589–606, 595.

[21] Rowe, MA, & Glover, JC (2001) 'Antecendents, descriptions and consequences of wandering in cognitively-impaired adults and the Safe Return (SR) program' *American Journal of Alzheimers Disease and Other Dementias* 16(6), 344–52.

[22] Ibid. In terms of intersectionalities—women and the elderly (generally spouses) bear the greatest burden statistically. Women generally report higher levels of caregiving burden as do older caregivers and those with less education who tend to be undervalued: Di Mattei et al (2008) 'The burden of distress in caregivers of elderly demented patients and its relationship with coping strategies' 29 *Neurological Sciences* 383–39.

[23] Suzanne Cahill, Director, Dementia Services Information and Development Centre Ireland, St James Hospital, Dublin (2003). Letters 386 *British Medical Journal* 280.

technology would give a false sense of security'.[24] The illusion of safety that technology tends to create can be dangerous, with caregivers lulled into laxity and resources consequently being withdrawn. This is borne out in the domestic abuse context: see below.

PART II

NOT ALL TECHNOLOGIES ARE CREATED EQUAL: CARVING OUT THE 'LEAST RESTRICTIVE MEANS'

In their important piece warning of the ills of certain assistive technologies in the dementia context, Hughes and Louw call for supervision by governments with a view to mitigating the ill effects of GPS tracking. That call resonates with the general complaint that 'unfortunately, the principles enshrined in existing legislation, though laudable, offer little practical guidance to the clinician faced with a wandering patient and who is considering the use of tagging technology'.[25]

As with new technologies more generally, the objective is to develop a more nuanced, contextual approach, mindful that the triumph of health considerations may be less helpful in a technologically dynamic setting. In so doing, it is important to recognize that not all assistive technologies are created equal. Any parameters must therefore distinguish between more intrusive or stigmatizing forms of tracking that tend to affect negatively 'older people's attitudes about themselves' and their more benign counterparts. Another important nuance that any regulation (whatever form it eventually takes) must capture is the *identity of the trackers*. In other words, who is doing the monitoring—police; family members; health care professionals? Who has access to the data (law enforcement; insurers?) and is the monitoring constant or intermittent?[26]

These issues have been considered in the establishment of a tracking programme offered by the Alzheimer's Association (entitled 'Safely Home')[27] which is the fruit of tripartite cooperation between caregivers, patients' advocates (the Alzheimer's Society) and the police (on whose database the patient's personal information is stored and who are ultimately responsible for the tracking). Involving the police undoubtedly presents special challenges, for it may give rise to undesirable stigma stemming from the use of this technology in the criminal setting—most conspicuously convicted sex offenders. Certainly,

> the use of such devices is well established for convicted criminals in some jurisdictions. Animals are also often tracked by means of electronic tags. Therefore extension of this

[24] Lyons and Thomson (2006).

[25] See Welsh et al, above (n 2).

[26] 'If someone was keeping an eye on you it would depend who it was. If it was your partner you might feel alright about it but you might not. You might not want your partner always to know where you were. It's the relationship you've got with the person who is keeping an eye on you' (Person with dementia 3 [number assigned to preserve anonymity]).

[27] See, eg: globalnews.ca/news/276691/gps-technology-id-bracelets-among-options-for-people-with-alzheimers-who-wander/.

> technology to people with dementia, as mentioned in the editorial by Hughes and Louw, evokes unfortunate associations: infantilisation, custody, and a subhuman existence.[28]

To make matters worse, the technology is being applied to track domestic abusers.

The association in the popular consciousness of sex offenders or domestic abusers and tracking technologies may, patient advocates and patients themselves fear, precipitate erroneous assumptions and even attacks, thereby ironically compromising patients' physical (or psychological) security.

Not all types of GPS technology raise identical concerns. A GPS tracking device embedded in a mobile phone may be inconspicuous and therefore not especially stigmatizing. Phones do, however, raise distinct worries among elderly dementia patients: they might be frightened of being robbed.

An example of a more 'humane' application of tracking technology is perhaps the 'Buddi' system, which is attached to a patient's keys or shoes. Although not infallible it appears not to bear the stigma of other devices and does not appear to expose the patient to theft or attacks, or the fear thereof. It is also significant that those doing the tracking are (to our understanding) family members. As the following anecdote recounts:

> Anne Grimshaw, 78, has become one of the first people in the UK to be equipped with the [new tracking] technology so her family can find her when she gets lost.
>
> The device—known as 'Buddi'—is attached to Anne's keys and shows her last known position on an online map daughter Joanne has access to.[29]

PART III

STANDARDS: HUMBLE BEGINNINGS

It seems prudent to enact standards to avert the risks of data mining, scams and the like. The UK Alzheimers' Society agrees. It proposes the following: 'Questions to think about when developing guidelines and a person-centred assessment:

- Why is the person with dementia walking? Is there a need that is not being met?
- What are the views of everyone involved about the use of technology and the consequences of using it or not using it?
- What is the actual and perceived level of risk?
- Is everyone involved aware of the pros and cons of this technology for the person and their carers?
- Does the situation really call for the use of technology? What are the alternatives?

[28] Hughes, JC and Louw, SJ (2002) 'Electronic tagging of people with dementia who wander' 325(7369) *British Medical Journal* 847–48.

[29] 'Dementia Sufferer Anne Gets Device to Stop her from Getting Lost' *The Sun* (2 April 2013). Available at: www.thesun.co.uk/sol/homepage/news/4870095/dementia-suffering-nan-gets-tracking-device-to-stop-her-getting-lost.html#ixzz2RO12uW1P.

Beyond this, certain lessons may be gleaned from proposed and enacted Radio Frequency Identification (RFID legislation in the US. While these norms are entirely divorced from the health context and mostly focus on financial institutions (consonant with the US sectoral approach to privacy), they are helpful in so far as they consider and seek to counter abuses commonly associated with similar 'risk technology'.[30]

The harms are mainly: massive data aggregation (collection and use); individual tracking and profiling by law enforcement and private parties with commercial interests (analytics and beyond).[31]

Any form of regulation (whether guidelines and protocols in the health sector or something more constraining) would therefore ensure that monitoring (both data collection and data use) is narrowly tailored to the immediate purpose, presumably promoting patient safety and mobility and reducing caregiver anxiety. To 'enable'[32]—rather than put at further risk.

Existing baseline privacy legislation (which exists in many jurisdictions as well as in the US) can also be applied to GPS in the dementia context and is valuable for the following reasons (as set out by analogy respecting RFID inter alia):

> Law can be evaded and it is difficult to design [specific] legislation that perfectly reconciles the sometimes competing interests of convenience and privacy. Still, law's ability to establish enforceable barriers to privacy invasions makes it a powerful contributor to consumer privacy. Comprehensive privacy legislation has emerged as privacy advocates' chosen strategy because it appears to counter the surveillance trend by encouraging a culture of privacy. The benefit of baseline privacy legislation is that it not only addresses privacy with respect to RFID but it also binds the implementation of emerging technologies in ways that respect privacy. CDT Counsel Paula Bruening explained her rationale when she said: Every time there's a new emerging technology that involves data collection, we find ourselves back in these hearing rooms talking about how to specifically address privacy and that specific technology. Our belief is that if we have legislation that addresses collection of information no matter what the technology, we will be way ahead of the curve when it comes to the next technology that emerges. Businesses will have a better sense of what the responsibilities are in terms of putting [in] privacy-implementing policies that are privacy respectful and consumers will have a better sense of what they can expect in terms of their rights and responsibilities and their own information.[33]

Baseline privacy legislation aside, specific protocols, proactively aimed at providing more direct guidance for GPS tracking in the dementia context (given the peculiarities discussed above) are separately useful, notwithstanding the above. Accordingly

[30] Consider Washington State's relatively new Bill targeting 'skimming' (data theft broadly speaking) off RFID technologies and the stiff penalties it foresees: www.rfidjournal.com/articles/view?3988; RFID by analogy more generally.

[31] Providers of GPS sell location data to third parties. See, eg, Federal Trade Commission, FTC Staff Report: Self-Regulatory Principles for Online Behavioral Advertising 45–47 (2009). Available at: www.ftc.gov/os/2009/02/P085400behavadreport.pdf.

[32] See, eg, the European initiative entitled 'project enable'.

[33] Hildner, L (2010) 'Defusing the Threat of RFID: Protecting Consumer Privacy through Technology-Specific Legislation at the State Level' 41 *Harvard Civil Rights–Civil Liberties Law Review* 133–76.

insisting on encryption (for example) to prevent data theft (a crime to which the elderly or dementia patients are presumably more susceptible) is a helpful start.[34]

What is ultimately required is a system to determine when and how GPS technology may be used in the dementia context. Protocols must deal both with data collection (which may itself constitute harm)[35] and data use. Norms, whether embodied in protocols or legislation, also educate: they foster public awareness and make violations realizable and enforceable.

[34] See, eg, Assem 290, 97th Leg, Reg Sess (Wis 2006) (enacted); HR 203, 159th Gen Ct, Reg Sess (NH 2005) (enacted); HR 185, 2005 Leg, Reg Sess (Utah 2005) (enacted); HR 258, 58th Leg, Reg Sess (Wyo 2005) (enacted); S 148, 2004 Gen Assem, Reg Sess (Va 2004) (enacted); see also 2006 Privacy Legislation, above; 2005 Privacy Legislation, above.

[35] Hildner, above (n 33).

Part IV

Social Aspects of Dementia

35

Discrimination

DOUG SURTEES

THE VERB 'TO discriminate' means to be able to perceive distinctions, or tell the difference between things, people or concepts. It can be used as a compliment; saying someone has discriminating tastes implies that the person has exquisite taste and is able to make fine distinctions, for example, in selecting the best wines or foods or identifying the latest fashion. The verb can also be used as a neutral statement of fact. Saying someone cannot discriminate between green lights and red lights is nothing more than an observation of colour blindness. Of course, neither of these meanings represents how the term is used in the human rights context.

In the human rights context we understand 'discrimination' not as an attribute of the person making distinctions, but rather as something which impacts another person or group. 'Discrimination' in this sense owes its existence to the creation of (negative) effects upon someone. It is something that is done to someone.

Discrimination occurs in many ways. It may occur by conscious choice. It may also occur as an unintended consequence of actions or systemic design. 'Adverse effect discrimination' can occur as a result of rules and systems created, or choices made, for other purposes. Since discrimination in the human rights realm is concerned with the effects visited upon another, it is possible for discrimination to occur in the absence of any intention to discriminate, and even in the absence of choice. Jurisdictions employ different regimes to mitigate discrimination and have different understandings of what constitutes discrimination. I conceptualize discrimination in more generic terms. Here, I want to create a common understanding of discrimination generally before examining this concept specifically in the context of dementia.

At a basic level we have common concepts regarding discrimination. Intentional discrimination provides a good starting point from which to examine these common concepts. Intentional discrimination is the easiest form to see, and provides a useful context for examining what we mean when we say something is discriminatory. Consider a law, which holds 'No person with dementia may vote'. How do we determine if such a law is discriminatory?

One way to answer this question is to determine whether or not the law violates any human rights legislation in force in the particular jurisdiction. One may think of human rights legislation at a basic level as being comprised of two lists. The first list is a list of decisions which will be made. For example, people make decisions as to who to admit to a university, who to hire for a job, who to serve in their restaurant and who to select as a tenant to rent a house. There are two variables with respect to this list. One is made up of the specific decisions that are regulated, and the other is made up of the specific decision-makers who are regulated. Some legislation regulates only government actors while other legislation regulates either some or all private actors.

The second list is a list of personal characteristics. Typical characteristics included are gender, race and age (or at least some range of ages). These characteristics are specific to individuals and may not be used by the decision-makers to make the types of decisions included in the first list. Of course, there will usually be exceptions and exemptions built into the legislation. This basic understanding of human rights legislation will be useful to see if discrimination will be found under the particular legislation in force in a particular jurisdiction. The choices as to which decisions, which decision-makers and which characteristics are included on the lists will be informed by spoken and unspoken moral, ethical, religious and political beliefs.

In answering the question: 'Is this discrimination?' this approach defines discrimination as a violation of the legislation, and so really answers a narrower question that is: 'Is this a violation of the human rights legislation in force in our jurisdiction?'

The answer will be 'yes' provided that:

1. The authority which passed the 'No person with dementia may vote' law is within the group of regulated decision-makers.
2. Decisions involving the voting are within the group of regulated decisions.
3. Dementia (or disability) is within the group of regulated characteristics.
4. No exceptions or exemptions apply.

A broader understanding of discrimination will lead to a broader approach in answering the question of whether or not something constitutes discrimination. Rather than define discrimination simply as a violation of human rights legislation, we can define discrimination as 'unjustified differential treatment'. Using this understanding of discrimination frees us from the specifics of any particular human rights legislation and requires us to apply a deep analysis as to whether there has been differential treatment and if so, whether that differential treatment is justified. Again, spoken and unspoken moral, ethical, religious and political beliefs will inform our conclusions.

This broader approach allows us to have less concern for who the decision-maker is. By shifting the focus from the human rights legislation to unjustified differential treatment, the cause of that treatment loses relevance. Therefore, in our example, it becomes unimportant whether that which prohibits persons with dementia from voting is a law, a rule, a practice, a result of organizational systems or something else. The difference between prohibition and practice shrinks. Practices, structures, unconnected rules and ways of doing things can prevent, without prohibiting, persons with dementia from voting. Where this is without adequate justification, these constructs can be as discriminatory as a law that prohibits the same thing.

In the 'No person with dementia may vote' example, the differential treatment is clear. It is presumably the purpose of the law. By changing the example we can demonstrate a situation where the differential treatment only becomes clear after some analysis. If the law (or under this broader approach, the rule, practice, structure etc) was 'No person who lives in a long-term care home may vote' our analysis would be different. The obvious differential treatment here is that people who live in long-term care homes are being treated differently from people who don't. Using the broad approach we would begin by examining the justification for type of residence as a basis for differential treatment. If there is sufficient legitimate justification for it, the law would not be discriminatory. If there is no such justification, the rule would be discriminatory despite the fact that type of residence is generally not considered as a characteristic leading to discrimination. The 'two list' human rights approach would lead at first to a conclusion that since type of residence is generally not a protected characteristic (list two) there is no human rights regime violation. This does not end the enquiry however. The law is not saved simply because it appears not to be aimed at using disability as the differentiating characteristic. This law would create a differential effect based on disability, simply because most people who live in a long-term care home have disabilities. Therefore, this law would discriminate on the basis of disability.

Where there is differential treatment we must carefully consider whether or not it is justified. We must also consider the cause of the differential treatment. The cause may be something as obvious as a law or a rule, but it may also be the result of a practice or organizational structure. It could also be an unintended consequence of an unrelated rule or way of doing things. Discriminatory effects caused by the interaction of seemingly unrelated factors is easy to visualize in a setting such as a long-term care home, which is a workplace for some and a home for others.

Consider how discrimination, understood in this broader sense, may affect people in three distinct spheres of their relationship to dementia. The first of these spheres, paradoxically, does not involve people with dementia, but rather people who are prone to dementia. The medical profession has long had an array of tests that are able to determine that one individual has a greater predilection for a certain disease as compared with the general population. The mapping of the human genome has opened possibilities never before available to mere mortals. Understanding the increased genetic likelihood that specific individuals will develop particular infirmities such as dementia could help researchers in developing harm prevention and harm reduction strategies. It could help public health officials to more efficiently and effectively allocate resources. This knowledge makes many positive developments possible. Access to this knowledge however also facilitates discrimination. It makes possible the arranging of private affairs to maximize individual (or individual shareholder, or service provider) benefit, to the detriment of individuals with certain characteristics.

Contract law is generally the mechanism for people acquiring things like a job, a place to live or insurance. Private ordering, which is a theoretical basis of contract law, has no dependable mechanism to alleviate discrimination. Unless regulated, contract law allows, and in fact presupposes, individual choice in the resultant bargain. While it may be true that the reality of contract is more and more that the stronger presents the weaker with what is basically an adhesion contract and the weaker party is only free to either enter the contract on the terms presented, or not at all (Preston and McCann, 2012), contracts are generally enforced as if each term is the result of an actual agreement between the parties. This ability for the parties (or perhaps for the stronger party) to organize their affairs, trade their rights and allocate risks, is not absolute. There are areas where we say we will not allow individuals to give up certain rights by contract. So, employees are generally not allowed to agree to work for less than specified minimum working standards. We generally do not permit individuals to 'contract away' human rights. Human rights legislation generally applies even when a party purported to give up their human rights. Contracts to purchase an organ for transplant, to hire a surrogate mother to deliver a baby, or bribe a public official are typically made ineffective or at least regulated within the contract law concept of 'public policy' or by statute. These are but a few of the areas where we regulate the right to contract in the name of public benefit. Left alone, contract law will have a difficult time preventing knowledge of a genetic predisposition for developing dementia from being used to discriminate against such individuals. It may be that eventually contract law will develop an internal workable way (such as the use of concepts like public policy) to limit the use of such knowledge. Without external controls these contracts will be drafted to benefit the more powerful.

External controls can take one of two forms. They may change the rules of contract law, such as by requiring that a particular clause is part of every contract, or by using anti-discrimination law to limit the parties' power to use genetic information. Alternatively, the use and distribution of individuals' genetic data could be protected by enhanced privacy legislation (Lemmens, 2000). A combination of these two approaches may hold the best hope for effective regulation. Some have suggested that countries with universal health care have been quicker to embrace restrictions on the use of genetic information in life insurance and additional health insurance contracts, perhaps because these countries are more likely to see access to such insurance as more of a necessity and less of a mere commodity (Lemmens, 2000).

The advantage of having specific legislation to prohibit genetic discrimination in a specific context is that we can be confident the law will apply in that situation. The disadvantage is that it may not apply when people are discriminated against in new, previously unthought of ways. Although anti-discrimination laws often have the flexibility to be applied in novel contexts, it is presently difficult to determine if they will be applied to protect a person who displays no symptoms and who actually may never develop the condition for which the genetic tests show a higher risk (Gin, 1997). Anti-discrimination legislation usually protects persons with a disability, as well as those perceived to have a disability. Those who are seen to have an increased genetic risk of developing a condition may not be within this protection. Tests for genes associated with Alzheimer's disease do not tell us that the person will or will not develop Alzheimer's disease; they simply result in placing individuals in various 'risk pools'. The results allow us to conclude only that some individuals will be more likely or less likely to develop Alzheimer's disease. With a large number of individuals, we can conclude nothing at all (Greely, 2001).

Insurance and anti-discrimination laws have an uncomfortable relationship. Justice Sopinka of the Supreme Court of Canada said: 'The underlying philosophy of human rights legislation is that an individual has a right to be dealt with on his or her own merits and not on the basis of group characteristics' (*Zurich Insurance v Ontario Human Rights Commission* [1992] 2 SCR 321 quoted in Lemmens, 2000). Indeed insurers have made the argument that only by obtaining full disclosure of risk, are they are able to place individuals in the appropriate premium category.

Insurers say that using this information allows them to ensure those with similar risks pay similar premiums (Lemmens, 2000).

In the absence of restrictions on the use of genetic information, full disclosure is the norm in the insurance field. Insurance contracts typically contain a clause that the insurer need not pay if the insured has not made full disclosure. In Quebec, a man named Tremblay was killed in a car accident. Following his death, the insurer discovered that when Tremblay had originally applied for life insurance, he had answered 'no' to a question asking if he had any physical or mental anomaly. In fact, although Tremblay had no symptoms, he knew that he had the genetic mutation for myotonic dystrophy, a condition his father and brother had developed. The insurer was able to refuse to pay the life insurance benefit because of the misrepresentation (*Audet v Industrielle-Alliance* [1990] RRA 500 (Sup Ct) referred to in Lemmens, 2000). Even where insurers cannot or do not require genetic testing, they can and do benefit from the results of genetic testing which has occurred.

In addition to life insurance, genetic information is relevant to travel insurance, health and disability insurance. Individuals may be required to obtain life insurance as a prerequisite to obtaining a mortgage or business loan. For example, in the UK, homeowners are required to obtain life insurance in order to obtain mortgages (Lemmens, 2000). The Association of British Insurers has agreed to extend a moratorium on using predictive genetic testing on life insurance policies under £500,000 until 2017 (Association of British Insurers (ABI), 2013).

Outside the insurance context, such information could affect access to employment, housing, adoption or any other activity where the other party perceives it to be in its interests to avoid entering into a relationship with someone at higher risk of developing Alzheimer's disease (Halliday et al, 2004). In the absence of legislation, it is an easy matter to require applicants to consent to genetic testing and to make the validity of the proposed contract dependant upon the presence or absence of certain genetic markers. This would certainly be differential treatment. Presumably, the justification for the differential treatment would be the presence of a genetic indication that the party has a greater likelihood of becoming a higher cost (or less convenient) tenant or employee. The issue here is whether such a justification should be seen as sufficient. This issue remains the same whether discrimination is based on actual knowledge, or merely a perception of dementia, as in the following example.

Beatrice Baum, a clerical worker for a community college in New York, alleged her employer discriminated against her based on perceived dementia. The parties were able to arrive at a mediated settlement agreement, but following that settlement agreement, the employer purported to require Baum to submit to an intrusive physical examination as a condition of returning to work. This requirement was found to be retaliation, either for Baum's original complaint of being discriminated against for perceived dementia, or for comments she made during the mediation which flowed from the complaint (Mental and Physical Disability Law Reporter, 2004).

A second sphere of a person's relationship with dementia where an individual may face discrimination is where the individual's memory and other cognitive problems have manifested themselves. Of course, human rights legislation would typically be triggered as such cognitive issues constitute a disability. Generally human rights legislation affords protection from discrimination based on disability. However, systemic decisions can and are being made which discriminate against people with dementia. For example, Britain's National Institute for Health and Clinical (now Care) Excellence has argued that the National Health Service (NHS) should not be permitted to supply dementia treatment drugs to NHS patients because they cost too much (Harris, 2005).

Dementia will bring about a profound change in the way in which some people interact with the world. Memory problems cause loved ones and places to be forgotten. Mood symptoms and definite changes in personality may occur (Holmes, 2012: 629). This challenges us to examine issues of discrimination in light of who the individual is, not who the individual was. We often long to have loved ones remain who they were, and not who they have become. W Somerset Maugham poetically put it this way: 'We are not the same person this year as last; nor are those we love. It is a happy chance if we, changing, continue to love a changed person' (Maugham, 1938). All of us change over time. Generally evidence seems to indicate that each of us recognizes changes in our own values, preferences and personalities that have occurred over time. In other words, we recognize that many aspects of the traits that make us distinct, that make us who we are in a sense, have changed. Paradoxically, we generally have difficulty imagining that we will continue to change into the future. We believe we 'have arrived', and that who we are, is who we will be. This phenomenon has been called the 'end of history illusion' (Quoidbach et al, 2013). To put it another way, 'present me' can recognize the difference between 'present me' and 'past me', but cannot foresee the difference between 'present me' and 'future me'. While we may recognize the significant changes that have occurred in ourselves, we live in the present. We exercise our autonomy based on who we are now. Our current wants, values, preferences and personalities inform our choices.

Changes in values, preferences and personalities can sometimes be dramatic and quick in individuals with dementia. Changes which occur quickly, and which are brought on by a medically labelled condition will be much more difficult for others to accept, as compared with relatively slow changes brought on by 'life experience' and 'normal ageing'. This raises a fundamental question regarding labelling actions and systems that do not respect the autonomy of individuals with dementia, as discriminatory.

Do individuals with dementia have a right to autonomy? Dementia has been characterized as 'a progressive loss of the capacities on which autonomy is based' (Defanti et al, 2007). Of course, there are many views as to what autonomy is, and in fact, as to how autonomous any of us really are. Autonomy may be related to capacity, but they are not twins. A loss of capacity does not necessarily mandate a commensurate loss of autonomy. It is uncontroversial to believe that 'those with capacity deserve autonomy' (or at least as much relative autonomy as the context in which they exist makes reasonable). It is a fallacy, however, to then make the logical mis-step that therefore those without capacity do not deserve autonomy. This fallacy is so common it has its own name. It is known as 'denying the antecedent', or 'fallacy of the inverse'.

Our right to autonomy must surely be based on our humanity, not our capacity. Capacity deals with the issue of whether or not the relevant legal system recognizes an individual's right to make particular decisions. Autonomy is more fundamental. It is generally concerned with our right to make and implement our choices. Of course, the range of choices we are able to make and implement varies according to the context of our lives. For some, autonomy is seen as a very individualistic concept, while for others it is a concept exercised only within a network of social and familial relationships (Herring, 2013: 71–73). Whatever the precise content of autonomy, our claim to it is based on our humanity. Whatever changes dementia has brought about in individuals, those individuals' humanity, and therefore their claim to some form and extent of autonomy, remains. Factors such as the stigma of dementia, our desire for our loved one to be how they were (and who they were) and our own fear of change which might be visited upon us, can lead to dehumanizing descriptions of individuals with dementia. People with dementia are recreated as the living dead; breathing but not really human any more (Behuniak, 2011). It is important, particularly for caregivers and others opposed to discrimination, to reaffirm the essential humanity of individuals with dementia. While the autonomy exercised by individuals with dementia will be limited and balanced with other ethical considerations, we must strive to respect an appropriate level and kind of autonomy.

A tenant who develops dementia may be troublesome, and not a particularly desirable tenant for a landlord or patient for a health care facility. Certainly residents in senior care facilities who develop dementia have additional needs and require additional resources from the care facility and staff. Care homes are typically subject to different regulations depending upon the level of care provided. There has been a 'blurring of the lines' between health care facilities—which have the right to legitimately make medical decisions based on disability—and private housing developments, which do not. As creative home care alternatives increase, it may become increasingly difficult to make meaningful distinctions between some types of housing (Kane, 1995). Private rental homes supported by a myriad of private and public home care services may be hard to distinguish from a care home. This may raise issues if private rental homes and care homes are subject to different regulations.

Health care facilities are often required to make medical decisions, which treat people differently because of their medical condition. Not every decision a health care facility makes however is a medical decision. Margaret Wagner had Alzheimer's disease, which was accompanied by symptoms including aggressive behaviour, screaming and agitation. She was denied admittance to a 900-bed care facility called 'Fair Acres' because of these behavioural manifestations. She was admitted to another facility that was located further away from her husband and children. Fair Acres said they were not staffed or set up to manage Ms Wagner's behaviour. They claimed that the decision not to admit Ms Wagner was a medical decision and therefore the relevant anti-discrimination legislation did not apply. The court determined that the admission decision was not a medical decision. They found Fair Acres could make changes to provide the care and supervision that Ms Wagner required, without incurring an undue burden or altering the essential nature of their programme. As a result, Fair Acres was required to admit Ms Wagner as a resident (Mental and Physical Disability Law Reporter, 1995).

In New Jersey, the son and caregiver of a woman named Viciliki Nicolas alleged a condo board had discriminated against his mother by refusing to allow her an appropriate parking space. Ms Nicolas had dementia (as well using a wheelchair and having sight and hearing impairments). In reviewing the case the court made it clear that condo boards must accommodate individuals with disabilities by providing them with parking spaces in appropriate locations. The issue in Ms Nicolas' case was simply whether the parking space which Ms Nicolas had requested (and which was assigned to another tenant but had been used by Nicolas prior to the sale of that unit) was the only one which would provide appropriate accommodation for her, or alternatively whether either of the two alternative parking spaces offered by the condo board were appropriate accommodation for Ms Nicolas. After stating the law, the court referred the application of the law in this case to a jury (as the finder of fact) (Mental and Physical Disability Law Reporter, 2007).

Decisions such as these are real world examples of trying to determine the appropriate level and kind of autonomy for people with dementia. Such decisions occur in a variety of contexts. Employees who develop dementia may well place additional burdens on employers or may make more extensive use of benefit plans thus representing additional costs to the employer. Landlords, care facilities and employers may financially benefit simply by refusing to 'do business' with individuals with a certain genetic makeup, or who display certain symptoms of dementia. This of course limits the autonomy of the person with dementia (or with the apparent predisposition towards dementia) by limiting their access to housing, care and employment.

Reasonable people may disagree on what it actually means to respect an appropriate level and kind of autonomy in specific circumstances. Consider, for example, the apparently widespread practice of caregivers covertly hiding a patient's or resident's medication in food or drink. Such a practice is surely forcibly medicating an individual. It is no different from applying a medicinal cream while the person sleeps, or secretly injecting a needle into the person (if it were possible to do so, such as where a person has no feeling in an area). Such actions by caregivers may be rightly condemned in some circumstances and ethically justifiable in others. If the choice of whether or not to take the medication lies with the patient or resident, such surreptitious medication is wrong. It is wrong whether the medication is administered by trick, by stealth or indeed by force. Such surreptitious medication may be ethical in a narrow range of cases, such as where the patient is temporarily incapable of exercising choice or foreseeing consequences, and there is a dire need for the medication (Jones, 2001). An example of this may be a temporarily irrational person who refuses an urgently required medication.

If we accept that individuals with dementia retain their claim on autonomy (given our different understandings of autonomy and our different understandings of the appropriateness of varying limitations on the exercise of that autonomy), we still must address another issue: to which self does autonomy relate? Is it the individual's past or present self? The very nature of changes to an individual's values, preferences and personality means that that individual will want different things and will value things differently. When the individual does not or cannot express choices, it makes sense to recognize their autonomy by ensuring that their choices are informed by the past self. Our knowledge of their past self in this context is the best guide to their current self. Without any conflicting information, it is reasonable to assume that someone who liked X in the past continues to like X in the present. Where the individual expresses desires or attempts to make choices which are inconsistent with those the past self would make, the individual's present choices should be respected, provided this is a choice the individual is free to make. The current self should not needlessly be a prisoner of the past self's values or wishes. Individuals with dementia will be discriminated against if they are assumed to lack autonomy generally. They will also be discriminated against where their present self is assumed to be a subject of their past self. Every person deserves the dignity of having their expressions of choice continually heard, and their choices respected within appropriate spheres. Instead, stigmatization and negative attitudes towards people with dementia has become embedded in our care systems to such an extent that they might go unnoticed (Chan and Chan, 2009). Autonomy withers in the face of such attitudes.

A third sphere of a person's relationship with dementia—where an individual may face discrimination—is when the dementia requires that the individual lives in long-term care. The need to live in long-term care imposes limitations on the choices and freedoms of all residents. Residents with dementia, however, can face discrimination beyond these generalized limitations on choices and freedoms. This discrimination can be by virtue of the design of long-term care facilities and the organization of the institution and its workforce.

Residents with dementia can require a different range of services from other residents. Often facilities must be locked and organized in such a way as to reduce the risk of harm to the resident and to other residents. Often residents with dementia are housed together, away from other residents. Some individuals with dementia become physically or sexually aggressive and it is essential that measures taken to protect some residents do not expose other residents to unjustifiable risk. Certainly providing long-term care to residents with dementia can be extremely challenging. At times residents with dementia will be treated differently from other residents because of their symptoms or behaviour—being required to live in locked wards is an example. However, facilities and organizational structures must be created or modified so that differential treatment imposed upon individuals with dementia is justified. For example, a long-term care home would certainly be expected to take risk minimization steps where a mobile individual with dementia is sexually exploiting, physically intimidating or assaulting residents of a long-term care home. However, simply moving that individual to a 'dementia ward' and thus exposing residents of that ward to the same risk would not be justified. Further measures would have to be taken to ensure, as far as possible, that those residents were not exposed to a higher risk simply because they have dementia. Similarly, simply because individuals have dementia, long-term care institutions may have to take additional measures in some circumstances to provide those residents with the same level of protection and benefits as other residents. Fair Acres was required to accept Ms Wagner as a resident. Had she been required to live in the other facility available to her, she would have been further away from her family. She would have been disadvantaged by not being able to live in the care home of her choice, and by being forced to live further away from her family (and therefore to make it more difficult for them to see her) simply because the administrators of Fair Acres wanted to accept residents who were easier to care for. Her autonomy would have been needlessly compromised.

Where separate facilities are justified they should be provided. The justification will usually relate to the safety and well-being of the individual with dementia, and sometimes to the protection of other residents. Such justification for separate facilities or wards does not carry over to justify differential treatment in other areas, such as the availability of programming, choice of food and so on. In areas where differential treatment is not justified, those who design care homes, organize its workforce, develop rules and procedures or deliver services, owe it to individuals with dementia to ensure that they are treated with an even hand with respect to other residents in care.

Discrimination against individuals with dementia occurs whenever they are afforded unjustified differential treatment. Some of this discriminatory treatment will be prohibited under human rights legislation in force in the jurisdiction; a great deal of other discriminatory action will not be. Preventing and stopping such discrimination will at times require additional legislation. Preventing discrimination based on the results of genetic testing is such an example. Sometimes stopping discrimination is best achieved by having recourse to human rights or other legislation. Often the path to ending discrimination begins by recognizing it for what it is. We must recognize that the way in which we choose to do everything we do as we interact with individuals with dementia, creates the potential for differential treatment in the form of negative effects on individuals with dementia. These negative effects may be the result of our actions, the way health services are delivered or the way home care services are organized. They may be the unintended consequence of rules designed to organize work places or for other purposes. Whatever the cause of the differential treatment, to correct it we first must recognize it, and then we must ask, 'Is this justified?'

REFERENCES

Association of British Insurers (ABI) webpage (2013). Available at: www.abi.org.uk/News/News-releases/2011/04/Insurance-Genetics-Moratorium-extended-to-2017.

Behuniak, SM (2011) 'The living dead? The construction of people with Alzheimer's disease as zombies' 31(1) *Aging & Society* 70–92.

Chan, PA and Chan, T (2009) 'The impact of discrimination against older people with dementia and its impact on student nurses' professional socialisation' 9(4) *Nurse Education in Practice* 221–27.

Defanti, CA et al (2007) 'Ethical questions in the treatment of subjects with dementia, Part 1, Respecting autonomy: awareness, competence and behavioural disorders' 28(4) *Neurological Science* 216–31.

Gin, B (1997) 'Genetic Discrimination: Huntington's Disease and the Americans with Disabilities Act' 97(5) *Columbia Law Review* 1406–34.

Greely, HT (2001) 'Genotype Discrimination: The Complex Case for Some Legislative Protection' 149(5) *University of Pennsylvania Law Review* 1483–1505.

Halliday, J et al (2004) 'Genetics and Public Health: Evolution or Revolution?' 58(11) *Journal of Epidemiology and Community Health* 894–99.

Harris, J (2005) 'It's not NICE to discriminate' (editorial) 31(7) *Journal of Medical Ethics* 373–75.

Herring, J (2013) *Caring and the Law* (Oxford, Hart Publishing).

Holmes, C (2012) 'Dementia' 40(11) *Psychiatric Disorder Medicine* 628–31.

Jones, RG (2001) 'Ethical and legal issues in the care of people with dementia' 11 *Reviews in Clinical Gerontology* 245–68.

Kane, RA (1995) 'Expanding the Home Care Concept: Blurring Distinctions among Home Care, Institutional Care, and Other Long-Term-Care Services' 73(2) *The Millbank Quarterly* 161–86.

Lemmens, T (2000) 'Selective Justice, Genetic Discrimination, and Insurance: Should we Single Out Genes in our Laws?' 45(2) *McGill Law Journal* 347–412.

Maugham, W Somerset (1938) *The Summing Up* (Garden City, NY Doubleday).

Mental and Physical Disability Law Reporter 19(4) (July/August 1995) 492–98.

Mental and Physical Disability Law Reporter 28(3) (May/June 2004) 421–22.

Mental and Physical Disability Law Reporter 31(1) (January/February 2007) 112–14.

Preston, C and McCann, E (2012) 'Llewellyn Slept Here: A Short History of Sticky Contracts and Feudalism' 91 *Oregon Law Review* 129–75.

Quoidbach, J, Gilbert, DT and Wilson, TD (4 January 2013) 'The End of History Illusion' 339(6115) *Science* 96–98.

36

Physical, Financial and other Abuse

RUIJIA CHEN, E-SHIEN CHANG, MELISSA SIMON AND XINQI DONG[1]

INTRODUCTION

ELDER ABUSE IS the abuse or neglect directed at a person aged 60 or above by a caregiver or another person in a relationship involving an expectation of trust (Center for Disease Control and Prevention, 2013). Elder abuse is a worldwide social and health issue that occurs across all racial and ethnic groups. According to the World Health Organization, the prevalence of elder abuse in developed countries ranges from 1% to 10%. The US National Elder Mistreatment Study, conducted with a representative sample of 5777 adults aged 60 years and older, reported that more than 10% of community-dwelling elderly people experienced abuse or potential neglect in the past year (Acierno et al, 2010). Elder abuse is associated with adverse health outcomes, and more importantly, it has been linked to an increased risk of morbidity and mortality (Lachs et al, 1998; Dong et al, 2009).

Abuse of the elderly takes multiple forms, including physical abuse, psychological abuse, sexual abuse, elder caregiver neglect, financial exploitation and elder self-neglect. Physical abuse refers to the force against an elderly person which results in physical pain, injury or impairment. Psychological abuse is defined as the use of verbal, written or gestured communication directed at an elderly person that causes emotional distress. Sexual abuse is any sexual contact with an elderly person without his or her consent. Elder caregiver neglect is the failure to provide basic necessary care or services when such failure may lead to physical or emotional harm or serious loss of personal dignity. Financial exploitation involves the illegal or improper use of an elderly person's funds or property. Different from other forms of abuse that have a perpetrator, elder self-neglect is the result of an older adult's inability to

[1] Dr Dong is supported by the National Institute on Aging grant (R01 AG042318, R01 MD006173, R01 AG11101 & RC4 AG039085); Paul B Beeson Award in Aging (K23 AG030944); the Starr Foundation; the American Federation for Aging Research; John A Hartford Foundation and the Atlantic Philanthropies. We are grateful to Community Advisory Board members for their continued effort in this project. Particular thanks are extended to: Bernie Wong, Vivian Xu, Yicklun Mo from the Chinese American Service League (CASL); Dr David Lee from Illinois College of Optometry; David Wu from the Pui Tak Center; Dr Hong Liu from the Midwest Asian Health Association; Dr Margaret Dolan from the John H Stroger Jr Hospital; Mary Jane Welch from Rush University Medical Center; Florence Lei from CASL Pine Tree Council; Julia Wong from CASL Senior Housing; Dr Jing Zhang from Asian Human Services; Marta Pereya from the Coalition of Limited English Speaking Elderly and Mona El-Shamaa from the Asian Health Coalition.

perform essential daily care tasks, including providing adequate food, water, clothing, shelter, personal hygiene, medication and safety precautions. Elder self-neglect is the most common category of elder abuse, representing between 40% and 50% of cases reported to Adult Protective Services (APS) (National Center on Elder Abuse, 2010).

Dementia is an umbrella term that describes a group of symptoms caused by brain disease or injury. Its features include loss of memory, communication and language ability and reduced capability in focusing and paying attention. With the 'greying' of the global population, the number of people with dementia is estimated to increase to 115.4 million in 2050 (Prince et al, 2013). Dementia has far-reaching personal and economic implications: it is likely to affect both caregivers' and recipients' quality of life and cause significant health and social issues.

Elder abuse in people with dementia is a pressing issue. It is estimated that a person with Alzheimer's disease is 2.25 times more likely to be physically abused than other older persons living in the community (Paveza et al, 1992). Prevalence estimates suggest that elder abusive behaviour towards demented patients ranges from 15% to 62.3% (Paveza et al, 1992; Cooper et al, 2009; Wiglesworth et al, 2010; Yan and Kwok, 2011). With the rapidly increasing ageing population around the world, it is imperative to improve our understanding of dementia and elder abuse.

RISK FACTORS ASSOCIATED WITH ELDER ABUSE IN DEMENTIA PATIENTS

Compared with abuse in older adults without dementia, elder abuse or neglect in the demented population is more likely to be directed by caregivers or by demented patients themselves (Burgess and Phillips, 2006). Existing literature on the association between dementia and elder abuse mainly focuses on individual pathologies of victims and perpetrators.

Victim Characteristics

Socio-Demographic Characteristics

Previous research has documented inconsistent results on the possible association between age and sex of dementia patients and the occurrence of elder abuse. A telephone survey of 82 community-dwelling caregivers reported that younger demented patients have a higher possibility of suffering from verbal abuse (Cooney et al, 2006). In contrast, other studies have not found any difference in terms of age and sex between elder abuse victims and non-victims (Cooney and Mortimer, 1995; Compton et al, 1997). Different research methodology and population settings may account for the inconsistency in findings.

Physical and Cognitive Functional Status

The prevalence and severity of elder abuse in people with dementia are associated with patients' functional status. Caregivers for demented patients with lower levels of physical functioning are more likely to report engaging in abuse (Coyne et al, 1993). Patients with lower functional status are in need of more intensive care, which in turn, may increase caregiver burdens and give rise to elder abuse. Similarly, lower cognitive function is associated with a higher possibility of abuse occurrence. In a population-based study of 238 community-dwelling older adults with elder abuse experience, Dong et al found that lower global cognitive function level (OR 4.18, 95% CI 2.44–7.15), MMSE (OR 2.97, 95% CI 1.93–4.57), episodic memory (OR 2.27, 95% CI 1.49–3.43) and perceptual speeds (OR 2.37, 95% CI 1.51–3.73) are associated with increased risks of elder abuse (Dong et al, 2011c).

In addition, the severity of cognitive function decline is positively associated with a higher risk of caregiver neglect in institutional facilities. A prior study found that nurses in long-term care facilities may feel no need to talk to demented patients due to the patients' communication problems (Ekman and Norberg, 1988). They tend to rank and devote their care according to the patients' degrees of capacity: the more severe the cognitive impairment, the less care may be provided (Ekman et al, 1991).

Psychopathological Symptoms

Agitation and aggression are among the most common and problematic symptoms occurring in dementia. As one of the most challenging aspects of dementia care, behaviour disturbance increases caregiver workload and stress and intensifies caregiver–patient conflicts (Leonard, 2006; Sloane et al, 2004). Studies have implicated a strong relationship between behaviour disturbance and elder abuse. In a study of 82 community-dwelling caregivers, demented elder abuse victims reported significantly higher behaviour disturbances than those non-victims ($t = -2.7$, $p < 0.01$). More specifically, overt behavioural disturbance and mood disorders have stronger associations with verbal abuse than apathetic withdrawn behaviours (Cooney et al, 2006). Another study with a convenience sample of 129 caregiver–care recipient dyads revealed that patients who direct physical assaults and psychological aggression towards their caregivers are more likely to be victims of elder abuse (Wiglesworth et al, 2010). Behaviour disturbances of demented patients may be more severe and more frequent in long-term facilities. Nurses may feel the need to resort to abuse in order to manage their frustration resulting from patients' disorderly conduct (Eriksson and Saveman, 2002).

Caregiver Characteristics

Socio-Demographic Characteristics

Studies on the relationship between caregivers' socio-demographic characteristics and elder abuse have yielded divergent results. One study suggests that being a male caregiver, lacking adequate economic resources and sharing living arrangements with a care recipient may be associated with an increased risk of exhibiting abusive behaviour towards patients (Cooper et al, 2008). However, there is also evidence that shows no significant difference between abusive caregivers and non-abusive caregivers in terms of socio-demographic characteristics (Cooney et al, 2006).

Caregiver Burden and Stress

Taking care of a demented patient is challenging and burdensome. Caregivers of older adults with dementia experience a higher level of burden because of great physical and time demands. As the disease progresses, patients' care needs also increase. Bearing a higher level of burden is associated with an increased incidence of abusive behaviours towards care recipients. Being a caregiver for more years, providing more hours' care per day and caring for patients with higher levels of impairment are likely to increase the occurrence of abusive behaviours (Coyne et al, 1993).

Caregivers' objective and subjective burdens are both associated with elder abuse. Compared with objective caregiver burdens, subjective burdens—including the perception of stress, caregivers' responses to the situation and the nature of the caregiver–recipient relationship—play a more crucial role in explaining abusive behaviours. Caregiver stress mainly stems from an overwhelming burden and ineffective coping strategies, and is likely to cause significant health issues (Son et al, 2007; Schulz and Martire, 2004). Higher levels of stress in turn reduce caregivers' coping abilities and trigger potential elder abuse. In institutional facilities, the burden and stress of dementia care are much higher and more difficult to manage given an excessive number of patients and a limited number of staff. Nurses may resort to abuse to deal with overwhelming feelings of being powerless and stressed (Eriksson and Saveman, 2002).

Psychological Well-Being

Caregivers' psychological well-being is closely correlated with abusive behaviours towards demented older adults. Depression—the most common psychological symptom in caregivers of demented patients—has been identified as a key risk factor for elder abuse (Paveza et al, 1992). As for the subtype of abuse, higher levels of depression in caregivers are associated with exhibiting physically abusive behaviours (Cooney and Mortimer, 1995).

Substance Abuse

Substance abuse also emerges as an important predictor of elder abuse. Under the influence of alcohol or drugs, caregivers are more likely to use violence as a conflict resolution strategy (Choi and Mayer, 2000). A study of 254 caregivers and 76 elders with Alzheimer's disease supports this view by showing that caregivers who abused alcohol are three times more likely to exhibit physically abusive behaviours towards dementia patients (VandeWeerd and Paveza, 2005). In addition, dependent caregivers with substance abuse problems may be more likely to be involved in financial abuse to provide money for drug or alcohol consumption.

Social Support

Social support is a strong mediator for elder abuse in demented patients (Lee, 2008). Social support reduces elder abuse occurrence through improving caregiver self-efficacy—the caregiver's belief in his or her ability to manage difficult tasks and deal with care recipients' behaviour problems. Increasing the availability and accessibility of social support is likely to improve caregivers' confidence in stressful caregiving situations, and thus reduce the chance of abuse. Social support also buffers the burden and stress on caregivers' well-being and reduces the incidence of elder abuse. Social isolation, on the contrary, increases the likelihood of caregivers directing abuse towards demented older adults (Cooney and Mortimer, 1995). Caregivers of demented patients are limited in their personal and social activities, which may exacerbate the sense of helplessness and loneliness and increase the possibility of admitting to abuse.

Premorbid Relationships

The quality of premorbid relationships between caregivers and demented patients also influences the likelihood of elder abuse occurrence. High premorbid relationship satisfaction reduces the care burden and enhances the quality of care, whereas a problematic premorbid relationship may lead to negative moods and abusive behaviours. Elder abuse in community-dwelling populations could be the consequence of long-term family violence. The experience of child abuse or domestic abuse may affect caregivers' reactions towards the problem behaviours of demented patients, increase caregiver burden and decrease communication efficiency and coping skills (Steadman et al, 2007). A study with a cohort from a psychiatry of old age service in rural Ireland has demonstrated that abusers had significantly poorer premorbid relationships with the patients than non-abusers (Compton et al, 1997)

OUTCOMES ASSOCIATED WITH ELDER ABUSE IN PEOPLE WITH DEMENTIA

Elder abuse in demented older adults may cause serious short-term and long-term health issues, including physical impairment, psychological distress and increased intervention and medical cost.

Elder abuse may result in immediate physical problems such as wounds and injuries, continued physical pain and nutrition and hydration issues, which exacerbate demented patients' functional problems and place them at a higher risk of morbidity and mortality. For instance, Dong matched data from the Chicago Health and Aging Project to suspected elder abuse cases reported to social services agencies in a 12-year period. The findings suggested that elder abuse and neglect in older adults with all levels of cognitive function is associated with increased risks of mortality (Dong, 2009).

In addition to impacting physical and psychological well-being, elder abuse may lead to increased social, economic and medical costs. Studies have demonstrated that elder abuse is associated with increased rates of nursing home placement, emergency department and adult protective services utilization (Dong and Simon, 2013; Lachs et al, 2002). Health departments and social agencies are required to develop interventions to combat elder abuse. Costs relating to social services, criminal justice, education and research increase as the number of elder abuse cases rises. The occurrence of elder abuse also adds burden and complexity to the management of institutional care.

DISCUSSION

Given the frailty of demented older adults combined with the sensitive nature of elder abuse issues, it is not unusual for researchers in the field of elder abuse and dementia to come across a wide range of salient methodological, ethical and cultural issues.

Methodological Issues

There are a variety of methods for assessing elder abuse, including record review, sentinel reports, criminal justice statistics translation and telephone or-in person surveys of victims, family or caretakers (Acierno, 2003). Detecting elder abuse among demented patients is more challenging than in general populations. Cognitive decline impairs older adults' ability to report abuse cases and impedes the detection of abuse. Traditional survey methods which require intact cognitive ability may therefore not be appropriate for demented patients. One common methodology used in the literature to assess elder abuse in demented patients is through interviewing caregivers directly. Despite the fact that the majority of caregivers are willing to participate and answer questions regarding elder abuse or neglect, the severity of the problems may be under reported. Therefore, the approach of collecting data from caregivers should be carried out with caution. A better way to approach caregivers with respect to elder abuse maybe to start asking questions about the difficulties of caring, then move on to any frustrations caregivers may experience and the abusive behaviours caregivers may direct towards patients (Cooney and Mortimer, 1995). It is also of great importance to build rapport with caregivers in order to collect more reliable data.

Ethical Issues

Investigators may encounter a wide range of ethical dilemmas while seeking to meet the requirements of the institutional review board as well as collecting the most reliable data. Informed consent is one of the major issues involved in studies with the demented population. Dementia is accompanied by a decrease in decision-making capacity, including the ability to communicate a choice, to understand relevant information, to appreciate how the information applies to one's situation and to give comprehensive reasons for a decision (Appelbaum and Grisso, 1988). Whereas demented older adults may have decision-making difficulties, obtaining proxy consent or asking for assent from demented patients is employed in several studies as a solution to this ethical issue (Black et al, 2013).

Another ethical issue concerns the confidentiality of studying elder abuse. Elder abuse is a sensitive topic. In some cultures, people perceive elder abuse as a private family issue and find it shameful to report (Dong et al, 2011a; Dong et al, 2007). Releasing personal information may cause worry and anxiety, and increase the risk of abuse recurring. Protecting vulnerable participants from potential harm therefore requires special consideration.

Furthermore, the study of elder abuse in demented patients involves the reporting of abuse. Mandatory reporting statutes require individuals to report injuries or cases of abuse or neglect to law enforcement, social services and/or a regulatory agency. The report of elder abuse in the US varies from state to state. Some require all parties to have the responsibility of reporting elder abuse, while others require only professionals to be the mandatory reporters. Elder abuse law in Illinois, for instance, requires clergy, doctors, nurses, nursing home aides, psychologists and social workers to report elder abuse cases. The mandatory reporting statute is controversial. Supporters claim that mandatory reporting helps victims identify the service they need and enhances health professionals' awareness. However, the motivation of reporting elder abuse may be impaired by the risk of retaliation by the perpetrators as well as the possible negative effects on the physician–patient relationship (Rodriguez et al, 2006). Moreover, opponents may cast doubt on the effectiveness of case investigation because of a lack of resources and staff training in Adult Protective Services (Pillemer et al, 2007).

Voluntary reporting is particularly recommended for friends, relatives or neighbours of demented victims who lack the ability to self-report. A study of 284 cases of elder sexual abuse suggested that only one out of eight elders with dementia was able to self-report compared with five out of eight of the elders without dementia (Burgess and Phillips, 2006). The inability of demented patients to identify abuse emphasizes the important role played by observers in verifying and reporting abuse. In addition, there are no mandatory reporting requirements for elder self-neglect, which further highlights the significance of voluntary reporting in detecting elder abuse and neglect in demented patients.

Cultural Issues

Notable cultural variations exist in the knowledge of dementia and elder abuse in minority groups. The studies of elder abuse and dementia are more challenging and perplexing in the Asian population, where the culture is dominated by the value of filial piety and family collectivism. As the guiding principle of intergenerational relationships, filial piety strictly dictates children's obligatory roles and caregiving responsibilities to older adults. The emphasis on filial piety will improve family relationships while at the same time increase children's burdens and inflict family conflicts.

Dementia care in Asian populations is typically shaped by its culture. In Chinese culture, for example, dementia is considered by some people as a type of mental illness, and is always referred to as 'crazy' or 'catatonic' (Elliot et al, 1996). Family caregivers tend to confine patients at home so as to avoid social stigma and this great burden, together with the enduring social stigma, places caregivers at a higher level of stress which may lead to abusive behaviours. A study of 122 family caregivers of demented older adults in Hong Kong found that 62% of the caregivers had directed verbal or physical abuse at patients in the past month (Yan and Kwok, 2011). A study of 1000 primary caregivers of disabled elderly in Korea further suggested caregiver burden as the main risk factor for elder abuse in demented older adults ($\beta = 0.246$, $p < 0.001$) (Lee, 2008).

Despite growing interest in the study of elder abuse in minority groups, the prevalence and the extent of elder abuse still remain under-explored in diverse ethnic/racial groups. Cultural norms significantly influence older adults' perception of elder abuse and help-seeking behaviours. For example, compared with their Western counterparts, Asian older adults are more reluctant to disclose elder abuse for fear of losing support and family reputation. A community-based participatory research (CBPR) approach is recommended as effective for addressing elder abuse in minority populations (Dong et al, 2014. CBPR refers to 'a systematic inquiry with the participation of those affected by the issue being studied, for the purpose of education and taking action or affecting social change' (Green and Mercer, 2001). CBPR not only facilitates the recruitment and retention of potential and existing participants, but also enables researchers to gain a deeper understanding of local perceptions of elder abuse and dementia. Through integrating the collaborative efforts of community stakeholders, culturally-appropriate research methodology contributes to the salience of prevention and intervention (Dong et al, 2011d).

Programmes and Intervention

Intervention in elder abuse can be broadly categorized into two types: community service intervention and legal intervention. Both types of intervention require participants to maintain intact mental capabilities. Due to the impairment in the mental state of dementia patients, interventions in elder abuse in demented populations are more likely to target caregivers.

Community Services Programmes

Support Groups

Given that social support plays an important mediating role in reducing the incidence and severity of elder abuse, it is valuable to employ the support group approach to intervention in elder abuse. Support groups enable patients and caregivers to break through isolation, share experience and learn how to solve problems with others during traumatic times.

Despite the success of support groups, studies have found that intervention that offers combinations of individual or family counselling, case management, skills training and behaviour management strategies is more effective than intervention that only utilizes a support-group approach (Beach et al, 2005). A five-element intervention model which included a Homecare intervention team, the Indicators of Abuse Checklist (IOA), an Expert Consultant Team, a weekly Empowerment Support Group and an autonomous Community Senior Abuse Committee was developed by Reis and Nahmiash (1995). The results indicated that medical, nursing and rehabilitation strategies, as well as abuser/caregiver strategies, such as individual counselling, were recognized as the most successful channels for raising self-esteem. The intervention programme described by Norton and Manson (1997) also combined support groups with other strategies. The programme involved home visits and a weekly family violence group. The authors claimed that participants of the intervention programmes were able to build relationships with the counsellor and benefit from active participation.

Educational Therapy and Programmes

Caregivers may not consider abusive behaviours towards older adults with dementia to be as serious as that directed towards those without dementia (Matsuda, 2007). Educational programmes that improve both caregiver and demented victim awareness of elder abuse are therefore useful in reducing elder abuse. Since the association between caregiver distress and elder abuse is explained by the level of burden and a lack of coping strategies, programmes providing coping skills and knowledge are effective in combating elder abuse (Matsuda, 2007; Cooper et al, 2010). Moreover, programmes teaching patients ways of managing problematic behaviours and advising caregivers about how to react to behavioural problems appropriately, will decrease the likelihood of elder abuse occurring.

Legal Intervention

Adult Protective Services (APS)

The Adult Protective Services department is mandated by state law to protect and investigate cases of elder abuse and neglect. After receiving an abuse report, APS will evaluate the case and provide an emergency service if needed; it is also responsible for developing specific intervention plans for individual victims. The majority of services provided require consent from victims. Involuntary intervention is allowed for clients, such as demented patients, who have decision-making difficulties.

The Long-Term Care Ombudsman Programme

The Long-term Care Ombudsman Programme was created under the Older Americans Act (OAA) to protect older adults' rights and promote quality of life in long-term care facilities. It is responsible for informing residents and their families of their rights, resolving complaints, providing information on residents' needs and advocating for better care. The programme serves as an effective tool for stopping elder abuse in acute care settings (Harris-Wehling et al, 1995).

FUTURE RESEARCH

In spite of the contribution of recent work, knowledge gaps in our current understanding of elder abuse and dementia still exist. First, current studies on the relationship between demographic variables and elder abuse are inconsistent and inconclusive. Clarifying the association is crucial for developing tailored interventions. Large population studies are needed to shed light on these divergent findings.

Even though there is a growing body of literature that examines elder abuse in demented patients, the association between the types, intensity and severity of elder abuse with different levels of dementia remains unclear. Prior research postulated that elder abuse may differ with the severity of cognitive impairment, with financial exploitation being the most common in the early stage of dementia, physical abuse in the moderate stage and elder neglect in the advanced stage of dementia (Burnight and Mosqueda, 2011). In addition, the incidence of elder abuse may also vary with the severity of the disease. A qualitative study in Sweden found that caregiver burden in the initial stage is associated with increased elder abuse. However, two years later, no abusive behaviours were detected among the perpetrators. This suggests that abusive behaviours may decrease as dementia progesses (Grafstrom et al, 1992). Longitudinal cohort studies are needed to further explore elder abuse at different levels of dementia.

In addition, elder abuse in the demented population may vary by the subtypes and/or multiple forms of abuse. The majority of studies have examined the association between physical abuse or psychological abuse and dementia. However, as the number of financial abuse and sexual abuse cases reported has been increasing in recent years, the risk factors and outcomes of these subtypes of abuse in the demented population should be assessed in future research.

Another limitation concerns the study of minority groups. The US National Research Council called for more rigorous research on elder abuse and cultural diversity issues (National Research Council, 2003). Research is needed to facilitate the understanding of cultural norms and expectations in relation to caregiving of dementia patients and elder abuse in different racial/ ethnic populations.

PRACTICE AND POLICY IMPLICATIONS

The prevalence of elder abuse necessitates the development of policies and programmes by professionals in a variety of disciplines, including case managers, health practitioners and social workers.

Close monitoring and improved understanding of the risk factors associated with elder abuse in demented patients enable clinicians to better incorporate efforts from family members, social workers and other health professionals to improve demented patients' health conditions. Improved training should be provided to staff working with older adults with dementia. Risk assessment tools, policies and protocols should also be adjusted to include the risk factors of elder abuse.

For community gatekeepers, programmes should be developed to improve the availability of home care service for families with demented patients. The association of caregiver burden with elder abuse points to the importance of reducing caregiver burden in elder abuse intervention. A lack of regular caregiver assistance from community programmes is identified as one main source of stress (Griffin and Williams, 1992). Studies have demonstrated the effectiveness of home care service in reducing caregiver burden and improving the quality of care in disabled older adults (Dias et al, 2008). Support should also be provided for institutional caregivers. Interpersonal conflicts, overwhelming workload and problematic behaviours exhibited by patients are key factors associated with elder abuse in institutional care. Increasing effort should be put into improving staff coping strategies as well as the availability of care in institutional facilities.

Special attention should be drawn to the development and implementation of policies in protecting demented older adults. The Elder Justice Act is the first comprehensive legislation addressing elder abuse. It requires the development of grants and programmes, the establishment of an elder justice coordinating council, an advisory board on elder abuse and forensic centres and the improvement of long-term care. It was designed to direct the US Department of Justice to prevent elder abuse. Three other relevant elder abuse Acts—the Violence Against Women Act, Elder Abuse Victims Act and Older Americans Act—may also have an impact on the field of elder abuse (Dong and Simon, 2011). In spite of recent developments, there are major gaps in policies targeting the population with dementia.

CONCLUSION

Older adults with dementia are especially vulnerable to elder abuse. Patient and caregiver characteristics, including socio-demographic factors, functional status, psychopathological symptoms, caregiver stress and burden, premorbid relationships, psychological well-being, substance abuse and social support, are associated with elder abuse occurrence. Elder abuse in older adults with dementia may lead to a variety of social, health and economic issues. Given demented patients' inability to make decisions, research on elder abuse in demented patients may encounter methodological, ethical and cultural issues. Health professionals, community gatekeepers and caring family members share a collective responsibility for elder abuse detection, intervention and prevention. Improved public health policies are needed to support caregivers and the demented elderly.

REFERENCES

Acierno, R et al (2010) 'Prevalence and correlates of emotional, physical, sexual, and financial abuse and potential neglect in the United States: The National Elder Mistreatment Study' 100(2) *American Journal of Public Health* 292–97.

Acierno, R et al (2003) 'Assessing elder victimization' 38(11) *Social Psychiatry and Psychiatric Epidemiology* 644–53.

Appelbaum, PS and Grisso, T (1988) 'Assessing Patients' Capacities to Consent to Treatment' 319(25) *New England Journal of Medicine* 1635–38.

Beach, SR et al (2005) 'Risk factors for potentially harmful informal caregiver behavior' 53(2) *Journal of the American Geriatrics Society* 255–61.

Black, BS, Wechsler, M and Fogarty, L (2013) 'Decision making for participation in dementia research' 21(4) *American Journal of Geriatric Psychiatry* 355–63.

Burgess, AW and Phillips, SL (2006) 'Sexual abuse and dementia in older people' 54(7) *Journal of the American Geriatrics Society* 1154–55.

Burnight, K and Mosqueda L (2011) 'Theoretical Model Development in Elder Mistreatment' US Department of Justice.

Center for Disease Control and Prevention (2013) Elder Maltreatment Prevention. Available at: www.cdc.gov/features/elderabuse/.

Choi, NG and Mayer, J (2000) 'Elder Abuse, Neglect, and Exploitation' 33(2) *Journal of Gerontological Social Work* 5–25.

Compton, SA, Flanagan, P and Gregg, W (1997) 'Elder abuse in people with dementia in Northern Ireland: Prevalence and predictors in cases referred to a psychiatry of old age service' 12 *International Journal of Geriatric Psychiatry* 632–35.

Cooney, C, Howard, R and Lawlor, B (2006) 'Abuse of vulnerable people with dementia by their carers: Can we identify those most at risk?' 21(6) *International Journal of Geriatric Psychiatry* 564–71.

Cooney, C and Mortimer, A (1995) 'Elder abuse and dementia: A pilot study' 41(4) *International Journal of Social Psychiatry* 276–83.

Cooper, C et al (2008) 'Screening for elder abuse in dementia in the LASER-AD study: Prevalence, correlates and validation of instruments' 23(3) *International Journal of Geriatric Psychiatry* 283–88.

—— (2009) 'Abuse of people with dementia by family carers: Representative cross sectional survey' 338 *British Medical Journal* 1–5.

—— (2010) 'The determinants of family carers' abusive behaviour to people with dementia: Results of the CARD study' 121(1–2) *Journal of Affective Disorders* 136–42.

Coyne, AC, Reichman, WE and Berbig, LJ (1993) 'The relationship between dementia and elder abuse' 150(4) *American Journal of Psychiatry* 643–46.

Dias, A et al (2008) 'The effectiveness of a home care program for supporting caregivers of persons with dementia in developing countries: A randomized controlled trial from Goa, India' 3 *PLoSOne* e2333.

Dong, X and Simon, MA (2011) 'Enhancing national policy and programs to address elder abuse' 305(23) *Journal of the American Medical Association* 2460–61.

—— (2013) 'Association between elder abuse and use of ED: Findings from the Chicago Health and Aging Project' 31(4) *American Journal of Emergency Medicine* 693–98.

Dong, X, Simon, MA and Gorbien, M (2007) 'Elder abuse and neglect in an urban Chinese population' 19(3–4) *Journal of Elder Abuse & Neglect* 79–96.

Dong, X et al (2009) 'Elder self-neglect and abuse and mortality risk in a community-dwelling population' 302(5) *Journal of the American Medical Association* 517–26.

—— (2011a) 'How do US Chinese older adults view elder mistreatment?: Findings from a community-based participatory research study' 23(2) *Journal of Aging Health* 289–312.

—— (2011b) 'Assessing the Health Needs of Chinese Older Adults: Findings from a Community-Based Participatory Research Study in Chicago's Chinatown' 2010 *Journal of Aging Research*. doi: 10.4061/2010/124246.

—— (2011c) 'Association of cognitive function and risk for elder abuse in a community-dwelling population' 32(3) *Dementia and Geriatric Cognitive Disorders* 209–15.

—— (2011d) 'Working with culture: lessons learned from a community-engaged project in a Chinese aging population' 7(4) *Aging Health* 529–37.

Dong, X et al (2014) 'Association of depressive symptomatology and elder mistreatment in a US Chinese population: Findings from a community-based participatory research study' *Journal of Aggression, Maltreatment & Trauma* 23(1), 81–98.

Ekman, SL, and Norberg, A (1988) 'The autonomy of demented patients: interviews with caregivers' *Journal of Medical Ethics*, 14(4), 184–87.

Ekman, SL et al (1991) 'Care of demented patients with severe communication problems' 5(3) *Scandinavian Journal of Caring Sciences* 163–70.

Elliot, KS et al (1996) 'Working with Chinese Families in the context of dementia' in G Yeo and D Gallagher-Thompson (eds), *Ethnicity and the Dementias* (Washington, DC, Taylor & Francis).

Eriksson, C and Saveman, BI (2002) 'Nurses' experiences of abusive/non-abusive caring for demented patients in acute care settings' 16(1) *Scandinavian Journal of Caring Sciences* 79–85.

Grafstrom, M, Norberg, A and Wimblad, B (1992) 'Abuse is in the eye of the beholder. Reports by family members about abuse of demented persons in home care. A total population-based study' 21(4) *Scandinavian Journal of Social Medicine* 247–55.

Green, LW and Mercer, SL (2001) 'Can public health researchers and agencies reconcile the push from funding bodies and the pull from communities?' 91(12) *American Journal of Public Health* 1926–29.

Griffin, L and Williams, O (1992) 'Abuse among African-American elderly' 7(1) *Journal of Family Violence* 19–35.

Harris-Wehling, J, Feasley, JC and Estes, CL (1995) *Real People Real Problems: An evaluation of the Long-Term Care Ombudsman programs of the Older Americans Act* (Washington DC, Institute of Medicine).

Homer, AC and Gilleard, C (1990) 'Abuse of elderly people by their carers' 301(6765) *British Medical Journal* 1359–62.

Lachs, MS et al (1998) 'The mortality of elder mistreatment' 280(5) *Journal of the American Medical Association* 428–32.

—— (2002) 'Adult protective service use and nursing home placement' 42(6) *Gerontologist* 734–39.

Lee, M (2008) 'Caregiver stress and elder abuse among Korean family caregivers of older adults with disabilities' 23(8) *Journal of Family Violence* 707–12.

Leonard, R (2006) 'Potentially modifiable resident characteristics that are associated with physical or verbal aggression among nursing home residents with dementia' 166(12) *Archives of Internal Medicine* 1295–1300.

Matsuda, O (2007) 'An assessment of the attitudes of potential caregivers toward the abuse of elderly persons with and without dementia' 19(5) *International Psychogeriatrics* 892–901.

National Center on Elder Abuse (2010) *A Response to the Abuse of Vulnerable Adults: The 2000 Survey of State adult protective services* (Washington, DC).

Norton, IM and Manson, SM (1997) 'Domestic violence intervention in an urban Indian health center' 33(4) *Community Mental Health Journal* 331–37.

Paveza, GJ et al (1992) 'Severe family violence and Alzheimer's disease: Prevalence and risk factors' 32(4) *Gerontologist* 493–97.

Pillemer, KA et al (2007) 'Interventions to prevent elder mistreatment' in LS Doll et al (eds), *Handbook of Injury and Violence Prevention* (New York, Springer).

Prince, M et al (2013) 'The global prevalence of dementia: A systematic review and metaanalysis' 9(1) *Alzheimer's & Dementia:* The Journal of the Alzheimer's Association 63–75.

Reis, M and Nahmiash, D (1995) 'When seniors are abused: An intervention model' 35(5) *Gerontologist* 666–71.

Rodriguez, MA et al (2006) 'Mandatory reporting of elder abuse: Between a rock and a hard place' 4(5) *Annals of Family Medicine* 403–09.

Schulz, R and Martire, LM (2004) 'Family caregiving of persons with dementia: Prevalence, health effects, and support strategies' 12(3) *American Journal of Geriatric Psychiatry* 240–49.

Sloane, PD et al (2004) 'Effect of Person-Centered Showering and the Towel Bath on Bathing – Associated Aggression, Agitation, and Discomfort in Nursing Home Residents with Dementia: A Randomized, Controlled Trial' 52(11) *Journal of the American Geriatrics Society* 1795–1804.

Son, J et al (2007) 'The caregiver stress process and health outcomes' 19(6) *Journal of Aging Health* 871–87.

Steadman, PL, Tremont, G and Davis, JD (2007) 'Premorbid relationship satisfaction and caregiver burden in dementia caregivers' 20(2) *Journal of Geriatric Psychiatry and Neurolology* 115–19.

VandeWeerd, C and Paveza, GJ (2005) 'Verbal Mistreatment in Older Adults: A Look at Persons with Alzheimer's Disease and their Caregivers in the State of Florida' 17(4) *Journal of Elder Abuse & Neglect* 11–30.

Wiglesworth, A et al (2010) 'Screening for abuse and neglect of people with dementia' 58(3) *Journal of the American Geriatrics Society* 493–500.

Yan, E and Kwok, T (2011) 'Abuse of older Chinese with dementia by family caregivers: An inquiry into the role of caregiver burden' 26(5) *International Journal of Geriatric Psychiatry* 527–35.

37

Driving and Dementia

DESMOND O'NEILL

A SCIENCE AT THE MARGINS OF CLINICAL PRACTICE

FEW AREAS OF clinical practice so entwine health, ethics and law as medical fitness to drive, yet the subject rarely features in journals of medicine, medical ethics or law. This may be because for most physicians the assessment of medical fitness to drive lies at the margins of their everyday practice. The specialism of traffic medicine[1] is in its infancy, and several studies show that doctors have a low level of awareness of guidelines on the medical fitness to drive (O'Neill et al, 1994), and few medical schools routinely incorporate instruction on medical fitness to drive in their curricula (Hawley et al, 2008).

DIVERGENCE BETWEEN LAW AND ETHICS

The boundaries between law and ethics are sometimes unclear. In certain jurisdictions, the law may routinely place practitioners in situations which test their professional ethics. As well as the mandatory reporting for driving of many illnesses in all Canadian provinces (see below) raising significant ethical concerns (McLachlan et al, 2007), there are similar concerns over mandatory reporting of elder abuse in all 50 US states—some considering it to be counter-productive and out of step with modern gerontological practice (Daniels et al, 1989).

There are clearly important links between law and ethics (Dickenson and Parker, 1999), and undergraduate and graduate education needs to be informed by medical jurisprudence. Many societal debates on ethical issues are aired and decisions achieved through law, albeit in a setting in which discourse may be constrained by legal protocols in court settings, where decisions in both judicial and legislative settings may be dichotomous in nature and where such decisions may be antagonistic to professional and deeper ethical principles. However, law is a separate discipline, and special skills are needed to clarify the interface between the law, ethics and professional practice (Madden, 2002). An important concern is the avoidance of 'legalism', whereby practitioners place an undue emphasis on the law (Appelbaum, 2004).

[1] A relatively new specialism embracing all those disciplines, techniques and methods aimed at reducing death and injury inflicted by traffic crashes, but which is also enabling/rehabilitative in trying to ensure that transport mobility is not hampered, or rendered unsafe, by remediable illness or functional loss.

A NEED FOR JOINED-UP THINKING

An increasing body of literature points to the imperative of steering as sure a path as possible between the three disciplines of traffic medicine, ethics and law, as the ability to drive is increasingly recognized as a critical factor in health and well-being. In addition, in the absence of informed and sophisticated debate among clinicians, there is a danger that legislators will implement laws on fitness to drive which may be removed from clinical reality (such as elements of the 2009 European Union Directive)[2], ineffective and/or harmful (as with much older driver regulations) or unethical (mandatory reporting of drivers).

It is precisely this dissonance which makes medical fitness to drive a very helpful educational topic for teasing out the differences between law and ethics, a differentiation all the more relevant to students as an example of upstream ethics, ie, not the drama of beginning-of-life/end-of-life scenarios but rather of everyday clinical exchange. Certain aspects of the research of fitness to drive also expose some unhappy research ethics issues, particularly the question of professional probity in pursuing lines of research which may unnecessarily add to the stigma of certain groups of patients (O'Neill, 2012).

LEGAL ASPECTS

The legal aspects of medical fitness to drive can be categorized into three types: specific regulations about driving and disease, mandatory reporting and concerns of liability and potential litigation.

Laws and legally-binding regulations generally cover a restricted range of conditions particularly, in most countries, relating to the use of alcohol or drugs, but extending to more specific directions on vision, diabetes and epilepsy in the 2009 EU Directive.[3] The strictures on alcohol dependency illustrate how a medical issue can spill over into a more defined legal scenario: a driver with alcohol dependency has a condition relevant to medical fitness to drive but can drive legally if abstinent or if under the legal blood alcohol limit. However, at the point that he or she drives a car while over the legal limit, a statutory offence has been committed.

In a limited number of jurisdictions, a further legal aspect is the requirement for mandatory reporting to driver licensing authorities of a range of medical conditions relevant to medical fitness to drive. It is increasingly clear that this approach is neither effective nor ethically sustainable (Simpson et al, 2004). In one study of epilepsy and driving, there was *less* reporting in the state with mandatory reporting than in that without (Drazkowski et al, 2010). Most mandatory reporting relates to the condition rather than to function, which is very much against current thinking on assessment of capacity.

Concerns over litigation are in general of three types: that of being sued (a) for not advising appropriately, (b) for not reporting an impaired driver who is considered

[2] European Commission (2009) Commission Directive 2009/112/EC of 25 August 2009 amending Council Directive 91/439/EEC on driving licences (Brussels, European Commission) 26–30.

[3] Ibid.

to pose a risk to others, and (c) being sued for breaking confidentiality over a driver with dementia who has not complied with advice to cease driving and whom the physician has reason to believe poses a substantive threat to other road users.

The most substantive risk lies with not advising patients appropriately who subsequently are involved in a crash. However, this is tempered by a recognition in many jurisdictions that drivers also have a responsibility to monitor and regulate their own health if it affects their driving ability. This was the case in Ireland where an insurance company sought to recoup an insurance payment by suing the driver's family doctor: the court determined that if the driver was suffering from dizzy spells, then the responsibility to stop driving also lay with him.[4]

The situation with reporting is more complex, and will be discussed in the context of clinical management of the driver with dementia.

DEVELOPING AN EVIDENCE BASE

Much of the practical literature on driving and illness has evolved from habit and practice, as relatively few high quality studies on the impact of illness on driving safety have been performed, and it is likely that earlier versions of guidelines were influenced by the more difficult cases seen in specialist practice by those involved in drafting the guidelines. A landmark study in 1991 showed minimally increased crash risk for drivers with diabetes and epilepsy: this was influential in generating a reconsideration of guidelines (Hansotia and Broste, 1991).

Over the subsequent two decades, three trends have become noticeable: a liberalization in terms of temporal restrictions (driving cessation advised after stroke in the UK dropped from three months to one month in this time period); a greater emphasis on clinician discretion; and more emphasis on function as opposed to diagnostic labels. This latter point parallels clinical thinking on capacity in other domains, and forms the backbone of assessment of driving capability in dementia, predominantly through on-road testing of driving ability.

It is also clear that an earlier focus on psychometric testing, vision and aspects such as reaction time was not helpful as it failed to draw on modern understanding of the driving task as a complex mix of behaviour, with a particular emphasis on self-regulation—termed 'risk homeostasis' by one of the leading researchers in the field (Fuller, 2005). Indeed, one of the key points of enquiry in traffic medicine is how prudent a patient will be—both in terms of management of his or her illness(es) and driving safety.

Negativity towards ageing (ageism) is widespread, reflecting in widespread false belief that older drivers are unsafe (Martin et al, 2005). Dementia is marked by what the pioneer of dementia care, Tom Kitwood, termed a malignant social pathology, whereby personhood, individuality and strategic responses may not be recognized (Kitwood, 1997).

[4] *McGarvey [a minor] v Barr* [2011] IEHC 461 (O'Neill J).

MOBILITY AND SAFETY

However, the most major change in the literature of transport and health in the last decade has been the recognition that any focus on medical fitness to drive must maintain a due equilibrium between mobility and safety. This may seem so obvious as to be banal, but the literature for the first one hundred years has been almost obsessively concerned with safety (Jones, 2014).

Transport is the invisible glue that holds our lives together—an under-recognized contributor to economic, social and personal well-being. Unfortunately, in public health terms, the medical profession has allowed itself to focus almost exclusively on the downsides of transport. This is exemplified by the chapter on transport in one of the key texts on public health, Marmot and Wilkinson's otherwise excellent *Social Determinants of Health* (Marmot et al, 1999). It makes for grim reading: accidents, pollution and the impact of cars on exercise, and no mention of how lack of access to transport is associated with impaired health and social inclusion—an emerging research issue (Hjorthol, 2013).

A major catalyst for change was the impact of injudicious policies on older drivers, and in particular medical screening policies in many jurisdictions. A series of gerontologists and human factors researchers undertook research which showed quite conclusively that: (a) older drivers are among the safest groups of drivers (Langford et al, 2006); (b) medical screening programmes of older drivers are associated with increased levels of death and injury among older traffic users (Siren and Meng, 2012); and (c) older people who cease driving are more likely to suffer from depression (Marottoli et al, 1997), enter nursing homes (Freeman et al, 2006) and die (Edwards et al, 2009).

MEDICAL FACTORS AND RISK

These findings in turn are congruent with an increasing recognition that medical factors have a relatively small role to play in accident causation (Marshall, 2008). Nonetheless, patients require advice for many medical conditions, not only to protect them and other road users from harm, but also to provide enabling and rehabilitative strategies which will facilitate continued and more comfortable driving, as has been outlined for a wide range of conditions, including stroke, arthritis, cataracts and Parkinson's disease as well as rehabilitation for general debility (O'Neill and Carr, 2006: 141–50).

The safety dividend from a systematic approach was outlined in a major Canadian study in 2012 whereby routinely giving medical advice on fitness to drive with conditions relevant to fitness to drive was associated with a 45% reduction in crashes (Redelmeier et al, 2013). A note of caution was also sounded, in that the study also found a modest increase in depression as well as of reduced attendance at return appointments.

That crashes were reduced but not eliminated is an important message for traffic medicine: as in many other areas of clinical practice, risk cannot be entirely eliminated but can be better managed. This study clarifies that traffic medicine functions more akin to a burglar alarm—which reduces but does not eliminate burglary—than to a watertight seal in the reduction of crashes.

In turn, it is also relevant that an often significant minority of drivers will not adhere to the advice given by physicians in terms of driving cessation, for example with epilepsy (Tatum et al, 2012) and transient ischaemic attack (McCarron et al, 2008). This is of course no different from most of our transactions with patients, but sometimes clinicians apply a rather simplistic prism to traffic medicine interactions when in fact they constitute clinical advice in the same complex manner as all other clinical advice.

THE IMPACT OF DEMENTIA AND DRIVING

In terms of the contemporary emphasis on mobility as well as safety, one of the important consequences of dementia is eventual driving cessation, and driving cessation in dementia is associated with a mismatch between transportation needs and available resources with consequent loss of mobility (Taylor and Tripodes, 2001).

The precise contribution of the dementias to overall crash hazard is uncertain, as exemplified by the range of risk (including none) associated with dementia in the survey of empirical research in 2010 (Carr and Ott, 2010). Although Johansson suggested a major role for dementia as the cause of crashes among older drivers on neuropathological grounds (Johansson et al, 1997), subsequent interviews with families did not reveal significant problems with memory or activities of daily living (Lundberg et al, 1999). The Stockholm group also showed that older drivers who had a high level of traffic violations had a high prevalence of cognitive deficits (Lundberg et al, 1998). Retrospective studies of dementia and driving from specialist dementia clinics tend to show a high risk (Friedland et al, 1988; Lucas-Blaustein et al, 1988; O'Neill, 1993), whereas those which are prospective and which look at the early stages of dementia show a less pronounced pattern of risk. In the first two years of dementia the risk approximates to that of the general population (Drachman and Swearer, 1993; Carr et al, 2000). The most carefully controlled study so far of crashes and dementia showed no increase in crash rates for drivers with dementia (Trobe et al, 1996). Likely causes for this counterintuitive finding include a lower annual mileage and a restriction on driving by the patient, family and physicians.

Quantifying and contextualizing risk, including the counterbalancing of competing risks, remains a problem for the literature on older drivers and cognition. For example, a search of ten years of media reports in the United States uncovered 32 deaths among drivers with dementia who became lost while driving and were subsequently found (Hunt et al, 2010): while any death is regrettable, this total is considerably lower than the number killed by spider bites in the US in a similar time period (Langley, 2005) and needs to be seen within the perspective of the known risk of social isolation and reduced access to a wide range of services associated with driving cessation (Taylor and Tripodes, 2001), as well as an increased risk of institutionalization (Freeman et al, 2006).

What is clear, however, is that at a certain stage in dementia driving is no longer possible. The key challenge for clinicians is to assist patients and their families in ensuring a transition that is timely and safe, and ideally which plans for transportation needs after driving cessation.

AN ETHICS OF COMPETENCE, CARE AND COMMUNICATION

The primary focus in the ethics of dementia and driving touches on the triad of competence, care and communication. In terms of competence, the engaged clinician should therefore be aware that: (a) transport, and in particular driving, is a key component of well-being with many illnesses; (b) driving skills may be preserved in the early and middle stages of dementia; and (c) protocols for the assessment and management of driving in dementia are increasingly available. From a care and communication perspective, the clinician needs to adopt a problem-solving approach, the essence of which is the need to recognize that the assessment of dementia provides the potential for a range of interventions, one of the most important being the establishment of a framework for advance planning in a progressive disease.

Just as this is commonly recognized for such practical matters as enduring power of attorney in many jurisdictions, so too do we need to start a process which encompasses an assessment, a commitment to maximizing mobility and also an awareness-raising process for the patient and carers that the progression of the disease will inevitably result in a loss of driving capacity. This latter component has been termed a 'Ulysses contract', after the hero made his crew tie him to the mast on the condition that they did not heed his entreaties to be released when seduced by the song of the sirens (Howe, 2000).

NEW STANCES IN DEMENTIA CARE

Developing this process incorporates some relatively new stances in dementia care, including a routine enquiry as to driving and transport as well as routine diagnosis disclosure—the patient who drives needs to be told that he or she has a memory problem that is likely to progress and hamper their driving abilities. In general, carers are fearful of diagnosis disclosure (Maguire et al, 1996) but older people seem to want to be told if they have this illness (Turnbull et al, 2003). There is also evidence that such a process may facilitate driver cessation by enhancing a therapeutic dimension to disease diagnosis and advance planning (Bahro et al, 1995). It forms the basis of a useful patient and carer brochure from the Hartford Foundation which is also available online (Hartford Foundation, 2000).

The commitment to maximizing mobility must focus first on as accurate an assessment as possible of the patients driving abilities, and second on exploring and planning alternative options for a future when driving is no longer possible. It is the promise of attempting to maximize mobility that is the key to this transaction. If this is not a central component, we are then faced with a dual ethical hazard. In the first instance, the therapeutic role of medicine is subjugated to an approach which inverts the standard mobility–safety ratio to which we are all entitled (Hakamies-Blomqvist and Peters, 2000). A further concern is that people with dementia may avoid assessment of the illness early in the course of the illness for fear of unreasonable restriction of their mobility, and as early diagnosis and treatment/management is often (but not universally) considered to be desirable, this would be an unwelcome development.

The very act of highlighting the potential of compromised driving ability may have a therapeutic benefit, promoting an increased vigilance on the part of the patient and carers that their social contract for driving privileges is not the same as that of the general public. Support is given to this concept by the success of restricted licensing for people with medical illnesses in the state of Utah (Vernon et al, 2002). While some of the effect might arise from the restrictions (avoidance of motorways, night-time driving) it is also possible that the very act of labelling these drivers may heighten their self-awareness—a clinical variant of the Hawthorn effect whereby workers in the control arm of a study of changing work practices increase their output as a consequence of being observed more closely.

The ethical component of risk is the onus on the physician to ensure that this has been assessed in the most accurate and professional manner possible—the greatest risk is to fail to refer on for full assessment, perhaps on the basis that such expertise is geographically distant. In essence, we would not let this deter us from arranging specialist neuroradiology for a suspected subdural haematoma or a ventilation/perfusion scan for a possible pulmonary embolus. We should apply similar criteria to the need for specialized assessments for impaired older drivers, particularly in view of the potential risk to other road users.

ASSESSMENT

The process of assessment of transportation and driving in dementia has been described in detail elsewhere (Breen et al, 2007). In essence, there are two stages of outcome: the first is an immediate risk assessment as to whether the driver should: (a) continue driving until a formal assessment in the near future (low risk); (b) stop driving until formal assessment (medium risk); or (c) stop driving immediately (high risk).

There is as yet no specific instrument to aid in this office-based assessment, which hinges on an overall assessment of the patient's condition, a collateral (informant) history of driving capabilities and any changes that might have occurred in these. In general, continued driving is most likely to be safe in those with mild dementia, where the collateral history does not report unsafe or marginal driving, where there have not been recent crashes or traffic violations and the patient does not show aggressive or impulsive personality characteristics (Iverson et al, 2010).

In terms of formal assessment, there is no substitute currently for on-road testing, which should take place at six-monthly intervals, or sooner if any change is noted. Most health systems do not fully cover the costs of such assessments, and this may be perceived as a barrier. However, if a mechanical element of the car fails, such as the clutch or timing belt, the driver generally understands that the associated repair costs are part and parcel of the maintenance of driving, so it is not completely unreasonable to apply this logic to maintenance of the human factors aspect of driving. However, as continued safe driving has clear societal and health benefits, a case can also be made for incorporating such assessments as integral to health care assessments (Rapoport et al, 2007).

One of the common challenges is where a patient refuses an on-road assessment and continues to drive. There is little guidance from the literature, but my own practice is that the social contract for continued driving would mandate that drivers should understand the potential implications of driving with dementia: if they do not agree to assessment, I advise the patient to stop driving.

SPECIALIST DRIVING ASSESSORS

Ideally such on-road assessments should be undertaken by a specialist driving assessor. Standards for this profession are currently under development, with recommendations from the PORTARE project, funded by the European Union, which have been widely welcomed (Hunter et al, 2009), and similar standards developed by the ADED in the US (Association of Driver Rehabilitation Specialists, 2009). In addition, occupational therapists in Canada and Australia have developed a postgraduate specialization in driving assessment. In the UK, the Forum of Driving Centres has developed this form of expertise.

Clinicians should liaise regularly with the specialist driving assessor as a minority of patients may perform significantly better in their driving tests than as reported by family, and in such cases clinical discretion should trump the on-road test.

ALTERNATIVES TO DRIVING

An overall ethical imperative remains that the assessment should provide enhancement of both mobility and safety. Although no studies currently exist on the impact of routine assessment of driving (Martin et al, 2009), it is clearly important that clinicians should also be able to direct patients and their families to alternative sources of transport when driving is no longer feasible. Driving cessation may be particularly challenging for those without family members available to provide transportation (Choi et al, 2012).

SHARED DECISION-MAKING

Many scenarios of driving and illness seem to paint a dyadic dialogue between doctor and patient, when in fact many elements contribute to decision making after assessment of fitness to drive. Not only are family or friends usually involved, but also other actors including insurance companies and the driver licensing agency. The discussion on driving should include the family/carers.

In general, the welfarist role of the physician extends to reminding the patient and carers that most insurance companies require disclosure by the driver of 'illnesses relevant to driving' such as dementia when they arise. In my own experience, insurance companies have not increased their fees for those drivers with dementia who are being assessed with regular on-road assessments; however, some drivers may give up rather than approach their insurance company.

The thorny question of mandatory reporting needs to be taken up by clinicians through their professional groupings, as has occurred already with a call for its removal by epilepsy specialists in Canada (Remillard et al, 2002). For individual practitioners in jurisdictions where such regulations exist, a twin-track approach is probably necessary –professional advocacy with law makers, and a considered approach on a case-by-case basis as to whether disclosure is in the patient's best interests.

If the physician is confident that the state or province has a mechanism for fair assessment and an enlightened approach to maintaining mobility, compliance is not difficult. If the assessment is cursory and aimed at unduly restricting mobility, physicians may be faced with a problem recognized with other laws which may put the patient's welfare at risk and where professional obligations may require non-compliance with an unfair law.

BREACHING CONFIDENTIALITY

The actual process of breaking confidentiality by a health care professional in the event of evidence of hazard to other members of the public is almost universally supported by most codes of medical practice. In general it is expected that the clinician will have tried persuading the patient and the family in the first instance, and that breaking confidentiality should only occur if both of these approaches have failed and the patient is deemed to represent a significant risk to other road users.

A grey area is the determination of what represents a significant risk to other road users. It is likely that a relatively low threshold is indicated for a progressive neurodegenerative illness where insight is often impaired: if a patient refuses an assessment or is reported by a third party to be driving erratically or in an unsafe manner, then it is probably appropriate to consider breaking patient confidentiality.

However, this is generally a last resort, and we may have laid too much emphasis in the literature on medical fitness to drive guidelines on the role and responsibility of the doctor, and not enough on the responsibilities of drivers and other citizens, and have thereby perhaps over-medicalized the response. At the point where concerns arise over continued driving by a driver with dementia and it is clear that the patient's driving habits are dangerous, it is a misguided kindness to approach dangerous driving as an issue which should be approached in terms of diagnosis and treatment of the underlying cause. As dangerous driving not only represents a hazard to the driver and other road users, and is a statutory offence, it should be reported to the police in the first instance.

This approach can lift a weight off a doctor's shoulders, as not uncommonly a relative will ask the doctor to do something about the dangerous driving the relative has witnessed in a driver with dementia. This is second-hand information, and the doctor should remind the relative that they have a citizen's duty to report the dangerous driving to the police: the medical aspects can be dealt with subsequently.

In addition, it is also inappropriate and unfair to expect doctors to be the sole conduit for reporting driving that poses a hazard to the general public, so this responsibility, in the absence of a family member or carer who can assist, should lie with the health care professional witnessing the behaviour.

To whom this dangerous driving should be reported poses some ethical reflection. It is important that this disclosure has some likelihood of impact and results in the least traumatic removal of the compromised older driver from the road. In such instances, the family may be able to intervene in terms of disabling the car and providing alternative modes of transport. In my own experience, we rarely have to invoke official intervention but find that a personal communication with a senior police officer in the patient's locality may result in a sensitive visit to the patient and cessation of driving.

The existing literature overly emphasizes reporting to driver licensing authorities which may have relatively little benefit in some jurisdictions—removal of a driving licence is likely to have little impact on drivers whose insight into deteriorating driving skills is poor. In the UK, the DVLA makes contact with local police forces if there is cause for concern, and this should provide some assurance to clinicians that their report will have some effect.

CONCLUSION

The inclusion of driver assessment into clinical practice represents a new departure for the disciplines of applied ethics and dementia and ageing studies. It presents both challenges and opportunities and affects not only clinicians but also public health professionals to ensure that our practice represents a judicious balance between benificence and non-maleficence, while at the same time keeping a true perspective on the major issue: that of impaired mobility. The critical elements of care, competence and communication are the fundamentals of clinical practice which help to illuminate and clarify this equilibrium.

The relevance of this background is that the framing of the topic is all-important, and needs to take into account the increasing realization of the need to ensure that people with dementia are accorded the same proportionality between mobility and risk that other age groups are afforded, with due recognition of the importance to their health and well-being of adequate transportation.

REFERENCES

Appelbaum, PS (2004) 'Legalism, postmodernism, and the vicissitudes of teaching ethics' 28(3) *Academic Psychiatry* 164–67.

Association of Driver Rehabilitation Specialists (2009) *Best Practices for the Delivery of Driver Rehabilitation Services* (Hickory, NC, The Association of Driver Rehabilitation Specialists).

Bahro, M et al (1995) 'Giving up driving in Alzheimer's disease – An integrative therapeutic approach' 10(10) *International Journal of Geriatric Psychiatry* 871–74.

Breen, DA et al (2007) 'Driving and dementia' 334(7608) *British Medical Journal* 1365–69.

Carr, DB and Ott, BR (2010) 'The Older Adult Driver with Cognitive Impairment: "It's a Very Frustrating Life"' 303(16) *Journal of the American Medical Association* 1632–41.

Carr, DB et al (2000) 'Characteristics of motor vehicle crashes of drivers with dementia of the Alzheimer type' [see comments] 48(1) *Journal of the American Geriatrics Society* 18–22.

Choi, M et al (2012) 'The impact of transportation support on driving cessation among community-dwelling older adults' 67(3) *The Journals of Gerontology Series B: Psychological Sciences & Social Sciences* 392–400.

Daniels, RS et al (1989) 'Physicians' mandatory reporting of elder abuse' 29(3) *Gerontologist* 321–27.

De Saint Martin, LB (1998) '[Teaching ethics in French medical schools: evolution or revolution?]' 27(20) *La Presse Médicale* 968–70.

Dickenson, DL and Parker, MJ (1999) 'The European Biomedical Ethics Practitioner Education Project: An experiential approach to philosophy and ethics in health care education' 2(3) *Medicine, Health Care and Philosophy* 231–37.

Drachman, DA and Swearer, JM (1993) 'Driving and Alzheimer's disease: The risk of crashes' 43(12) *Neurology* 2448–56 (published erratum appears in (1994) 44(1) *Neurology* 4).

Drazkowski, JF et al (2010) 'Frequency of physician counseling and attitudes toward driving motor vehicles in people with epilepsy: Comparing a mandatory-reporting with a voluntary-reporting state' 19(1) *Epilepsy & Behavior* 52–54.

Edwards, JD et al (2009) 'Driving status and three-year mortality among community-dwelling older adults' 64(2) *Journals of Gerontology Series A: Biological Sciences & Medical Sciences* 300–05.

Freeman, EE et al (2006) 'Driving status and risk of entry into long-term care in older adults' 96(7) *American Journal of Public Health* 1254–59.

Friedland, RP et al (1988) 'Motor vehicle crashes in dementia of the Alzheimer type' [see comments] 24(6) *Annals of Neurology* 782–86.

Fulford, KW et al (1997) 'Ethics and the GMC core curriculum: A survey of resources in UK medical schools' 23(2) *Journal of Medical Ethics* 82–87.

Fuller, R (2005) 'Towards a general theory of driver behaviour' 37(3) *Accident Analysis & Prevention* 461–72.

Hakamies-Blomqvist, L and Peters, B (2000) 'Recent European research on older drivers' 32(4) *Accident Analysis & Prevention* 601–07.

Hansotia, P and Broste, SK (1991) 'The effect of epilepsy or diabetes mellitus on the risk of automobile accidents' 324(1) *New England Journal of Medicine* 22–26.

Hartford Foundation (2000) *At the crossroads: a guide to Alzheimer's disease, dementia and driving* (Hartford, CT, Hartford Foundation).

Hawley, CA et al (2008) 'Medical education on fitness to drive: A survey of all UK medical schools' 84(998) *Postgraduate Medical Journal* 635–38.

Hjorthol, R (2013) 'Transport resources, mobility and unmet transport needs in old age' 33(7) *Ageing and Society* 1190–1211.

Howe, E (2000) 'Improving treatments for patients who are elderly and have dementia' 11(4) *Journal of Clinical Ethics* 291–303.

Hunt, LA et al (2010) 'Drivers with dementia and outcomes of becoming lost while driving' 64(2) *American Journal of Occupational Therapy* 225–32.

Hunter, J et al (2009) *Handbook of disabled driver assessment* (Ljubljana, PORTARE).

Iverson, DJ et al (2010) 'Practice parameter update: Evaluation and management of driving risk in dementia: Report of the Quality Standards Subcommittee of the American Academy of Neurology' 74(16) *Neurology* 1316–24.

Jacobsson, L (1998) '[The faculties should have units of medical ethics]' 95(25) *Lakartidningen* 2964–66.

Johansson, K et al (1997) 'Alzheimer's disease and apolipoprotein E E4 allele in older drivers who died in automobile accidents' 349(April) *Lancet* 1143.

Jones, DS (2014) 'Doctors and the dangers of driving' 370(1) *New England Journal of Medicine* 8–11.

Kitwood, TM (1997) *Dementia Reconsidered: The Person Comes First* (Buckingham, Open University Press).

Langford, J et al (2006) 'Older drivers do not have a high crash risk – A replication of low mileage bias' 38(3) *Accident Analysis & Prevention* 574–78.

Langley, RL (2005) 'Animal-related fatalities in the United States – an update' 16(2) *Wilderness & Environmental Medicine* 67–74.

Lehmann, LS et al (2004) 'A survey of medical ethics education at US and Canadian medical schools' 79(7) *Academic Medicine* 682–89.

Lucas-Blaustein, M et al (1988) 'Driving in patients with dementia' 36(12) *Journal of the American Geriatrics Society* 1087–91.

Lundberg, CL et al (1998) 'Impairments of some cognitive functions are common in crash-involved older drivers' 30(3) *Accident Analysis & Prevention* 371–77.

—— (1999) 'Follow-up of Alzheimer's disease and apolipoprotein E E4 allele in older drivers who died in automobile accidents' in *The Older Driver, Health and Mobility* (Dublin, ARHC Press).

Madden, D (2002) *Medicine, Ethics and the Law* (Dublin, Butterworths).

Maguire, CP et al (1996) 'Family members' attitudes toward telling the patient with Alzheimer's disease their diagnosis' 313(7056) *British Medical Journal* 529–30.

Marmot, M et al (1999) *Social Determinants of Health* (Oxford, Oxford University Press).

Marottoli, RA et al (1997) 'Driving cessation and increased depressive symptoms: Prospective evidence from the New Haven EPESE. Established Populations for Epidemiologic Studies of the Elderly' 45(2) *Journal of the American Geriatrics Society* 202–06.

Marshall, SC (2008) 'The role of reduced fitness to drive due to medical impairments in explaining crashes involving older drivers' 9(4) *Traffic Injury Prevention* 291–98.

Martin, A et al (2005) 'A bad press: Older drivers and the media' 330(7487) *British Medical Journal* 368.

—— (2009) 'Driving assessment for maintaining mobility and safety in drivers with dementia' 1 *Cochrane Database of Systematic Reviews* CD006222.

McCarron, MO et al (2008) 'Driving after a transient ischaemic attack or minor stroke' 25(6) *Emergency Medicine Journal* 358–59.

McLachlan, RS et al (2007) 'Impact of mandatory physician reporting on accident risk in epilepsy' 48(8) *Epilepsia* 1500–05.

O'Neill, D (1993) 'Driving and dementia' 3(3) *Alzheimer Review* 65–68.

—— (2012) 'More mad and more wise' 49 *Accident Analysis & Prevention* 263–65.

O'Neill, D and Carr, D (2006) 'Transport, ageing and driving' in JS Pathy and A Sinclair (eds), *Principles and Practice of Geriatric Medicine* (London, Wiley).

O'Neill, D et al (1994) 'Physician awareness of driving regulations for older drivers' 344(8933) *Lancet* 1366–67.

Rapoport, MJ et al (2007) 'Sharing the responsibility for assessing the risk of the driver with dementia' 177(6) *Canadian Medical Association Journal* 599–601.

Redelmeier, DA et al (2013) 'Physicians' warnings for unfit drivers and risk of road crashes' 368(1) *New England Journal of Medicine* 87–88.

Remillard, GM et al (2002) 'Epilepsy and motor vehicle driving – A symposium held in Quebec City, November 1998' 29(4) *Canadian Journal of Neurological Sciences* 315–25.

Simpson, CS et al (2004) 'Mandatory physician reporting of drivers with cardiac disease: Ethical and practical considerations' 20(13) *Canadian Journal of Cardiology* 1329–34.

Siren, A and Meng, A (2012) 'Cognitive screening of older drivers does not produce safety benefits' 45 *Accident Analysis & Prevention* 634–38.

Tatum, WO et al (2012) 'Disobedience and driving in patients with epilepsy' 23(1) *Epilepsy & Behavior* 30–35.

Taylor, BD and Tripodes, S (2001) 'The effects of driving cessation on the elderly with dementia and their caregivers' 33(4) *Accident Analysis & Prevention* 519–28.

Trobe, JD et al (1996) 'Crashes and violations among drivers with Alzheimer disease' 53(5) *Archives of Neurology* 411–16.

Turnbull, Q et al (2003) 'Attitudes of elderly subjects toward "truth telling" for the diagnosis of Alzheimer's disease' 16(2) *Journal of Geriatric Psychiatry and Neurolology* 90–93.

Vernon, DD et al (2002) 'Evaluating the crash and citation rates of Utah drivers licensed with medical conditions, 1992–1996' 34(2) *Accident Analysis & Prevention* 237–46.

38

Voting and Political Participation

NINA A KOHN

INTRODUCTION

IN DEMOCRATIC SOCIETIES, the right to vote is one of the most fundamental rights a citizen can have. The right to vote is a critical source of political power and a powerful symbol of one's membership in a society. Persons with dementia, however, face significant barriers to exercising the right to vote. This chapter describes those barriers and explores the extent to which they are consistent with international law and human rights norms. After showing how many are not, it suggests how jurisdictions might adopt voting-related laws and practices to enable persons with dementia to more fully engage in the political life of their societies.

BARRIERS TO VOTING BY PERSONS WITH DEMENTIA

Persons with dementia face significant limitations on their ability to vote. Some of these limitations are functional in nature: having dementia can make it difficult—even prohibitively difficult—to perform voting-related tasks. Other limitations are categorical: persons with dementia may be denied the right to vote because they fall within a category of persons who are believed to be incapable of voting or ill-suited to voting.

Functional Limitations

The fact that an individual has dementia does not mean that he or she is unable to vote. Research suggests that many—perhaps most—persons with dementia remain interested in voting and do in fact vote, although those with more severe levels of dementia are both less likely to be interested in voting and less likely to actually do so (De Cauwer, 2005; Ott et al, 2003; Karlawish et al, 2002).

Having dementia, however, can undermine an individual's ability to vote. In part, this is because dementia can make it harder for individuals to comply with election procedures. For example, persons with dementia may have difficulty remembering when or where to vote or following instructions for completing a ballot.

The extent to which dementia interferes with an individual's ability to comply with election procedures is a function of both the individual's cognitive state and a jurisdiction's voting procedures. The more confusing or complex polling technologies or procedures are, the less likely it is that those with dementia will be able to comply with them. Confusing ballots may make it more difficult for the individual to record his or her voting choices, and increase the likelihood that the individual will either 'under-vote' (record too few voting choices) or 'over-vote' (register more votes on an issue or an office than permitted). Poorly lit polling places, or polling places where there is an abundance of noise, may increase the cognitive demands of exercising voting rights. Vote-by-mail or absentee balloting systems designed to increase the accessibility of the vote may themselves disenfranchise such persons as a result of unduly complex application or ballot return procedures. Moreover, as procedures become more complex, there is a greater likelihood that an individual with dementia will need assistance to vote. Such assistance, while essential, increases the likelihood that the person with dementia will be subject to undue influence or, at the very least, be unable to cast a secret ballot.

Dementia can also undermine the ability to vote because it can make it more difficult for individuals to make voting-related choices. Those with moderate or severe dementia may be incapable of making knowing and informed voting choices, and of deciding for whom or what to vote. As it becomes more severe, dementia may even prevent an individual from understanding the nature and consequences of the act of voting. This is significant because an understanding of the nature and consequences of one's act is often cited as the threshold level of capacity one must have in order to engage in a legally binding act, and thus is sometimes described as the threshold level of capacity one must have in order to vote.[1] A key factor affecting whether a person with dementia is able to vote, despite the difficulties that dementia creates in complying with election procedures and making voting-related choices, is the availability of voting-related assistance. Persons with dementia may not only need help getting to a polling place, but may also need help obtaining and completing a valid ballot. In addition, not unlike their fellow citizens but to a greater extent, persons with dementia may need help obtaining information about candidates and ballot measures and weighing that information in order to decide for whom and for what to vote. Thus, where governments limit who may assist voters or the ways in which assistance may be provided, they may effectively disenfranchise some persons with dementia who would otherwise be capable of voting.

Categorical Limitations

Formal Categorical Limitations

Most democratic countries allow individuals to be disqualified from voting based on mental incapacity (Massicotte et al, 2004: 27). A 2010 survey of the then 27 members of the European Union found that all but six restricted the voting rights of at least some persons with cognitive disabilities (European Union Agency for Fundamental Rights, 2010).

[1] See, eg, *Doe v Rowe*, 156 F Supp 2d 35 (D Me 2001); Appelbaum, 2005, Karlawish et al, 2004.

Some countries permit disenfranchisement based on mental capacity without any formal court process. For example, a voter can be removed from the voting rolls in Australia based only on a third party's objection to that person's inclusion and a certificate from a medical practitioner indicating that the voter is of 'unsound mind' (Karlawish and Bonnie, 2007). Similarly, the European Union Agency for Fundamental Rights reports that certain European Union Member States permit disenfranchisement when a medical practitioner finds that a person with a cognitive disability lacks capacity, even though there has been no court-based finding of incapacity (European Union Agency for Fundamental Rights, 2010).

Although some jurisdictions thus allow disenfranchisement on the basis of mental incapacity without a court process, countries that restrict the right to vote based on mental capacity typically deny the right to vote to those who have been adjudicated to be incompetent. Notably, these countries differ as to whether they require a court to make a specific assessment that the individual lacks voting capacity in order to disenfranchise him or her, or whether it is sufficient that the would-be voter has been appointed a guardian or otherwise found to be broadly incapacitated by the court.

There is, however, a trend away from such status-based disqualifications. Canada led the way towards abolishing capacity-based requirements when, in 1992, it simply eliminated its mental capacity requirement for voting. In 2006, the United Kingdom followed Canada's lead and eliminated its prohibition of voting based on 'intellectual or mental state' (Redley et al, 2012). More recently, Croatia abolished its restriction on voting by persons subject to guardianship (Mental Disability Advocacy Center (MDAC), 2012).

To the extent that countries retain formal restrictions, there is also a trend towards requiring individual assessment before disenfranchisement. Much of this trend has been prompted by court rulings invalidating such restrictions. For example, in *Doe v Rowe*, a United States federal district court struck down a state law disenfranchising all persons subject to guardianship as both unconstitutional and a violation of the Americans with Disabilities Act because it disenfranchised persons subject to guardianship regardless of whether they understood the nature and effect of voting.[2] Similarly, in 2010, the Czech Constitutional Court held that a guardianship action could not deprive a ward of the right to vote without an individualized assessment of the ward's voting-related capacity (Alternative Report, 2011). Likewise, in *Alajos Kiss v Hungary*, the European Court of Human Rights ruled that the government of Hungary violated the European Convention on Human Rights by automatically denying the right to vote to a person under guardianship without an individualized assessment of his capacity to vote.[3] More recently, after a Japanese court found the country's public elections law unconstitutional because it automatically denied voting rights to persons subject to guardianship, Japan amended the law to eliminate the restriction on voting by such persons.[4]

[2] *Doe v Rowe*, above (n 1).

[3] *Alajos Kiss v Hungary*, App No 38832/06, EurCtH.R (2010). Available at hudoc.echr.coe.int/sites/eng/pages/search.aspx?i=001-98800.

[4] 'Wards win back their right to vote' *Japan Times* (17 July 2013). Available at: www.japantimes.co.jp/news/2013/07/17/national/wards-win-back-their-right-to-vote/#.UgBXwYzD_IU.

Moreover, even within countries which fully retain their legal restrictions on voting by persons with cognitive disabilities, there appears to be movement towards expanding the franchise. For example, the European Union Agency on Fundamental Rights has reported that Cyprus no longer enforces its restrictions (European Union Agency for Fundamental Rights, 2010). The United States—the author's home country—has retained significant capacity-based limitations on the franchise: 37 states' constitutions limit the franchise based on mental capacity or permit their state legislatures to impose such limitations (Hurme and Appelbaum, 2007). However, even in the United States, there has been some effort to move away from capacity-based disenfranchisement. Not all state legislatures restrict the vote to the extent permitted by their Constitutions (Hurme and Appelbaum, 2007). Moreover, there was a brief flirtation in the United States in the mid-2000s with the idea of imposing capacity-testing on residents of long-term care facilities (an idea sparked by a suggestion made in an article that appeared in the prominent *Journal of the American Medical Association* (Karlawish et al, 2004)); however, the idea was soundly rejected in 2007 by a group of experts convened by the Borchard Foundation Center on Law and Aging, the American Bar Association Commission on Law and Aging and the Capital Center for Government Law and Policy at the University of the Pacific, McGeorge School of Law (Symposium Recommendations, 2007), and it has not been seriously considered since.

Informal Categorical Limitations

Not all categorical exclusions from voting and political participation result from formal legal rules or processes; many such exclusions are instead the result of informal processes by which citizens with disabilities are disenfranchised based on third-party judgements about their suitability for such participation. Individuals who rely on others for assistance with mobility or communication may effectively be disenfranchised by being denied voting-related assistance from those upon whom they depend. Such denials may reflect a care provider's deliberate decision not to assist or simply the care provider's (perhaps unconscious) beliefs or stereotypes about persons with dementia. For example, a care provider may simply not think of people with dementia as the type of people who vote and thus may not think to ask care recipients about voting or to assist with the voting process.

The most significant research on informal disenfranchisement by care providers has been conducted in the context of voting by persons in long-term care institutions. This research indicates that individuals with dementia or other cognitive impairments who reside in long-term care facilities may effectively be disenfranchised when facility staff do not inform them of elections or deny them assistance with voter registration and balloting. The most significant study to date of long-term care facilities' practices regarding resident voting surveyed 246 long-term care facilities following the 2006 mid-term elections in the State of Virginia. The study found that it was 'commonplace' for long-term care facilities to disenfranchise residents based on diagnoses of dementia or staff's subjective impressions of their cognitive abilities or level of awareness. Among other ways, facilities wrongfully disenfranchised residents by (1) limiting assistance with voting procedures (for example, registration) to 'residents whom the staff think can vote'; (2) by limiting assistance based on staff's assessments of residents' voting capacity—assessments that were often based on factors that bore little relationship to the State's legal standard for disenfranchisement; and (3) excluding all residents with certain diagnoses from receiving voting assistance. Notably, the study found that some facilities screened residents for mental capacity in order to determine if they had capacity to vote even when those residents had affirmatively expressed interest in voting (Bonnie et al, 2013).

The Virginia study built on earlier surveys of long-term care facilities in Pennsylvania (Karlawish et al, 2008) and Virginia (Bonnie et al, 2005) that also found that many such facilities engage in some form of screening to determine which of their residents should be permitted to vote or be assisted with the voting process. In the Pennsylvania study, for example, almost two-thirds of the facilities surveyed 'assessed' whether their residents had the ability to vote (Karlawish et al, 2008). A variety of techniques were used by facility staff to assess voting capacity, including asking residents election-related questions (for example, asking residents to name current political officer holders), conducting a Folstein Mini-Mental State Exam (MMSE) or looking to prior assessments of residents' mental statuses (Karlawish et al, 2008; Bonnie et al, 2005). As with the larger Virginia study, the researchers in the smaller studies found that the screening tests staff used did not comport with the legal standards for when a resident could legally be disenfranchised.

Thus, as the studies of voting in long-term care facilities illustrate, non-state actors may restrict voting by persons with dementia even in situations in which they clearly lack legal authority to do so. Accordingly, ensuring that persons with dementia can vote to the full extent to which they are capable will require more than simply scaling back or even eliminating formal capacity requirements.

IMPLICATIONS OF THE CONVENTION ON THE RIGHTS OF PERSONS WITH DISABILITIES

In 2006, the United Nations General Assembly adopted the Convention on the Rights of Persons with Disabilities (CRPD). The Convention represents a new recognition of and commitment to the human rights of persons with disabilities. The CRPD is an ambitious, sweeping document that envisages a world in which persons with disabilities fully enjoy the same rights and privileges as all other persons.[5] As of August 2013, the CRPD had 156 signatories, of which 133 had accessed or ratified it.[6]

The CRPD dramatically limits the ability of countries that are parties to the Convention to deny voting rights to persons with dementia and other cognitive disabilities. Specifically, Articles 29 and 12 of the CRPD and the requirement that states reform their laws to comply with them as articulated in Article 33 of the CRPD, directly limit the ability of states to restrict voting by persons with dementia or other forms of diminished cognitive capacity. Notably, these provisions build

[5] United Nations Convention on the Rights of Persons with Disabilities 2006.
[6] United Nations Enable (August 2013). Available at: www.un.org/disabilities.

upon Article 21 of the Universal Declaration of Human Rights, which recognizes the right to vote as a human right.

Article 29 of the CRPD, which concerns the right of persons with disabilities to engage in political and public life, requires that parties ensure that persons with disabilities have 'the right and opportunity' to vote. It also requires that 'voting procedures, facilities and materials are appropriate, accessible and easy to understand and use' and that states protect 'the right of persons with disabilities to vote by secret ballot'. Article 29 also specifies that persons with disabilities are entitled to assistance with voting 'by a person of their own choice', and that states must facilitate 'the use of assistive and new technologies where appropriate'.

Article 29 thus clearly prohibits signatories from categorically restricting persons with certain diagnoses or conditions from voting. Whether it also limits states from restricting the franchise based on individual assessments of voting capacity has, however, been the subject of considerable debate (Redley et al, 2012). The language of the CRPD would seem to disallow such assessments as Article 29 does not permit any disability-based barriers to voting. Moreover, since assessments are triggered by a person's disability or alleged disability, such assessments could themselves be seen as a form of impermissible discrimination on the basis of disability.

Article 12 of the CRPD does not speak directly to voting, but it limits states' ability to restrict voting by persons with cognitive disabilities because it states that parties 'shall recognize that persons with disabilities enjoy legal capacity on an equal basis with others in all aspects of life.' Article 12 is thus clearly inconsistent with restrictions on voting that categorically bar voting by persons with certain diagnoses or conditions. Like Article 29, Article 12 is arguably inconsistent with limiting the franchise to persons based on individual assessments of voting capacity. Article 12 also requires parties to the Convention to affirmatively support persons with dementia and other forms of diminished cognitive capacity with exercising their right to vote. Specifically, it states that parties 'shall take appropriate measures to provide access by persons with disabilities to the support they may require in exercising their legal capacity'.

Adoption of the CRPD has spurred significant advocacy around reforming election laws to enable voting by persons with intellectual disabilities, mental illness and other forms of cognitive disability including dementia. Disability rights organizations, such as the Mental Disability Advocacy Center (MDAC) based in Budapest, have used the adoption of the CRPD as an opportunity to push for broad reforms of election laws, including the wholesale elimination of capacity requirements for voting. Such advocacy has led to some significant reforms to make voting more accessible to persons with cognitive disabilities. For example, although Kenya's Constitution prohibits voting by persons of 'unsound mind', as a result of advocacy efforts that drew support for their position from the CRPD, the country has taken affirmative measures to facilitate voting by persons with intellectual and mental disabilities (Redley et al, 2012).

Notably, the efforts to use the CRPD to expand the franchise are also supported by other forms of international law. Most notably, in Europe, such reforms are also supported by the European Union's protections against disability discrimination including Articles 21, 26 and 39 of the Charter of Fundamental Rights of the

European Union. Other relevant European Union documents include the Council of Europe's Disability Action Plan for 2006–2015 (Action Line No 1) and the Venice Commission's Revised Interpretative Declaration to its Code of Good Practice in Electoral Matters on the Participation of People with Disabilities in Elections.

POLICY RECOMMENDATIONS

As the previous section has shown, legal and extra-legal systems, interacting with an individual's internal cognitive abilities, can combine to disenfranchise persons with dementia in ways that are inconsistent with the CRPD and emerging international legal norms.

Such disenfranchisement should be a significant concern for democracies not only because it runs contrary to the CRPD and emerging international legal norms, but also because it undermines the human dignity of persons with cognitive challenges. The right to vote is not just a source of political power; it is also a powerful symbol of an individual's membership in a society and a source of identity. When jurisdictions create barriers to voting by persons with dementia and other cognitive impairment, they signal that such persons are not full members of the community and promote stereotypical thinking about persons with such disabilities.

Furthermore, democracies should be wary of restricting the right to vote of persons with dementia because, as the author has previously argued, selectively disenfranchising persons with cognitive disabilities can actually weaken democratic systems of government. Specifically:

> Selective disenfranchisement of distinct groups of citizens with shared interests reduces the likelihood that elected officials and democratically enacted initiatives will reflect the will of the people. This is particularly likely where the selectively disenfranchised group is otherwise politically marginalized. For cognitively impaired citizens, who face a myriad of other barriers to full participation in the political community, the right to vote is not only their primary mechanism for exerting political power, it may also be their only mechanism for doing so. When unable to exercise their right to vote, they are less likely to be able to promote and protect their common interests (eg, enhanced interests in high quality health care or disability accommodations), and thus the government as a whole may be less representative of the general population (Kohn, 2008; internal citations omitted).

Notably, the ability of persons with dementia to give voice to their political preferences may be especially important when the communities and countries in which they live experience an economic downturn, as is currently the case in many parts of the world. Economic turmoil tends to prompt greater political scrutiny of the public benefit programmes upon which many persons with dementia depend, giving rise to a greater need for them to be politically active to protect their common interests.

In short, both as a matter of human rights and as a matter of practical politics, democracies should avoid disenfranchising people with dementia who are able to form voting choices. Democracies should instead strive to design and implement voting systems that increase the cognitive accessibility of voting. This section proposes four key ways in which they may do so.

Eliminate Formal Capacity Requirements

At first blush, capacity requirements seem consistent with the laudable goal of ensuring that voters are able to intelligently and rationally evaluate candidates and issues. A more penetrating look, however, suggests that such requirements are not only inconsistent with the emerging human rights norms embraced by the CRPD, but are counterproductive in that they create more problems than they solve. Thus, as Linda Barclay has argued, although capacity is not morally irrelevant in determining who should have the right to vote, capacity testing is not justified because the benefit of detecting that a 'vanishingly' small number of people lack capacity comes 'nowhere near to justifying the cost' of that detection (Barclay, 2013). Barclay identifies these costs as including not only the resources required to create a 'credible' testing programme, but also the damage to people's self worth and the reinforcement of prejudice that occurs when people who do not in fact lack capacity are singled out for testing (Barclay, 2013). Such perpetuation of prejudice is an inevitable feature of capacity requirements in part because such restrictions suffer from selective enforcement as no democracy screens all potential voters for capacity (if only because doing so would be prohibitively costly).

The greatest cost imposed by capacity requirements, however, is that they can disenfranchise persons who are able to make voting choices and who wish to vote. This excessive disenfranchisement can occur when the law allows voting rights to be stripped without an individual assessment of voting capacity, when assessments of voting capacity are made based on cursory examinations of the individual or rely heavily on prior diagnosis, or simply when the existence of a capacity requirement causes would-be voters or those upon whom they rely to erroneously conclude that they cannot or should not be voters.

The benefits of such testing, by contrast, are minimal. In the absence of undue influence or other forms of voting fraud, voting by persons who in fact lack the capacity to understand the nature and consequences of doing so is unlikely to cause more than 'statistical noise' in election results, in part because the numbers involved are small and in part because there is no reason to believe that such persons would vote in a particular pattern. Indeed, although the notion of persons with cognitive disabilities voting may be unsettling to others, such persons pose far less of a threat to a democratic system of government than the ill-informed or irrational voters without such disabilities whom democracies do not attempt to disenfranchise. As Professor Pamela Karlan has explained, 'a large number of citizens' views and choices are driven by a range of irrelevant factors and fortuities—such as a candidate's height, whether he uses a nickname, or the format of the ballot' (Karlan, 2007). Yet democracies do not disfranchise persons because they make voting decisions based on such irrational or unintelligent factors.

The real concern raised by voting by persons with cognitive disabilities is that unscrupulous electioneers, or simply misguided family or friends, will take advantage of the cognitively disabled and cause (through undue influence, coercion, or other inappropriate mechanisms) such persons to vote in ways that do not reflect their own preferences. Addressing such concerns does not require disenfranchising persons with cognitive disabilities, but rather creating systems that reduce the likelihood that third parties will successfully engage in such behaviour.

Accordingly, jurisdictions with formal capacity requirements should give serious consideration to eliminating those requirements. If they are unwilling to do so, they should, at the very least, refuse to disenfranchise any person without a specific, probative assessment of that person's voting capacity and clear and convincing evidence that the person lacks the level of capacity required of all voters, regardless of whether or not they have a disability. Since, as a practical matter, democracies typically allow non-disabled citizens to vote if they wish to do so (subject, in some cases, to a bar on voting by persons convicted of certain crimes), democracies that wish to retain a capacity requirement should consider adopting the capacity requirement favoured by the 2007 symposium of experts convened by the Borchard Foundation Center on Law and Aging, the American Bar Association Commission on Law and Aging and the Capital Center for Government Law and Policy at the University of the Pacific, McGeorge School of Law. That Symposium recommended:

> If state law permits exclusion of a person from voting on the basis of incapacity, a person should be determined to lack capacity only if the person cannot communicate, with or without accommodations, a specific desire to participate in the voting process (Symposium Recommendations, 2007).

By only disenfranchising persons who cannot communicate a desire to vote, and not allowing disenfranchisement based simply on a person's cognitive state, the Symposium's recommended approach limits disenfranchisement to situations that raise a legitimate fear of vote stealing or other forms of electoral fraud that might affect election outcomes.

Prioritize Cognitively Accessible Election Procedures

As discussed earlier, the ability of a person with dementia to vote may depend in part on how complex, confusing, or distracting election procedures and polling places are. By designing procedures and systems that simplify procedures and reduce unnecessary distractions (such as reducing ambient noise and improving lighting) democracies can increase the likelihood that all voters, and particularly those with cognitive challenges such as dementia, will be able to successfully record their voting choices. As part of such efforts, democracies should consider using 'vote-by-mail' systems and 'mobile polling' (ie, moveable polling) systems to allow at least some voters (for example, those living in long-term care facilities or other institutions) to vote at their residence because being in a familiar setting may reduce distractions and allow would-be voters to function at a higher level.

Although voters with cognitive challenges such as dementia or intellectual disability are likely to disproportionately benefit from cognitive accessibility of election procedures, all voters potentially stand to benefit from such changes. For example, confusing ballots can lead both those with and without such disabilities to incorrectly register their voting preferences, and thus to either under-vote or over-vote. Similarly, complex voter registration can confuse—and thereby cause the disenfranchisement of—voters with a wide range of abilities. In addition, increasing the cognitive accessibility of election procedures may reduce voter fraud and undue influence by reducing the need for third-party assistance.

Of course, in simplifying election processes, governments need to be sensitive to the fact that some methods of increasing the cognitive accessibility of elections may undermine other goals. For example, voters with memory deficits may find it easier to vote when candidates' photos appear alongside their names (Ott et al, 2003) and yet this may increase racially-based voting (Banducci et al, 2008). Similarly, mobile voting may increase the physical and cognitive accessibility of voting but may increase opportunities for undue influence or ballot tampering, and 'may reduce the sense of community as voting becomes a personal rather than a public act, and may reduce the public visibility of persons with disabilities if such persons disproportionately elect to vote at home' (Kohn, 2008). Likewise, voting systems that seek to achieve proportional representation by requiring voters to rank different candidates may result in more complex ballots than systems that do not seek proportional representation. Thus, while governments should strive to make voting systems cognitively accessible, they may need to balance that priority with competing goals.

Provide Support for Decision Making

Consistent with the CRPD's requirements that countries help persons realize their legal capacity, democracies should take affirmative steps to help persons with dementia to vote. First and foremost, this means that democracies must ensure that persons with dementia are entitled to receive assistance recording their voting choices and that they have ready access to persons who can provide this assistance.

It is important to recognize that in order to exercise their right to vote, persons with dementia may require assistance beyond that of just help with voting procedures; they may also require support making voting-related decisions. Like those without identified dementia, individuals with cognitive challenges may be better able to make choices that reflect their values and principles if they discuss and weigh potential options with others. Countries should consider how they might design and implement policies that also promote this deeper form of assistance. In doing so, they must, however, be cognizant not to permit others to substitute their preferences or choices for those of the person with a disability in the name of providing assistance. Thus, countries should not, as some have advocated (see, for example, Nussbaum, 2010: 79), permit surrogate decision-making in the context of voting.

Educate the Public about Voting Rights of Persons with Cognitive Challenges

Countries should also respond to the voting needs of persons with dementia by affirmatively educating the public about the voting rights of those with cognitive impairments. Such education should be targeted, at least in part, at both paid and unpaid care providers because, as discussed earlier, research suggests that care providers screen out individuals from voting even when they have no authority to do so. In addition, education of election workers should be a priority because they too serve as gatekeepers to the vote.

CONCLUSION

This chapter has explored how legal and extra-legal systems, in combination with an individual's internal cognitive abilities, can work to disenfranchise persons with dementia. Such disenfranchisement should be a significant concern for democracies because it runs contrary to the CRPD and emerging international legal norms, undermines the human dignity of persons with cognitive challenges and weakens the democratic system of governance.

Democratic governments should therefore take affirmative steps to create systems that embrace and respect the right of persons with dementia to engage in the voting process, and that provide individuals with dementia the support they need to do so. This does not mean that everyone with dementia will be able to vote; rather, it means that democracies should strive to ensure that the only barrier preventing a person with dementia from voting is that person's fundamental inability to make voting-related choices even if he or she has robust support.

REFERENCES

Alternative Report for the UN Committee on the Rights of Persons with Disabilities, Czech Republic (November 2011).

Appelbaum, P, Bonnie R and Karlawish J (2005) 'The Capacity to Vote of Persons with Alzheimer's Disease' 162(11) *American Journal of Psychiatry* 2094–2100.

Banducci, S et al (2008) 'Ballot Photographs as Cues in Low-Information Elections' 29(6) *Political Psychology* 903–17.

Barclay, L (2013) 'Cognitive Impairment and the Right to Vote: A Strategic Approach' 30(2) *Journal of Applied Philosophy* 146–59.

Bonnie, R et al (2005) 'How Does Voting Occur in Long-Term Care'. Interview Script and Responses (unpublished manuscript, on file with the author).

Bonnie, R et al (September 2013) 'Voting by Seniors in Long-Term Care Facilities' 12(3) *Election Law Journal* 293–304.

De Cauwer, H (2005) 'Are Cognitively Impaired Older Adults Able to Vote?' 60(3) *Geriatrics* 13–14.

European Union Agency for Fundamental Rights (2010) *The Right to Political Participation of Persons with Mental Health Problems and Persons with Intellectual Disabilities* (Vienna).

Hurme, SB and Appelbaum, PS (2007) 'Defining & Assessing Capacity to Vote: The Effect of Mental Impairment on the Rights of Voters', 38 *McGeorge Law Review*. 931.

Karlan, PS (2007) 'Framing the Voting Right Claims of the Cognitively Impaired' 38 *McGeorge Law Review* 917–30.

Karlawish, JH and Bonnie, RJ (2007) 'Voting by Elderly Persons with Cognitive Impairment: Lessons from Other Democratic Nations' 38 *McGeorge Law Review* 879–916.

Karlawish et al (2002) 'Do Persons with Dementia Vote?' 58(7) *Neurology* 1100–02.

—— (2004) 'Addressing the Ethical, Legal, and Social Issues Raised by Voting by Persons with Dementia' 292(11) *Journal of the American Medical Association* 1345–50.

—— (2008) 'Identifying the Barriers and Challenges to Voting by Residents in Nursing Homes and Assisted Living Settings' *20*(1) *Journal of Aging & Social Policy 65–79.*

Kohn, NA (2008) 'Cognitive Impairment and the Right to Vote: Rethinking the Meaning of Accessible Elections' 1(1) *Canadian Elder Law Journal* 28–52.

Massicotte, L, Blais, A and Yoshinaka, A (2004) *Establishing the Rules of the Game: Election Laws in Democracies* (Toronto, University of Toronto Press).

Mental Disability Advocacy Center (MDAC) (December 2012) *Croatia lifts voting prohibition for people with disabilities*. Available at: www.mdac.info/en/14/12/2012/croatia-lifts-voting-prohibition-for-people-with-disabilities.

Nussbaum, MC (2010) 'The capabilities of people with cognitive disabilities' in EF Kittay and L Carlson (eds), *Cognitive Disability and its Challenge to Moral Philosophy* (NewYork, Wiley-Blackwell).

Ott, BR, Heindel, WC and Papandonatos, GD (2003) 'A Survey of Voter Participation by Cognitively Impaired Elderly Patients' 60(9) *Neurology* 1546–48.

Redley, M et al (2012) 'The Voting Rights of Adults with Intellectual Disabilities: Reflections on the Arguments, and Situation in Kenya and England and Wales' 56(11) *Journal of Intellectual Disability Research* 1026–35.

Symposium on Facilitating Voting as People Age: Implications of Cognitive Impairment, Recommendations of the Symposium (2007) 38 *McGeorge Law Review* 861–69.

Part V

Patient and Carer Perspectives

39

This is My Life

PETER JS ASHLEY

This is my life
And I don't give a damn for lost emotions
I've such a lot of love I've got to give
Let me live
Let me live
This is my life.

THE DIAGNOSIS

THE DATE WAS 20 July 2000, the time approximately 11:40 in the morning, the place the Cerebral Function Unit, Greater Manchester Neuroscience Centre, Manchester Royal Infirmary/Manchester University.

My wife and I were called into a consulting room to see my neurologist and psychologist. The desk was covered with the results of tests carried out during the preceding three months. These included an intense battery of psychological cognitive tests, my physical performance analysis and various specific motor coordination and functional tests, my MRI and SPECT scans, the reports of the neurologist, psychiatrist, psychologist and other staff who interviewed me at various times, along with reports from my GP and psychiatric consultants at our local mental health hospital where, for several years, I'd been both an inpatient and outpatient.

My neurologist stated: 'Mr Ashley: we have come to a diagnosis. We believe you are suffering from Lewy body syndrome'. My immediate reaction was naturally one of shock as I realised that this was a dementia from the research I had already undertaken on the internet.

Whilst both my wife and I suspected that my condition was serious, the shock of receiving such a diagnosis was immense. However, we recovered our composure quite quickly and looking back on these events, were surprised at how intense our questioning had been of the two professionals present.

We studied all the reports and examined the scans, asked many questions and I even asked for copies of the scans which I still have to this day.

My recollection is that the consultation took quite a long time following which we sat in the hospital café having a cup of tea to try and recover prior to leaving the hospital for the 10 miles or so drive home. Later that day, as we sat on the patio in the sunshine, we literally wept to think of the consequences that we assumed would take place from all we knew of this diagnosis.

In the many subsequent presentations and lectures I have given over the years I've characterised our emotions during the ensuing six months as sequentially falling into the following five categories.

— Utter shock: trauma, grief.
— Disbelief.
— Mourning—for me!
— Realisation.
— Resurrection.

I felt shocked that something so dramatic as a terminal illness, rather like cancer, had happened to me, but which, unlike cancer, would divest me of my ability to recognise my wife, my family and my friends and in addition would rob me of all those skills which I had acquired during a happy and fulfilling personal and business life. Thereafter, an inability to communicate verbally—something I have done effectively throughout my life. The utter despair and inability to enjoy all those things that had gone before, such as my leisure interests: reading, debating, listening to music, sailing, sub-aqua diving, playing the piano and organ, etc. The steady erosion of my memory.

These feelings were followed by total disbelief that this could happen to me. Like most of us I had put to one side my mortality as a member of the human race and regarded myself, rather naïvely with hindsight, as living for many more years, for in 2000, at 64, I'd just achieved one of my major ambitions by becoming a founding shareholder and Group Technical Director of a computer graphics public company. As far as I was concerned my future was clear and I had it all mapped out. I was never going to retire. Perhaps I would take it easy, but in my dotage I would still do what I'd always done—work in my professional calling of computing, electronics and mathematics.

All the efforts I'd put into achieving my goals of providing our family with an enjoyable and fulfilling life were for nothing. The sacrifices I had made when missing many holidays, seeing my children grow up and enjoying the rewards I had achieved so far, were all for naught. The fruits of my labour were lost at a stroke and my entrepreneurial skills were now to be wasted.

The dictionary defines mourning as an expression of deep sorrow. It is this feeling that consumed my wife, me and our children following my traumatic diagnosis; it was as though a living death had arrived. For my part, whilst I had suffered from bouts of intense depression all my life, this was far worse.

Eventually, *realisation* came as a consequence of receiving a diagnosis; then trying to come to terms with it and reconciling all that you have gleaned from the information you have read and which has been given to you by others—information which, at the time, you assumed was provided by people far more knowledgeable than perhaps they really were. This goes both for people with a dementia and their carers and somewhat surprisingly many so-called professionals. Your realisation is more often than not based on what you subsequently learn is an averaging of the realities surrounding all the different types of dementia. I have learnt there are more than a hundred types. Dementias cannot be normalised, as you begin to realise with the passage of time. No two sets of conditions, let alone their related circumstances, are ever the same.

Resurrection is a word which occurred to me in December 2000 but I suspect and regret may not occur to the majority of other people having a diagnosis of a dementia.

It is my fervent hope that things will change and that this philosophy will be seen as potentially beneficial in leading some from their initial diagnosis to enjoying a better life—certainly in the early phases of the condition. Not the magic elixir we all eventually long for, but a form of remission for a few more years.

MY RESURRECTION

In January 2001, more or less six months from the date of my diagnosis, I suddenly realised that I had to make the best of my life and channel all my efforts and whatever resources were left to help myself, my wife and my family. My feelings were that this would help me, but in doing so, if I could share what I was planning with others in a similar position, it might help them as well.

I determined to strive and not allow my physical and mental attributes to degenerate in the manner that had been predicted by all the professionals I'd seen. I would not give in to my condition. What better way than to start learning about my condition in as great a detail as possible But in doing so I knew I must not lose sight of the fact that this was not just about me and my family, but about the 700,000 people in the UK alone who had received a diagnosis of a dementia.[1] If I could serve myself and at the same time work in the interests of everybody affected by dementia—the person with dementia, the family carers, all the professionals who work hard to identify the genesis of our conditions—this would become my life's work for whatever period I had left. A challenge perhaps, but if successful, what wonderful rewards. On the basis 'you never know until you try' I ventured forth in January 2001 with, I will now admit, some fear and trepidation, on my New Year's Resolution!

Not known for being slow at identifying an opportunity to explore my strategy, I targeted first a small group of professionals I had come to know and respect in the previous six months, and secondly the Alzheimer's Society—a leading body supporting at least, as their name implies, people suffering from the most numerically significant form of dementia. I rapidly learnt that the Alzheimer's Society, in spite of its name, covers the full spectrum of dementias.

The professionals I approached were only too willing to help, although many of them found it strange that a person with any form of dementia, let alone dementia with Lewy bodies, should want to take this course of action. I will be forever grateful to these individuals for the faith they put in me and for their unlimited cooperation. Sadly there is no room to name them all but it would be remiss of me not to mention and thank Harry Cayton OBE the then Chief Executive of the Alzheimer's Society and Dr Nori Graham, who at that time was Chairman of Alzheimer's Disease International.

[1] This figure has now been reassessed in 2014 to be nearer to 880,000.

My greatest breakthrough occurred during 2001 when I became a member of the Alzheimer's Society and became heavily involved not only with the Alzheimer's Society itself, but with Alzheimer Europe and with Alzheimer Disease International. At this point I'd like to go back in history, before picking up this story again in 2002. In stepping back, my observations are more to do with my early adult life and more particularly to the latter part of the 1990s.

MY PAST: MATTERS PRIOR TO MY DIAGNOSIS WITH DEMENTIA

Throughout my adult life I could have been categorised as a total workaholic, being very intense and highly strung in all that I do. I am obsessive with attention to detail.

After serving in the RAF as a regular (four years), I completed my education graduating in the late 1950s in electrical engineering, computing (still in its infancy), electronics and mathematics. Subsequent to this, a progressive career developed working in numerous sectors of the electronics industry and academia until I achieved the significant position of a major shareholder, founding member and Group Technical Director of a public limited company, as well as being the director of several related subsidiaries. Throughout this period I spent much time travelling abroad in pursuit of technical innovation and to study the developing areas of computing and its potential application.

All my adult life my health had been pretty good, with a couple of exceptions. I have regularly suffered from clinical depression. I also have mild OCD, which results in me being meticulous and fastidious. I have a preoccupation with the number three and multiples thereof and also the subject of prime numbers.

LIFE AFTER MY DIAGNOSIS

I now want to return to January 2001, from when I date the start of my 'resurrection', and life as it has evolved to the present.

My vow at that time was to ensure that I would make the best of my life and endeavour to work hard to this end. This was first and foremost for my own survival and to fight what I thought might be the inevitable consequences of developing a dementia ('*If you don't use it, you'll lose it*', I thought); but secondly, to try and work in a way which would give back to the community of people that I was now a part of as much as I possibly could.

As a consummate professional I knew that this couldn't be achieved without a much more comprehensive understanding of the subject with which I was dealing, my own condition and of those related to it. In my mind, I drew up a plan which would necessitate befriending as many professional experts as I could find in the medical, scientific and voluntary areas. Little did I realise at that time how welcoming many of these people would be, and I was heartened as I carried out my task to find just how cooperative people were.

I was elected as a trustee of the Alzheimer's Society, and served for four years. It appears that this was the first occasion on which any person with a diagnosis of a dementia had been elected to the governing body of the relevant national society anywhere in the world.

I worked closely with two staff members of the society—Rachel Litherland and Nada Savitch—to develop a 'Living with Dementia' group within the Alzheimer's Society. We coined the phrase 'Living with Dementia' which I'm delighted to say has become universally used as a descriptor for people who have such a condition. I also started carrying out presentations to both national and international audiences, people with dementia, carers, volunteers and professionals of all callings to try and spread the message that we were trying to convey. And I always rounded off my presentations by including the phrase: *I am living with dementia, not dying from dementia.*

During the last 14 years, my condition has taken its toll in some respects; my motor functions are the worst hit and I can no longer write, play the piano or organ and have extreme difficulty walking so I tend to spend much of my time in a wheelchair. My tremors, although well controlled, can sometimes be a nuisance. But, and it's a very big 'but', most important of all I do not appear to have lost my intellectual competency nor is my memory greatly impaired. I guess it is through sheer determination and 'exercising the brain' that I am able to lead an active and productive life. Through studying my condition and the organic causes I have a fundamental belief in the principles of neuroplasticity and neurogenesis and whilst these are poorly researched there is, in my opinion, great opportunity for their investigation in much more detail.

During this period I have undertaken more than 200 presentations in the UK and internationally on all aspects of dementia and related subjects. Building on my role as a trustee of the Alzheimer's Society, I went on to become one of their ambassadors (a role which I have recently relinquished). I was involved in the formation of the Lewy Body Society (now affiliated to Parkinson's UK) and am an ambassador. I am also an associate of Innovations in Dementia CIC.

In 2004, I joined the Guideline Development Working Group commissioned to produce the NICE/SCIE Dementia Guidelines CG42 (published 2007) which subsequently became the definitive work on supporting people with dementia and their carers in health and social care. I was one of a team of 28 which comprised 25 professionals working in the field of dementia, two carers and myself. It can be said without fear of contradiction that it was this document that set the scene for all subsequent developments in the dementia area.

The publication of the Mental Capacity Act 2005 was a major step forward in determining the rights of people with mental illnesses, and more specifically dementia. I was a member of the drafting team; I took part in much of the associated promotional work thereafter.

It has to be said that this was an extremely difficult subject to address, and whilst we made enormous progress in its original form, even following a redrafting exercise in 2007, it contained many contentious issues, most of which are down to ethical matters of concern and disagreement between all the related parties.

February 2009 saw the publication of *Living Well with Dementia: A national dementia strategy* and I was again a member of the working group on this proposal. The work group comprised 41 professionals and five carers/people with dementia of which I was one.

This document, more so than the Dementia Guidelines, tends to be quoted as the foundation for current thinking, but in reality it uses much of the work in the Dementia Guidelines and adds more of a political imperative to the subject.

I have served on numerous other bodies concerned with health and social care. These have used my professional skills in computing, electronics and IT.

'SO WHAT ABOUT ETHICS?'

This book is about ethics and the law and all I've done is to write about me! This is not borne out of some great egotistical dream, although I am producing an autobiographical work from which much of this chapter has been drawn.

I am trying, in the context of my own 'success' of 'living with dementia', to engender in the minds of readers that in many (I admit, not all) a good life is still possible. You have to work at it very hard if you are to succeed. Traditionally, being given a diagnosis of dementia meant the end: all the collective consequences of all the dementias were heaped on you in an instant and your illness was immediately compounded in its severity.

And this is where the ethics come in. Those around you assume the worst and impose on you their interpretation of your condition. They assume that they know far better than you do. Even medically this is not always the case, as you have to experience and 'live' with a condition to be an expert; you are an expert by experience. When I get hallucinations, nobody, no matter how professionally trained they are, can explain what it's really like. In this situation I'm the expert and it *must* be recognised.

In a care situation a carer who imposes their will in place of yours is ethically incorrect. Don't get me wrong: carers are worth their weight in gold, but to remove the individuality of a person prematurely is wrong in every way.

A friend of mine was leaving a day centre and his wife (his carer) said: 'Have you said thank you?' He was just as clear thinking as me and could decide for himself whether he wanted to say thanks or not. His carer was being ethically incorrect. There's no doubt his wife loved him dearly, but she was wrong.

But I can't put my pen down (metaphorically speaking) for in my case, it's my voice recognition software that physically writes this for me—there are ways around everything.

I started by quoting the words of 'This is my life'. I can hear Dame Shirley Bassey singing in my head as I write *This is my life, and* with the help of my wife Ann and my family, and all my friends and professionals around me, it will remain so!

> Funny how a lonely day, can make a person say:
> What good is my life?
>
> Funny how a breaking heart, can make me start to say:
> What good is my life?
>
> Funny how I often seem, to think I'll find never another dream
> In my life
>
> Till I look around and see, this great big world is part of me
> And my life

This is my life

Today, tomorrow, love will come and find me
But that's the way that I was born to be
This is me
This is me

This is my life
And I don't give a damn for lost emotions
I've such a lot of love I've got to give
Let me live
Let me live

Sometime when I feel afraid, I think of what a mess I've made
Of my life

Crying over my mistakes, forgetting all the breaks I've had
In my life
I was put on earth to be, a part of this great world is me
And my life

Guess I'll just add up the score, and count the things I'm grateful for
In my life

This is my life
Today, tomorrow, love will come and find me
But that's the way that I was born to be
This is me
This is me

This is my life
And I don't give a damn for lost emotions
I've such a lot of love I've got to give
Let me live
Let me live

This is my life
This is my life
This is my life.

40

Dad's Dementia

ANDREW BILLEN

IT IS SAID that the terrifying thing about dementia is its evisceration of personality. The lights are on but no one is at home, or, as distressingly, there has been an eviction and the longstanding owner-occupier has been replaced by a squatter—often a belligerent one. In my father's nursing home, an old woman, once, we are told, perfectly benign, patrols the corridor scolding the staff and ranting about a conspiracy against her. She stands at my father's door demanding answers to questions he is incapable of understanding, even grammatically.

For Dad's dementia, now entering its last days as lung cancer beats it to the finishing post, has had only one symptom: it has made him stupider and stupider. His decline has been disturbing enough, and sad enough, but Dad's 'dadness' has been a constant, and for that my family is grateful. Mercifully too, it has also been, until the last six months, a mostly gradual, medicated, descent down the intelligence quotient with only the occasional dizzy-making scurry.

Medically, I imagine, apart from the problem of knowing exactly what kind of dementia the patient is facing—apparently no diagnosis is definitive until you chop into a brain post-mortem—the greatest difficulty is in deciding when it began. When did general ignorance about times no longer really your own, absent-mindedness, nominal amnesia and the associated indignities of age give way to disease?

In my father's case I am tempted to go back a dozen years, to his mid-eighties, although I am sure that as a cocky graduate I complained even before then of the intellectual laziness of someone who had been thrown out of university after a year (a decorated career as a wartime bomber pilot bought you only so many credits at St Andrew's). His lacklustre attempts, for instance, to master French—honoured, in his later years, by a daily desk calendar of phrases—embarrassed me, not least because in this area, at least, I had inherited his stupid gene.

As a younger man, however, he was sharp; sometimes cuttingly so. He referred to a neighbour's 'dubious profession': she was a graphologist. A morose drinking buddy 'responded', he wrote in the diaries he kept for years, 'well to alcohol'. And although he knew rather little about what interested me—literature, politics and their meeting point in journalism—he knew rather a lot about what didn't—birds, flowers and nature. Artistically, he expressed himself in muddy pastels of Northumbrian landscapes. Personally, he had charisma. He used sensitivity to coax things out of people, and outspoken candour to make them laugh. I inherited more than his stupid gene.

By his eighty-fifth birthday, however, we children were beginning to make excuses for him. Round a table, he became lost in a discussion. One to one, he missed the point. On holidays, a day's outing elaborately outlined the night before would be big news for him by the morning. We excused it as deafness and persuaded him to buy an expensive hearing aid (which he then refused to wear). But there were other things too. On holiday in Italy, he spent hours searching for his binoculars and wallet, before finding them in his bum bag (which he was wearing). Television plots proved inscrutable. Train journeys were trips into the unknown. Conversations became circular and the circles became smaller. Favourite phrases were 'I have never seen anything like it in my life', indicating that forgetfulness at least offers the benefit of making the world fresh to you each day, and 'no bloody idea', in response to a direct question.

But by now he was approaching, and then speeding past ninety. What was more, he was doing so from behind the wheel of a car (he bought a new one as a ninetieth birthday present to himself). Generally, he was doing remarkably well.

Then one morning, four years ago, a friend came to take him to art class and he did not recognise him. Dad panicked. My sister booked him an appointment at a neurological clinic. On the cognitive scale, he scored in the high twenties out of thirty, but he momentarily could not recognise my sister in the waiting room and, when asked if he had other children, replied in the negative. At the follow up, she begged them not to use the inevitable word 'Alzheimer's'. The NHS said he had the right to know. Happily, the consultant's accent allowed him to miss it when it came—another blessing of decrepitude. So his medicines were from then on his 'memory pills'. For more years than we were advised to hope for, they did their job. There were moments of distress, including one brief and immediately forgotten weekend in which he said he wanted to go into a care home; but his increasing frailty was well managed, by the drugs, by our visits and by increasingly frequent visits by Age UK to the cottage where he still lived alone.

My father covered for himself well. Like many who fought in the War, he had rarely spoken of his service record. Now as his short term memory faded, he reopened those memories. Some were hair-raising. Other stories about his relationship with our mother were almost equally so, and possibly medically symptomatic of disinhibition. Later, even the RAF and his marriage became inaccessible to him. In his last few years he never mentioned my mother, who had died way back in 1985. I once asked directly if he remembered her. 'Who could forget your mother?' he asked. It sounded like a reply he had prepared earlier. His conversational gambits became either very specific: 'Do you see that boat on the horizon?' or unanswerably wide: 'Anyone any idea how clouds are made?' Dinner conversation ranged as far as the knick-knacks on the kitchen shelves and eventually ventured no further than the food itself ('bloody marvellous'; 'muck!'). Over one meal, perhaps nine months before he left his cottage for the hospital and then a nursing home, he explained to me in a matter-of-fact way I still found pathetic, that conversation was now 'very difficult for him'.

This tumble down Mount Mental Competence had its moments of tragi-comedy as his intelligence bowed to greet my infant daughter's coming up. 'What is a tractor?' he asked on a car ride, after we had pointed one out to the three-year-old. One night he insisted on finding out how much he had in the bank and embarked on a mad phone call to First Direct in which he failed to negotiate a single password: 'Memorable place? Well, where I live! It's memorable to me'. My brother later told me he had been through exactly the same rigmarole on his last visit. He asked me about my sister, his most favoured child. 'Has she a boyfriend at the moment?' He had managed, conveniently, even wilfully, to forget her husband of 20 years. On one of her visits, she confided about some anxieties that had been tormenting her, one of them being his decline. 'Don't worry about me. I'm 95', he answered acutely (he clung on to the clear fact of his age as if to a life buoy). 'Who are your parents, anyway?'

We would report back to one another at the end of visits. My sister was most optimistic, or most in denial. I was most pessimistic. My brother seemed to catch him at his worst: his last New Year was celebrated by defecating in his bedroom wastepaper basket. By April, however, he could not remember by the afternoon that morning's visit by the woman we would later employ to live with him for, as it turned out, only a few months.

From his armchair, he confronted me, and perhaps himself, with what was happening. I asked him if he knew where he lived. After an agonising period of thought, he named the town he had moved from 22 years before. I recorded the conversation on my phone because I thought it would be the last proper one I would have with him, and I was right. The next time I visited, he and I spent ten minutes hopelessly wrestling with the meaning of two sentences I had, at his request written on paper: 'Andy Murray is a British tennis player. He may win Wimbledon'. I recorded this conversation too, and my tone of rising irritation does not make me proud. (The patience—even, in a generalised sense, the love—of the nurses was miraculous to me.)

Yet throughout this process of stupefaction, Roy Arthur Billen had not actually gone anywhere far. In some ways he was even more himself. His lifelong neatness became obsessive. His outspokenness upgraded to outrageousness: he asked my svelte teenage niece where her breasts were. But he was also still able to make me, and others, laugh. One brutal February day on the Northumbrian coast, a dull neighbour recalled how as a child ice had formed on the inside of his bedroom windows. 'It was the same where I grew up', Dad replied, 'except the ice was on the sheets'. Towards the end, drowsily drooling over a plate of unwanted food, a carer asked if he would like it taken away. 'Take it away, kid,' he chirped. In his room, decorated with some of his landscapes, the bed-maker said: 'I didn't know you were an artist'. She got the reply: 'Nor did I'.

I have no wish to enter into the pro-life/pro-euthanasia debate and have only commonsensical opinions on it, but in my father's case it would be a lie to say that by his final months the real man was already dead. After we were told—a few days after his ninety-seventh birthday—that he had only a short while to live, my brother and I wondered by email why, when his death had loomed for so long, its proximity was still a shock. It was, he concluded, because although Dad's body was now a thin, hunched, semi-comatose thing, and his face drooped with Bell's Palsy, Dad was still somehow 'in there'.

Saying goodbye is hard. At least we have someone to say goodbye to.

41

Lewy Body Disease: A Carer's Perspective

SUE BERKELEY AND ROB BERKELEY

I STILL CANNOT sleep on his side of the bed. Nor can I see it cold and empty, so it is my snack bar and bookshelf. The television chatters constantly to muffle the silence of the hours without him.

My loved one Tony is not dead, nor far away. I take the daily pilgrimage to his nursing home. He looks like an older version of the charming man I met decades ago, though his broad shoulders are now hunched over his shuffling frame. I can still hold his taut body, but those blue, searching eyes are now glazed, impassive and indifferent to my approach. Cocooned in his own agitated and paranoid world, Tony has gone where I cannot follow. Bizarrely, he sometimes returns for a short while, in unpredictable remission from this relentless neurological onslaught: the battle for his mind, Lewy Body disease (LBD).

There is currently no known cure for LBD, but accurate diagnosis is vital to avoid the life-threatening complications that can result from misguided treatment with anti-psychotic drugs. Early in Tony's illness, I was confronted with the dilemma of administering such a drug—haloperidol—to Tony, by exasperated geriatricians who, after several years of trying, were unable to explain his aberrant behaviour within the existing Alzheimer's disease framework. A toxic overdose was the result.

Eventually, four years ago, I wheeled Tony into a neurologist's office. Slumped, confused, agitated, doubly incontinent and virtually deaf and mute, Tony's LBD was finally confirmed by a DAT scan. Very clinically, I was told that he may live for two to three months. Haloperidol was withdrawn. He needed full-time nursing care; I was burnt out and disillusioned.

Part of me died too when, a month later, I took Tony to the nursing home to stay. His dignity was laid bare by the necessary insult of sewing name tags on to his clothes, reminiscent of sending a child to school for the first time. Instead of childhood developing autonomy though, this marked Tony's growing dependence and institutionalization.

With a host of dementia-like symptoms taking over Tony's psyche, our youngest son Rob was to spend a number of his teenage years witnessing his father's decline within the dehumanizing mental health system. We made harrowing trips to mental health wards where Tony was 'incarcerated' in mood disorder asylums—here, patients were then inmates, often found wandering in drug-induced states down cold, bare, locked corridors.

Concepts such as the best interests of the patient (termed the 'service user'), choice, dignity, self-worth and respect were all seemingly forgotten in the context of this environment. Drugs, a significant part of hospital culture for dementia patients, were routine; alternative treatments were never discussed—why not try art therapy until diazepam was truly needed, for example? The dangers of traditional anti-psychotic drugs were never mentioned either, despite this information being easily obtained through the internet.

Patience and kindness can confer dignity, but understanding and empathy tend to typify a close, personal and permanent relationship, so often impossible for staff to attain in this setting. Recently a new geriatrician arrived to assess Tony in his nursing home and, after ten minutes with him, decided to scale down his medication significantly on the grounds that there were simply 'too many tablets'. Bearing in mind that this combination had been carefully designed over many years in order to maximize quality of life and to minimize side effects I offered my opinion, but my viewpoint was ignored.

Our GP felt unable to override this change from 'on high'. However, when I exaggerated a recent downward spiral in Tony's health as a result of the tablet withdrawal, the decision over tablets was reversed. I felt no ethical dilemma over massaging the truth in Tony's best interests—but should it have been necessary?

Most of the symptoms of LBD can be relieved with medication, through close monitoring by me, nursing home staff and an excellent GP. Cholinesterase inhibitors to relieve symptoms of Alzheimer's disease were never available to us on the NHS until Tony was too ill to benefit from them. Political uncertainties, postcode lotteries and shifting financial goalposts became a regular hindrance to obtaining the most appropriate treatment.

Atypical anti-psychotic drugs have been effective in relieving anxiety, but we only obtained access to these after research on efficacy and risks by me and LBD experts elsewhere.

Diazepam (Valium) has a cautionary role in controlling agitation, but I have an ongoing worry about its use 'on demand' in the nursing home setting. This rare element of choice can result in falls from having too much, or being bedridden with anxiety from having too little and being at risk of vascular complications and chest infections. At home, I would regulate the dosage according to Tony's state of mind and behaviour on an almost hour-by-hour basis; a system impossible to implement in the nursing home. Tony's regular medication, for sleep disturbance, depression, urinary infections and other ailments, is handed out daily by the staff—he has no choice in this as his wildly fluctuating executive functions make informed decision-making impossible.

Now, at least a decade after the start of Tony's decline, his palliative care in a supportive, risk-controlled environment—where I can be involved in joint decision-making—has finally improved the overall quality of his twilight years living with LBD.

There are, however, times of conflict in this collaborative decision-making. Recently, I asked for Tony's urine to be checked—a urinary tract infection could sometimes mimic some of the dementia symptoms—but the nurse did not agree, and it was three days before my suspicion was confirmed and treatment of the urinary tract infection could begin. This is inevitable when dealing with human fallibility;

many decisions that I have taken over the years, seemingly in Tony's best interests, have not worked out that way. We can only do our best.

When Lewy 'takes a sabbatical' Tony and I still share close times. I ride the rollercoaster of the illness alongside Tony; this can sometimes distort my view of the situation, so I am always grateful for the doctor's perspective. The doctor and I constantly try to make the best of a less than perfect living environment in which to strive for Tony's happiness, in spite of a restriction in his independence.

The spiritual dimension in care is also vital—in Tony's case, living in a home with a Christian ethos. This is provided in a formal sense with prayer and worship; when Tony is able, we go to church, as well as art galleries, music recitals, parks and gardens. Even simply sitting outside the home amongst the flowers can bring joy, however fleeting.

When doors close in life, others inevitably open. Discovering that even with hearing aids Tony could no longer make sense of the dialogue in a play left that cultural door shut, but this will hopefully push open the door to a visual alternative.

As the disease progresses and avenues of opportunity become cul-de-sacs, so his ability to meaningfully participate in the decision-making process in his life declines. I find my role even more essential to his continued well-being: fighting his corner to ensure dignity and comfort; calming his irrational fears; maintaining the core values in his life in these last months or years and preparing to do so at the end of his life. Dignity and respect in dying should be available to all of us, irrespective of illness and capacity.

Finally, dying will open a 'Pandora's box' of choices in the palliative care of those with dementia, one which will no doubt create its own set of dilemmas for the carer. Having Power of Attorney for Tony's welfare does not allow me to ride roughshod over his end-of-life wishes. However, this issue remains complex; Tony's fear of death, and indeed his denial of the possibility, prevents him from discussing it with me.

As he avoids the topic, choices and decisions are left open for the moment. Even those choices he has made can be in doubt; Tony's prior decision to leave his dementia-affected brain to medical science has recently been reversed, apparently 'in case God requires the body intact to go to Heaven'.

Previously stated funeral preferences have changed radically—from a green eco-friendly affair with a willow coffin, jazz band and real ale, to a solemn High Church service complete with a mahogany coffin and traditional funereal trappings. However, the most significant element—the decision on a 'do not resuscitate' order—remains absent from his care plan. This represents a true conflict in our joint decision-making ethos, as Tony appears to have no understanding of the consequences of this choice. If the choice is simply to live or die, he chooses life—of any quality. In contrast, I fear a permanent vegetative state more than the finality of death itself.

Whatever the advance directive—even with the form left blank—I shall continue to strive for a dignified end for my lifelong soul mate and friend. For all of us, care and respect is imperative in the quality of our death, as in life.

42

Our Journey

SHIRLEY NUROCK

THE ISSUES AND dilemmas we as carers have to face when looking after a loved one with dementia are overwhelming. As we embark on our journey, many of us have little idea what to expect and I for one was totally unprepared for the problems and challenges that would arise over a caring career that was to last some 15 years.

It all began when my husband, a GP in London, was diagnosed with probable Alzheimer's disease. He was in his fifties, and our three children were in their early 'teens. Although we were both aware that he had been increasingly forgetful over the last couple of years I accepted his explanation of stress at work and depression, but when the diagnosis came nothing could have prepared me, in my forties, for what lay ahead and the devastating impact the illness was to have on his life, my life, the children's lives and the wider family.

I read books (this was before the era of universal internet access) and slowly it dawned on me that there was no cure: this was a terminal illness with no defined rate of progress; it was different for everybody. All those years ago, dementia was little spoken of and, if it was, was usually referred to as senility.

With hindsight I went through all the well-charted stages of denial, anger, sadness and acceptance of sorts, but the challenges of maintaining well-being and quality of life for my husband to the best of my ability and trying to guide children through turbulent teenage years, the choices they faced over schools, universities, careers and ultimately partners, was more than I could cope with. I felt helpless watching my kind, caring, handsome husband slowly reduced to a shell, as if I were, being torn apart, and in the end I don't think I was terribly good as a wife or mother.

The early practical issues centred on whether it was really safe for my husband to drive. He had been advised against it. Eventually, however, he chose for himself, probably having had a 'near-miss': one day he simply hung up the keys. Was it safe to leave him at home on his own while I went out briefly to work? Would he leave taps running, let the kettle boil dry, go out and forget to shut the front door, or forget his keys? Would he get arrested in Waitrose for picking up a sandwich and walking out without paying because either he had no money or couldn't remember what it was for? And worryingly, would he get lost? If he did, would he remember that he had a slip of paper in his jacket pocket with his name and address and telephone number, or remember to show someone his bracelet?

We had always been open with each other, and the concept of lying or 'being economical with the truth' was not something I was used to. But I found myself making up excuses for locking the front door and 'losing' the keys; reasons why friends seemed to have vanished; why his medical friends never got in touch; why it would be a good idea to go and visit the new GP when he was adamant there was nothing wrong with him; why the nice 'friend' (a private carer I had found) wanted to come and visit him every week.

Then there was the agony of school parents' evenings, trying to make sure he didn't ask inappropriate questions, covering up if he did and trying desperately not to embarrass our children. It was a losing battle. Our daughters rarely brought boyfriends home. Our son, the youngest, lived his secondary school years under the shadow of Alzheimer's disease, and never brought friends home. Being shy, he was in a permanent state of embarrassment. When we were together or on family outings it was for our son to take his father to the toilet, and I recall often standing outside the gents asking strangers to look for my husband and guide him out to where I was waiting.

All these incidents faded into insignificance compared with what came later. Over all these years I had tried to do everything possible that would be in my husband's best interests and give him the best quality of life—for instance finding a suitable day centre where he could go for two days a week. He refused to go initially until, lying, I said that he was going as a doctor and the patients would benefit by him talking to them. Being on the other side of London, it meant me driving him there through London's rush hour traffic, swearing at every red light. By the time I deposited him there, too exhausted to get home, I would spend those two days a week wandering round the local shopping mall or reading psychology textbooks in the local library.

When he went through a stage of extreme agitation, endlessly walking, wandering, never sitting down, even to eat, I would sleep on a mattress on the floor by his side of the bed so that when he got up to wander every hour or so he first trod on me so I woke up and could prevent him from tripping down the stairs and coax him back to bed.

When the unsympathetic geriatrician finally agreed to visit my husband, (being under 65 he was not strictly eligible for 'elderly services') his verdict was 'a hopeless case'. He prescribed an antipsychotic, haloperidol, to control the agitation. I wish I had known then what I know now. When I complained every week that it was making him worse and causing shuffling gait and drooling, the dose was increased. No one listened. It was as if I didn't exist.

A few months later he was admitted to long-term care. I went through agony trying to decide what was in his best interests ... and mine. I was told there was only one suitable home with a bed for him and that I would feel only relief when he was there. Well, I didn't. That was the start of nearly five stressful years, spending hours with my husband each day, shocked at the poor quality of life and the lack of activities. He suffered two fractured hips and a broken knee, all on different occasions. Eventually he was admitted to NHS continuing care in a private nursing home near where we lived. My immune system worn down, I subsequently spent weeks in hospital recuperating from legionella and have never felt quite well since.

At the care home I tactfully tried to change things, left post-it notes all over his room for the staff and brought in food I knew he liked. I found private carers to be with him when I couldn't be, particularly at meal times, or to push the wheelchair to the park on sunny days. I worried constantly that I would be seen as a troublemaking wife and told to move him elsewhere. By then, having completed a psychology diploma at night school and being half way through an MSc in Social Gerontology, I knew care could be better but my offers to advise staff informally on caring for residents, and on relatives' expectations of care, were ignored by the manager.

My husband developed large blisters which were ignored by the GP. Eventually I called in a dermatologist I knew privately who immediately diagnosed bullus pemphigoid and prescribed steroids. I was told he would have died the most agonizing death within hours. It wasn't that I was trying to save my husband at all costs, but when he still enjoyed some quality of life I wasn't about to say 'do nothing'. The months he spent on steroids to clear the condition, strangely enough, were the best for years. He temporarily regained some speech, smiled and looked cheerful always. When the medication was due to be stopped completely I pleaded for him to remain on a small dose as it appeared to be so beneficial to his well-being. I was told 'no, it wasn't ethical'. But since my husband had been unable to walk for years, or do anything much for himself, I thought, why? So much of the treatment meted out to people with dementia is unethical.

He acquired MRSA, I have no idea how, and from then on his quality of life deteriorated. He was prescribed endless antibiotics for chest infections, urinary tract infections and sores. He slept most of the time. He looked so pitiful. Eventually it was me who pushed the protesting nurse out of the room and pleaded with the new young GP who had taken over to 'let him go'. For his last days I was viewed with disapproval by the staff, but he died peacefully, surrounded by family and having seen his first grandchild. I doubt he was aware it was his, but I treasure the photo of him with the baby on his lap.

My parents are still alive. My father is 102. Fond of him though they were neither of them was very sympathetic when my husband was ill. They probably blamed him for ruining their daughter's life. And I also have responsibility for my father's 98-year-old sister. All are confused, and still living in their own flat with 24-hour care. I am sorry to say I have less patience than previously. Most of their friends have died and, given all their concomitant medical conditions, their quality of life is low. More and more I find myself addressing the issue of a 'fair innings'. I worry too about my children inheriting Alzheimer's as all these years on there is still no meaningful symptom relief or prevention let alone a 'cure'.

43

The Power of Imagination

PETER RICHARDS

'ALARM RISING, ANNIE struggles awake, trying to make sense of the dampness she can feel on Katie's side. Katie is still apparently asleep. Turning on the bedside light, Annie registers the dark red across the bed. Terrified, she sees the trail of blood on the carpet leading towards the door. Her heart freezes when she remembers the spare razor blades in the bathroom cabinet'.

Then, in the mid-1950s, Annie was a young woman of 25 and caring for her sister, Katie, who was suffering from severe postnatal depression and talking of 'ending it all'. Katie couldn't be left on her own whilst her husband was away overnight taking their baby on the long journey to stay with its grandmother. Although Annie had removed all of the potential means of suicide she could think of, she hadn't thought of the spare razor blades in the bathroom.

I am the older of Annie's two, now middle-aged sons. This is how I now imagine—in clichéd terms, admittedly—the traumatic incident which may have triggered our mother's lifelong struggle with depression, anxiety and obsessive thoughts of death. Our mother told this story to my brother and me when we were teenagers and she explained that it was why our Auntie Katie always covered her wrists and neck to hide the scars. It also explained why she, Annie, needed her tablets and the occasional stays in hospital (I later discovered for electro-convulsive therapy (ECT)) to make her feel better. In recent years I've realised that she was probably already emotionally very fragile at that point: she had just lost her first husband to the chronic illness he contracted as a prisoner of war. Annie hadn't included this in her story, perhaps out of loyalty to our father, her second husband, or because she hadn't made the connection. I'm not a mental health expert, but it seems plausible that the shock and stress of that night may have triggered mental illness in someone already vulnerable.

'Clinical depression' was the initial diagnosis; food allergies were explored as causes, and various drug combinations and ECT were used in treatment. Twenty-five years later (my brother and I had both left home and moved away by then) a period of improvement began. She became an evangelical Christian after years of not really believing. But then came a sudden, dramatic lapse, and the diagnosis became 'manic depression'. Newer drugs kept her depression and anxiety manageable, but she was becoming less and less able to carry out everyday tasks such as making a cup of tea. An Enduring Power of Attorney (EPA) was arranged. Aged only 65, 'irreversible dementia-like symptoms' of confusion and forgetfulness were added to Annie's diagnosis and our father activated the EPA. I read up on dementia and, given that historically her drugs had included barbiturates and benzodiazepines, speculated to my father about polypharmacy as a possible cause. With a new psychiatrist and a different combination of milder drugs, Annie's mood improved, although not her functioning and she remained under the care of the GP. But our father's health was beginning to fail: a degenerative, terminal health condition was diagnosed, which of course caused us all stress and anxiety, and which became the focus of the family's attention. At the handover of Annie's care to my brother and me shortly before our father died we arranged another assessment which produced a diagnosis of 'Alzheimer's dementia'. That was seven years ago. Annie is now 85 and lives in a care home, and my brother and I are her Property and Affairs Deputies.

Our family rarely talked openly of our mother's condition. Our father played it down. We knew it was deeply upsetting for her, since mental illness was surrounded by misunderstanding, fear and shame in those days. My father concealed the later dementia diagnosis from her, fearing the knowledge would cause her more anxiety and obsessive worrying. It is possible her psychiatrist advised this strategy, and although today's attitudes favour telling a patient her diagnosis, my brother and I still think it best to follow our father's example. The handover psychiatric assessment confirmed that she had little insight into her anxiety. We don't refer to her memory loss—she remembers little of her life after the age of 30; and meals for example are forgotten 15 minutes later. Neither do we refer to her inability to carry out everyday tasks such as dressing, but we do explain—truthfully—that the increased anxiety she experiences every few months is a symptom of the urinary tract infections (UTIs) she contracts because she doesn't drink enough. Our mother has no other visitors to whom we need explain this approach, there being no surviving close relatives or family friends. The care home staff know about our strategy, and I suspect they, and the health care professionals who visit, follow suit. For two reasons, then, I am very reluctant to ask her directly about that time with Auntie Katie, but imagine it instead: if she were to remember it, the distressing memories might cause more anxiety; if not, she might worry about why she couldn't remember it, and about her diagnosis.

Creating this story helps me interpret her behaviour and anticipate her needs. A gregarious person in her youth—surviving photographs of her and her girlfriends in the early 1950s confirm this—Annie now spends her time in her room with the curtains drawn, reluctant to interact with the staff. On bad days, she shouts at staff and visiting health care professionals to leave the room. It's very likely she doesn't recognise or remember them. People she doesn't recognise, devices powered by batteries or electricity and most new experiences 'frighten' her—her word. Or she gets stuck on bizarre ideas she dreamt or imagined, no longer distinguishable from reality. I realise she needs reassurance or a distraction, like one of the simple crossword puzzles she enjoys—she's said more than once about the puzzles, 'they stop me thinking about dying'. When she has a UTI and her dementia symptoms are heightened (so-called toxic dementia), and there happens to be some pain in her body, however minor, she persistently asks, 'am I going to die?'; copious reassurance is needed. This is the crux of her condition, I think: the persistent anxiety and obsessive thoughts of her depression is aggravated by the confusion and memory loss of her Alzheimer's.

Another story I've imagined concerns Annie's eating. I remember our mother describing how her own mother was very strict and made her sit and eat all her food when she was young, even the things she didn't like. She wasn't allowed to leave the table until her plate was empty and it could be very late afternoon before her mother relented. This would have been during the 1930s Depression when I know for a fact the family was poor, so I imagine they struggled to buy food sometimes. I observe Annie's increasing anxiety towards mealtimes and her consistent refusal to eat any main course, to the point that desserts, sandwiches and cereal are the only foods she will eat (she is prescribed fortified drinks). We have tried to tackle this with her many times, but frustratingly she appears to be completely unable to explain it. Ruling out problems with her dentures and/or chewing as potential reasons, I imagine her childhood mealtimes as a possible explanation. I've noticed she is completely disdainful—appalled even—by the idea of drinking soup, again with no explanation when asked; I imagine its connotations, the judicious use of leftovers, the poverty of her childhood.

Of course, these imagined histories are spurious. I haven't shared them with anyone else—not even my brother. But persuading others of their veracity is not necessarily the point; they perform a further, important function for me. Caring for our mother, a role which neither my brother nor I asked for (although we did prefer to become Deputies ourselves rather than have a professional take this on), and which feels like a pretty thankless task sometimes, is demanding. Often my energy runs low: trying to keep my visits to Annie upbeat when I'm running out of patience with her repeated questions and obsessive irrational thoughts; the time-consuming Deputyship administration; and the occasional frustrations with the care system—for example, lost NHS records on one occasion that no one else was chasing, disagreements between professionals over who should fund Annie's additional nutrition on another. Re-running these stories reminds me again of my mother's difficult life, and so it renews my compassion for her, tops up my caring energy.

Turning to the future, my imagination comes into play again. Sometimes I catch myself entertaining words and phrases to say to Annie when she no longer recognises me, or when her language no longer makes sense. For important decisions made on behalf of our mother, though, I need to imagine in a more focused way, weighing up the likelihood of different outcomes. For example, should her confusion and hence her anxiety increase as her dementia progresses, her old-age psychiatrist has asked if we would agree that it is in her 'best interests' to administer ECT. Even if this is done more humanely nowadays, I am concerned it may trigger painful memories of the locked psychiatric wards she stayed in during the 1970s with disastrous consequences, plus it goes against her stated wish of never wanting to go to hospital again whenever she remembers her last stay on a (general) hospital ward five years ago to treat a gastric ulcer. On the other hand, some medical evidence suggests the treatment could be very successful. A more straightforward example is the administration of CPR: she would have only a small chance of surviving it anyway, and if she were to survive she may well have broken ribs (she has osteoporosis) and would have to deal with the consequences of dealing with whatever caused her heart or breathing to stop. I've persuaded my brother to tell the care home that, as next-of-kin, we think that Annie should not be resuscitated.

There is one last use of my imagination, and it concerns the present. Caring for a person with dementia requires time, energy and patience, even when the cared-for person is in a care home. I'm extremely lucky, though. I can manage my time to make regular visits and to research the care issues as and when they arise. My brother and I work well together, sharing the work and talking through any disagreements. I've heard friends' stories in which long-standing family tensions are aggravated, sometimes into open hostility, when the adult children disagree over the care of their parent(s), making what is always a difficult situation infinitely worse. I can imagine that not all carers are as fortunate as I am.

44

Dementia Care: Workpoints

U HLA HTAY

THE EARLY STAGE

At a support meeting with the carer, the carer proposed that we should 'deal without deceiving' in our caring journey.

The patient refuses to take medicine. The carer explains the benefit of taking the medication and delivers medicine with food and drinks.

Verbal aggression persists while attending a hot summer wedding. The carer administered 50% more than the regular dose of Aricept to moderate her behaviour.

The patient shouted at neighbours. The carer told her to stop. It went on and on. The patient says it was not her, but the other woman, who was causing trouble. The carer agreed, and went along with the patient's story.

If the patient was disoriented, or used rough language, the carer would correct and reprimand with a jovial jibe. The patient's behaviour got worse.

At social gatherings with friends and family, and at clinic appointments, the carer would finish the patient's sentences. This annoyed the patient.

The patient wandered outdoors. The carer would not lock the door or tell the patient not to wander. Instead the carer followed at a discreet distance.

The carer favoured attaching a GPS to the patient instead of using medicine to subdue her.

During night time wandering at home, the lights were kept on. When finally exhausted, the patient ended up in a different room. The carer had fallen asleep.

At a social meeting, the patient's favourite music was playing. The patient started to dance. The carer tried to stop her dancing.

The carer took the patient along to his own (the carer's) clinic appointments. The patient had to wait for two hours at reception.

The carer encouraged the patient to eat as much as she enjoyed, in order to build up a store of energy for the very long haul as the disease progressed. The patient became obese.

DURING THE MIDDLE STAGE

The carer continued to administer medicine covertly to the patient, along with food and drink.

Whatever the behaviours and misconceptions of the patient, the carer goes with the flow, instead of correcting or orienting the patient.

The carer insists that the health care assistant takes the patient on daily walks, come rain or shine. (The patient knows where she is, and is concerned about her safety when she is outside.) The carer's reason is that this will improve and maintain the patient's bowel function. Before commercial domiciliary care was arranged, the carer (the spouse) left the patient for three days in the care of their three teenage sons while he attended the Alzheimer's Society annual conference.

The carer suggested to the patient that they should have joint bank accounts.

DURING THE LATE STAGE

The patient was given what the carer considered to be a sufficient amount of food and drink.

Despite the patient wanting to rest, the carer insisted on taking the patient on regular daily walks.

Toileting was at set times, whether or the not the patient was ready.

The patient was kept in the living room until midnight, and then taken to the toilet and put to bed.

To keep the patient stimulated, the carer put on the patient's favourite videos. There was little response. The carer then laughed exaggeratedly and made excited gestures. The patient then joined in.

During the patient's sleep, the carer suspected that she was wet but failed to check. In the morning the bed was sodden.

The carer took the patient to the wedding of her sons. The patient was dressed for the proceedings, but not fully aware of what was happening.

Index

Lightning Source UK Ltd.
Milton Keynes UK
UKOW07n0944150917
309169UK00014B/391/P